D0586501

THE LIFE AND DEATH OF
SHERLOCK HOLMES

MATTIAS BOSTRÖM is a Sherlock
Holmes expert. He was elected into the
exclusive Sherlock Holmes association
Baker Street Irregulars in 2007. He
lives in Sweden.

First published in the US as *From Holmes to Sherlock* in 2017 by
Mysterious Press, an imprint of Grove/Atlantic, New York

First published in the UK in 2017 by Head of Zeus Ltd

A version of this book was first published in Sweden by Piratförlaget, 2013

9 7 5 3 1 2 4 6 8

A catalogue record for this book is available from the British Library

ISBN (HB): 9781784977733
ISBN (E): 9781784977726

Printed and bound by CPI Group (UK) Ltd, Croydon, CR0 4YY

Head of Zeus Ltd
First Floor East
5–8 Hardwick Street
London EC1R 4RG
WWW.HEADOFZEUS.COM

THE LIFE AND DEATH *of* SHERLOCK HOLMES

Mattias Boström

Translated from the Swedish
by Michael Gallagher

A Mysterious Press book for
Head of Zeus

Illustration Credits

Contents

THE LIFE AND DEATH *of* SHERLOCK HOLMES

1

IT ALL STARTED on a train.

That's where the idea came to Steven Moffat and Mark Gatiss. They were going to modernize one of the world's most renowned literary characters—remove the filter of a misty London, full of hansom cabs—and bring Sherlock Holmes up to date, placing him squarely in our high-tech, contemporary world. Sir Arthur Conan Doyle's creation would go from Victorian gentleman detective to modern, eccentric genius—from Holmes to Sherlock.

This, of course, was sacrilege. Such a television show was bound to be controversial among the fans, as Moffat and Gatiss were aware. Nevertheless, the more they discussed it, the stronger the idea seemed to grow. They wanted to do away with the classic symbols—the deerstalker, the pipe, the magnifying glass—all the nostalgia that was getting in the way, all those things that made Holmes seem more like a well-defined silhouette than a complex human being. The changes would, however, need to be made with great love for the original stories. The pair wanted to bring viewers really close to the original friendship between Sherlock Holmes and Dr. Watson, closer than anyone had brought them since the figures were born in the author's imagination well over a century before.

This was just a few years after the turn of the millennium, and for the time being their plan was no more than a tiny seed—just a topic of conversation during Gatiss and Moffat's commute from London to their script-writing jobs at BBC Wales in Cardiff.

But there were lots of train journeys. And the idea kept on growing.

A short time later, on January 7, 2006, Mark Gatiss and Steven Moffat found themselves at the Sherlock Holmes Society of London's annual dinner. Gatiss had been invited to speak, and Moffat was there as his guest.

Gatiss had also attended the previous year. He had been invited by a friend, Stephen Fry, a member of the society already in his early teens, who had been guest of honor and after-dinner speaker on that occasion. Gatiss had asked the society's chairman for an invitation for the 2006 dinner.

So there he was, in his tuxedo and black bow tie, about to make a speech in front of the assembled members—Holmesians, as they called themselves, or Sherlockians, for those who preferred the more widespread American term.

They were seated in a dining room in the House of Commons, a magnificent and thoroughly fitting venue for a Victorian flight of fancy, with its carved oak panels and beautiful evening views across the Thames to the lights of Lambeth on the opposite bank. Slightly to the left was the London Eye, the symbol of modern London and thus of an updated version of Sherlock Holmes, too.

It was an anxious moment. That evening Gatiss and Moffat would float their idea before a broad audience for the first time—and these particular guinea pigs were among the most critical, circumspect subjects you could imagine.

Mark Gatiss was coming to the end of his speech. He had told the members of his long-standing interest in Holmes and had arrived at the train conversation with Moffat.

"We began to discuss the question: could Holmes be brought alive for a whole new generation?" Gatiss said. He described the scenario: "A young army doctor, wounded in Afghanistan, finds himself alone and friendless in London." That detail about Afghanistan had been crucial for Gatiss and Moffat. The tale of Sherlock Holmes could in fact be introduced in the same way, regardless of whether it was set around 1880 or in the present. Those regions that were ravaged by war in the late nineteenth century remain conflict zones to this day.

"Short of cash," Gatiss went on, "he bumps into an old medical acquaintance, who tells him he knows of someone looking for a flat-mate. This bloke's all right but a little odd. And so Dr. John Watson—wounded in the taking of Kabul from the Taliban—meets Sherlock Holmes, a geeky, nervous young man rather too fond of drugs, who's amassed a lot of out-of-the-way knowledge on his laptop." Gatiss looked out over the assembled Sherlock Holmes enthusiasts. "It's only a thought. A beginning."

The Sherlockians were a hardened bunch. Many attempts at recasting Sherlock Holmes had been made through the years. Some had succeeded, others had not. Would Gatiss and Moffat's idea of bringing Holmes into the present find fertile ground?

"But to prove Holmes immortal," Gatiss continued, "it's essential he's not preserved in Victorian aspic—but allowed to live again!"

The general opinion among those present seemed to be that this was, well, controversial. It was also, nonetheless, intelligent, funny, and stimulating—much like Gatiss himself.

The mood in the dining room was cheerful. Mark Gatiss and Steven Moffat no longer had to hold their breath. Stage one was complete.

Every era had its own Sherlock Holmes. For over a century the famous detective had been reimagined to fit contemporary trends and ideals. Perhaps Gatiss and Moffat, with their new approach, would be the ones to ensure that yet another generation discovered Sherlock Holmes.

"Ladies and gentlemen," Gatiss concluded, "I give you Conan Doyle, Sherlock Holmes, and Dr. Watson. Forever."

Part 1

1878 – 1887

2

It was a Friday in late autumn 1878. Edinburgh's Royal Infirmary had moved to new premises at Lauriston Place, surroundings that benefited from significantly cleaner air than the old location toward the center of town. Although the slum clearances around High Street and the steep alleys of the Old Town had been under way for almost a century, mortality was still much higher there than in the more prosperous New Town neighborhood.

With its new Royal Infirmary, Edinburgh was now home to the largest and best-planned hospital in Britain, containing as many as six hundred beds. It was also a place where a new generation of doctors undertook studies in modern, clinically based medicine.

A man hurried down one of the hospital's corridors, waving a towel enthusiastically. This was a familiar sight to his colleagues and to his students, who always arrived on time for his lectures. He held his head high; his steel-gray hair stood on end; his gait was jerky and energetic; his arms were like two great pendulums.

He went through a small anteroom laboratory and then straight into Ward XI, his operating theater. The terraces of wooden benches that surrounded the amphitheater were packed: the Friday lectures delivered by this thin, gangly man were among the most popular on offer. The flickering gas lamps cast a bluish light; down where the light was strongest, the man sat on a chair and unfurled the towel across his lap. He then got under way.

"This, gentlemen, contains a most potent drug." He instructed his assistant to pass around a vial filled with an amber-colored liquid. "It is extremely bitter to the taste. Now I wish to see how many of you have developed the powers of observation that God granted you. But sir, you will say, it can be analyzed chemically. Aye, aye, but I want you to taste it—by smell and taste. What! You shrink back? As I don't ask anything of my students which I wouldn't do alone, wi' myself, I will taste it before passing it around."

His voice was high and discordant, and his lowland Scots was evident in every word. He dipped his finger into the liquid and looked up at the students. The young men on the benches watched as he popped his finger into his mouth, sucked, and grimaced.

"Now you do likewise."

Student after student tasted the liquid, displaying all manner of facial contortions before passing the bottle along. When it had made its way up to the top row, to its last tormented taster, a hearty laugh came from the floor.

"Gentlemen, gentlemen," he chortled. "I am deeply grieved to find that not one of you has developed his power of perception, the faculty of observation which I speak so much of, for if you truly had observed me, you would have seen that, while I placed my index finger in the awful brew, it was the middle finger—aye—which somehow found its way into my mouth."

The man with the towel was Dr. Joseph Bell, forty-one-year-old instructor of clinical surgery. His unorthodox methods were well known at the university. This was not the first cohort to have fallen for his vial trick, designed to give the young men their first great insight into the importance of observation.

Bell wanted to demonstrate that the treatment of illness and injury was largely dependent on thorough, quick understanding of the small details that separated the patient's condition from one of good health. To wake the students' interest in this approach, Joseph Bell demonstrated the extent to which a person who has trained his powers of observation can discover relevant, mundane details that will in turn reveal such information as the patient's history, nationality, and occupation.

"Well, my man, you've served in the army," Bell said to the first patient of the day, a man in civilian clothes who had just entered the theater after waiting in an adjoining room. Bell's assistants were extremely well organized, and no time was lost as the patients were brought in, one after the other, given their diagnoses, and then led away.

"Aye, sir."

"Not long discharged?"

"No, sir."

"A Highland regiment?"

"Aye, sir."

"A noncommissioned officer."

"Aye, sir."

"Stationed at Barbados."

"Aye, sir."

"You see, gentlemen," he explained to the students, "the man was a respectful man but did not remove his hat. They do not in the army, but he would have learned civilian ways had he been long discharged. He has an air of authority and he is obviously Scottish. As to Barbados, his complaint is elephantiasis, which is West Indian and not British."

The students took notes by the light of the gas lanterns. Bell's assertions, which had at first seemed miraculous, appeared perfectly logical after his explanation.

During another lecture, an elderly woman was led into the theater. She wore dark clothes and carried a worn black handbag. Bell glanced at her and said: "Where is your cutty pipe?"

The woman drew her bag closer.

"Don't mind the students," Bell said to the embarrassed old lady. "Show me the pipe."

Sure enough, the woman pulled out a clay cutty pipe.

"Now," Bell said, turning to the students. "How did I know she had a cutty pipe?" No answer. "Did you notice the ulcer on her lower lip and the glossy scar on her left cheek indicating a superficial burn? All marks of a short-stemmed clay pipe held close to the cheek while smoking."

Bell often tried to involve the students in the diagnoses, but their powers of observation were not sufficiently well honed. A young, mustachioed man in the third row was among those to whom Bell paid particular attention. The young man, named Arthur Conan Doyle, seemed to be noting down every single word Bell said.

Another patient entered Ward XI.

"What is the matter with this man, eh?" Bell asked. He focused his stare on one of the students. "No, you mustn't touch him. Use your eyes, sir, use your ears, use your brain, your bump of perception, and use your powers of deduction."

"Hip-joint disease, sir," spluttered the student.

Bell leaned back in his chair and placed his fingertips together underneath his chin. "Hip nothing! The man's limp is not from his hip but from his foot. Were you to observe closely, you would see there are slits, cut by a knife, in those parts of the shoes where the pressure of the shoe is greatest against the foot. The man is a sufferer from corns, gentlemen, and has no hip trouble at all. But he has not come here to be treated for corns, gentlemen. His trouble is of a much more serious nature. This is a case of chronic alcoholism, gentlemen. The rubicund nose, the puffed, bloated face, the bloodshot eyes, the tremulous hands and twitching face muscles, with the quick, pulsating temporal arteries, all show this. These deductions, gentlemen, must however be confirmed by absolute and concrete evidence. In this instance my diagnosis is confirmed by the fact of my seeing the neck of a whisky bottle protruding from the patient's right hand coat pocket. . . . Never neglect to ratify your deductions."

The lecture was over. In the third row, Arthur Conan Doyle collected his notes and rose to his feet. He was tall and athletic, barely twenty years old. He made his way down from the audience and walked toward the exit.

3

Arthur Conan Doyle grasped the pen and began writing a letter to his mother.

> Just a line to say that I move into my house tomorrow, No. 1, Bush Villas, Elm Grove. I am wedged in between a church and a hotel, so I act as a sort of a buffer. I have, though I say it, managed the whole business exceedingly well. There is nothing I put my mind to do that I have not done most completely. I have a few shillings left to live on and have put £5 by for the rent. My furniture is A1. Let me know when Connie comes. Any old carpeting or oil cloth most acceptable.

It was June 1882. Arthur Conan Doyle had turned twenty-three a few weeks earlier and had just moved to Southsea, a contiguous suburb of Portsmouth on the Channel coast of England. He wrote to his mother, Mary Doyle, about everything, and he did so often, sometimes almost daily. He described small, everyday things, all kinds of difficulties, and his innermost thoughts. His relationship with Elmo Weldon, who was still living with her parents in Ireland, had been patched up once more, in spite of the fact that the great distance meant that they almost never saw each other. Mary was kept comprehensively informed of the situation. If all went well in Portsmouth, he would marry Elmo. Until then they would have to make do with exchanging letters.

It wasn't long before a brass plaque was mounted outside his door, and Conan Doyle eagerly awaited the first patients at a medical practice all his own. His suggestion that his fourteen-year-old sister Connie should move down to Southsea to keep him company was not well received. But he continued to send wheedling letters, and eventually his nine-year-old brother, Innes—or Duff, as he was known—moved in to act as a kind of servant boy. Conan Doyle was of the opinion that a doctor's prestige was undermined if he had to open the door to visiting patients himself. And, as he pointed out in a letter to his mother, the air was much healthier in Portsmouth. "This is a far healthier town than Edinburgh. Our death-rate is only 13." This compared favorably with Edinburgh's rate of a little over twenty deaths per thousand annually.

The house was simply furnished but its layout practical. A hall led to a reception room with a desk and two chairs, and then a waiting room with a bench and a further few chairs. One flight of stairs led up to the room where patients were treated. His own living room was immediately adjacent to that, and he had furnished two bedrooms up on the top floor. The curtains came from Aunt Annette. His mother had sent a large chest filled with books, ornaments for the mantel-piece in the reception room, and blankets for the bedrooms. He was grateful for the opportunity to display the objects he had collected after his studies, during the time he spent as ship's doctor on a whaling vessel in the Arctic.

As for his studies, it was during his third year at the University of Edinburgh that he had begun attending lectures by Dr. Joseph Bell. He had, it would seem, somehow made an impression during those lectures, because Bell had offered him a role as his outpatient clerk. Conan Doyle had been assigned the task of receiving the patients in a room adjoining the operating theater, noting their complaints, and preparing them so that the consultation in Ward XI could be conducted as quickly as possible. Sometimes he would take care of as many as eighty patients before a lecture. He showed them in, one by one, and Bell would always manage to ascertain more information with a sin-gle glance at the patient than Conan Doyle had managed to garner through his questioning.

As Bell's assistant, Conan Doyle became even more inquisitive as to the methods of his lecturer. He would often ask about various details after the lecture and check that his notes were accurate.

"But how could you tell that the patient had arrived in town from the south and that he had walked across the links?"

"On a showery day, such as it had been," Bell answered, as Conan Doyle made notes in his little book, "the reddish clay at the bare parts of the links adheres to the boot and a tiny part is bound to remain. There is no such clay anywhere else around the town for miles."

* * *

In Southsea, Conan Doyle sat and waited. So far no patients had rung the doorbell. But in less than half an hour on the Wednesday evening, no fewer than twenty-eight people had stopped to read the brass plaque, and the following day the results were even better: twenty-four people in just fifteen minutes.

On Mondays, Wednesdays, and Thursdays, the poor were offered free consultations between 10:00 a.m. and 1:00 p.m. Conan Doyle had arranged to have this written on the plaque. A batch of medicines had arrived from London—at a cost exceeding eleven pounds! Nevertheless, this was still cheaper than sourcing them via local chemists. And all craftsmen need the tools of their trade.

He had ended up in Portsmouth and Southsea purely by chance. He had made a failed attempt at running a practice with a colleague in Plymouth the previous spring. He had then moved on to Tavistock in Devon to see whether there were any openings for a young doctor. There were not.

So he took the steamer to Portsmouth, where he found himself now, eager to start practicing the profession he had trained in, and with a serious need to earn some money.

Innes boiled the last six potatoes over the open fire. They had some candles but no gas.

The small income Conan Doyle did have was mainly thanks to the stories he wrote for various periodicals. As usual, he told his mother all about them: "I have a wonderful story on hand 'The Winning Shot' about mesmerism and murder & chemical magnetism and a man's eating his own ears because he was hungry."

Conan Doyle had written his first story at the age of six, on paper folded in the folio format. Each line had space for four words, and the author had also provided illustrations in the margins. The plot centered on the meeting of a young man and a tiger. Conan Doyle described the man's untimely death with a great deal of realism. However, once the tiger had consumed all the man's body parts, one problem remained: What was the rest of the story going to be about?

It would be four years before he created another work. In the intervening years he had developed his talents through reading. He was allowed to borrow one book at a time from the library. Rumor had it that the library committee had called an extra meeting on the subject of young Arthur, at which it was decided that no member be allowed to change his or her loan more than three times per day.

The books took him to the prairies where herds of buffalo roamed, to the great waves of the Pacific Ocean, and to chivalrous knights and comely maidens.

Arthur's classmates at Stonyhurst College boarding school discovered just what a storyteller he was. On rainy days outside term time, he could be found on a bench, an audience of small boys sitting on the floor in front of him, as he regaled them with tales of his heroes' fates and adventures. Week in, week out, his heroes went on fighting, struggling, and grunting, to his classmates' great amusement. They would bribe him with biscuits, willing him to continue, although sometimes he would stop just as the excitement peaked. He would later recall that after delivering a line such as, "With his left hand in her glossy locks, he was waving the bloodstained knife above her head, when—," he knew he had his audience in the palm of his hand. That was how his second book was created—not written, but told.

In Southsea, the adult Conan Doyle was still waiting. In between the visits of a handful of patients, however, he was able to dedicate himself to writing. He got a lot done.

Three years earlier, at the age of twenty, Conan Doyle had had his first short story published. An Edinburgh magazine had paid three pounds for a story that was not far removed from his childhood tales of adventure. Another magazine had since published several of his short stories, and it was the payment for them that had enabled him to purchase that parcel of expensive medicines from London.

Conan Doyle continued to write, preferring supernatural phenomena as subject matter, and sent off cylinders containing the rolled-up manuscripts. First, he turned to the most popular periodicals—the *Cornhill Magazine*, *Temple Bar*, and many others. The cylinders came back, only to be sent on immediately to other publications. It was an endless cycle of constant rejection and new attempts. After a long struggle, he began to succeed, and more and more of his stories appeared in print. This success did not result in any praise whatsoever, though, since the magazines had a policy of not publishing the names of their authors. When one of his short stories was published in London's most influential literary monthly, the *Cornhill Magazine*, one critic was convinced that it had to be the work of Robert Louis Stevenson. It was written in the same adventurous style, and was at least as good, as Stevenson's submissions. In fact, the reviewer went as far as to compare the tale to the work of the master of the short story, Edgar Allan Poe. It was incredibly flattering, yes, but for an anonymous author, terribly frustrating.

4

IF THERE WAS one thing Conan Doyle loved besides writing, it was sports. He had been fascinated by athletics from a very young age, and Portsmouth gave him many opportunities to engage his interest.

It was January 9, 1886, and England was experiencing the harshest winter in living memory. Temperatures were below freezing, and those who could do so stayed indoors. The nation was at a standstill. Electric trams could not cope with the ice and slush; passengers longed for a return to their trusty horse-drawn predecessors. Out in the country, where roads were impassable, many sheep were feared to have perished in the colossal snowdrifts.

In Portsmouth's North End, however, men played football.

Portsmouth Association Football Club was still in its infancy but had already seen success. One of the fullbacks in particular, A. C. Smith, drew the plaudits, and his powerful punting was praised in the press. Once a goalkeeper, Smith had later progressed to right back. Deep down he was a rugby player, but he had quickly adapted to kicking rather than carrying the ball. At six foot one and 225 pounds, he was a cornerstone of the team and an increasingly popular Portsmouth athlete.

It had become clear to Conan Doyle that he wasn't going to get any patients by simply putting up a brass plaque and then sitting back and waiting. An unwritten rule decreed that doctors did not advertise their services. Conan Doyle though, found a loophole. In one of the local newspapers, under the heading "Miscellaneous Wants," he submitted a short notice: "Dr. Doyle begs to notify that he has removed to 1, Bush Villas, Elm Grove, next the Bush Hotel."

He would change his name to suit the occasion. Sometimes he would shorten it, becoming simply Doyle; otherwise he used Conan Doyle as his surname. Doyle was his father's family name and Conan came from his godfather, Michael Conan, his grandfather's brother-in-law. In the case of the "Miscellaneous Wants" notice, newspapers usually charged by the word, and choosing a shorter name was a question of being economical.

He published the notice several times, to make sure that the citizens now knew of his existence.

There were also other ways in which to raise the profile of the practice. One November day an accident occurred in the street outside; a man fell from his horse after one of his stirrups broke, and the horse then fell on top of him. Conan Doyle rushed out to attend to the injured party. After taking him inside and declaring that the man had suffered nothing more serious than some nasty bruising, Conan Doyle did what any doctor in his position would do. He hurried over to the *Portsmouth Evening News* to recount the day's events. The story of the doctor's intervention appeared in the evening edition that same day.

To simply sit and wait for further good fortune of the sort would be rather too optimistic. No, the twenty-three-year-old newly qualified doctor would have to get out and meet, and get to know, the people of Portsmouth.

He began to exchange services with tradesmen in the town. A grocer came to see him, seeking treatment for his incipient epilepsy. Conan Doyle received butter and tea in return. The poor grocer never suspected the doctor's delight upon hearing of further seizures a short while later—more butter and tea.

It was not merely potential patients that he needed to become acquainted with. It was customary in the medical profession for newly qualified doctors to pay visits to older colleagues in the neighborhood. Despite his young age and inexperience, Conan Doyle had no difficulty making an impression on his fellow physicians. One sent patients on to him, while another was a member of the cricket club, which Conan Doyle also joined. He played for Portsmouth Cricket Club as a batsman, and his on-field exploits were often reported in the local newspapers. Cricket was the kind of sport that doctors were expected to participate in, while the same could not be said for association football, or soccer. While his teammates and indeed the press surely knew who he was, an alias to protect his good name as a doctor could do no harm. So, when he took to the football pitch to belt the leather sphere in all weathers, he was no longer Conan Doyle but the rather more anonymous A. C. Smith.

Conan Doyle's social sphere continued to expand. He was elected a member of the Portsmouth Literary and Scientific Society, which arranged lectures every other Tuesday evening during the winter months. Many of Portsmouth's most influential people were members, and for Conan Doyle it represented another rung on the ladder of social advancement.

Membership in the society was restricted to men. Women were welcome to attend the lecture evenings as guests but were not permitted to ask questions or participate in discussions. The editor of one of the city's newspapers wondered whether something could be done about the women's incessant engagement in handicraft during meetings. It was, he felt, annoying.

The listings featured lectures on a huge range of subjects, from the tampering with foodstuffs and how it could be revealed with the help of a microscope to the archaeology of Hampshire to the movement of the earth. The society's chair, Major General Alfred Drayson, recounted his personal recollections of South Africa, and on another occasion it was the turn of Surgeon Major G. J. H. Evatt to give his account of the medic's role in the theater of war. Portsmouth's status as a military town was obvious, both in the membership of the society and in the city as a whole. The town harbored Britain's largest naval base and was home to many army as well as navy personnel.

A few weeks after being made a member, Conan Doyle gave a talk about the Arctic sea, based on his own experiences as ship's doctor on the whaler *Hope*. Two hundred and fifty ladies and gentlemen listened intently; it had the second-best attendance of any lecture of the whole season. The young speaker was accorded great respect, and he was surely a great hunter. The table in front of him was heaving with stuffed Arctic birds.

The following day, Conan Doyle returned the borrowed objects to the local taxidermist.

A. C. Smith morphed after each football match, becoming his true self once more, twenty-six-year-old physician A. Conan Doyle, MD. That was the suffix on his brass plaque since he had gained the higher qualification by virtue of his paper on tabes dorsalis, a neurological manifestation of syphilis resulting from spinal deterioration.

The football team headed off to the Blue Anchor for a meat tea. A light meal was just what was called for after ninety minutes of struggle in high winds and biting cold.

It was then time for Conan Doyle to make his way home, a few miles south, to the streets of Southsea. He did not mind a long walk.

Back at the practice, things were improving all the time. His annual income topped £300—nothing to be sniffed at. It was, though, still somewhat short of the salaries commanded by his more senior colleagues in the city. In his first tax return, he declared that he had earned so little that he was not liable to pay any tax at all. The form was returned with the comment, "most unsatisfactory." Conan Doyle promptly resubmitted the form, with the response, "I entirely agree."

He remained at Elm Grove, although the household had changed somewhat. His little brother, Innes, had moved out of Bush Villas the year before and was to attend boarding school in Yorkshire until he was old enough to enlist in the navy. For the past few years Conan Doyle had employed a housekeeper, who doubled as his receptionist and was responsible for giving patients the impression that Dr. Doyle was a supremely busy man. He was, in fact, a man with plenty of time on his hands, who spent his days reading and writing.

Conan Doyle walked home at a brisk pace. The icy winds continued to blow ashore, and it was a relief to cross the threshold into the house.

He took out new blank sheets and dipped his quill: back to the writing.

5

CONAN DOYLE FELT as though his writing was getting nowhere.

Since that first published short story, he had successfully submitted a further twenty-five stories to various magazines—not a bad result by any means. Even if his fee for the stories was sometimes only a few pounds, he had in fact been paid thirty pounds by James Payn, the editor of the *Cornhill Magazine*. Almost a year's rent for a single short story, it was the same sum he would earn from two hundred paying patients.

The pride Conan Doyle felt upon receiving Payn's approbation was enormous. He had even been invited to the *Cornhill Magazine*'s end-of-year supper. Arriving early at the restaurant in Greenwich, he made use of a little side room to change out of his traveling clothes and into his tailcoat. Twenty-five authors and illustrators were present, including Grant Allen, a former science writer who was establishing himself as a novelist. Best of all, Conan Doyle got to meet the editor, James Payn, an author in his own right and one of Conan Doyle's favorite writers. Taking him to one side, Payn warmly praised his short story and explained that their best draftsman had been given the task of illustrating it. It was to be published in the January 1884 edition.

Conan Doyle was delighted. His first literary dinner had given him a taste for more. Of course, even great pleasures subside eventually, and it had been almost two years since then.

The fact that almost everything was published incognito was hugely frustrating—no one ever knew that he had written those stories. In Portsmouth he was renowned as an athlete and, to some extent, one would hope, as a doctor. For the people of the city to realize that he was also an author, he would have to tell them himself. Even his alias, A. C. Smith, gained more attention than his literary persona.

After that wonderful dinner in Greenwich, Conan Doyle had been full of enthusiasm and drive, so much so that he wrote to his mother telling her that he wanted to concentrate on his writing. He was in a hurry to write something really big, something that would result in three-figure checks.

If he was ever going to get anywhere, he would need to write a longer story. The only way to gain recognition as a writer was to get your name attached to a proper book. "Only so do you assert your individuality," he once declared. The short stories would have to take a backseat; he was going to become a novelist. The year 1886 was only one month old; he was to turn twenty-seven that spring, and something had to happen soon. His erstwhile passion for writing was about to return.

It was not his first attempt at book writing. Two years earlier he had set to work on an ambitious novel. At first the work had impinged on the time available to write his lucrative short stories, so for a while he had to live frugally. He explained to his mother that his tale, about the employees of the Girdlestone business firm, would be either a laughable failure or a great success.

He threw himself into the novel writing, but periods without significant progress on the manuscript soon occurred and grew ever greater. The novel was not completed until toward the end of 1885.

There was no interest from publishers. Conan Doyle realized that this manuscript did not, in fact, assert his individuality but rather relied too heavily on the work of others. He soon came to accept publishers' refusals and stuffed the manuscript away in a drawer.

Writing one's first novel, he learned, was not easy.

Actually, though, this had been his second. He had already written a novel, *The Narrative of John Smith*, but it had got lost in the post. He had been attempting to rewrite it from memory ever since.

Despite the obstacles he met with these two attempts, Conan Doyle saw them as good practice. He felt ready to start another novel—one that would definitely be published. Yes, he was certainly ready. A chance event the previous year had provided him with the missing piece of the puzzle, one he so badly needed after several years of writing.

One day in March 1885, a Portsmouth colleague, Dr. Pike, who lived just a few hundred yards away, wondered whether Conan Doyle might examine one of his patients. Named Jack Hawkins, he was a young man, the same age as Conan Doyle himself, who had recently been struck by increasingly frequent seizures.

Both doctors arrived at the same diagnosis: meningitis. There was no cure. All they could do was ease the patient's suffering.

As the seizures became progressively more frequent, the young man's domestic arrangements became increasingly untenable. Since moving to Southsea some six months previously, he had shared a flat with his widowed mother and his sister, two years his senior. Neither of the doctors was able to offer him a satisfactory treatment regimen in his current accommodation.

Conan Doyle suggested that Hawkins should move into one of the attic rooms at Bush Villas. He and his housekeeper would thus be able to keep a constant eye on the patient, and Mrs. Hawkins and her daughter would be welcome to visit as they pleased.

The young man's condition progressed faster than anyone could have predicted. On March 25 the resident patient died. Two days later the short funeral cortege left Bush Villas for the cemetery, proceeding slowly along the avenue of elm trees. The first horse pulled the hearse, while a second drew a carriage transporting the mourners: Hawkins's mother, his sister, and the young doctor.

In the weeks that followed, Conan Doyle and the Hawkinses continued to meet, united in their feelings of guilt. The doctor was distressed at not having been able to do more. The mother and sister were similarly distraught at having put the doctor in such a position.

The sister, with her pale complexion and quiet manner, was reserved and feminine—and beautiful. Her name was Louisa, but before long the doctor was given permission to call her Touie.

She had an income of £100 per annum from her father's estate. She was amenable and acquiescent, not to mention polite and respectful toward Mrs. Mary Doyle, who had rushed south to inspect the woman that her son had chosen as his wife-to-be.

The piece that had been missing was now in place. After the wedding Conan Doyle felt sharper. His imagination was much improved, and he felt far more articulate. He had rediscovered his enthusiasm for writing.

That piece was Touie. Everything about her put him back on course. His bohemian, bachelor lifestyle made way for a salubrious daily routine. She knew what mattered to him, and with her mother's help she organized a study in one of the small rooms on the top floor.

Until now, his primary goal in life had been a career in medicine. Now though, with the regimented lifestyle and his increased responsibilities, alongside his expanded intellectual capacity, the literary side of his personality grew steadily, before long precluding everything else.

He wanted to become an author; he was sure of it.

His thoughts turned to writing a detective story.

6

C ONAN DOYLE FILLED notebook after notebook with ideas for stories he wanted to write. He had the title for one of them, "A Tangled Skein," but for the time being it consisted of nothing more than a few ideas about a cabman and a policeman.

He constantly made notes, as he had done for many years, jotting down things he had done, things he had read, ideas that popped up—small details and fragments that might one day grow into stories, articles, or lectures.

He wrote notes about the books he read. He thought that the French novelist Émile Gaboriau's police stories were very good. The mysteries concocted by English writer Wilkie Collins were better still.

Conan Doyle, though, wanted to make his own mark. Since childhood, he had counted Poe's masterly amateur detective C. Auguste Dupin among his heroes. Perhaps it wasn't a policeman he should write about after all, but rather a detective operating outside the conventional police force. He crossed out "A Tangled Skein" and wrote a new title instead, "A Study in Scarlet." What was needed was some kind of content to create the fresher, crisper, and more workmanlike tale he felt so ready to write.

How might one develop the detective role into something new? He wanted a more scientific detective, one who solved crimes through his own attributes, not thanks to criminals' blunders.

Conan Doyle thought of his medical-school lecturer, Joseph Bell. That's what a detective should be like! He would be a detective who— just as disconcertingly as Bell—would notice the tiniest details and, with the help of his powers of observation and deduction, go on to solve the case. Had Bell himself been a detective, he would surely have transformed the fascinating yet disorganized occupation into something more closely resembling pure science.

Bell had demonstrated that something akin to scientific detective work was possible in real life, so it had to be possible to make it credible in fiction too. All that was required was to fill the story with various examples of the detective's observational skills, just as Bell had done several times in the course of each lecture.

Conan Doyle began making notes. At the top of the page, he wrote "A Study in Scarlet" once more. He was taken with that title. Who would be his leading characters? The detective, of course, but Conan Doyle preferred to tell his stories in the first person, and allowing the detective to narrate would remove too much of the suspense. He needed a companion. Conan Doyle invented a name, and made a note of it: "Ormond Sacker—from Soudan." He would be a military man. For years, the Mahdi uprising had attempted to liberate Sudan from British colonial Egypt. Actually, come to think of it, he would set the story a few years earlier, so it would have to be another war zone. He crossed out the second part, and wrote "from Afghanistan" instead.

He went on: "Lived at 221b Upper Baker Street."

On the next line, he penned a single word: "with."

Another new line. Well, with whom? What would he call his detective? From an early age, Conan Doyle had been a fan of the work of the American doctor and author Oliver Wendell Holmes. Holmes was a good name. Underneath "with" he wrote: "Sherrinford Holmes." That would do for now. Ormond Sacker, though . . . he would have to give that a bit more thought. His companion really ought to have a more ordinary name. That would have to wait; he had to get his ideas about the detective down on paper:

The Laws of Evidence

Reserved—sleepy eyed young man—philosopher—Collector of rare
Violins—An Amati—Chemical Laboratory
I have four hundred a year—
I am a Consulting detective—

The ideas flowed. Conan Doyle could certainly feel his brain working faster nowadays, and he was really exceeding his previous output. Thank you, beloved Touie, for that missing piece! This felt far more original than his previous attempt at a novel, *The Firm of Girdlestone*.

Back to the note-taking. He had a line in his head that he wanted to write down:

"What rot this is" I cried—throwing the volume petulantly aside. "I must say that I have no patience with people who build up fine theories in their own armchairs which can never be reduced to practice—"

He managed to commit another to the page:

Lecoq was a bungler—Dupin was better. Dupin was decidedly smart—his trick of following a train of thought was more striking than clever but still he had analytical genius.

Now, though, it was time to put the paper to one side. Apparently there was a patient waiting.

7

Conan Doyle managed to finish his novel quickly, and for a time that was as far as it went. Several publishers turned it down; yet he did not give up. He wanted his name on the spine of a book. After all, it would take only one person to like the story to give him the chance of becoming a published novelist.

Before long, that person appeared.

Jeannie Gwynne was ten years old, when suddenly, completely unexpectedly, she saw her mother lying dead in the White Room.

This was unexpected primarily because Jeannie was not even in the house but was on a gravel track out in the countryside, reading a book about geometry.

For several minutes, the surrounding countryside faded away and then disappeared completely. She found herself in the White Room, an unused bedroom at home. Her mother lay lifeless on the floor, with a lace handkerchief by her side.

Gradually the gravel track returned, hazy at first but before long crystal clear once more.

The ten-year-old did not doubt that the vision was true, not even for a second. So rather than making straight for home, she went directly to the family doctor, who lived close by. She persuaded him to come with her, but he received no direct answers to the questions he posed— since when Jeannie had left home, there had been nothing the matter with her mother.

Once there, Jeannie led the doctor, and her father, straight to the White Room. There they found her mother, lying exactly as her daughter had seen her, with the lace handkerchief just as she had expected. Her mother had suffered a heart attack and, had it not been for the doctor's timely arrival, she would soon have taken her final breath.

Jeannie grew up with her father, a mathematician, as her only teacher. She went on to university, got married, and had three children with her husband, Cambridge science professor George Thomas Bettany. A geologist, biologist, and botanist, Bettany spent his free time writing a tome about Charles Darwin. He also worked for the publisher Ward, Lock & Co. as an editor of several different series of books.

Jeannie was twenty-nine years old; George was thirty-six. One day in September 1886, he came home and said to his wife: "You have published a novel, and have contributed stories to *Temple Bar*, the *Argosy*, and *Belgravia*, and are likely to be a better judge of fiction than I. So I should be glad if you would look through this, and tell me whether I ought to read it."

He pulled the manuscript from its cylinder. It looked well thumbed. It had probably been through several publishers' hands before arriving at Ward, Lock & Co.

Jeannie Gwynne Bettany read the manuscript and saw something that no one else had seen. "The writer is a born novelist. I am enthusiastic about the book, and believe it will be a great success."

Professor Bettany trusted his wife's judgment, and planned to recommend it to the publishing house.

"This is, I feel sure, by a doctor," she added. She had once hoped to become a doctor, and had attended lectures and studied medicine. "There is internal evidence to that effect."

Bettany had faith in her. They had been married for eight years, and he knew exactly what she was capable of.

Ward, Lock & Co. decided to publish the book, and a letter to the author was composed at the company headquarters in London's Salisbury Square. Among the steady stream of refusals, bringing joy to an aspiring author with a simple "Yes" was rather enjoyable.

Dear Sir,
    We have read your story and are pleased with it. We could not publish it this year as the market is flooded at present with cheap fiction, but if you do not object to its being held over till next year, we will give you £25 for the copyright.

Yours faithfully,
Ward, Lock & Co.

The author was not satisfied with the offer, replying that he wished to be paid royalties from future sales instead. No, unfortunately, no royalties would be paid. A one-off payment of twenty-five pounds was the publisher's final offer.

This unknown author, who, it turned out, was indeed a doctor, ought to be grateful for the chance to get his name on a book. Although, in fact, "book" might have been overstating it somewhat. It was the publisher's seasonal offering, *Beeton's Christmas Annual*, which was to be published in November 1887, for the twenty-eighth successive year. It cost one shilling, sold out within a fortnight, and after reading made an ideal fire starter.

The annual was padded out with two drawing-room plays, and a renowned illustrator had been commissioned to provide four illustrations to accompany the main feature, A. Conan Doyle's novel, *A Study in Scarlet*.

An advertisement was inserted in the industry magazine the *Bookseller*:

> This story will be found remarkable for the skilful presentation of a supremely ingenious detective, whose performances, while based on the most rational principles, outshine any hitherto depicted. In fact, every detective ought to read "A Study in Scarlet," as a most helpful means to his own advancement.

The publishers chose to draw particular attention to the book's lively scenes played out among the Mormons of Salt Lake City, in the United States. Detective novels were a relatively new genre and published mainly as cheap railway literature, so it was far safer to market the title as a swashbuckling adventure about people in peril in an exotic, threatening milieu. No one was to be left in any doubt when it came to the publisher's unparalleled expertise in identifying precisely what the readers wanted:

> The publishers have great satisfaction in assuring the Trade that no Annual for some years has equalled the one which they now offer for *naturalness, truth, skill, and exciting interest*. It is certain to be read, not

once, but twice by every reader; and the person who can take it up and
lay it down again unfinished must be one of those rare people who
are neither impressionable nor curious. "A Study in Scarlet" should be
the talk of every Christmas gathering throughout the land.

It was time for the readers to meet the world's first consulting detective, Sherlock Holmes.

Part 2
1888–1893

8

Sunnyside was a magnificent building, reminiscent of a great manor house, set in the Scottish countryside. A somewhat elderly man by the name of Charles Altamont Doyle was sitting on a bench outside. He was tall and ungainly, and his great wild beard dominated his appearance.

He raised his gaze from the sketchbook in his lap. He could hear someone nearby yelling and causing a commotion. It was probably some poor cretin.

With a shake of his head, Charles Doyle returned to the task in hand, drawing. His late father had been well known for his political cartoons, while Charles's brother, who had by now also passed away, had been responsible for giving *Punch* magazine its distinctive appearance. Artistic traits, then, ran in the family.

Doyle sat surrounded by a great garden. On a map, he was a couple of inches north of Dundee, a little way inland from Montrose. In the middle of that garden was Sunnyside. Eighty-seven windows were visible on this side of the house.

His sketchbook was filled with fairies: fairies and rose petals, fairies in wheat fields, a fairy holding an earthworm behind its back to protect it from a large magpie. But now the fairies would have to take a backseat. He had a commission, his first in quite some time.

He had been charged with creating six illustrations for a book. The first was to depict three men standing in a room studying a corpse. The man in the center was the story's main character, the detective Sherlock Holmes. He had drawn him as a tall, ungainly man with a great wild beard. One must, after all, be allowed some artistic license. The word RACHE was to be written on one wall. He had no idea why.

The work had been commissioned by his son Arthur. After the publication of the Christmas annual, the publishers were planning a separate edition in the form of a real book.

Charles Doyle did his best to keep abreast of his son's successes, but not much made it into the Scottish papers, which were all he had access to at Sunnyside. And, sadly, except when Mary sent parcels of Arthur's cast-off clothes, Charles had little contact with his wife; she was the one who always found out all the news about Arthur. That was just the way things were; there are some things beyond one's own control.

Charles had spent three years at Sunnyside, or, to give it its proper name, Montrose Royal Mental Hospital. His problem was the bottle. In the end it had affected his good sense. And now it was giving him epileptic seizures to boot—or, rather, the absence of alcohol was.

There were three hundred people living at Sunnyside. Some could afford to pay their own way and lived in great comfort. The others had a decent lifestyle too, if only they had been sufficiently sound of mind to realize it. This was not one of the old-fashioned asylums—which were more like workhouses or prisons—but was rather modern and well organized, which was all due to the director, Dr. James Howden.

Each year, Sunnyside was inspected by Scottish members of the Commissioners in Lunacy. Their praise was always high. Here things were far more peaceful than in the old type of asylum, and there was no call for any corporal punishment. Patients often participated in healthful physical work and other such pastimes, which brought them great joy, as well as picnics and long walks.

Charles Doyle was able to attend plays and concerts, performances by illusionists and dance troupes, and magic-lantern displays. There had even been a visit from the D'Oyly Carte Opera Company. He was a regular contributor to the institution's own magazine, the *Sunnyside Chronicle*, which, alongside reports of events at Sunnyside, featured patients' poetry, articles, and illustrations.

Much of the time, he felt very good. Other times he felt worse, much worse. On his arrival here from his previous institution—after yet another escape attempt in search of alcohol—he had apparently been unable to say how many children he had. There were seven, named, in descending order: Annette, Arthur, Lottie, Connie, Duff, Ida, and Dodo. It was not difficult to remember at all. And then there were two poor wretches who never got to grow up, but that was a long time ago.

Charles continued his sketches for the commissioned illustrations. Arthur had explained in his letter that one of them should depict the detective leaning back in an armchair, with his companion sitting at the desk next to him, and then a row of five young street urchins saluting them both. Charles Doyle's experience of children was limited; his recollections of the years spent with his own offspring were often rather vague. At its worst, the alcohol had such a tight grip on him that he spent months able only to crawl around on the floor.

He began drawing the boys' faces. Perhaps they should have some of his own children's features. He tried to recall their faces. He would draw Arthur perhaps, with his round cheeks and slightly droopy eyes.

One must, after all, be allowed some artistic license.

9

CONAN DOYLE WAS on his way to London. It was Friday, August 30, 1889, a sunny and perfectly warm day.

London was not a city he knew particularly well. While writing the novel about Sherlock Holmes he had had to make do with a map of the capital and a healthy dose of imagination. He had, on the other hand, even less knowledge of Utah and Salt Lake City. Attending a lecture on the Mormons had helped, and reading some articles in the *Nineteenth Century* magazine had too, and, after all, the *Encyclopaedia Britannica* had articles about most things. To be perfectly candid, he had borrowed some details in his Utah scenery from his great literary idol, Robert Louis Stevenson. That loan could of course always be considered a tribute to the popular author.

He had made his first visit to London at the age of fifteen, lodging with his Uncle Dicky—Charles's brother—and Aunt Annette. To ensure his aunt would recognize him on his arrival at Euston Station he had written ahead, explaining that he was five foot nine and fairly stout, and would be wearing dark clothes and, most important, a bright red woolen scarf.

From the station they traveled first by underground to Earls Court and then, for the last leg, by cab. He was to stay for three weeks. Uncle Dicky was able to borrow a theater box from his boss at *Punch* so that Arthur could see *Hamlet*; a young Henry Irving played the lead. They visited Westminster Abbey, the Crystal Palace, and the Tower of London, with all its instruments of torture. They went to the zoo, and best of all, they visited Madame Tussaud's, which at the time was still housed in cramped premises above the Baker Street Bazaar.

Conan Doyle had since visited London on three further occasions. His most recent visit had been the previous November, just two weeks after Jack the Ripper had mutilated his fifth victim. The purpose of that visit had been to discuss abridging the manuscript for his historical novel *Micah Clarke*, his greatest masterpiece to date. It received almost exclusively positive reviews, and the first edition of one thousand copies had soon sold out. Sales may have been helped by the letters he had sent to all his relatives and acquaintances, asking them to buy the book.

Now he was sitting on the train, once again bound for London on literary business. An American magazine editor wanted to buy him dinner.

The journey between Portsmouth Town station and London Victoria station took two hours and forty minutes. The train rolled through the countryside, probably at about sixty miles per hour, and called at Fratton, Havant, Chichester, and Horsham. Conan Doyle had studied Bradshaw's railway guide.

The Sherlock Holmes novel had been a one-off, as had *The Mystery of Cloomber*, a novel he had published at the end of 1888, which owed a lot to the sensational literature of the time, especially to Wilkie Collins. Neither of the books was in a genre that really appealed to him. He had decided, in fact, that his future lay in writing historical novels. It was less than two weeks after he had started work on his latest, *The White Company*, so he knew what would occupy his time during that autumn and the following spring. *Micah Clarke* had been set in the seventeenth century, but this time he was going to travel even further back, a few centuries earlier, to the Hundred Years' War and a brave company of archers.

His medical career had also taken a new course, and he had begun specializing in ophthalmology. He spent three hours a day at the eye hospital correcting astigmatism and ordering spectacles. The future for an ophthalmologist looked lucrative. Of course, one could make money treating disorders of the ear, but the eyes were a gold mine. Patients would grumble over the smallest sums to treat a throat complaint, or a pain in the chest, yet when it came to their eyes they were prepared to spend every last penny.

After his short shift at the hospital he would walk home. Everything had changed there too since the arrival of Mary Louise, who had turned seven months old two days earlier. She was named for her mother and grandmother, but she had not yet been formally baptized.

In a compartment on the train, Conan Doyle leaned back in his seat. It would soon be time for a pleasant dinner, and tomorrow he would return to Southsea to continue working on the historical novel. On the mantelpiece was a list detailing everything he was going to do over the next six months. It was nice to have a plan.

10

THE TABLE WAS laid for four. Three were already seated and waiting for the missing guest—the doctor.

The candelabra glittered, and the crockery, glass, and cutlery gleamed. The magnificent Renaissance-style marble pillars cast broad shadows over the walls' muted tones of cream, green, and gold. This was the dining room at the Langham Hotel, though one might easily have mistaken it for a conservatory, so strong was the scent from the hundreds of rare and exceptionally well-kept plants, purchased without the slightest regard to cost, neatly arranged along the row of large windows.

The Langham was an oasis for Americans in London. It just didn't get any more American than this, at least not in a hotel outside the United States itself. One could come and go, even as a nonresident, without having to explain to the porter where one came from, who one was, or indeed the reason for visiting. And here, some ninety-five feet above the Thames's high-water mark, the air was much healthier than down in the less salubrious area of Belgravia, where many hotels were located. The usual marketing trick was deployed: the area purportedly had low mortality rates.

When the hotel opened in 1865, in a ceremony led by the Prince of Wales, it went some way to addressing the great shortage of hotel rooms in the capital, and not least a shortage of rooms of a high standard. At the time, travel agent Thomas Cook considered only two hotels in the whole city adequate to accommodate his guests. For his wealthier clients, he was able to arrange lodgings in private homes.

Langham was the most modern hotel in London, featuring air-conditioning; hot and cold running water in each of the six hundred rooms, sourced from an artesian well deep beneath the hotel, from which the water was pumped up to great iron tanks in the domed tower; and last but by no means least, England's first hydraulic elevators, or "rising rooms" as they were known. There were electric lights, at first only in the entrance lobby and the courtyard, but soon extended throughout the building, and the hotel had its very own post and telegraph office.

Two decades after opening, the Langham had lost none of its luster.

One of the gentlemen at the table was Thomas P. Gill. Irish Home Rule had been Gill's great passion in life ever since his uncle had introduced him to the idea during his third year of study for an engineering degree in Dublin. Gill soon became a politician and journalist, just like his uncle. Everything had happened so fast. Despite his ongoing studies at Trinity College, he had been sent to the west of Ireland to write a series of articles on the effects of the famine. The articles' reputation quickly spread, and Gill became coeditor of a weekly newspaper that would later play a significant role in the struggle for Irish self-determination.

During a lull in his campaigning he went to the United States, where he traveled the country researching the widespread landlordism, which had also caught his attention at home in Ireland.

Now, at the age of thirty, he was himself in the ranks of the ruling class, elected to the House of Commons for the Irish constituency of South Louth.

Gill might have been well known in Parliamentary circles, but the man next to him was truly famous. His name was Oscar Wilde.

The preceding two years had transformed Wilde's life. He had secured a steady income, as editor of the *Woman's World*, and a life dominated by routine. Three days a week he would take the underground from Sloane Square to Charing Cross to spend an hour with his magazine colleagues. Beyond that, he had his obligations as a husband and father to attend to.

Gone were the heady days of the early 1880s, when Wilde's likeness featured regularly in *Punch*. Back then he had been a long-haired poet and aesthete with the whole city at his feet. He had been dedicated to self-promotion and spent many an hour sharpening witty retorts, which he would use when the opportunity arose. And arise it did; he made sure of that.

In 1882 Wilde went to America on a yearlong lecture tour and returned with $6,000 in his pocket.

Since then, journalism had become his vocation, and he was an undoubted success.

But enough was enough; the October issue of the *Woman's World* would be his last.

Where had the doctor got to? The host of the dinner, Joseph M. Stoddart, glanced down at his watch. He was a quarter of an hour late. Both the other guests at the table were becoming similarly impatient.

Something had to be done. Stoddart excused himself and made for the elevators. Earlier that day he had met with Conan Doyle, who had just arrived in London. He had brought the novelist doctor to the Langham Hotel and ensured that everything was to his liking. Conan Doyle had retired to his room for a short rest. Why had he still not joined them in the dining room?

It was months since Stoddart had arrived in Europe, on a voyage that combined business with pleasure, and he certainly had wanted to meet Conan Doyle. Indeed that was the reason for inviting the Portsmouth physician to be guest of honor at the evening's meal. At home in Philadelphia, Stoddart published *Lippincott's Monthly Magazine* and he was planning a British sister publication. He leaped at the chance to engage some of the country's authors.

Stoddart had entered the world of publishing at an early age and had turned out everything from operatic libretti to a book on Ireland's struggle for freedom. He even published an American edition of *Encyclopaedia Britannica*, which his competitors smeared as pirated.

Publishing was all a rather tricky business. The United States was still not among the signatories of the international convention agreed upon in Bern in 1886, which guaranteed an author ownership of the rights to his own work, even when it was published in other countries. As it stood, anyone in the United States could republish a book from the United Kingdom, or some other country, with no payment whatsoever to the author. At *Lippincott's Monthly Magazine*, however, Stoddart made sure foreign authors received payment. Among respectable publishers, that was the done thing.

It should be acknowledged that one of the reasons that Stoddart— like so many other American publishers—was busy trying to sign deals with British authors was to tie their hands in case of any changes to American copyright law. *Lippincott's* distinguished itself by publishing a new novel in each edition, hence its great interest in securing a steady supply of accomplished authors—even those authors who didn't have the good grace to turn up on time when invited to dinner.

Conan Doyle's clothes lay strewn across the room and in the middle of the chaos sat the man himself, looking thoroughly distraught, with uncombed hair and a wild stare.

"For heaven's sake man, what's wrong?" asked Stoddart.

"The button," Conan Doyle cried, between breaths. "The button, back one, the back button!"

He had managed to rip open the back buttonhole of his shirt, where the detached starched collar attaches to the neckline. Neither the button nor the collar could be affixed to the shirt. Stoddart realized the gravity of the situation and without hesitation brought Conan Doyle, the shirt, and the collar across the corridor to his own room. Before Conan Doyle knew what was happening a young housemaid was standing in front of him. Stoddart gave her hurried instructions, and the next time Conan Doyle looked up she had returned, equipped with a needle and thread; she quickly set about the task in hand.

At that moment Conan Doyle appeared perfectly helpless, as only a shirtless Englishman can.

The dinner proved to be a wonderful one for Conan Doyle. Stoddart turned out to be a capital fellow, but what else could he be after his earlier intervention? Gill, the Irishman, was very entertaining, even if Conan Doyle took a different view on the Irish question. But above all it was Oscar Wilde, that great proponent of aestheticism, whom Conan Doyle really admired. Stoddart had been involved in Wilde's American tour, so they had known each other for some years. Wilde's conversational skills left a lasting impression on Conan Doyle, and despite the fact that Wilde's intellect towered above everyone else's, he remained most adept at giving the impression of being interested in what each of them had to say. To Conan Doyle's great surprise, Wilde had read his novel *Micah Clarke*—and enjoyed it!

So there he was, in the extravagant dining hall in one of London's most luxurious hotels, in the company of an eminent American publisher, a controversial member of Parliament, and one of London's most famous cultural figures. And he felt that he somehow was their equal.

Conan Doyle lapped up every second of that evening. Oscar Wilde had such finesse, such tact, he wasn't at all one for monologues—since a man who engaged in such behavior could never be a true gentleman. He expressed himself with absolute precision, his humor was perfectly judged, and he underlined his spoken words with measured hand gestures. This last was a small trick but effective nonetheless.

All in all, it had been a golden evening for the thirty-year-old doctor from Portsmouth.

Joseph M. Stoddart too was very pleased. He had hoped to persuade both Conan Doyle and Wilde to write a forty-thousand-word novel each for publication in *Lippincott's*. The contract with Conan Doyle was drawn up that very same evening.

Stoddart hadn't actually known much about Conan Doyle in advance, despite the success in America of pirated editions of *Micah Clarke*. The English edition of *Lippincott's* was, however, to be published by Ward, Lock & Co., and when Stoddart had asked George Bettany and his wife to come up with names of potential novel writers, they had given Conan Doyle's.

Stoddart was even more convinced that Conan Doyle was his man after hearing the *Cornhill Magazine*'s James Payn mention his name. Payn had, admittedly, turned down both *A Study in Scarlet* and *Micah Clarke*, but he remained optimistic that Conan Doyle's talent would soon bear fruit.

At the beginning of December, Stoddart received a new manuscript written by Oscar Wilde in a style reminiscent of Hans Christian Andersen's "The Little Mermaid." It was far too short, at just fifteen thousand words. Stoddart needed at least twice that for *Lippincott's*, so he rejected it. Perhaps Wilde wasn't a novelist after all, never having written a long story before. The only problem was that in the previous issue the magazine had announced that it had secured a novel written by Oscar Wilde.

Two weeks later, Stoddart could once again breathe easily.

"I have invented a new story, which is better," Wilde wrote. "I am quite ready to set to work on it at once."

Stoddart was to receive it in March. There were no such difficulties with Conan Doyle. Just a few days after their meal, Stoddart received a letter from the doctor:

> As far as I can see my way at present, my story will either be called *The Sign of the Six* or *The Problem of the Sholtos*. You said you wanted a spicy title. I shall give Sherlock Holmes of *A Study in Scarlet* something else to unravel. I notice that everyone who has read the book wants to know more of that young man. Of course the new story will be entirely independent of *A Study in Scarlet* but as Sherlock Holmes & Dr Watson are introduced in both, I think that the sale of one might influence the other. I wish therefore that your firm would reprint *A Study* in America and give me some dollars for it.

By September 30, Conan Doyle had finished his story, which now went under the title *The Sign of the Four*. By late spring Oscar Wilde had also submitted his manuscript, entitled *The Picture of Dorian Gray*. Joseph M. Stoddart was more than pleased with his dinner initiative.

11

CONAN DOYLE'S NOVEL didn't require a great deal of editing; Stoddart essentially just adjusted some spellings to fit American conventions.

Conan Doyle had further developed his leading character. In the first book, Sherlock Holmes had been self-obsessed and constantly seeking attention. A few years older in the new novel, he had matured. Conan Doyle had matured too, and *The Sign of the Four* was a far more thought-out piece of work. With its stimulating setup—the lost treasure, the wooden-legged villain, the exotic links to India, and the climactic steamboat chase down the Thames—it was modern and a quick read yet still a strong adventure in the classic style.

Beyond that, *The Sign of the Four* was the novel that made Holmes a truly complex figure. Right at the start, the reader was confronted with the detective's intravenous use of a 7 percent cocaine solution, an attempt to deal with the boredom brought on by a dearth of challenging cases to solve. There was nothing illegal about his drug use, and Holmes would presumably have acquired his cocaine at the nearest Baker Street apothecary. Nevertheless, Dr. Watson was concerned about the potential effects of the drug on his companion's health.

Conan Doyle's stroke of genius was not in fact the creation of the detective, Sherlock Holmes, but rather that of his faithful companion, Dr. Watson. Through the use of this particular narrator, the author had devised a very clever way of describing the course of events in the Holmes stories.

Dr. Watson gave voice to the concerns of the reader, posing the questions the reader wanted to ask, while also acting as a sounding board for Holmes during the development of a case. In this way, Watson played a crucial role, representing the reader and the heart of the story, while the more eccentric and fascinating detective provided the brains of the pair. In this latest novel, Watson had become even more human, by virtue of falling in love, something the emotionally detached Holmes regarded with great suspicion.

The Sign of the Four was published in the February 1890 edition of *Lippincott's Monthly Magazine*, in both America and England. It would later be rechristened with the shorter title *The Sign of Four* in Conan Doyle's homeland. The author wrote to Stoddart in March, thanking him, and adding:

> By the way there is one very obvious mistake which must be corrected in book form—in the second chapter the letter is headed July 7th, and on almost the same page I talk of its being a September evening. Again in the first chapter the same post office is called Wigmore Street & Seymour Street. The first is correct.

Stoddart would try to remember this.

That same month he published the first American edition of *A Study in Scarlet*. Before long he received another letter from the author.

> I was so glad that *The Sign of Tom* as the *New York Herald* called it made some friends. It seemed to be fairly fortunate over here also. I did not see a single review out of 30 or 40, which my Press Agency sent me, which was not very kind, from "This is the best story I ever read in my life," of one priceless critic, down to more discriminating & less flattering reviews. It's a triumph ever to get a rise out of you shrewd people on the other side, but a Philadelphia tobacconist actually wrote to me under cover to you, to ask me where he could get a copy of the monograph in which Sherlock Holmes describes the difference in the ashes of 140 different kinds of tobacco. Rather funny, isn't it?

12

ARTHUR CONAN DOYLE quietly read the text he had written: "She was a blond young lady, small, dainty, well gloved, and dressed in the most perfect taste. There was, however, a plainness and simplicity about her costume which bore with it a suggestion of limited means."

The paragraph continued with his description of her appearance. Her plain dress; a somber grayish beige, and her face, which he found sweet and pleasant, despite her lack of classic beauty. He described her "singularly spiritual and sympathetic" blue eyes.

Conan Doyle was alone in the room. Touie was somewhere else in the little house. It was March 1890 and their daughter, Mary, had just turned one. He recalled his daughter's countless laughs at only a few weeks old; she seemed to laugh if he so much as looked at her. Clearly there was something irresistibly comical about his appearance.

He returned to his text: "My mind ran upon our late visitor—her smiles, the deep rich tones of her voice, the strange mystery which overhung her life. If she were seventeen at the time of her father's disappearance she must be seven-and-twenty now—a sweet age, when youth has lost its self-consciousness and become a little sobered by experience."

Twenty-seven years of age. That's how old Touie had been when they first met, in such tragic circumstances, and when they had traveled together to her brother Jack's funeral.

His eyes fell on the page once more. The text described a woman in a carriage, a woman bravely trying to negotiate the tumultuous events in her life. At her side sits a man with an apparently cool and reserved exterior, whose mind, however, is struggling with the feelings he has for her. He cannot let it show. He must not exploit the situation at this point, when she is weak and vulnerable.

Conan Doyle was very pleased that he had asked Touie to be his wife. Perhaps there was no glowing passion between them, but love comprises many parts, and Touie was as good a housewife and partner as a man could possibly desire.

After a while Conan Doyle put down the February edition of *Lippin-cott's Monthly Magazine*. Seeing *The Sign of the Four* in print brought him a pleasant feeling, and he had taken the opportunity to read it again. He wasn't usually satisfied with his own texts, but this one was quite good. More intricate than *A Study in Scarlet*, it was not complicated by the device of a prolonged flashback and was a far more cohesive story altogether. Holmes himself was in great form throughout—no longer merely a great thinking machine, he was now a learned man, and more human, too.

Conan Doyle was satisfied with his reference within the new novel to *A Study in Scarlet*—it might help sales of that book in the United States. His agreement with *Lippincott's* for *The Sign of the Four* was far better than the one with his English publishers, who had even moaned about the fee for his father's illustrations. After quite some time, they eventually relented, paying Charles Doyle five pounds, which Arthur forwarded to his mother, Mary. *Lippincott's*, on the other hand, paid £100 for the full American rights, including three months' rights in England, so that the novel could be serialized in a number of provincial newspapers there. He would find a publisher for the book format himself. And he would make sure to secure himself healthy royalties.

The author was certainly pleased with *The Sign of the Four*. Some members of his social circle would probably recognize his relationship with Touie when they read the love story that developed between Dr. Watson and the client, Miss Mary Morstan. Because surely it was Touie he'd described in those paragraphs. He had a habit of drawing inspiration from his surroundings.

Conan Doyle was content with many aspects of his life. His career as an author was going very well; the success was a result of his decision to move from short stories to the longer form. *Micah Clarke* had been reprinted several times and had sold a nearly unbelievable ten thousand copies. He had become a critics' favorite and was referred to as one of the country's leading authors of fiction. An anthology of his best short stories was about to be published. Even his old novel *The Firm of Girdlestone* had been rewritten and was soon to be released in book form. He had already received £240 for the serial rights. This was an enormous sum, which for once he invested, in stocks and shares, rather than spending it on day-to-day necessities.

Conan Doyle spent the spring and early summer finishing off the historical novel *The White Company*. He felt that it was his magnum opus. He would never be able to write better than this. On completing the story's last sentence he was so excited that he cried out—"That's done it!"—and flung his quill pen across the room, where it struck the wall, leaving a great black stain on the duck-egg-blue wallpaper. He felt so confident in himself and in his writing that he even signed a deal with a literary agent, who was to represent him.

The summer came and went. He strained his back playing cricket. He bought a secondhand Remington typewriter. Autumn arrived. He participated in lecture-society events, wrote a short story, and did his best to cure patients. Autumn was almost over. And life, quite simply, went on, according to its usual routine.

Until one day in the middle of November, when he was struck by an idea. The word "suddenly" can seldom have been used in a more appropriate context. He decided that he would travel to Berlin and attend a presentation of a supposed new cure for tuberculosis. This was by no means his specialty; he could not for the life of him explain why he wanted to go. He simply had to do it.

Within a matter of hours, his bag was packed; he said farewell to his wife and daughter and ensconced himself on the train for the journey to Berlin. It was like a real adventure. Conan Doyle was energized.

On the train to Berlin he happened to talk to a compatriot. He too was a doctor and on his way to the same event. His name was Malcolm Morris; a onetime country doctor, he was now a skin specialist with a practice at London's premier medical address, Harley Street.

The two talked well into the early hours of the morning. What Malcolm Morris had to say prompted Conan Doyle to move away from Southsea within a matter of weeks, sending his life into a whole new turn.

13

I<small>N</small> M<small>AY</small> 1891, in one of the many bookshops in central Stockholm, a postman arrived with the third delivery of the day. It comprised lots of book orders, as usual—the result of sustained advertising in the provincial press.

Thirty-year-old bookseller Viktor Josephson thumbed through the latest issue of the Swedish booksellers' journal, which contained the release dates for upcoming titles.

His eyes were drawn to a little advertisement, the contents of which left him somewhat ill at ease.

Three months earlier, in Leipzig, Germany, Bernhard Tauchnitz had taken on a new author.

Baron Tauchnitz had built a literary empire. He was barely twenty when, in 1837, he founded the publishing and printing business that bore his name. His plan was to republish the works of British and American authors and then sell these editions to English-speakers throughout Europe and elsewhere around the world. The only restriction to the rights Tauchnitz secured was that the books were not to be imported to the United Kingdom or any British colony. This stipulation was routinely ignored by Britons, who bought the cheap and convenient paperback editions while traveling on the Continent.

In 1869 Baron Tauchnitz had published his one-thousandth title. Over the years, he had gotten to know many of his authors. His closest British friend was Charles Dickens, who would always send him a manuscript early on—with the result that on more than one occasion the international edition of Dickens's book was released before the domestic version.

By February 1891 Baron Tauchnitz had reached book number 2,698. The author was new to him. Baron Tauchnitz did not take any risks, and rarely took on an author who had not completed at least three or even four books and also been well received by the critics. Thanks, though, to his network of contacts, and regular correspondence with many leading authors, Tauchnitz would often be tipped off about which new authors and books might be worth investing in. Number 2,698 was just such a book.

Viktor Josephson had started working in the book trade as a young man. Once he had garnered the necessary experience, he and a colleague, Ernst Nordin, decided to open their own bookshop. Nordin was two years older and the son of a bookseller. Like many others in the trade, he had spent a yearlong apprenticeship in Leipzig—the metropolis of the European book business. Their Stockholm shop, Nordin and Josephson, had immediately earned a reputation for being both attentively run and well organized.

The bookshop was not the only venture demanding their attention. Booksellers were often publishers too. They knew what customers wanted, and what the market was not currently offering, and they had access to the ultimate sales channel—their own store.

For Nordin and Josephson the publishing arm began on a small scale, in 1887, with the publication of academic papers, large and small, ranging from a treatise on glue and gluing to a massage handbook. A thirty-eight-page booklet depicting a future in which Sweden had lost the northern half of its territory to the giant in the east sold briskly and was reprinted several times. Russophobia was apparently widespread.

In spring 1891 they decided to expand their operations and begin publishing fiction. Nordin had come across the Tauchnitz publishing house during his time in Leipzig—it was the leading operator in the field after all. Nordin and Josephson made sure to import and sell Tauchnitz books in their shop.

Among the many novels by popular authors that were given this international distribution, they found book number 2,698, a novel about an English detective.

Meanwhile, in another part of the Swedish capital, Danish-born Ejnar Cohn, twenty-four, was working in his printing shop, which specialized in ephemera. It was located in the house in which he lived with his parents and two brothers, Axel and Olof. Axel was a stonemason, but he was seriously considering becoming a bird seller instead. Their father, Carl, was a bookkeeper. Several businesses coexisted under one roof, and yet another was added to the list, as Ejnar and his father started a publishing company. Their great coup was persuading one of Sweden's most popular authors to compile an anthology featuring fifteen of the country's most promising young writers. They had also decided to publish two foreign authors in translation, one of whom was from Great Britain.

Publishing translated works was not an expensive affair. The translator had to be paid, but no moneys were payable to the author, as long as he or she wasn't from Norway, Denmark, France, or Italy—Sweden had bilateral agreements with those countries. The Swedish publishers' union preferred to see Sweden remain outside the Bern Convention's international copyright agreement. Signing it would simply make publishing translated literature more expensive, and on the other side of the equation it would make no difference—Swedish writers were, according to the publishers, so seldom translated to other languages that it was hardly a great loss to them to forgo compensation from abroad.

Perhaps the Cohns had heard a rumor; maybe they knew exactly what their competitors Nordin and Josephson were planning, or else they had no idea—no matter. Ejnar Cohn and his father published a small advertisement in a trade journal:

> To avoid any collision, we hereby announce that *The Sign of Four* by A. Conan Doyle will shortly be published in translation by Ejnar Cohn's, Stockholm.

Publisher Viktor Josephson was somewhat perturbed by Ejnar Cohn's advertisement. How quickly could the translator deliver? How quickly could the printers come up with the books? Naturally, he wanted to be first out with his edition of *The Sign of Four*, not that it mattered, in legal terms, which of them came first. Both publishers had an equal right to the title. Whoever did make it first, though, could expect better sales.

★   ★   ★

Before long it would be clear who had made it first. In June 1891 came Ejnar Cohn's publication of the previously announced translation of *The Sign of Four*.

However, just as May drew to a close, Viktor Josephson and Ernst Nordin had managed to release their own edition.

Without realizing—and by only a matter of weeks—they had published the world's first translation of a Sherlock Holmes book.

14

CONAN DOYLE HAD received unexpected praise, and he could not get over it. The content of Dr. Lawson Tait's letter was, in many ways, sensational, and it turned everything upside down.

It was January 5, 1891, and he and Touie had arrived safely in Vienna. They had felt the biting cold only once or twice during their journey, but had not needed to wrap themselves up in the travel rugs. It was no worse than an ordinary frosty day in England, fortifying and healthful.

They had spent the day looking for a place to stay. The hotel was merely a temporary address while they inspected the city's lodging houses. A guesthouse on Universitätsstrasse appealed to them. It was situated close to both the university and the hospital. The landlady's name was Bomfort, and there were already fourteen residents, Americans and Englishmen, for the most part. The room they had chosen had a view over one of the main roads in the city. It was furnished with two funny little beds, and there were a desk for Conan Doyle's use, a couch, several chairs, and an ordinary white-tile stove. They would not be cold. The mealtimes were communal, and there appeared to be no shortage of food.

It was to cost four pounds per week, plus supplements for lighting, firewood, beer, and wine. It was rather expensive for their budget, but it was of great importance that he be able to sit and write.

Writing was not the main reason for their presence in Vienna. Conan Doyle was to retrain as an ophthalmologist, something he had been thinking about doing for more than two years, which now was to become a reality. This was part of the plan he had hatched with his colleague—now friend—Malcolm Morris, in the compartment on the train that had taken them across Europe to Berlin. Morris had convinced Conan Doyle to hesitate no longer.

The trip to Berlin had resulted, among other things, in an article for a medical journal, in which Conan Doyle had explained that he didn't believe in the new cure for tuberculosis that had been presented there.

After his return to England, everything had been dealt with very quickly: the winding up of the practice in Southsea, an interview in the *Portsmouth Evening News* about his new plans, a farewell party with thirty-four friends, the handing over of the almost two-year-old Mary to Touie's mother on the Isle of Wight, and then finally celebrating Christmas at his own mother's house, up north.

The list of things he would be doing over the next six months was removed from the mantelpiece to be completely rewritten.

He and Touie soon got used to their new daily routine. He had to be at the university by eight in the morning for Dr. Bergmeister's lecture, and a cup of coffee before he left home and another when he returned kept him warm and alert. He would then write until lunchtime, after which they would go for a walk, exploring the city. Another writing stint followed, until five, when he would rush off to the second lecture of the day. After dinner he would write for another couple of hours, before retiring for the night at half past ten.

Every Sunday they went to a café to drink a glass of beer and watch the passersby. They went ice-skating and dancing. At the guesthouse they would socialize with the other guests, albeit perhaps not too much with the globe-trotting American lady. Despite her friendly disposition, she was rather too vulgar.

Touie settled easily in Vienna, and her husband succeeded in writing copiously. He completed a few short stories, the sort of thing he could produce almost without thinking. Within a few weeks he had written a short novel and sold the serial rights, and then got down to work on a more ambitious historical novel. His latest venture in the genre, *The White Company*, had proved to be a great success and was being serialized in the *Cornhill Magazine*—at long last, James Payn had approved of one of his novels.

One thought still played on Conan Doyle's mind. He really ought to be able to exploit the monthly magazines more efficiently. As things were, he wrote both stand-alone short stories and novels, which were published in serial form. Suppose he were to write a series of short stories featuring a regular leading character: if such a character could be made sufficiently engaging, readers would remain loyal to that particular magazine. It was odd that no one had done it earlier.

He recalled again the letter from Dr. Lawson Tait. His thoughts were constantly returning to it.

Conan Doyle didn't know Tait, but he did know of him—he was the surgeon who had revolutionized abdominal surgery. In a letter to Conan Doyle, Tait had professed that both he and Lord Coleridge—John Coleridge, the lord chief justice!—were great admirers of *A Study in Scarlet* and *The Sign of Four*.

That both of these men, two of England's leading figures in their chosen fields, known as far away as America, would even have read this kind of literature was really quite remarkable. These editions were—it had to be said—cheap books, sold almost exclusively at railway stations, the kind of stories often referred to as shilling shockers or penny dreadfuls. Not only that, the two novels had hardly been great successes. And yet Dr. Lawson Tait and Lord Coleridge had somehow found them. What is more, they liked them! They had even gone to the trouble of writing to the author to inform him how much they liked them, and that they wanted to read more about this consulting detective Sherlock Holmes.

So it was settled then. He would write a series of six short stories about the same central figure. He didn't even need to invent the character.

Alexander Pollock Watt was a reserved man, with a very discreet manner. Originally from Glasgow, he was fifty-seven years old. He had an innate dignity about him and was deeply religious.

The number of writers in England who were not aware of the name A. P. Watt could probably have been counted on the fingers of one hand. His office, at 2 Paternoster Square, had played host to many of England's most significant authors in the decade since he had started his operation. It was in the first-floor office here that all the agreements were drawn up. These were contracts that enabled the most important magazines in Britain, Australia, the United States, and many other countries to access what was their lifeblood—short stories and serialized novels.

A. P. Watt was a literary agent—the first of his kind.

Watt's career path had begun while he was in the employment of his brother-in-law, a publisher. Watt had noted all the changes taking place in the world of publishing, in particular the increasing commercialization of literature. He saw how publishers were able to increase their revenues by exploiting new, untapped markets but also saw their failure to exploit countless other opportunities. Most publishers were active in both the book and the magazine sectors, and he saw that his brother-in-law's quality magazines were being squeezed out by the new illustrated weeklies—of which George Newnes's magazine *Tit-Bits*, first published in 1881, was a perfect example. A different format, design, and type of paper made these new periodicals cheaper to print and more popular with readers. These were magazines produced with the intention of entertaining their readership.

As George Newnes wrote, in a letter to his former associate W. T. Stead:

> There is one kind of journalism which directs the affairs of nations; it makes and unmakes cabinets; it upsets governments, builds up Navies and does many other great things. It is magnificent. This is your journalism. There is another kind of journalism, which has no such great ambitions. It is content to plod on, year after year, giving wholesome and harmless entertainment to crowds of hard-working people, craving for a little fun and amusement. It is quite humble and unpretentious. That is my journalism.

The competition from *Tit-Bits* and its ilk proved too much, and Watt's brother-in-law's magazine company had no choice but to conform to the new way of doing things and yield to the demand it had created among readers.

When A. P. Watt invented his own profession he already had great knowledge of the book and magazine market and had established a broad network of contacts. Ten years later, he was at the very center of the English literary industry, even if he, in his modesty, would never have put it in quite those words.

At first Watt had charged a flat fee for various tasks, such as writing a letter, sending a telegram, or drawing up a contract. This fee would often prove to be disproportionate to the amount of work he had put in. Instead, he began to apply the principles he had learned during his time as an advertising salesman for his brother-in-law. Under that system, his work was rewarded with a 10 percent share of any revenues resulting from the contracts he drew up.

As much as Watt sought to please his clients, he also understood the publishers' situation. He had indeed increased many authors' rates, but a good deal was not a good deal if no publisher was able to turn a profit.

This, then, was the man who had been Conan Doyle's literary agent for a few months. A manuscript from Conan Doyle had arrived at Watt's office with the morning post.

A. P. Watt read the tale, counted the number of words, and wrote back to his client:

> I am in receipt of yours of today's date and will take the story which has also arrived to the *Strand Magazine*, as none of the other periodicals can use more than 7000 words at the outside. I note that you propose to write a series, and that you will entrust the sale of it to us.

Over the years, Watt had acquired a good knowledge of the various periodicals and their editors' preferences and selection criteria, and as a result he always knew where to turn. He was also well aware of just what he could demand of the authors he represented. It wasn't unheard of for him to suggest alterations that might improve the stories and their salability.

Now he hoped to complete the chain by writing another letter, this time to the *Strand Magazine*.

Editor Herbert Greenhough Smith rushed—as much as a man of his unshakably calm temperament was capable of rushing—into his boss's office.

The *Strand Magazine*'s proprietor, George Newnes, was of course keen to find out what was going on. Greenhough Smith held a manuscript in his outstretched hand.

As Newnes read, thoughts flew around Greenhough Smith's head. This had to be the greatest short-story writer since Edgar Allan Poe. What a godsend to an editor jaded by wading through reams of impossible stuff—the ingenuity of plot, the clarity of style, the perfect art of telling a story!

His expressionless face, however, gave none of this away.

Newnes finished reading and nodded his approval.

This they would most certainly publish.

A few days earlier, in Vienna, Conan Doyle had pulled shut the guest-house door for the last time.

He was very pleased indeed with the Sherlock Holmes short story he was in the process of writing, a story in which the consulting private detective would find himself trumped by a woman, the adventuress Irene Adler. He would send it to A. P. Watt as soon as he was back in London.

The sojourn in Vienna had left its mark on the story. It was called "A Scandal in Bohemia"—after all, why not seize the chance to write about the northwestern corner of the Austro-Hungarian Empire while spending time in another part of the realm? As usual Conan Doyle enjoyed inserting small details from his own life into his stories. It might be a place-name from some relative's address, the subject of a conversation he had overheard, a book he had recently read, or simply a surname he had happened to notice.

Arthur Conan Doyle and his wife, Touie, thanked Frau Bomfort, their hostess at the guesthouse, and set about carrying their cases down the stairs. It was time to enact part two of the plan that he had decided upon in concert with his fellow medic Malcolm Morris.

15

B Y FRIDAY, APRIL 10, 1891, the second Sherlock Holmes short story, "A Case of Identity," had reached agent A. P. Watt, sent by Conan Doyle himself. Ten days had passed since Watt had received the first, which to his and his client's delight had been accepted by the *Strand Magazine*, the most widely circulated monthly magazine in Britain.

A week and a half later the third short story, "The Red-Headed League," was complete and lay on Watt's desk, ready to be sent on to *Strand* editor H. Greenhough Smith. Conan Doyle certainly wrote at a blistering pace, despite being simultaneously engaged in his career as an ophthalmologist in London. How did this man manage it all?

Another week or so later "The Boscombe Valley Mystery," the fourth of six promised short stories, reached the agency.

After that, not a word came from the prolific author.

Andrew Lang was seventeen when he first came to Saint Andrews, Scotland. Even though he spent a lot of time in London, Saint Andrews was the place he loved.

He loved lots of things in life. He loved his wife, Leonora. He loved being an author—the list detailing his books ran to over a page. He loved golf and fishing. And he loved fairy tales. Lang collected fairy tales from all over the world and, together with Leonora, translated them and compiled them into books.

One day in early 1889 Lang received a visit from S. S. McClure, who was visiting Europe and had taken a detour and gone up to Scotland. McClure was an American, born into poverty, who had resolutely and deliberately bettered himself. Some five years earlier, he had founded McClure Syndicate, a business based on buying up leading authors' short stories and novels and then selling them to newspapers across

America. At the time, this had been a completely new concept, but several competitors had since established similar enterprises.

In McClure's syndicate, the papers could rest assured that they had first refusal on short stories and serials, which were offered at very low prices. McClure and the authors made their money through the sheer volume of sales achieved.

The conversation between Andrew Lang and McClure touched on a wide range of subjects. Lang was a renowned literary critic, and McClure was by now a significant figure on the American literary scene, so they were not short of discussion topics. Lang was employed as, among other things, a literary advisor to a publisher, and it was in this role that he had recently read the *Micah Clarke* manuscript by an author named Conan Doyle. He had instructed the author to abridge the text, and they had even met for lunch at London's Savile Club. Conan Doyle had previously had a shilling shocker, what the Americans called a dime novel, published. The author was certainly one that McClure would be well advised to keep an eye on, on the syndicate's behalf.

Later, while McClure was standing at the station waiting for the train back to London, he caught sight of a book in one of the racks at the station. It was Conan Doyle's shilling shocker, *A Study in Scarlet.* He promptly bought a copy and read it.

A little more than two years had passed since that train journey. S. S. McClure was at his office in New York, and had just received a letter, dated April 14, from London's leading literary agent, a man with whom McClure often did business.

"I understand," wrote A. P. Watt, "that you are willing to give the sum of £50 (fifty pounds) for a series of six stories of a detective nature relating to the experience of a Mr. Sherlock Holmes."

Yes, of course! McClure had been waiting for this.

Samuel Sidney McClure generally had only one method of testing a story—namely, to see whether or not it appealed to him personally. He judged literature via his solar plexus rather than his brain. He needed to feel that the story grabbed something inside him. To avoid being overly influenced by external factors—such as being in an unusually good mood—he would read each story three times within a seven-day period. He had, on several occasions, missed his station when traveling home by train, so engrossed was he in a story he had already read twice that week.

When it came to the new Sherlock Holmes stories, he knew he would like them before he had even read them once.

A. P. Watt had negotiated a rate of four pounds per thousand words from the *Strand Magazine* to secure the British rights. This represented a significant increase from three pounds per thousand words, which was Conan Doyle's usual rate. Watt had already accepted a check for thirty-six pounds for the first short story, and had taken out his commission before sending the remainder on to Conan Doyle.

He had also informed Conan Doyle of the implications of America's new copyright law. After years of lobbying from British authors, among others, the United States had agreed that foreign authors' rights should also be protected by American law. This applied only to works published after the law took effect on July 1. So Watt made sure that the *Strand*, or indeed McClure, would not be publishing any short stories until July at the earliest.

Everything went according to plan.

His only concern was why the author had not yet contacted him with the fifth short story. It was now nearly the middle of May.

Herbert Greenhough Smith was in the editorial offices at the *Strand Magazine*, sitting at his imposing desk. It was here he would select and arrange the material for the magazine, under the supervision of the owner, George Newnes. Proofs and manuscripts filled the bookcases that surrounded him. A spare chair for any visitors was placed next to the desk, while an open fireplace provided warmth.

Loose leaves were strewn across the office. This was patently a room where work was done. Greenhough Smith stood up from his chair and walked over to the spot where W. H. J. Boot sat. Boot was the magazine's art editor.

The desk and other surfaces in Boot's corner were not dissimilar to those in Greenhough Smith's own side of the office, but in place of manuscripts were piles of illustrations, lithographs, India-paper proofs, pens, and paintbrushes. A large magnifying glass sat mounted in a wooden frame. The room was also furnished with a large chest with many numbered drawers, each one full of drawings.

Greenhough Smith wanted to consult Boot about suitable candidates to provide illustrations for Conan Doyle's six Sherlock Holmes stories. Each story called for between five and ten illustrations, and no spread was to be without one. George Newnes had invested in modern printing techniques, and the magazine was jolly well going to use them.

Greenhough Smith and Boot pondered the choice of illustrator for a while, riffling through the piles of sketches for inspiration.

Boot had a suggestion: that illustrator who had accompanied the expedition sent up the Nile to rescue the British army general Gordon in the Sudan, the one who worked for the *Illustrated London News*. Name of Paget, wasn't it? He would be just the man.

They decided to go ahead. The work on Conan Doyle's stories was proceeding swimmingly. The only thing puzzling them was the fact that A. P. Watt had so far delivered only four of the six promised stories.

Boot sat at his desk and wrote an order for the illustrations.

He addressed the envelope simply to "Mr. Paget."

16

Besides being his home and artist's studio, Sir Frederic Leighton's great brick-faced house was half statement of intent, half billboard. As chairman of the Royal Academy of Arts, and one of England's leading artists to boot, he understood the value of showcasing the classical and aesthetic artistic direction he promulgated.

His home's two-story Arab Hall, lined with mosaic tiles he had collected on trips to the Middle East, the calming indoor fountain, the large collection of artwork, and the musical soirees up in the artist's enormous studio—these things all combined to make Leighton's home an artist's palace known throughout London. It was just what he had hoped for when he began construction in the mid-1860s.

Leighton's private quarters within the house were, on the other hand, small and Spartan. After all, a bedroom is merely for sleeping in. He was sixty years old, unmarried, but had a wide circle of friends. A virtual colony had grown up around him; his part of Kensington was crawling with artists. There were eleven on Holland Park Road alone. The Pre-Raphaelite Val Prinsep was Leighton's next-door neighbor; Phil May, the *Punch* cartoonist, had recently moved in a few doors down the street; and four artists shared the studio space at number eleven.

And it was outside number eleven that a messenger boy stood waiting to deliver a note.

"Letter for Mr. Paget," the boy said.

"Is that for me?" one of the artists in the house asked. He always had to ask, just to make sure.

The messenger boy looked at him. Artists were a strange bunch. Yes, if he was Mr. Paget, then the letter was for him. He handed over the letter and disappeared just as quickly as he'd arrived.

Mr. Paget tore open the letter and read what Boot, of the *Strand Magazine*, had to say.

★   ★   ★

Something along those lines occurred the day Sidney Paget received
the order for the illustrations to accompany six new short stories by
A. Conan Doyle.

Sidney Paget was turning thirty-one that October. Among the Paget
siblings, three of the brothers had ended up being artists. At the age of
twenty-one Sidney had embarked upon six years of study at the Royal
Academy, winning several prizes along the way, and was expected to go
on to do great things. His oil paintings and watercolors were exhibited
early on at the Royal Academy's summer exhibition. He painted portraits, and landscapes too—waves whipping against fishing boats out
on the high seas and other panoramic scenes in which humans were
completely at the mercy of the forces of nature. And then he did lots
of work for newspapers, magazines, and books.

Prior to this, he had worked for the *Strand* on only four occasions. The market for magazines, however, was in a period of frenzied
growth, and Sidney Paget would receive more and more of these com-
missions. The rise of the magazines was the result of three factors:
the Education Act of 1870, which meant that far more people were
able to read; the reduced tariffs on the imports of newsprint paper;
and not least, the latest innovations in printing and binding, which had
increased the speed of production many times over. Furthermore, the
expansion of the railway network meant that more and more people
traveled by train to their workplace and were ripe to buy something
to read during the journey.

Paget was to produce ten illustrations for the first short story in
the series, "A Scandal in Bohemia." According to the manuscript, the
main character, Sherlock Holmes, was tall and thin. Sidney Paget was
not able to discern much more than that from the text, so he deployed
his usual method, drawing from a combination of imagination and
elements inspired by reality.

As luck would have it, Sidney Paget shared a studio with one of his
brothers, Walter. What could be simpler than getting Wal to model for
him for a moment? Sidney decided at that point that his brother in fact
had the perfect traits for an astute detective. Dr. Watson, meanwhile,
borrowed several features from one of his old friends from his student
days, who had become an architect.

Sidney Paget took out a stiff, white leaf, roughly six by eight inches. He would produce the illustration in monochrome, using a water-based technique.

He began sketching out the image in pencil. The tall, thin detective—with his brother Walter's profile—stood in front of the hearth, dressed in a morning jacket, waistcoat, and black-and-gray-striped trousers. Dr. Watson, sitting in an easy chair beside him, was still—since it was only a flying visit—wearing his overcoat. A glimpse of the medic's formal attire was just visible underneath: morning dress, a high, starched collar, and a cravat. This was the uniform of the urban middle classes: the epitome of style and professionalism.

Paget had Holmes standing, feet apart and with his hands in his trouser pockets, visibly self-assured. He then filled in the background with a light color wash and started painting the dark parts of the scene with black watercolor. He left it to dry for a while.

While it may well be the case that Paget was no Leighton, or even Val Prinsep, once he had added the final details, with sharp black and white strokes, the result was truly striking. By tilting the paper slightly and holding it up to the light, one could make out the exquisite pencil drawing on which the whole piece was built.

It was then up to the publisher to decide which engraver would be charged with reproducing this illustration. Some of the magazine's engravers could transform a beautiful work into something ugly and unrecognizable, while others had truly mastered the art of producing woodcuts. Paget, though, was hardened to such vagaries. Besides, he would be paid regardless of the engraver's talent, or lack of it. This time the fee was a little over twenty-six pounds for the ten illustrations.

Summer arrived in Kensington. Sidney Paget continued working on the illustrations for the Sherlock Holmes stories. Time was beginning to run out, as the publication of the stories was to start in the July issue. The *Strand Magazine* had decided to change the order in which the stories were to appear, which meant that Paget had to produce drawings for "The Red-Headed League" before those for "A Case of Identity," despite the fact that the former contained a reference to the latter.

Paget was paid just over thirty pounds for the ten illustrations for "The Red-Headed League." "A Case of Identity," being a little shorter, warranted only seven illustrations, which meant a fee of twenty-two pounds.

In the fourth story, "The Boscombe Valley Mystery," the author had described the detective as wearing a "close-fitting cloth cap" on the train when he and Watson headed out into the countryside. What could Conan Doyle possibly mean by that? It didn't matter; Paget knew what he himself liked to wear on jaunts out in the country. He decided that the detective's headgear was in fact a deerstalker—a cap with a peak at the front and the rear. Besides, it was rather fitting that Holmes should wear a hunting cap; he was hunting after all—albeit his quarry was criminals and not deer.

Naturally Holmes always wore a hat when he found himself out of doors; Paget would usually sketch a top hat, but occasionally he would get the urge to let Holmes wear something else entirely. He would, on the other hand, never depict Holmes wearing a deerstalker around London. Such wildly inappropriate headwear would be sported only by fools and recently arrived Americans.

The deerstalker wasn't the only effect that was actually Paget's own. Some of the furniture depicted in the illustrations could be found in his studio or at his home. In one of the illustrations accompanying "A Scandal in Bohemia," Holmes was to be dressed as a stable hand, so Paget clad the detective in a waistcoat that he had hanging in his own wardrobe, a blue-and-green-striped affair. He did take the liberty of adding an extra button, to make up for Holmes's taller stature.

Sidney Paget put down his brush. He glanced sharply over at his brother. His eyes then took on a misty glaze. Maybe he was thinking of Miss Edith Hounsfield, who had nursed him so tenderly after a riding accident out in the country the previous summer.

At the other end of the studio Walter Paget was also illustrating, for essentially the same employers. Publishers had mixed up the brothers on more than one occasion. When Walter Paget sent home his illustrations from the mission to free the hostages in the Sudan, the lummox of an engraver had even managed to add his brother Sidney's signature in the bottom corner.

So it was perhaps not so surprising that art editor W. H. J. Boot's letter, addressed simply to "Mr. Paget," had ended up with the wrong brother, Sidney instead of Walter.

Yet Walter had given Sherlock Holmes something after all: his appearance.

17

There was a reason literary agent A. P. Watt had not heard from his new client.

In a small flat on Montague Place, just around the corner from the British Museum, Conan Doyle lay confined to his bed. He had been struck down by a life-threatening influenza, the same type of ailment that his sister Annette, three years his senior, had caught the year before. She had been working as a governess in Portugal, sending home all of her wages to her mother to help the family to pay for their brother Duff's schooling. The influenza had claimed her life just when Conan Doyle's finances were improving and the family could have afforded to move her back home.

Annette had had two doctors call upon her, and Mary Doyle had traveled to Portugal to be at her daughter's side the last three days. By then Annette was so ill that she did not even recognize her own mother.

Conan Doyle was barely conscious. But he understood that his time had come.

He was wrong. The illness relinquished its grip. Eventually he recovered enough that he was able to write "The Five Orange Pips," the fifth Sherlock Holmes short story.

The final story, though, was going to have to wait. Conan Doyle had had an idea. During the worst period of his illness, the room around him had appeared almost to be filled with fog, and although his body was still weak, his head was perfectly clear. This meant that all he could do was think. He contemplated his new circumstances: how he would see patients in the morning, would spend the rest of the working day at the hospital, and only in the late evening would find time for writing. The tempo and the sheer volume of work would surely be the end of him. With each Sherlock Holmes story he had completed that spring, his health had deteriorated further.

Eventually, while still lying in his sickbed, Conan Doyle arrived at an important decision. His joy and relief at this were such that he wanted to throw something, as he often did at such moments. A towel on top of his quilt lay close to hand, and with strength he barely possessed, he flung the towel up toward the ceiling. Conan Doyle had, quite simply, decided to relinquish his medical career and concentrate solely on his writing. From then on, he vowed, he would live off the proceeds of his books, short stories, and articles. As for the cunning plan devised on the train to Berlin—a scheme in several stages that would give him a successful medical career in London—it would guide him no more.

As soon as he was able to get out of bed, Conan Doyle began consulting estate agents in the search for a property that would be more fitting for his little family, as well as a good base from which to launch his new full-time writing career. He wanted to get away from the city center, away from the noise and the unhealthy air, yet still be only a short train ride away, so that he could remain in easy reach of the country's literary hub.

He settled on the suburb of South Norwood, about six miles south of the River Thames. A redbrick house at 12 Tennison Road became the family's new home in the summer of 1891. Conan Doyle immediately joined the local cricket club, wrote a light satire about life in the suburbs, and once again took up his old hobby, photography.

In August that year he finally managed to send the sixth Sherlock Holmes short story to the expectant A. P. Watt.

In New York, syndicate owner S. S. McClure had a problem. The Sherlock Holmes tales were not at all popular among the editors of America's local press. Usually such syndicated stories came in at around five thousand words, but Conan Doyle's short stories, at around eight thousand or nine thousand words, took up far too much space. Sometimes the solution was to publish the stories in abbreviated versions. McClure had, however, paid for them and was utterly convinced of their quality, so he tirelessly continued supplying them to reluctant editors.

The *Strand Magazine*, on the other hand, had no such problems. The whole magazine was structured in such a way as to allow the inclusion of longer stories. Conan Doyle's work soon became popular with the readership, and once the magazine had published three or four stories, it tried to persuade the author to pen more, over and above the planned series of six. Not to put too fine a point on it, the magazine begged him. In the middle of October, Conan Doyle informed the *Strand* that, yes, he could be persuaded to produce another six stories—but demanded a payment of fifty pounds for each and every one, regardless of length.

Conan Doyle quite unexpectedly found himself in a situation where the offers were flooding in. He turned down the chance to write a serialized story in a major journal. Needless to say, he also said no to Ward, Lock & Co. when they asked him to write the foreword for a new edition of *A Study in Scarlet*—he had no intention of helping them out after their refusal to honor his request to earn royalties on his creation. He declined even to allow them to add a subtitle to the book—they wanted to include Sherlock Holmes's name, now that he had become so popular in such a short time.

The author's greatly increased demands to the *Strand Magazine* might also have been interpreted as a no. It was by no means certain that they would accept his terms.

But accept them they did, without so much as a pause for thought. H. Greenhough Smith could see the value of the Holmes stories. So Conan Doyle got straight to work on new ones. Within a week he had managed to finish both "The Blue Carbuncle" and "The Speckled Band." He did not anticipate any problems completing the remaining four. In a letter to his mother, he let it be known that he would be using the final story to kill off Sherlock Holmes, once and for all. Conan Doyle felt that the detective took time and creative energy away from other, better endeavors. Holmes had been useful in making his author famous, but that goal had now been reached.

Strangely enough, just a few years after Conan Doyle had abandoned short stories completely in order to get noticed at all, it was now the short-story form that made his name. When he wrote novels, his name was getting about, but it was only when he went back to short stories that he became quickly established as one of England's most successful and talked-about writers.

Twelve Tennison Road was a veritable writing factory. A relentless tapping could be heard through the open window. The author's twenty-three-year-old sister Connie had moved in with the family. Back when he had been a young doctor in Southsea, Conan Doyle had harried his mother to send his younger sister to live with him but without success. Like their sister Annette, Connie too had traveled to Portugal to work as a governess, but she was back now and was certainly earning her keep. Connie was tasked with typing up the Holmes short stories on the Remington typewriter from Conan Doyle's handwritten manuscripts. His plan was that his sister Lottie should also move down, so that he could dictate new stories to her while Connie typed away at the finished one. In that way, Conan Doyle would be able to double his productivity while resting his hands and his eyes. Many of his author friends had worn themselves out or been struck with writer's cramp in their working hand.

Conan Doyle was busy planning the final Holmes stories when he received a letter from his mother. She was furious. He was not to kill off Sherlock Holmes under any circumstances. Besides that command, she provided him with the bones of another Holmes story, about a woman with a rather particular hair color.

His mother's words won the day. He was even able to use the idea, which became "The Copper Beeches," the twelfth and, as far as Conan Doyle was concerned, concluding, Sherlock Holmes story. He finished writing it over Christmas 1891.

While the detective may have escaped with his life intact, as far as Conan Doyle was concerned, this was a farewell to Sherlock Holmes.

In the United States, S. S. McClure was delighted by the growing interest in Conan Doyle's detective stories among newspaper editors. Demand was increasing.

And at the *Strand Magazine*, Sherlock Holmes was certainly considered one of the most important features of the publication. In February 1892 the magazine wrote to Conan Doyle again with another request for even more Sherlock Holmes stories. The author responded with a demand for a total of £1,000 for a further twelve stories—a rate more than three times the fee he had been paid for the first ones.

The staff at the magazine perhaps did not realize that the author's huge demands were made in the hope that the *Strand Magazine* would turn him down.

Editor Greenhough Smith and his boss George Newnes had no need for a period of reflection. They accepted the demand. Sherlock Holmes was not finished yet.

18

No sooner had Conan Doyle's short stories been published than the first Sherlock Holmes parody emerged. Conan Doyle and his publishers could not have wished for a more resounding confirmation of his creation's instant success.

"My Evening with Sherlock Holmes" appeared in the *Speaker* at the end of November 1891. The short text described a dinner, which the anonymous author claimed to have attended with Conan Doyle and Sherlock Holmes, during which the anonymous source and Sherlock Holmes tried to trump each other with clever deductions. Neither Holmes nor Conan Doyle was directly mocked; this was more of an exaggerated version of the art of deduction. It was like a Sherlock Holmes scene, but in heavily concentrated form, which is how the tone, one of gentle parody, was achieved.

Something had certainly happened to the Sherlock Holmes stories when Conan Doyle took the detective from the novel to the short-story format—something that made the detective an easy target for satirists. The short stories were completely focused on a crime, and the solving of that crime; any subplots or background stories were rendered unnecessary. Increasingly, the stories revolved around Sherlock Holmes's detective specialty: powers of observation coupled with the art of deduction.

Most of Conan Doyle's stories followed a defined template. Usually they began with Sherlock Holmes and Dr. Watson each sitting in an easy chair in the flat at 221b Baker Street. A client would arrive and be received by the landlady, Mrs. Hudson. Sherlock Holmes would make quick deductions after observing small details about the person in question—something about his or her clothes, hands, or posture. Watson and the client would be astounded by his perceptive capacity, but only until he explained to them just how simple it had been to arrive at that conclusion. The client would then present his or her case, which was often a sequence of events so odd, or else seemingly insignificant, that the police would simply have laughed at it. On occasion it was in fact Scotland Yard that had referred the client to Sherlock Holmes. Once Holmes had taken on the case he would head out to begin his inquiries, sometimes alone, sometimes accompanied by Dr. Watson; these inquiries might take him all over London or indeed to the countryside beyond. Sometimes he would wear a disguise so convincing that not even Watson could recognize him. All that remained then was the solution, and the capture of the perpetrator. Holmes did not feel bound to hand over his captives to the police and thus would allow, often as not, the criminal to avoid the justice system altogether. His reasons for doing so tended to have varying degrees of moral justification. In the final scene Holmes explained to Watson exactly how he had arrived at the solution.

The short stories were not usually about murder. Theft, fraud, and even simple misunderstandings were more commonplace. It wasn't merely a series of brainteasers featuring a detective sitting in an armchair and working out just what had happened—quite the opposite in fact. Holmes and Watson were always out on adventures, some dangerous, others less so. This was also reflected in the story titles, which in unabridged form almost always began with the words "The Adventure of."

Even if it was the sense of adventure that captured readers' interest, it was the powers of deduction, and indeed the personality of Sherlock Holmes, that helped the stories stick out from the crowd of contemporary popular literature. The parodies would focus on these traits. During the course of 1892, the parodies flourished, with more and more appearing as the year went on. They were sometimes accompanied by the author's real name, and sometimes appeared under a pseudonym.

The author of "My Evening with Sherlock Holmes" was a mystery to Conan Doyle.

The year 1892 was just a few days old and Conan Doyle was invited to a dinner.

The men around the table were dubbed the "new humorists" in the British press. Even they had no idea why; they had no intention of revolting against any "old" humor.

The overwhelming majority of these writers were young men, and their natural habitat was soon to become the monthly periodical called the *Idler*. Like many other magazines of the time, it contained a mixture of short stories, serials, autobiographical pieces, interviews, travel writing, and book and theater reviews. But it was the humorous element that set it apart from its competitors. The tone was one of light satire, the humor quite risqué and very much of the moment.

Robert Barr, a Canadian who had been a London resident for some ten years, was the figure behind the magazine. Barr had chosen as his coeditor the author and journalist Jerome K. Jerome, who had made his name three years earlier with the novel *Three Men in a Boat*.

Jerome was an industrious character, yet his writings extolled the life of a daydreamer, above all in his collection of humorous essays *Idle Thoughts of an Idle Fellow*. Barr could not imagine a better colleague at the *Idler*. Jerome thought himself a rather dull person, and he was certainly shy, yet his humor had reached a large audience, making him an influential man. In the year following the publication of *Three Men in a Boat*, the number of registered private boats on the Thames increased by 50 percent, and the river became a major tourist attraction in its own right.

Even before Robert Barr established his magazine, many of his soon-to-be-colleagues socialized at the Idlers' Club, which would later lend its name to the publication. It was at such a dinner that Conan Doyle found out just who had parodied him so skillfully.

Since moving to London and deciding to make writing his living, Conan Doyle had begun exploring the social life on offer in the city. The Reform Club was one of the gentlemen's clubs he frequented, another being the Idlers'. He even played cricket on a team composed almost entirely of authors and journalists. None of the others really knew how the game was played, so any hope of scoring was laid firmly at Conan Doyle's feet.

The captain of the team made a rather unlikely cricketer. He was Scottish, around five feet tall, and acquainted with the rules of the game only theoretically. Fun was had in countless games played against the local team in the picturesque Surrey village of Shere. The cricket captain of limited stature was J. M. Barrie, who had latterly earned a reputation for his nostalgic writings on Scotland.

When Conan Doyle met him at a dinner with the Idlers, Barrie explained that he was the anonymous author responsible for parodying Conan Doyle in the *Speaker*.

★   ★   ★

The friendship between Conan Doyle and Barrie flourished in the spring of 1892. Barrie would stay with Conan Doyle on his visits to the capital, and Conan Doyle visited Barrie in Scotland. They pondered writing a book together. They also talked about plays. Barrie had started writing scripts, and that spring Conan Doyle wrote a one-act play for the great actor Henry Irving. After his manager read the script and was very enthusiastic Irving agreed to do the play.

Parodies of Sherlock Holmes continued to emerge. *Idler* founder Robert Barr attempted a parody of his friend Conan Doyle's stories in his magazine's May 1892 issue, finding the humor in Sherlock Holmes's improbable powers of deduction.

Conan Doyle did not really mind the parodies. On the contrary, he was quite fond of some of them and not only those written by personal friends. Later in the year, a local newspaper sent a story in which the author had used Sherlock Holmes as one of the main characters. Conan Doyle read it, emphatically pronounced it good, and gave it his blessing. Naturally, the newspaper played on this endorsement in its advertising of the short story.

The parodies of the detective had created a parallel Sherlock Holmes. This detective, even more so than Conan Doyle's version, was built upon the characteristics most associated with Holmes. Increasingly, people could be heard using "Sherlock Holmes" as a synonym for detective, or indeed for someone astute in general. Despite all kinds of protection from the copyright law, Conan Doyle's creation was no longer his alone.

Nevertheless, the original lived on, thanks to the mercy of his creator.

19

M ANY YEARS HAD passed since Joseph Bell had instructed a young
Conan Doyle up in Edinburgh. Bell remembered the tall, mustachioed lad well and followed his literary success from afar, just as he
had followed another former student, Robert Louis Stevenson, who
had published several best-selling books over the preceding decade and
become one of the world's most renowned authors.

Bell had been forced to give up his post as a surgeon before turning
fifty, since hospital rules prevented any doctor from remaining in the
position for more than fifteen years. Those responsible for the ordinance had presumably been seeking to avoid the prospect of elderly
surgeons, yet owing to the fact that Bell had achieved the position
much earlier than might be expected, he was still very much at the
peak of his powers.

He missed those days at the hospital. Equally, his former colleagues
missed him. A long list of nurses who had worked with Bell over the
years, including Florence Nightingale, organized a collection, raising
enough money to send him a beautiful oak desk, with matching chair, as
well as writing materials, paperweights, and a pair of silver candlesticks.

Soon enough, though, Bell found himself occupied again. He became
a consulting surgeon at the infirmary, and the children's hospital
employed him as head surgeon. The reason for this latter appointment
was his exceedingly good manner with children; he truly understood
them and was greatly respected by their parents.

Bell was fifty-five years old when, one day in 1892, he was reading
the May issue of the *Bookman*. He surely never imagined that his life
would take another significant turn once his formal working life had
come to an end. He was a famous figure on the streets of Edinburgh
and could often be seen walking, having left the horse and carriage at
home. Still, he was not looking for any more recognition than that.

As Bell read the interview with his former student he was indeed surprised. Conan Doyle did not mention him directly, but when he told the interviewer about the inspiration for the Sherlock Holmes character, he explained that it was a professor of medicine at the University of Edinburgh—a professor with the ability to diagnose patients after only the most cursory of observations.

Bell sat at his beautiful oak desk and wrote a letter to Conan Doyle. They had exchanged letters earlier that spring, so he knew the address.

Might it somehow be possible, Bell wondered, that the person referred to in the interview was in fact Bell himself?

Conan Doyle immediately wrote a reply.

> My dear Bell,
>
> It is most certainly to you that I owe Sherlock Holmes, and though in the stories I have the advantage of being able to place him in all sorts of dramatic positions, I do not think that his analytical work is in the least an exaggeration of some of the effects which I have seen you produce in the out-patient ward.

Bell was taken with the Sherlock Holmes stories and certainly had nothing against being the model for the master detective. Conan Doyle even expressed his desire to include a dedication to Bell in the upcoming collection of the first twelve short stories, to be published as *The Adventures of Sherlock Holmes*. That too, was acceptable. And the professor provided the author with a photograph of himself, ahead of an interview the *Strand Magazine* was about to conduct with Conan Doyle.

When journalist Harry How arrived at 12 Tennison Road, he had no idea of the revelation that awaited him. Conan Doyle had begun to lift the shroud concerning the real-life inspiration for Sherlock Holmes, but in the interview that followed he went as far as to mention Joseph Bell by name.

Conan Doyle felt almost guilty about having named Bell, despite the surgeon's having agreed to it. Bell would probably be subjected to the great numbers of correspondents who assumed that Conan Doyle could solve crimes just as effectively as Holmes himself. The young man from Glasgow would surely be in touch, as would the American lady with a curved spine, the Liverpool merchant who "burns to know who Jack the Ripper is," and of course the many folks who believe their neighbors are starving maiden aunts to death in hermetically sealed attics.

That worry aside, the interview went well. They talked about Conan Doyle's sporting prowess—in football, tennis, bowls, and cricket—and Conan Doyle showed off the large tricycle on which he and his wife covered so many miles. Harry How found Conan Doyle's wife charming—at least that was the opinion he expressed in the final article. Did it look as though she might be pregnant again? Their daughter Mary was by now almost three and a half; a sibling would surely complete their domestic bliss. Needless to say, there would be no mention of his suspicions about pregnancy in the published article.

Harry How was given a guided tour of the Conan Doyle home. In the study hung paintings by the author's father, while the mantelpiece was home to a signed portrait of J. M. Barrie and a sketch by Conan Doyle's grandfather depicting a six-year-old Queen Victoria as she rode through Hyde Park in a carriage.

The journalist and his interviewee took afternoon tea, served in the parlor by Louisa Conan Doyle. They each held a cigar as they took their seats in the study and talked about how Conan Doyle's writing had begun in his youth and about the lectures by Joseph Bell. They then slipped into a discussion on Conan Doyle's favorite subject—his historical novels.

After a while Harry How managed to steer the author back to Sherlock Holmes, which was what the *Strand*'s readers really wanted to know more about. Conan Doyle revealed that he normally started the process of writing by coming up with the ending. The art then lay in writing his way to the end while managing to conceal the finale from the reader. Each short story took a week to complete, and the ideas came to him in all manner of situations—when he was out walking or cycling or playing cricket or tennis. His working day started with a writing session between breakfast and lunch, and he would sit down to write again from five until eight in the evening. He would usually manage three thousand words a day.

Harry How moved quickly when he got back to his office. He wrote to Bell straightaway, asking what those lectures Conan Doyle had attended had really been like. Bell responded, explaining his methods—how he taught his students the power of observation and the art of deduction.

Harry How liked Bell's letter so much that he decided to publish it in its entirety in the August edition of the *Strand Magazine*.

That was how the general public started to associate Joseph Bell with Sherlock Holmes.

Many probably believed that he *was* in fact Sherlock Holmes.

20

CONAN DOYLE'S EDITOR at the *Strand Magazine*, H. Greenhough Smith, was a tall, thin man. His strawberry-blond mustache was perfectly matched by the freckles on his pale skin. He observed the world through rimless pince-nez. That his expressionless face made him a first-class poker player was no surprise to anyone.

Each morning Greenhough Smith would stroll from his home in Queen Anne's Mansions, London's tallest privately owned building, the construction of which blocked Queen Victoria's view of the Houses of Parliament from Buckingham Palace. She had not been amused, but her protests were to no avail, since there were at the time no restrictions on building heights.

The editor would take a diagonal path through Saint James's Park, crossing the bridge over the lake with its resident swans; emerging on the north side of the park, the Mall; and continuing through Admiralty Arch and on toward Trafalgar Square. After that only the stroll along the Strand remained, until he reached the left onto Southampton Street.

On the right side of Southampton Street, just south of Covent Garden, was a wide building of red and white brick, the home to all of George Newnes's publications. It stretched right back to the next street, where the goods entrances were located. The deliveries of paper and the collection of newly printed issues made the back entrance a hive of activity throughout the day.

If one peered in through the large windows to the right of the entrance on Southampton Street, one could, with a little luck, or if it was a Thursday, witness the packing of the latest issues of *Tit-Bits*, *Million*—complete with color illustrations!—and the *Strand Magazine*, and maybe even some of the hardcover books Newnes also published.

The very first edition of the *Strand* had sold an incredible three hundred and fifty thousand copies. That was two and a half years ago, and the print run had been extended considerably, thanks in no small measure to the Sherlock Holmes stories. Greenhough Smith was pleased that he had agreed to Conan Doyle's somewhat inflated fee for a further twelve stories. They had been featured in every edition since December 1892, and now, in August 1893, the idea of the *Strand Magazine* without Sherlock Holmes was almost inconceivable. By this point Conan Doyle had already said that the intrigues were running out. But that was probably nothing to worry about. Very few authors in England were as accomplished at writing short stories as Conan Doyle.

Huge volumes of the magazine were printed each month, and packing and sorting them for delivery to the railway stations across London, and on to the rest of the country, were a time-consuming process.

To the left of the entrance was the countinghouse, a spacious room that breathed mahogany. This was as businesslike as could be, an impression reinforced by the sight of a very large double-door safe and heavy accounting ledgers.

To reach the first floor, one could take the stairs or the lift. It was there that George Newnes and his secretary sat, and that the editorial assistants for *Tit-Bits* gathered, in the White Room, as deadlines drew near. The art gallery was just across the corridor, comprising two rooms full of illustrations from the company's various titles; it was even open to the public. The room next door housed the editorial team for *Million*.

Two flights up sat Greenhough Smith and picture editor Boot of the *Strand Magazine*. One summer's day, Greenhough Smith sat working in his shirtsleeves, surrounded by galley proofs and articles. "You could tell that he loved the job," a colleague observed. "You also knew that he would have resigned rather than admit it."

This floor was also home to the two gents responsible for editing *Tit-Bits*, as well as Harry How, a journalist for several of Newnes's magazines.

At the opposite end, the composing room was visible. A virtual forest of electric lights hung above the small army of typesetters and the double cases in front of each of them. The upper case held capital letters, the lower the small letters. The most frequently used letters were kept closest to hand. It was here that an article by Harry How or another exciting Conan Doyle short story would emerge, letter by letter.

The resulting galley would then be run through a hand press, producing a proof, and it was these proofs that filled Greenhough Smith's room. He would send them on to the author, for a final approval. When all the errors had been corrected, and all the illustrations rendered the correct size—no small task—the type and the illustration-block would be fixed in iron frames, making pages, which were ready for the next stage of the process.

On the top floor lay the dirtiest workshop in the building, the electrotyping department, with its array of twenty-two machines. The dirt was graphite dust, which, while not dangerous, found its way onto every conceivable surface. The graphite was crucial to several of the stages that followed: the production of a wax mold, the electrolyzing bath to which copper was added, and finally the production of the printing plate itself. This was carefully scrutinized, and if the slightest imperfection was found, the team would restart the whole process from scratch.

The printing plates were then transported down to the cellar, where the *Strand Magazine*'s three printing presses were located. The first was the only press in Europe capable of printing sixty-four pages of illustrated copy in a single revolution; the second press could not only print but also fold the sheets as required; and the third was used mainly for precision work.

After the magazines were bound—at a rate of several hundred copies per minute—they were ready for distribution. Nearly fifty people were employed in the ground-floor locale, where passersby could observe them through the windows. One hundred and fourteen tons of the *Strand Magazine* were to be shipped every month.

Up in Greenhough Smith's office, the noise of the printing presses wasn't quite as noticeable as it was farther below, which was just as well when concentration was required.

His work was crucially important to the magazine, even if he himself would be loath to say as much. It was in fact he who had suggested the idea of the *Strand* to George Newnes. This happened in the wake of an aborted magazine project that Newnes had abandoned after recruiting a full editorial team. Newnes had followed the development of American magazines, so Greenhough Smith's idea had been well received. It would include lots of illustrations, and it would use short stories, not just serializations of novels, as was common in most other magazines. These would be interspersed with exciting articles across 112 pages of print monthly.

That the venture was a success was soon obvious. The *Strand Magazine* focused on the educated middle-class reader, a notch above the *Tit-Bits* readership, and much of the content also appealed to readers whose social status was higher still.

The authors employed at first were generally not terribly well known, even if the magazine tried to give the impression they were. Above all, Greenhough Smith wanted good-quality, readable stories, suitable for their intended readership. The early content was aimed primarily at male readers: thrilling detective stories, gripping tales, short stories translated from French and Russian, articles about veterinary hospitals or a night with the Thames Police, and a regular feature with portraits of celebrities at different times of their lives. Even reading material for children was included. Two and a half years later the composition was essentially unchanged.

The writers themselves appreciated the *Strand Magazine*. Normally, when working for other magazines, they would be paid upon publication. Yet the *Strand* paid on submission of the text—one of Greenhough Smith's absolute rules. He also preferred to make quick decisions. Either he accepted the text or else he dismissed it immediately. No author would be made to wait.

On this particular August day, however, it wasn't a rejection that preyed on Greenhough Smith's mind. A missive had arrived from Conan Doyle, and Greenhough Smith realized that the pages of the *Strand Magazine* would never be quite the same again.

He was holding in his hand the last Sherlock Holmes story—unequivocally the last, ever.

21

CONAN DOYLE STARED out across the waves of the North Sea. There was no turning back. His decision was final.

Sherlock Holmes must die.

Conan Doyle no longer wished to be associated with his popular detective. His literary reputation was at stake.

In April 1893 he wrote to his mother, explaining that he was halfway through the final Sherlock Holmes story, in which Holmes disappears, never to return. He was sick of hearing the name Sherlock Holmes. Word had reached him that Holmes was doing very well in America, so that money ought to be able to finance other activities for a while.

This time he would not let his mother persuade him. No fee, no matter how high, would persuade him to continue with Holmes.

Fortunately, he had the support of his friends. Not least among these was J. M. Barrie, who lived in Scotland, but with whom Conan Doyle tried to meet regularly; they played cricket and recently Conan Doyle had helped Barrie to compose the libretto for a comic opera, which was to be performed in May. It was Barrie who had been sitting beside him on the beach at Aldeburgh, in Suffolk, when he realized that Sherlock Holmes must die.

By now Conan Doyle had a whole list of author friends, people he might easily have turned to, who would understand his decision. Brothers-in-arms, they could put themselves in his shoes. Had he had even the slightest of doubts, he might have talked to Jerome K. Jerome, who was himself increasingly associated with a single work.

Jerome had become a close friend and had even joined Conan Doyle and a few of his family members on a summer holiday in Norway the previous year. Conan Doyle had attempted to learn to speak Norwegian, practicing his newfound skills at every opportunity. This interest did have its risks, a fact made plain when they met a Norwegian at a cottage high in the mountains. Conan Doyle and the man spoke to each other, but on their departure they realized that Conan Doyle had inadvertently given away the pony that was pulling their coach. After that attempt he barely spoke Norwegian at all.

So Conan Doyle had no shortage of friends. And the hard part wasn't in fact deciding to kill Holmes but rather the short story itself, the writing of which was no walk in the park. How would it end? Something was missing: something fateful, something irrevocable.

Sidney Paget worked hard to deliver seven to eight illustrations a month to W. H. J. Boot, the art editor at the *Strand Magazine*. On June 1 Paget took a well-earned break—it was, after all, the day of his marriage to his beloved, Edith Hounsfield.

At breakfast, he opened one of the wedding gifts that had arrived. Inside was a beautiful silver cigarette case, engraved with the words "From Sherlock Holmes, 1893." He realized at once who the sender was: an author with whom he had had the pleasure of working for over two years. Paget wrote in his diary that he could not imagine a more delightful present.

In his mind's eye, the author had seen Holmes as rather less attractive, with an even more pronounced hook to his nose, his eyes more closely set. Instead, he'd been given the rather more prepossessing features of Sidney's brother Walter Paget, which the author seemed rather pleased about. As early as the summer of 1891, editors Greenhough Smith and Boot had conveyed the author's praise to Paget.

As for Walter, yes, he did tend to get recognized from Sidney's illustrations. While attending a concert at London's Bechstein Hall, he had heard a woman say, "Look, there's Sherlock Holmes!" Such was the status the stories had achieved.

It would be the end of the summer before Conan Doyle came up with the solution. A man like Sherlock Holmes cannot simply die from a pinprick or a nasty flu; he must be disposed of violently, with great drama.

At the same time, Conan Doyle was preparing for a life in which he would be occupied by other work. The foray into Gilbert and Sullivan–style opera had been a failure for him and Barrie; their play, *Jane Annie*, had run for less than two months—and some critics had opined that even that was far too long. It was at this time that an actress who wanted to put Sherlock Holmes on the stage approached Conan Doyle. He said no. He was of the opinion that Holmes's deductions and reasoning would be all too tedious onstage.

It was plays, and lectures, that he really wanted to concentrate on. Although the former hadn't gone entirely according to plan, the latter still held promise. Conan Doyle decided to go on tour that autumn, lecturing about the well-known English novelist George Meredith. That author, now elderly, had long been a role model for Conan Doyle; by the fourth short story about Holmes he had had the detective mention Meredith's name. By then Sherlock Holmes had become a far more cultivated and literary person than he had been in the first novel.

Conan Doyle also planned a short lecturing tour to Switzerland. Touie was to accompany him, but Mary, four, and their son, Kingsley, born the previous November, would stay with Touie's mother.

They reached Lucerne at the beginning of August. After a few days lecturing, Conan Doyle and his wife, along with a few others, set off on a long hike in the mountains. All Conan Doyle could think of was killing off Sherlock Holmes. His companions on the trip did their best to help him. Perhaps Holmes could come here, to Switzerland, and fall down a ravine, they suggested.

After a while they reached the beautiful Hasli Valley, and Meiringen, a little village that had twice been damaged by fire in recent years but was being rebuilt to attract tourists. An inn nestled some way up in the mountains was to be the traveling party's next stop.

They heard the sound at some distance, a noise that could be caused only by nature at its most powerful. The water thundered over a ledge and down into a huge cauldron, giving rise to a great cloud of water vapor. A narrow trail wound upward, right alongside the abyss, and anyone who dared look down would not be able to make out the bottom. The noise was an absolutely deafening din.

The memory of that torrent, the Reichenbach Falls, etched itself in Conan Doyle's mind.

No sooner was Conan Doyle back home at 12 Tennison Road than he quickly set to work on the piece. He had decided where Holmes was to meet his end. All that remained was to lure him there. This would require a degree of inventiveness, and the invention was Professor Moriarty.

If anyone were to challenge, let alone break, England's leading detective, then it must surely be England's leading criminal. What would such a person be like? He would need to be as intelligent as Holmes, the kind of chess player capable of planning countless moves ahead. A man of such intelligence would never risk being apprehended by Scotland Yard. He would never be associated with minor crimes. He must, therefore, be at the head of a criminal organization with wide-reaching branches. He has a respectable facade, in this case as a professor of mathematics with a particular aptitude in the field of analytical reasoning. The police, naturally, have never heard of him. Sherlock Holmes, however, has him in his sights and is threatening to uncover the whole organization. This could not lead to anything other than a life-and-death struggle.

For George Newnes, owner of the *Strand Magazine*, Holmes's imminent death was a terrifying prospect. It was to occur in four issues' time, hopefully without any premature leaks. Newnes somehow had to secure a future for the magazine without Sherlock Holmes, as impossible as that seemed. He felt responsible not only to his readers but also to his shareholders. Among the latter, ironically, was Arthur Conan Doyle.

By a month later the news had leaked. A daily newspaper printed a short announcement revealing that Conan Doyle was to kill off his detective. The identity of the article's author was not revealed, nor was the source. Just a few days earlier, however, Conan Doyle had attended the wedding of his sister Connie and journalist Willie Hornung. It was not inconceivable that Conan Doyle had told his friends there that he was, finally, free. They all knew one another—most of them played on Barrie's cricket team—so the rumor would have quickly spread.

Newnes wasn't the only one for whom Sherlock Holmes had assumed great importance. In a few short years, the fictional detective had become a famous name in many places around the world. A judge in the South African city of Pietermaritzburg told local police that they would be well advised to immerse themselves in the Sherlock Holmes stories in order to improve their success in following leads.

Back in London, two actors were busy writing a single-act performance to be staged at the Court Theatre that autumn; it was a satire about the events of the year, with Sherlock Holmes and Dr. Watson as the main characters. It emerged that another theater entrepreneur planned to stage a four-act play about Sherlock Holmes, which was set to open after Christmas.

The murder of a butcher's wife in the seaside town of Ramsgate hit the headlines. Private individuals asked Conan Doyle for help. The newspapers asked: Where is Sherlock Holmes? Will the police really be able to solve this case on their own? The same questions arose in the aftermath of such sensational events as the Hampton Rocks mystery, the Bathgate murders, and the trial of the Dutchman accused of murdering both his wives. Sherlock Holmes was needed more than ever. The gap between fact and fiction had rarely been so small.

In an Edinburgh courtroom, Joseph Bell had been called as an expert witness regarding the Ardlamont mystery, which revolved around a suspected murder and a case of insurance fraud. Reams of reports on the story filled the newspapers, never failing to name Joseph Bell as the original inspiration for Sherlock Holmes. Eventually he was so tied to that name there was no longer the need for any explanation. The journalists in the gallery waited for the real Sherlock Holmes to give his testimony. First, though, Bell's colleague, a renowned ballistics expert, was called to the witness box. Inevitably, the waiting press corps loved him, too. Bell's colleague's name was—by sheer coincidence— Dr. Watson.

For Conan Doyle, Sherlock Holmes was no longer important; in fact, he was scarcely even concerned about writing. That autumn, darkness had come very quickly. On the couple's return from Switzerland, Touie had complained of an incessant cough and pain on one side. Her symptoms soon got worse, and the doctor diagnosed consumption. She wasn't given long to live. Conan Doyle had to quickly draw up plans to ensure her as healthy an environment as possible. The mountain air in the Alpine resort of Davos would be just the thing.

Meanwhile, in a Scottish mental hospital, a man of about sixty unexpectedly rose from his bed to hand the attending doctor a blank sheet of paper. The man explained that the sheet contained gold dust, which he had managed to collect from the rays of sunshine that had found their way to his bed. He was most grateful for the doctor's services. A week later, Charles Altamont Doyle suffered a fit during the night and died. Arthur Conan Doyle was now the head of his family.

In the second week of December 1893, more than one hundred tons' worth of the year's final issue of the *Strand Magazine* was transported to railway stations near and far. The main draw was "The Final Problem," the last Sherlock Holmes story, in which the master detective pits his wits against Professor Moriarty—"the Napoleon of crime"—and in which both meet a grisly end by the Reichenbach Falls in Switzerland.

The response was immediate. One woman who wrote to Conan Doyle began her letter with "You Brute!" Many readers were brought to tears. Twenty thousand canceled their subscriptions. The Prince of Wales, it was said, was completely distraught.

Rumor had it that young men in the City tied crepe bands around their hats. Surely that could not be true. Sherlock Holmes was, after all, just a fictional character—how could people regard him as anything else?

Conan Doyle couldn't for the life of him understand the reaction. He was completely unfazed by what he had done. Sherlock Holmes was his invention, and he had the right to do with him as he pleased. At last, he thought, there would be no more talk of the detective.

For Conan Doyle, one simple thing mattered. Finally, Sherlock Holmes was dead!

Part 3

1897–1930

24

22

THE GROUND SHOOK under the hooves of the galloping horses. Over ditches and hedges and through the English countryside they thundered. Ahead of them, the slathering hounds could be heard as they chased down the elusive fox.

There were almost forty men on horseback, all wearing scarlet or black coats depending on their role in the hunt. Some stayed close to the hounds, others formed small groups at the fringes of the pack, and others still rode some distance away, hoping for the fox to dart off in their direction.

Lord Leconfield's hunt took place six days a week for the duration of the season. Some days were absolutely perfect, with no wind to blow away the scent, no rain to wash it away, only a crisp December damp that captured the scent and made it easy to trace.

Sidney Paget had arrived in Hindhead, Surrey, the previous day. He was no stranger to horses, and even had experience with them in the most unfortunate of circumstances. It was, after all, a riding accident that had brought him and his wife together all those years previously. He had depicted the odd hunt over the years. This, though, was his first fox hunt with Arthur Conan Doyle.

The author himself was new to the business. Who would have thought, two years earlier, that he would be spending his days fox hunting? When Conan Doyle put his mind to something, it tended to consume all his spare time. One of his recent interests was teaching himself to play the banjo, at which he would spend hours at a time. Now, though, musicianship was far from his thoughts. The only thing on his mind was the hunt for the fox.

The hunters rode across fields and through small woods. The woods were sparser than they used to be, at least according to the old hands on the hunt. The old fellows would gladly explain—as the post-hunt port was imbibed—how the foxes were cleverer than before. It was vital to drive the fox out into the open; otherwise they might end up riding across the whole county. This was something that the older members of the hunt had experienced, of course. Each new tale they told was more outlandish than the one before.

Sidney Paget rode a majestic chestnut steed, lent to him by Conan Doyle, while the author himself sat astride his trusty Brigadier, a well-disciplined and phenomenally powerful horse of the Norfolk breed, which he had acquired at the beginning of that year. Suddenly, the yapping gave way to a howl. The hounds had found the scent. The illustrator and his author friend found themselves far from their desks—the game was afoot!

The road up to Hindhead was steep and winding. It was perhaps one of the most beautiful spots in England, the views in every direction calling to mind the paintings of J. M. W. Turner. The area was known as Little Switzerland, for its clean air and rolling hills. Conan Doyle; his wife, Touie; and their children, Mary and Kingsley, now called it home.

The Conan Doyles had lived something of an itinerant life ever since Touie had been diagnosed with the fearful condition known as consumption, or tuberculosis. For the most part, they had lived in resort hotels in the Swiss town of Davos, although they had been able to visit their old home in South Norwood during the summers.

Two years earlier, during a homeward journey to England in 1895, Arthur had met fellow author Grant Allen for lunch. Allen had himself suffered from TB and revealed that his recovery had been aided by a move to the healthier climate offered by the area around the little village of Hindhead, Surrey. Conan Doyle had wasted no time. He traveled to Hindhead and bought a plot of land in a charming little spot, chose an old friend from Southsea as his architect, and selected his firm of builders. He then returned to Switzerland and brought Touie southward with him to winter in Egypt. He did everything possible to increase her chances of a longer life. She had already confounded the autumn 1893 prognosis giving her only a short time to live.

Only two months had passed since they had finally been able to move in, after a year's delay in Conan Doyle's original plans, as the construction of the house had taken much longer than anticipated. It was a wonderfully spacious home, and everything was just as he wanted it. All visitors to the house were immediately besotted with the place.

Darkness had fallen over Hindhead when Paget and Conan Doyle returned from their day participating in Lord Leconfield's hunt. The house was easy to reach, lying at the junction of the roads leading in from Haslemere and Portsmouth, almost on the brow of the hill and set on its very own little plateau. To the north and east, where the nearest neighbors were situated, the shrubbery was so dense that privacy was ensured in both directions, while the side of the house facing the valley below had an open vista. The vegetation also ensured that the house was completely sheltered from chill winds. And, although it had been damp on the hunt, the air up here was perfectly dry. Even if Conan Doyle had been able to instruct nature to design a place for his family to live, it would have been impossible to improve on this location.

The lights were on inside the house. Its sheltered location allowed the architect to add far more windows than were standard. By day the house was flooded with natural light, and in the evening the lamps hinted at the snug and enticing interior that awaited the returning huntsmen.

The following day was Sunday. There was less than a week to go until Christmas. Sidney Paget was free to do as he pleased, whether that might be some preliminary sketching or something else entirely. He walked around the house, admiring its reception rooms and common areas. It had the smell of a newly built home, from the fresh wooden joists and all the recently bought furnishings. Yet Undershaw—as Conan Doyle had christened the house—was a hive of activity. The family's social life had quickly been established after they moved in. Good friends were often invited to visit, and not a week went by without a dinner, an afternoon tea, or a large gathering of some description. Fellow authors and relatives came from far and wide; new acquaintances from the area stopped in. The family—not least Conan Doyle himself—had gotten to know, among others, a charming young lady by the name of Jean Leckie. She soon established herself as one of their frequently invited guests.

From his base at Undershaw, Conan Doyle had access to all kinds of distractions when relaxing or taking a break from writing. If he wished to visit old friends in Portsmouth, it could be reached in just an hour. He had his own billiard table, could play golf nearby, and found plenty of opportunities to play cricket or go riding, hiking, or fishing in the large lake close by. Sometimes, when passing the nearby boarding school, he would join the student football games for a bit of fun. The boys—still no more than striplings—were somewhat wary of the tall and powerful man. Those who plucked up the courage to tackle him somehow always ended up colliding with the chunky bunch of keys he carried in his pocket. Conan Doyle just laughed. A few hard knocks on the field of play hadn't done him any harm as a youngster.

The boys knew no more about Conan Doyle than that he was a doctor, new to the area, and wore a walrus mustache. Imagine their surprise if someone had told them that the man with the clucking laugh was none other than the creator of the literary world's most famous sleuth, Sherlock Holmes.

Sherlock Holmes was supposed to be dead—not forgotten, necessarily, but sufficiently rooted in the past so as not to obscure Conan Doyle's other creations.

But the author was no longer in control of the situation. Sherlock Holmes had ceased to be a mere literary character—he was unquestionably the most distinctive of his time. He had become an icon. He popped up all over the place. When a Constable Avenell of Reigate successfully tracked down two potato thieves by noting the missing studs in their boot prints, the newspaper, sure enough, called him "a Sherlock Holmes." The same moniker was conferred upon his London colleague who had noticed a man, whose shoes were perfectly clean, approaching on a bicycle that was far too big for him and covered in mud. The thief was sentenced to six months penal labor and probably cursed the author who had inspired so many servants of the law to suddenly deploy all of their powers of observation.

It was not only in the newspapers that the character and his qualities had become established, but rather throughout modern society as a whole, in daily speech and, indeed, even as an accepted contrivance among other authors. To be a Sherlock Holmes was to be perceptive. And, by the same convention, it didn't take a Sherlock Holmes to work that out.

The name Sherlock Holmes started appearing in advertisements for everything from ladies' magazines to laxatives. Conan Doyle tried to speak up for his creation, but controlling all the unauthorized usage was becoming more and more difficult.

American author John Kendrick Bangs released a humorous novel in 1897 featuring a deceased Sherlock Holmes living on a houseboat on the River Styx in the realm of the dead. Bangs even dedicated the work to Conan Doyle, thanking him for the detective's untimely death, which had made the events of his book possible.

Bangs was a friend of Conan Doyle, so his borrowing of the Holmes character was not a contentious issue. They had gotten to know each other during the latter's two-and-a-half-month lecture tour of the United States in 1894. Conan Doyle had carried three separate presentations in his suitcase across the Atlantic. One was about his favorite literary contemporaries; another was the tried and tested lecture on the author George Meredith; and completing the set was a talk on his own authorship, with references both to Sherlock Holmes and to his other works, which he considered to be less ephemeral.

By the end of the tour, a tally showed that Conan Doyle's hosts had asked him to give the talk on his contemporaries once, the Meredith lecture not a single time, and the one concerning Sherlock Holmes on thirty-four occasions.

Conan Doyle had been accompanied on the American journey by his younger brother, Innes, by now grown up and serving as an army lieutenant. As soon as they arrived in New York, stepping onto the pier extending into the Hudson River, waiting journalists approached the author. In the newspapers they described Sherlock Holmes's creator as tall and athletic, with an erect posture. They wrote that his blue eyes, indeed his whole face, radiated energy. His appearance was positive, alert, and inquisitive.

Naturally, they asked politely about his other literary work, but there could be no doubt that when it came down to it, Sherlock Holmes was what they wanted to know more about. The pattern was set for the whole of his American journey. Sherlock Holmes, Sherlock Holmes, Sherlock Holmes . . .

The illustrator Sidney Paget was one of the relatively few people involved with the stories' publication who did not mourn the passing of Sherlock Holmes to any great degree. Upon completing the illustrations for "The Final Problem" four years earlier, he had considered it merely another job done. It had been one of many, and since then he had had the pleasure of illustrating other short stories and novels by Conan Doyle. Paget had become the author's preferred illustrator at the *Strand Magazine*. And it was the *Strand* that had first refusal on pretty much everything Conan Doyle wrote.

The success of the Sherlock Holmes stories had also led to other opportunities for Sidney Paget. In the wake of Holmes, a whole derivative genre had emerged, written by epigones and featuring detectives who bore a striking resemblance to the great role model. They were not exact copies, however, and the authors often went to great lengths to emphasize the differences in physical appearance between their creations and Holmes. Paget was given the task of illustrating the most successful of these series, Arthur Morrison's tales about the detective Martin Hewitt, which had begun appearing in the *Strand Magazine* immediately after Conan Doyle had killed off his own master detective.

Sidney Paget was a busy man. But when Conan Doyle invited him to Undershaw he accepted, not merely for the pleasant company but also for his latest assignment: to paint Conan Doyle's portrait.

Undershaw was a large house, and lots of wall space remained bare. A man of Conan Doyle's standing ought to have his portrait hanging in a prominent place.

Yes, Undershaw was a big house, and it had had a price tag to match. Its size meant certain other expenses: servants, electric light, horses, carriages—and the coat of arms featured on both the coaches and the horses' harnesses. When Conan Doyle was a boy, his mother had told him of the family's eminent background, descending from the royal House of Plantagenet.

The author's fortune had taken a huge hit in the building of the house, and he had even been forced to ask Greenhough Smith for an advance on the fee for a novel that was then being serialized. Conan Doyle needed to put money in the bank in double-quick time to keep up the new lifestyle to which he was becoming accustomed. How, though, could he generate a large enough income?

In the weeks before Paget's visit to Undershaw, rumors had begun circulating in the newspapers. Conan Doyle had once again begun writing about Sherlock Holmes, they claimed. But the detective had not risen from the dead; indeed there was no new novel or short story. He was, nonetheless, writing about Holmes.

Conan Doyle had returned to his love of the theater and decided to write a play about his most famous character. In fact, he had already finished writing it, though the newspapers did not yet know that. Writing about the detective had never been a particularly time-consuming activity.

Conan Doyle adjusted his position in the wing chair in which he sat and stretched himself. In one hand was an open notebook, in the other a pen. His mustache was elegantly waxed and his hair neatly groomed. At first he had planned to wear his cricket kit, but he thought better of it and plumped for a slightly more formal look, wearing suit and tie. He did his best to sit as still as possible.

Opposite him, Sidney Paget made his first strokes on the canvas.

23

THE GREAT AMERICAN actor William Gillette—also a playwright and director—was nervous before his meeting with Dr. Conan Doyle. How might the British author react to what Gillette had done to his play?

More than eighteen months had passed since Conan Doyle had completed his play about Sherlock Holmes and sent the manuscript to a theatrical agent, who in his turn had approached Herbert Beerbohm Tree to see if this leading English actor and theater manager might take on the production. Sure enough, Tree had been interested. Only a few tweaks to the script would be required. They were trifling things; for instance, Tree wanted to play both Sherlock Holmes and Professor Moriarty himself. But they appeared in the same scene, Conan Doyle objected. Exactly; that was why the script required adjustments. But would the audience see the difference? Would it not be confusing? Of course not; Sherlock Holmes would have a beard throughout the piece—an ingenious solution!

Herbert Beerbohm Tree wanted, in other words, to alter great swaths of the manuscript. What was Conan Doyle to do? He suspected that the play would earn him bags of money, not least in America and the colonies. Undershaw was in great need of those bags. But desecrating his script did not sit well with the author.

Conan Doyle declined Tree's offer. He instead made contact with Sir Henry Irving, then sixty years old, who had already produced one of Conan Doyle's plays and was an institution in the British theatrical world. Irving had already shown some interest in the idea.

As he had in the earlier transaction, Conan Doyle dealt with Irving's manager. His name was Bram Stoker, and he was a man with his own ambitions of making it as an author. He had published the novel *Dracula* the year before, but it had yet to be a success in terms of major sales.

Conan Doyle was quite taken with it. He considered it to be the best book about "diablerie" that he had read for many years, and he wrote to Bram Stoker to tell him so.

No contract was sealed with Henry Irving. The actor was busy with another production, and was not feeling fully fit.

Conan Doyle seriously considered stuffing the script into a desk drawer. It would seem that Sherlock Holmes wasn't meant to be on the stage—just as he himself had thought when he had refused to allow an actress to dramatize the detective's stories many years earlier.

William Gillette was one of the biggest stars on the other side of the Atlantic. When he had begun his career at the age of twenty, back in 1873, old-fashioned plays about exaggerated heroic and mythical figures who recited blank verse onstage had been very much in vogue. But now there were signs that a change might be on its way. Increasingly, theaters produced new French and German plays. They depicted real men and women in realistic, credible situations. Gillette loved modern theater.

His stage acting was naturalistic. He didn't raise his voice, except when the script demanded it. His emotions and gestures remained within the confines of what one might see in everyday life. This was a new method, and Gillette was at the forefront. Since he also wrote plays, he was able to tailor his leading characters accordingly. He always made sure that his characters spent some time on the stage without speaking; the silence served to heighten either the suspense or the comic effect. His plays had to be thrilling, or funny; after all, the point was to entertain the audience.

Gillette had achieved a lot in his stage career, and he owed much of his success to those around him. He had grown up in the Nook Farm area of Hartford, Connecticut, and a neighbor had secured him his first role and supported him financially when necessary. The neighbor was Samuel Langhorne Clemens, known in literary circles as Mark Twain. Nook Farm was an interesting community to grow up in, bursting as it was with creativity, ideas, and intellect. Next door to Clemens lived Harriet Beecher Stowe, whose novel *Uncle Tom's Cabin* was considered one of the most important books of its time.

Another, even more important influence on Gillette's career was Charles Frohman. No other producer held such great sway both in

London's West End and on New York's Broadway. Frohman was Gillette's close friend and employer.

Frohman met with Conan Doyle, who told him he was willing to sell the rights to the stage production of Sherlock Holmes. He had only one condition: any form of romantic involvement for Holmes was out of the question. The contract was a handshake. Frohman was famous for never using written agreements.

Gillette, who was on tour at the time, received a telegram from Frohman advising him to find an understudy who could take over his role so that he could spend six weeks "resting." What Frohman actually meant was spend time amending Conan Doyle's play.

Gillette checked into a swanky hotel. Among other books he brought a British edition of *The Adventures of Sherlock Holmes*, and he began making notes. He found passages that could usefully form parts of the plot, and interesting descriptions of Sherlock Holmes's personality; and he cut out some of Sidney Paget's illustrations—they could prove useful for the production's costume designer. Paget's drawings were virtually unknown in the United States, where other illustrators had been used.

In one of the short stories, reference was made to Sherlock Holmes's headgear, a "close-fitting cloth cap," and it could be seen in the illustrations. It was one of those English hats with flaps that could fold down over the ears. Gillette was taken with that. It was just right for the play.

Conan Doyle's original script changed, slowly but surely. Gillette removed lines and events, replacing them with his own ideas. Professor Moriarty was retained, however; Gillette didn't want to lose such a source of intrigue. And then he turned to the element that all modern plays required: love. It was at this point that Frohman recalled the agreement with Conan Doyle, whereby any love interest was simply not permitted.

With a certain trepidation, Gillette wired Conan Doyle: "May I marry Holmes?"

He need not have worried. Conan Doyle had either forgotten his earlier conditions, or ceased to care. He replied immediately: "You may marry or murder or do what you like with him."

Gillette could breathe easily again, and before long the first version was ready. He then handed it over to his secretary. The whole theater company was in San Francisco, yet Gillette and his secretary were staying at different hotels. In the middle of the night, an exhausted Gillette was awakened by a persistent knocking on his door. It was his distraught secretary. There was a fire! The only copy of the Sherlock Holmes script had been destroyed when the hotel burned down!

"Is *this* hotel on fire?" Gillette inquired.

"Oh, no, not at all," replied the secretary.

"Well, come and tell me all about it in the morning," Gillette said, before going back to sleep. He had all the lines in his head and was able to reproduce the script within a week.

One day in May 1899, William Gillette was on a train on his way to meet Conan Doyle. That he had left the bustle of London behind was quite apparent from his fellow passengers' attire. Frock coats and top hats made way for Norfolk jackets, deerstalkers, and ankle-length cloaks. This was tweed country, and Gillette fitted right in.

The train squealed to a halt, and Gillette stepped out from his compartment. Conan Doyle, standing there on the platform waiting to meet him, was dumbfounded. Walking toward him was none other than Sherlock Holmes himself, exactly as he had imagined the detective: tall, with angular features, even dressed in clothes Sherlock Holmes might have worn on an excursion to the country. The American approached Conan Doyle and whipped out a magnifying glass. He examined him carefully before saying, in just the sort of tone that Sherlock Holmes might have used, "Unquestionably an author."

Before long the author and the actor had made their way to Undershaw, where Gillette was to spend the weekend. The hospitality was, as usual, first class, and with eleven bedrooms upstairs and as many bathrooms, there was no shortage of space. It was a peaceful home. Conan Doyle's wife Louisa's piano playing was audible from one of the downstairs rooms. Admittedly, the children were raised strictly and at times a little scared of their father, just as in so many other families. Yet they had the freedom to roam as they pleased in their spare time. As long as they made sure to be home in time for meals, they were free to explore the great outdoors around Undershaw.

Gillette had worried about the reception his play would receive, but he need not have. The two men sat in a room with a broad vista over the valley below, and Gillette read the whole script aloud for the detective's creator. After a few small alterations were made, the whole thing met with Conan Doyle's approval. He was taken with it. Sherlock Holmes was back—the creation he had tried so many times to leave behind. All his old reservations had evaporated.

He was even heard to say, "It's good to see the old chap again."

24

A YOUNG BOY, known to his family and friends as Kit, stood, paint-brush in hand, in front of a clubhouse. He had altered the sign, so it now read "T.S.O. 4"—to be read as "The Sign of Four." Kit was not yet in his teens, and it felt like a very long time before he would be. Born on May 5, 1890, he had recently noted that Sherlock Holmes had died the day before his first birthday. According to the short story "The Final Problem," the detective had fallen into the Reichenbach Falls on May 4, 1891. Kit had been just a few years old when Conan Doyle had stopped writing his Holmes stories, which meant that he was too young to have experienced the hysteria that erupted when the author killed off his hero, although he had experienced the same reaction when reading the story in question some years later.

There were four boys in the club. Earlier, they had had another club and had all had aliases, but now everything was about Sherlock Holmes. Three of them had just been to see a play about the detective.

"I'm Holmes," said one.

"And I'm Dr. Watson," said another.

"Then I'll be Lestrade," said Kit, referring to the Scotland Yard inspector who made frequent appearances in the Sherlock Holmes stories.

The fourth member of the club had to settle for Professor Moriarty.

"Put him in the gas chamber," Holmes, Watson, and Lestrade shouted in unison. Moriarty didn't know what was going on, as he was the one of the quartet who had not seen the play. He had no way of knowing what kind of unpleasantness occurred in the gas chamber. The other three pushed him into the old henhouse. The smell in there was far from pleasant.

Kit's family had recently moved to Baltimore. His parents were originally from England, and his father was a professor of mathematics. Kit spent most of his free time in the Enoch Pratt Free Library. When the school day ended, he would head there immediately. He read piles and piles of books—by Jules Verne, Rider Haggard, Kipling, Stevenson—but he was particularly fond of Conan Doyle, and not only his Sherlock Holmes stories. As soon as he spotted a Conan Doyle he had not read before, he would borrow it and begin reading as he trudged home. It was a long way from the library, and Kit had mastered the art of walking slowly. He would often have finished a large part of the book before he got home.

He did not simply read the books; he studied and pondered them carefully. He would then force his younger brothers, Felix and Frank, to read them as well, and then follow up with an oral exam as home-work. He did not want them to simply skim through the stories, so he formulated tricky questions about details in the text. This would ensure that his brothers were left in no doubt as to the greatness of Conan Doyle's creations.

In the henhouse, Moriarty began to show signs that he was not altogether enjoying the aftermath of that Sherlock Holmes play. The mess left behind by the hens stank of ammonia.

The play had been fantastic. It had everything. Kit recognized lots of details from the two novels and twenty-four short stories that Conan Doyle had written about Holmes. The play had comprised five acts, set variously in, among other places, Sherlock Holmes's flat (with Holmes in his dressing gown), Professor Moriarty's underground office, and the notorious gas chamber in Stepney. The point at which Holmes and Moriarty met had been even more exciting than it had been in Conan Doyle's short story.

According to the program notes, William Gillette and Conan Doyle had written the play together. Gillette had been perfect as Holmes. He had one of those hats with a peak at the front and the back, and he smoked a pipe, too. It would seem that that was how a detective should look. In Conan Doyle's stories, however, Holmes always used a pipe with a straight stem, whereas Gillette used a curved one, to avoid obscuring his mouth as he was delivering his lines.

The newspapers had reported that Gillette's production had run for full houses in New York for thirty-six weeks earlier that year. The show had then been taken on the road, and was playing in Baltimore every evening for a week, plus a Saturday matinee. One article claimed that this role was the high point of Gillette's career, and for Kit it was certainly the highlight of the Baltimore theater season.

Kit and his companions had of course committed several lines to memory. Just as in the play, the club's young Holmes turned, stony-faced, to his equally young colleague, Dr. Watson, and pronounced the words, "Elementary, my dear fellow."

The most exciting part of the production was, according to the audience, during the act that took place in the gas chamber when, without warning, the stage was plunged into darkness. The only thing visible was Holmes's glowing cigar.

"Follow the cigar!" cried one of Moriarty's men. The audience could not see anything, but the dialogue and the cursing hinted at the violence unfolding on the stage. Then, just as suddenly, the lights came up, revealing that Holmes had succeeded in fooling the crooks by placing his cigar on a window ledge while he made for the exit. That this was scarcely credible was not a problem for anyone concerned. Everything else felt plausible: the actors wore ordinary clothes, Gillette's Holmes was realistic, and there was nothing overly theatrical about the play's performance. It was simply impossible not to get caught up in the suspense, both for Kit, a regular theatergoer, and for his friends. Not even the fact that Sherlock Holmes had gone and fallen in love with the female lead was enough to ruin the experience for the members of T.S.O. 4. That detail, though, simply could not be the work of Conan Doyle. Gillette must have been the one who came up with that.

Eventually, the members of T.S.O. 4 showed mercy. Moriarty did not have to stay in the henhouse. Their friend no longer had to play the Napoleon of crime. Now he could play the landlady, Mrs. Hudson.

As the play made its way across America, Sherlock Holmes increasingly turned up in all kinds of situations. Photographs and drawings showed Gillette in his deerstalker, with his curved pipe, and his characterization was becoming the accepted depiction of Sherlock Holmes. New American editions of the Holmes stories took their inspiration from Gillette; he was pictured wearing his dressing gown and holding a pistol in his hand.

The Mutoscope was beginning to make its appearance around the country, and it was possible to watch a Sherlock Holmes "movie" in one of these devices. The user looked into the machine while simultaneously cranking a handle and enjoyed the appearance of a rudimentary motion picture. The Mutoscope series of images, which had been recorded on a cinematograph, was entitled *Sherlock Holmes Baffled*. It showed a burglar getting his mitts on a variety of silver objects. A man wearing a dressing gown over his ordinary clothes entered the room, a cigar in his mouth, and then tapped the thief on the shoulder. The villain disappeared from one frame to the next, leaving his loot behind. The man in the dressing gown lit his cigar, which exploded. Out of nowhere the thief reappeared, and the startled man fired a shot at the villain, who all of a sudden was behind him. Just as the man seemed to be holding the booty, it turned out it was the thief who had it. He was able to climb out the window at the far end of the room and disappear.

The whole thing lasted only half a minute or so. It may not have had any connection to Sherlock Holmes, but that name in the title attracted paying customers, and the moving images were impressive, especially with the trick photography. The series of images had been recorded in 1900 on a Broadway rooftop, as recording such a scene without natural light was impossible.

Gillette's success in America with Sherlock Holmes may have inspired the actor's old friend Mark Twain to write the 1902 novel *A Double Barrelled Detective Story*, in which Sherlock Holmes turned up in a Californian mining camp and attempted to solve a crime. "Attempted" is the appropriate word since—because this was Twain's satirical take on the genre—Holmes did not emerge triumphant. Another American, Bret Harte, had also written about the detective quite recently, in a magazine spoof called "The Stolen Cigar-Case." Early in Conan Doyle's writing career, Harte had been a big inspiration to him.

A copy of Twain's book surely found its way to the Enoch Pratt Free Library in Baltimore, where it was no doubt read by a young boy as he made his way home from said library, even if it was so short that he would surely have finished it before getting home.

Nothing, though, could beat the original, as far as Kit was concerned. And, in the autumn of 1901, the original was back, with the *Strand Magazine*'s publication of Conan Doyle's new Sherlock Holmes novel—about a legend of a terrifying hound.

25

C ONAN DOYLE WROTE a letter to his mother from Rowe's Duchy
 Hotel in Princetown, Devon, in late spring 1901.

Here I am in the highest town in England. Robinson and I are exploring the moor over our Sherlock Holmes book. I think it will work out
splendidly—indeed I have already done nearly half of it. Holmes is at
his very best, and it is a highly dramatic idea—which I owe to Robinson.

We did 14 miles over the moor today and we are now pleasantly
weary. It is a great place, very sad & wild, dotted with the dwellings
of prehistoric man, strange monoliths and huts and graves. In those
old days there was evidently a population of very many thousands
here & now you may walk all day and never see one human being.

Conan Doyle had spent the autumn of 1899 waiting for the New York
premiere of Gillette's play, *Sherlock Holmes*. Success would mean a handsome reward, money that could finance so many other things. Not least,
he had decided to travel to South Africa to participate as a volunteer
in the war that was breaking out—a decision completely against his
mother's wishes, despite everything she had taught him about being
a patriot. Time was short, since the war would soon be over. It was
after all mere farmers—the Boers—taking on the well-drilled soldiers
of the British army.

The war, though, was dragging on, as the Boers proved to be far
tougher than their opponents had anticipated. Conan Doyle decided
to go. His mother, Mary, did not mince her words: this would end
badly. Tall and broad as he was, her son would make an easy target.
She pleaded with him, as son, husband, and father, not to go. Not only
that, his impact as an author and intellectual back home was far more
significant than any contribution he might make on the battlefield.

Word of outstanding reviews of the play in America reached Conan Doyle. He imagined the play being produced by a list of touring companies for many years to come, both in English-speaking countries and on the Continent. He expected to make £10,000 from the venture, with the first payments coming immediately and further disbursements on a weekly basis thereafter.

Above all, though, his thoughts were of war. In a letter to the *Times* of London, he suggested that the government should call on all the country's hunt marksmen to join up as volunteers. The powers that be actually responded to his suggestion. Conan Doyle signed up at once. He knew that such men as he and Rudyard Kipling were among those best able to influence the young men of Britain and young sportsmen in particular. At forty, he wanted to be their clarion call, to show them what true patriotism meant.

Military authorities did not want Conan Doyle. He was a civilian and had no place on the battlefield. In the end, in the final tremulous month of the century, Conan Doyle found a way to get to the war. He signed up as a surgeon in a private field hospital financed by a friend.

It was not patriotism alone, nor indeed the heat of battle that appealed to him. He wanted, quite simply, to get away.

"I have lived for six years in a sick room," he had admitted in a letter to his mother. "And O how weary of it I am! Dear Touie! It has tried me more than her."

He wrote his will and testament and then boarded the ship that would take him to the center of events. For the first time, Conan Doyle would experience a real war. While in South Africa, he wrote in his diary that the way to Bloemfontein from Modder, the site of a bloody battle, was easy to find—it was simply a matter of following the stench of dead horses.

Working at the field hospital plunged him into the midst of death. The Boers cut off the fresh water supply, and typhus was soon rife. Even Conan Doyle caught the disease. He recovered.

At the field station he was Dr. Doyle, a hardworking doctor, nothing else. Sherlock Holmes was far away. Conan Doyle continued to write nonetheless. In his spare moments he was able to write almost a complete book on the conflict in South Africa.

After just a few months it was time for Conan Doyle to return home. The private field hospital closed down after half the staff members contracted typhus and were no longer able to carry out their duties. The military hospital had plenty of beds and did not require any further assistance.

On the SS *Briton* from Cape Town to Southampton it took sixteen days to reach home. The boat was full of people returning from the war. A French major claimed, in Conan Doyle's presence, that the British had used dumdums, dangerous hollow-point bullets, in South Africa. Conan Doyle was enraged by the accusation, and the war correspondent for the *Daily Express* had had to intervene to prevent the pair from coming to blows.

The war correspondent turned out to be agreeable company, just as interested in sports as Conan Doyle himself. His name was Bertram Fletcher Robinson, and he hailed from a small village in Devon, not far from the great wilds of Dartmoor.

Back on British soil, Conan Doyle was once again able to devote himself to the important things in life—cricket, above all.

Willie Hornung loved cricket too. He had married Conan Doyle's sister Connie a few years earlier, and the couple lived in London. He had supplemented his journalistic endeavors with a literary career. The previous year he had dedicated his collection of short stories about Raffles, the gentleman thief, to his brother-in-law. Raffles was a sort of inverted Sherlock Holmes character. Hornung and Conan Doyle had become good friends over the years, and Hornung probably felt that he knew his relative very well.

One Tuesday in August 1900, Hornung happened to visit Lord's Cricket Ground in London, and whom should he bump into but his brother-in-law—accompanied by a woman fifteen years his junior. The woman was Jean Leckie, who up to that point had been referred to only as a friend of the family.

Later the same day, Mr. and Mrs. Hornung had a visit from Conan Doyle, who wanted to explain the situation. His relationship with Miss Leckie was purely platonic, he emphasized.

Hornung was of the opinion that it made no difference whether in fact it was platonic or not. Conan Doyle protested that it made all the difference between guilt and innocence. He felt that he had always been so loyal to all the members of his family—why should he now have such allegations thrown in his face?

★ ★ ★

The Boer War dragged on stubbornly. The conflict had become a guer-
rilla war. Against this backdrop Conan Doyle released his historical
tome *The Great Boer War*. By the end of the year it had sold thirty
thousand copies in England alone, as well as nearly twenty thousand
in America and the colonies.

The war maintained its grip on Conan Doyle in more ways than one.
The typhus returned in 1901, and he was bedridden. He was certainly in
need of recuperation. It was decided that he and Fletcher Robinson, his
new friend, would spend a weekend away at a seaside hotel in Norfolk.

Recuperation meant, in this case, playing golf. One day, though,
was so cold and windy that they decided to stay indoors. The subject
of conversation turned to the myths about demonic hounds that were
widespread around Dartmoor. Robinson knew a lot about the tales and
began recounting them for Conan Doyle. Before long, they realized
that this could easily form the basis of a novel. Indeed, they decided to
write a book together. It was to be a real thriller and would be called
The Hound of the Baskervilles. Robinson had the original idea and the
local knowledge, and a short time later when Conan Doyle told Greenhough Smith of the *Strand Magazine* about the project, he pointed out
that both he and Robinson were to be credited as authors. This was
despite the fact that he was going to be the one to write it. He asked
for his usual fee of fifty pounds per thousand words.

Back home at Undershaw, Conan Doyle threw himself into writing, but before long he realized that the story needed a strong central
character, someone capable of changing the whole sequence of events.
Why invent such a person, when he already had Sherlock Holmes?
The detective was dead, after tumbling into the Reichenbach Falls,
but Conan Doyle could easily set the tale in the time before Holmes's
demise. Conan Doyle watched as the money rolled in from Gillette's
play, a production that would soon be opening in London. The master
detective would be the talk of the town once more. The author could
certainly command double his usual rate if the story were to feature
Sherlock Holmes.

Greenhough Smith went along, as usual, with Conan Doyle's
demand—he knew what it would mean for the magazine. The *Strand*
paid £6,000 to buy the rights to the British serialization, which was as

much as Undershaw had cost to build. On top of that, Conan Doyle could reckon with royalties from future book editions and the fees for the American rights.

As the story was changed into a Sherlock Holmes tale, Robinson's involvement was reduced. In the end the novel was published with a dedication from Conan Doyle to Robinson, nothing more.

The first episode was to appear in the August 1901 edition of the *Strand Magazine*. The subscriptions began flooding in once more.

The touring William Gillette production of *Sherlock Holmes* had had its triumphant London premiere a month before. Holmes's image was beginning to change in England too—the detective was increasingly coupled with the deerstalker and the curved pipe. A few short quotations from various Holmes stories by Conan Doyle and a few illustrations by Sidney Paget had, on the far side of the Atlantic, been transformed into character-defining objects, which were now being imported back to England.

Sherlock Holmes was still dead; nothing had changed on that score. And yet no one could deny that he was very much alive.

26

I‍T WAS THE end of an era, and the British Empire was in mourning. On January 22, 1901, at half past five in the evening, Queen Victoria had passed away. She had written detailed instructions for her funeral. Although she had dressed only in black since the death of her husband, Prince Albert—a display of mourning lasting over forty years—she decreed that her funeral should be a white affair. She was lowered into her coffin wearing a white dress; on her head she wore her wedding veil, which she had last worn as a young woman of twenty. At her side were one of Albert's dressing gowns and a plaster cast of his hand. In her left hand, in accordance with her instructions, she held a lock of hair from her personal servant John Brown, as well as a picture of him. Both were tactfully hidden from the family's view by a strategically placed bouquet.

The Prince of Wales was to become King Edward VII, but the coronation was not planned to take place until the following year. Tradition dictated that mourning should last for a whole year, during which time the prince was not expected to attend any public amusements. Several members of the royal family had—incognito—seen William Gillette's Sherlock Holmes play at the Lyceum in the autumn of 1901. The family's biggest Holmes enthusiast—the king-to-be—had had to make do with the content being recounted for him.

Within a week of the end of the year of mourning, King Edward and his queen, Alexandra of Denmark, arrived in the royal box at the Lyceum. The prime minister, Arthur Balfour, was also in attendance, as were Conan Doyle and his wife, Louisa.

The first act ended, and the audience streamed out to purchase refreshments. Indeed, there were those for whom socializing during the intermission was the main attraction of a night at the theater. The Lyceum was Henry Irving's home stage, and it had for many years played host to plays featuring Britain's foremost actor and actress, Irving and his opposite number, Ellen Terry, in the leading roles. Times, though, were changing. New owners had taken over, and Irving would soon be giving his farewell performance at the theater that had been his home for three decades.

Slowly, the *Sherlock Holmes* audience returned from the intermission. They waited for the second act. And they waited. Shouts could be heard from the stalls. The audience reaction escalated with every minute that passed. Still, on the stage there was nothing. The crowd demanded to see the remainder of the play. The critics had been subdued in their reviews when the play had premiered in London, but this had had no impact whatsoever on attendance. What had been billed as a six-week special appearance had now been running for five months.

Among those unperturbed by the long intermission was the king. He had invited Gillette up to his box after the first act and was deeply interested in discussing the royal parallels in the plot of the piece. When the protests from the seats became a clamor, and the intermission had run to over an hour, he realized that it might be best if Gillette continued with his acting—not least because His Majesty himself wanted to know what would happen to Holmes.

London was such a success that Gillette and his producer, Charles Frohman, decided to establish two touring companies that could take the play around England. One company took the northern counties, while the others played the south. Frohman made sure that the sets were exact copies of the London original and that the sophisticated electrical equipment required for the advanced lighting effects arrived from America. Gillette himself oversaw the rehearsals of the traveling companies.

H. A. Saintsbury, taking the role of Sherlock Holmes, led the northern tour. He had an eye for talent. During the tour he needed someone to play Billy, the page boy, and hired a fourteen-year-old for the part, recognizing the boy's exquisite timing and talent for mimicry. Saintsbury put in extra work with the young actor, so that he might learn to use his talent to best effect. Sure enough, despite playing only a minor role, the boy became an audience favorite. His humor, above all, shone through. His name was Charles Spencer Chaplin, and this was his first real job in the theater.

During the early part of 1902 word spread about the Sherlock Holmes play, not just in England but over on the Continent too. The first translated version opened in Amsterdam in January. The Dutch actors had come to London for three weeks and spent evening after evening at the Lyceum studying the performances of their English counterparts. And just as he had with the English touring versions, Frohman made sure that all elements of the set were built in London and then shipped over to the Netherlands. Similar productions were prepared for Germany, France, Austria, Belgium, and Russia.

If Conan Doyle had not had Europe at his feet before, he certainly did now. On every little stage Sherlock Holmes struggled against Professor Moriarty. For those who had not known who Moriarty was—he had featured in only a single short story after all—it was now absolutely clear. Moriarty became the archetypal master criminal; his was a name that would strike fear into the hearts of children.

There was one country, however, where Gillette's play need not bother to extend its tour: Denmark.

Walter Christmas was Danish. His father was a chamberlain and master of the royal hunt, his mother a baroness. At fourteen he joined the navy, signing on for a career that would soon take him on adventures to the four corners of the earth. He joined an expedition to Greenland; traveled up the Amazon to Peru in order to prepare a possible Danish trade route; and went to Siam, on Danish orders, to help the country's navy, but was eventually discharged after getting involved with the independence movements in the French colonies of Indochina. He then took up employment with the Greek navy instead, joining in the battles against the Ottoman Empire. Christmas wrote several books about his experiences and when commitments allowed also spent time writing a country-house novel. During the periods when he happened to be in Denmark, he had time to marry, father a daughter, divorce, and remarry.

In 1899 Walter Christmas found himself in New York. He had been involved in an attempted sale of the Danish West Indies to Germany, which had ended in failure. Now he was trying to sell the colony to the United States instead.

One evening he went to see the play that everyone was talking about. He immediately saw its potential and contacted Charles Frohman to secure the rights to a Danish version. Frohman demanded a huge sum of money, but Walter Christmas had never let such details get in his way. He found that it was far cheaper simply to buy tickets for a number of successive performances and then set about filling the cuffs of his shirt with annotated lines from the piece.

Using Gillette's play as a base, and with a good portion of imagination, Walter Christmas created his own version. The lines were more direct, the language was coarser, and all the action was even more exciting. Where Gillette had withheld mysterious details, Christmas decided to reveal them at once, to demonstrate how exciting or suspenseful it all was. Christmas took the play back to Denmark, where he persuaded the Folketeatret in Copenhagen to stage it. The premiere took place on December 26, 1901. The critics may have had their opinions, but the audiences loved it. The play had verve and action and it ran for five months. Walter Christmas got all the credit. William Gillette's name was never mentioned.

On the morning of October 24, 1902, in a room inside Buckingham Palace, Conan Doyle was knighted, becoming Sir Arthur Conan Doyle and receiving the office Deputy Lord Lieutenant of Surrey. Afterward, he felt like a newlywed bride who did not really know what to call herself. "Sir Arthur" did not appeal. He instructed the *Strand Magazine* to continue to credit his stories to "A. Conan Doyle," just as before.

Conan Doyle had been knighted for his writings about the recently concluded Boer War. That, at least, was the official line. For King Edward VII, who had recently asked to be seated next to Conan Doyle at a dinner, the whole business probably seemed a formality. Conan Doyle was, after all, Sherlock Holmes's creator.

27

CONAN DOYLE WAS positively swamped with letters. His study at Undershaw was beginning to look like a small post office. Some of the correspondence was addressed to "Sir Sherlock Holmes," or "Sherlock Holmes, Esq." Other letters were addressed to the author but with a request that they be forwarded to the detective himself. The writers would ask for Sherlock Holmes's autograph or a signed photo, or inquire about the detective's family history and coat of arms. Conan Doyle received tobacco, pipe cleaners, and violin strings—all accompanied by requests that he hand them over to Holmes.

This was, of course, completely absurd. When the *Strand Magazine* had published the novel *The Hound of the Baskervilles* two years earlier, there had been appreciation from readers, yes, but none of these letter-writing madmen. For Conan Doyle sensed that some of these letters were not written as jokes but in fact were quite serious. There were people who genuinely believed that Sherlock Holmes existed.

Almost ten years had passed since Conan Doyle had killed off Holmes. He was of the opinion that had he not done so, Holmes would have killed him off instead. The years had mellowed the author's feelings about his creation. This was thanks first to the play, which Gillette had reworked, but more recently to Holmes having proved useful in Conan Doyle's telling of the tale of the terrifying hound of the moorlands. Conan Doyle was never paid as well as when he wrote about Holmes—up to three times as much as he received for other work. So why not, frankly, give in to temptation? With a family, a large house, and a range of expensive pastimes, he had plenty of holes that could swallow money.

In spring 1903 the editor of the American magazine *Collier's Weekly*—an old acquaintance of Conan Doyle—sent a request to him. Was there any possibility he might bring Holmes back from the dead—not merely by writing new stories set in the time before his death but rather by actually resurrecting him? Conan Doyle was offered $25,000 for six short stories; $30,000 for eight; or $45,000 for thirteen, regardless of length.

Conan Doyle sent his reply on a postcard: "Very well, A.C.D."

He got straight to work, and it was not long before the new series' first short story, "The Empty House," was complete. He had come up with an ingenious explanation for Sherlock Holmes's disappearance. He had in fact never died but rather had left the field for three years, spending time with, among others, the Dalai Lama in Tibet.

Jean Leckie was the one who had actually come up with the plot for "The Empty House." Conan Doyle's life was complicated, and its complexities had taken a toll on him. He wanted to be loyal, and faithful, to his wife, Touie. He was duty-bound to suppress his feelings for Jean, despite being sufficiently creative to engineer plenty of opportunities to meet with her. Mary Doyle, her son's constant correspondent, knew everything about him and Miss Leckie and even chaperoned many of their meetings. Increasingly, other family members and friends were brought into the couple's confidence or else had their suspicions. Touie was to be spared this knowledge. Conan Doyle was absolutely sure that she had no idea. He could sometimes be a bit naïve.

It was not a demand as such, but the Americans hoped that the new stories would include some connection with the United States. Perhaps Sherlock Holmes would even cross the Atlantic in the name of fighting crime. Conan Doyle gave the idea serious consideration and made contact with a Long Island, New York, hotel that was actually open only during the winter. That detail notwithstanding, he wanted to rent the entire hotel over the summer season in order to conduct the necessary research. The news about Conan Doyle's imminent arrival was wildly exaggerated but this did not hamper its spread. It was not long before S. S. McClure, owner of the syndicate that had sold so many of Conan Doyle's stories, received a letter. It had come from one of Conan Doyle's countless admirers, wanting to know when the author would be arriving. If Conan Doyle was going to be in the country, the admirer wanted to meet him. This was not the kind of admirer that one could easily ignore. He was Theodore Roosevelt, the twenty-sixth president of the United States.

The journey to Long Island never took place, nor was the American element particularly discernible in the new stories, published under the name *The Return of Sherlock Holmes*. While the rumor of the Long Island trip was still making the rounds, it was seized upon by a young writer and humorist, twenty-two-year-old Pelham Grenville Wodehouse. His first two names were normally abbreviated to their initials, while his friends knew him simply as Plum.

Holmes in America presented a prime opportunity for comedy. P. G. Wodehouse wrote a short parody involving a chance meeting between the detective and Watson after Holmes's long absence, in which Watson could scarcely recognize him, for whatever Holmes said was inflected with an American drawl.

P. G. Wodehouse loved Sherlock Holmes; indeed he loved everything Conan Doyle wrote. As schoolboys, he and a friend used to hang around the railway station on the day each month when the *Strand Magazine* was due to arrive. Wodehouse often referred to Sherlock Holmes in his own works. He had even met the author himself: the meeting was not thanks to Wodehouse's own writing success; it occurred when they played cricket together. The game took place on May 22, 1903, on Conan Doyle's forty-fourth birthday. The Artists took on the Authors in sweltering heat, as temperatures rose into the mid-eighties. Wodehouse was on the same team as Conan Doyle, his brother-in-law Willie Hornung, and of course J. M. Barrie. Even if Hornung had arranged the match, Barrie was a central figure in any cricketing contest featuring the great and the good of the literary world. Barrie had gradually become rich and famous, thanks for the most part to his plays. The year before he had also written a book based on his own adventures in Kensington Gardens, where he had not only played cricket but also gotten to know a group of young siblings. Inspired by these children, he had created a tale about a boy who never grew up, named Peter Pan.

Willie Hornung's writing career was also going well. He had published two collections of short stories about Raffles, his gentleman thief. Conan Doyle was not pleased with his brother-in-law's choice of hero—a criminal, albeit a refined and cricket-playing one. Bones of contention would occasionally arise between Conan Doyle and Hornung, but as close relatives, they continued to socialize in spite of such disagreements.

Hornung had created Raffles using Holmes as his template. Raffles even had his own companion and narrator in the Watson mold. In 1903, the usual roles of the brothers-in-law were quite unexpectedly reversed. This time it was Conan Doyle who turned to Hornung's writings for help. Conan Doyle read the Raffles stories thoroughly, looking for inspiration for the eight stories he had undertaken to deliver. It was not easy to invent new scenarios, and he was aware of the danger that these new stories might seem like repetitions of earlier Holmes stories. Conan Doyle was able to find in the Raffles stories plot ideas that he could borrow; he ran his ideas past Hornung first.

Another sounding board was Fletcher Robinson, the man behind the idea for *The Hound of the Baskervilles*. Several of the basic plots that they discussed, and which Conan Doyle later used, also found their way into Robinson's own detective short stories.

The promised eight short stories became twelve. In September 1903, the first of them, "The Empty House," was published in *Collier's Weekly* in the United States and pretty much simultaneously in the United Kingdom in the *Strand Magazine*.

Conan Doyle continued writing at his usual pace, sending off the completed short stories to his agent, who would in turn send them on to the magazines for publication. On the content of this new collection, *Strand* editor H. Greenhough Smith was less than satisfied, finding the lack of crimes in some of the stories of particular concern. He had reservations about both "The Norwood Builder" and "The Solitary Cyclist." Conan Doyle defended himself when it came to the first—even ranking it among his best works—but had to agree that the second was not particularly accomplished. He edited it as best he could, hoping to tighten the plot. His fourth submission, "The Dancing Men," on the other hand, was a much stronger story, and Conan Doyle suggested that Greenhough Smith publish it between the other two so as to separate them. The idea for the dancing figures had come to him during a visit to the Hornungs' country house, after he had seen some stick-figure drawings a child had done. As usual, Conan Doyle sucked up real-life details and transformed them into fiction.

Ten years earlier, S. S. McClure, the owner of the syndicate responsible for distributing Sherlock Holmes stories across America, had embarked on an ambitious publishing project. In June 1893 he had published the first issue of a new monthly magazine, *McClure's*, the contents of which ranged from fiction to articles of a more political character. Thanks to his impressive network, McClure was able to publish works by all the major authors: Kipling, Stevenson, Jack London, Conan Doyle. The journalism the magazine undertook was of an investigative nature, and *McClure's* in many ways became a sort of ethical watchdog of the time.

Competition from low-budget monthlies would soon hit McClure hard. After one year of publication he owed the British authors $3,500, and was losing $1,000 a month. He decided to temporarily cut the number of pages and to reduce the size of the illustrations. These moves improved the finances of the magazine, but they were not enough. The debt owed to the authors soon reached $5,000. Up-front payments from advertisers did not stretch far enough, and credit from facilities linked with the paper suppliers and printers was already at its limit. McClure's business partner had even persuaded his father to remortgage his house.

Every day was like trying to walk through a granite wall. The autumn of 1894 had been so hard on McClure that he had not been fit to set up a meeting with Conan Doyle, who was then in the United States on his lecture tour. One morning McClure decided to put this right. He caught the train in from Long Island, with a manuscript under his arm to read on the way, and upon reaching New York City made straight for the Aldine Club, where Conan Doyle was staying.

He then went as far as to reveal the extent of his financial woes.

"I would gladly put some money into the business," Conan Doyle said. "If you need it."

If he needed it? It would be like a gift from above!

Conan Doyle believed in the magazine—and above all he believed in Samuel Sidney McClure. He had also earned a substantial sum from his American tour, money that was ripe for investment. The two men ate lunch before going together to McClure's office, where Conan Doyle wrote a check for the exact sum owed to the British writers.

McClure was back to his affable, enthusiastic self. His monthly magazine was to become one of the most important in the decade that followed.

It was now November 1903, and McClure was on a visit to London. Lunch with Conan Doyle was booked in his diary. He simply had to ask: Might Conan Doyle be able to write a further twelve Sherlock Holmes short stories when he was finished with his current series? McClure was prepared to pay $75,000. Or he would offer $25,000 for a novella that could be split into three or four parts for publication in the magazine.

Conan Doyle turned down the offer of a full series, since he really had exhausted all sources of potential inspiration for plots. *McClure's*, though, had been the US publisher of the short story about the death of Sherlock Holmes ten years earlier, and he felt that he might be able to write a separate story for the magazine that would be the conclusion of the whole Holmes saga. This would have to wait until all the short stories he was writing for *Collier's Weekly* had been published.

Entitled "The Second Stain," this was intended to be the last Holmes story ever. Right at the beginning of the story, Dr. Watson explained that Sherlock Holmes had retired to Sussex to become a beekeeper.

When it came to the crunch, *McClure's* declined to publish the story. S. S. McClure's business partner put a stop to it. A single short story would not be enough to encourage more subscriptions, and besides, this was no cheap short story for which they could afford to buy the rights. *Collier's Weekly* bought the story instead, and in England it was published in the *Strand Magazine*, as usual. The twelve stories that made up *The Return of Sherlock Holmes* had become thirteen.

The last story reached the public in the winter of 1904–5. Two letters reached Conan Doyle. One was from a lady on the Isle of Wight offering her services as a housekeeper, now that he had moved to a country cottage. The other letter was written by an expert in apiculture, who was more than happy to provide advice.

The letters were not, then, intended for Conan Doyle. He was merely the messenger who could reach their intended recipient.

28

Frederic Dorr Steele was a prodigy among the illustrators of New York City in the 1890s. When, at the age of sixteen, he caught a train to the great global metropolis, it had been with a single aim: to carve out a future as an artist.

Steele's mother was an accomplished watercolorist and oil painter—and a grandmother was a poet and authoress—so his chosen career was hardly surprising. Art was in his blood. He was not, though, the only young man with such dreams drawn to New York, the center of the publishing world. For most, the dream soon yielded to reality, often a cold, hungry existence in drafty lodgings somewhere in the city. Young Fred Steele had no such problems. He got a great start in the world's second city. New York was creaking at the seams, so fast was its growth, as immigrants by the thousands poured off transatlantic steamers. It would not be long before it would overtake London in terms of population.

Steele immediately found employment at an architectural firm, and for a while was forced to suppress his more artistic side in favor of the straight line. The set square became his best friend. He took evening classes in drawing to improve his technique in subjects requiring more than straight lines. Before long, Steele managed to find a job in the publishing world, at the monthly magazine *Harper's*. Each new issue called for dozens of small illustrations, and he and a few other youths were paid fifteen dollars per week to provide them.

Without a trace of anxiety, Steele decided one day to become a freelancer. The 1890s were the golden era of illustration. Almost all fiction was accompanied by illustrations, and the artists were often just as revered as the authors. Improvements in printing techniques did justice to the illustrators' handiwork; these changes were particularly important for Steele, since he often worked in crayon. One of his major employers was *McClure's*, which—after a period on the ropes, resulting in smaller illustrations—had managed to find a financier and had played a significant role in Frederic Dorr Steele's career. *McClure's* reproduced its illustrations through photographic techniques, meaning that artists did not have to see their work mutilated by the old engraving method.

Steele had a gentle and quiet manner, yet he was still the sort to seek out social situations. Despite his young age, he was soon accepted by his much older colleagues and was invited into their circle, a clique comprising the country's illustrating elite.

Slowly but surely Steele began illustrating the magazine's main attractions—the short stories and serials. He was often given the freedom to choose the subjects of his illustrations. The feeling of being among the very first to read these stories, written by some of the giants of English literature, was quite wonderful. But Steele understood that the opportunity to give these fictional characters a face was a huge responsibility that required in-depth study of the texts. Many readers were interested to see what their favorite character looked like.

The years went by. One summer day in 1903, an Englishman named Robert King arrived in the little village of Deerfield, Massachusetts. He was a very expressive man, and indeed expressiveness was a requisite quality for his profession. His task was clear: to play Sherlock Holmes, as people imagined him to look, which is to say, rather like the actor William Gillette. Robert King did not possess a hooked nose, but at least his eyes were rather deep set. And, crucially, he owned a frock coat.

King's assignment was to model for the by-now-famous illustrator Frederic Dorr Steele. Steele had been asked to deliver illustrations for *Collier's Weekly*, which had bought the rights to a series of new Sherlock Holmes stories currently being written by Sir Arthur Conan Doyle. The first adventure was to be published in the September issue.

Sherlock Holmes, as far as Steele was concerned, looked like William Gillette. In place of the actor himself, Steele had hired look-alike model Robert King. In America, where the image of Gillette as the detective was so widespread, the idea of presenting a Holmes who bore no resemblance to the actor was simply impossible. Steele had not seen the play before illustrating *The Return of Sherlock Holmes*, but was able to rely on the wealth of photographs in circulation. In the play, Gillette wore a deerstalker, even though the story was set in London. Steele chose to deploy the headgear only when Holmes was in the country-side. Since this was a regular occurrence in the new short stories, the deerstalker featured heavily in their pages right from the start.

For the color illustration for the cover of the issue containing "The Empty House," Robert King was to pose kneeling on his left knee, with his left hand on the ground to support himself, while pretending to gaze out over the Reichenbach Falls. This was to accompany Sherlock Holmes's explanation of how he had managed to survive his meeting with Professor Moriarty. King was required to hold the uncomfortable pose for long enough to allow Steele to sketch his facial expression as well as all the creases in his suit. Some illustrators used models only for the composition of the image, while Steele made use of the model for much more than that.

The illustrator liked to gather inspiration for landscapes and back-drops from the surroundings close to home. The Swiss Alps, however, were an altogether more difficult proposition. He had no choice but to use photographs and illustrations of the places concerned, and he was particularly conscientious about getting such details right. Once, when he had been unable to decipher the era in which a Mark Twain story was set, he decided without further ado simply to visit the author at home, calling on him at lunchtime. He had found the famous author in bed, surrounded by breakfast plates forming small islands on his bedclothes. In his booming voice, puffing on his everlasting cigar, Twain had given Steele a cryptic, vague answer. Steele managed to draw some kind of conclusion from the response and was later rewarded with a letter from Twain, who thanked him for a job well done.

After the cover illustration was sketched out, King and Steele con-tinued their collaboration for the remaining illustrations to accompany "The Empty House." King struck various poses while Steele sketched. To the casual observer, Steele was his usual calm self—he was never a man to raise his voice—but those who knew him well could no doubt sense his anguish. In February of that year, back home in New Jersey, he and his wife had momentarily lost sight of their three-year-old son, Jack, who had toddled off toward the river near their house. An hour later, the boy's lifeless body was found half a mile downstream.

Steele finished off the illustration of the Reichenbach Falls that was to adorn the cover. There was no sign of water anywhere in the image.

★   ★   ★

In a little village in Hertfordshire in England, Sidney Paget was busy creating the corresponding illustrations for the British publication of the stories in the *Strand Magazine*. He had built a studio in one corner of the orchard surrounding his house. He preferred, however, to spend sunny summer days toiling in the garden itself. This meant that when the deadline for the next batch of illustrations approached he often had to spend half the night finishing them off.

Although separated by the Atlantic Ocean and unaware of each other's work, Paget and Steele chose the same motifs for more than half of the illustrations accompanying the two versions of "The Empty House."

Paget delivered ninety-five illustrations for the new stories in total, and his fee was more than ten times what it had been ten years before. He led a happy life with his wife, Edith, and their four daughters and two sons, the youngest of whom had arrived only recently. Sidney Paget was on top of the world and could indulge his great affection for fun and games.

One beautiful, crisp winter evening, Paget invited his old friend Alfred Butler—an architect who had lent his features to Dr. Watson—to the Art Workers' Guild, where the members themselves provided the entertainment. The evening's theme was somewhat unclear, yet the show as a whole resembled some kind of vaudeville revue. The star of the show was a thoroughly captivating ballerina, played by Sidney Paget, wearing a huge lampshade as a skirt and a corset around his torso. Edith had taken her husband to all the dressmakers in the area in search of a suitable garment. To top it all, he wore teardrop rhinestone earrings and a black wig, which provided the perfect backdrop to his muscular shoulders and slender neck. Edith had powdered his shoulders white before he took the stage.

Paget arrived onstage on a pantomime horse, performed his dance, and then blew kisses and threw flowers to the audience. His performance proved a huge success among his artist colleagues—a veritable showstopper. The finale of the show saw Paget, by now wearing only the lampshade, run out the door, into the snow, and off toward his dressing room. His delighted friend Butler followed hot on his heels, like the good Dr. Watson he was. Paget might reasonably have been expected to catch a cold after a finale like that.

Sure enough, he was soon struck by a cough. At first it was rather chesty, but before long his lungs were affected. It was not tuberculosis, but nevertheless affected his capacity to work and left him suffering in silence. Eventually his lungs gave up, and he died, at age forty-eight, on January 28, 1908.

29

O N THE NIGHT of July 4, 1906, tuberculosis had finally claimed Louisa "Touie" Conan Doyle's life. Thirteen years had passed since she had been told that she had only months to live. She had done all she could during those years to make the most of the time she had left, and she had seen her children grow up. Mary, who had turned seventeen, and Kingsley, thirteen, had been summoned home from their schools, as their mother's condition had worsened. Together, they sat with their mother during the final hours of her life. Their father was also at the bedside. Tears streamed down his cheeks as he held Touie's pale little hand in his fist.

Shortly afterward, when the children went back to their schools, and Conan Doyle was alone at Undershaw, he became depressed. Still, he had to take care of his family responsibilities, and he was expected to deliver the stories he had undertaken to write. Eventually, what would drag him from the depths of despair turned up, quite unexpectedly, in the form of a nearsighted lawyer, an expert in transport law for railway passengers, who had spent the last three years in prison for mutilating a horse.

In late autumn 1906 Conan Doyle had started plowing through months' worth of unopened mail. In the pile of letters he found one from a George Edalji, recently released from prison after serving half of his sentence. Although he was free, try as he might, he simply had not been able to clear his name. He was innocent. His alibi was watertight, and the evidence against him entirely fabricated.

George Edalji's father, an Anglican priest, had been born in Bombay and was of Parsi descent. Since settling in England, the family had struggled with hate campaigns against them in the village in the West Midlands where they had lived for many years. Anonymous letters and absurd accusations were almost everyday occurrences. Even the local police were against them.

In 1903, sheep, cows, and horses had been subjected to a wave of nocturnal mutilations in the pastures surrounding the Edaljis' village. George, who was twenty-seven and still living with his parents, and who commuted daily by train to chambers in Birmingham, was accused of the awful deeds, and in particular the last act, in which a pony had been maimed.

In court, George Edalji found his alibi being turned against him. He shared a bedroom with his father, the vicar, and George explained that being a light sleeper, his father would surely have noticed had he attempted to sneak out in the dead of night. The accomplished prosecutor managed to twist the alibi in such a way as to make the accused seem even more suspect. The trial continued in this vein. The description of George's overcoat, which had been hanging in the freezing-cold porch when the police came to arrest him, went from "damp" to "wet." Every single piece of evidence that he felt supported his version of the events ended up being discredited.

Edalji had finally been released, but the guilty verdict, strangely enough, remained. He wanted nothing more than to clear his name and in so doing regain his legal accreditation.

Over the years, Conan Doyle had been approached any number of times with questions about various legal cases. People confused him with his fictional hero. Usually he would politely yet firmly decline. This time was different. He was fascinated by the case. He also had more time on his hands than he had had for a very long while and was bored. And so he decided to arrange a meeting with George Edalji at the Grand Hotel near Charing Cross.

When Conan Doyle arrived he noticed a man of Persian appearance reading a newspaper, with the page just inches from his face. Up to that point, Conan Doyle had not been completely certain that Edalji's protestations of innocence were genuine. Ophthalmologist that he was, however, Conan Doyle recognized at once that a man with such severe astigmatism would never have been able to negotiate fields, ditches, and fences in the dead of night and then conduct complicated surgical procedures on a pony or indeed any other animal. Conan Doyle realized that this was an innocent man. All that remained was to immerse himself in studying the case and then chip away at the evidence against Edalji.

Conan Doyle wrote to the Home Office straightaway, pointing out the grossly unfair manner in which the local policemen had acted. Not only that, he traveled to the West Midlands to meet with the policeman who had made the initial accusations against Edalji. At first, the policeman misunderstood the situation, believing Conan Doyle to be on his side. He even repeated his allegation that Edalji and his father engaged in unnatural acts in the bedroom they shared.

Conan Doyle then went on to describe the case in newspaper articles, deploying every technique in his literary arsenal in order to provoke the reactions he was seeking. He met with the home secretary, Herbert Gladstone—surprising him by proffering the name of the man whom he presumed to be the guilty one—and the minister promised to set up an inquiry.

The inquiry, however, did not go as Conan Doyle had intended. The man in charge of the investigation turned out to be a cousin of the stupid West Midlands policeman. Still, they had no choice but to quash Edalji's conviction for maiming the horse. Another charge—that Edalji had written the anonymous letters he claimed had terrorized him and his parents—remained, even though the accusation had been exposed as completely absurd in light of the evidence Conan Doyle had presented for the Home Office. Furthermore, the officers and other authorities involved in the case never received any kind of reprimand, and Edalji did not receive a penny in compensation for the time he had spent in prison.

At an early age, George Edalji had realized that he could not avoid the spitting and the blows that prejudiced neighbors subjected him to. Therefore, the inquiry's conclusion that he had written some of the letters had not come as a surprise. He was well aware of the fact that life was not fair. Conan Doyle continued to struggle in his name, not least in the wake of a new wave of anonymous letters, for which Edalji was blamed again. After this turn of events, the author conversed about the case with the new home secretary, a friend of his, Winston Churchill. In the end, George Edalji succeeded in the most important thing—being reinstated as a practicing lawyer. For that he was eternally grateful to Conan Doyle.

★ ★ ★

September 18, 1907, was a significant day for both Conan Doyle and George Edalji. It was the date of Conan Doyle's marriage to Jean Leckie, and Edalji was among the smattering of guests invited to attend the service.

The couple wanted a simple ceremony in the presence of their immediate family and closest friends, and their choice of church, Saint Margaret's in Westminster, had been kept secret from all but the guests themselves. Edalji sat in a pew, straining to discern as much as possible of his surroundings. The church was beautifully decorated in light tones, the chancel flanked by two great palms. As the ceremony began, the bride's father led her to the altar. Her gown was made of silver tissue veiled with silk lace and embroidered in pearls, with a long crepe de chine train turned back at one corner with a large lover's knot in chiffon and a horseshoe of orange blossom. Two bridesmaids and a four-year-old boy—Conan Doyle's nephew—followed her down the aisle. The brother of the groom, Captain Innes Doyle, was best man, and the celebrant was Conan Doyle's brother-in-law—his sister Dodo having married a priest.

The nearsighted Edalji, though, could not see much of what was going on. He felt rather out of place. Aside from the family, the other guests, all accompanied by their spouses, composed a veritable literary elite. J. M. Barrie was there; his play about Peter Pan had become one of the great theatrical successes of the time. Jerome K. Jerome was still a big name, even if he hadn't been able to match the success of *Three Men in a Boat*. The author Coulson Kernahan and his wife were also in the church—Jeannie Gwynne had been her name when she was younger, and it was she who had discovered Conan Doyle's unique brand of literature via the handwritten manuscript for *A Study in Scarlet*. Humorist Robert Barr of the *Idler* was also among the guests, along with Bram Stoker, who had recently published a major interview with Conan Doyle. At least Edalji could feel some kinship with Bram Stoker, since he too was now only partially sighted.

The reception was a rather larger affair, with two hundred invited guests, at the Hotel Metropole in London. Before leaving for their continental honeymoon, the newlyweds had time to open their wedding gifts. Conan Doyle gave his new wife a diamond tiara and received a gold watch in return. The servants at Undershaw gave Conan Doyle a silver inkwell. One thing was sure—he would keep writing.

The following day George Edalji's name was featured prominently in the newspaper, first on the list of eminent guests. Life in the spotlight did not suit him. He returned to the West Midlands and lived as normal a life as was possible. All he ever wanted was to be a lawyer, preferably an expert on matters of law for railway passengers.

30

Harald Thornberg was on the warpath. Besides being the proprietor of Scandinavia's first literary agency for English authors, he was also the Swedish representative for Curtis Brown of London, one of Europe's oldest literary agencies.

On January 5, 1909, he picked up his pen and began a letter to Mr. G. Herbert Thring at the British Society of Authors.

> Dear Sir:
>
> Will You please inform Sir Conan Doyle, that it is necessary he should make some protest against the use of the name of "Sherlock Holmes" on books not written by him. The trash, made in Germany, is overflowing this country. Our newspapers are making war on it, but—no one tells of Sir Conan Doyle not being the author. I send You to day a false "Sherlock Holmes," made in and circulating in Denmark. Also there a protest ought to be given.

The trouble had begun in 1905 when a German publisher in Dresden acquired the rights to two American weekly dime-novel series, one about Buffalo Bill and the other featuring Nick Carter. A new story was released each week, and these exciting yarns for the masses were an instant hit. The venture was such a success, in fact, that the publisher translated and distributed the stories in France, Spain, Holland, Belgium, Russia, Italy, the Balkans, and Scandinavia. Everything was produced in his printworks in Dresden and then shipped to the foreign markets in great quantities.

The Dresden publisher established an international publishing group —the first of its kind—with offices in several countries. Such success did not go unnoticed by the other German publishers, and before long competition had begun to enter the market. The different series were always about a lead character with an English-sounding name, but the stories themselves were in fact all written by anonymous German authors. It was work that put food on the table, no more, no less.

In January 1907 another weekly series appeared. Each issue featured thirty-two pages of text, and the format was the same as that of most other weekly or monthly publications. Published by the Berlin-based Verlagshaus für Volksliteratur und Kunst, it was entitled *Detectiv Sherlock Holmes und seine weltberühmten Abenteuer* (Detective Sherlock Holmes and his world-famous adventures). After a complaint from the Robert Lutz publishing house, which owned the German publishing rights to Sherlock Holmes and had recently reissued all the original stories, the series name was changed after eleven weeks of publication to the less provocative *Aus den Geheimakten des Welt-Detektivs* (From the secret files of the world detective). The stories themselves were still about Sherlock Holmes. This Holmes, though, bore no resemblance to Conan Doyle's creation. Powers of deduction were rarely deployed, but rather the anonymous authors solved the cases with a combination of unlikely coincidences or brute force. Dr. Watson was sidelined, replaced as Holmes's assistant by the young Harry Taxon. Titles such as "The Moneylender's Daughter," "The Blood-Stained Jewels," and "Interred with the Infernal Machine" were intended to persuade young readers to break into their piggy banks.

Conan Doyle had seen a couple of the issues and wrote to his literary agent:

> I return the Copenhagen "Sherlock Holmes." It is entirely a fake, just as a Spanish one was. I should dearly like to prosecute these infernal villains. Please say so to Thring.

Conan Doyle faced insurmountable problems guarding his character on the Continent. In his own social circle he allowed friends to write parodies and pastiches, but he never envisaged perfect strangers making a living on the back of his creation. When the French novelist Maurice Leblanc inquired as to whether he might use Sherlock Holmes as a secondary character in his stories about a gentleman thief named Arsène Lupin, Conan Doyle at least had had the opportunity to say no. And say no he did. In response, Leblanc had simply renamed his character Herlock Sholmès, but he did not make any other alterations.

The arrival of film had served to further complicate matters. In 1908 an unauthorized Sherlock Holmes film suddenly arrived in British cinemas; after Walter Christmas's theft of Gillette's play, it may have come as no great surprise that the film turned out to be Danish. Something was indeed rotten in the state of Denmark. The film, called *Sherlock Holmes i Livsfare* (Sherlock Holmes in mortal danger), ran for just over fifteen minutes. During that time, Sherlock Holmes (played by Viggo Larsen) managed to prevent the thief Raffles from stealing a pearl necklace, avoided capture by Professor Moriarty, and ultimately ensured that the two villains were brought to justice. The film, which had borrowed Willie Hornung's antihero Raffles as a character, owed more to Christmas's play than to Conan Doyle's original tales. It was only the first in a series of Danish films with essentially the same structure. Conan Doyle had cause for alarm.

Yet, the author's main concern remained those awful dime novels. In early February 1909, Harald Thornberg wrote to Mr. Thring once more. They had been in regular contact over recent months. Thornberg was reluctant to take the matter to court, believing instead that a more effective course of action would be for Conan Doyle himself to write a protest, which could then be published in both the Danish and the Swedish press. People would at least understand that he was not the author of these dreadful stories. If Conan Doyle was prepared to send Thornberg such a statement, the Swede would take care of the rest.

Several weeks passed, and nothing happened. Conan Doyle had undergone a minor operation in mid-January and spent February convalescing in Cornwall. By early March he was back on the case and had by then decided to go ahead and publish a protest letter. Before he did so, he asked a Danish legal firm to take a closer look at the series. The lawyers concluded that the text on the back of the publication did in fact imply that the main character was the world-famous detective Sherlock Holmes.

At the Society of Authors, meanwhile, Thring continued forwarding foreign Sherlock Holmes booklets to A. P. Watt, Conan Doyle's literary agent. An irritated Conan Doyle complained to his agent, "These things cover Europe and entirely elbow out the real S. H. stories."

Conan Doyle's anxieties were well founded. This proliferation was not merely a threat to the survival of his previous work—he had started writing new Sherlock Holmes stories, in spite of having solemnly sworn in 1905 that "The Second Stain" was to be the very last. He was not compiling a regular series this time but rather issuing the occasional short story now and then. He had managed to complete "Wisteria Lodge" and "The Bruce-Partington Plans" during the course of 1908.

While Thring continued writing to the Danish lawyers representing Conan Doyle, the author was provided with something of a distraction. On March 17, 1909, Jean gave birth to their first child, a son, Denis Percy Stewart Conan Doyle. The impending birth had been the reason behind Conan Doyle's unwillingness to commit to a whole new series of Holmes short stories. He wanted, for once, to spend time with his family.

Conan Doyle had rented out Undershaw the previous year, and the newlyweds had moved to a new property, Windlesham in the Sussex village of Crowborough, close to Jean's family home. Conan Doyle dubbed the pile "Swindlesham," on account of the sums of money he had been forced to spend on unforeseen repairs. The reason, then, for his writing Sherlock Holmes stories at all was really quite simple: once again, he needed the money.

Conan Doyle's Danish lawyers advised against any form of legal action, since the publishers had in fact never claimed that the texts had been written by Conan Doyle. And so, finally, in early September 1909, Conan Doyle's protest letter was published in the Danish newspapers.

Sir! Would you have the great kindness to state that I have no connection with the cheap illustrated stories about Sherlock Holmes which are published in Denmark and other countries. I leave it to your readers how fair it is just to steal the name of a character in such a fashion. Yours faithfully, Arthur Conan Doyle.

The author both lost and won the fight. The German originals—the root of the problem—were untouched and went on being published for two more years, in the end comprising 230 stories.

Conan Doyle's Danish lawyers had convinced him that it would be hard to wage and win a legal battle. There was, however, a way to stop the publication of these low-quality series about Sherlock Holmes, Nick Carter, and other dime-novel heroes. In Sweden, where it turned into a political issue, the publishing of the stories came to an end after an extensive boycott against retailers selling them.

Conan Doyle's own involvement in the matter highlighted the hopelessness of the situation for the creator of the master detective. There was only one way to keep control of Holmes—to write even more stories about him.

Half a year later, in February 1910, owing to a murder committed by two young Swiss farmhands—who claimed to be under the influence of the fascinating stories they had read about how murders were committed—the Swiss railway authorities decided that no publications of the Sherlock Holmes type were to be sold at railway bookstalls.

Once again Conan Doyle's stories had been mixed up with those German dime novels that he hated so much.

31

KIT WAS NO longer the little boy who had locked Moriarty in the henhouse in Baltimore. His playfulness and a great love of the written word remained, but in so many ways he had grown. Increasingly, the nickname Kit made way for Chris. At the age of twenty, he graduated at the top of his class at Haverford College in Pennsylvania. He gave the valedictory address at graduation—in Latin, of course. He had been editor of the yearbook; the college newspaper had been his second home for several years; and he had written, produced, and starred in the drama society's performances. In addition, he had played on both the soccer and the cricket teams and had been a board member of more student societies and committees than could be squeezed into his yearbook entry. That this was a student who would fit right in at the University of Oxford—once the Atlantic steamer *Friesland* had brought him to England—was not in any doubt.

The ceremony welcoming Chris and the other new students to the historic university took place on a Saturday afternoon in October 1910. All the young men wore dark suits, white bow ties, mortarboards with tassels, and traditional gowns. Chris was not alone in having arrived on a Rhodes Scholarship; a young man named Elmer Davis from Indiana was there by the same graces. One by one, the students were given the large blue book *Statuta et Decreta Universitatis Oxoniensis*—essentially a rule book to guide Oxford students on matters of good academic practice and etiquette, all written in seventeenth-century Latin. Reading the book, Chris realized that he was part of something ancient, with rituals going back much further than any he had ever come across in the United States. He had spent many childhood summers in England, and he loved the country and its traditions. He found wonderfully British the notion that the old Latin rule book could be applied to any new element of a contemporary life. Even the arrival of the first airplanes in Oxford was seemingly covered by a suitable paragraph—*De Vehiculis*—which could be applied to govern students' use of such machines.

Oxford was full of wise men. One such man was Ronald Knox. His father was the Anglican bishop of Manchester. From the age of fifteen, Ronald had become increasingly High Church in his ways, while his father had made the opposite journey and was now ever closer to the evangelical strain within the church. During his years at boarding school, Ronald had been renowned as the brightest boy ever to have attended, and his success continued at Oxford. In 1910 he completed his undergraduate degree and was immediately offered a readership at Oxford's Trinity College. The plan was for him to become a Church of England priest and then take up the role of college chaplain at Trinity.

Despite being only two years older than Chris, Knox lectured the students under his aegis on everything from logic to the writings of Homer and Virgil. He was renowned for delivering lively, entertaining lectures, and none of his colleagues came close to equaling his prodigious talent for bringing his subjects to life. Just as for many other Oxford readers, one of his duties was to give talks before the myriad of student societies. He had quickly realized that there really was no need to write a new presentation on each occasion, since each new audience was listening to him talk about the subject for the first time. He would give the same talk again and again, until he was bored with it, at which point he would have it published.

Knox decided at first to write two lectures: one that was suitable for the theological societies and another for the secular clubs. He wrote the latter first and, having delivered it, realized that it was perfectly acceptable even in a more theological setting. The lecture was called "Studies in the Literature of Sherlock Holmes," and in spite of its subject matter, it was, in fact, an intervention in a religious debate.

One of the most keenly discussed theological questions at Oxford at the time concerned what students of the Bible called "higher criticism," whereby the books of the Old Testament had been examined in terms of their origins and historical context and—based on detailed scrutiny and analysis of the texts—ascribed to different authors. Homer had received the same treatment, and parts of his *Iliad* had been attributed to other authors as well. Ronald Knox was critical of such thinking. In terms of the Bible, he felt that faith was of primary importance, not some modernizing of theological instruction with the help of textual analysis. His approach to the subject was sharply satirical. And he used Sherlock Holmes to illustrate it.

As youngsters, Knox and his brothers had written to Conan Doyle, inquiring as to why Dr. Watson's first name had changed from John to James in one of the stories. An editorial mistake, Conan Doyle had replied. All these years later, Knox was able to deploy the anecdote, noting that inconsistencies in the use of John/James were fundamental to Backnecke's theory of a proto-Watson and a deutero-Watson, elaborating which stories had been written by the earlier and later versions. Knox then went on to take isolated details from the Sherlock Holmes stories and explain how they had formed the basis of studies by internationally renowned experts such as Binsk, Bilgemann, Ratzegger, Sabaglione, Sauwosch, Papier Maché, and Piff-Pouff.

Of course neither Backnecke nor Piff-Pouff, nor indeed any of the others, actually existed. There was certainly no actual research based on Sherlock Holmes. None of the audience, however, could be under any illusions as to the fact that the whole thing was a satire on Albert Schweitzer and his near-identical speculation surrounding the prophet Isaiah.

It was, nonetheless, an undeniably entertaining and incisive lecture about Sherlock Holmes.

Everyone at Oxford in 1911 knew who Ronald Knox was—his tour of student societies was renowned. Chris's interest in the detective might not have been as fanatical as when he had interrogated his brothers up in the attic, but the young American was undoubtedly struck by this new way of approaching the old favorites, dismantling them into component parts, and then playing a sort of academic game with Holmes. If one treated the stories as if they were true, this provided a pleasing intellectual puzzle, as one could then seek to explain inconsistencies and errors.

After a year, Ronald Knox was so tired of his own lecture he decided to publish it in a student newspaper. One summer day in 1912 he received a letter—from Sir Arthur Conan Doyle.

The famous author had been in the spotlight even more than usual that spring. The *Strand Magazine* had begun publishing a new novel he had written, *The Lost World*, about an expedition that discovers not just living dinosaurs but an entire prehistoric world high on a mountain plateau in South America. The first part was released just as the RMS

Titanic sank to the bottom of the North Atlantic. Conan Doyle had become embroiled in a public dispute with George Bernard Shaw, who had been critical of the crew's actions and indeed their competence.

Conan Doyle was also busy in other areas. As the chairman of the Amateur Field Sports Association, he was following all the reports of British performances at the Olympic Games, which were then under way in Stockholm.

On July 5, Conan Doyle had, however, a quiet moment and after reading Knox's article, which its author had sent to him, he replied.

> I cannot help writing to you to tell you of the amusement—and also the amazement—with which I read your article on Sherlock Holmes. That anyone should spend such pains on such material was what surprised me. Certainly you know a great deal more about it than I do, for the stories have been written in a disconnected (and careless) way, without referring back to what had gone before. I am only pleased that you have not found more discrepancies, especially as to dates.

Conan Doyle continued the letter in Knox's own style, referring to Piff-Pouff and the other imaginary greats in the field. He made no reference to the fact that the text actually referred to something else. Perhaps he missed that altogether, or perhaps the context disappeared as soon as one took the article out of Oxford. For Ronald Knox, though, who had been ordained an Anglican priest that autumn, that no longer mattered. The presentation about Sherlock Holmes was a closed chapter, one that might now slowly be slipping into the mists of time.

32

O N WEDNESDAY, SEPTEMBER 2, 1914, the heat of summer still hung over London, but a chill sent a shudder through the nation. *London Opinion* was putting the finishing touches on Saturday's front page, which was to feature the pointing minister of war, Lord Kitchener, framed by the words, "Your country needs YOU."

The National Insurance Commission's offices were located in Wellington House, on Buckingham Gate in central London. This was a state authority charged with administering the system of welfare that had been ratified by Parliament a few years previously. The chair of the commission was the politician and journalist Charles Masterman.

At that address, a gathering of Britain's most well-known authors was under way. J. M. Barrie was seen passing through the gate, as was his friend Conan Doyle. The universally gifted G. K. Chesterton, known, among other things, for his Father Brown stories, arrived soon afterward. His characteristic Falstaffian bulk was unmistakable. John Galsworthy had torn himself away from working on the novels that would later be published as *The Forsyte Saga*—or perhaps something else from his broad oeuvre—and Conan Doyle's old acquaintance H. G. Wells, writer of fascinating futuristic scenarios, had also accepted the invitation. Even old Thomas Hardy, loved for *Tess of the d'Urbervilles* and other works, was there, and many, many others were besides. If not for the serious nature of the matter at hand, such a meeting might have been rather collegial and pleasant. The host, Charles Masterman, was pleased with the turnout. His only cause for concern was the presence of Rudyard Kipling—that could certainly cause problems later on.

One month earlier, on the same evening that war had broken out, Conan Doyle and other residents of Crowborough had established a volunteer home guard. His idea was that every citizen, young or old, would be assigned to such a unit and trained in the use of weapons. A few days later he wrote a letter about his initiative to the *Times*, and the idea spread rapidly across the country. Lord Kitchener, though, soon put a stop to it, decreeing that civilian reserve organizations were forbidden. Conan Doyle did not give up. He so desperately wanted to be part of the effort. This was of course a war, and wars are problematic by nature, but war could also result in virtuousness among the combatants and a chastening that might lead Europe on to greater things. It would surely not be a long war, a year at most. The outbreak of war was widely expected—looking back, one could see that the path to war had been clearly staked out long before. Conan Doyle sought his brother Innes's advice. Was it at all conceivable that the army would have use for a fifty-five-year-old, albeit one who was still in good nick? He would learn the other things quickly. If he were allowed to sign up, this would surely encourage other men his age to do the same.

Innes, who had by now attained the rank of major, was still in England. Conan Doyle's secretary, Alfred Wood, whom the author had known ever since he lived in Southsea, was a reserve officer and had been called up. Jean's younger brother Malcolm Leckie was an army doctor, and Conan Doyle's twenty-one-year-old son Kingsley had voluntarily enlisted with the City of London Royal Army Medical Corps. Conan Doyle's nephew Oscar Hornung had signed up at the age of nineteen and had even urged his uncle to use his influence to ensure that he was sent to the front without delay.

Conan Doyle felt as if he were the only one not able to go. Any family member he had asked whether there were a way had said no. In the cold light of day he could see why; he had both responsibilities and duties, particularly now, when besides his grown-up children, Mary and Kingsley, he also had sons Denis and Adrian Malcolm, five and four years old, respectively, and daughter Lena Jean (or Billy, as she was known), who was almost two. In their nursery Conan Doyle had, as an act of patriotism, hung a large photograph of the Earl Jellicoe, admiral of the Grand Fleet.

The responsibilities and duties were one thing; Conan Doyle's emotional response, however, was quite another. He realized that he had only one life, and that an opportunity had presented itself that could provide him with an incredible experience as well as the prospect of being of service to others. In the end he could not resist and sent off his application. "Though I am 55 years old," he wrote, "I am very strong and hardy, and can make my voice audible at great distances which is useful at drill." The army said no.

At least now Conan Doyle would be doing something useful. The room at Wellington House was filled with nervous tension in antici-pation of what was to come. Everything had been arranged in the utmost secrecy, and the goings-on at Buckingham Gate were known to only a select few in the nation's governing elite. After the discovery that Germany had long been busy preparing an advanced propaganda apparatus, Charles Masterman was tasked with quickly establishing its British counterpart, the War Propaganda Bureau. His first action was to summon the country's leading authors. Two weeks later he would meet with suitable publishers and, not least, A. P. Watt, who was to be the bureau's agent.

The main purpose of the propaganda effort was not in fact to spread information within the country's borders but rather to reach allied nations and, in particular, neutral countries. Among the latter was the United States, the most important of those nations yet to be drawn into the war. The bureau sought to avoid the mistake Germany had made in directing propaganda at the great mass of the population. No, it would focus squarely on the elite, the commentators, the well-educated: influ-ential politicians, academics, teachers, journalists, and business leaders. For the propaganda to be effective, it had to be seen to be something other than propaganda. That, then, was the reason those authors had been invited to Wellington House. The message would be disseminated via well-formulated, almost academic explanations of the great ques-tions posed by the war. It was clear to everyone involved that Rudyard Kipling was a potential liability in such a context, especially since he was scheduled to undertake a lecture tour of the United States. Rabid warmongers were just what the propaganda bureau did not need.

Conan Doyle, on the other hand, completed his assigned task imme-diately. His pamphlet *To Arms!*—already written before the Wellington House meeting—was published within weeks. Before long it was also being spread on the other side of the Atlantic. Continuing in the same vein, he then produced a series of articles and other writings about the war.

After three decades as an author, Conan Doyle remained an influential figure, nowhere more so than in America. That June, he and Jean had toured the United States and Canada, after being invited by the Canadian government. From the moment he stepped off the boat, he had been hounded by journalists wherever he went. His popularity seemed to have grown every bit as much as the skyscrapers had since the last time he had visited New York. He was at a loss as to why but was delighted by the reception given to Jean, who was referred to as "Lady Sunshine" in the New York press. It was a great pleasure to see her in the spotlight, not least because she herself seemed to appreciate it so much. She enjoyed everything she saw and all that she experienced. The couple's schedule was packed almost to bursting, and as they crossed the Canadian prairie toward the end of the trip, they were completely exhausted. Returning to England was positively restful.

Conan Doyle was enormously popular at home too, both for his writings (he wrote up to a dozen short stories or longer stories each and every year) and for his incisive commentary on a range of issues, encompassing both the national and the personal spheres. In July 1914, the *Strand Magazine* published a story of his with a wartime theme, in which only a few enemy submarines bring England to the brink of defeat. More and more experts were warning of the potential danger posed by these lurking vessels. Whether they would turn out to be a factor remained to be seen. The war, however, had arrived.

Conan Doyle's great fame, nonetheless, was based on the master detective, and he no longer harbored any thoughts of retiring him. He knew that most of his literary career was behind him. Holmes was no longer a threat, able to overshadow something more significant. Any resentment the writer might once have felt toward Holmes was long gone—after thirty years in each other's company they were like old friends. Along the way, Holmes might have lost some of his more eccentric features, but he had grown as a human being.

Conan Doyle had, over the last few years, managed to write roughly a short story a year about Sherlock Holmes, and every occasion had been treated as supremely newsworthy. This reduced rate of output seemed about right to Conan Doyle at the time, and it was sufficient to ensure that public interest in the detective never died out. Some readers, however, wanted more. One of them, a young architect named Arthur Whitaker, sent Conan Doyle a completed Sherlock Holmes short story, "The Man Who Was Wanted." Whitaker proposed they publish it as coauthors. The story, though, was not particularly good, and Conan Doyle knew that his fee would be reduced by 75 percent as soon as any other writer was credited with a Holmes creation. Instead, he did as he had done with others before—namely, he suggested that he pay Whitaker ten guineas for the idea, which did not necessarily mean he would use it. Whitaker agreed to this, the ten guineas were paid, Conan Doyle placed the short story in a drawer, and that was the end of that.

Even if Conan Doyle's output of detective stories was now somewhat sporadic, Sherlock Holmes had nevertheless proved to be a knight in shining armor. In 1910, Conan Doyle had rented the Adelphi Theatre in London, at his own expense, in order to stage a production very close to his heart, a play about professional boxing in the early nineteenth century. At first all went well, and the crowds flocked to see it. But interest in seeing a theatrical boxing match quickly waned, particularly among women. On May 6 the final blow had been delivered—King Edward VII passed away, less than a decade after ascending the throne. The nation was in mourning. The theater closed for a month, and by the time it reopened, the play had met with the same fate as the late monarch—it too was dead and buried.

Conan Doyle was left with the theater he had rented but no show to put on. Instead of subletting the theater, he came up with the idea of filling the remainder of the season with a staging of a Sherlock Holmes tale.

When Conan Doyle set about writing something he had no difficulty in shutting out the world around him and simply letting the inspiration flow. He would often write without taking a break, and it looked as though he never even needed to pause for thought. Sometimes he managed to write an entire Sherlock Holmes story while sitting in a room full of people, all chatting away. He had also done so on a train and even on the floor of the cricket pavilion when rain had stopped play.

Within a week the script was finished. A week after that, the entire cast was busy in rehearsals. The play, *The Speckled Band*, was based on the short story of the same name, which he had written almost two decades earlier. Using a preexisting—and popular—story was rather practical, certainly compared with inventing something completely new, even though Conan Doyle reworked and deepened the plot quite significantly in order to transform it into a play that would last a whole evening.

Sherlock Holmes was to be played by H. A. Saintsbury, who had been touring England with Gillette's play for several years and would soon celebrate his one-thousandth performance in the role of the detective.

The respected Shakespearean actor Lyn Harding played the story's cruel stepfather. Harding, though, was not altogether taken with Conan Doyle's traditional melodramatic interpretation of the character and expressed a desire to insert lines and actions that would add rather more idiosyncratic effect to the role. Conan Doyle, who supervised rehearsals, was not at all convinced. But Harding was an actor for a reason. Before long the stepfather—with a blink here, a trembling leg there, and even a quick tug at a lock of hair on his forehead—was transformed into the neurotic figure Harding had been aiming for. Conan Doyle was none too happy, but Harding was also the director of the piece, which left the scriptwriter able to do no more than point out that the whole thing had become rather burlesque. Their relationship had been good at first but was now strained.

It was at this point that one of the production staff came up with an agreeable middle way: let J. M. Barrie—a good friend of both men, as well as a leading dramatist—decide.

Barrie came, Barrie saw, and Harding conquered. "Let Harding have his own way," Barrie whispered to Conan Doyle out in the auditorium.

The play premiered on June 4, 1910. It was a triumph, presenting good old Holmes and Watson in fine form, and audiences loved it. As Conan Doyle and Saintsbury took the stage after the performance, the applause was deafening.

The real success story was Lyn Harding. He took no fewer than twelve bows before the audience had had enough. The critics, too, loved his interpretation of the stepfather role. "One of the sensations of the present season," one of them wrote of Harding's performance. Conan Doyle, proved wrong, sent a delicate letter of congratulation to the great actor.

The success continued, through 169 performances at the Adelphi, after which a provincial tour and foreign versions awaited. Once again, Conan Doyle had hit the bull's-eye with Sherlock Holmes. It was not surprising that his attitude toward the detective had changed—he had an awful lot to thank him for.

Now, four years later, Conan Doyle was again on the verge of another Sherlock Holmes milestone. In September 1914, the *Strand Magazine* and the American *Sunday Magazine* began publishing installments of a new Sherlock Holmes novel, *The Valley of Fear*. Readers were reintroduced to Professor Moriarty, with a description of the man and his home. Despite having appeared in only two of Conan Doyle's short stories—and uttering a total of ten lines—he had become the ultimate criminal, king of the underworld. His notoriety was due to William Gillette's huge success of a play, still touring both the United States and many European countries.

As with *A Study in Scarlet*, much of the new story looked back at events that had taken place in America. What had been a novice author's solution to plot making was now a skilled craftsman's precise deployment of a literary device. As a crime thriller, the story also offered something new—a murder in a manor house, with a limited number of suspects and the escape routes blocked. The conundrum itself was far too complex to be fitted into a short story. All the clues were there, in full view, and they led the reader to the solution at exactly the same pace as Sherlock Holmes himself. It was less about powers of deduction and more about logical brain activity.

The American part of *The Valley of Fear* revolved around a secret gang of Irish coal miners in Pennsylvania. Conan Doyle's inspiration for these characters came from a book about their real-life counterparts by Allan Pinkerton, who had, back in the 1850s, opened the world's first private detective agency. Conan Doyle had also played host at Windlesham to a former Pinkerton detective, who had provided him with plenty of material to expand upon.

In contrast to his appearances in *The Hound of the Baskervilles*, Sherlock Holmes was present throughout the whole investigation into the case in *The Valley of Fear*. Holmes, though, had changed over the years. While the story was set a few years before Holmes and Moriarty's struggle by the Reichenbach Falls, the eccentric traits Conan Doyle had once given him were nowhere to be seen. Gone were the strange chemistry experiments and the disguises, as was the monotonous violin playing. His use of a 7 percent cocaine solution definitely was no longer featured. For a readership that was increasingly familiar with the detective genre, he became a more credible figure.

Conan Doyle had never invested such a significant amount of time—four months—in writing a Sherlock Holmes story. This, though, was to be his literary swan song, as he explained to H. Greenhough Smith at the *Strand*. He did not plan to write any more novels. Conan Doyle was also apologetic at having delivered something so trivial at a time when the country faced such a grave threat.

Greenhough Smith, though, was pleased to have a real treat to offer his readers. There were enough war reports in the ordinary newspapers. The war also inspired Conan Doyle to make some last-minute changes to the manuscript for British publication. He changed the nationality of one of the families in the second half of the book from German to Swedish. The family remained German in the American edition; there was no cause to change anything, since the United States was not engaged in the war at the time.

The war had an obvious effect on Conan Doyle, right from the outset, not only in his writing, and it even more palpably affected his closest friends and relatives. In the very first battle, near the Belgian city of Mons, Jean's brother Malcolm, who so often had acted as a chaperone for Jean and Conan Doyle's meetings during those secretive years, was reported missing. The family lived in uncertainty well into autumn, until the message arrived. Malcolm Leckie was dead.

Conan Doyle realized that he had been wrong. This was to be a long war.

33

In Washington, DC, as 1914 was drawing to a close, the situation grew more and more complicated. America's active attempts to avoid being dragged into the war, it seemed, might not be enough. Diplomatic intrigue had become a fact of life. The German ambassador, Johann Heinrich von Bernstorff, was doing everything in his power to prevent the United States from entering the war.

At the US Department of the Navy, thirty-two-year-old assistant secretary Franklin Delano Roosevelt sat at his desk, a tall, lean, stylish man with an air of intelligence and an appealing nature. He was somewhat athletic and adventurous, having been part of an expedition only five years earlier whose goal had been to recover Captain Kidd's lost treasure from a Canadian island. He shared a name with a previous president, though they were only distantly related. Roosevelt was a favorite among the news-hungry reporters who filled the city when they were looking for a story.

One such correspondent, Vincent Starrett, from the *Chicago Daily News*, had a habit of perching on a corner of Roosevelt's desk after cadging a cigarette. The two men enjoyed talking to each other, whether the conversation concerned work or something else entirely. Roosevelt was a keen philatelist and, to a lesser degree, a book collector, who often scoured the many antiquarian bookstores in Washington for titles concerning the maritime world. The newspaper correspondent, four years Roosevelt's junior, was also a bibliophile, but his collection focused squarely on detective stories.

"Sherlock Holmes?" said Roosevelt. "I think I have read all the Holmes adventures ever written. I hope there'll be more some day. They don't come any better."

Starrett agreed. Sherlock Holmes was his favorite, too. It was clear that Roosevelt was happy to discuss the subject further.

"What was that story about the red-headed man who got a job copying the Encyclopaedia by hand?"

"The Red-Headed League," Starrett replied. "It's the one nearly everybody remembers first."

"But I'm not sure the snake story wasn't a better yarn," Roosevelt remarked, as he tried to recall which other Sherlock Holmes stories he had particularly enjoyed.

"It's Conan Doyle's own favorite," said Starrett, who diligently followed everything that was written about the British author. Earlier that year, during the summer, there had been a lot of coverage when Conan Doyle had honored the United States with a visit.

"I see we have a lot in common," Roosevelt said. "Drop in when you care to. When the cigarettes aren't on the desk, they're in the left-hand top drawer."

Roosevelt's wish for more Holmes stories would soon be realized. Even if he had not followed the serialization in the *Sunday Magazine* between September and November, he did not have to wait long for the book. The American edition of the new Sherlock Holmes novel, *The Valley of Fear*, was published by February 1915, a whole three months before the *Strand Magazine*'s readership on the other side of the Atlantic even discovered how the story ended.

That particular novel made perfect reading for Roosevelt. Not only was it about Sherlock Holmes; it also had an American dimension and a clear political element. Something had to be done about the miners' working conditions. As for the title, Roosevelt was of the opinion that the only thing we have to fear is fear itself.

34

On January 8, 1915, G. Herbert Thring, of the Society of Authors, received a letter from the London law firm of Wake, Wild & Boult about a copyright matter. Progress in the case had been painfully slow—it had been going on since the previous January, which felt like an eternity for Thring. London had been another world back then. One's gaze had not constantly met recruitment posters encouraging men to sign up. Men had not been forced to wear armbands indicating their readiness to act as soldiers when the need arose. Women had not doled out shaming white feathers to men not in uniform.

The letter concerned the film *A Study in Scarlet*. The argument had begun when Ward, Lock & Co.—which thirty years earlier had bought the comprehensive rights to the book of the same name—sold the film rights to Samuelson Film, a British company led by twenty-six-year-old George B. Samuelson. He had established himself as a filmmaker after producing a newsreel of the funeral of King Edward VII.

The problem was that on June 28, 1912, Conan Doyle had himself signed a contract with the French filmmaker Éclair, giving that company exclusive rights to the use of his Sherlock Holmes stories for the production of films, both in monochrome and in color. The exclusive rights applied within France and abroad. Éclair had paid the sum of 12,000 francs for the rights, equivalent to around £500.

Via their London lawyers, the Frenchmen complained that Samuelson had simultaneously been able to purchase the rights to a Sherlock Holmes story. As a consequence, their own film project would be severely disadvantaged.

Conan Doyle found the punctilious attitude of the French rather irritating. They had the rights to forty Sherlock Holmes stories and were quarreling about the fact that a single story turned out not to be covered by the arrangement.

Éclair had a studio in Paris, but operated from its London head-quarters under the name of the Franco-British Film Company. The Franco-British operation began work on transforming eight Sherlock Holmes short stories to films, each about twenty minutes in length, immediately upon gaining the rights during the summer of 1912. The company chose a large amusement arcade in the English seaside town of Bexhill-on-Sea for the erection of its studio, in part because of Bexhill's proximity to London. Additionally, the surrounding Sussex countryside—which was not far from Conan Doyle's own home—was suitable for their outside work. The French actor-director Georges Tréville, who also produced the films, took the part of the famous detective and was joined by a party of about fifteen English actors and actresses, most of whom had appeared on the musical comedy stage in London. Conan Doyle had insisted that the films be made with English artists.

Over the previous few years, a succession of Holmes films had been shown in cinemas, although none had been based on Conan Doyle's original stories. Most were produced in Denmark and frankly had very little to do with Sherlock Holmes. The only company holding valid rights to make a film was the Vitagraph Company of America that had bought the rights in 1905 from S. S. McClure, who was responsible for Conan Doyle's work in the United States.

Thring dearly hoped that the dispute with Éclair could be brought to a satisfactory conclusion. The Frenchmen were irritated about something that ought really to have been a trifling matter, and it ought to be possible to quickly bring it to a close. The Society of Authors existed to assist its members in cases such as this, usually on legal matters. In the end, Conan Doyle, beginning to lose patience with Éclair, offered the company twenty-five pounds in compensation.

Thring, though, realized that the process would take time. In the letter from Wake, Wild & Boult, he was informed that the firm had been attempting to contact its clients for some time, without success. All the senior staff members of the French film company were away in battle and could not be reached.

Cinema was a strange phenomenon. Movies were silent, but the shows were punctuated by audience applause, just like any other performance. Sometimes the cinema managers would undertake to enhance the illusion. If someone was being beaten on screen, the manager might loudly smack his cane around, or when something was smashed in the film, tumbling and crashing sounds could be heard in the auditorium. But it was the accompanying music that brought thrills to audiences. If the cinema was unable to afford a complete orchestra, a chamber ensemble would suffice, or perhaps even some exotic quartet of purported Turkish, Indian, or African players—in coarse robes and dyed black hair and beards that gave just the right impression—whose origins could normally be traced to somewhere rather closer to home. Occasionally the film's accompaniment was a lone pianist, who would pound the keys with all his might to accentuate the on-screen effects.

Samuelson's ambitious version of *A Study in Scarlet* was a feature film, coming in at over an hour and a half. The outdoor scenes had been filmed in June 1914 amid the dramatic limestone cliffs of Cheddar Gorge in Somerset. One of the country's most spectacular landscapes, it was also the one that most closely resembled the Utah mountain setting where the novel's Mormon scenes took place. The indoor shooting had to wait until July, by which time Samuelson's new, modern London studio would be ready.

The film concerned itself mainly with the adventurous scenes in Utah. In the role of Sherlock Holmes was an Englishman by the name of James Bragington—the first English actor to play the role on film. Bragington had never acted in a film before, but he worked at Samuelson Film's offices and was the spitting image of Sherlock Holmes as imagined by Sidney Paget.

The film was such a huge success that George B. Samuelson decided to make another ambitious feature-length film about Sherlock Holmes. This was no easy task against the backdrop of an ongoing world war raging outside the studio. There was a constant fear that Germany might send its new Zeppelin airships to drop bombs on England.

Since Éclair owned the film rights to everything Conan Doyle had written up to 1912, there was only one long story available. Samuelson therefore chose *The Valley of Fear*, making it into a film only two years after its original publication. This time the role of Sherlock Holmes was given to the actor who had played the detective onstage more than anyone else, H. A. Saintsbury. The London *Times* opined that Saintsbury had been born to play the role. Saintsbury found transposing the detective from the stage to the silent screen a difficult challenge and felt that he was unable to deploy Holmes's inscrutable face and passive attitude in the new medium. During filming, he had no choice but to do just the things he had left out onstage.

Six months earlier, in America, the most famous, internationally renowned player of Sherlock Holmes, William Gillette, had stood in front of a film camera for the first time. He had developed a silence onstage that had become his trademark. This was now a real advantage.

Where others were terrified by the presence of cameras and the limitations of silent film, Gillette was utterly at home. His interpretation could reach his audience without the need for words.

The film was called, simply, *Sherlock Holmes* and was a straight adaptation of his own play. Several actors from Gillette's productions of the play were featured in the film version.

The American film-industry magazine *Motography* wrote, "The name William Gillette is synonymous with Sherlock Holmes." Hundreds of thousands of people had already seen him perform his signature role on the stage. Now, he was about to reach countless others—both in the United States and on the far side of the Atlantic—and thanks to the recording, his performance would also be saved for posterity.

The image of the deerstalker-wearing, curved-pipe-smoking master detective was reinforced still further.

35

"My creation of Holmes did, after all, a small bit of war work," Conan Doyle explained, employing a booming voice to ensure that he would be heard throughout the Balmoral ballroom. One hundred and thirty guests had been invited to Stoll Picture Productions' convention dinner at the Trocadero in London, and all of them were interested in the guest of honor's speech. Recently Conan Doyle's reputation had suffered, and some critics had even gone as far as to ridicule him, but in spite of that the writer, now in his sixties, remained one of the country's most well-known and well-respected personalities. It was a September evening in 1921. The world war had ended several years earlier, and the future was bright.

"I had a friend," said Conan Doyle, "who was shut up in the Magdeburg Military Prison in Germany. As he and his brother officers were getting no news from England, I took a volume of Sherlock Holmes and in it I pricked out all the news letter by letter, beginning with the third chapter—pricking under each letter of the message with a needle. I sent the book to him with a note saying: 'This may relieve your prison captivity and afterwards be placed in the prison library. It is slow but perhaps you might find the third chapter to be a little more interesting.' I thought that would be good enough for him, but as a matter of fact he missed it. There was, however, another officer, Capt. the Hon. Keppel, of the Guards, who, with extraordinary sagacity, 'got on' to it. The result was that the British officers in captivity got the whole of the news of England at that time. I then got another letter saying, 'Please send us another Sherlock Holmes story.' I continued to send them with all the news pricked out in them to those officers until I learned that they were actually being allowed to have English newspapers."

The room filled with laughter. Conan Doyle was an accomplished speaker, and his voice put his audience at ease. The Scottish accent could still be discerned, four decades after he had left the city of his birth.

Stoll was the latest company to produce films about Sherlock Holmes. Conan Doyle had eventually lost patience with the French filmmakers and decided to buy back the rights. They had cost him ten times as much as he had originally received, but the transaction had been worth it. The new films that Stoll produced were closer to what Conan Doyle had hoped for. That year, they had made film versions of fifteen of the Holmes short stories as well as the novel *The Hound of the Baskervilles*.

The only criticism the author had to make of these new films was that they were full of telephones, motor vehicles, and other modern conveniences that the Victorian Holmes could only have dreamed about. The films had simply brought the stories up to date, moving them into a contemporary setting. In the light of the films' success, these criticisms were insignificant. Conan Doyle was particularly taken with the actor chosen for the lead role, Eille Norwood. He was so taken, in fact, that he had honored Norwood with a gift of a large-patterned dressing gown, which the actor would later wear in many of the films.

Eille Norwood was not the actor's real name. Born in 1861, he was originally named Anthony Edward Brett; he had chosen his stage name in honor of his sweetheart, Eileen, and then added the name of the London suburb in which he was resident.

When Sir Oswald Stoll had started his film company in 1919, Norwood was one of the first actors to work for him. Stoll had developed a theater empire around the turn of the century, comprising theaters all over the country. After the war, he foresaw the declining interest in music-hall entertainment among his compatriots and decided to enter the world of film. His approach had been two-pronged: on the one hand he opened many cinemas, and on the other he started his own film company, with shooting facilities housed in a former airplane factory that by now had become Britain's largest film studio.

The director of the forthcoming films had one day asked Norwood whether he might consider auditioning for the role of Sherlock Holmes. Norwood had retreated to his changing room, returning just minutes later. The director was dumbstruck. Norwood had used barely any makeup, and had not selected any accessories, yet the transformation was convincing. This *was* Sherlock Holmes standing in the doorway.

Norwood completely immersed himself in the role. He studied all of Conan Doyle's stories in great detail, making sure that Sherlock Holmes's passion for tobacco, disguises, and music made it into the films. To be as credible as possible, he also learned the basics of playing the violin, since, even though it would not be heard, it still ought to look right. He even shaved his hairline to accentuate the character's prominent forehead. And, when the time came to record the scenes, he did his utmost to recall Sidney Paget's illustrations as far as humanly possible.

Above all, Norwood, who always applied his own makeup, proved himself to be a master of disguise, which was a major asset in the filming process. One day, during the filming of *A Scandal in Bohemia*, a cabdriver with a blank expression was standing inside the studio waiting for his fare. People felt that this was a distraction, and as the company's manager tried to shoo him away, the whole thing threatened to end in a fight. At that moment, a call went out for Mr. Norwood to come to the set. The cabdriver struggled free from the manager and promptly took his place in front of the camera. The manager's assertion that Norwood had trouble adopting the posture and appearance required of him for each scene was thereby completely disproved.

Conan Doyle was bowled over by Eille Norwood's disguises. He was also impressed that the film company had constructed an exact replica of Sherlock Holmes's sitting room. Not content merely to construct the room and use one-sided sets for the outdoor scenes, they had built the entire house in the old airplane factory. Upon entering through the door, one met a flight of stairs leading up to a flat laden with ornaments and curiosities, dusty books, used pipes, ancient tobacco tins, and chemistry equipment. It was all in a state of disarray, as might be expected of a bachelor's abode. When the arc lights were extinguished and the sounds of the film crew went quiet, one could easily forget that this was in fact a film set. It was easy to believe that Sherlock Holmes was real.

The Holmes films proved to be a great success for Stoll, so there was every cause for celebration at the Trocadero that night. The company's leading staff members had taken the opportunity to give speeches about the other successes they had been responsible for. The director of the film company was able to reveal that the new Holmes films had been sold to interests in the United States for one of the largest fees ever paid for films in America. Not only that, the films had been exported to such far-flung places as Australia, Japan, and some other countries in the Far East.

It was a great honor to have the author of these stories in their midst, not least because he had not attended a public dinner for more than seven years, since August 1914. The director went on to add that he had just been informed that the prime minister, Mr. Lloyd George, had been among the first to have read the latest Holmes story, published in the October issue of the *Strand Magazine*, and that he considered it to be among the very best he had ever read. The prime minister was a great admirer of both Sherlock Holmes and Brigadier Gerard, the hero of another of Conan Doyle's series of stories.

The guests applauded, despite the fact that others who had read the new short story, "The Mazarin Stone," might well have questioned the prime minister's verdict. The story was hardly one of the best; in fact, quite the opposite was true. But this was an evening of celebration, not the time or the place for grumbling. The story itself was something of a curiosity, in that it was narrated not by Dr. Watson but in the third person. The explanation for this probably lay in the fact that it had been based on a short, one-act play Conan Doyle had written for the stage. On the other hand, *The Valley of Fear* had been intended to feature a third-person narration throughout the story, not merely in the second half of the book, as had eventually come about. Conan Doyle's approach to writing Holmes stories was becoming increasingly experimental.

They had arrived at the high point of the evening, Sir Arthur Conan Doyle's speech. Conan Doyle began by apologizing for the rather boastful quotations that accompanied his name on the list of speakers that had been distributed to the audience. "He was, I take it, the most perfect reasoning and observing machine that the world has seen," had been quoted from "A Scandal in Bohemia" and naturally referred to Sherlock Holmes.

"You must remember," he implored his audience, "that these are the words of a certain gentleman named Watson whose opinions were not generally very weighty ones."

He went on:

"If my little creation of Sherlock Holmes has survived longer perhaps than it deserved, I consider that it is very largely due to those gentlemen, who have, apart from myself, associated themselves with him. In the early days it was Sidney Paget who illustrated those stories so well that he made a type which the whole English-reading race came to recognise, and I may say here that in his premature death English art lost a very great asset. Afterwards there came along William Gillette, with his wonderful impersonation in the play written entirely by himself—so entirely that I remember his sending me a cable from America in which he said, 'May I marry Sherlock Holmes?' I had such confidence in him that I cabled back 'You may marry him, murder him, or do anything you like with him.' Then there came Mr. Saintsbury with his excellent personation in *The Speckled Band*, and now, finally, but not least important, there comes Mr. Eille Norwood, who has carried his extraordinarily clever personation of Sherlock Holmes, not only all over Great Britain, but, as I learn with very great pleasure, over the United States of America as well."

Conan Doyle nodded toward Eille Norwood, who performed a humble bowing gesture. After Conan Doyle's speech, it was Norwood's turn to respond. He was to tell the audience about how he had dreamed of playing Sherlock Holmes for many years. He was to mention how he had received hundreds of letters from book lovers, at home and abroad—in fact, he had received so many letters that film stars must now be a significant source of revenue for the Royal Mail. And he would say that, if Conan Doyle were to write any more stories about Holmes, then he dared say that Stoll would be keen to produce more films about him. In actual fact, plans for the filming of a further fifteen stories were already under way. He did not, though, want to say so in public.

Conan Doyle continued his speech:

"I suffer sometimes from some little confusion between the author and the character. I am afraid that in my own personality I rather represent that gentleman already quoted—Dr. Watson. But the psychologists tell us that we really are very multiplex people; that we are like a bundle of faggots, or rather a rope with many strands, and that sometimes in the most commonplace rope there may be one single strand which, if you only isolate it, produces unexpected effects. There may be represented in my being some strand of Sherlock. If so all the villains I have created may be also represented by strands in my personality."

In recent years, Conan Doyle had given a great deal of thought to the human self. Not, perhaps, so much to the brain, or psychology, but rather to the soul.

Many people of the time participated in séances or other forms of spiritualism, and these fads had entertained Conan Doyle's mind since before the turn of the century. Since the death of his brother-in-law Malcolm Leckie, however, his interest had taken a different turn. Although his wife, Jean, was deeply skeptical, he arranged séances at their home, Windlesham. One of Jean's friends who participated in the séances had also lost a brother in the first months of the war. Another of her four brothers was the officer imprisoned in Magdeburg to whom Conan Doyle had sent books. According to the participants, at one of the séances it had been discovered, quite unexpectedly, that Jean's friend—a rather ordinary, sickly woman—was a highly sensitive psychic medium with a talent for automatic writing.

Before long, even the skeptic Jean was receptive to the messages. Conan Doyle watched as the two women apparently made contact with more and more of their loved ones who had died in the war. They even sent reports of how the war would develop over the coming period. With great enthusiasm, Conan Doyle sent these prognoses on to his brother, Innes, who was very tactful in his reception. War did things to people, and it was hard to tell someone not to look for a ray of hope in the darkness.

On July 6, 1915, Oscar Hornung, the son of Conan Doyle's sister Connie, was killed at Ypres. Three weeks later, his sister Lottie's husband met the same fate. His son Kingsley almost died from pneumonia. The darkness intensified.

Conan Doyle wrote whatever he could to contribute to the war effort. He wrote pamphlets for the War Propaganda Bureau, a history of the war, and letters to the editors of various newspapers. He was full of ideas as to how lives might be saved out on the battlefields.

Now he was finally going off to war, as he had wanted to do for so long. He had been invited by the Foreign Office to travel to the front line in Italy and write about the situation there. He availed himself of the title bestowed upon him when he was knighted, Deputy Lord

Lieutenant of Surrey, and commissioned a suitable uniform for a man with such a title. He was transported down through France, meeting Innes, Kingsley, and his secretary, Major Alfred Wood, on the way. He visited the trenches on numerous occasions, experiencing the combat at very close range.

Traveling home, he happened to meet a French general, who wondered what contribution Sherlock Holmes had made to the war effort. Conan Doyle could only reply that Holmes was a bit too old for any active participation. Back at Windlesham, though, he sat down and wrote a story set in the early days of the war, in which a Sherlock Holmes of advancing years captured a master German spy. The short story was published in the *Strand Magazine* as "His Last Bow: The War Service of Sherlock Holmes."

On July 1, 1916, Kingsley was wounded in the neck during the first day of the Battle of the Somme. The injury was not fatal, but it kept him away from the front for two months. The impact of the son's injury was felt keenly by his father. Conan Doyle, who had up until then stood only on the edge of the unknown, made the leap and allowed himself to be enveloped in spiritualism. What had been his private thoughts he now made public. And when Conan Doyle went public with something, he always did so wholeheartedly. On November 4, 1916, he spoke out in the press, declaring his new conviction. He considered spiritualism to be a religion, a mixture of the ancient and the modern. He was no longer in any doubt; he was convinced that there was indeed a life after death. It was not so very far removed from other religions; it was really only the rituals that differed. For Conan Doyle, a whole new world opened up—one in which he, with his pen and his standing, could do so much good.

The war did not claim the lives of any further family members. But the Spanish flu did. In late October 1918, just days before the official end of hostilities, Kingsley died. He had not yet turned twenty-six. Four months later the flu also took Conan Doyle's brother, Innes, the forty-five-year-old brigadier, who had once been known as Duff and who had happily boiled the last six potatoes over an open fire in the house in Southsea some thirty-six years earlier.

Conan Doyle mourned them, but knew that he would soon be in contact with them again.

*   *   *

The speech in the ballroom at the Trocadero was nearing its conclusion. Conan Doyle had touched on a whole range of issues with some connection to Sherlock Holmes. He had explained how the brothers Sherlock and Mycroft Holmes had gotten their first names from cricketers he had played against. He had praised his editor, H. Greenhough Smith, who had also been invited to the dinner. Even the Russian lady who wrote to him about Sherlock Holmes so often, always opening her letters with the greeting "Good Lord," had been given a mention.

"I think of all the little incidents that have pleased me in connection with Holmes," Conan Doyle said, in conclusion. "The most pleasing was when a party of school boys from the Paris lycees were brought to London, crammed into charabancs; asked what they would like to see first, and, when everybody thought they would say Westminster Abbey, all replied 'Baker Street.'"

Conan Doyle proposed a toast to Eille Norwood, the Sherlock Holmes of his age, and the 130 guests present filled their glasses and joined him in the salutation.

36

"THIS IS THE world's happiest museum," Conan Doyle said, as he welcomed the young woman. It was a spring day in 1925. They were on the first floor of the building that housed the Psychic Book-shop, the author's recently opened London store. He had fitted out the space above the shop as his own spiritualist museum. There were written messages from the spirit world, photographs of ghosts, and small objects that had been moved around by spirits during séances and turned out to have come from faraway lands. Most fascinating were the plaster casts of spirits' hands. When mediums entered a trance, they would ask the spirits to put their hands into liquid paraffin, and when a cast was made later the hands were found to have fingerprints that were different from those of the medium. Furthermore, the casts were so narrow around the wrist that no human hand could possibly have been pulled out of the hardening lump of paraffin. Conan Doyle considered spiritualism to be fact, rather than faith. He had seen the evidence, at séances, with his own eyes; there was simply no room for doubt. Not only that, there were few scientific experiments subjected to such scrutiny as spiritualist ones. It was unfortunate that far too many fraudsters had given spiritualism a bad name.

Birgit Th. Sparre, just twenty-two years old, found Conan Doyle to be a friendly old man with a glint in his eye. Birgit's mother had gotten to know one of Conan Doyle's friends through spiritualism back in Sweden, and when her daughter had expressed an interest in meeting the famous author, the personal invitation from Sir Arthur had arrived soon afterward, asking her to visit him and his wife at Windlesham.

After visiting the museum, they headed south in Conan Doyle's car, first leaving behind the hum of London life and then heading into the wonderful English countryside. Doubtless it was all a big change from back home. She had to concentrate to avoid getting motion sickness.

Conan Doyle loved motorcars and found great amusement in traveling at high speed.

Birgit loved Windlesham, from its well-kept garden where Sir Arthur tended his flowers daily to its billiard-table lawns. The house itself was cozy and inviting, with coal fires in the hearths, brasses polished to a high shine, and armchairs upholstered with cretonne. Lady Conan Doyle, maternal and gray-haired, led them through to the table, groaning with scones and delectable cucumber sandwiches, that had been set for afternoon tea.

There was another guest that weekend, the French astronomer Camille Flammarion. "Astronomy has brought us closer to other worlds," he explained to Birgit. "Spiritualism, though, will take us all the way." He stroked his silver beard, adding, "The proliferation of the telegram, the telephone, spectroscopy, and electromagnetism does not give us humans the right to seal the portal to the unknown."

The Conan Doyles—it seemed to Birgit—were a happy family. Everything about their home was harmonious. Nevertheless, she found it not a little strange that the house was inhabited by various noble spirits. Sir Arthur did not do anything until ordered to do so by his Arabian guardian spirit, Pheneas. The spirit communicated through Lady Conan Doyle, who in a state of trance would fill page after page with compact rows of handwriting. At teatime, she would read through a daily roundup from the spirit world. This would often include direct instructions concerning important family decisions that were to be made. Sir Arthur followed them slavishly.

The famous author was a naturally inquisitive person. He was always looking to expand his knowledge of everything to do with the spirit world, and as soon as he found positive proof he would publish his discoveries. A few years earlier, he had planned to write an article about fairies. It was intended to be nostalgic and folkloric in character, since he had never seen a fairy himself, except in his father's paintings, and didn't really believe in them. He then came across a series of photographs taken by two girls in Cottingley, West Yorkshire. The pictures clearly showed the small, winged creatures surrounding the girls. Conan Doyle brought in a photography expert, who was unable to prove that the images were false. With such scientific proof, not to mention the testimony of the innocent lasses, Conan Doyle had little choice but to publish this astonishing discovery in the *Strand Magazine*.

The magazine's readership was not convinced. Such setbacks, though, seemed not to trouble the author anymore. He redoubled his efforts, pouring even more money into spiritualism. He was the face of the movement, as well as its most significant financial backer.

As soon as Birgit had the opportunity to talk to Sir Arthur undisturbed, she steered the conversation to the subject of Sherlock Holmes. Her father, Earl Sparre, would often read aloud for the family and their guests. In the library of their manor house, in front of a roaring birchwood fire, one of Conan Doyle's exciting crime stories would often be the book of choice.

Sir Arthur, it seemed, was not interested in talking about Sherlock Holmes. Birgit had a feeling that he regretted ever creating the detective, for he would never be free of him. He told her that he had taken the lives of countless characters in his writings, but that Sherlock Holmes was the only one he could not kill.

There was ambivalence in this attitude toward the detective, for Conan Doyle continued writing stories about Holmes. Quite recently, two Holmes short stories had been published in the *Strand Magazine*. Considering the expenses involved in his forays into spiritualism, he certainly needed income. He had, however, refrained from projecting his spiritualist convictions onto Holmes—that, presumably, would be going too far. A follow-up to *The Lost World* did, however, see Professor Challenger convert to the spiritualist faith.

Evening arrived at Windlesham, and the group moved into the library, where a supper of Scottish delicacies—everything from roast lamb to Scottish apple pie, warm toast with blackberry jam, dollops of sour cream, and whisky-dipped pistachios—was laid out. Afterward, Camille Flammarion and Sir Arthur stretched out in their wing chairs and spoke of dear friends who had lived centuries before.

Things, though, were not quite as they seemed. Both parents had spoiled Denis and Adrian from a young age. The couple's daughter, Billy, on the other hand, had chosen her own path and lived away at school for much of her childhood. Her father's friend—later adversary—Harry Houdini had described her as a tomboy. The boys attended schools closer to home but had never shown any great scholarly interest or aptitude; they had undergone long periods of absence from their studies while accompanying their parents on lecturing tours all over the world.

Unlike their half brother, Kingsley, they were not remotely interested in Eton, preferring to choose schools that would not put them under such great pressure. Their father found their attitude irritating, yet he wanted to give them freedom. This was a commodity they couldn't get enough of.

When their aunt Connie died in 1924, the siblings inherited a significant sum, and Denis in particular adopted an increasingly hedonistic lifestyle. On his seventeenth birthday he was given a motorcar, in addition to the motorcycle he already owned.

Adrian, meanwhile, was often absent from school and was generally unruly. His father threatened to send him to Switzerland unless he pulled himself together. At about that time he was charged with reckless driving. When he was home, at Windlesham, Adrian would cause his mother such distress that his father felt he had no choice but to tell him not to visit as often. Conan Doyle knew very well how it felt to have dark days but believed that they should be endured alone, not taken out on others.

Conan Doyle's eldest child, Mary, who had recently turned thirty-five, had always ended up on the fringes of the family. Her stepmother, Jean, naturally showed less interest in her than in her younger half siblings. But Mary had recently found an occupation that brought her closer to her father—running his spiritualist bookshop and museum in London.

Family life had become far more difficult for Conan Doyle himself. When the children were small he had played with them—American Indian games with tall feathers and tomahawks—and tried to be a good father. He never achieved the same success in that field as he did in the literary and celebrity worlds. Over the last few years, he had had no one to consult on family matters. His dear mother had passed away, at age eighty-three, the day before New Year's Eve 1920. Conan Doyle had been in Australia at the time. Without her, and his brother, Innes, he had no one left to listen to.

His only guide in life was an Arab from Ur, Mesopotamia, who had lived before Abraham, and who was now a spirit by the name of Pheneas. Conan Doyle always listened to him.

37

Herbert Greenhough Smith was an old man; his seventieth birthday had come and gone a long time ago. He had been the editor of the *Strand Magazine*, surrounded by piles of manuscripts, galley proofs, and correspondence, for almost four decades. In fact he *was* the *Strand Magazine*.

George Newnes, the magazine's founder, had been dead for years. Greenhough Smith's own son, Cyril, had also passed away. The boy's mother, Greenhough Smith's first wife, had died back in the 1890s. The only one he had left was Dorothy, the ice-skating princess who, at the age of eighteen, had accepted his proposal and become his second wife, despite their age difference (he was twenty-seven years her senior). He was still proud of her bronze-medal-winning performance at the 1908 London Olympics. He had known her father very well—he wrote detective stories under the nom de plume Dick Donovan and had stepped in to save several issues of the *Strand* to which Conan Doyle had not contributed a Sherlock Holmes story.

Greenhough Smith still lived in his flat in Queen Anne's Mansions. The sitting monarch in Buckingham Palace, whose view the building obscured, was King George V. By now, though, there were several other buildings blocking the king's view toward the Houses of Parliament. Greenhough Smith's route to work was unaltered since the 1890s; it was merely the surroundings that had changed. The horse-drawn carriages had disappeared, replaced by the motorcar. Now the ladies wore short skirts, their hair neatly bobbed.

In nearby Marconi House, a stone's throw from Greenhough Smith's place of work, a sign saying "2LO" had appeared a few years earlier. This was the somewhat cryptic name for the operations of the British Broadcasting Corporation, which had permission to broadcast radio programs, but only seven minutes at a time.

At the Savage Club, at least, Greenhough Smith still had his favorite table, with a view overlooking the River Thames. For many years he had kept himself entertained there, playing the word game Spelka with an editor from the *Daily Express*, an orthopedic surgeon friend, and the actor Eille Norwood. He would sit there chain-smoking cigarettes through the long holder resting in the V formed by his spindly fingers. His other hand held the cards, all featuring single letters, that one after another would be placed on the table in order to form a word. That word could suddenly turn into another, depending on the other players' plans.

Now, though, it was time for some editorial duties at the office. Greenhough Smith leaned forward in his worn office chair, staring down at the document in front of him.

It was irrevocably and finally over. Not the job itself—he could probably manage that for a few more years—but Sherlock Holmes. The last story was about to be published; it had, after some debate, been named "Shoscombe Old Place." Frank Wiles provided the illustrations. Ever since Sidney Paget's death, a succession of different illustrators had been tasked with portraying the detective and his colleague. All of them based their illustrations on the look that Paget had etched into the minds of the readers, though they were not all as good as Paget. Frank Wiles was one of the few who could claim to be in the same class as his predecessor. After Wiles had provided the cover illustration for the September 1914 issue of the *Strand Magazine*, depicting the detective in a dressing gown, with a coded message in his hand, Conan Doyle had said that it was the closest thing he had seen to his own idea of what Holmes looked like. Another of Paget's successors was his own brother, Walter Paget, who finally got the job that should by rights have been his from the start.

Conan Doyle had written a farewell to his readers. The text was to appear in the *Strand* and to serve as the foreword to *The Case-Book of Sherlock Holmes*, a collection comprising the short stories he had written during the course of the 1920s, up to and including the current year, 1927. The short stories written from 1910 to 1920 had already been released as *His Last Bow*, named after one of the stories in the collection.

Greenhough Smith had provided the idea for one of the stories written in the 1920s, "Thor Bridge," drawing his inspiration from a real-life scenario. Sadly, the quality of Conan Doyle's short stories had declined during the 1920s, and parts were rather too brutal for an elderly gentleman like Greenhough Smith. Maybe the brutality was an effect of Conan Doyle's emotional sufferings during the war. Some characters were mutilated, while others met with fates of an equally gruesome nature.

Sherlock Holmes remained popular, but other authors dominated the world of crime fiction. Agatha Christie's books about Hercule Poirot and Dorothy L. Sayers's series about Lord Peter Wimsey were among the best sellers. Reading the Poirot mysteries, one could certainly see the impact that the first half of *The Valley of Fear* had had on the genre and how it had presaged the kind of crime novels that would follow.

At one point, Conan Doyle had told Greenhough Smith that the readers had probably lost that sense of novelty that had once characterized Sherlock Holmes and his methods. He believed that this was in large part due to the plethora of Holmes parodies that existed. Even if he had been able to maintain the quality of his writing, he still would not have been able to elicit the same response.

Greenhough Smith read through Conan Doyle's parting letter one last time before taking it down to the composing room.

I fear that Mr. Sherlock Holmes may become like one of those popular tenors who, having outlived their time, are still tempted to make repeated farewell bows to their indulgent audiences. This must cease and he must go the way of all flesh, material or imaginary. One likes to think that there is some fantastic limbo for the children of imagination, some strange, impossible place where the beaux of Fielding may still make love to the belles of Richardson, where Scott's heroes still may strut, Dickens's delightful Cockneys still raise a laugh, and Thackeray's worldlings continue to carry on their reprehensible careers. Perhaps in some humble corner of such a Valhalla, Sherlock and his Watson may for a time find a place, while some more astute sleuth with some even less astute comrade may fill the stage which they have vacated.

Greenhough Smith could well imagine this literary Valhalla. Sherlock Holmes and Dr. Watson deserved their places there more than any others. As far as their readers were concerned, no other fictional characters came close to being their equal in reputation and fame. Hamlet did, perhaps, but then he was a rather tragic young man.

As Greenhough Smith read on, he reflected on the fact that those boys who had read the first Sherlock Holmes stories in the *Strand* way back in prehistory had become parents themselves, and that their children had also grown up with the same detective, in the same magazine. And even their children, grandchildren, and great-grandchildren might one day open *The Hound of the Baskervilles* and shudder at the thought of "the footprints of a gigantic hound" and the horrors that took place up on the moors.

Conan Doyle's farewell piece went on, well written as always. The author recounted how, in *The Return of Sherlock Holmes*, he had brought the detective back from what everyone assumed was death. He wrote:

> I have never regretted it, for I have not in actual practice found that these lighter sketches have prevented me from exploring and finding my limitations in such varied branches of literature as history, poetry, historical novels, psychic research, and the drama. Had Holmes never existed I could not have done more, though he may perhaps have stood a little in the way of the recognition of my more serious literary work.

Finally, Conan Doyle wrote:

> And so, reader, farewell to Sherlock Holmes! I thank you for your past constancy, and can but hope that some return has been made in the shape of that distraction from the worries of life and stimulating change of thought which can only be found in the fairy kingdom of romance.

Greenhough Smith picked up the sheet of paper, left his room, and headed off down the corridor, toward the next stage in the publication's never-ending run.

Conan Doyle, too, was an old man. He had not given up, though, not yet. He was no longer full of vim and vigor, but he would continue disseminating his message until he dropped dead. He could no longer count the number of lectures he had given on spiritualism, or even which countries he had delivered them in. He had also written countless articles and books on the subject. And now, in 1929, he had agreed to yet another lecture tour. The spiritualist community of Scandinavia wanted him to come. Naturally, Jean was at his side.

They started in Holland and then continued by train up to Denmark. He received a respectful welcome, and the journalists' questions were actually about important issues and not only about Sherlock Holmes. There was, however, one journalist in Copenhagen who could not help himself:

"What do you think Sherlock Holmes might say if he were to meet with the phenomena of spiritualism face-to-face?"

Conan Doyle smiled for the first time in the interview, pointed to his heart, and said: "Sherlock Holmes is, of course, a part of me. Do you not think that he, with those great powers of observation at his disposal, would approach the phenomenon with the same eyes as I? I know so."

The journey continued.

38

A LARGE CROWD gathered on the platform at Stockholm Central Station one Sunday morning in late October to greet Arthur Conan Doyle, traveling by sleeper from Copenhagen, when he arrived. There were men and women with bouquets of flowers, press photographers, and a man with a newsreel camera. Carl A. Carleson, who had published several translations of the author's spiritualist works, was there to meet the famous visitor. Carleson was the man responsible for inviting Conan Doyle to Sweden, and he and several members of the Stockholm Spiritualist Union had formed the welcoming committee. The train glided into the platform, and Conan Doyle stepped down from the sleeper car. "His presence was part Norse chieftain, part lion," wrote one of the newspapers.

The party headed for the Grand Hôtel, where the interviews were to take place. Interest in Conan Doyle was huge, among both ordinary Swedes and journalists. There was even a revue ditty written about the visit.

Beneath the hotel window, the churning waters of Stockholm's Ström channel appeared dreary and gray in the October rain.

"London weather!" Conan Doyle boomed. "I appreciate that you would like me to feel at home." He answered the journalists' questions politely, with his attentive wife at his side, but at the mention of Sherlock Holmes he would give the shortest possible answers or avoid the subject altogether. In every interview when the detective was mentioned, Lady Conan Doyle interposed that her husband had solved criminal cases himself, cases that the police had failed to bring to a solution.

The subject of one of those cases was the unjustly convicted Oscar Slater, a petty criminal of Glasgow. Twenty years earlier he had been accused of murdering a rich elderly spinster. The main evidence against him had been that he had tried to pawn a brooch similar to the only item that had been taken from the scene of the crime and that he had left the country for New York five days later. Conan Doyle had shown that the brooch was not actually the stolen one, but that fact had led to nothing. Then the world war had come, and it wasn't until it had ended that Conan Doyle and a few others again tried to get Slater's conviction reversed. Finally, in 1927, they managed to get the case into the public mind once more; Slater had by then been imprisoned for eighteen years. It was revealed that the police had influenced witnesses and withheld evidence in order to get Slater convicted. He was released, and Conan Doyle helped him launch an appeal and put up the money to pay for it. Slater's conviction was vacated, and he was compensated by the government, but he refused to repay any money to Conan Doyle, since the author had shown distaste for the low life Slater had led earlier.

It was now October 1929, and Slater had come around and agreed to pay back the money to Conan Doyle. The author was still irritated, and Slater was a subject that he and his wife repeatedly discussed during this tour to Scandinavia. Lady Conan Doyle maintained that her husband had received more gratitude from their dog at home. She meant to use all the influence in her power to prevent her husband from ever again taking up the case of any person suffering unjustly.

Conan Doyle felt that he had never been so well received as in Stockholm. The Swedish newspapers were full of long articles concerning his visit. He had great plans for this lecture tour—after Stockholm and Oslo he would head south, bringing spiritualism to capital city after capital city until he reached Rome, or Athens, or perhaps even down as far as Constantinople, or Istanbul, as it was beginning to be known.

Later that evening the Stockholm Concert Hall's great auditorium was full to the rafters. Fifteen hundred people fixed their gazes on the podium as the world-famous author made his entrance at a few minutes past eight. A tall, imposing, and elegant man, he had friendly eyes and a powerful voice that was audible in every corner of the hall. The seventy-year-old and his wife, accompanied by their friends Mr. and Mrs. Ashton Johnson, sat in armchairs arranged around a small table in the center of the stage. The chairman of the Stockholm Spiritualist Union stepped forward and welcomed the audience to the lecture, "Life after Death—As Illuminated by Modern Psychic Science."

Any further introduction of the evening's speaker was unnecessary. Everyone in the audience knew that this man was the creator of Sherlock Holmes.

Conan Doyle walked over to the podium. His wife and their two friends remained seated in the armchairs—that was their only task.

Afterward, Conan Doyle was very pleased with the presentation. During the next few days he and his wife went to a big luncheon arranged by his Swedish publisher and to a reception at the British Legation, went sightseeing, and saw a play at a theater.

And then he gave a new lecture, "The Results of Psychic Research," accompanied by a large number of slides. Once again the concert hall was full. Conan Doyle was heartened by the great interest in his mission, particularly as he saw Sweden as the home of spiritualism, since the great Emanuel Swedenborg had hailed from there. He had talked about this eighteenth-century scientist and mystic on Swedish radio the evening before—an experience he had thoroughly enjoyed.

Now, though, he was tired, almost exhausted. He had felt sharp chest pains in Copenhagen, but had refused to abandon the remainder of the lecture tour. While addressing the public in the concert hall, he had to steady himself against the lectern to keep his balance. At the next destination, Oslo, he was so worn out that he could not muster the strength to remove his overcoat unaided. The tour absolutely devastated Conan Doyle's brittle health and on his return to England he had to be carried ashore.

His final words to Carl A. Carleson in Stockholm had been to encourage him to try to unify the two denominations within Swedish spiritualism so that they might form a single congregation and to help them in their struggle for truth. A while later, he wrote to Carleson: "You say that I left my mark on Sweden. That may be so, but Sweden has left its mark on me. My last exertions were too great—they have left me a wreck."

During the spring that followed, Conan Doyle's condition continued to worsen, and on the morning of July 7, 1930, he passed away. His funeral was bright and beautiful, and no tears were reported among the mourners. They were all to be reunited on the other side, when the time came.

"Believe me," Conan Doyle had concluded his lecture at the Concert Hall, "the age of miracles has not yet passed."

Part 4

1930–1955

39

In London, almost two decades earlier, an American girl wandered around among the instruments of torture at Madame Tussaud's. She saw the guillotine, with its original eighteenth-century blade, responsible for the decapitations of the French Revolution. She was fifteen years old, and found the whole thing perfectly delightful. Small scenes, in which the murderers stood, ready to carry out their gruesome tasks, were illuminated in the darkness. She couldn't help shuddering with contentment. At first, the collection had been known simply as Madame Tussaud's Separate Room, but it had since been rechristened the Chamber of Horrors by those enterprising gentlemen at *Punch*. The name was fitting, since it was exactly that. There were rumors of a great reward for anyone brave enough to spend a night in the room. A few years earlier, and without explanation, Madame Tussaud's had begun receiving letters, thousands of letters, in fact, from those volunteering for the task. They came from widows, soldiers, a man describing himself as an absolutist, and a woman who made it clear that she was not applying for amusement or enjoyment but rather was interested only in the money, nothing else. For the young American, no such incentive had brought her to the Chamber of Horrors; she simply very much wanted to see it. She had explored the exhibits for hours, reading every explanatory text and lapping up the eeriness that the room conveyed. The girl had already visited the waxworks with her mother and sister earlier in their trip, but her sister was too young to go down into the Chamber of Horrors, so now she, with map and a Baedeker travel guide in hand, had set off exploring London on her own.

The attendants struck the gong. It was closing time. The girl made her way up from the chamber and before long found herself out on Marylebone Road, where Madame Tussaud's had been located for many years. A thick fog had enveloped London, as was so often the case. The sounds around her were muffled, and she was careful to avoid stepping out into the road, since a carriage or a dray or a motorcar could appear at any moment. That accidents were not more commonplace was a miracle. She followed the pavement and spotted a road sign ahead. She could scarcely believe her eyes. Baker Street! Good heavens above, she was on Baker Street! She was *there*!

She had traveled to Europe two years earlier on a small ship called the SS *Bremen*. The seas of the North Atlantic had raged, and there were no treatments for seasickness. Her mother, concerned that the girl might become seriously unwell, asked the purser whether he had an exciting book that might keep her daughter's mind occupied. Like many other children, she was a bookworm—her daily life was rather devoid of other amusements that might distract her. The purser managed to find a copy of the first Sherlock Holmes book, and the girl read and read, giving not so much as a thought to the world around her. She did not notice even the slightest nausea. It was a fantastic book!

And now here she was, on Baker Street. She began looking for the house numbers, no easy task in the foggy gloom and with dusk approaching. Eventually she found herself outside a house that matched her idea of Holmes's address and decided that this must be 221b. She was so excited that she very nearly stepped out into the path of a horse pulling a two-wheeled carriage, which appeared from out of nowhere. It was a hansom cab, just the sort in which Holmes and Watson traveled so often.

The carriage door opened and—the girl could not believe her eyes— out climbed a man wearing a deerstalker and a flapping Inverness cape. Tall and thin, he quickly strode over to the door of the house and went inside.

No one would believe her. But she knew. She had just seen Sherlock Holmes.

40

"ELEMENTARY, MY DEAR Watson, elementary," Sherlock Holmes said, for everyone in the auditorium to hear.

For Dr. Watson, it was anything but elementary. His daughter's fiancé had disappeared, and he was also accused of murder. She had then asked her father's friend Sherlock Holmes—by now retired—for assistance. Holmes had agreed to help and before long was hot on the heels of none other than Professor Moriarty and his gang. The hunt was leading them toward New York.

This was *The Return of Sherlock Holmes*, an American film, and the audience in the cinema was spellbound—perhaps not entirely by the film itself, although it was exciting, and there were more light moments than usual. Clive Brook had landed the role of Holmes mainly by virtue of having established himself in America as the "perfect Englishman." The plot bore little resemblance to Conan Doyle's Sherlock Holmes stories, but this did not noticeably bother the audience. The stories were widely regarded as rather dusty and old-fashioned, so the filmmakers' decision to set events in the present day was just as well. What was most modern about the film, what left audiences dumbstruck, and what the cinemas themselves promoted heavily in their advertisements in autumn 1929, was the actors' voices.

This was the first talking picture to feature Sherlock Holmes, and when he uttered the immortal words "Elementary, my dear Watson," it was the first time that line had been heard in a cinema. The audience recognized it nonetheless. It was Sherlock Holmes's most famous line. As soon as a company used Sherlock Holmes in any kind of advertising, that phrase would be deployed. With a pipe, a magnifying glass, some sort of Holmes headgear, and that famous phrase, the detective could be used in the marketing of just about anything. In fact, the phrase alone was sufficient, even without the accessories, it was so well established in the lexicon of the day.

When Holmes was to be parodied, the same thing applied. No humorous tale featuring the detective that graced the pages of the newspapers was complete without the phrase.

"Here," said Sherlock Holmes, in one such humorous newspaper piece, "sits the loneliest man in the world. Unmarried, unloved, no brothers or sisters, no little children to call him uncle; not even a landlady's child to smile at his return."

"Wonderful," gasped Dr. Watson. "How do you know all this?"

"Elementary, my dear Watson," replied the great detective. "He opened a package of cigarettes and threw the picture card away."

Newspaper articles, causeries, and even books regularly employed the phrase. When P. G. Wodehouse published his novel *Psmith, Journalist* as a serial in 1909, he used the line. In several hundred other instances throughout his works he inserted references to his cricketing teammate's stories. Not only that, he had created his own pairing that owed much to Holmes and Watson: Jeeves and Wooster.

By the time Wodehouse borrowed the line in 1909, it was already Sherlock Holmes's most famous phrase, at least if the newspaper notices of the day were anything to go by. That was strange, since it did not appear anywhere in a single one of Conan Doyle's tales.

Conan Doyle had used "elementary" just a handful of times in the Holmes stories, while "my dear Watson" featured very regularly indeed. Once, in the 1893 short story "The Crooked Man," both "elementary" and "my dear Watson" *had* appeared—but there was the small matter of fifty-two other words separating them. Nowhere were the two combined in a single phrase. Despite its murky origins, "Elementary, my dear Watson" was so well known in conjunction with Sherlock Holmes that by 1901 a parodist had written a newspaper story in which his detective, Shylock Combs, said to his colleague, "Elementary, my dear Potson."

There is no smoke without fire and no parody without something to send up. The line must have come from somewhere. Since it was not seen at all until after the turn of the century, and had in the subsequent years spread quickly across England and the United States, there was only one conceivable source. Only one large, successful phenomenon had encompassed both continents. It was not a book, nor something that had appeared in the press. It was William Gillette's play, *Sherlock Holmes*. In the script, the detective has the line, "Elementary, my dear fellow." Although the American playwright had used "my dear fellow" in that particular line, throughout the play he seemed to use "my dear fellow" and "my dear Watson" interchangeably. It would have been a natural thing for the "elementary" line, gradually, over the course of hundreds of performances, to have turned into a "my dear Watson" line.

It was through this spoken line that the phrase had been coined; in one way or another, its association with Holmes was attributable to William Gillette.

The deerstalker had been placed on the detective's head by the illustrator Sidney Paget and then taken on by Gillette and, in turn, the American illustrator Frederic Dorr Steele.

The curved pipe was William Gillette's idea, with the aim of making it easier to deliver his lines.

William Gillette, then, had rather a lot to answer for in terms of the received image of Sherlock Holmes.

Conan Doyle himself could actually take credit only for the large, round magnifying glass, since Sherlock Holmes had carried just such a device in *A Study in Scarlet*.

This was just as well, since Conan Doyle could be said to have had at least a finger, if not a whole hand, in shaping the myths surrounding his own character.

41

IN NEW YORK, in the 1920s, Christopher Morley was writing a postcard. His message was brief. It was an invitation to the Three Hours for Lunch Club.

He continued addressing cards to his acquaintances until he had invited another six or seven people for lunch. That ought to be a suitable party.

Morley had originally been a journalist but had established himself as a book author in the late 1910s. His 1919 novel *The Haunted Bookshop* was a long-lasting, national success. Novels alternated with essay collections, at least one book every year, several becoming genuine best sellers. As a very young child, in fact as soon as he had been able to hold a pen, Morley had scrawled block capitals on paper. Since the age of nineteen, he had regularly submitted his work to publishers for appraisal, hoping that it might perhaps get published. Three years later, while he was still a university student, a newspaper had published one of his poems; he had been bowled over by seeing his own words in print. It gave him the confidence to submit a whole collection, and despite the publisher's very specific criticism of the absence of commas—a straightforward issue to rectify—he was finally published. Admittedly the print run was a modest 250 copies, but one had to start somewhere. Exceptionally modest in his approach, Morley often attached a card containing an apology to copies of the book he gave away.

That was more than a dozen years ago. He no longer apologized for his writing. He wrote books, and a weekly column, and had been involved in starting the *Saturday Review of Literature*, to which he was also an influential contributor. Christopher Morley was an intellectual of his day, a man of letters, just as he had hoped to be from such a young age. It was a description that could easily be applied to so many of his boyhood idols.

What really set Morley apart, though, was his social skill. He had the gift of gab and was not afraid to use it. Other, similar characters were drawn to him, and together they endeavored to do the most important thing in life: eat lunch.

Morley was a master of the art of eating lunch. Each and every lunch was an adventure in its own right. All were hearty, spontaneous events, filled with humor and madcap skits, rewarding conversations, and good food. There were other, similar groups in New York, but Morley had never felt drawn to any of them. In particular, he had no interest in those gatherings that involved the famous critic Alexander Woollcott—Morley could not abide the man.

The Three Hours for Lunch Club was dissolved after each completed lunch, to be reconstituted once again when it was time for a new meeting. Morley considered it an excellent way to bring together individuals who he felt ought to get to know each other.

Meanwhile, a little distance away in Manhattan, the atmosphere at Broadway's Garrick Theatre had become somewhat tense. The police had turned up to get the theater to cancel the day's two performances. It was Sunday, and the Sabbath League had made a complaint, that it was breaking the ban on performances on the day of rest. In the end, the actors were able to persuade the police that they were putting on a charitable function, arranged by the prestigious Theatre Guild. Or rather two charitable functions, since the second performance was to be given later that evening, and never again after that.

The audience flocked into the nine-hundred-seat auditorium, and what was known as *The Garrick Gaieties* could begin. It was a sketch show. The other theaters were closing for the season, so what could be more apt than parodying their shows? A group of energetic young men and women took the stage.

It was a success. When the reviews arrived the next day, there was no doubting it. The show had to continue. The theater was due to close for the summer break, but the young cast returned to the stage and was able to entice audiences despite the sweltering heat. One cast member hired a limousine and drove around with the whole gang to

cool off on a hot summer night. They were young, and they sang like
lunatics. They drove out to Long Island to watch the sunrise, went
home, and got up again just in time to get to the theater in the evening. That was the life!

For one of the troupe's leaders, twenty-seven-year-old Edith Meiser,
The Garrick Gaieties meant a great leap forward in career terms. The
company gave a total of 211 performances.

Christopher Morley had founded a new club, Grillparzer Sittenpolizei Verein (Grillparzer morals police association). There was nothing
odd about that; Morley founded new clubs as often as some people
changed their shirts. They had ludicrous names like Nassau and Suffolk
County Deviled Ham and Ronkonkoma Association. And he would
dissolve these clubs just as suddenly as he had founded them. They
were, ultimately, merely excuses for having a good time. The Three
Hours for Lunch Club was almost unique in having survived over the
years. Now he had founded Grillparzer Sittenpolizei Verein, simply
on the basis of having happened to pick up a book about the works
of the Austrian dramatist Franz Grillparzer on his way to the lunch.
New members of the group had to open the book at a random page,
underline a sentence or paragraph that seemed to fit the mood, add
their signature, and finally affix a note, or whatever they might have on
their person, to the page. As grand master of the group, Christopher
Morley would then—often in Latin—approve the initiation in the book.

The difference between the Grillparzer and the Three Hours for
Lunch Club was soon obvious—not least because women were allowed
in the Grillparzer. There was even some advantage to being accompanied by a woman—perhaps one of the young women from the newspaper offices. Any man who brought female company did not have
to pay her full share of the bill; it would be divided instead among
all the men present. Prohibition was in place, and the group's meals
were eaten in a speakeasy. The particular establishment the Grillparzer
frequented was decorated with submarine landscapes, and soon the
women in the group—especially those working at the *Saturday Review
of Literature*—were referred to as "the mermaids."

In 1927, Edith Meiser and her husband, Tom McKnight, were touring
with a vaudeville troupe, when something happened that changed the

entire industry forever. The first talking pictures arrived, and the vaudeville establishments wanted to show films rather than live performances.

Edith and Tom, both talented writers for the stage, headed for
another new medium—radio. Most people involved in radio were
complete beginners, and before long the married couple had become
genuine experts. They formed a production company together and
hired actors themselves, and then sold the material to radio stations.
Edith and her husband divided their workload between them; he wrote
variety, comedy, and music programs, leaving her to concentrate on
crime and mystery. The first radio program Edith wrote was a series
of fifteen-minute mysteries, presented once a week by the National
Broadcasting Company's radio network. The villain was called "the
man with the pointed ears," and the show was a big hit with young
listeners across the country.

The couple soon had several shows running concurrently, even if
none were particularly significant. One day Edith Meiser had an idea
that she thought would make an extraordinary show: Sherlock Holmes.
She sharpened her pencil, picked up a lined pad, and crawled up into
bed, which was very high to prevent her Scottish terrier, Dr. Watson,
from jumping up onto it. She could have typed out the story, but she
did not like writing dialogue that way. She set about dramatizing two
of Conan Doyle's stories. But that was it: there was simply no interest
in the radio series.

A year or so later, everything changed. The old actor, director,
and playwright William Gillette had, in autumn 1929, at the age of
seventy-six, begun a farewell tour with his thirty-year-old Sherlock
Holmes play. Edith Meiser had watched him onstage as a five-year-old,
when her parents had taken her to the theater. Gillette was still superb
in his signature role, and upon seeing him again she was inspired to
give her idea for a radio series featuring the detective another go. A few
weeks ahead of Gillette's opening night, the Wall Street stock exchange
had crashed, and the United States was heading for a depression. People
stopped going to the theater. Radio audiences grew, and so did interest
from sponsors, and it was thanks to them that producers were able
to sell their programs to radio stations. Edith Meiser's sponsor was
George Washington, the owner of G. Washington Coffee, the first
commercial instant coffee. Washington loved Sherlock Holmes, too,
as did the chairman of his company's board.

Finally, Edith Meiser's dream was becoming a reality. Her circle was complete. Ever since she had been given the book to stave off seasickness on the liner to Europe, she had loved the detective. For her, he would no longer be merely a figure in the fog on Baker Street. He was going to be real.

Christopher Morley had not given Sherlock Holmes much thought in recent years. Slowly but surely, however, the detective was once again coming to the fore. Morley's knowledge of the subject from his Baltimore childhood had not been forgotten. Upon his meeting with a kindred spirit, the conversation would soon, and quite inexplicably, become a competition in Holmes trivia.

"What was the name of the doctor in 'The Speckled Band'?" an acquaintance once asked.

Morley countered: "Which mystery was it that was solved by the ash of a Trichinopoly cigar?"

His opponent was not to be outdone: "Who was the fellow who had the five orange pips sent to him?"

Morley fired again: "What was the adventure they cleaned up early enough in the evening to go and hear a concert at Queen's Hall?"

This could have gone on for hours, were it not for the fact that others in the party were beginning to feel rather left out.

In his column in the *Saturday Review of Literature*, Morley increasingly referred to occurrences relating to the Sherlock Holmes stories. It was not then perhaps altogether surprising that he was approached when he was.

On July 8, 1930, all the newspapers carried the report that Sir Arthur Conan Doyle had died the day before. Soon afterward, Morley found himself in a speakeasy, not far north of Fiftieth Street. Standing at the bar, he met a group of acquaintances who worked at Doubleday publishing. The company had been established in the previous century as Doubleday and McClure—the latter name belonging to S. S. McClure, the syndicate owner who owed so much to Conan Doyle for having saved his magazine. Later, a rash of mergers and takeovers had shaken the publishing world and also reached Doubleday, which was now known as Doubleday, Doran. Morley had worked there himself upon his return from England, but that was a long time ago.

An unspoken rule the friends were following during Prohibition was to avoid mentioning work until after the third round of drinks. It did not, on the other hand, take an awfully long time to get there.

Conan Doyle was dead, and there would be no more Sherlock Holmes stories. The Doubleday people felt that it was the perfect time for a complete edition. Maybe they also had got wind of the fact that there was to be a new Sherlock Holmes radio series, which would mean renewed interest in the books.

They planned to release a new, two-volume edition comprising all of Conan Doyle's fifty-six short stories and four novels about Holmes and Watson. Might Christopher Morley consider writing the preface?

"If the fee would be generous enough for me to go to Baker Street and back I'd do it," was Morley's reply.

The publishers agreed and in so doing committed themselves to paying the highest fee for a preface that Morley had ever heard of. On July 25 he submitted "In Memoriam Sherlock Holmes," an outstanding essay, the likes of which could be produced only by a genuine man of letters who also knew a great deal about Sherlock Holmes.

On July 30 he received the check, and at six minutes to midnight, on August 1, 1930, the RMS *Caronia* set sail for England, with Christopher Morley on the passenger list.

For Christopher Morley, too, the circle was complete. His childhood passion for Sherlock Holmes had been reignited. Sherlock Holmes had been a common thread running through his life, from Moriarty in the henhouse in Baltimore and Ronald Knox's Oxford lectures to this preface about to be published in New York, considered one of the finest essays ever written about Sherlock Holmes.

He looked back, full of nostalgia, at his childhood idol. To the world at large, he was Christopher Morley; to his family, though, he was still Kit.

42

On Baker Street in London, in 1921, an American radiologist made his way slowly along the pavement. He was on a brief visit to the metropolis but was determined to do one thing. He was going to find 221b Baker Street. Or rather, he was going to discover which house lay behind the fictional 221b, since the Baker Street of the 1890s did not run to such high numbers, having been more abbreviated at the time.

His approach was very methodical. He had drawn a map, on which each house was represented by a rectangle, and he set about checking which of the buildings best matched Conan Doyle's descriptions and directions—because such existed, in minute detail.

Dr. Briggs had the Holmes adventures in his briefcase. In "The Empty House," Holmes and Watson approached their former home with great caution, because it was under surveillance. After picking his way through the maze of streets to the east of Baker Street, Holmes, with Watson in tow, had turned down a narrow alley, stepped through a wooden door, crept across a small backyard, and then gone through a back door, before ending up in a long corridor, which led to an entrance adorned with a fan-shaped glass transom above the door. Holmes explained to Watson that they were now inside Camden House, directly opposite their abode.

Dr. Gray Chandler Briggs of Saint Louis, Missouri, continued his methodical promenade along Baker Street, looking for a house on the eastern side of the road matching Conan Doyle's description. If he succeeded, he would then simply have to turn around and see which house stood opposite. He had found support for his theory that Holmes's house was on the western side in other stories. One by one, he crossed off all the houses that could not be contenders: opposite one was a crossroads rather than a house; some had no back door, while others had no fanlight above the door. There were many grounds on which to reject them.

He had just begun the process of examining the houses around the street's junction with Portman Mansions, when he discovered a narrow alley behind the houses. Dr. Briggs turned down the passage and was met by two gates that both opened in the right direction, one made of wood, the other cast iron. Needless to say he chose the wooden one—because that would match Conan Doyle's story—and found himself in a small backyard. On the other side of the yard was a house, 118 Baker Street, if his map was to be believed. The hands in which he held the map still bore the scars of an experiment he had performed while at school with X-rays, a new discipline, and as such, a difficult one to master. The injuries, however, had not been sufficiently severe to prevent him from pursuing a career in the field.

Dr. Briggs peered through a pane in the back door, and at the far end of the hall he could see how the light seeped in through a window above the door. It was a fanlight!

This was too good to be true. Dr. Briggs found his way back out through the alley, turning left at the corner and back toward the heavy traffic of Baker Street. Looking up at the numbers of the houses, he proceeded three doors down, in a southerly direction, before finding number 118. He prepared himself and his Kodak camera. He had to preserve the memory of the house opposite Sherlock Holmes's quarters, the house that Conan Doyle had called Camden House in "The Empty House." He would also photograph number 111 Baker Street, across the road, the house that must have held the famous apartment.

It was then he noticed a sign, directly above the door of number 118. No X-ray was needed to decipher it. The sign read "Camden House."

The following day, Dr. Briggs met Sir Arthur Conan Doyle. He told him of his discovery, and the author was clearly taken aback. What an incredible coincidence!

"How did you find it?"

"By the description."

"Do you know," said Conan Doyle, "I don't think I've ever been in Baker Street in my life. And, if I have, it must have been so long ago that I have forgotten."

★　★　★

By 1929, Frederic Dorr Steele was fifty-six years old. He had gone on illustrating the Sherlock Holmes stories right up until Conan Doyle had written his last story about the detective two years earlier. Over the years, the magazine business had changed, new editors had taken charge, and different publications had been issuing the short stories.

The world war had all but ruined Steele's life. Prior to the war, Steele had been one of America's most renowned magazine illustrators. His pictures had been seen by millions, and his version of Sherlock Holmes was the one generally accepted in the United States. The war had brought shortages of paper and staff. The magazines shifted the emphasis of their contents from largely illustrated fiction to photographic reports from the war. By the time of the peace treaty, everything had changed—bringing new owners and nothing but radical new ideas. Steele's old friends in the magazine world had disappeared.

One of these new editors had even missed the fact that Steele normally illustrated the Holmes stories and had given the job to another artist. When Steele started illustrating for *Liberty* magazine, the editors wanted to decide just what he should illustrate—pointing out the modern reader's appetite for speed and excitement. The *Liberty* editors also had rather a lot to say about the order of the illustrations; their concern was less with following the plot than maximizing the potential value of advertising space. They also liked to split the illustrations in two and publish them on facing pages, which Steele hated. He had to be quick, too—now whenever he found an assignment, he had to work on it in his studio seven days a week, from morning till night, to meet the deadline.

Over the years, Steele had continued to use models for his illustrations. When he was required to depict an ape-like pose for "The Creeping Man," he had asked his son to assume the uncomfortable position until he had captured all the fine details in his drawing.

The deerstalker that Gillette had worn for his play had, with time, become a sort of shorthand for Sherlock Holmes, which explains why Steele deployed it with increasing regularity.

Even if Steele no longer felt quite as appreciated as he once had, his memories brought him great enjoyment. Just before the Great War, the Steele family had moved to New York. He had become a member of the Players, a gentlemen's club for actors and performers and people in literature, the fine arts, and music. It was there, in the billiard room, on a March day in 1922, that he had met the actor John Barrymore.

"There's a film I want you to see that I've just finished," said the famous actor. "*Sherlock Holmes*. Think you'll be interested." It was a film version of William Gillette's play, in which Barrymore was the big star—though, if truth be told, he was rather the worse for wear throughout the filming.

"Indeed, I will," said Steele. "I used to make pictures of Sherlock."

"Why, hell," Barrymore said, flashing his movie-star smile. "We had all your old pictures out on the lot. You're more to blame than Gillette!"

Steele had met Gillette once, a few years after he had begun illustrating the Holmes stories. He had gone to see the play *Sherlock Holmes* and had had the opportunity for a pleasant conversation with Gillette in his changing room during the intermission. And now, twenty-four years later, Steele had the chance to sit down with Gillette once again. He would, for the first time, sketch a portrait of Gillette from life, rather than from photographs, as he had done so many times before.

Steele had been charged with producing a souvenir program for Gillette's farewell *Sherlock Holmes* tour, as well as a great deal of other promotional material for the show. Steele also wrote an essay for the program, about his colleagues who had illustrated Sherlock Holmes and how he himself had set about the task. He even managed to squeeze in an anecdote about how an acquaintance of his, Dr. Gray Chandler Briggs, had managed to find 221b Baker Street while visiting London.

Steele and Briggs had first begun corresponding after the doctor's trip to London. Briggs was absolutely fascinated by Sherlock Holmes and expressed his interest in purchasing one of Steele's original illustrations. Later, he continued to buy original drawings, amassing a number of them, which helped Steele's increasingly parlous financial circumstances.

The first time Vincent Starrett wrote about Sherlock Holmes had been in 1917, a few years after he had perched on the desk of US Navy assistant secretary Franklin D. Roosevelt and scrounged cigarettes. Since then Roosevelt had run for vice president, caught polio, and become the governor of New York State. Starrett, while continuing his career in journalism, had moved back to Chicago and in recent years had established himself as a literary author.

Starrett's 1917 article had been a review of Conan Doyle's short-story collection *His Last Bow*. He had sent a copy to the author and received a friendly letter in reply. Three years later, when he wrote and published a Holmes pastiche titled *The Unique Hamlet*, he once again sent a copy to Conan Doyle in England. He had also met the author, albeit briefly, when he had had the chance to pose a few questions during a stop in Chicago on Conan Doyle's 1923 spiritualist tour of America.

Vincent Starrett had always enjoyed Conan Doyle's stories. At school, a teacher had once told the class: "Remember now, you may read and report on any book you like—all except Vincent, who must not report on any more Conan Doyles."

As a teenager, Starrett had seen William Gillette's play about the master detective, and during his first years as a journalist he had happened to share a train compartment with the great actor. Starrett had had a whole battery of questions, since the play was never very far from his thoughts. In particular, he was curious about the cigar. In the gas chamber scene, Gillette's Holmes had lit a cigar as he was in the clutches of the crooks. Holmes had then smashed a light, plunging the theater into darkness, apart from the glowing tip of the cigar. "Follow the cigar!" screamed one of the crooks. But, needless to say, Holmes was not where the cigar was.

"What would happen to the play if the cigar should happen to go out?" wondered Starrett.

"I'm always careful to puff it up into a fine red glow—perhaps you've noticed that—and I can't recall that it ever did go out. However, the possibility has not escaped me. There's always a stagehand close by in the wings, puffing like mad at a second cigar."

And now, there Vincent Starrett was, in the auditorium for the premiere of William Gillette's farewell tour. The curtain was about to be raised on *Sherlock Holmes*, and he was flipping through the souvenir program he had bought. He collected whatever he could pertaining to Sherlock Holmes and was indeed the proud owner of an excellent collection of first editions and all manner of things written by other authors about Holmes. He was even writing a book on the subject. His interest had become an obsession with the stories' tiniest details. Unfortunately, he did not have anyone to share this obsession with.

Starrett's gaze settled on a particular paragraph in Frederic Dorr Steele's essay, concerning a certain Dr. Gray C. Briggs—a dedicated Sherlockian from Saint Louis—and his discovery on a trip to London.

Starrett decided at once to write to Steele and ask for Dr. Briggs's address.

He wasn't alone, then. There was another one.

43

IT WAS ONE minute to ten, on the evening of Monday, October 20, 1930. In a newly equipped radio studio, eleven stories up, in the rooftop auditorium of the New Amsterdam Theatre in New York, six hundred people sat and waited. The audience largely comprised employees of G. Washington Coffee and their associates. The studio, near Times Square, was close enough to Broadway to allow the big stars to get there to make a quick contribution, just as evening radio listeners reached peak numbers. The audience was smartly dressed; tuxedos were the order of the day for men in attendance at the theater and at live radio broadcasts. Edith Meiser had allowed the audience to be present during the evening's broadcast, something she normally avoided, since the actors tended to perform to the audience in the room, rather than the wider audience across the country. And what an audience it was—NBC's station WEAF had a potential reach of as many as twenty million listeners. Within the past ten years, radio had become huge, the first genuine example of mass media, uniting Americans and shaping their view of the world.

The man who was to play Sherlock Holmes was almost eighty, so Edith Meiser had arranged for a chair, a table, and a tabletop microphone. The actor, though, would not hear of it. The broadcast was thirty minutes long, and he was quite determined to stand for the duration.

It was due to get under way within the next thirty seconds. The audience was separated from the stage by a six-ton curtain of steel and glass, lifted into place to prevent any audience reactions from being audible in the broadcast, while still allowing the audience to see the actors. Speakers were placed about the auditorium to allow the spectators to hear what was being said. The wires needed to link all the technology, including those connecting the twenty-two microphone outlets to the control room, which was located above the audience in the lighting booth, stretched over thirty-two miles.

None other than William Gillette, America's most prolific Sherlock Holmes portrayer, approached one of the microphones, inspiring the audience to burst into spontaneous applause, although the noise did not of course reach the actor. Gillette, dressed in a tuxedo, as were all the other men onstage, had taken a break from his farewell tour and was able to become the first man to play Sherlock Holmes on the radio in any significant broadcast.

The story Edith Meiser had adapted was "The Speckled Band." Gillette's participation was a one-off, and after the evening's performance the role would be taken over by Richard Gordon for the remaining thirty-four episodes of the season.

Precisely when the hands of the studio clock reached 10:00 p.m., another man approached the microphone. By strange coincidence, he shared the name Joseph Bell with the original inspiration for Conan Doyle's Sherlock Holmes.

"Tonight the makers of the new G. Washington Coffee present the first of a series of dramatizations from *The Adventures of Sherlock Holmes* by Conan Doyle," Bell announced, crisply and clearly, into the large microphone, before going on to introduce William Gillette. This was followed by a few words from the sponsor.

"As you enjoy the thrills and quick action of tonight's story, remember that there is as great a thrill waiting for you when you discover coffee made by the new G. Washington way—coffee made in the cup—without work or waiting. And now we will begin by calling on the genial Dr. Watson—Dr. Watson without whom the outside world would never have heard of the master detective, Sherlock Holmes. We find the doctor in his study. A cheerful fire is burning in the fireplace, and the fragrance of after-dinner coffee still hangs in the air. Everything looks calm and peaceful—everything that is except Dr. Watson. The good doctor seems a bit flustered—this is the first time he has addressed a radio audience. Ladies and gentlemen, we take pride and pleasure in introducing—Dr. Watson."

Bell added, in a hushed tone, "Yes, over here, doctor—that's right."

Dr. Watson was played by Leigh Lovell, an elderly monocle-wearing Englishman, who had once been very famous indeed and was now already in position at the microphone. Before Bell handed the broadcast over to Lovell, he asked, "And what incident are you going to start us off with this evening, Dr. Watson?"

"I . . . ," Lovell began. "Uh, that is, I haven't quite decided. Suppose we—"

He was interrupted by a crash. This had come from the men responsible for the program's sound effects. Prerecorded sounds were not used, and all the sound effects—be they pigeons' coos, rushing trains, or the fall of Babylon—were provided then and there. The sound-effects team was often placed behind the actors, so as not to distract the stars or cause them to burst out laughing. It was undeniably comic to see, for example, a sound-effects man wrestle himself to the floor, making various grunting and groaning noises, to provide the sound track to a bout of fisticuffs. After the most sound-intensive passages, the stage sometimes resembled a battlefield, covered in smashed-up props.

"What was that?" said Lovell, as Watson, reacting to the bang. "Oh, yes, the fire—the top log has fallen. M-m, where did I put that poker? Oh, yes—here it is. There . . ."

The men behind the actors provided the sound of a log being scraped around the hearth. Watson was pleased with the resulting fire, and said, "That's better."

"What a curious old poker, Dr. Watson," said Joseph Bell. "It looks as though it has seen many years of service."

"And so it has, my dear fellow—so it has," said Lovell. "It belonged to Sherlock Holmes himself in the days when we were sharing rooms in Baker Street. Dear, dear. You know, I lived there with him before I was married—and I couldn't do any better than to tell you the incident of 'The Adventure of the Speckled Band.'"

It was a story in which the poker had played a significant role.

"'The Speckled Band'—what does that mean, Dr. Watson?"

Lovell, in the role of Watson, laughed so hard that his monocle almost popped out.

"You're supposed to find that out from the story itself."

So began the story of how Helen Stoner had come to Sherlock Holmes early one morning seeking his help. Her twin sister had died, and she now feared for her own life. Edith Meiser, who also produced and directed the whole program, and another actress played the sisters.

William Gillette was exceptional in the role of Holmes. His was not the voice of an elderly man; it was sharp and clear, and Gillette was alert and followed the action unfailingly. The actor had made some adjustments to Meiser's script, so that it would more closely match his own interpretation of the detective. Sherlock Holmes was, after all, his alter ego; he knew exactly how the detective would react at any given instant. Indeed, Gillette was so sharp and alert that the broadcast was completed with a minute to spare, leaving Meiser to hurriedly instruct the orchestra to fill the remaining airtime—but not before Joseph Bell and Dr. Watson, while taking leave of the audience, made sure to mention the sponsor once more.

It had been a very good radio play, and Edith Meiser was pleased. The radio critics though, were not. "Who needs all this old-fashioned stuff?" they wondered. The sponsor took Meiser's side, and the series continued. At the end of the first season—which was to be followed by several more—the country's leading radio critic conducted a survey of American radio editors, to establish what had been the year's best radio show.

The Adventures of Sherlock Holmes received 94 percent of the vote.

44

O N DECEMBER 16, 1931, Vincent Starrett wrote a letter to Dr. Briggs on a typewriter that was definitely in need of a new ribbon.

> Who is H. W. Bell? Do you know? Have you any notion what form of book—what kind?—he plans to bring out? God knows, I have no wish to copy him, or steal even an idea, but I should like to avoid writing a duplicate of a book that—I gather from your letter—is likely enough to appear before mine does.

The correspondence between the two Sherlock Holmes enthusiasts had become increasingly animated. Starrett had shown an interest first in Briggs's discovery of the house on Baker Street and then in Briggs's enthusiasm for illustrations by Frederic Dorr Steele. The conversation had gradually become a discussion about the book Starrett was planning. And now rumors were rife that another book, by the mysterious H. W. Bell, was also in the offing.

Dr. Briggs felt that they could simply ignore Bell and concentrate on Starrett's book. Thanks to Briggs's collection, the book would include at least ten unpublished Holmes illustrations, something that Bell would never be able to offer.

Starrett and Bell were not the only ones writing books about the Holmes canon, and a pattern had been made clear. There were more essays and nonfiction books concerned with Sherlock Holmes than there were dealing with Conan Doyle. This was a strange development; modern literary characters did not normally attract greater interest than their creators.

The trend had started in England in 1928, with a publication by Ronald Knox. Since delivering his Sherlock Holmes lectures at Oxford in the early 1910s, he had given up his Anglican faith and converted to Roman Catholicism. He had, in fact, become one of the country's most well-known Catholic priests. So, when he released his collected *Essays in Satire*, which included the Holmes text, the latter was greeted with far greater interest than it had been when originally published by a relative unknown in the student newspaper sixteen years earlier.

The *Cambridge Review*, published in the rival university town of Cambridge, wanted to review Knox's book, so the editors commissioned it to one of the university lecturers, S. C. Roberts. They also sent him a newly published collection of Conan Doyle's Holmes short stories.

The first thing S. C. Roberts did was flip through Knox's book to the Sherlock Holmes essay. As a child, Roberts had read the stories in his father's bound editions of the *Strand Magazine*, and he had even met Conan Doyle on one occasion, although sadly they had not spoken about Sherlock Holmes. Now and then, Roberts would get word from Oxford about Knox's lecture on Holmes. But reading it himself for the first time, and forced to find some way of reviewing the essay, he was struck by the idea that he could do something similar himself. To rebuff the fictional scientists Backnecke, Piff-Pouff, and Papier Maché, he created his own experts, whose research he could use in his analysis. Before long, though, the review had become a rather more detailed study into the chronological problems presented by the Holmes stories.

The review was published. Some of his friends asked him for copies of the text, so Roberts printed a hundred copies, in a little eight-sided pamphlet titled *A Note on the Watson Problem*, which he then sent to friends and acquaintances by way of a Christmas greeting.

It might all have ended there. Yet somehow Dr. Watson continued to fascinate him, so Roberts wrote a second essay, about Watson's early life. This was published in a literary magazine and later in a collection of the best essays of the year.

Now that he was under way, it was just a case of keeping going. Roberts wrote another essay, this time concentrating on Watson's later years. He was reluctant to bother any editor with something that might simply be seen as a continuation of the second essay, but a Holmes-loving publisher suggested that Roberts combine the two essays into a single text, which he would publish as part of a series of pamphlets on a range of subjects. *Doctor Watson* was released in 1931. The publisher worked at the newly established Faber and Faber, where he had a colleague who was equally taken with Holmes—T. S. Eliot.

The publisher was Frank Morley, who at the age of four had been forced to read Sherlock Holmes in the attic of his childhood home, ahead of interrogations on the subject by his older brother Kit.

Ronald Knox had not been the first to carefully analyze the Sherlock Holmes stories and treat them as though they were about real events. As far back as 1902, the *Cambridge Review* had featured an article by Frank Sidgwick that took the form of an open letter to Watson on the subject of the inconsistencies and oddities in *The Hound of the Baskervilles*. It fell to the author A. A. Milne—also a Holmes enthusiast—to point out Sidgwick's efforts when he felt that the *Times* had given Knox rather too much credit for having launched the discipline.

There were others, besides Frank Sidgwick, who had started early. In the United States, an editor at the *Bookman* had regularly pointed out similar flaws and other details in the Holmes stories.

Regardless of whether Sidgwick was first, Ronald Knox was the starter for S. C. Roberts, and the latter's research in turn encouraged others to write on the subject. The year after Roberts's pamphlet about Dr. Watson, an English publisher released a somewhat thicker volume about Sherlock Holmes, in a limited edition of 350 copies. The author was a reserved and quiet man in his early thirties by the name of Thomas S. Blakeney. The book referred to Knox but above all was concerned with Holmes—the man, his career, his relations with Scotland Yard—and included a run through the essays, articles, and other texts that had been written about the detective. Unlike his predecessors in the Holmes genre, T. S. Blakeney had not had the benefit of a university education, having taken employment at a City firm of timber importers on leaving school. His great interest in life was alpine mountaineering, and in 1928 he had been part of an expedition that had climbed Mont Blanc, although he did not make it to the summit, falling ill during the climb. Thanks to the bleak economic situation, Blakeney lost his job in 1932 and thereafter supported himself with a series of casual jobs while writing a book, *Sherlock Holmes: Fact or Fiction?* After its publication, he decided to emigrate, and cycled through Europe to Constantinople. He continued on via Egypt and eventually settled in Ceylon, becoming an assistant manager on a tea estate.

Meanwhile, Dr. Briggs and Vincent Starrett followed events on the other side of the Atlantic with interest. In the *Saturday Review of Literature*,

Christopher Morley heaped praise on S. C. Roberts's piece, which his brother Frank had published in Britain. Starrett and Briggs continued writing to each other, discussing such developments in great detail.

By March 1932, Starrett had begun to finalize the structure of his book and had managed to jot down two of the book's twelve chapters. He searched high and low for every conceivable text on the subject of Sherlock Holmes and Conan Doyle's writing of the stories. He wrote letter after letter to gather more facts, and every day he received new pieces of the puzzle that was to be put together in the book itself. This required a great deal of dusty trawling of the archives—both his and Briggs's personal collections and those maintained by archivists and librarians—to find out exactly what had been published in newspapers and books a few decades earlier. Unlike the books that had gone before, this was to be a complete overview of the Sherlock Holmes oeuvre. The book was taking shape, thanks in large part to the correspondence with Dr. Briggs, Starrett's tireless sounding board and constant advisor.

The pair's only cause for concern was this H. W. Bell. Before long, Briggs was able to put Starrett at ease. He had found out that Bell's book was concerned only with listing all the Sherlock Holmes cases, including those named only in passing, in chronological order. Bell's book, then, was only about dates and years, although his method had revealed the fact that Watson must have married three times.

H. W. Bell, it turned out, was an American archaeologist, whose book was being published by a British firm in a limited run of five hundred copies. Bell's book would never have come about had it not been for S. C. Roberts's pamphlet about Dr. Watson; Bell made a point of this in his acknowledgments. Among the names of others to whom he expressed his gratitude was that of Dr. Gray Chandler Briggs.

In late August 1932, Starrett told Briggs the title of his book: *The Private Life of Sherlock Holmes*. In 1933 the book was finally released. It was dedicated to William Gillette, Frederic Dorr Steele, and Gray Chandler Briggs.

In December the same year, the *Saturday Review of Literature* published a review of Starrett's book, written by Elmer Davis, whom Christopher Morley knew from their time together at Oxford.

The members of the small clique of dedicated Sherlock Holmes enthusiasts from around the world had begun to find one another.

45

Two MEN EMERGED from the doorway: the first was sharp-featured and wearing a deerstalker and carrying a magnifying glass, the other a rather more portly figure. It was a cold December evening, and a thick fog enveloped the big city. It didn't get any better than this. The man in the deerstalker, to his surprise, noticed two hansom cabs waiting for them. The first drove away at once, empty. As the men climbed into the second one, the more rotund of the two exclaimed, "The first may be dangerous!"—before hurriedly instructing the driver, "Follow that cab!"

It was December 7, 1934, and the evening's gathering in New York was set to be rather special.

At Christopher Morley's lunches, Sherlock Holmes was mentioned with increasing regularity. To Morley and his friends, it seemed as though, all of a sudden, the world revolved around the English detective. The way this had come about was not straightforward. William Gillette's farewell tour, which had by now been going on for years; Conan Doyle's death; the wide circulation of Doubleday's complete edition of the Holmes stories (with Morley's preface); and the nostalgia surrounding all things Victorian all had to do with Sherlock Holmes. There were, too, the books that had been released in England. In the *Saturday Review of Literature*, Holmes had made ever more regular appearances in Morley's column.

It was, then, not all that surprising that the group's lunches toward the end of 1932 were increasingly taking on the character of a Sherlock Holmes quiz; the attractive prize on offer was an exemption from buying the next round of drinks. Competition had squeezed prices at New York's speakeasies, so a loss was not too hard to bear. A run of poor performances, however, could quickly empty one's wallet. This meant that Morley's friends were increasingly dedicating their free time to the study of the Sherlock Holmes stories, in part hoping to find really tricky questions to ask their lunch companions but also to bone up for the challenge of similar brainteasers.

Some of the group went further still. To support their arguments in the hotly contested discussions, they prepared themselves with even more rigorous study of a range of Holmes-related subjects. Not having to buy a drink was worth several hours of preparation. Something analogous to the quasi-academic studies undertaken by their English counterparts was beginning to take form.

Competing for something as important as a drink meant that toasts were proposed very frequently. If, for example, someone failed to recognize a quote from Colonel Sebastian Moran, from "The Empty House," then it was only proper to raise a glass in his honor. Here's to the second most dangerous man in London! Certain toasts were soon regular features and eventually became traditions. To begin with, this occurred under the auspices of the Three Hours for Lunch Club, but before long it had spread to the Grillparzer Sittenpolizei Verein. After all, the two clubs contained essentially the same members.

As 1933 drew to a close, Vincent Starrett's book was published. It was glowingly reviewed by Elmer Davis in an article that also served as a summary of the recent new wave of Sherlock Holmes research that had emerged.

At about the same time, it so happened that the owners of Hotel Duane, on Madison Avenue, wanted to market their restaurant as the perfect lunchtime meeting place for the inhabitants of the publishing and literary world. This coincided with the end of Prohibition in the United States, in December 1933. After thirteen years of clandestine drinking, the consumption of alcohol was legal once more. Christopher Morley decided that this would be the perfect opportunity for a birthday party. In January 1933 he had used one of his columns to proclaim that January 6 was Sherlock Holmes's birthday, on rather tenuous grounds. January 6, 1934, happened to fall on a Saturday and was now just a few weeks away. His old friend, head of sales at Doubleday, was in on the scheme, as was the Duane Hotel management, which agreed to let Morley hire the entire restaurant.

Morley invited his regular lunch companions from Grillparzer—including a number of women—and a few people from Doubleday.

The event, which Morley wrote about in his column, was a success. It was much like a Grillparzer lunch but slightly more extravagant and with the addition of repeated birthday toasts to Sherlock Holmes. Perhaps what most made the whole thing memorable was what happened immediately after lunch: they played "sardines" with the women.

Sardines was a sort of inverted hide-and-seek. Whoever was "it" went and hid, and the others set about looking for him or, even better, her. Everyone who managed to find the person who was hiding joined him or her in the hiding place. By the end, only one or two were left, looking for the others, who were packed into the hiding place like, well, sardines. If there was a good mix of men and women, it was a lot of fun.

It was the first meeting of what Morley referred to in his next column as the Baker Street Irregulars—the name Sherlock Holmes had used for the street urchins who sometimes assisted him. In his column two weeks later, Morley revealed that the group's first toast had been raised to "*the* Woman"—Irene Adler, a character in "A Scandal in Bohemia," of whom Watson writes: "To Sherlock Holmes she is always *the* woman. I have seldom heard him mention her under any other name." Other toasts were proposed to Mrs. Hudson, Mycroft Holmes, the second Mrs. Watson, the second most dangerous man in London, and the quotation "The game is afoot!"

It was also agreed that the venue for their meetings must always be located seventeen steps up from street level, just like the famous flat on Baker Street. That no such discussion had actually taken place during the meeting did not stop Morley from making this claim. In his column, fiction was never very far away.

Morley continued placing Sherlock Holmes snippets in the magazine, now under the heading "The Baker Street Irregulars." He regularly inserted material written by others, in one case printing a letter from Vincent Starrett to the editor, concerning Professor Moriarty. At the end of February, Morley's friend Elmer Davis had given him a document, which was also published in the column. Davis had, entirely of his own accord, written a constitution for the club. It explained that the purpose of the group was "the study of the Sacred Writings"— Conan Doyle's stories about the master detective—and that anyone who managed to pass a test and was otherwise considered suitable would be initiated into the group. The annual meeting was to be held on the sixth of January. Other paragraphs were chiefly concerned with the consumption of alcohol—including detailed guidelines as to who should buy the next round of drinks, according to the level of Sherlock Holmes knowledge displayed by the participants—or how men and women ought to behave toward one another when only a single representative of either sex was present. The penultimate point was: "All other business shall be left for the monthly meeting." The final was: "There shall be no monthly meeting."

Elmer Davis did not intend all of his points to be taken seriously. Among other things, it soon became clear that women were not intended to become members. This was a gentlemen's club. It was, in effect, simply another of Morley's ordinary lunch clubs.

The entry test, mentioned in the constitution, was printed in the May 1934 issue of the *Saturday Review of Literature*. It took the form of a crossword, and all the clues pertained to Sherlock Holmes in some way. The puzzle was signed "Tobias Gregson," which was also the name of a Scotland Yard detective featured in the Holmes stories. This alias belonged to Christopher Morley's younger brother Frank, who had been so bored on the boat journey back to his publishing job in England that he had used the time to construct the elaborate crossword. He had not had any Sherlock Holmes stories with him on the journey, but managed to retrieve all the necessary facts from memory. Anyone able to complete the crossword within one month was welcome to join the Baker Street Irregulars. Among the very first correct submissions was that sent by Vincent Starrett of Chicago.

Everything about the Baker Street Irregulars had rapidly become much bigger than Christopher Morley had ever intended. He also, to some extent, was having problems directing the club, since many people had begun acting on behalf of the Baker Street Irregulars.

Before long, news reached Morley's group that some people in England were planning to found their own club, the Sherlock Holmes Society. Their first dinner was scheduled for June 6. While the Baker Street Irregulars had held their first January lunch, they had not yet actually had a formal meeting. They had to maintain their head start over the English. Invitations were sent to anyone Morley considered eligible—those men who had successfully completed the crossword as well as other acquaintances he felt belonged in the club. Women who had managed to submit a correct crossword solution might yet be considered for membership at a later date, but he wanted this first meeting to be a men-only affair. The dinner was to be held a week later, on June 5, at an establishment called Christ Cella's, one of Morley's favorite speakeasies during Prohibition, now a proper restaurant, where they could have exclusive use of a separate room—a room exactly seventeen steps above ground level.

The dinner took place, toasts were made, and talks were given on the subjects "Was Sherlock Holmes American?" and "Sherlock Holmes and Music." It was a pleasant evening, although perhaps not unforgettable. A minor benefit was that they had beaten the Englishmen to it.

The following day in a restaurant on Baker Street, two dozen men and women met. Many were crime writers with a special interest in Sherlock Holmes, in particular Dorothy L. Sayers, who had also been inspired by S. C. Roberts and Ronald Knox to write investigative essays about Conan Doyle's creation. Roberts himself was present, as was H. W. Bell, while T. S. Blakeney had sent his apologies from overseas. Frank Morley came too, becoming the primary connection between the Sherlock Holmes Society and the Baker Street Irregulars.

At Christ Cella's, the members of the Baker Street Irregulars were gathering once more. Six months had passed since their previous meeting, and this Friday in December was to mark the first of what would be their annual dinners.

Twenty or so gentlemen were in the private room. Some had solved the crossword; others were long-standing friends of Morley's. Elmer Davis was there, and H. W. Bell happened to be in the country and also attended. Another guest from Europe was a leading member of their English equivalent, the Sherlock Holmes Society. Dr. Gray Chandler Briggs had traveled all the way from Saint Louis. Frederic Dorr Steele had had a rather less arduous journey—from his club, the Players, which lay two dozen blocks to the south.

Morley had scoured half of Manhattan—or maybe he just went to a Woolworth's—looking for a convincing fake jewel that could represent the blue carbuncle. Now, just as in the short story of the same name, the stone lay hidden inside the Christmas goose that was to be served. The restaurateur was rather taken aback by Morley's instructions that the bird be roasted with the jewel inside.

The men sat at a long table, anticipating the three-course meal and the fine wines awaiting them. The room was thick with smoke. On the street outside, an old hansom cab turned up in the midst of the evening traffic. There must have been only a few of these old carriages left in New York. And wouldn't you know it—another turned up. Vincent Starrett and the critic Alexander Woollcott emerged from the second cab. Starrett had traveled from Chicago to New York for the purpose of attending the dinner. Woollcott was a different proposition altogether; he was the type who liked to be noticed, and many felt he was rather too much, in all sorts of ways. Starrett had met him earlier that year, and they had stayed in touch. When Woollcott had realized Starrett was attending the dinner, he had made sure that Starrett invited him along as his guest. It had been Woollcott who had arranged the two carriages. Grandiose entrances were very much his style, even if photographers for some reason hadn't turned up to preserve the moment for posterity. What should he write about the soiree in his magazine column in the *New Yorker*—surely it wasn't too much to say that he was a founding member of the group?

Before the journey, Woollcott had given Starrett a deerstalker and a magnifying glass, but he had now reclaimed the double-peaked hat. They went over to the door, still unmarked, as it had been since the days of Prohibition. If you didn't know about the establishment, it simply looked like any other door on the street.

After ascending the seventeen steps, they both entered the room. Upon noticing whom Starrett had dragged along, Morley mumbled something rather louder than good manners would dictate.

The dinner progressed smoothly. The talk was of Sherlock Holmes, in great detail, and considered and learned comments were made. Dr. Briggs was praised for his Baker Street discovery. They toasted *the* woman, Mrs. Hudson, and Dr. Watson's second wife. H. W. Bell of course knew that there must have been a third, if one studies the stories in chronological order.

Woollcott was not Starrett's only guest that evening; he had also invited someone else, who, it seemed, was not going to turn up. It was already getting late. And then, the sound of footsteps ascending the seventeen stairs was followed by the door opening into the room where the Baker Street Irregulars were halfway through their meal. There he was, the guest Starrett had invited: William Gillette.

He had turned eighty the previous year, this Nestor of American theater.

"Splendid, Mr. Gillette!" someone exclaimed. "We'd given you up. It was good of you to leave your other party to join us."

"Other party? Certainly not. I've been four hours on the way from Hadlyme, Connecticut, and I'm damned hungry."

William Gillette had spent many years living in the rather odd stone castle that he had built for himself in southern Connecticut. He had amassed great wealth over the years, and the castle housed a number of ingenious mechanical devices that Gillette himself had worked out. The building was a monument to the art of rustic engineering, right down to the locks, no two of which were alike, on the castle's many doors.

Illustrator Frederic Dorr Steele, meanwhile, was moved almost to tears by the sight of the aging actor. Sadly, he didn't get many chances to speak to him. Alexander Woollcott made sure that Gillette stayed at his side throughout the meal.

When they had finished eating, the elderly actor rose to his feet and told the story of how, long ago, he had become Conan Doyle's detective.

That was as close as one could get to Sherlock Holmes.

46

"LONG LIVE LENIN! Long live the revolution!" the mob in the square was shouting, loudly enough to be heard above the rat-a-tat sound of machine guns and the clattering of the Red Army through the streets. The year was 1921, the place Batum, the second-largest city in the Transcaucasian land of Georgia.

The gates to a governmental mansion were opened, and a car rolled through but was blocked by the mob. A frightened girl jumped out, leaving her mother; her younger brother, Alexis; and the family's chauffeur behind.

In the midst of the mob, the Bolshevist leader stood on his red-painted car. The girl, whose name was Nina, pushed her way toward him.

Her father, a general, who had been aide-de-camp to the tsar, had gone to Constantinople to organize the White Army in a last great effort to win back Russia from the Bolshevists. Suddenly he had realized that his family was no longer safe at home and had fired a wireless message to an Italian steamer that was still in Batum. A lieutenant had volunteered to go back into the town to the rescue. Five minutes: that was how much time Nina, Alexis, and their mother had to leave the house, their home.

Fifteen years later, Princess Nina Mdivani (the M was silent) crossed the threshold of Windlesham, the large house in Sussex that was still home to Jean Conan Doyle. Six years had passed since her husband's death, but for Lady Conan Doyle and her family, Sir Arthur wasn't far away.

Nina had been there several times before, accompanied by Lady Conan Doyle's oldest son, Denis, who was a few years Nina's junior. This time it was different, however. The divorce from her former husband had at last been finalized, and she had come straight from the courtroom negotiations in The Hague. She would soon be allowed to marry her beloved Denis, with his film-star looks and warm personality. She was rather attractive herself, so they made a perfect couple.

On her first trip to Windlesham, when Denis had wanted to introduce her to his mother, she thought the house was a rather ramshackle Victorian pile. A tour of the rooms left her completely astounded. It was as though the family had never thrown away so much as a wrapper; she had lost everything when her family had been forced to flee its native country of Georgia during the Russian Revolution. Denis's rocking horse, which he had ridden as a five-year-old, remained in his old room, minus the tail, which had worked loose and disappeared somewhere along the years. The children's christening robes were covered in little mementos that her mother-in-law-to-be had attached to them decades earlier. And there were the handkerchiefs that Billy, soon to be her sister-in-law, had had as a three-year-old. The house was full of memories, an alien world for Nina. She was one of the modern nomads, those constantly moving between Paris, Venice, and Newport—from one hotel to the next, with the exception of the odd night spent on a luxurious yacht or in the palatial home of an industry baron. Since fleeing Georgia, she had spent most of the 1920s in Paris, so if she was at home anywhere, it might have been there. But she did not have a proper home.

Nina and Denis had met through her brothers. Conan Doyle's sons moved in the best social circles and shared an interest with the Mdivani brothers, motorcars. All they ever talked about had to do with cars: rev counts, brakes, horsepower, cooling vents, and suspension. Despite the fact that Adrian was about to turn twenty-six, and her future husband Denis was already twenty-seven, the interest the Conan Doyle brothers had discovered in their teens remained intact. They had got it from their father. Sir Arthur Conan Doyle had been an enthusiast ever since motorcars began to appear in England; he had purchased his first one in 1903.

While they were still in their teens, their father had given the brothers an expensive gift—a race car. Adrian and Denis claimed that it was the only dirt-track race car in England, and they were hoping to score in competitions with its colossal acceleration and enormous wheel track. It took them two hours every morning to go through the long starting procedure to be able to drive it at all. Their elderly father had loved to ride in it, and in their other cars, during the last years of his life, preferably at speed—up to one hundred miles per hour.

After his father's death, Denis acquired the original, renowned Chitty Bang Bang race car, famously powered by an aircraft engine and capable of an unbelievable 120 miles per hour. The two brothers, dressed in black silk shirts and black hooded pullovers, had participated in a land-speed record attempt in Cambridge, gaining a lot of attention in the process. A large group of spectators helped them get a push start, and after that the driving had gone well—until Denis decided to do the circuit in reverse, and managed to relocate part of the barrier in the process. A truck was called to extricate Chitty from the scene.

That was not the only time Adrian and Denis managed to crash a car. On one occasion in Oxford they were in a collision with a lamp-post, but managed to solve the problem this caused by buying a new car on the spot in which to continue their journey.

In 1932 the brothers bought a pair of supercharged Mercedes-Benz SSK roadsters, so each could have a car in which to compete at Monza, Nürburgring, and the other great continental circuits. Those who chose this pursuit were always close to death. Many of the siblings' friends had been killed or injured in car accidents. This did not seem to affect them, perhaps because they had inherited their father's spiritualist faith as well as his interest in cars. As far as they, and their mother, were concerned, life after death was a certainty.

It wasn't always easy for Nina to take her mother-in-law-to-be seriously. Sometimes it felt very much as though the messages from the other side were her way of keeping the boys from going out with dancing-girls or young actresses from the Drury Lane Theatre. The sons took heed—these were messages from their father, after all.

Having a father-in-law in this world could be tricky, but having one in another world was quite an experience. Now that Nina's divorce had been finalized, Lady Conan Doyle summoned Denis's intended to her boudoir. The older woman peered over her glasses, which had slipped down her nose, and said in a friendly, if somewhat flat tone: "I have received a message from my beloved. The marriage must be postponed for six months."

To this statement Princess Nina, who had been born a Muslim, replied in her Russian-toned accent: "I have received a message from Mahomet that the marriage must be done at once."

Nina got her way. The engagement was announced in June 1936, and Denis and Nina were to be wed later that same summer, on August 18. They planned a civil ceremony at a registry office in the Welsh town of Bridgend. The date was widely known to the public, but the time was kept secret in an attempt to prevent the turnout of large crowds. It wasn't, after all, just Conan Doyle's son who was to be married but also, and more important, one of the famous "marrying Mdivanis," as Nina and her siblings were known. Over the previous decade they had often been gossip columnists' favored quarry.

The Mdivanis' marital circuit had started with the marriage of the youngest brother, David Mdivani, to the much older Hollywood star Mae Murray, who had regularly played opposite Rudolph Valentino and was much loved by fans of the silent era. David persuaded her to leave her movie studio, MGM, a decision she later bitterly regretted, and before long they divorced. The oldest brother, Serge, had found himself an even more famous film star, Pola Negri, one of Hollywood's great femmes fatales, who had previously been romantically involved with both Charlie Chaplin and Valentino. When Negri lost her fortune in the Wall Street crash of 1929, Serge abandoned her to marry one of the world's leading opera sopranos instead. The middle brother, Alexis, targeted heiresses. First came Louise Astor van Alen, but Alexis soon divorced her to wed one of the richest women on the planet, Barbara Hutton, the sole heir to the Woolworth empire. She had been dubbed the "poor little rich girl" after having enjoyed an incredibly extravagant debutante ball during the worst depression in memory. Alexis was able to exploit this great wealth, while Barbara bathed in a little reflected royal glory. Finally Nina's fourth sibling, her sister Roussadana, an accomplished sculptor, married the Spanish painter José María Sert.

It had all been an unparalleled marriage merry-go-round. Nina's former husband—an international lawyer—had always arranged the necessary paperwork his in-laws needed for entering and indeed leaving marriage.

Things had come to the saddest imaginable pass. For Nina, the past few years had been grueling. First had come the death of her brother Alexis in Spain, killed in a car crash at great speed as he drove his latest conquest, a young German baroness, to the Paris train. Though the car had rolled over several times, miraculously the baroness had survived after being flung out of the passenger seat. Prince Alexis was only twenty-six. Their sister Roussie was inconsolable and had yet to recover from her brother's death. Not long after that, Serge was honeymooning in Long Beach, having remarried, this time taking his brother Alexis's first wife, Louise, as his bride. He was playing polo with some other Russian émigrés and in the desperate effort to score he steered his horse directly toward that of an opponent. His speed was so great that a collision was inevitable. The eight thousand spectators, including his new wife, watched as he fell to the ground, and then attempted to get to his feet, before he was struck squarely in the head by a hoof. Louise rushed onto the pitch. Prince Serge Mdivani, though, was already dead.

It was time for the next marriage in the family. Nina and Denis had Saint Donat's, a medieval castle in southern Wales, at their disposal for the honeymoon. It had been lent to them by Nina's friend, the American actress Marion Davies, who had been given the castle by her lover, the newspaper magnate William Randolph Hearst. Unfortunately, they had not been able to arrange the ceremony itself in the adjoining eleventh-century chapel, as the vicar had refused to officiate. Instead, Nina and Denis drove the six miles into Bridgend. Accompanied by his brother, Adrian, the groom arrived in a streamlined cream-and-silver sports car. He wore a gray pin-striped suit and a black homburg hat. The crowd—numbering many hundreds, maybe a thousand—had spent hours waiting for the couple, and the police struggled to hold them back. A few minutes later, the black car containing Princess Nina arrived. Her simple dress was embroidered with blue and white silk, and was paired with a large white straw hat. Bouncing on its brim was the largest emerald the women of this county town had ever seen. In the princess's hair was a cluster of diamonds. The neckline of her pale dress was weighted with jeweled clips.

She was not carrying any flowers, but the interior of Mr. Jenkins's little registry office was festooned with Madonna lilies, blue hydrangeas, gladioli, and carnations, purchased at a cost of £100. It had been a nervous, restless morning for Jenkins and his assistant, Mr. Isaac. Jenkins had brought his wife to the office. Isaac couldn't stop shaking, so he went to the chemist's shop and took aspirins for the first time in his life.

The marriage witnesses were Adrian, whose fiancée, Rita Cooper, was also in attendance; the brothers' younger sister, Billy, whom the papers called Miss Jean Conan Doyle; and two of the couple's friends. Denis's mother, Lady Conan Doyle, did not attend, nor did his half sister, Mary.

Adrian had become engaged to Rita nearly four years ago—directly following the end of his prior engagement, to Miss Isabelle Bridges—but the new engagement hadn't been announced until quite recently. There were no marriage plans yet, and they did not plan to give up their chosen careers. Adrian had just got a new race car, and Rita was a West End musical-comedy actress, having had great success at the Drury Lane Theatre.

The ceremony lasted less than five minutes. As Nina and Denis posed on the steps for the photographers they were showered with confetti. The police helped them to their waiting car. On the outskirts of the town, the bride was transferred to a fast sports car and was driven to the castle, while the groom grabbed the chance to sneak off to a nearby post office and send some telegrams.

Nina could relax. Finally, the Mdivani family had something to be happy about. Ever since the death of their father some years before, they had been subjected to a steady stream of great misfortune. The gossip didn't help. It was claimed that the family was not royal at all, since the Mdivanis didn't appear in any registers, but this was just because the critics did not know how things worked in Georgia. Their father had in fact had connections to the tsar, and in the years following their flight the siblings had come to realize what a door opener a royal title could be. Their father hadn't made things easier for them, however. He had always referred to himself only as General Mdivani. When people telephoned, asking to speak to Prince Mdivani, he would answer that they were probably looking for one of his sons. He once told a journalist that he was the only person in world history to have inherited a royal title from his children.

No, it wasn't easy being a Mdivani. Right now was, however, a joyous moment. Princess Nina Mdivani Conan Doyle knew how to get what she wanted, for herself and for her family, and this August day she felt nothing but happiness.

Back on that day in 1921, the girl and the Bolshevist leader had stood there, in the middle of the mob. Somehow—was it something she said? or the way she looked?—the Bolshevist had been touched by her entreaty.

"There is only one way," he told her, against his own conviction. "Go quickly back into your car. I will drive through the crowd. They will open up for me. Tell your driver to keep his motor so close to mine that the crowd cannot get between and block you off."

She rushed back to the car, and they followed the red-painted vehicle through a town in chaos. She saw dead men on the side streets. Finally they reached the waterfront and the Italian steamer, which would bring them to safety in the temporary quarters of their father.

47

At Windlesham, Lady Conan Doyle spent much of her time with her deceased husband. She made no decisions without first consulting him through a medium. For her, and the children, this was perfectly natural. In interviews and in her own published writings, Jean promoted her husband's achievements within spiritualism while still in this world, augmenting his successes with his latest messages from the other side. She also had another mission: seeking to demonstrate that Conan Doyle had used himself as the model for Sherlock Holmes. She meant that her husband had possessed a real Holmes brain, having succeeded several times in solving cases when the police had been bamboozled. The case of the wrongly convicted railway lawyer George Edalji was just one example of his brilliant brainwork.

Lady Conan Doyle was dedicated to propagating her own version of her husband's character. In 1931, when the family decided to commission Conan Doyle's biography, the man charged with the task was the Reverend John Lamond. He wrote from a broadly spiritualist perspective, since he shared the family's beliefs. Lady Conan Doyle authorized the biography and also contributed a long chapter. The book clearly presented the picture of her deceased husband that she wanted to spread, while simultaneously covering the history of spiritualism.

Lady Conan Doyle had no interest in further exploiting Sherlock Holmes. The money in the estate was plenty for her. If anyone wanted to buy rights, she simply referred the applicant to A. P. Watt, the literary agency. Alexander Pollock Watt had died in 1914, but his son had taken over the company. Jean's eldest son, Denis, was also involved in the Conan Doyle family business, although he spent most of his time on the Continent. He loved his mother and wanted to see her as often as possible, but his wife, Nina, and his mother did not get on well.

Conan Doyle's will had named Lady Conan Doyle and Denis as the executors. She had inherited the contents of the house, including all books, illustrations, and manuscripts. What she chose to do with them, whether she wished to keep them or sell them, was entirely up to her. Upon her death any remaining artifacts were to be shared among Conan Doyle's surviving children, Mary, Denis, Adrian, and Jean.

Conan Doyle's other assets had been sold and formed the estate. Two thousand pounds went to his daughter Mary; this, along with any maintenance payments she had already received and her share of the artifacts, was the full extent of her inheritance. A few other relatives were also remembered, as well as Conan Doyle's former secretary and some friends from the spiritualist world.

The remaining estate was divided between Conan Doyle's wife, who received half, and the couple's three children, who shared the remaining 50 percent. The two executors were responsible for issues around copyright, plays, film rights, and unpublished manuscripts—on condition that they cooperated with the agency of A. P. Watt. Conan Doyle had not left any more detailed instructions than that as to how his manuscripts were to be dealt with. The annual proceeds of the literary estate were to go to his wife and their three children.

Lady Conan Doyle's life began to slip away. In the mid-1930s, after she had just turned sixty, she was diagnosed with cancer. She underwent a series of operations, and her condition temporarily improved. She would not be reunited with her husband quite yet.

Keeping on top of the family's affairs was becoming increasingly difficult. Adrian spent a lot of time at home at Windlesham and was frustrated at the absence of Denis, who was always away in some far-flung corner of the world. Adrian, having no formal role in the execution of the will, could not make any decisions, yet he was still able to take care of much of the administrative work.

Adrian put literary agent Watt to work trying to sell film rights in the United States, primarily for those works that were not about Sherlock Holmes. In early 1938 he began a complete review of his father's old share certificates, which had not provided any dividends in recent years. The portfolio definitely needed to be rethought. Improving the finances of their father's estate was crucial for the brothers, since they were completely dependent on that money. The family had no other

income. Adrian pleaded with Denis to return home, as he did not wish
to involve his ailing mother. Denis said he would come home soon and
promised that together they would do whatever they could to sell the
rights to a film or two, because that was where the real money was.

During the 1930s, several English Sherlock Holmes films had been
made, with Arthur Wontner playing the lead.

"Surely no better Sherlock Holmes than Arthur Wontner is likely
to be seen and heard in pictures, in our time," Vincent Starrett had
written in his 1933 book *The Private Life of Sherlock Holmes*.

Arthur Wontner really did look like the Sherlock Holmes of Sidney
Paget's illustrations. Even Conan Doyle had said so, when he met
Wontner in 1920 to discuss a possible dramatization of a Holmes story.
That project never got off the ground, but a little more than a decade
later Wontner had landed the role.

The first film to feature Wontner as Holmes was *The Sleeping Cardinal*.
It was a talking picture of course. Like all the earlier Sherlock Holmes
films, this new picture was updated and set in a contemporary world.
Unimpeded by the modernization, Wontner played the quintessential
Englishman—upper class, self-assured, and rather mature. The film was
adapted from two of the most famous short stories, "The Final Problem"
and "The Empty House," a combination that allowed Holmes to be pitted against two of his enemies—Professor James Moriarty and Colonel
Sebastian Moran. The filmmakers exploited this plot device with gusto.

The film had been a success, in both England and America, and a
sequel was expected. It arrived the following year, under the title *The
Missing Rembrandt*, and was loosely based on Conan Doyle's short story
"Charles Augustus Milverton." Wontner's success in his first appearance
had made Hollywood aware of his talents. He found himself in great
demand, to the extent that a rival film company employed him that same
year to play Holmes in their production, a film version of *The Sign of Four*.

Vincent Starrett praised Wontner to the skies. The films that had
already been produced were good, certainly, but if a major studio were
to produce a really big Sherlock Holmes film, then Arthur Wontner
would be perfect for the role.

Wontner went on to appear in another two Sherlock Holmes films,
and although he was clearly the 1930s' incarnation of Holmes, none
of his films was the great Holmes movie that Starrett had hoped for.

48

RUNNING A LUCRATIVE literary estate was no easy task against the backdrop of the war looming over the Continent. Adrian Conan Doyle was shaken. It was September 28, 1938, and the past few days had tested him and those around him quite severely.

It was the deepest crisis to hit Europe since the Great War. The madman in Germany had demanded to be allowed to incorporate the German-speaking parts of Czechoslovakia into the German state. A war between the two nations was at hand, one that might see even more countries dragged into conflict. British prime minister Neville Chamberlain sought to negotiate a continued peace. Londoners had, at first, kept calm; by mid-September there were still no outward signs of anything being amiss. London's working people went to their jobs as usual, while those who were so inclined hurried to the early-autumn sales in the shops. The summer heat had made a brief return, and the sun shone in a clear blue sky.

The threat from the Continent rumbled on, leaving no Englishman in peace. The population's mood flipped between hope and despair from one day to the next. As soon as the newspapers arrived at the news-stands, small groups assembled on the streets to read the latest reports together. People gathered around their wireless sets for bulletins.

The military made preparations. Adrian saw trenches being dug in Hyde Park and on Clapham Common, and military convoys were on the move day and night. Passing a hotel, he could not fail to notice the reflection in the window of what he guessed was anti-aircraft artillery, illuminated by the hotel's lanterns.

The people of London began streaming out of the city and into the countryside. Everybody kept his or her gas mask at hand. The English were ready to take on the Germans once again.

Adrian noted that many wealthy families had quickly fled the country to settle in neutral regions. All flights were full for the next three weeks. He was relieved that Denis and Nina were in Switzerland. At the same time he knew that fleeing did not display the courage his father had taught him. Adrian himself was to join the Royal Marines if the war became a reality.

Regardless of the threat of war, there were certainly a few Germans whom Adrian very much wanted to obliterate. Ufa, a film company, had made an unauthorized film, *Der Mann, der Sherlock Holmes War* (The man who was Sherlock Holmes), which was about two men claiming to be Holmes and Watson. Adrian, Denis, and their mother agreed to sue Ufa. Denis was even convinced that a legal wrangle would be excellent publicity for his father's books.

The film industry was indeed where the money was. The family had employed the Rudolf Jess agency in London to represent them in negotiations with foreign film companies. Most of the interest was for motion pictures based on the Sherlock Holmes stories, although Adrian and Denis did try to raise interest in other books written by their father.

Simultaneously in Hollywood, film agent Paul Kohner also followed the news closely every day. Kohner spoke six languages fluently and was something of an expert on the European film market. As an eighteen-year-old, he had come from Czechoslovakia to New York, and had found employment in Universal Studios' European department.

Kohner noted that the British prime minister had traveled to Germany to negotiate. Chamberlain wanted peace at any price. The price proved to be an agreement between Germany, France, Britain, and Italy that Czechoslovakia should cede the area to Germany. The Czechs themselves were not consulted.

On October 1 the Germans had annexed their new territory. In Britain, the nation's leader was lauded by many as a hero who had preserved peace.

Paul Kohner, who had grown up in the now occupied region, did his utmost not to let the strife in his homeland affect his concentration at work. Many of his ongoing negotiations were at a critical stage. That year he had established a talent agency, through which he already represented several of the biggest movie stars. He also had an arrangement with Rudolf Jess, the London film agent.

Kohner spent a year and a half trying to arouse interest among the film companies in making a movie version of Sir Arthur Conan Doyle's *Hound of the Baskervilles*. For a long time Metro-Goldwyn-Mayer was interested. The negotiations went well, and MGM was even interested in a contract covering other Sherlock Holmes stories. In the end, however, it all came to nothing.

At a dinner in early autumn 1938, the president of Twentieth Century Fox, a relative newcomer to the movie business, was chatting with two of his colleagues—a scriptwriter and a director.

"You know," the scriptwriter said, out of nowhere, "someone ought to film Conan Doyle's classics, *The Adventures of Sherlock Holmes*."

The president agreed. It was an excellent idea. But who would play Holmes?

The scriptwriter did not pause for thought, replying, "Basil Rathbone—who else?"

The director agreed. He could see it now; Rathbone would make a superb Holmes. He had generally played the sophisticated villain in period dramas, but he certainly had the look and the sharp profile needed to play the detective.

"We will need a Watson too," the director said. "To complete the team."

"Nigel Bruce," the scriptwriter shot back.

Once again, there was no hesitation. Rathbone and Bruce as Holmes and Watson: one could scarcely imagine a more suitable pair. Both were members of the large English colony of actors resident in Hollywood— or rather arch-English, since no one was more interested in the drinking of tea and the game of cricket than these men and women in the movie capital of the world.

The contracts with both men were sealed by the end of October. Rathbone looked forward to leaving the villain roles behind and thus circumventing the danger of being typecast. The $5,000 a week he received during shooting didn't hurt either.

When Fox had bought the rights to the most famous Sherlock Holmes story through Paul Kohner's agency, MGM was apparently furious—but had it not already turned Kohner down? In any case, it was the signed agreements that mattered. Fox had paid $27,000 for seven-year exclusive film rights to *The Hound of the Baskervilles*.

* * *

Denis Conan Doyle gazed over toward Mont Blanc. The weather was so beautiful, so clear, that it seemed as though the great peak was just a few miles away. He had seen a lot of Mont Blanc on his many wonderful drives with Nina during their time in Geneva. He had had so much to do, with all the correspondence and business papers, that those drives were a very welcome relief—he needed all the relaxation he could get. But his hard work had paid off. All his dealings with the London agents had resulted in a signed film contract for *The Hound of the Baskervilles* with a Hollywood studio. It was significant income for the family.

Now he had some time to prepare his lecture. He was planning a speaking tour of the United States, which would get under way two months later, in January 1939. Since his father's death he had become increasingly well known in spiritualist circles, and he was keen to share his father's discoveries with his fellow followers in America. As soon as the threat of war subsided he planned to travel to England. He needed to return home to Windlesham to examine his father's spiritualist-themed slides through the Sciopticon projector, and see which of them were most suitable for public display. He also wanted to read his father's articles on the subject and to hear his mother's memories, which he might be able to use. He would do whatever it took to make a success of this tour.

He planned to arrive in England in mid-December, but first he needed to travel to Paris with Nina to update her wardrobe for their American trip. The tour was to last up to ten weeks; at its finish, in April, they would return to England. He hoped that his mother's intended surgery could be postponed until their return in the spring.

Things did not turn out as Denis had intended. His father, through a medium, had left specific instructions that his mother's operation was to be carried out on or around December 20. Adrian was happy to go along with that. He had secretly been holding séances twice a week in his London flat with astonishing results. His father had managed to impart a whole host of messages, on top of such communications as tapping and levitating the table. The transmission had even included a message in Danish for Adrian's wife, Anna.

The daughter of a Copenhagen shipowner, Anna had come to London in May 1937 to see King George VI's coronation. At a party that evening she met her future husband. They married a year later. They went to Cameroon on their honeymoon, though they spent much of their time on board a ship in the Gulf of Guinea. Upon their return Adrian had twenty-five snakeskins in his luggage; he had killed all the snakes himself.

Adrian told Denis everything about the séances, including, most important, that his father had given his unequivocal blessing to Denis's marriage to Nina. It was nice that at least one of their parents approved.

49

NIGEL BRUCE WAS a very busy man. Twentieth Century Fox had begun shooting *The Hound of the Baskervilles* just days after Christmas, two months after he and Basil Rathbone had signed their contracts, and the schedule was tight, to say the least. In half a day's filming, they might manage nine different scenes, some of which even included horses, carriages, and special effects. Some days, they would be in makeup at six thirty in the morning and not finish until ten o'clock at night. There wasn't much time, then, for tea and cricket.

This was the first Sherlock Holmes film to be set back in the Victorian era. Up until then, over three decades, each of the Holmes films had been updated to the contemporary world, but this time, turn-of-the-century clothes, backdrops, and objects were the order of the day. The Fox filmmakers were understandably concerned that Conan Doyle's Holmes stories might be considered old-fashioned, which led them to describe *The Hound of the Baskervilles* primarily as a horror film rather than a mystery.

Some of Fox's employees had traveled to England, specifically Dartmoor, to get a feel for the place. The film company then spent months erecting a three-hundred-by-two-hundred-foot English moor, with a painted backdrop giving the illusion of an even larger landscape. The moor was so large and full of dead-end tracks that it was easy to get lost in it.

The scenographers had placed a number of stone blocks in the center of the area, although they were actually made from plaster. When Nigel Bruce traversed the landscape, he had to keep a careful eye out for the streams and concavities in the ground. He had a back injury from a previous film, and it was a welcome relief not to have to film any terribly violent scenes. He didn't have to jump over the streams either; there were little bridges dotted around. He and Basil Rathbone spent eight weeks on the fake moorland with the other actors and some of the film team, and conditions were trying. Dartmoor was to be shrouded in fog at all times, so a new artificial mist was pumped in after each take.

Despite the difficulties, Rathbone and Bruce, who had been good friends for a number of years, remained in good spirits. Their director was known for his short temper, and he did indeed throw a few tantrums early on, but the two actors greeted him each morning with wide smiles, and each kissed his furrowed brow. After each take, the two leading men would shake hands and congratulate each other on an "excellent performance." The set, in the middle of an American film studio, was all rather British. In fact, the majority of the actors involved hailed from across the pond.

Nigel Bruce really did love working with Basil Rathbone. There was no one as kind, generous and considerate as Rathbone, who was always selfless and cooperative during filming. Rathbone, meanwhile, might never have fully understood how much it had meant to Bruce when he had received his telegram a few months earlier, after being involved in a failed Broadway production.

"Do come back to Hollywood, Willie dear boy, and play Doctor Watson to my Sherlock Holmes. We'll have great fun together." Rathbone always called him Willie.

Basil Rathbone had been married, to Ouida, four years his junior, since the mid-1920s. She was careful to explain to people that she had been a successful actress and scriptwriter before meeting Basil but had given it all up for true love. Basil was head over heels in love with her, and perhaps a touch submissive. She was a very ambitious woman—even grasping and brash, some might say. That could have been her exotic bloodline. She had been raised by her grandparents in Madrid, the story went, while her Spanish father and Anglo-French mother traveled the globe. When her parents finally returned home, she did not understand a word her mother said—the latter spoke English, while Ouida understood only Spanish.

Rathbone had been born in South Africa, but the family had fled to England in the 1890s after his father was accused by the Boers of being a British spy. He grew up in England and became an actor, specializing in Shakespeare plays. Film also appealed, and since the 1920s he had traveled back and forth across the Atlantic and had appeared in major film productions. He was forty-six years old, but even now, as Sherlock Holmes, he still was not given top billing. Instead, the posters gave prominence to the young actor playing Sir Henry Baskerville, and to the picture's female starlet. Love and horror were an unbeatable combination.

It was a turbulent time for the film agent Paul Kohner. He and his wife, Lupita, who was in her eighth month of pregnancy, worked hard to help the European film workers who were arriving as refugees from a Europe in turmoil. Kohner continued negotiating with Twentieth Century Fox. He hoped the company would buy the rights to all of the Holmes stories, and go on to shoot films with Rathbone and Bruce for many years to come.

At the same time he secretly attempted to resurrect negotiations with Fox's competitor MGM, whose interest had been piqued once more. MGM had requested an exclusive deal giving the studio the rights to the remaining Holmes stories. It was prepared to pay $15,000 per short story and $25,000 each for the novels. Kohner had the prices approved by the Conan Doyles through Rudolf Jess, their representative in London. All of this happened in December 1938. Countless transatlantic telegrams had been exchanged. The MGM deal was as good as done.

At that point Kohner heard that Lady Conan Doyle was seriously ill and was in the hospital awaiting an operation. She was not to be disturbed with business matters under any circumstances. He sent the occasional telegram to Rudolf Jess to see whether there was any news. There wasn't.

Parallel negotiations with Fox about further film versions came to an end immediately before Christmas. The studio's final response was no. Six years earlier, Fox had bought the film rights to William Gillette's *Sherlock Holmes* and intended to make its second film with that as the base. Fox did not need Conan Doyle's stories when it had another way to access the detective.

Everything, therefore, came down to the MGM deal. Paul Kohner could not help wondering what Rudolf Jess was up to over in London. Why was nothing happening?

Rudolf Jess answered. He asked Kohner not to underestimate all the work he had put into this particular affair. If Kohner had known the Conan Doyles at all, he would have realized just how difficult they were to deal with.

In the end, Rudolf Jess decided not to wait for Lady Conan Doyle's recovery but to travel to Paris instead, to meet the other executor of the will. A signature on the contract was a necessity.

In Denis Conan Doyle's life, nothing turned out as he had been promised. Plans were altered, and most things were postponed, saved for a later date. It was early April 1939, and he was with Nina in a hotel in Morocco. He had not gone on his planned lecture tour of America. But that January he had at least visited Paris, where he had met with agent Rudolf Jess. Denis, however, had not wanted to sign the contract for a film deal with MGM, preferring to try to squeeze a few thousand dollars more from the deal.

At that point Rudolf Jess had had to contact Paul Kohner, who in turn spoke to MGM. The studio replied that an increase was out of the question.

More than two months had passed since then. To Denis, the whole thing seemed to be at a standstill. Literary agent A. P. Watt wrote that the delay was being caused by MGM, which wanted to check the copyright situation for each story that was to be included in the contract. In England, this business was all perfectly straightforward, while in the United States it was a big mess. Numerous mistakes had been made by the American publishers who had released the Holmes stories—such as neglecting to submit a copy of the story for registration of the copyright, or forgetting to extend the copyright as it expired.

The only good news for Denis had been the reports concerning the success of the film version of *The Hound of the Baskervilles*—it had been an instant success in movie theaters. The filming had finished only a few weeks before, yet the premiere had already been screened.

Disaster was imminent. Paul Kohner could feel it. Yes, things had been rather shaky before, especially when Denis Conan Doyle had quite without warning tried to raise the agreed price at the Paris meeting with Jess, and again when the family was rumored to be involved in secret negotiations in Hollywood via Prince David Mdivani. And now the whole MGM deal was at stake. Kohner had got word of a completely ridiculous paragraph in a 1932 agreement. When Twentieth Century Fox made the deal for the play *Sherlock Holmes* with William Gillette and Conan Doyle's heirs, it had also been given permission to make an unlimited number of versions based on the play. Provided it made just enough adjustments each time, Fox could make as many sequels as it wished, without paying a single dollar to the copyright holder.

This made MGM's demand for exclusivity impossible to implement, which in turn caused its interest to cool off immediately.

Almost a month later, the Conan Doyle family decided to sue Fox if the studio were ever to make more Holmes films than the two for which it had explicit contracts.

Nina and Denis eventually made it to America, in October 1939. Denis had kept the trip a secret from almost everyone. Besides his spiritualist engagements he had decided to go to Hollywood to deal with the film contracts himself.

He had not even told his family that he and Nina were traveling by boat to New York. He did not want them to worry during the journey. After all, war had broken out and Denis and Nina feared that the seas were no longer safe.

50

ILLUSTRATOR FREDERIC DORR Steele stepped through the door of the Murray Hill Hotel on Park Avenue, between Fortieth and Forty-First Streets in New York, and was immediately surrounded by an air of faded Victorian grandeur. It was a Tuesday evening in January 1940, and for the first time in four years a dinner of the Baker Street Irregulars had been convened. The group would no doubt have gone extinct had it not been for a senior executive at General Motors, Edgar W. Smith, his great interest in Sherlock Holmes, and his impressive ability to build an organization from something that in truth was merely a thinly veiled excuse for eating and, above all, drinking.

Steele had received a written invitation from Smith, and the evening seemed well organized. Free copies of Vincent Starrett's new Holmes anthology, *221B: Studies in Sherlock Holmes*, featuring the writings of the society's members, were to be distributed, and one of Christopher Morley's brothers was to give a talk.

The hotel dated from Sherlock Holmes's era, and the atmosphere inside really got the party in the mood. For Steele, this was a welcome break from a daily life that wasn't as rewarding as it once had been. He was approaching seventy; his children had long since left home and gotten married. He and Polly should have been enjoying their twilight years together, but instead they had separated. Steele had moved into his artist's studio in Greenwich Village. It was a large room, admittedly, but drafty and cold. His food came from a nearby restaurant. His health was poor, and his finances were, if that was possible, even worse. A decade before, when he and Polly had still been married, they had emptied their bank accounts and borrowed money in order to realize their dream journey to Europe, to visit the old civilizations and cities. They had, finally, stood on Baker Street, which for so many years had been the key location in his illustrations.

Steele had heard barely anything from any magazine since the Depression and had had no indication that anyone wanted to hire him. Twentieth Century Fox, though, had asked him to provide a few illustrations for the publicity material for *The Hound of the Baskervilles*. He had also drawn an image of Holmes for the menu that evening, and a copy had been laid at each seat. At first he hadn't been able to get the likeness without a model, but on his third attempt he had donned his dressing gown and sketched what he saw in the mirror.

Steele greeted his friends in the Baker Street Irregulars. The party of almost thirty men sat down for dinner. In accordance with the established tradition, toasts were raised to three of the Holmes stories' female characters: *the* woman, Mrs. Hudson, and Dr. Watson's second wife. Then it was time for one of the evening's highlights, and Christopher Morley introduced Denis Conan Doyle, who had just arrived in New York, and who now was ready to give a lecture, "My Father's Friend, Mr. Sherlock Holmes."

Denis was astonished. This really was a very original dinner. The attendees were nice chaps and seemed pleased at his presence. Nonetheless, it was all rather strange that everything was about Sherlock Holmes.

He turned to Edgar W. Smith and whispered, "I don't understand this! My father's name has not been mentioned."

Smith replied that he would explain the whole thing later, and added that it was probably the highest compliment ever paid in the history of literature.

Denis continued listening to these men, who were going on as though Sherlock Holmes had been a real live person.

"No other writer, not even Shakespeare," Smith said a short while later, "can boast of creating a character so vivid that people believe in the character rather than the author."

"But what role is my father supposed to have played in all this?" Denis asked. "Surely, no one could believe that Dr. Watson . . ."

"Dr. Watson wrote up the cases, of course. They were all quite factual. Sir Arthur was—so to speak—the literary agent." The General Motors executive explained that Conan Doyle, according to the society's take on the Holmes stories, was a struggling young doctor who had been only too happy to market his colleague's narrations.

Denis was confused, to say the least. He really didn't know what to think.

When he wrote to his mother, his description of the dinner was a positive one. He wrote even more about the lectures that had brought him to America in the first place. In all kinds of venues, in places all over the country, he held talks about his father and spiritualism. He was homesick throughout the trip. As soon as he and Nina returned to London they planned to move into the little house that they had bought and furnished from afar. The previous autumn they had finally seen the end of the drawn-out inheritance struggles that followed the deaths of Nina's brothers.

Denis had also decided what he wanted to do with his life. He had turned thirty the year before, so it was time. He set his sights on a political career, in both domestic British politics and international affairs. His American tour, he felt, had been excellent practice, having involved a great deal of public speaking, as well as meeting so many people of note.

He also had his family's finances to consider. None of the film agents they had employed seemed to be doing their jobs, so he had no choice but to become involved. Instead of the useless Paul Kohner, he planned to collaborate with the Orsatti brothers. A friend in Hollywood had told him that they were the agents everyone wanted. He had also hired the best movie lawyer around in an attempt to bring the Fox dispute to an end. Part of the case rested on the interpretation of that particular paragraph, as well as the claim that Fox had breached copyright in some way by calling its second film *The Adventures of Sherlock Holmes*. That was, after all, the title of one of his father's short story collections.

When it came to radio, Denis had withdrawn the agreement with NBC and renegotiated it. He had not been satisfied with the fifty dollars payable for each new episode broadcast. Throughout the 1930s, in season after season, Edith Meiser had both adapted his father's original works for broadcast and written original stories. In the end, Meiser felt that interest in Holmes was waning and decided to mothball the series. This lasted until the Fox films gave the detective new life once more. Meiser moved to Hollywood and started production of a series of live broadcasts there, featuring Basil Rathbone and Nigel Bruce in the leading roles. While both Holmes films had been seen by large audiences, it was in fact the radio series that really introduced Rathbone's Holmes and Bruce's Watson to millions of Americans.

Denis was also trying to get a Broadway show off the ground. Edith Meiser was to write the script, and he dearly hoped to recruit Rathbone and Bruce as its stars. But would their film company allow them to be dragged off to New York?

For Denis, every day brought a new query. He did not want to leave a single stone unturned. There were dozens of meetings, letters, and telegrams. One day, in June 1940, came the telegram he least wanted to receive, yet had expected for some time. The woman he loved most on this earth had died. His mother, Lady Conan Doyle, lived no longer.

Adrian was quite clear about one thing. Denis had to come home. This war was not like the last. The British had begun seeing themselves as a single, unified nation in which class differences were being erased. People had already begun to speak in unflattering terms about the men who had fled the country and thereby avoided military service. Denis could wave good-bye to any aspirations he held of a political career if he had not done his duty for king and country. It was convenient to have him there in the United States, close to the film-rights negotiating tables, but now, for his own sake, there was no doubting where he ought to be. Nina was nervous about Denis's safety if they were to return, but considering the poor state of his health over the past few years, the risk of his being called to the front line was nonexistent. He would surely be given a desk job back in England. Meanwhile, seven doctors had examined Adrian for two hours, and thanks to his fine physique he had been accepted into the Royal Marines. He was now waiting for the draft.

At Windlesham, Adrian and his wife had attempted to tidy up after Lady Conan Doyle's death. Her boudoir and study had been transformed into habitable rooms once more, and ten years of dirt and damp had been aired out. Many rooms had been locked for years, and only now did Adrian realize the state the house was in. He did not want anyone from outside to see it, not even the servants, so he and Anna worked hard tidying and cleaning the place. Adrian had been responsible for most of the household even before his mother's death. He had sat at her bedside day and night for four days. Their sister Billy could not leave her duties in the women's unit of the Royal Air Force, where she had been serving since mid-1938, and Denis was a long way away. Toward the end, their mother returned to being as loving as she had been before her illness had taken hold. She had long conversations with her late husband. She held on for twenty-four hours longer than the doctors had predicted, but then, finally, after ten years of loneliness, she was reunited with her beloved Arthur. It happened in silence, like a leaf falling slowly to the ground. Adrian saw the beauty of that moment. It was not death, but triumph.

51

IT WAS MIDNIGHT, and Adrian and Anna were walking along a road not far from Windlesham. A low-flying German bomber passed overhead, but this was such a regular occurrence that they barely noticed anymore.

This time, however, the whistling sound of falling bombs followed. Adrian and Anna dived to the ground and lay prone on the road. They saw a flash of light and heard the bang. The bombs must have fallen close to Windlesham.

They hurried home in the darkness. An incendiary had pierced the roof of their gardener's cottage and landed in the bedroom. Anna immediately set about helping the gardener to fight the blaze. She ran off to find a spade, returning to scoop up the bomb, carry it down the steps, and sling it out into the garden.

In the meantime Adrian came across another bomb, which had fallen just beyond the hedge. Flames were flickering around it, threatening to ignite the whole device and thereby light up the surroundings. The bomber could still be heard overhead in the pitch-black October night, and Adrian had to act fast if the Germans were not to catch sight of Windlesham in the light from the fire. His only option was to strike the back of the bomb casing as hard as he could with a spade. It exploded immediately. Shrapnel filled the air and flew past his ears, covering parts of him in burning carbide. Adrian realized that he had got off lightly, burns to his hands being his only injury. He managed to extinguish the flames by shoveling sand over the fire.

It all ended fairly well, this time around. The newspapers were full of reports from the Blitz in London, but the countryside also received its fair share. Sussex, over which almost all German planes flew, was particularly susceptible. And around Windlesham there were no protective batteries of anti-aircraft guns, no searchlights scanning the sky, not even any bomb shelters—individual households had to make do. Earlier that same evening, when the Conan Doyles had been eating dinner in a makeshift shelter in their coal bunker, the windows in the house had rattled as five highly explosive bombs had obliterated the road to Eastbourne. Within a two-mile radius, six houses had been destroyed in the past month, and several families had lost their lives. As the sun set, people prayed that they might see it rise again.

Adrian's sister, Billy, had enlisted in the Women's Auxiliary Air Force. Their half sister, Mary, who had passed fifty, served as an air-raid warden. Adrian himself was waiting for a call-up from the marines. He felt that Denis was the only one not doing his duty. The family had heard hardly a word from him for months. There may have been a reasonable explanation—perhaps the letters were lying on the seabed. Until his return, Denis was encouraged to write more regularly, but not to include news of the great parties he had attended, descriptions of Nina's newest purchases, or newspaper clippings featuring his name in the society columns.

Over in Hollywood, Nigel Bruce was greatly enjoying playing Dr. Watson on the radio. He and Basil Rathbone had recorded a first season in a period stretching from October 1939 to March 1940. Now, a year later, it was full steam ahead with the second. Edith Meiser wrote all the scripts, and her husband, Tom McKnight, was the producer. Meiser's scripts provided Nigel Bruce with more of a challenge than the films, because Watson was to appear rather more intelligent. Bruce had to up his game.

The broadcasts, live from the studio, came on each Sunday evening and lasted thirty minutes. The cast would rehearse for two or three hours on Saturday and put in as well a short stint on Sunday afternoon. Bruce received $500 a week for his trouble.

Nigel Bruce had taken a shine to Edith Meiser straightaway. A tall, stylish woman, she possessed not only a sense of humor but also a great knowledge of acting. Her husband, Tom, was harder to make out. His sarcastic manner belied the fact that he was actually a very kind and generous person.

The radio studio was so pleasantly quiet, not at all like a film studio, where the sweltering arc lamps and the never-ending retakes could drive you mad. And Bruce got to work with Rathbone. They had become even closer friends, and when they were not busy making films or radio shows they loved playing golf on the Riviera and Bel Air courses. They had some great rounds, both men playing off a handicap of ten.

The radio studio featured a sponsor's box, to which the sponsoring company could bring guests to watch a recording. It was not unheard of for Denis Conan Doyle to drop in during a broadcast. Meiser, though, had made an embarrassing gaffe on one occasion. She had, before transmission—not in a script, but merely in passing—happened to call Basil Rathbone's character "Sherlock."

"What did you say?" asked Denis.

Meiser repeated what she had said.

"We always call him Mr. Holmes," said Denis.

That aside, Edith and Denis enjoyed a good working relationship. As soon as she finished writing the script for a new series of radio adaptations, she would send it over to Denis for approval. She had even offered to write a cameo role for Denis's wife, Nina, a female character who would suit Nina's accent. Sadly, this never happened, since Denis and Nina soon moved on.

For Nigel Bruce, there was a lot going on in the Sherlock Holmes field. The idea of a Broadway play was still being considered. He and Rathbone had also met a producer who was keen to make new films. Meiser's husband was involved in that project. The plan was to begin filming a movie version of "The Speckled Band" just three months later, in March 1941. All that was needed was an agreement between the Orsatti brothers and Denis Conan Doyle. Rathbone had written directly to Denis, explaining that he would like to arrange a meeting when Denis next returned to Hollywood. There were a few wrinkles to be ironed out; rumors were flying about which film company had the rights and which might actually be given the go-ahead to produce the film. Both Nigel Bruce and Basil Rathbone were keen to be involved.

One June day in 1941 Denis and Nina were driving north in California to spend a few days at the palatial home—"the ranch," as its owner called it—of their friend, the newspaper tycoon William Randolph Hearst.

On the road between Oakland and Berkeley, not far from San Francisco, an enormous roadside billboard caught Denis's eye. It was an advertisement for New Golden Glow Beer. To his horror and astonishment he saw that the figure in the drawing was depicted with a

deerstalker, pipe, and magnifying glass. He was examining a beer tan-
kard, and the words he was uttering made reference to Watson. The
shock almost sent Denis careering off the highway.

It was a flagrant breach of copyright. And, as if that weren't enough,
it was using Holmes and Watson in a beer advertisement. This was
clearly undermining the value of the characters. As soon as he arrived
at Hearst's residence, which had the look of a Spanish cathedral, he
wrote to H. William Fitelson, his new lawyer in New York. The posters
had to go, and compensation would be sought.

It transpired that the copyright issue was not altogether straightforward. The brewery argued that Sherlock Holmes appeared regularly in
advertisements for all manner of companies, so the family could not
reasonably expect people to ask permission. Once again, the vague and
complex rules regarding copyright in the United States worked against
Conan Doyle's heirs.

For Denis, however, it was perfectly simple. No one else should be
making money from Sherlock Holmes unless the estate was, too. A
steady stream of income was necessary to pay for his and Nina's incidental expenses. Adrian explained in his letters that the other money
that had come in had been used for the upkeep of the family's various
houses. It had been thought that Denis would take on Windlesham
when he returned to England, but he and Nina were not terribly interested, and had become even less so since they had begun planning
their London abode.

On the film front, a potential collaboration with Warner Brothers
Pictures had emerged, and it had progressed to the point that the studio was going through the endless copyright issues. Denis had tired
of the Orsatti brothers. They had been employed as agents since 1939,
and nothing had happened. At this rate, there would never be another
Holmes film.

52

Franklin D. Roosevelt put his elbows on the Oval Office desk. He felt the heavy burden of responsibility. The war was in a critical phase; it had been ever since December of the previous year, when the Japanese had attacked Pearl Harbor.

Operation Watchtower, as the Guadalcanal campaign had been dubbed, was being launched. American troops were heading for the Solomon Islands, east of Papua New Guinea, to try to prevent the Japanese from establishing bases there. Were the Japanese to succeed, there would be dire consequences for the Allies' transport convoys. In two days' time, American forces would launch their first ground offensive against one of the Axis powers.

The war was present at home, too. Only the day before, eight German saboteurs had been sentenced to death in Washington, DC. Roosevelt had appointed the commission that had investigated the case.

Among all these grave decisions, there were chinks of light. A few days earlier he had received a letter, dated July 27, 1942, from an executive at General Motors. It was an invitation to become an honorary member of the Baker Street Irregulars. His old cigarette-bumming friend Vincent Starrett was a leading member of the society, and a founding member was the director of the Office of War Information, Elmer Davis, who had written the society's constitution.

Roosevelt had finished his answer. He gratefully accepted. He was pleased to put his name to any movement that wished to keep the memory of Sherlock Holmes alive. He was also able to reveal a snippet concerning the secret retreat where he would often spend a Sunday recuperating from the week's work. There was a row of small cabins for the Secret Service men, Roosevelt explained, and that little row was called "Baker Street."

★   ★   ★

Meanwhile, in Los Angeles, Denis Conan Doyle had met with Tom McKnight, who had informed him that Universal Studios was exceptionally pleased with its first film, *Sherlock Holmes and the Voice of Terror*. In addition to producing the radio programs, McKnight had been working as an expert Sherlock Holmes consultant for the new series of films.

After years of negotiations with various film companies, it was Universal with which the family reached an agreement for a series of films about the master detective. Everything proceeded quickly once the contract had been signed. Universal had come with a draft agreement in January 1942, and by the end of February negotiations had been complete and the contract signed. Just five months later the first three films were in the can. That was the annual quota, which the studio was obliged to fulfill for the contract to be extended for a further twelve months. The contract would last for a maximum of seven years.

One of the three films per year was permitted to be a new story, while the others were to be based on original Conan Doyle short stories. The film company was entitled to substantially revise the stories, even to modernize them, which was exactly what it did.

Sherlock Holmes and the Voice of Terror was not completely without Conan Doyle's influence—the antagonist of the film, German agent von Bork, was someone whom Holmes had encountered in the short story "His Last Bow," set on the fringes of the First World War. This time, though, it was a different war, and the opponent was not merely a country but a whole ideology.

All the major studios had received letters from Elmer Davis's Office of War Information during the spring of 1942. The gist of the message was that new films that reflected the current situation would be welcomed. There was a long list of questions in response. Could a film help the war effort? How was the war to be portrayed? Would a film's portrayal be regarded as plausible or just dismissed as propaganda? A close collaboration between the office and the film companies began. The war was woven into a number of film series that were already under way—regardless of whether they were about Tarzan or starred the comedy duo of Abbott and Costello.

Bringing Sherlock Holmes and Dr. Watson lock, stock, and barrel into the modern age was a part of this patriotic effort but also had other, coincidental advantages. Audiences were drawn to war-themed films and to modern crime stories. And sourcing sets and costumes was quick and straightforward.

Universal wasn't among the biggest film studios at the time, and the company's financial constraints almost gave the production the feel of a B movie. Shooting took just two or three weeks, and the films were not particularly long, either, often running just over an hour.

Denis supported these new films wholeheartedly. They were said to have been based on various Holmes stories, but the odd plot element aside, little of the originals remained. Denis and his siblings had other details on their minds, however. A clause in the contract stated that the film company was not permitted to change either Sherlock Holmes's or Dr. Watson's personality. Above all, the family wanted to preserve the respect audiences felt toward Holmes and to avoid parodies turning him into a joke. On the other hand, it was acceptable for Dr. Watson to deliver the film's light relief, a welcome feature in those hard times.

Denis felt that bringing the story into the present day had been a daring experiment but a successful one. Holmes and Watson had become immortal over the years, and their trademark features made them easy to transpose to any era. Rathbone and Bruce, who expressed their opinions regularly during the shooting, had at first objected to the modernization. The producer had managed to convince them that it was actually the only way to reach a young audience.

President Roosevelt had recently tried to contemplate what Sherlock Holmes's coat of arms might look like. The present situation made it, however, difficult to get to the bottom of the subject; it would have to wait till a more peaceful time. Fortunately no war would ever threaten the everlasting existence of Sherlock Holmes and Dr. Watson. Or, as his old friend Vincent Starrett had put it in the two finishing lines in his sonnet "221B," published earlier that year, "Here, though the world explode, these two survive, / And it is always eighteen ninety-five."

While Hollywood had Sherlock Holmes fighting the Germans on the silver screen, the situation in the White House was very real indeed. President Roosevelt had ignored his military advisors and issued a direct

order to the generals involved: the Allies were to land sixty-five thousand men on the coast of French North Africa.

It was October 1942. A tall American major general, Mark W. Clark,
was on board a British submarine, accompanied by a few of his closest
aides. The officer was clearly not built for such a vessel, bumping into
dials and levers each time he tried to move. The commander of the
troops in the Mediterranean region, General Dwight D. Eisenhower,
had nominated the major general as his deputy during the operation.
The small group of Americans was to land on the Algerian coast in
order to secretly prepare for the North African operation alongside
French forces. Until then, the men would keep themselves busy by
playing bridge.

It was in the middle of the Mediterranean night that the submarine
surfaced and several small dinghies were launched. The lead boat contained an American colonel, who was to wade ashore and make the
first contact. Major General Clark and an aide followed in one of the
others. Over on the beach, a light was visible against the backdrop of
the dark cliffs. It was a signal from the welcoming party, or it was a
trap. There was no way of knowing until they were there.

They were almost on the beach. The colonel jumped down into the
water. A French captain waded out to meet him. The Frenchman had,
despite his nationality, inherited a name from his English forebears;
when he introduced himself, he did so as "Watson."

"Holmes," the American colonel replied, since that was his name.
Standing up to his waist in water, and with the most collected demeanor
imaginable in such grave circumstances, he quipped, "I have an impression, dear doctor, that we have met before."

53

O N THE SAME day that Edgar W. Smith sent the Holmes society's invitation to President Roosevelt, he had also written to his fellow Sherlockian Vincent Starrett. A rumor concerning something quite fantastic had begun circulating, and Smith wanted to talk things over with his friend. In an English newspaper article, Adrian Conan Doyle had revealed that an unpublished and previously unknown Sherlock Holmes short story had been unearthed among his father's papers.

Smith sat in his office at General Motors in New York, beside himself with excitement. For him, this discovery had an almost cosmic significance. Yet he was also distraught, since it seemed that Conan Doyle's heirs did not intend to publish the work.

Why on earth would they not publish? Why?

Denis was bombarded with letters from Sherlockians across the United States. Since the founding of the Baker Street Irregulars in the 1930s, several smaller groups had emerged, all taking their name from a Sherlock Holmes–inspired source; there were, for example, the Five Orange Pips, and the Speckled Band of Boston. It was as though all of them had come together with a single common purpose: to get the newly discovered story published.

It had been found in Windlesham, inside an old chest full of forgotten family documents. After his mother's death, Adrian had gone through all the books and papers that had been secreted in nooks and crannies throughout the big house. The idea was to get all the papers organized before the siblings got together to divide the inheritance among them.

The short story had been in an envelope, the front of which had been marked with a note in Lady Conan Doyle's handwriting. It stated that her husband did not intend for the story to be published, because it did not meet the standards set by his other Holmes stories. The

American Sherlockians—several of whom were leading lights in literary circles—clearly felt that the short story should be published regardless.

Adrian had informed the press that nothing would happen before Denis returned to England. This was a family decision, and Denis was the sole executor of the will since their mother's death.

The brothers had another reason for waiting. As soon as the war ended they would be able to publish the story in all the English-speaking countries simultaneously, which would be considerably more lucrative than if they were to publish at once.

In the meanwhile, they could still benefit from the huge interest surrounding this new story. In a few weeks' time, Denis would be traveling east, first to Washington, DC, and then on to New York. From there—after more than three years in the United States—he would finally travel home to England. A few days earlier he had had a long meeting with the director of publicity at Universal Studios, drawing up grand plans for Denis's own participation in the publicity to launch the new films, since he would be on the East Coast anyway. They had already exhausted all promotional avenues available on the West Coast.

Although the films strayed from his father's stories, Denis felt that they were good entertainment. Introducing the well-loved character to a new generation of both American and British audiences could only be a good thing. It might even strengthen the bond between the two nations, a notion that he held dear, just as his father had.

As an official representative of the films, Denis had been given the title of production consultant. He was only too happy to participate in radio interviews, both for American stations and for broadcast across the Atlantic by the BBC. The excitement surrounding the newly discovered short story ensured that interest in his father's work was at a peak. The director of publicity at Universal, knowing that the heirs had not yet decided whether the short story was of sufficient quality for publication, proposed that a few members of the Baker Street Irregulars should form a committee to make the decision. Denis revealed that President Roosevelt was a newly recruited member, and that perhaps he might be persuaded to make his position public. That would surely increase the public's interest in all things Sherlock Holmes. Denis also explained that he counted the Sherlockian Elmer Davis, director of the Office of War Information, among his closest friends. Davis would turn the town upside down for Denis. If Davis and a few of the other famous names who were members of the Baker Street Irregulars were prepared to give endorsements, then the premiere party for the film *Sherlock Holmes in Washington* would be a very impressive shindig. Perhaps they might even be able to involve the president in some way.

Finally the director of publicity asked Denis whether he might be able to come up with a story about how his father predicted the outcome of the war. Denis balked at the suggestion. Asking questions of his father was difficult. Contact with him wasn't something that could simply be switched on and off. He made contact with Denis only through a medium, and there was no way of knowing when that might happen.

With his capacity to enter business agreements severely restricted, the best Adrian could hope for was to see that one third of the earnings Denis reported made its way to his account. Sometimes there would be a delay, and he would need to remind Denis. Neither Adrian nor his younger sister had seen a trace of their share of the $1,000 Denis had received from the brewery, for example, or of a similar sum received from another company that had used the image of Sherlock Holmes. There had been no payments in regard to the radio contracts for a year now. Probably this was just an oversight on Denis's part.

Adrian's existence had become gray and uneventful. His health was failing. War, though, could not stop the changing of the seasons. The world around Adrian was once more transformed by the arrival of the spring bloom; it gave him renewed energy with which to address the finances of the literary estate. He was not averse to being involved in the war effort, but he wanted to avoid what he saw as a meaningless clerical job. He asked the authorities for an exemption, in order to be able to continue concentrating on the correspondence surrounding film rights instead. That would generate far more tax revenue for the state.

He put pressure on his brother to, in turn, put pressure on the American publishers to step up their promotion of the Holmes books in each of the forty-eight states. He was on the warpath against the British publishers, who blamed the fall in sales on the shortage of paper brought about by the war. Adrian would not stand for it.

The American radio contract needed a new sponsor. Surely Denis could meet Edgar W. Smith of General Motors and ask if he might be interested in a deal?

Then there was the American tax problem. Deductions on income earned in the United States were always problematic. Denis had been troubled by double taxation for the several years he had been an American resident. Adrian looked forward to one day making the estate into a company. In order for that to happen, Denis was going to have to come home, even if his work in America did mean a great deal to the family.

In November 1943, after a further six-month delay, Adrian's prayers were answered. Denis and Nina were on board a ship heading back across the Atlantic.

54

THE WAR ENTERED its fifth year, and Adrian finally became a seaman, in the Royal Marines. He was called to the training center in the summer of 1943. One thousand new recruits arrived every third week to undergo a ten-week period of training. He was in charge of more than forty men, and keeping this company of ruffians from London's grimmest slums in line was no easy task—they did not even know how to hold a conversation in English. Adrian and his platoon marched, exercised, and rowed. They kept it up for eighteen hours a day, before they would all collapse into their bunks.

Adrian had barely finished his training before he was taken seriously ill and found himself in the hospital. That was where he lay now. The nurses were preparing him for surgery.

On the table next to his sickbed lay a book he had just been given, a recently published biography, written by Hesketh Pearson. The subject of the book was Adrian's father.

The doctors had forbidden him to read anything that might upset him or even to speak about anything that might have that effect. It was a wise move, since Adrian had something of a short fuse. The staff kept an eye on him, and he had managed only to dip into the book a few times before he heard a nurse's footsteps approaching. What he had seen of the biography thus far was very much to his liking.

Adrian had met Pearson a number of times over the years, and had talked with him about his father. He had also given Pearson access to many old documents, and it was actually thanks to this research that the newly discovered short story had been found. Pearson had explained that his book was to be more of a literary critique of Conan Doyle's entire body of work than a straight biography, and that it would restore him to his rightful place among the literary greats. Adrian had no problem endorsing that vision.

A nurse came in, and he placed the book back on his bedside table. His body was weak, and before long he dozed off. When he woke up, the book had been confiscated.

Five thousand miles away, the filming of Universal's fifth Sherlock Holmes production was complete.

When Nigel Bruce took the role of Watson in the Universal Studios films he was paid $850 per week and guaranteed forty working weeks a year. That was somewhat less than he was used to, but both he and his wife, Bunny, were glad of the sizable and stable income it provided. With the money from the radio shows as a bonus, they were able to live comfortably despite the troubled times.

Each passing year, Bruce's weekly pay would increase by $100. His friend Basil Rathbone earned significantly more, but then he was also the major star. Rathbone received $20,000 per film, the equivalent of one seventh of the total budget.

After releasing three war films about Sherlock Holmes in the first year, Universal decided to change tack. The new films were also set in the modern world, but the plot and the atmosphere more closely resembled the original era of Sherlock Holmes, around the turn of the century. The war had been going on for years, and the studios noticed that audiences wanted to see something else, something that might give them a brief respite from reality. The director, Roy William Neill, was a recognized talent in the horror genre, and the films were now imbued with a sense of mysticism and gothic imagery.

Denis Conan Doyle maintained some involvement, although it was not nearly as significant as his participation during the first year. He had suggested that Pola Negri—an ex-wife of one of Nina's late brothers— play the female lead in one of the new films, *The Spider Woman*, but the studio felt it had too many other talented actresses on hand.

When Denis finally left Hollywood, and the United States, his involvement in the films ceased. He was still involved in the radio series with Rathbone and Bruce, but eventually he withdrew from that, too. In January 1944 he let it be known that he no longer needed to approve the radio scripts, as long as they were still written by Edith Meiser.

Adrian was not able to continue reading Pearson's book, but he did have access to the newspapers, which had begun writing about it. These writers' descriptions of its contents nearly drove him mad. Clearly there were outrageous allegations in the book that his hasty skimming had not revealed. He immediately dictated a letter from his sickbed to the editor of the London *Times* to expose Pearson's fraudulent intentions. The notion that his father had lacked enormous powers of deduction, for example, was clearly absurd. He had, after all, succeeded in solving cases that the police had failed to close, as Adrian's mother had pointed out on numerous occasions in the last decade of her life. The medical school instructor Dr. Joseph Bell might well have helped Arthur Conan Doyle to develop his famous talent, but the assertion that Bell had been the inspiration for Sherlock Holmes was simply not true. It was time for the truth to emerge—namely, that the inspiration for Sherlock Holmes had in fact been Sir Arthur Conan Doyle himself.

Adrian was discharged from the hospital, and spent some time in Cornwall convalescing before returning home. He had been put on sick leave from the marines for a few months. He now had the opportunity to read Pearson's book in its entirety. The more he read, the angrier he became. Pearson was attempting to present his father as a perfectly ordinary man, "the man in the street." This was despite the fact that all who had known him agreed that he was unique. Adrian felt that the whole portrayal was a grotesque caricature. One way or another, Adrian was going to knock Pearson off his perch.

There was also a new issue that had come up. Adrian had been told by an acquaintance at the BBC that an American book was on the way. His contact thought, mistakenly, that Adrian would like it. The crime writer Ellery Queen, actually a pseudonym for a pair of cowriting cousins, had edited an anthology, *The Misadventures of Sherlock Holmes*, featuring parodies and pastiches by a whole range of authors.

Adrian threatened Ellery Queen's publisher with legal action. If this went uncontested, it would set a dangerous precedent for all kinds of future cases. The United States would be awash with books of the same ilk, which would in turn undermine the value of the rights to Sherlock Holmes.

One of the Ellery Queen cousins, Frederic Dannay, was well connected to the Baker Street Irregulars. Denis turned to Edgar W. Smith and made it clear that from that moment forward, no member of the BSI would be allowed to publish any book or article with a direct or indirect connection to the characters of Sherlock Holmes and Dr. Watson without the express consent of the Conan Doyle family.

After drawn-out negotiations—it was now July 1945—Ellery Queen's publishers gave way. They paid the legal costs and damages of $500. They also undertook not to distribute any further books, apart from the 388 copies that remained in the warehouse from the book's run of thirteen thousand copies. The collection had been loved by many members of the Baker Street Irregulars and had been lauded in the press as a great tribute to Conan Doyle's creation.

With the Ellery Queen book, the friendly links between Conan Doyle's sons and the American Sherlockians were broken. In the wider world, the war was over, but in this smaller one, the first troop maneuvers were being carried out. Their war was just beginning.

The Baker Street Irregulars were still led by Christopher Morley, although it was Edgar W. Smith who had transformed the BSI into a functioning organization. It had evolved into an external operation, with various kinds of publications, and an internal one, with its annual meetings. The US president's membership had been a closely guarded secret for three years. It was the kind of information that could, if it fell into the wrong hands, be used against Roosevelt.

Unfortunately, the president was unable to physically participate in the BSI's meetings, although he did make written contributions. His theory that Sherlock Holmes not only had been born American but also had even had a criminal career was a subject of great discussion among the members.

In March 1945, a few weeks after returning from the Yalta Conference— his meeting in Crimea with Winston Churchill and Joseph Stalin to plan their final moves against Nazi Germany—and at the same time as he was writing some forcefully worded follow-up messages to Stalin, the president wrote what was his last letter to Edgar W. Smith. A few weeks later Roosevelt was dead.

The incoming president, Harry S. Truman, gave his opening address to the US Congress. Smith felt he could sense a connection between some of the phrases Truman used to describe Roosevelt and those used by Watson to describe Sherlock Holmes. Smith wrote to the president, informing him of his predecessor's membership. If it happened to be the case that Truman shared Roosevelt's Sherlockian interest, then the society would be delighted to accept him as an honorary member.

The response came two weeks later. The president had been a Sherlockian for as long as he could remember, and it would be his great honor to accept Smith's invitation.

55

THE ILLUSTRATING WUNDERKIND of the 1890s had been forgotten, except by his nearest friends and the small group of admiring Sherlockians that made up the Baker Street Irregulars. He sat in his drafty Manhattan studio, his physical decline accelerating, and he felt that dying might not be altogether a bad thing.

Then something happened that Frederic Dorr Steele had long since given up hoping for. For years, a few of the members of the BSI had talked about a fantastic project, a collection of all the Sherlock Holmes stories, illustrated by Steele. It was a dream, and was perhaps expected to remain so, until a small publisher, the Limited Editions Club, decided to join the project. It was to be a special edition, limited to just fifteen hundred copies. Edgar W. Smith, ever the dynamo, had proofread the stories—"collating the text," as he called it—and corrected old printing errors, many of which were quite serious, to produce a definitive, error-free edition.

Since Steele hadn't been hired until around the turn of the century, well into the run of the Sherlock Holmes stories, there were plenty of stories for which he would need to produce new illustrations. He was now tasked with doing so.

Reinvigorated, he set about his assignment immediately. But the offer that he had waited decades for had come too late. The more he exerted himself in the pursuit of his absolute favorite pastime—drawing Sherlock Holmes—the more punishment his body was subjected to. He was so busy doing the sketches that he would forget to eat. His memory was failing.

Frederic Dorr Steele entered a bubble containing only himself and the master detective.

56

In England in 1945 Adrian recalled the last time he had seen Denis. It had been on an autumn day, near Hyde Park Corner, and he had sensed somehow that they would not see each other again for some time. That had been five and a half years and a whole world war ago.

Denis had not returned to England after all but had traveled directly to a hotel in the southern Spanish city of Granada. This was no great surprise, considering his fragile health, and the fact that he had returned to Europe in November—not the healthiest season of year to be spending time in England. Spain had been a neutral nation during the war, which made the decision an even easier one.

Denis was still in Spain, and Adrian was worried that the siblings' financial future was threatened. They needed to convert the estate into a limited company in order to do away with old worthless contracts and adapt to the new realities. As things stood, they earned almost nothing from the books. During the previous year, the American publishers had sold twelve thousand copies of *The Hound of the Baskervilles*, Adrian mentioned in a letter to his brother. The estate's share of the cake? Nine miserable pounds!

Everything was determined by ridiculous contracts from the Victorian and Edwardian eras. The terms given to the publishers by old A. P. Watt would stand in perpetuity if they did not succeed in canceling them. Watt's heirs at the firm were not much better. Adrian felt that they had to be the worst businessmen in London. As soon as the limited company was launched, the brothers would jettison Watt; they would become their own agents.

The situation was not improved by the fact that Watt had made deals with bunglers. The American publisher who, in 1920, should have renewed the copyright on the earliest short stories had contrived to overlook half a dozen of them, which meant they were now out of copyright altogether in the United States. Adrian and Watt had concluded that the fewer people who knew about that, the better. They would simply continue to pretend that they did own the American copyright for those titles.

An American crime writer named John Dickson Carr had been living in London for many years, working as a scriptwriter for the BBC. He had recently come to know Adrian and had predicted that the end of the war would be followed by a boom in sales of Sherlock Holmes stories. If he was right, it was vital that the siblings have all the contracts in place, to make sure they got their slice of these larger revenues. This was especially important if the boom was to be further fueled by the release of the newly discovered Conan Doyle story.

Edgar W. Smith was worried. Progress on the new collection was painfully slow. Conan Doyle's sons were against it. And his friend Frederic Dorr Steele had been taken to the hospital while working on the illustrations, only to pass away a few weeks later. The dream was under threat from all directions.

Smith wasn't going to give in. There were other projects in the pipeline. Next on the list was the production of a quarterly magazine for the society—not a profit-making venture, merely a place where the ever-increasing number of articles, written by the ever-expanding membership, could be collected in print. The articles covered Sherlock Holmes and his world, as well as Sherlockian theories that attempted to fill or at least explain the gaps in the fifty-six short stories and the four novels. The magazine would be called the *Baker Street Journal*.

The American author August Derleth had received a threatening letter from a law firm in New York, addressed to Mycroft and Moran, publishers of his latest book. The publisher was in fact Derleth himself—he had created the entity for the sole purpose of releasing the first collection of short stories about a detective named Solar Pons.

In 1928, when he was nineteen, Derleth had understood that Conan Doyle was intent on not writing any further Sherlock Holmes stories. Derleth loved writing exciting short stories himself and could not understand why Conan Doyle no longer felt the same way. Derleth had written to Sir Arthur Conan Doyle from his home in Wisconsin expressing his disappointment.

Derleth had another matter he wished to raise in his letter. Would the author object to Derleth's continuing to write about the London detective? Otherwise, would it be acceptable for him to write about his own creation, the detective Solar Pons, resident at 7b Praed Street, whose cases were narrated by Dr. Parker? This was no parody of Holmes, but rather a pastiche that was built upon the Holmes stories and stood very much on its own merits.

Conan Doyle replied: Sherlock Holmes, no, he must not. Solar Pons, certainly, get to it.

Following Conan Doyle's approval, Derleth quickly produced and published a handful of Solar Pons short stories. He had barely left his hometown, but through his reading of other writers' works he was able to write knowledgeably and in some detail about London, setting his stories there in the 1920s. He had also written a long list of potential titles for forthcoming Solar Pons adventures. He always came up with a title first and then created a story around it.

Then the Great Depression arrived, and Derleth had other things on his mind. But Frederic Dannay, the half of Ellery Queen belonging to the Baker Street Irregulars, got in touch, reminding Derleth of his old stories. Dannay was busy collating *The Misadventures of Sherlock Holmes*, and he liked what he saw of a 1928 Solar Pons story he was including in the collection. Dannay encouraged Derleth to write even more stories and compile them into a whole book.

Derleth followed Dannay's advice and submitted his completed manuscript to various American publishers. Most of them were positive in their response, but none wanted to take the book on. They all knew what had happened to their colleagues in the industry who had published Ellery Queen's Holmes anthology. Nobody wanted to clash with Conan Doyle's mad sons.

The only one who had really succeeded in writing a Sherlock Holmes pastiche without being attacked by the Conan Doyle brothers had been the author H. F. Heard. His *A Taste for Honey* from 1941 sold half a million copies. To avoid copyright problems he had masterfully disguised his Holmes as the retired beekeeper Mr. Mycroft.

In the end Derleth decided to publish his book himself, and asked Vincent Starrett to write the foreword. The book, entitled *In re: Sherlock Holmes*, was released in a limited run. He was hardly surprised when the letter from the sons' lawyers, Fitelson and Mayers, turned up.

He couldn't help laughing. They were seriously contending that his little publication would constitute a material threat to the distribution of Sherlock Holmes in film, radio, and print. The only part of the book that mentioned Sherlock Holmes was the title, which used a name that surely could no longer be protected by copyright in the United States. The risk of confusing the book with one of Conan Doyle's was nonexistent.

It was a shame, then, that he could not find the old correspondence from Conan Doyle, which would have enabled him to prove his case, but no matter. Derleth continued selling his book, continued writing short stories about Solar Pons, and disregarded the repeated threats coming from Conan Doyle's lazy, good-for-nothing sons. He knew that what he was doing was right. He had Conan Doyle's word on it.

The Conan Doyle brothers' relationship was strained. Denis's claim that Adrian's work consisted in nothing more than managing contact with Watt and sorting press cuttings was a direct insult. Adrian spent up to eight hours every day, year in, year out, managing the literary estate's affairs. Never had it been less than three hours. Indeed, even as he underwent his training with the marines (before he was discharged because of his failing health) and when he lay in the hospital, he spent as much time as he could taking care of his father's legacy. How many hours a day had Denis himself spent on that?

Adrian regretted his decision to give up his hobby, oil painting, in order to take care of all the correspondence. One ordinary day, as he left for London for meetings with publishers, the postman had arrived with sixteen letters, each requiring a prompt response.

It was late evening before Adrian returned home. The following day, a further seventeen letters arrived, an average amount. He spent hours at his desk replying to them all. A long letter from the new accountants required an equally long reply. The family's lawyer had sent an invoice, and Lloyds Bank had dispatched a statement. He wrote to a Norwegian publisher, attempting to extricate the estate from a badly negotiated fifty-year-old contract. It was of the utmost importance to formulate such letters carefully. He sent letters to Egypt and Chile, also concerning publishing issues. The BBC was sent two letters: one was about the contract for a forthcoming radio adaptation; the other was the script itself, which Adrian had approved.

In America, Edgar W. Smith, once the brothers' close associate, had defied their warning and started the *Baker Street Journal*. Adrian considered this to be the most significant copyright infringement ever. He wrote to Smith, threatening him with a lawsuit unless the magazine was canceled immediately. The brothers intended to publish their own Sherlock Holmes magazine in the United States and definitely did not want to see any competitors.

Adrian's days were full of that sort of thing. Only a few of the letters he received were written to him personally; the vast majority concerned the running of his father's written legacy. Unless Denis was prepared to nominate him as co-executor of the will, thereby giving him an equal say in the matter, Adrian did not intend to continue taking care of everything for his brother and sister. The only cause for optimism was that Denis had finally returned to England and was now in London. With the advent of new taxation rules between Britain and America, Denis and Nina no longer needed to worry about spending time at home.

57

Anthony Boucher had been one of the authors whose work had been included in Ellery Queen's *Misadventures of Sherlock Holmes*. Among Boucher's many books was *The Case of the Baker Street Irregulars*, a novel featuring his imagined version of the society, written before he actually got to know the real BSI and became a member.

Now he was attending a cocktail party in San Francisco for Nigel Bruce and Basil Rathbone. During the war the two actors had been on tour, broadcasting the Sherlock Holmes radio series from a number of West Coast theaters to support the country by promoting war bonds. Rathbone and Bruce were immensely popular, and their effort had raised over a million dollars.

Boucher caught sight of a woman he knew from college. She was married to Denis Green, one of the scriptwriters who had taken over the Holmes radio series. Edith Meiser had left the show following a dispute with a sponsor about the level of violence in the program. She did not want it raised, regardless of how popular such a trend might be. Nowadays Denis Green wrote the scripts, together with Leslie Charteris, the author of the books about the thief known as the Saint. However, Charteris wanted out. He was tired of writing weekly radio scripts and was finding it difficult to come up with new plots for the show. They had long since run out of original Conan Doyle stories to adapt.

Boucher just happened to be in the right place at the right time; one thing led to another, and soon he had replaced Charteris and teamed up with Denis Green to write the Sherlock Holmes radio episodes. Boucher wrote the synopses and Green then filled in the dialogue.

★   ★   ★

So many things had changed in Nigel Bruce's life. First of all, he missed
Edith Meiser. Meiser nowadays wrote other radio series and continued
with her acting career.

She had had no time for the Universal films or their contemporary
setting. She was a stickler for the traditional. In January 1942 she had
even been invited to the opening hour of the Baker Street Irregulars'
annual dinner, for the cocktail service. This was significant, considering
that the society was otherwise open only to men. Christopher Morley
and Vincent Starrett were both friends of hers and supported her in
her work on the radio shows. When the time came for the all-male
dinner, however, she had to leave.

Since then Edith Meiser and her husband, Tom McKnight, had
divorced, and her closest companion was now Dr. Watson, her dog.

Most of all Bruce missed the film shoots with Basil Rathbone and
all the others. Universal had made twelve films, the last of which had
just finished filming. Some of them had turned out very well indeed.
Much of the credit was due to the director, Roy William Neill, or
Mousie, as they called him. Neill had had a major influence on the
development of the film series and had been trusted by all involved.
He was extremely disciplined on set and had a sharp eye for aesthetics,
a trait instilled by his years in the European film industry.

Perhaps people saw the Sherlock Holmes films as B movies, but some
of them were much better than that. Neill's conscientious approach
to the smallest detail in those films raised them to a higher level. The
series was a commercial success, even if it left the critics divided.

Bruce would gladly have filmed several more, but when Rathbone
let it be known that he was moving on, the whole thing wilted. Rathbone had spoken of his great frustration at always being associated
with Sherlock Holmes. He no longer wanted to hear people shout after
him, "Hi there, Sherlock! How's Dr. Watson?"

Nigel Bruce, though, had his suspicions about where this all came
from: Basil Rathbone's wife, Ouida. She wanted to see Basil back playing
more romantic roles, as he had done in the Shakespeare performances
that had formed the platform for his career. And Basil never said no
to Ouida.

Despite attempting to conceal his true feelings, Nigel Bruce could
never quite forgive Rathbone for calling time on their partnership.
Deep down inside, a flame of hope that there might yet be more films

still flickered. That hope was extinguished in December 1946, when their beloved director, Mousie, suffered a fatal heart attack while on a visit to England.

Nigel Bruce loved the Dr. Watson role and knew that he had been loved in return. During his and Rathbone's time on the radio, he had always received more fan mail, great piles of it. Edith Meiser had persuaded him to keep quiet about it, so as not to upset Rathbone.

A new radio series was under way. Bruce continued in the role of Dr. Watson, but Rathbone had been replaced by an actor whose voice was so similar that many listeners did not realize he had left.

Try as he might, for Basil Rathbone there was no escaping Sherlock Holmes.

58

UNIVERSAL'S DECISION NOT to produce any further Holmes films was a great blow to the Conan Doyle estate's finances. At the time, however, Adrian had even more important issues to deal with. He was going to restore his father's honor.

It was that damned Pearson's fault. His biography was a disgrace, and Adrian had a good mind to tell the Society of Authors to give him an official warning. Adrian had written a rebuttal—a twenty-four-page booklet, *The True Conan Doyle*, in which he called Pearson's book "a travesty"—but more needed to be done.

Adrian and Denis had been working for some time with a new biographer, a man who could deliver an accurate and truthful account of their father. He was a German by the name of Emil Ludwig. His last project had been an acclaimed biography of Beethoven, and when Denis met him in America, Emil Ludwig had expressed interest in writing about Conan Doyle. If Ludwig were to succeed in writing the definitive Sir Arthur Conan Doyle biography, Adrian felt, it would surely become the best and most sensational thing written in the last hundred years. Their father had had it all. He had been a fifteenth-century knight incarnate, an author, politician, adventurer, sportsman, detective, missionary, defender of the weak, doctor, and descendent of great artists of ancient noble stock. With Adrian's help, Ludwig would be able to write a biography that others could only dream of. Had Pearson not been motivated by his envy of a man more successful than he was, he could have had access to all this and made history.

Adrian was convinced that they needed to persuade Emil Ludwig to write the book. He asked Denis to contact Ludwig, who was in Switzerland at the time, and give the impression that they were in the process of signing new deals for Conan Doyle's books across Europe.

Adrian himself was in Italy, on the lookout for a suitable castle that he and Anna could make their home.

Unfortunately, it wasn't to be—no castle, at least not on that journey. Back home in England, Adrian continued to work around the clock to sort his father's documents in anticipation of the planned biography. By the end of November 1946 there were only six trunks left to go through, perhaps six weeks' worth of work. It was important to get a definite answer from Ludwig, since they would have to find someone else if he turned them down. Either way, Adrian knew that he had prepared the ground for a complete success.

A fortnight later, Adrian had changed his mind. The best man for the job was no longer Emil Ludwig. The man's knowledge of his father and his works was almost nonexistent, and any biography he wrote would have to be translated from German into English.

No, the best person for the task was in fact an American living in England whom Adrian had gotten to know. They had collaborated on a radio script about Sherlock Holmes and had met several times over the course of the past two years. This was a man who had a unique understanding of his father's books and who loved his work. He was also extremely diligent in his own writing and was one of the leading crime writers on both sides of the Atlantic.

His name was John Dickson Carr, and Adrian had not yet said a word to him on the matter.

59

THE TRAFFIC POLICE, sitting in their patrol car, were having a quiet day at work—until a woman roared past them in a fast sports car. The police car gave chase and eventually pulled alongside the sports car. The window opened, and a male passenger leaned out.

"Viper bite!" he screamed.

The police overtook the roadster and then escorted the vehicle, assisting the driver, the man's wife, to reach the nearest hospital quickly and safely. The patient was given an injection and later that night had recovered sufficiently to be able to tell the newspapers about the incident.

It was not the first time that Adrian Conan Doyle, youngest son of the famous author, had made the press in a snake-related story. Ten years earlier he had sparked a police search lasting several days for his missing python, Tiko. In the end, Londoners need not have worried. The snake had never left the house but had merely evaded its owner by hiding in the chimney.

In December 1946 John Dickson Carr had been asked to write Sir Arthur Conan Doyle's biography. Six months had passed since then, and Adrian was eager for the book to be ready for publication. A new edition of Hesketh Pearson's biography was on the way, and Adrian's ire increased with each passing day that his father was not defended from Pearson's malignant allegations that Sir Arthur had been an ordinary fellow. The new book would put Conan Doyle up on the pedestal he deserved.

Carr and Adrian were sitting in their armchairs at the former's Hampstead home. Adrian was upset that the country's current paper shortage was still affecting publications, which in turn affected the income he and his siblings received. He was flailing his arms, so much so that sooner or later he would certainly knock something valuable to the floor. His character had its good side, but he was prone to have outbursts over trifling matters, completely without warning.

The two men worked very closely together on the biography. Adrian read and edited every page of the manuscript. For the most part, they met at Adrian's home, since Carr's home had been damaged in bombing raids and only recently rebuilt. Adrian was then living at Bignell Wood, one of the houses Conan Doyle had owned before his death. It was very close to the New Forest outside Southampton, and the woodlands surrounding the house had the feel of the Middle Ages, where some of Conan Doyle's fictional writing was set. Occasionally an inexplicable sound could be heard in the old house.

"Oh, that's Daddy prowling around in the library," Adrian would explain.

Carr had been given access to a majority of Conan Doyle's surviving documents. There were a lot of them, and it was almost an impossible task to take them all in. Adrian had spent more than two years sorting them, and they were all stored in his Bignell Wood home. Carr had not yet told anyone that he had taken on the project. He wanted to be sure that he could see it through first. He had, however, sought recollections or correspondence from newspaper readers, hoping to complete the picture of Conan Doyle.

Adrian's plan was for Winston Churchill to provide the foreword. But he had to ask Churchill first.

A year later the biography was finished. What John Dickson Carr had written was exactly what Adrian had hoped for. He had asked Carr to revise one chapter, but aside from that things had gone swimmingly. While it was Carr's name on the spine of the book, Adrian knew that if not for his own hard work in sorting the papers it would not have been a success.

Things were happening on the film front. It was a shame that Alfred Hitchcock was so busy with other things, since he had expressed interest in making a film version of one of Conan Doyle's short stories, one that was not about Sherlock Holmes. Another Hollywood studio wanted to film Conan Doyle's favorite novel, *The White Company*, but when the biography appeared the heirs would be able to demand even more money for the film rights, which was why they wanted to stall negotiations a little longer.

There were dark clouds on the horizon too. A journalist had written a lead story for the *Saturday Review of Literature* that claimed Dr. Joseph Bell in Edinburgh had been the inspiration for Sherlock Holmes. Adrian had spent countless hours and filled yards of newspaper columns to discredit Pearson when he had made the same claim. Once again he had to pull out the evidence that supported his counterclaim that his father and Sherlock Holmes were in fact the same person. He would use the opportunity to simultaneously promote Carr's biography.

The heirs had sealed the most important of their recent deals a few months earlier, after six months of negotiations. Their father's unpublished short story, "The Case of the Man Who Was Wanted," would finally be presented to the waiting world. An American magazine, the *Cosmopolitan*, had paid $5,000 for the right to print it, and it was due to appear in the August 1948 edition. A further five months later, English readers would also be able to read it. This story was not as accomplished as Conan Doyle's other works, but if an undiscovered Sherlock Holmes story by Conan Doyle himself couldn't bring the money rolling in, then what could?

Arthur Whitaker was a pensioner living with his wife in the small rural village of Sheepscombe, not far from the Welsh border. Once upon a time, as a young, newlywed architect with too much time on his hands and too little money in his wallet, he had penned a few detective stories in the hope of earning a few pounds.

That was a long time ago. His career and his family had taken over. When he retired, he had moved from Sheffield to Sheepscombe. Now he had only one interest in life—birds—and before long he had established a reputation among the local ornithologists and been made the bird recorder for the entire county of Gloucestershire. He had recorded every nest he had come across in the past thirty years, and felt that this information could be used in a handbook on British birds.

Sitting at the kitchen table at home in January 1949, Whitaker had the *Sunday Dispatch* in front of him, open to the newly discovered Conan Doyle story that was being so heavily promoted. He found its presence unfortunate—for he knew that the short story was not by Conan Doyle. Whitaker had written it himself, some forty years earlier.

Whitaker had sent his story to Conan Doyle long ago, hoping that the author might be able to base a new Sherlock Holmes story on it.

This had not worked out, but Conan Doyle had kept hold of it and paid him ten guineas for his trouble.

Perhaps Whitaker ought to have made more of a fuss a few years earlier, when he had written to Hesketh Pearson, pointing out that his biography contained an error. Pearson had written that the unpublished story was the work of Conan Doyle. It might have been reasonable to expect Pearson to pass this information on to the heirs. Now, as Whitaker wrote to Denis Conan Doyle, he pointed out that this mis-understanding could not possibly be construed as his fault. He had actually explained the truth of the matter to Pearson. How was he to know that Pearson and the Conan Doyle brothers did not get along?

Adrian could no longer bear to live in a country governed by the Labour Party. He and Anna had moved to the Moroccan port of Tangier, which had become a tax haven since the Spanish forces had hastily abandoned their positions there at the end of the Second World War. Situated close to the Strait of Gibraltar, the city was a self-governing territory, a multinational zone renowned as a center of international subterfuge.

Adrian and Anna had sold Bignell Wood, his father's old house. Living cheaply and indeed more comfortably in the warmth was very pleasant. The business about a castle in Italy had been forgotten—it was far too expensive a country to live in.

The city's proximity to the sea was also a plus. Adrian was con-templating buying a boat for angling and could hardly wait for the swordfish season to start.

At that moment, however, thoughts of leisure could not have been further from his mind. Adrian sat in the shade of a palm tree and was incandescent with rage. Some elderly bastard claimed to be the author of "The Case of the Man Who Was Wanted." And, to make matters worse, he hadn't contacted the family directly. No, the treacherous so-and-so had written to Pearson and to the American Vincent Starrett. Pearson was a rogue of the worst kind—Adrian was already convinced of that—and the members of the Baker Street Irregulars were increas-ingly troublesome. Those were the kind of people that Whitaker had thrown his lot in with. If Whitaker was not able to produce some conclusive proof of his claim of authorship, then Adrian would sue him, as well as Pearson and Starrett, if they uttered so much as a word that seemed to call the authenticity of the story into question.

He had just instructed the family's London lawyer to move against Whitaker and Pearson but to be a little more cautious with Starrett. Adrian had never been so angry in his life.

Did he have evidence? Arthur Whitaker regretted even attempting to clear up the misunderstanding surrounding the authorship of the story. He did not really have much in the way of evidence. He had once had a letter from Conan Doyle in his possession, which would have explained everything, but that letter had disappeared.

He did have a carbon copy of his original typed manuscript, however. Perhaps that would suffice.

The letters Whitaker received from the lawyers were harshly worded, and it was never very long before the next threat arrived. Eventually he remembered that he had given the old Conan Doyle letter to a relative who collected autographs. Fortunately, the relative still had the letter. Finally, they would be able to bring this unhappy episode to a close.

Arthur Whitaker had no desire whatsoever to appear in any publicity or indeed to earn any money from the issue. He just wanted to see the back of it. It was completely distracting him from the birds.

The matter was quickly hushed up in England. The *Cosmopolitan* never published a correction, and many American readers remained convinced that Conan Doyle had written a sixty-first tale about Sherlock Holmes and Dr. Watson. The *Cosmopolitan* attempted to recover the money it had paid for the story, but Adrian Conan Doyle fought the request. In the end, £500 was paid to the magazine, plus a further £150 in legal costs.

Summer came along, and in July 1949 Arthur Whitaker died at home in the little English village. During the last six months of his life, he had turned the world upside down for the legions of Sherlock Holmes fans. His contribution to the handbook of British birds, on the other hand, never materialized.

The spring of 1949 had seen the release of John Dickson Carr's biography, *The Life of Sir Arthur Conan Doyle*. Edgar W. Smith voiced his enthusiastic approval in a review, as did Vincent Starrett, Elmer Davis, and Christopher Morley, all of whom wrote for major newspapers. As members of the Baker Street Irregulars, they were also keen to advertise their organization in their reviews.

Carr's book was published more or less simultaneously in America and Britain. Advertisements were placed in the big American newspapers. Carr made public appearances and did interviews. Within a few weeks, the book had made it onto best-seller lists in America.

Carr gave a speech at the Baker Street Irregulars' annual dinner. "Let us just imagine, for once, that there really *was* a man named Sir Arthur Conan Doyle," he began.

With the exception of the odd sneering critic—whom Adrian pledged to hunt to the ends of the earth—there was only one person who was not happy with the book. When Mary Conan Doyle, the brothers' elder half sister, read the biography, it came as a shock to her. Her mother was portrayed as a negative and insipid individual, a woman who had not had any discernible influence on her famous husband. That was as far from the truth as it was possible to get. Mary's stepmother, Lady Conan Doyle, meanwhile, had been depicted in an incredibly flattering light. It was not fair. Mary wrote a letter to the editor of the *Daily Telegraph* to expose the book's inaccurate description of her mother.

John Dickson Carr had interviewed Mary about life at Undershaw, but he had asked questions only about her father, nothing about her mother, Louisa. Denis, who was hunting big game in India with the Maharaja of Mysore, wrote to Mary expressing his sympathy. Denis had thought that Adrian would have made sure to consult Mary about everything in the book. Not only had Adrian let Mary down; he had also failed to change a number of details that Denis had protested about early on. Denis promised Mary that he would make sure that these things were revised in the next edition. With Denis, however, the suspicion was always that this would not happen.

Mary was very angry with John Dickson Carr, but deep down she knew that the guilty party was actually a lot closer to home. The incident caused an even greater rift between her and her half brother Adrian.

Seventeen stories up, in an air-conditioned skyscraper on Broadway, Edgar W. Smith allowed his mind to wander away from automobile exports for a while. He spent many hours in the office, so it was not unreasonable for him to take care of some private matters there. He was also a serious family man, and it was difficult for him to fit all his activities into his schedule.

He opened a desk drawer and pulled out a thick pile of manuscripts. These were articles for the next edition of the *Baker Street Journal*—the final issue. It had been brought down not by Conan Doyle's sons but by the unsustainable losses.

Smith's other pet project, the publication of the book by the Limited Editions Club, had still not been given the green light. Adrian and Denis had all but stopped the sale of Sherlock Holmes books in America. These actions were just so very strange. They had withdrawn the rights to Conan Doyle's last series of short stories in order to negotiate a better contract, which meant that it had not been possible to sell any complete editions for three years. They had also forbidden the sales of the popular twenty-five-cent editions, the only ones that ordinary people could afford. The sons had effectively killed off reading Sherlock Holmes in the United States. They had probably lost $10,000 into the bargain.

It was not surprising, then, that some American Sherlock Holmes societies had introduced a new toast over the last year. The toasts were no longer limited to characters from the Holmes stories; others could be honored as well. Edgar W. Smith could not, despite his instinctive diplomacy, help agreeing.

To the adder that bit Adrian Conan Doyle!
May it do so again!

60

O N A WINDY October evening, the rain whipped the windows of
Marylebone Town Hall, just a stone's throw from Baker Street.
In a room inside the building, the borough council was meeting.

It had been five years since the end of the Second World War, but
the British were still feeling its effects. Rationing was still in place, and
the people were in need of cheering up. It was decided that a great celebration of Britain and the British spirit—the Festival of Britain—would
be staged the following year, 1951. It would occur exactly one hundred
years after the Great Exhibition of 1851, an excellent opportunity to
reawaken the nation's pride.

It went without saying that part of the plan was to stage something
that would bring visiting tourist dollars to Britain.

Each of the boroughs of London had been tasked with organizing
events and activities that demonstrated the British spirit. It was this
task that the Labour and Conservative members were debating about
in the council chamber. The proposal from the local Labour politicians
was an exhibition detailing the borough's success in eliminating slums
and making Marylebone a far more healthful place to live. They felt
that such a demonstration would be both educational and inspiring.

Unfortunately, the proposal met with resistance from the library
committee, which was in charge of organizing the whole thing. Was
this really the sort of thing that would draw Americans to London?
That the idea was born of noble intentions would not necessarily make
it a tourist magnet.

The library committee had a proposal of its own. It was well known
that foreign tourists often asked about the house on Baker Street where
Sherlock Holmes lived. Jack Thorne, who worked in the reference section of the library, suggested an exhibition about the detective, featuring copies of the *Strand Magazine* and other items that could easily be

associated with the library's everyday operations. The idea had come to him during a conversation in the library with a journalist, James Edward Holroyd. When the *Strand* published its final issue, Holroyd had decided to reread the old Sherlock Holmes stories that he had loved so much as a child. He had become fascinated once more. He plowed through the stories, but he wanted to see what Paget's illustrations had looked like in the original issues, which was what had brought him to Marylebone Library. Unfortunately, the library did not have them, but he did discover that it had a few years' worth of an American magazine called the *Baker Street Journal*. This publication had revealed a whole new world for James Edward Holroyd. There were Sherlock Holmes enthusiasts, even overseas! Surely some of them would want to come to England to visit an exhibition, were it to take place.

At the council meeting, the library committee's proposal was greeted with skepticism. The Labour politicians did not like the idea, preferring the exhibition to be about the progress in eliminating slum housing. Not only that, they protested, but a Sherlock Holmes exhibition could be arranged at any time, not necessarily as part of the Festival of Britain. Did the council really want to announce to the world that the most significant thing about the borough was that it had once been home to a fictional detective? Besides, he had lived at an address that did not even exist until recently, when York Place and Upper Baker Street had been combined, making Baker Street more than twice the length it had been in Holmes's day. In Holmes's time the numbers of the houses had gone up only to 85, and all the buildings had since been renumbered.

The chamber united against the handful of voices in support of the Sherlock Holmes exhibition, and once they had been silenced, a majority of the Conservative councillors agreed to Labour's proposal. The decision was rubber-stamped, and the council moved on to the next point on the agenda.

And all the while, the rain had whipped constantly against the windowpanes.

A few days later, observant readers of the *Times* might have spotted a letter to the editor from a certain John H. Watson, former military doctor. Since his good friend Mr. Sherlock Holmes had moved to Sussex and become a beekeeper, he wrote, he could hardly be expected to keep abreast of the reports from council proceedings. Therefore

Dr. Watson felt duty-bound to express his great disappointment at the council's decision. There were of course a great many worthwhile and health-improving slum clearances around the city, but there was only one Sherlock Holmes.

Next it was the turn of actor Arthur Wontner to write in. Since Mr. Holmes had been unwilling to play himself on-screen, Wontner had had the great honor of doing so on five occasions. Wontner could vouch for the enormous interest in Holmes's adventures, and above all that the interest was also strong on the other side of the Atlantic. On the matter of whether Americans might be drawn to such an event, he echoed Dr. Watson's words, already printed in the same newspaper. The council would have to think again.

The letters to the editor continued to appear. They were not just from the city's dignitaries, but also from illustrious figures who had temporarily stepped out from the pages of fiction: Mycroft Holmes, Inspector G. Lestrade, and Mrs. Hudson. As a taxpayer and resident of the borough, living at 221b Baker Street, Mrs. Hudson felt she had a perfect right to make her voice heard on the matter.

The pressure on the council became irresistible. It had no choice but to tear up its previous decision and agree to host a Sherlock Holmes exhibition.

Jack Thorne, who had been put in charge of the exhibition, was overwhelmed. Ever since the plans had been made public, he had received a steady stream of letters from people offering to help or to lend objects to the exhibition. This would not be the little book exhibition the library had planned. It grew and grew. His enjoyment was increased still further when people who had been involved in the success of Sherlock Holmes, or their relatives, contacted him. Dr. Joseph Bell's family contributed photographs and letters from Conan Doyle explaining that his teacher had been the inspiration for Sherlock Holmes. Winifred Paget not only lent out some of her father's original illustrations for the Strand Magazine but also sent his wicker chair and dressing gown, which looked exactly as they did in his drawings. Adrian Conan Doyle wrote to the organizer from somewhere in the Indian Ocean, where he was aboard a schooner exploring undiscovered islands. In return for his travel expenses, or 25 percent of the ticket sales, he would dig out some of his father's most important Holmes-related objects and ship them from Tangier. He was, according to his letter, the only expert on the subject, aside from John Dickson Carr.

Unfortunately, the exhibition budget did not stretch to Adrian Conan Doyle's requests. The entry fee was to be so small that it would hardly cover any great excesses. The organizers were keen to avoid making any kind of profit, since that would attract an entertainment tax.

Luckily, Adrian Conan Doyle had siblings.

Jean Conan Doyle, thirty-nine years old, was no longer known as Billy. She had continued her career in the Royal Air Force after the war ended and had been made an Officer of the Most Excellent Order of the British Empire by the queen. One day in March 1951 she found herself standing in front of an outbuilding in Crowborough, near Windlesham, where she had grown up.

Jean looked around. Apart from her sixty-two-year-old half sister, Mary, who had offered to keep her company, there was not a soul to be seen, although they had arranged with others to meet them there. Eventually the building's owner turned up and unlocked the door. There was still no sign, though, of the men who were to help Jean and Mary lift the large chests and remove their lids.

Jean obstinately climbed a ladder and began to sift through the objects that made up her share of the inheritance. Just then a car pulled up outside. In it were Jack Thorne and one of his colleagues, who had come to lend a hand. They had brought an entire wish list.

The men took down packing case after packing case. Jean dived into them, looking for first editions, early translations, and any other valuable documents or objects. She worked quickly and concentrated on the task in hand. She knew exactly what she was looking for. Mary followed her, putting back the items that she had pulled out. Jean wondered how she would ever have managed without Mary, who was a great help and every bit as tactful as the situation required.

After Jean had gone through her own possessions, she moved on to a dozen of Denis's packing cases. It would have been so much easier if Denis had been able to help, but the last Jean had heard, both Denis and Nina were in Egypt. Before that they had toured Venice, Geneva, and Paris. That was typical of Denis. He was supposed to have returned to England in November. That was changed to January, later becoming February. Then he had appeared, out of nowhere, but disappeared just as quickly. Jean worried about him—not just about his heart, but also about the fact that he had put on so much weight. He and Nina looked terrible, both scruffy and overweight, and he was still only forty-two. Denis did not seem to have any goals whatsoever in life, and the only thing that might improve matters would be an anonymous visit to a medium and a few choice words from his father.

Denis did not seem to realize that he would have to do anything ahead of the exhibition. Jean was devoted to her brother and did not want to hurt him by being too direct. He was a fragile soul. He had promised to help, of course, but how he intended to do so from Egypt was anyone's guess. It seemed inevitable that Jean would have to spend all of her limited free time on the preparations.

The main thing was that Adrian was thousands of miles away. If he returned to England he would take over the whole exhibition. He had already sent a letter to the organizers, a missive full of "I, I, I." That was a shame, because he could be a pleasant chap too. Now they just needed to make sure he stayed away.

The doors to the Sherlock Holmes exhibition were to open on Conan Doyle's birthday—May 22—and then be open six days a week for the subsequent four months of the festival. The organizers kept to a hectic schedule to get the exhibition ready on time.

Jack Thorne had a team of very talented people. A prominent theater designer had been given the task of re-creating Holmes and Watson's sitting room. A college lecturer assisted with the more scientific aspects of Holmes's career, providing five glass specimen jars, each containing a snake that might potentially have been the species featured in "The Speckled Band." Help came from institutions, companies, and private individuals, particularly after the organizers had appealed for help in the newspapers. Scotland Yard donated a paw print from its very largest police dog, which stood guard at the queen mother's London residence. The Science Museum lent out test fonts from various typewriters, and a tobacconist delivered as many kinds of tobacco ash as he could smoke his way through.

There were late nights for the exhibition team. One Tuesday evening in February, at around nine o'clock, they realized they needed something to eat and drink, at which point they crossed the road outside the library and went into Allen's Bar. The group comprised Jack Thorne, his colleague Freda Pearce, the lecturer Bill Williams, Colin Prestige—who had been among those writing letters to the *Times*—and finally a young lawyer by the name of Anthony Howlett, who possessed the vital combination of a burning interest in Sherlock Holmes and rather a lot of free time. The fact that he had fallen for library assistant Freda Pearce did not diminish his enthusiasm.

Under the influence of their liquid refreshments, the team came upon what they felt was a brilliant idea. They would create a Sherlock Holmes group. Such an organization, the Sherlock Holmes Society, had existed in the 1930s, but just like the Red-Headed League (in the story of that name) it had one day simply ceased to exist.

A few weeks later they met again, but on this occasion they had a more formal meeting in the children's section of the library. Further members had joined: Ivar Gunn, who had been a member of the original society; Sidney Paget's daughter Winifred; journalist James Edward Holroyd; and a few others. A month later the society was founded. To distinguish it from its predecessor, it was to be known as the Sherlock Holmes Society of London. A straightforward name for the society, it was rather more British than the playful, sometimes outlandish names adopted by many of the American societies.

Meanwhile the work on the exhibition continued apace. It grew larger; the twelve-hundred-square-foot exhibition space was going to be a tight squeeze. The rooms had been lent by the Abbey National Building Society, whose offices occupied 219–229 Baker Street and thereby encompassed the famous address.

Thorne and his collaborators did everything possible to make sure that the exhibition was correct, down to the tiniest details, in particular when it came to the replica of the sitting room. Only one thing was missing. Thorne knew where to find it. He went to the British Museum and asked to be shown to its most neglected room, and to the corner of the room where no museum attendant or indeed any of its staff had set foot during the last fifty years. This request turned out not to be difficult to fulfill. There were plenty of hidden nooks in the building, and Thorne was brought to one. He bent down to collect something that had lain there, undisturbed, for decades. He now had the very last piece of the meticulously assembled exhibition in his possession—genuine Victorian dust.

★ ★ ★

A few days before the exhibition's opening, Jean made a telephone call to Mary. Jean had already been asked to give the opening address. Actually, Denis was supposed to do it, but since the best guess pertaining to his whereabouts was somewhere on the Upper Nile, the chances of his making it in time were rather small. His name had been used in the publicity materials, but as Jean said to Mary, that meant nothing.

The organizers wanted a long speech, so Jean had spent a lot of time compiling one. Now, though, they had changed their minds and required only a ten-minute address. Mary thought that Jean should not worry about it and should talk for as long as she liked. People would be only too happy to hear what she had to say about their father.

The night before the opening came around. Who should arrive, when all the hard work had already been done? It was none other than Denis Conan Doyle.

Mary was pleased. Her little brother had made it home in time. Both Jean and Denis delivered wonderful speeches during the ceremony. Mary did make it into some of the photographs alongside her siblings, but nobody seemed to know who she was, and she was not mentioned in the newspaper reports. This was not so very surprising, considering the fact that the books her father had written about his children had not mentioned her. The existence of a fourth Conan Doyle sibling was by no means common knowledge.

The exhibition was a great success. The re-created sitting room was the attraction that everyone wanted to see. There was the violin in the corner. The Persian slipper where Holmes kept his tobacco was hung by the fireplace. There were the cigars in the coal scuttle, the bearskin rug, the unanswered correspondence transfixed by a jackknife to the wooden mantelpiece, the photograph of Irene Adler, and the bullet holes in the wall spelling the initials V. R., for Victoria Regina. Yes, even the wax bust of Holmes from "The Empty House" was in place. Every tiny detail mentioned by Dr. Watson had been re-created here, and every object carefully examined to ensure it belonged to the era in question.

The visitors stood behind a rope. A small, elderly woman turned to the man who happened to be standing next to her. "Excuse me," she asked. "Is this his very room?"

The man contemplated his answer for a while, having no desire to divest her of her illusion. "I am told that that is so," he said, finally.

The organizers had thought of everything. They wanted to give the impression that Holmes and Watson had just left the room, in a hurry. On the table were two half-eaten muffins, each on its own little plate. Muffins tended to be rather scarce in the summer months, but a bakery had agreed to make two fresh muffins before each day of the exhibition. The organizers also realized that eagle-eyed visitors might notice if the same teeth marks were in both muffins. So, each morning, two separate members of the staff each took a bite of a muffin.

One day in July, Queen Mary, the widow of George V and mother of the reigning king, George VI, came to visit, wearing a floral dress, a pearl necklace, and a hat adorned with a large round bobble. Jack Thorne quickly ordered for the sign explaining the provenance of the paw print to be hidden away. The queen mother detested large dogs, and therefore was not to find out that such beasts were used to guard her house.

Queen Mary walked around the exhibition. She showed particular interest in a walking stick that doubled as a violin, and a Humber bicycle that, according to the manufacturer, was the very one that Violet Smith had ridden in "The Solitary Cyclist." The company's director had managed to establish that Miss Smith had sold the bicycle back to the manufacturer after her marriage.

"How interesting," the queen opined, "and amusing."

A British queen was, in fact, amused—an honor indeed.

By the time the exhibition closed its doors on September 22, more than fifty-four thousand visitors had seen it, and countless tourist dollars had been enticed to Baker Street.

One of the visitors, though, had not needed to travel far. From his legal chambers on Argyle Square it was a mere thirty-minute walk, but as age had taken its toll, a taxi might have been in order. He came there with his sister—who had been present thrice—and walked slowly around the exhibits and historical artifacts. For him, though, this was more than mere history.

He was nearly blind, so his sister had to read the signs aloud to him. They looked at Conan Doyle's original notes from the birth of

Sherlock Holmes, the illustrations by Sidney Paget and Frederic Dorr Steele, parodies and pastiches in hard-to-find collections, such as *The Misadventures of Sherlock Holmes*, a long row of reference books that treated Sherlock Holmes as a real person, and orchids and butterflies from Dartmoor that perfectly matched the descriptions in *The Hound of the Baskervilles*. They watched images from cinematic and theatrical productions. From an unidentified source somewhere in the room, they could hear the recorded sounds of a barrel organ, horse's hooves from a hansom cab, and a paperboy shouting the latest headlines.

The old man and his sister stopped by exhibit forty-three. His face was wrinkled, but his Persian features were still apparent. The small print of the newspaper article was impossible for him to read, but that did not really matter. He had read it many times before. The article was taken from the *Daily Telegraph* of January 11, 1907, and was written by Sir Arthur Conan Doyle. The headline read "The Case of Mr. George Edalji." It was the case that had made Conan Doyle famous as not merely an author but an accomplished solver of crimes.

The exhibition catalog covered 243 exhibits, some of which featured several objects. This meant that it took quite some time for the elderly man to reach the room everyone was talking about, Holmes and Watson's sitting room.

A while later, before heading back out into the glorious sunshine on Baker Street, the aging George Edalji dwelled for a moment on exhibit forty-three, one last time. Many years had passed since those events. For him, though, Sir Arthur would always be Sherlock Holmes.

61

Songo Mnara was a fairy-tale island. An isolated, elongated coral reef in the Indian Ocean, close to the coast of Tanganyika and not far from Zanzibar, it was covered with feather palms and impassable undergrowth.

Adrian, Anna, and Jum-Jum, their bulldog, had just come ashore to explore the interior of the island. Thirty feet long and with a harpoon platform aft, their boat, the *Gloria Scott*, was bobbing with the waves a little way out from the shore.

They had not come far up the beach before they encountered the impenetrable limbs and roots of a mkoko tree. There had to be a way around it. After an intensive search, they did find a path trodden by animals, just a foot or so wide. It took them farther in among the tree trunks, bushes, and tangled vines. When they could not follow the path, they used their machetes. On the branches above sat honeybirds with scarlet bodies and iridescent blue heads, extending their tail feathers so that the exploration party could almost reach up and touch them. The birds were not scared of the strange visitors to the uninhabited island.

The track was getting narrower. Adrian and Anna were sweating, and the humid atmosphere made breathing heavy work. It had been quite some time since they had left the beach. A dense thicket blocked their path, but in the end they managed to squeeze around it.

There, beyond the undergrowth, was an entrance, just as the legends described it—the gateway to a palace.

It occupied an area the size of a castle. It was almost as though Hampton Court or the Tower of London had been moved to the jungle and abandoned to nature for a thousand years. Walls and pillars were still standing, but the undergrowth, the vines, and the roots of fat-bodied baobab trees had taken over.

Adrian and Anna were dumbstruck as they wandered around the ruin. This was the palace from the East African sagas, the one known as the House of the Devil, where no living person dared tread. It had once belonged to history's greatest queen, the one so impressed with King Solomon's wisdom in the first Book of Kings. It was the queen of Sheba's palace.

Six months later, Adrian was in Paris. He had revealed his discovery to the press as soon as he came ashore in Marseille, and the news had spread quickly around the globe. Adrian and Anna had spent only three weeks on the island but hoped to be able to return for a two-year study. Adrian also explained that he intended to write a book about the whole expedition.

For now, however, it was not the African jungle that occupied his thoughts. For the third day in succession, he was with his brother Denis at *l'hôtel* Trianon Palace Versailles, hammering out plans for the future.

They planned to take advantage of the hugely successful Sherlock Holmes exhibition in London. They had decided to send an equivalent exhibition to America. Anna was to be in charge of the project and would accompany the exhibition wherever it went. They would need to spend some money initially, perhaps as much as $1,000, for the construction of a fold-up room and to fill it with Victoriana and ship it over to America—as well as to cover Anna's travel and accommodation costs. Once that money had been recovered from admission fees, though, the rest would be sheer profit. Adrian estimated that they ought to be able to pull in $250,000.

The project was soon under way. Jack Thorne, of the Marylebone Library, promised to help them as soon as the London exhibition was over. Edgar W. Smith indicated that the Baker Street Irregulars would assist as best they could. The family's New York lawyers were briefed to prepare the venture right away.

Neither Adrian nor Anna was looking forward to their six-month separation, but the benefits to the estate's finances—and by extension their own—were too great to ignore.

Anna would begin by bringing the exhibition to New York and after that she would tour the largest American cities. As a young woman Anna had been employed as a traveling sales executive for Elizabeth Arden, so Adrian felt she had precisely the business acumen the situation required. Then of course there was her talent for organizing, not to mention her beauty, which would bowl everyone over.

This exhibition tour would really change everything! Adrian pictured all the positive effects. Book sales in the United States would rocket. The TV contract they had sought for so long would come through—their negotiating partners would not be able to say no, with the exhibition tour as an incentive. He and his siblings would need to be tough and give an ultimatum: either climb aboard the cash express, or get off right away if it doesn't suit you.

In a few years' time they would no longer hold any copyrights in the United States, so it was now or never in terms of earning substantial sums. This would be their hour of greatness.

62

THEY HAD DONE everything just right. A year had passed since Adrian, Denis, and Anna had begun planning for the American exhibition tour. Everyone they contacted supported the project and was convinced it was going to be a success: the publishers, the New York lawyers, the organizers of the London exhibition, and the Baker Street Irregulars. The American press was supportive.

Anna was to be paid 10 percent of the profits for her endeavors. The siblings would divide the remainder among them. Jack Thorne had taken a sabbatical year in order to accompany the exhibition to America. Anna had traveled to England from Tangier and with Adrian's directions had gone through the family's treasure troves, discovering yet more objects and documents that were to be included in the exhibition. They had also been able to borrow much of the material that had been featured in London for the American tour. Adrian felt that the new exhibition would be immeasurably more impressive than the first.

The estate had tax arrears in the United States, so to avoid any Internal Revenue Service involvement, Adrian arranged the exhibition privately. An interested party had made contact with H. William Fitelson, the New York lawyer, with a view to arranging the tour itself.

Jean's departure from the project had been no big deal. That was her choice and would mean a greater payoff for the brothers. Denis's absence, and lack of input—he was away in India, hunting big game—was a source of irritation but ultimately not all that significant for the exhibition.

The problems began as soon as Anna and Jack Thorne landed in New York. Fitelson had done absolutely nothing to prepare for the triumphant parade. Instead, he had managed to send an excellent tour manager packing by allowing greed to take over and attempting to extract twice as much payment. He had not even found a suitable venue for the exhibition. Adrian's opinion was that Fitelson, whom Denis had brought into the estate affairs, had been their biggest handicap over the last ten years.

The only person who had been unfailingly polite and helpful toward Anna was Basil Rathbone. Without him, she would not have managed the first weeks in America. Anna had been sad, because her bulldog Jum-Jum had died on the way over on board the luxury liner SS *America*.

Eventually Adrian joined Anna in New York. The British Embassy helped him to employ a public-relations man—whom he promptly fired two weeks later. He then hired, and fired, another, before deciding to deal with all publicity himself. The embassy staff was of no use to Adrian; staff members made promise after promise, perhaps with good intentions, but they never delivered. The Baker Street Irregulars were also useless. And when it was discovered—only as they were about to assemble the exhibition—that an entire wall of the fold-up room had been left in London, Adrian laid the blame squarely at Jack Thorne's feet. Whether the accusations were well founded or not mattered little for a man constantly searching for scapegoats.

Since they did not have a suitable venue, everything was delayed. The places were either too small or too expensive. They eventually ended up at the Plaza Art Galleries in Manhattan. Denis had emerged from slumber, writing to express his disagreement with both the timing and the choice of venue. The grand opening had been scheduled for July 2, 1952—Adrian told Denis that everyone knew that there were more people in the city over the summer than at any other time. Eleanor Roosevelt was to attend the opening. Despite earlier difficulties, it looked as though everything was in place. The only thing that could stop them was the money running out. Just in time, a successfully renegotiated publishing contract was signed, and the $10,000 advance went straight into the exhibition's budget—even if the advance was estate money, to be shared with the siblings. All in all, the cost of the project had reached $20,000. A new wall had had to be built, and all the joiners, electricians, warehousing, and removal costs had been hugely underestimated in the original budget.

Adrian was satisfied with the media coverage. He appeared on American radio and television twenty-three times, and he estimated the value of the publicity to be in the region of $50,000. The opening was a success, and everybody who attended seemed to love the exhibition.

Jack Thorne, who had been so involved in its London incarnation, told Adrian that this one was much better—or at least that was what Adrian chose to hear.

Then the real problems began. The temperature in New York started to rise. The malaria Adrian had contracted on the Zanzibar expedition flared up, confining him to his bed. Adrian heard someone mention that it was the warmest summer in thirty-seven years and that people were most likely dying like flies in the great city. The heat was so overwhelming that nobody so much as wanted to leave the house. The quadrennial political conventions got under way in Chicago, giving people even more reason to stay at home, where they could watch them on television. Instead of the expected two thousand visitors a day, the Holmes show was averaging just one hundred.

Worst of all during his New York visit, Adrian realized the full extent of the Baker Street Irregulars' endeavors. It was necessary to combat their shameless exploitation of Holmes by any means available. On top of everything else they had restarted production of that horrid magazine the *Baker Street Journal*.

Adrian had already begun public attacks on behalf of his family. When speaking at a meeting of the Mystery Writers of America during his time in New York, he gave the group short shrift and revealed its true character—as he saw it. He had noted the presence of several BSI members in the audience, so his harsh words would surely be passed on to the society's leadership.

Meanwhile the New York exhibition was short-lived. Adrian and his team carried on for six weeks before packing the exhibits away and placing them in storage, ready for the tour that they still hoped to arrange.

Adrian was back in his villa in Tangier, on a slope of the Nouvelle Montagne, where most of the city's Europeans lived. He looked out the window, down onto the whitewashed neighborhoods that were home to the Arab population. In spite of the failure in New York, he still had hope for the future. American interest in Sherlock Holmes had increased, thanks to all the publicity, and Adrian had taken the opportunity to establish contacts for a whole range of new business opportunities.

That was precisely why he could not be anything other than absolutely furious with Denis.

Adrian had had his suspicions as far back as September 1951. There were all sorts of strange messages reaching him from various directions, about missing money, conflicting versions of events, and other gossip. In the end, Denis had come clean. For several years, he had kept large sums of the estate's royalty payments for himself. The checks were payable to him, since he was the sole executor of the will, and he had simply not paid Adrian and Jean their shares.

There was nothing left of the money. His and Nina's hotel bills and extravagant lifestyle had swallowed the lot.

Worst of all, Denis had been paid a deposit of $10,000 by a television producer, a Mr. Shapiro, who was planning a television series about Sherlock Holmes. Denis had assumed that the deal would go through and had immediately squandered every penny. Now Shapiro was demanding his money back, putting Conan Doyle's estate on the verge of bankruptcy.

Not only that, Denis owed several thousand dollars to a hotel in Paris for an unpaid bill. The hotel manager was threatening to go to the press, to start an international manhunt for Denis. That would truly drag their father's name through the mud.

And, if all that wasn't enough, Universal Studios was considering legal action to recover the $40,000 it had been forced to pay in taxes after Denis had persuaded it to pay him in full, without deducting taxes. The American tax authorities were after the family, too. All the estate's US assets and incomes had been frozen until the tax bill was settled. Just before leaving America, Adrian had been shadowed by Secret Service agents before being pulled in by the Internal Revenue Service for interviews.

Adrian was convinced that Nina was to blame for the luxurious lifestyle and the countless mad excesses that lay behind all these expenses. She could do the right thing and sell some of her jewels or other possessions. Why did she and Denis need to travel the world and stay in the most expensive hotels? It was a blow to Adrian's heart each time he opened a letter from Denis to be greeted by the letterhead from some Grand Hotel in some new place.

The best solution would be for Denis to relinquish his role in the family business and hand it all over to his brother. Adrian had at least managed to persuade him that new contracts would require both of their signatures.

Now, however, it was time to look ahead. Denis owed Adrian a lot of money, but they could deal with that later. If only his brother could lie low for a while, then Adrian would be able to sort this out. There was big money on the way, which would mean Denis could start afresh—preferably without Nina.

Wherever he went, Adrian heard gossip about Denis and Nina, gossip that further tarnished the family's good name. For the past year, Denis and Nina had had a constant companion, a young man named Tony Harwood. Adrian suspected that Denis was not entirely happy with Nina and Tony's relationship, so he offered to come to Venice and throw Tony into a canal. If Adrian wasn't mistaken, Tony had even said he would like to marry Nina!

Luckily, Adrian had a plan to save the family finances. It was already being put into action from his desk in Tangier. At the moment there was a power outage, but he was well used to that. The electricity came and went.

He tried to let go of his internal fury. He had made up his mind, and nothing would stop him.

He was going to write new Sherlock Holmes stories.

Denis was in his hotel room in Versailles, sitting in front of the typewriter. He was so weak that the long letter he was writing to his brother would take him days to complete.

He had spent two months in the American Hospital of Paris, hovering between life and death. Even with his recent improvement, things were still very serious. Nina had battled for his recovery, paying for the best doctors by selling assets and managing to persuade Europe's leading heart specialist to board a flight from London with only a few hours' notice.

Denis could well understand Adrian's anger. What he had done to his brother and sister was unforgivable. He was ashamed and did not deny any of it. He would do whatever he could to repay Adrian and Jean every last penny.

But could Adrian please stop bringing it up? With Nina's help, Denis was in the process of tidying up the mess and making amends. Adrian seemed to think that the blame for Denis's occasionally extravagant lifestyle rested with Nina. That was about as far from the truth as it was possible to get. Nina was a victim of the dire situation, not the cause. In fact, she had saved him time and time again, thus severely depleting her own fortune.

Adrian's exhortation—that Denis leave Nina—was nothing short of shameful. Besides, he had completely misunderstood the situation with Tony Harwood. Yes, both Denis and Nina found him irritating at times, yet they cared for him. Nina had told Denis that if he did find Tony's presence to be a disturbance, then she would ask him to pack and leave within twenty-four hours. She had said this regardless of the fact that Tony had taken such good care of her during that awful time when Denis was in the hospital.

Adrian had heard gossip? Well, it goes with the territory, surely. And Adrian wasn't really in a position to be moralizing over such things. If one of them had tarnished the name of Conan Doyle, surely it was he, through his adulterous affair with that Turkish woman—the one who had gone around telling her friends all the intimate details of their lovemaking. It was Nina who had used her private savings to pay the woman off and get rid of her. Nina had also persuaded Anna to stay by her husband's side. That was not the first time that Denis had had to hush up Adrian's involvement in some scandal.

Perhaps Adrian was right, and he should be the one in charge of the estate. Denis did not doubt his honesty, integrity, intelligence, and energy for a second. What he did doubt was his judgment, which was dreadful. He routinely misjudged situations and people.

And he was unmoved by Adrian's inflated predictions of future profits. They had never once come to pass.

Brotherly love was at a low ebb. The last thing Denis had heard from Adrian was that his letters were disturbing the production of new Sherlock Holmes stories and that it might be best for the brothers to go their separate ways.

Well, perhaps it was for the best, in which case, so be it.

63

ADRIAN CONAN DOYLE and John Dickson Carr had stayed in touch since their collaboration on Sir Arthur's biography. In the summer of 1950 Carr had visited his friend Adrian in Tangier, and he had returned the following year with his family to live in the North African port over the winter.

When Adrian had gone to New York for the exhibition, Carr had decided to keep him company. Carr had seen the London exhibition and had even used it as the setting for the closing scene of his latest crime novel.

One evening, as they sat drinking coffee in Adrian's New York hotel suite, they chatted about Arthur Conan Doyle's predisposition for including American characters in the stories. They had talked about writing new Sherlock Holmes stories together a few years before, while working on the biography, but nothing had come of it. Now the idea popped up again.

"Well, why don't we get down to it?" Adrian wondered.

Carr concurred, continuing, "For some time I have had an idea involving seven clocks." And so he began the process of sketching out how the idea might be transformed into a short story about Sherlock Holmes.

Both men began studying old Holmes stories in depth, hoping to teach themselves Conan Doyle's manner of punctuation, sentence structure, and vocabulary, so they might produce absolutely perfect pastiches. As starting points Adrian and Carr chose cases that Conan Doyle's characters had mentioned in passing in the original stories, and they set about fleshing out these stories with appropriate plots. The combination of one of the world's most renowned crime writers and the name Conan Doyle—albeit Adrian instead of Arthur—surely guaranteed that the tales would bring in welcome dollars and pounds.

Carr accompanied Adrian to Tangier so that they could continue working on the short stories. They had told the press that they were essentially writing alternate lines, and that no one—not even themselves—could tell who had written what. In practice, that was not what happened. That the two had discussed the contents at length was true, however.

They had finished off the first story that summer in New York and had immediately set about writing the second. Adrian had always hated other authors' Holmes pastiches, but he considered his contribution to be merely an extension of his father's authorship. These stories truly were in the spirit of his father.

Denis hadn't seen things that way. He felt that the idea of new stories diluted their father's works. He was against the whole project. On the other hand he objected to whatever Adrian did. Denis had agreed not to make his reservations public. Jean, meanwhile, had refused to have anything to do with the stories and therefore would not receive any of the revenues. Adrian felt that it really was a shame to fall out over such trifling matters.

Adrian's attitude toward Sherlock Holmes pastiches in general was unchanged. Earlier that year, it had come to his attention that a new Swedish book had been published containing a series of newly written Sherlock Holmes stories. No author was mentioned on the book itself, leading one to believe that Conan Doyle could have written the stories. Adrian instructed his lawyers to threaten to sue the publisher, who was also the book's author, and he was forced to destroy his stock. No one was to earn money off the back of Sherlock Holmes unless he deserved to. And there were very few people in that category.

There was no formal agreement with Conan Doyle's estate about Adrian and Carr's new stories. That would have required Denis's signature. When the first of them appeared in *Life* magazine, Adrian still squeezed in a fabricated note claiming that the short story was indeed approved by the estate. It was a warning to other authors about what was required in order to gain permission to write about Sherlock Holmes.

The close collaboration between Adrian and Carr worked only in the beginning. After the first two short stories they decided that they should each take responsibility for one story at a time. The series had been given the title *The Exploits of Sherlock Holmes* and was to comprise twelve short stories in total. Adrian's new literary agent in New York, the young René de Chochor, had looked sharp and had managed to sell the first story for $10,000, while another magazine, *Collier's*, bought the remainder for a total of $40,000.

Adrian was delighted with René de Chochor. He was the best thing to have happened to him in a long time.

The happiness did not last. Carr did not deliver stories at anything like the rate Adrian wanted him to. This meant that Adrian was forced to increase the pressure on his writing partner. Carr, however, was also being pulled in other directions—hounded by publishers and agents wondering when his own books might be ready, nagged by the BBC about a radio series for which he had already received a healthy advance. Then there was his poor health—after two unsuccessful bouts of eye surgery he was on the edge.

On January 2, 1953, Carr drank his first drop of alcohol. He didn't stop until two months later, when his wife traveled to Tangier in a desperate attempt to save his life. By that time he weighed less than 110 pounds.

Adrian was furious. Carr had let him down, and Adrian would have to write the last six stories himself. He even wrote to his brother, asking Denis whether he had any suggestions for plots. Their relationship had thawed and was good once more. The final stories were published under Adrian's name alone.

The book was mentioned in the *Baker Street Journal*. It was explained that on March 30, 1954—"a day that will live in infamy," the journal interjected—a book entitled *The Exploits of Sherlock Holmes* had been released. *Sherlock Holmes Exploited* would have been a more fitting name, the review asserted. It could be summarized in just two quotes from Conan Doyle's original stories:

Art in the blood is liable to take the strangest forms.
A child has done this horrid thing.

64

Nigel Bruce had heard a rumor. A new Sherlock Holmes television series was in the offing, and the rumor also had it that Basil Rathbone was to play Sherlock Holmes. But who was going to play Watson? No one had asked Nigel Bruce.

He sent a telegram to his old friend Denis Conan Doyle. Denis had always approved of his acting—wouldn't he be able to insist that Nigel Bruce play Dr. Watson? Surely it would help the success of the project if the old pair were to be reunited. He dearly wanted to play his favorite old role again.

A young man was waiting in the offices of Fitelson and Mayers on Fifth Avenue, and he had no idea why.

Opposite him sat H. William Fitelson himself, who was still wearing his overcoat and kept answering the telephone, which rang at least every other minute.

The young man, literary agent of the Conan Doyle heirs, was René de Chochor. He sat in silence, wondering when he might discover the reason for his having been summoned there.

More time passed. Fitelson finished off one of his calls and put the phone down. He turned his gaze to de Chochor and said: "We are having a difficult time selling Sherlock Holmes on television and we also have to appease Mr. Shapiro to whom Denis sold TV rights for $10,000, so we may have to pay him back soon if you want to keep TV rights."

That was it—one long sentence. René de Chochor did not say another word, nor did Fitelson. They shook hands, and de Chochor left.

Adrian had initially engaged René de Chochor to take care of only the book rights, but he had been impressed with the young lawyer's business sense and had begun to employ him for all kinds of tasks.

De Chochor, who was now in sole charge of any television negotiations, still did not understand what that meeting had been about.
Fitelson ought to have been out of the picture by now. It would not
work if both of them were negotiating simultaneously. Fitelson had
primarily been Denis's contact, and de Chochor had been Adrian's ever
since the younger brother had taken over most of the business after
his time in New York.

Selling the television rights was racked with difficulties. Shapiro's
threat to claim the rights if his deposit was not repaid was just one of
the many problems.

The Conan Doyles' plan was to have a producer make a series of
twenty-six half-hour episodes. The first step was to find a sponsor—
always required to fund a series for one of the more popular networks.
They also needed to ensure that no other company made television
adaptations of the Sherlock Holmes stories that were no longer under
US copyright. The solution to that was quite simple. Broadcasts by
major American networks had a wide reach and could even be picked
up and viewed in both Canada and Mexico. And if any such program
could be watched in those countries, it would constitute a breach of
copyright there, meaning that the producer would have to pay for the
rights.

The biggest problem was that René de Chochor had already made
contact with pretty much every television company in America—even
Walt Disney had expressed an interest—and discovered that there was
always a catch. Often, the producers did not want to pay the sums
demanded by the Conan Doyle brothers. There had also already been
an American series in the making, which was to have been shot in
England with Basil Rathbone in the lead role. As usual, the negotiations
had come to nothing.

Not only that, time was now of the essence. The brothers had been
attempting to secure some kind of contract since 1948. Five whole
years had passed, and with each passing year it became even more
difficult to keep the parlous copyright situation a secret. No television
company wanted to buy the rights to Sherlock Holmes if it could not
be guaranteed exclusivity. Added to this was the fact that an increasing
number of sponsors were withdrawing support from various television
series as the competition within the television sector became tougher.

René de Chochor had managed to seal a smaller television contract. To Adrian's great pleasure, it concerned a live, half-hour adaptation of one of the new stories he had written with Carr, "The Black Baronet." Or rather, it was a story of which he had written 90 percent, even if Carr had come up with the plot. Adrian was convinced of the program's strategic importance and was certain it would increase the audience's appetite for televised Sherlock Holmes. The program was to be broadcast just three days after the story was published. One part of the plot would have to be altered, however. It was not OK for American television programs to show criminals escaping unpunished.

De Chochor suggested that they hire Basil Rathbone as Sherlock Holmes. Nigel Bruce, who had been such a popular Watson, was apparently on holiday in Mexico, so another actor was called upon to play the role. For Rathbone it was great public relations—his new play was about the master detective, and the premiere was only a short time away.

To Adrian, the Holmes properties and their manifestations were all connected. If René de Chochor could secure just one big television contract, it would generate interest, which in turn could bring the Holmes exhibition out on the road. It had been locked in a New York warehouse for almost a year. Whereas Adrian had been convinced that the exhibition's opening would create interest in Sherlock Holmes, he had been forced to reevaluate after the unsuccessful summer the show had endured. Clearly, there would have to be a television series instead.

And if interest in Sherlock Holmes were to increase, he would be able to launch his huge merchandising operation, the bones of which he had already set out. He had been in touch with a man closely connected to the monetizing of Disney's various trademarks, and for a fortnight or so Adrian had positively drowned the man in Sherlock Holmes material. The merchandising man was enthusiastic about the idea of cashing in on the famous detective. They planned Sherlock Holmes shoes, hats, toothbrushes, beer glasses, and toys. They also planned to license Sherlock Holmes for use in advertising for all kinds of everyday products.

The real money in America, however, lay elsewhere: in comic books and newspaper strips. This was strange, considering that this market barely existed in England. The comic-strip pages of the newspapers were far more profitable than the television rights could ever be, so Adrian and René de Chochor had begun negotiations. Rather than simply selling the rights, they planned to produce the strips themselves. They had employed some of the best illustrators and scriptwriters in America to do the job. This deal could, according to Adrian's calculations, be worth $50 million a year! Sherlock Holmes could become the next Roy Rogers.

65

Basil Rathbone had become a brand. He had quit the Universal films and the radio series and moved to New York. He had attempted to land serious roles in the theater and had finally succeeded, even winning a Tony Award for his role in *The Heiress*. At the same time, many people had trouble seeing him as anything but Sherlock Holmes.

During his time in Hollywood, Rathbone had redefined the role of Holmes. He had sanded off the detective's most eccentric edges. His Holmes was not an introvert. His interpretation of the role was free of melancholy. This was a Sherlock Holmes the public could love, and want to relate to—a real Uncle Sherlock.

For a long time after the Hollywood years Rathbone resisted his fate, before eventually softening and giving up. He accepted that he *was* Sherlock Holmes. He missed the camaraderie with Nigel Bruce and recalled how much their collaboration had meant to both of them. One December day in the late 1940s, he wrote to Edgar W. Smith of the Baker Street Irregulars and asked whether he might give a subscription to the *Baker Street Journal* to Nigel Bruce as a Christmas present. The magazine was unfortunately defunct at that time.

Rathbone had toyed with the idea of a Broadway production of Sherlock Holmes for several years. He had been in touch with his Sherlockian friends Christopher Morley and Vincent Starrett to test the waters and to see whether they might be able to write such a play. At the same time, a rival playwright had started work on a script of his own, although neither the Conan Doyle brothers nor Rathbone thought much of its content. The same writer had also been involved in another Holmes play meant for Rathbone and Bruce that had been planned some ten years earlier, but nothing had come of that either.

Was there no one who could write a decent play about Sherlock Holmes?

Arthur Conan Doyle in his study at Norwood (1894)

Louisa Conan Doyle

Jean Leckie

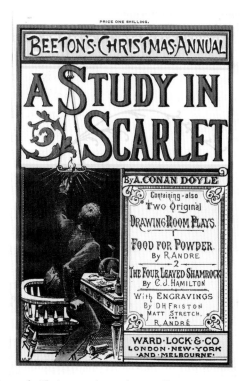

Beeton's Christmas Annual 1887 (facsimile edition)

Joseph Bell

H. Greenhough Smith

Above: Sidney Paget and one of his illustrations for "Silver Blaze"

Right and below: Frederic Dorr Steele and his cover illustration for "The Empty House" in *Collier's Weekly*

Below right: William Gillette

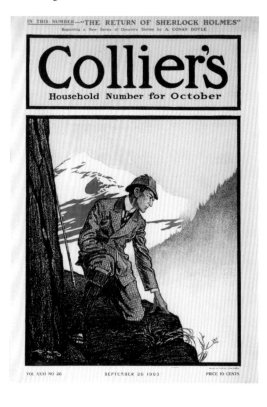

Eille Norwood and Sir Arthur Conan Doyle

Edith Meiser

Vincent Starrett

Edgar W. Smith

Christopher Morley

Left: Basil Rathbone in *The Hound of the Baskervilles* (1939)

Below: Nigel Bruce (reading S. C. Roberts's *Doctor Watson*) and Christopher Morley

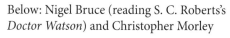

Above left: Adrian Conan Doyle

Above right: Nina Mdivani and Denis Conan Doyle arriving in the U.S. in 1937

Middle right: Anthony "Tony" Harwood

Below: The Sherlock Holmes Exhibition in London (1951)

SHERLOCK HOLMES EXHIBITION, LONDON, 1951
LIVING ROOM, 221 B. BAKER ST., RECONSTRUCTED BY MICHAEL WEIGHT

Left: Nicholas Meyer

Middle right: Mitch Cullin at the time he wrote *A Slight Trick of the Mind*

Below right: John Bennett Shaw in his library

Below left: John Bennett Shaw and teenage Mitch Cullin together with Mitch's parents at a meeting of the Brothers Three of Moriarty (the last one Mitch ever attended)

Middle left: Cover for Michael and Mollie Hardwick's novelization of the movie *The Private Life of Sherlock Holmes* (with the artwork from the movie poster)

Jeremy Brett and Edward Hardwicke during the shooting of
the river scenes in *The Sign of Four*

Dame Jean Conan Doyle at the
opening of the Sherlock Holmes
Museum in Meiringen

Vasily Livanov and Vitaly Solomin
in the Lenfilm TV series

Steven Moffat and Sue Vertue at the Sherlock Holmes, Northumberland Street, London

Mark Gatiss at the annual dinner of the Sherlock Holmes Society of London (2006)

Benedict Cumberbatch and Martin Freeman on location for "The Reichenbach Fall"

Above left: Poster for *Sherlock Holmes* (2009) with Jude Law and Robert Downey Jr.

Above right: Writing on the wall in a train underpass in Bryn Mawr, Pennsylvania, during the #believeinsherlock movement

Above left: Douglas Wilmer in front of Sidney Paget's oil painting of Sir Arthur Conan Doyle at the Sherlock Holmes exhibition at the Museum of London

Above right: Jonny Lee Miller and Lucy Liu in *Elementary*

★   ★   ★

Ouida Rathbone had not told those around her the whole truth. Even Basil had been misled on occasion. She was not actually four years younger than her husband but was in fact seven years his senior. Her exotic childhood in Madrid with her Spanish and Anglo-French parents was infinitely preferable to the truth—she was born in Little Rock, Arkansas. Her maiden name had not been Ouida Bergère or Ouida DuGaze, as she usually claimed, or even Ida Berger. She was originally Eula Branch.

This was the world of film and theater, where it turned out that most of what seemed real was in fact just a set.

If Basil was contemplating playing Sherlock Holmes in the theater, his wife wasn't about to stop him. Indeed, she would help him, and promised to make use of her old script-writing skills. She had after all been one of the highest paid American screenwriters of the early 1920s, and she had written a number of plays for her husband before. No one could say that she didn't have enough experience. Putting together a play about Sherlock Holmes couldn't be too difficult. It was simply a case of getting out the old stories and lifting as much plot and dialogue as possible. That, if anything, would endear it to Adrian Conan Doyle.

Ouida based the script primarily on two of the short stories, "The Second Stain" and "The Bruce-Partington Plans." She combined them with plotlines from another three short stories, stuffing them all into the script. Several characters from the various stories joined in, and the play became more and more complex. There were two fake American double agents, a fake French spy, a dead extortionist, a real German spy, Mycroft, Holmes, Watson, Moriarty and his accomplice Moran, Mrs. Hudson, Inspectors Gregson and Lestrade, and a whole succession of complicating circumstances. And of course—the Reichenbach Falls had to be brought to the stage! They would simply have to work out the details of how to re-create the roaring falls.

Wherever in the fifty-six short stories and four novels Ouida found dialogue, she copied as much as she could and pasted it into the script. Ninety percent of the dialogue in the opening scene set in the Baker Street flat came straight from various passages of Conan Doyle's original work. His son would like that. Some scenes might need a bit of polishing, but surely Basil would be able to enlist Vincent Starrett for that. Basil himself was delighted with the script. He had even helped her to write a few of the scenes.

Unfortunately, there was a delay in getting Starrett's help, and then Starrett had become ill. Morley did not have time to assist them either. But what did that matter when Adrian Conan Doyle had read the script and considered it the best Sherlock Holmes play ever?

As Basil sought a producer and financial backers, Ouida rewrote and rewrote the piece. There were so many scenes that could be improved. Changing one act often meant changes later on in the complex plot. When an event proved too difficult to stage, she would have the characters recount it instead. An eight-minute confession from one of the guilty parties at the climax of one of the acts solved the problem of explaining what had already happened.

And so the night of the final dress rehearsal arrived. Four railway carriages full of decor, props, and electrical special effects had been shipped from New York to Boston, where the out-of-town opening was scheduled for the following day, October 12, 1953. It was the biggest show ever staged at Boston's Majestic Theatre, despite the fact that it wasn't a huge musical but rather a traditional play.

The real premiere would come later, on Broadway, but the cast needed to do a couple of performances to see whether any tweaks or adjustments were necessary.

Terence Kilburn had been a young boy when he played Billy the page boy opposite Rathbone in one of his very first Holmes films. Rathbone had apparently taken a shine to him, since he had also been featured in the radio series and now, as a twenty-seven-year-old, had been given a role in the play. Sadly, Rathbone's old friend Nigel Bruce was not able to play Dr. Watson, as he wasn't altogether in good health.

Terry liked Basil Rathbone and his wife, Ouida, although he knew that many people did not care for her. He couldn't, however, claim to like the play. It simply wasn't very good. There was so much scenography, and so many costume changes, that it was hard to follow what was going on—and why.

The rehearsal was supposed to start at six, so the producers could avoid having to pay overtime to the light and sound people after midnight. They hadn't even unpacked all the sets by then, and it was eight o'clock before they got going. The scenography was impressive but far too impractical.

The cast comprised almost thirty members, and the lighting was so complicated that it was difficult to keep track of who was supposed to enter with which spotlight.

By 2:00 a.m., actors from other theaters around the city began turning up. While out drinking, they had got wind of the disaster unraveling at the Majestic, and they wanted to see it for themselves.

"No!" came a voice from in front of the stage. "That's the wrong set!"

No, no it wasn't.

"I'm telling you, that's the wrong set! What are you doing?"

It must have been a full hour before that was settled.

The stage manager was then found unconscious at his desk behind the stage. He had suffered a mild heart attack.

At three in the morning, they reached the scene where Moriarty entered the play. The actor's first action was to tread right on a nail. "I've got to have a tetanus shot immediately," he hissed. "I *refuse* to take another step."

Some poor soul was landed with the task of calling and waking a doctor who could come and attend to the evil criminal professor.

At eight o'clock in the morning, the exhausted actors said their closing lines.

It was well known that a hopeless rehearsal bodes well for the premiere. Still, Terry Kilburn knew that there were limits to how far you could stretch old theatrical superstitions.

He was quite right. It might not have been a catastrophe, but neither was it much good. Sitting in the auditorium at the opening were members of the local Sherlockian society, the Speckled Band of Boston. The cast need not have worried about whether the Sherlockians might find factual flaws in the play. It was more a question of whether the gentlemen and their wives would be able to follow the plot at all.

To top it off, Basil Rathbone was somehow no longer his old self. The man who had been the American audience's Sherlock Holmes for almost fifteen years had lost his touch. It was the end of an era. And when it was time for Watson's lines, they were not delivered by Rathbone's old friend Nigel Bruce, in his mumbling voice or with his contagious laughter. No, that laugh would never be heard again. The news had reached Rathbone on the day of the rehearsal. Out in California, Nigel Bruce had died of a heart attack.

Three weeks later, the play opened on Broadway. Every review was negative. When Basil Rathbone arrived at the theater to prepare for the second day's matinee performance, he was met by a note on the ticket window. That evening's performance would be the last.

66

FIVE CRITICS: THAT was all it took to kill off what Adrian Conan Doyle considered to be a fantastic play about Sherlock Holmes. Five critics, in so doing, had denied the Conan Doyle heirs their just deserts.

Adrian scarcely dared think about what this would mean for the television deal with Sheldon Reynolds. For six months Adrian, Denis, and René de Chochor, each from his own corner of the world, had negotiated with the young American scriptwriter, director, and producer. In his studio in France, Sheldon Reynolds had for some years been recording a popular television series for the American market, and he was perfect for the brothers' plans. Denis had made the initial contact and then flown on to Tangier, where he and Adrian hatched plans they hoped would shake the television world to its core. Once the contract was signed it would open so many other doors.

Since the Broadway production had been canceled, neither of them had heard a word from Reynolds.

By the light of the old desk lamp in his Versailles hotel room, Denis read the latest letter from the estate's literary agent, René de Chochor. The pair had exchanged letters about the play. Denis had never liked the play and, much like de Chochor, had had his doubts about whether it would be a success.

Now, though, it was time to sort out the television contract. That Reynolds had been interested was due entirely to Denis. He was the one who had been in touch with Reynolds in Paris and taken him to lunch, bought him cocktails, and invited him to the city's finest venues. The courtship had lasted several weeks. In the end, Reynolds could not help being overwhelmed by the idea of bringing Sherlock Holmes to television.

Denis leaned over his desk in order to carefully study what the agent had sent him. This was good, very good. In front of him lay a few sheets of paper covered with comic strips. These were the first samples from the new illustrator. The first illustrator they had turned to had been good, but this one was even better. Thank goodness they had changed. These images were more sympathetic, somehow warmer, more human, more charming. The artist's name was Frank Giacoia. The script had been written by Denis's acquaintance from his days in America, Edith Meiser, and it was good.

Edith Meiser was curled up in bed, at home in New York, with a pad, a pencil, and Conan Doyle's stories. She was working once more on Sherlock—sorry, Mr. Holmes, of course. Meiser smiled to herself. She had not worked on any Holmes stories since 1948, when she had completed her last radio script about the detective. She had left the production a few years before that, but when the series returned to New York after a decade in California she had taken on writing duties again, bringing the detective and his companion new, perplexing problems that could be solved during a thirty-minute radio broadcast. For tens of millions of Americans, her Sherlock Holmes was the real one.

It was now 1953. In recent years she had worked mainly in the theater but also in film and television. Friends of hers at the *New York Herald Tribune*'s comic-strip syndicate had approached her to write the script for a strip about Sherlock Holmes. She had no idea how to go about writing a comic strip but had accepted the challenge. She soon realized just how demanding it was. That Adrian Conan Doyle took issue with various aspects of what she produced was one thing. Such details could always be changed. No, the hard part was to piece together the elements of the story in a way that suited this particular medium. The strip was to be featured in newspapers for years to come. The plot was developed in the strips that appeared in the newspapers' weekday editions. In the Sunday editions she was obliged to merely tread water; some of the newspapers did not have a Sunday comics page, while others did not publish at all on Sundays. The readers had to be able to follow the story without Sunday's episode. And there were lots of readers. Before long more than three hundred newspapers worldwide were publishing her and Frank Giacoia's strips. It would not have been possible without Giacoia's great skill. Meiser always wrote the text first, and Giacoia then had the task of attempting to draw speech bubbles big enough to accommodate her dialogue.

Everything seemed to happen at once in René de Chochor's life. He could barely keep up with all the contracts and the new sales ideas that Adrian and Denis provided him with. They also wanted to be kept informed about all of it. He had no choice but to spend Sundays writing long letters.

Adrian had asked him to put a gun to Universal's head. This latest problem had come to light during dinner one evening, when de Chochor's wife told him she wanted to see Basil Rathbone in the Sherlock Holmes film being shown at the cinema across the street. De Chochor had immediately put down his knife and fork and rushed out onto the street to see what she was talking about. Sure enough, Universal was showing one of its old films. It no longer had any right to do so. Adrian felt that this misdemeanor could be used to blackmail it into purchasing the television rights to its own back catalog.

That meant Adrian, Denis, and de Chochor needed to get the deal done without delay. Color television was to be launched the following year, and the industry expected to complete a general switch over to the new medium within three years. After that, Universal's old black-and-white films would hardly be worth very much at all.

Sheldon Reynolds was working late at his home in France. He barely had time to respond to the correspondence from the Conan Doyle estate's representative. This was an enormous project and such a contract could not be drawn up in a matter of weeks. If possible, he wanted to shoot a hundred TV episodes about Sherlock Holmes, and in the shortest time frame feasible. He preferred to shoot in color, so that the installments could be shown in black-and-white first but could continue their run after the introduction of the new color sets.

He was perfectly prepared to abandon his other projects in order to make the series. He had started the casting process and was looking for scriptwriters, even though the contract had not yet been signed. He hoped that René de Chochor and the Conan Doyle brothers would be able to fly to London to approve all the actors. He would have liked to do the filming in England, since that was where the actors were, but the problem was that the available studios were either far too big or much too small. Therefore he planned to shoot the series in his own studio in France, the same studio that had once belonged to the film company Éclair when it was producing Sherlock Holmes films in the 1910s.

The sun had set over Tangier, and the Strait of Gibraltar was a great black void.

Adrian sat in the darkness.

It was frustrating that the contracts never quite made it all the way. Everything hinged on René de Chochor now. As far as Adrian was concerned, the young man had grown in stature with each passing month. Adrian was convinced that his father had sent de Chochor, and that this wasn't the only help their father had sent.

The new Sherlock Holmes stories Adrian had written had brought in large sums, and they had finally been able to tackle some of Denis's debts. This was a thankless task, not least since Denis had revealed that he had accumulated another $5,000 worth of debt for his recent stays at the hotel in Versailles.

The American tax arrears, too, hung over them like a dark cloud. It was bizarre that the tax authorities had recently begun chasing debts dating all the way back to the second decade of the century. Adrian knew there must be some mistake. His father had always been so conscientious. There was simply no question of any debt from that period.

Adrian was fortunate to have his income from the new Holmes stories, since they were beyond the reach of the tax authorities, which had now seized any US assets or incomes connected to the estate.

In a moment of clarity, Adrian had the thought that the income wasn't actually due to him. This was their father's gift. Adrian knew that he was not capable of writing those stories. No, it was his father, by the grace of God, writing them through him.

A few months later, in producer Sheldon Reynolds's studio in France, Scottish actor Archie Duncan, who played Inspector Lestrade, looked at his wristwatch.

"Sorry," he said, at precisely the moment the second hand indicated that it was 4:00 p.m.

They were midway through shooting a scene with him, but Reynolds knew that there was no point arguing. It was like this every day. They would simply have to wait for the fifteen minutes it took Duncan to enjoy the specially blended tea that was shipped to the studio from London.

It had been touch-and-go for a while as to whether there would even be a television series. Conan Doyle's sons had suddenly sold television rights to Universal, after having been offered $90,000—the family's biggest contract ever. Reynolds had believed all along that his contract with the estate had been a done deal—or rather Denis had led him to believe that. Reynolds had set about preparing a writ against them before everything was solved in the best possible way. Universal was allowed to rescreen its old black-and-white films while Reynolds got the nod for his television series, which comprised thirty-nine half-hour episodes under the title *Sherlock Holmes*. Some of the episodes borrowed freely from the original stories, but for the most part these were newly written adventures, composed by Reynolds as well as other scriptwriters.

The set designer who had been responsible for Holmes's sitting room at the London exhibition had created the room that stood in the Paris studio. Reynolds's uppermost desire was to make his films substantially different from the Basil Rathbone pictures. The easiest way to do so was to go back to the source and the portrayals in the original stories. Reynolds realized that Sherlock Holmes had been a young man in the early stories, not at all like the rather mature gentleman Rathbone had played. Reynolds decided to go for a youthful actor, Ronald Howard, who was known solely for being the son of actor Leslie Howard. Rathbone gave his view on the matter to the press: Ronald Howard was far too young for the role. Like many others, Rathbone had never considered that Sherlock Holmes was, in fact, young in the stories.

The choice of actor proved to be a masterstroke. Ronald Howard's Sherlock Holmes, a young man primarily concerned with success in his profession, was a thoroughly decent and personable character with great appeal in 1950s America. And Watson, for once, was portrayed not as a bit of a blathering fool but rather as Holmes's intelligent conversational partner. Instead, Inspector Lestrade provided the television program's light relief.

Considering the pace of filming, Reynolds was happy with the results. The budget was tight, and the cast and crew had only four days in which to record each episode. The launch of the series in the

United States, in October 1954, gave them every reason to celebrate. It was an instant success.

Sherlock Holmes was in demand in America once again. Unfortunately, that meant that Adrian could not sell the rights to his own newly written stories. Sheldon Reynolds owned the television rights for Sherlock Holmes at the moment. In the grand scheme of things, however, that was a minor setback.

67

THE NIGHT DENIS died, Nina felt that she died with him. She lay in the maharaja's guesthouse for hours, burning inside, a wild tigress who had lost her lifelong companion. It was March 9, 1955, and Nina was mad with grief.

She barely understood what was going on around her. The light of the full moon flooded in through the window, throwing itself like a drape over her deceased husband. She sent a message to the maharaja, but throughout the day that followed, no one came from the palace. Denis lay at her side, motionless.

Nina and Denis had come to India for the first time several years earlier. The maharaja's guesthouse was Victorian in style, and the garden featured a pond. Nina had been enchanted because the nighttime chorus of frogs sounded like Caruso.

She hadn't wanted to go; the journey was too long and tiring. Denis, though, was very excited at the prospect of meeting the maharaja, seeing wild elephants, and shooting a tiger.

It had been an emotional experience. They were met in Bangalore, where a little girl had given Nina an adorable bouquet before the maharaja's adjutant had taken them to Mysore.

Their room was beautiful and had a great high ceiling. Both beds were draped with tulle netting to protect against mosquitoes. Indian attendants ensured that all sixty of their Louis Vuitton trunks ended up in the right place. They also made sure that their French maid, Valentine, and Denis's bearer were shown to their quarters; that their dachshund was given something to drink in the sweltering heat; that the canary was brought in; and that their Rolls-Royce was properly parked.

Nina had looked at the people around her. There was something about Indians: their faces, their turbans, and the way they moved.

Their walk was quite different from that of Europeans—they glided across the floors.

A few days had passed before the maharaja summoned them to the palace. He was a young man, somewhat portly, with a beautiful face. She liked men who were slightly pudgy; that only added to their appeal. He was barefoot and wore sparkling emerald rings on his fingers. One of the rings represented a cow. His forehead bore several white painted stripes; he had probably come straight from the temple.

She was wearing a dress from one of Paris's leading fashion houses. It made her feel like an interesting woman, because that's how people saw her back home in France, and when she talked, people listened.

The young maharaja seemed shy. Nina sat down opposite him and started talking. She told him about Paris, French elegance, French poets, and French theater, all about the French way of life that she so admired. She told him about the perfumes and about the interesting people she knew.

The maharajah had lifted his head and looked at Nina. He had asked, "Don't you think that silence is also conversation?"

Nina and Denis had returned to India some years later. Denis wanted to shoot a wild elephant. They waited in Mysore for months for someone to catch a glimpse of one. Finally a message had come from the palace—a wild elephant had been terrorizing nearby villages.

It was one of those beautiful evenings for which Mysore was so well known. The full moon illuminated the entire landscape. Nina could not enjoy her surroundings, however, since she was constantly worrying that something would happen to Denis and his poor weak heart. All the terrible things that had happened in her life had happened at a full moon.

Early the next morning they had set off, accompanied by servants and beaters. Denis kissed her good-bye in the car, sat himself on an elephant, and disappeared into the jungle.

Nina stayed in the car and could hear the strength of the wind in the trees. She heard the sounds of jungle birds, screeching monkeys, a tiger's roar, and, at the same time, the complete silence.

She jumped when the first shot rang out. The rifle went off thirteen times—an unlucky number. She was terrified. And then silence followed, like the silence of the grave.

Eventually the party returned. The leader of the hunt approached Nina and said, "He killed him." Nina started to cry.

Denis climbed down from his elephant and got into the car.

Nina looked at him.

"Did you come to India to kill?"

He said nothing. He could not explain.

He never did anything she did not approve of. He was always sweet, always looked after her. It was just that this time, there was nothing to say.

He became ill later that day. The maharaja's doctor arrived and ordered Denis to take a long rest.

He lay there, in bed, for two weeks. And Nina knew there wasn't long left.

It would soon be a full moon again.

Part 5

1958–1970

68

I N THE SMALL Surrey village of Frensham, in the fall of 1958, someone
who looked very much like Sherlock Holmes was relaxing at the
Mariners, drinking a glass of pineapple juice at the bar. His Inverness
cape and deerstalker were laid aside.

"Mr. Cushing," the landlord said to the man. "I have something for
you." He had fetched it upstairs; it had been in his possession for years.

"Would you please accept this as a present?" The landlord handed
over a Conan Doyle first edition with Sidney Paget's illustrations.

The forty-five-year-old actor Peter Cushing was ecstatic and thanked
the landlord.

"I've based all my costumes on the original *Strand Magazine* pictures,"
Cushing told the man next to him, a drama critic who had come down
to Surrey to interview him about the film they were in the middle of
shooting. "Fortunately my father left me a whole set."

The wild heathland near Frensham Ponds was standing in for Dartmoor. The story, being turned into a movie for the seventh time, was
The Hound of the Baskervilles.

"Everything is accurate," Cushing continued, "right down to the
famous old 'mouse-coloured' dressing-gown which I charred with cigarettes to get the burns Holmes made during his experiments."

It was to be the first Sherlock Holmes movie in color, produced by
Hammer Films, a company that had made lavishly colored and classy
exploitation films its specialty. Hammer had, during the last few years,
made its reputation in horror, and the classic tale about the hellhound
on Dartmoor fitted its profile perfectly. It was not Holmes the filmmakers were after, it was the chills that would be sent down the spines of
filmgoers. Hammer's chairman had also asserted that the actor playing
Holmes needed to sex it up a bit.

Cushing had finished his pineapple juice. "The producers had some absurd idea that I should not wear a deerstalker. I told them you might as well play Nelson without a patch over his eye!"

Eight years earlier, one night at the main train station in Munich, Henry E. Lester looked out through the window of his compartment. Where was the baron? If he didn't deliver the cash to Lester it would jeopardize the whole film production.

A whistle was sounded by the stationmaster. Still no baron had appeared, and the train pulled out of the station. Lester, who was the German coproducer of this Italian mafia western noir film, *Amore e sangue*, had to complete the Italian financing in a hurry to keep the American coproducer from taking his stars and walking out. Everything was as chaotic as it habitually was in those European productions in which Lester happened to be involved.

Henry E. Lester had been born in Berlin but had an American passport after having served in the US army. He came from a German family of bankers. Leipziger was their name, and they were often involved in financing film projects, which had led Lester to enter the entertainment industry in 1937.

The train slipped into a smaller station on the outskirts of Munich but soon made ready to depart. Lester saw someone in the darkness. There he was! Baron Wolf Dieter von Oppen, Lester's noble secretary, came running hell-for-leather, waving a fat attaché case.

The moment Baron Wolf Dieter von Oppen reached the window, the train started to pull out. He tried to pass the case through the window of the moving train. It burst open, and 200,000 illegally converted dollars—the baron knew some things about money changing in the Munich black market—were scattered around the platform.

Somehow the baron managed to scoop up most of it, jam it into the case, and shove it through the window while running alongside the train.

Lester collapsed on the seat. Next to him sat a beautiful German actress who would shoot some scenes for the film in Italy.

"How do you expect to get that out of the country?" she inquired, nervous.

"I'll think of something," replied Lester, leaning back in his seat.

That was the man who six years later became Adrian Conan Doyle's right hand, working as the agent for the Conan Doyle estate.

Polish-born producer Gene Gutowski came to London for the first time in 1959 in order to set up production, together with his New York friend Henry E. Lester, of a television series about Sherlock Holmes. Lester had known Adrian Conan Doyle for a long time and had also been acquainted with Adrian's late brother, Denis.

The summer of 1959 was hot in London. The cinemas had posters for Hammer's *The Hound of the Baskervilles*, stating, "It's the Picture with That Bone-Chilling Howl!" and "It's Ten Times the Terror in Technicolor!"

The Hammer film had earned the Conan Doyle estate $20,000 and the heirs wanted new projects. Lester's provision when he was the agent for a contract was always 10 percent. There was big money coming in—Twentieth Century Fox was making *The Lost World*, the Professor Challenger story, for which it paid almost five times as much as Hammer had done for the Holmes movie. Unfortunately, the budget wouldn't accommodate stop-motion for the special effects, so the dinosaurs were lizards with plastic horns and spikes attached to them.

In the end, nothing came of Gutowski and Lester's Holmes TV series. Gutowski had, however, fallen in love with London and decided to stay. In 1961 he became director of a new British-based film company, CCC-Film London Limited. Its parent company was based in Berlin and owned by Artur Brauner, a man who hated spending money—even on simple things in his daily life—and always tried to make intricate territorial sales and obtain various subsidies before starting to produce a film. Gutowski, who had worked in the American film and television industry but lately had been Brauner's main talent scout and negotiator in Britain, had persuaded Brauner to form the English company with him so they could coproduce international films that were eligible for British government subsidies.

During the last two years Brauner had produced a number of Dr. Mabuse films, based on the character introduced in Norbert Jacques's 1921 novel *Dr. Mabuse, der Spieler*, and he was now thinking of making a similar series about Sherlock Holmes. The films should be in English and a dubbed version made for the German market. The Conan Doyle estate agreed to a payment of $10,000 for the first film, plus a share of the profit. The estate also had to approve the story line, a contract clause that made things slightly more complicated.

Lester, representing the estate, did not approve the first script. He also complained about the actor chosen to play Sherlock Holmes, Christopher Lee. The casting of such an unknown would imply this was a B movie. True, Lee had played Sir Henry in Hammer's *The Hound of the Baskervilles*, but an actor who had numbered Count Dracula, the Mummy, and Frankenstein's creature among his previous roles was not what Lester had in mind. Brauner didn't care about Lester's views on the casting, but he had to create a new script.

Brauner wanted the film to be about Professor Moriarty, that villain he had heard so much about. Lester told him that it was not possible, since the rights for the Moriarty stories, "The Final Problem" and "The Empty House," had just been sold to an American producer, who was going to put up a musical based partially on them and who also had the option to sell the film rights of the musical.

Lester then remembered that Moriarty was also mentioned in *The Valley of Fear*, and it was agreed that the film could be based on that novel to bring the evil professor into the story.

It was the spring of 1962, and in his East Ninety-Third Street office in New York, Henry E. Lester was working busily on the musical project. Vincent Starrett had seen the book and the lyrics and liked both, and Lester hoped that they would be able to get further help from Starrett to fashion a truly Sherlockian image.

Lester's friend Gutowski was having a difficult time; Brauner wanted to make all the decisions for CCC-London, yet all payments were to be done by the Berlin office. Lester was also worried that no contracts had yet been drawn up with the director Terence Fisher (who had directed Hammer's *Hound*) or Christopher Lee and that no money had been paid in advance to them, as had been promised.

Then Lester received the new script. The fact that the story had nothing to do with *The Valley of Fear* was maybe not the worst problem. Brauner and his scriptwriter wanted to update the story to a more contemporary setting, putting female actors in miniskirts and bringing in a popular German comedian to play Watson. It was slowly turning into a very German production instead of the British film series it was supposed to be. It lacked all Sherlock Holmes spirit. Adrian and the estate's literary agent, René de Chochor, wanted someone else to do the script. Lester agreed that it should be revised, and de Chochor instructed Michael and Mollie Hardwick to do it. Michael Hardwick had done a series of BBC radio adaptations of the Holmes stories.

The Hardwicks needed just a few weeks to write a script according to de Chochor's instructions, and Lester heard from de Chochor that it was excellent.

It was not—nor was it a revision of the previous script. The director said he couldn't make a film of it. It was an almost verbatim adaptation of the first part of *The Valley of Fear*, maybe suitable for radio, but definitely not for film. The estate had gone much further than the contract permitted; it had almost taken over the position of producer from Brauner.

"To hell with Brauner!" Lester heard de Chochor saying on the phone. That sounded like a quote from Adrian, who meanwhile wrote to Brauner saying he was not going to permit a blood-and-thunder film to be made. Adrian's worst fear was having a director who had made so many Hammer movies. What would CCC-London's next Holmes film, *Sherlock Holmes versus Jack the Ripper*, become in the hands of such a man? Michael Hardwick had already been instructed to write an outline for it.

This was the situation at the beginning of June 1962. Ten days later the shooting would commence in CCC's German studio. Some of the location shots would be done in Ireland—Christopher Lee could not work in England because of tax problems. Gene Gutowski, who had been little involved in the film, which should have been entirely a CCC-London production, at least joined the filming in Ireland.

In the end Terence Fisher, Christopher Lee, and Henry E. Lester reworked the Hardwicks' script so it could be melded together with the previous script. It was all sent to the film company. For some reason the wrong parts were pieced together, and the finished result consisted of the bad parts from the two versions. The revisions continued even after the filming had started.

The film was named *Sherlock Holmes und das Halsband des Todes* (*Sherlock Holmes and the Deadly Necklace*), and instead of being an English production, it became a German-Italian-French coproduction. Most of the actors were German, and Germany became the main market for the film in its dubbed version. When the film was released in England six years later, all the voices had been dubbed back to English, including the ones belonging to Christopher Lee and Thorley Walters, who played Watson. Though they had spoken their lines in English originally, they were now over-dubbed by other voice actors.

In August 1962 Brauner sent a story outline of *Sherlock Holmes versus Jack the Ripper* to the Conan Doyle estate. Three months later a first script was written and had been approved by the estate. The production was to start in January 1963. It was then postponed, and after that Adrian quickly lost interest in the new German film project. He and Lester had other plans for Jack the Ripper.

69

IN 1848 NASTY old Uncle Harry had been just an eight-year-old boy, getting into the grounds of the Duke of Wellington's castle. The duke, who was a superb horseman, chased him, but young Harry knew how to run and how to climb trees. At last the duke was right beneath him.

"All right, young shaver, all right," he shouted. "You've given me a good run for the money. Now come on out, I won't hurt you."

The boy climbed down, and the duke gave him a four-penny piece.

A whole lifetime later, nasty old Uncle Harry leaned back in his great big saddlebag of an armchair, with a glass of whiskey in his hand. He was vile, vicious, and self-centered, and he had a stick with which he suddenly lashed out. The young relative in front of him was breathlessly listening, with the four-penny piece in his hand, and standing exactly at a distance at which the stick whizzed past him just a few millimeters short of his nose. It drove the old man mad, but he seemed to appreciate that young Michael Harrison always liked to listen to his stories about bygone times.

In Michael's father's library there was a complete run of the *Illustrated London News* from 1843 onward, as well as *The Boy's Own Paper* and many other bound volumes of old Victorian magazines. Michael always had his nose stuck in them. As the years went by he came to know more and more of the Victorian era. He became, by mere accident, a gossip columnist, mostly because he owned a tailcoat, which meant he could go out to dinners. He befriended another gossip writer—"Call me Don," said the man—and he started writing novels, until the great boom for novels during the war had petered out around 1950. After that he concentrated on crime fiction and nonfiction. He signed a seven-book contract with a publisher, and for the final one the publisher wanted some sort of "In the footsteps of . . ." account—there was a whole genre of such titles at the time. All you had to do was get a biography of somebody, and a gazetteer, and a map, and a guide—it was all so easy, thought Harrison. They tried to come up with a person he could write about. He was the kind of author who could write about pretty much anything, especially if he could use his knowledge of the old days.

"How about Sher—" began Harrison.

"That's it!" the publisher cried. "You were going to say Sherlock Holmes!"

That was true.

"I can hardly wait," said the publisher. "Get on with it straightaway."

"There's a certain amount of preparation first," Harrison pointed out.

"Don't you know anything about it?"

"Very little."

So Harrison rang up his old gossip-columnist friend Don, or Lord Donegall, since he was the sixth Marquess of Donegall. He also held a long list of other titles, such as Viscount Chichester and Baron of Belfast and Hereditary Lord High Admiral of Lough Neagh. Lord Donegall was the editor of the *Sherlock Holmes Journal*, published by the Sherlock Holmes Society of London.

They were old friends, but there was something in Don's voice. It was a bit terse, rebuking, maybe even disappointed. Harrison was an outsider, a commercial writer, who got in on something that any of the members in the society could have done but had not.

Using Sir Arthur Conan Doyle's collected stories about Sherlock Holmes and a fairly good knowledge of England and Victorian London, Harrison managed to write a book that was well received. And then he went on writing books about other Victorian-era matters. Sherlock Holmes was merely a subject for him, not a fascination.

A few days after *In the Footsteps of Sherlock Holmes* had come out in 1958, Harrison received a letter, in a blue envelope with a Swiss stamp on it. Harrison recognized the address. It was from Adrian Conan Doyle, and a letter from that man could mean only one thing.

Michael Hardwick had also had somewhat complicated relations with some of the members of the Sherlock Holmes Society of London, at least initially. He and his wife, Mollie, had been working at the BBC, in adjoining offices, before they became a couple and later married.

Michael had felt that the BBC had done too little over the years with the Holmes stories, and so he had written radio dramatizations for the actors Carleton Hobbs and Norman Shelley, which had been highly popular.

Now the Hardwicks had written what they thought was quite a simple book, *The Sherlock Holmes Companion*, a compilation with the plots of the stories, thumbnail sketches of the characters, and other information of a similar nature. It took them only six months to finish it, and the first edition sold out in twenty-four hours upon its release in 1962. They felt that they should join the society, and after having done so, they found out that there were members who had been doing exactly the same type of compilations—making notes for ten, fifteen years—and hoping one day to publish a book. Among the members it was sometimes hard to understand that there really could be an attraction for Sherlockian matters also among normal people—that there could be something commercial about their quasi-academic universe.

In the United States there was one Sherlockian, a member of the Baker Street Irregulars, who had struck gold: he had written a landmark mainstream book that was well reviewed and well received and helped generate renewed interest in Sherlock Holmes.

The book was *Sherlock Holmes of Baker Street: A Biography of the World's First Consulting Detective*, published in 1962, and the Sherlockian was William S. Baring-Gould. In a time when the common reader's perception of the famous detective was mostly influenced by the Basil Rathbone movies, it drew attention to the original Victorian Holmes. It presented him as a full character, with a whole life story, rather than the series of fragments that could be found in Conan Doyle's stories. The book was soon to be seen as the definitive biography of Holmes.

To make a complete book out of very scattered information, Baring-Gould had been forced to make some things up. He decided that Holmes's full name was William Sherlock Scott Holmes, and that Rex Stout's armchair detective Nero Wolfe was the love child of Sherlock Holmes and Irene Adler (*the* woman). He had Holmes battling Jack the Ripper. And he gave Holmes an itinerant childhood, basing it on the childhood of his own grandfather, the Reverend Sabine Baring-Gould, the famous English clergyman and writer. Some of William S. Baring-Gould's theories and invented facts became almost accepted as knowledge added to what was known from Conan Doyle's sixty stories. To find the equivalent of such an honor one had to go back to Dorothy L. Sayers's old theory regarding John H. Watson's middle name: she claimed to have very good proof that it was Hamish, something that over the years and through literary osmosis had become regarded as truth.

Michael Harrison held the letter from Adrian Conan Doyle in his hand. He had reason to worry.

In the early 1950s, Harrison had prepared a half-hour talk on the origin of Sherlock Holmes, to be broadcast by the BBC.

"We are taking a very great chance," said the radio producer to Harrison. "But we are so impressed with your theory that we are prepared to take you on."

"What is the difficulty?" Harrison had asked.

"To be honest with you, Conan Doyle and Sherlock Holmes are subjects on our blacklist. We never talk about them. We decline to discuss them at all because of the trouble we have had with Adrian already."

Nothing had happened that time, but on another occasion Adrian had threatened to sue a magazine that had published an article by Harrison, in which he congratulated Adrian Conan Doyle and John Dickson Carr on writing the new series of Sherlock Holmes stories. Adrian was furious that Harrison had made it sound as if the two authors had written all of the stories together, when Adrian in fact had written half of them himself. Harrison had sent a letter to Adrian, and then nothing more had been heard from Conan Doyle's son—until this day.

Harrison opened the envelope, read the letter, and passed it over to his wife without a word.

"Well, well, well," they both said, after she had read it.

Adrian Conan Doyle had done something unusual. "How wonderful your new book is," he wrote. "May I congratulate you? It is the first time that my father's noble creation has been handled with dignity."

Harrison wondered what Adrian was after. Nothing, it seemed. In the end Harrison thought that Adrian had decided that Harrison was a bit too prickly and he'd better make friends with him. Harrison's name came from *hérisson*, French for "hedgehog," and he could indeed be very prickly at times.

70

THE HARVARD LAW professor Harold J. Berman left Boston for Moscow on September 20, 1958. His mission: to sue the Soviet Union for $500,000. The reason: it had neglected to pay royalties for at least ten million copies of Conan Doyle's works.

If the Russians would allow Berman to go to court, he would be the first foreigner ever to try a civil suit in a Russian court.

In the early part of the 1950s, the Conan Doyle estate's annual income averaged around £6,000. That was not much to live on, and had it not been for the newly written stories, Adrian would certainly have struggled. It was a shame that Denis had not lived to see the fantastic increase that had occurred in the subsequent ten years. The income had multiplied by four.

Adrian was proud. It was all due to his relentless hard work. Renewed book contracts, film rights, television and radio series—he had been involved in negotiating all of them. There was even a Sherlock Holmes musical on its way to Broadway.

Since the mid-1950s he had been battling the Soviet Union. In 1955 he had tried to get to Moscow in order to personally discuss the question with the Soviet authorities, but bureaucratic inefficiency between the Soviet embassies in England and Switzerland made it impossible for him to get a visa. He had to find another way.

In 1956 he filed a complaint with the Soviet premier Nikolay Bulganin but it had been turned down. After that Professor Berman at Harvard had worked out a new plan. Since the Soviet Union wasn't a signatory to the international copyright convention, the claim was not for royalties but would be a suit against the publishers and the USSR Ministry of Culture under an article of the Soviet civil code that provided that any person or organization that was unjustly enriched at the expense of another was obliged to make restitution.

The Soviets regularly used to provide Adrian with figures on the number of books they printed, although they never mentioned any payment. The detective was constantly popular—at the end of the Second World War there had even been published a Red Army edition of some Holmes stories in a print run of five million copies. Adrian had seen some of the Russian editions, which had been widely sold in the Russian-occupied zone in Austria until the last troops left in 1955.

Berman's trip to Russia, unfortunately, was not successful, but in a last attempt he tried to appeal to the Supreme Court of the Soviet Union. In August 1959, the Moscow city court—a panel of two lay assessors, one a male foundry worker and the other a female rubber-shoe gluer—ruled that Berman was allowed to appeal.

Berman appeared in the Supreme Court and pleaded the case in Russian, but the judge refused to reverse the decision of the Moscow city court, which said in effect that foreign authors had no right to royalties.

Adrian kept working on trying to find new income sources. In the beginning of the 1960s, he and his agent, Henry E. Lester, had, during an autumn week in Cannes, come up with what seemed to Adrian to be a really smart way to increase income. Why limit themselves to earning money on the sale of film rights, when they could be producing films themselves, thereby earning big bucks? Not only that, but all the UK copyrights on his father's works would expire in 1980, so he would have to move quickly; there was no time to wait for potential inquiries.

Just before the end of 1962, Adrian and Lester started a company, Sir Nigel Films. Adrian's sister, Jean, did not want to invest in the venture.

By 1963 the company already had several film projects in the works. One of them was a collaboration with the film company Mirisch and the director Billy Wilder, who was set to make a film called *The Private Life of Sherlock Holmes*. He had signed a contract with the estate some six years earlier, but that had been for a musical.

"I would have preferred doing it as a movie but, at that time, you couldn't show on the screen the things about Holmes I wanted to show," Wilder said. He found no backers for a stage production, so he changed his mind, first deciding to make it into a musical film before finally realizing that he actually wanted to make an ordinary feature film—even if he didn't intend the film to be particularly "ordinary."

Sir Nigel Films had not actually been in a position to sell any rights. The estate was the only entity that could do so. Adrian would soon establish an international company based in Liechtenstein that would take care of such matters on behalf of its sister company, Sir Nigel Films, and only at that point was it time to sign a contract with the estate. It was a little complicated, but it was financially advantageous. Since Adrian rode both horses it was merely a formality.

Then came strong objections from Nina.

Adrian had tried to support his sister-in-law after Denis's death. It wasn't easy. Her constant overreaction was difficult to contain. He had helped her to settle a debt to an orchid farmer by selling a few of her imported orchids for the sum of twenty-five pounds. She had been absolutely distraught when she found out. Apparently Denis had found them, in some jungle on the Tibetan border; he had always tried to find rare orchids for her.

She had then proposed that they sell the whole estate. It didn't take much imagination to see who was giving her these ideas: Tony Harwood, the young man who had followed Denis and Nina around for years. He had been with her in India. A few years after Denis's death, she had married him—a man who was many years younger than she. She explained that he had selflessly taken care of her in the terrible aftermath of Denis's passing.

If Nina wanted out of the estate—Denis's third had passed to her—then she was welcome to pay the $190,000 that Denis had owed Adrian and Jean. It was the amount he had frittered away during the wartime years in America.

In the end, Adrian did not want to wait any longer and went to court to recover his and Jean's money from Nina. The press got hold of the family feud. At home in England, their half sister Mary reacted very badly to the news. What was the point in creating a memorial to their father when the press was portraying his son as a simple thief? Nothing could be more harmful to their father's image. Her inheritance had been modest, but she retained her loyalty toward her father.

Mary ceased all contact with Adrian after that.

To speed up Nina's repayment of the debt, Adrian refrained from paying her one-third share of the estate's income to her. By doing so, he was gradually reducing her debt. She responded by suing him.

She had a lot to complain about. He had not provided complete documentation for all the contracts being prepared. She received no income reports and was therefore unable to determine how much money she should claim.

Good lord, Adrian thought, wasn't it sufficient that she got her money?—which she would get as soon as Denis's debt to his brother and sister had been cleared.

Nina also wanted to stop any new contracts from being signed with Sir Nigel Films. She claimed that Adrian, as sole executor of the estate, would favor his own production company.

She succeeded in getting her demands agreed to by the court, which stopped all development of Sir Nigel Films. All the company was permitted to do was to continue with those deals that had already been signed: *The Private Life of Sherlock Holmes*, another Holmes film called *Fog*, and a further two films based on Sir Arthur Conan Doyle's other stories.

71

THERE WAS A man sitting in a public library, studying literature about Victorian England. Day in, day out, he sat there. He was searching for something.

Suddenly, it leaped out at him: Queen Victoria's Diamond Jubilee parade and festivity in 1897! That was the perfect event—the biggest one in Europe at the time—that could tie the different stories together. The sixtieth anniversary of Queen Victoria's reign would be the background for his musical.

Jerome Coopersmith had been writing television scripts for fifteen years, but was trying to expand his work to the theatrical stage. He had come to think of Sherlock Holmes as a great subject for a musical, and it was one that had never been done before. He chose to base the musical on "A Scandal in Bohemia," because it was the only story that had a dramatically viable woman in it. He added "The Final Problem" and "The Empty House" to include Moriarty. The resulting plot had Holmes going after Irene Adler, then teaming up with her, and the pair together chasing Moriarty, who was planning to steal Queen Victoria's jewels.

Coopersmith presented his book for the musical to the theatrical producer Alexander H. Cohen, who liked it and acquired the stage rights from the Conan Doyle estate in November 1961. The world premiere was planned for one year later.

When Cohen first made contact with the Conan Doyle estate it had refused to give him permission to use Conan Doyle's stories, since the American producer Kenneth Hyman had already been granted the exclusive rights to make a Sherlock Holmes musical. The estate had signed a contract with Hyman after Billy Wilder had decided not to do a Holmes musical after all. The novelist Richard Condon, author of *The Manchurian Candidate*, wrote the book for Hyman—incidentally also a story with Irene Adler and Professor Moriarty. Hyman had been in the Holmes business before—he had previously acquired the rights to *The Hound of the Baskervilles* and suggested to United Artists that they should coproduce a movie of it with Hammer Films. They had accepted and made the film with Peter Cushing as Holmes.

Not having permission didn't stop Cohen. He continued to prepare for his musical, which was to be called *Baker Street*, but when his plans were announced in the *New York Times* in the spring of 1961, the estate reacted immediately, threatening to institute a suit to stop the musical. Such litigation would unfortunately also involve and hold up Hyman for a time. Hyman, however, seemed to have lost interest, and Cohen got his contract. Both Henry E. Lester and René de Chochor found Jerome Coopersmith's work of excellent quality.

Meanwhile, Hyman had not at all lost interest. He was of the opinion that Sherlock Holmes was in the public domain, and he sought a $5 million policy trust from Lloyd's insuring himself against damages from a possible lawsuit. In the end, however, nothing came of his musical plans.

Cohen and the estate agreed that certain changes were needed in the proposed book of the *Baker Street* musical and, after both parties listened to an audition, that a substantial portion of the music and lyrics would have to be rewritten; probably, this would require engaging a new composer and lyricist. It was stated in the contract that the estate should be consulted in advance with respect to all changes in the book, music, and lyrics, and also all artistic decisions. Lester represented the estate in all matters. He sent Cohen a list of actors he approved to perform the role of Sherlock Holmes: Sir Laurence Olivier, Sir Michael Redgrave, Sir Alec Guinness, Trevor Howard, and Christopher Plummer—the last, Plummer, got to read the manuscript. Christopher Lee was interested but was not considered famous enough. The producer also tried to get Gregory Peck or Peter O'Toole for the role.

Furthermore, Lester had detailed ideas for some new numbers to be written, to replace inferior songs. He also suggested that the production should make use of all the colorful and amusing Victorian-era props possible, especially of the sort that had not already been used in the musical *My Fair Lady*. For background about these things he suggested a newly published book, *In the Footsteps of Sherlock Holmes*, by Michael Harrison, and he gave Cohen a copy of Michael and Mollie Hardwick's *Sherlock Holmes Companion*.

During this period of all the correspondence between the Conan Doyle estate and the producer Cohen—and in the midst of the preparation of the CCC film *Sherlock Holmes und das Halsband des Todes*—there were dramatic goings-on with the estate. Lester and Adrian fell out, after a few months of disagreement and hard words, and Lester was forced to leave his position as representative for the estate. Two months later, however, when he and Adrian had solved the problems in their business relationship, he was reinstated.

At the end of 1962, the parties to the musical agreed with the original composers that a pair of new composers should rewrite the entire score. The book was also revised—though partly, Lester felt at least, for the worse.

In 1963 Rex Harrison became extremely interested in playing the role of Holmes. He had had a successful run playing Professor Higgins in *My Fair Lady* on Broadway in 1956, as well as in the film version, and had been poised to play the detective when Billy Wilder had been planning a Holmes musical.

Suddenly, one day, Harrison let it be known he was no longer interested. Cohen sent a cable to Lester: "Rex Harrison's refusal to further consider *Baker Street* is directly attributable to your stupidly ill-timed announcement of Wilder's film."

Having lost Harrison, Cohen wrote to Lester a few days later: "If I'm lucky now, I may be able to get Fritz Weaver to do this role. That would save our apples. He opens next week as the star of the musical version of *Around the World in 80 Days*."

Cohen *was* lucky, and finally had his detective: Fritz Weaver was chosen to play Sherlock Holmes.

The show had been delayed—and for each year the producer had postponed it he was forced to pay an additional $5,000 in advance to the Conan Doyle estate—but finally it was getting close to the premiere. Cohen just had some preparations to take care of, to make people talk about Sherlock Holmes again, particularly the musical *Baker Street*.

In one of his many letters to Cohen, Lester revealed, "We are going to do a 50-minute Sherlock Holmes TV series with BBC."

Enter Douglas Wilmer. An experienced British television actor, he had landed the role of Sherlock Holmes in the BBC's new series, having previously played the detective in a pilot episode.

The BBC had negotiated with Lester, whose preferred option was a coproduction with an American television company. The BBC was afraid that such a collaboration would heavily involve Lester in its production, and that his involvement would spell disaster. The less influence Lester held, the better. Lester had also informed the network that Adrian Conan Doyle would prefer to see scriptwriters Michael and Mollie Hardwick involved in the creation of the series. In an amendment to the contract Adrian added that his and John Dickson Carr's Holmes stories should be among those available for adaptation.

The BBC could adapt anything except the three short stories that were being used for the *Baker Street* musical and *The Hound of the Baskervilles*, which was still under license to Hammer Films. The most important thing for the estate was that a fidelity to the original stories be kept—a demand the estate always seemed to have regarding BBC productions, but seldom when other companies, especially American ones, made adaptations or wrote totally new scripts.

The BBC had a long tradition of Sherlock Holmes adaptations, primarily on the radio rather than television. Since 1952, Carleton Hobbs and Norman Shelley had been—for British listeners—the voices of Holmes and Watson, respectively. Other actors, such as Sir John Gielgud, had also been heard as Holmes, but Hobbs and Shelley had more or less made the roles their own. Just as had been the case in America in the 1930s and 1940s, the detective's popularity in England was thanks to radio.

The radio series had begun as part of *Children's Hour* on the BBC Home Service. The Sherlock Holmes stories were increasingly going the same way as many other literary classics—they were seen as children's stories. For the last decade, however, the series had been broadcast for adults. So now it was time for a television series. The BBC did what was the normal thing to do when Henry E. Lester started making demands on behalf of his employer—in this case on the matter of the Hardwicks' involvement. It chose to ignore them.

Douglas Wilmer was not altogether happy with how he had played the detective in the BBC's pilot episode earlier that year. He had been too smooth, too urbane, too civilized. Having been given a second chance, he wanted to portray a more primitive, inconsiderate man. Holmes should not be the typical Victorian gentleman—that was not how Conan Doyle had described him, Wilmer felt.

Wilmer had plenty to say about the script for the television series. It always arrived late, often just days before the shoot—nowhere near the three weeks in advance he had demanded. Once in hand, many of the scripts were in a terrible state, so Wilmer rewrote them, often working into the small hours. His character had to be as sharp as a knife, precise in all his utterances; otherwise the whole thing fell apart. Six different writers had been involved in the episodes, but nobody in the production team had bothered to smooth out these scriptwriters' varying styles and vocabulary. The number of directors was greater still, and half of them were fresh from the BBC's director-training program. Some of them had no idea how they might re-create the Victorian era. The BBC was highlighting the nation's literary classics in their original environments, so there would be no updating, no bringing the stories to the modern day. Based on the behavior of the drama department's employees, however, it seemed almost as though the series was more about fleshing out the schedule than anything else. Wilmer was almost alone in taking the whole thing seriously.

When Wilmer thought that things couldn't get any worse, he began reading the script for the episode entitled "The Red-Headed League." The scriptwriter wanted, quite seriously, to begin the episode by showing the bank director in bed with his mistress, improper images on the walls, and a comic policeman, who would climb first in, then out of, the window.

Douglas Wilmer called the production managers. "I do not have the smallest intention of appearing in such drivel," he said.

Panic bubbled up among the producers. "But we start rehearsing next week."

"Not with me, you won't," he told them. "It's found a suitable home: in the waste-paper basket. You can tell the script editor to get off his arse, have a good look at Doyle, and just copy out the excellent dialogue, as written."

For once, Wilmer did not have to do the work himself. The script was rewritten, and the result was satisfactory.

Some critics felt that Douglas Wilmer had made Holmes far too arrogant and unsympathetic. That, however, was how he saw the character. This was not to be some sanitized version, but more like Conan Doyle's intention. Holmes was a thoroughly unsentimental character in a most sentimental era.

*   *   *

It was the most mysterious casting assignment of the Broadway season. The producer Alexander H. Cohen had put out a call for an actor
whose main qualification would be a close physical resemblance to
Fritz Weaver, the performer who had been chosen to play Sherlock
Holmes in Cohen's musical.

Two months later, on December 18, 1964, the American bookdealer
Lew D. Feldman paid $12,600 at auction in London for the original hand-
written manuscript of "The Greek Interpreter," the Sherlock Holmes
story in which Mycroft Holmes is introduced for the first time. It had
been sold by a member of the Woolworth family. Feldman had been
acting on behalf of Adrian Conan Doyle. Never before had anyone
paid so much for a short-story manuscript by any author.

The newspapers wrote about this extraordinary event and reported
as well that the manuscript, according to Adrian Conan Doyle, would
be exhibited in New York at the Broadway Theater for the opening of
the musical *Baker Street* in February.

The premiere was getting closer, and the Fritz Weaver double, wearing a deerstalker, was turning up here and there around town, drawing
stares. When that scheme grew tame, Cohen ordered the actor to
unexpectedly stroll across the stages of other shows in performance.

Above the marquee of the Broadway Theater rose a $40,000 mechan-
ical sign with a number of moving cartoon figures, including a man
who climbed up the wall only to be clobbered on the head by a woman
in a window.

A sudden impulse inspired Cohen to dash over to Paris and persuade Richard Burton to make a recording of one of the show's songs
and Elizabeth Taylor to make another. The first five bars of Burton's
song—which became a commercial hit—were also used as a radio plug
for the musical.

In the theater lobby, an array of memorabilia, insured for more
than $75,000, was displayed in six locked cases. Among the forty items
the theatergoers could see were copies of *Beeton's Christmas Annual*
from 1887 and the extremely rare 1888 *A Study in Scarlet* with Charles
Altamont Doyle's illustrations. The highlights of the exhibition were
the original manuscripts of "A Scandal in Bohemia" and "The Greek
Interpreter."

For Cohen, promotion was the thing, and his productions were spectacles rather than run-of-the-mill shows. He was a man who piped champagne into the water coolers just because it would be the talk of the town. If a musical didn't thrill the critics, he would just ramp up the promotion.

In the end, the *Baker Street* musical, which had had record advance sales of $1 million, had a respectable run of 311 performances and was nominated for three Tony Awards, winning one of them.

72

In the beginning of June 1965, Dame Jean Conan Doyle was finally to marry, at age fifty-two. She had been made a dame in 1963, in recognition of her career in the Royal Air Force. Her husband-to-be was Air Vice Marshal Sir Geoffrey Bromet, and she was to become Lady Bromet. Her brother had come from his home in Geneva to give her away.

Adrian was in the oak-paneled coffee room of Brown's Hotel in Mayfair talking to a journalist. He had good reasons to do so, because next year looked as if it would be the best year ever for the Conan Doyle estate in terms of royalties, and he knew how to use the press. Tall, slim, and elegant in his gray suit, with a south-of-France tan and a red carnation, Adrian would have had a perfect Sherlock Holmes profile had he smoked a pipe instead of a cigar. During his London stay he had taken the opportunity to do some advising on the script of the new Holmes film with John Neville as Holmes and Donald Houston as Watson.

"They were going to call the film *A Study in Terror*," he told the journalist. "What a foolhardy title. *Fog*, I said, is much better. So *Fog* it is."

Previously, the American horror-movie producer Herman Cohen (no relation to the musical producer Alexander) had come for a visit to the set of a Compton Films production in England. He brought with him a German, who spoke impeccable English and was elegantly dressed, handsome, charming, and erudite, though slightly arrogant and pompous. His name was Henry E. Lester. They had come to meet the producer, Tony Tenser, and they wanted to ask him only one thing: "Would you be interested in doing a Sherlock Holmes movie?"

Tenser thought about it for a while. He was not interested in making one of the old stories. He wanted to do something new, more in line with the kind of movies he used to make—with horror, nudity, and violence.

"Yes," he answered. He did want to do a Sherlock Holmes movie. "I will think about how we can do it."

"Can you do a *Black Torment* on Conan Doyle?" Tony Tenser asked the two screenwriters, brothers Derek and Donald Ford, who had come to his office at Compton Films. *The Black Torment* was a gothic horror film the brothers had scripted recently.

Tenser even had a great idea of what the movie could be about. "The fictitious Sherlock Holmes is at the same period as the real Jack the Ripper," Tenser continued. "So why not have Sherlock Holmes discovering who Jack the Ripper was?"

Had Tony Tenser come up with the idea of combining Holmes and Jack the Ripper? No, it had come from the Ford brothers, the screen-writers. The American producer Herman Cohen was sure about that. And Tony Tenser and his business partner, Michael Klinger, had already been thinking about doing a Sherlock Holmes film when Cohen dis-cussed it with them.

Did he say the Ford brothers? Sorry, Herman Cohen corrected himself. It was actually he, Cohen, who had come up with the Jack the Ripper idea. By the way, Lester had talked to Tenser and Klinger in London, and Cohen had not been involved in that at all—which meant there had been no meeting during the shooting of that other Compton film.

Tenser? The Ford brothers? Cohen? Henry E. Lester knew the whole prehistory of the film. Sherlock Holmes and Jack the Ripper had already been the theme for the planned sequel to *Sherlock Holmes und das Hals-band des Todes*. And the title *Fog* had already existed in May 1963 when Sir Nigel Films had been founded and the newspapers reported on its future projects. In those notices, the filming of *Fog* was said to be starting in June the same year.

If there was administrative chaos concerning this new film project, it was no more than Lester was used to.

The Ford brothers got the screen credit for having written the film, but they didn't write it. Another writer, whom Adrian and Lester liked very much, was hired to do that.

James Hill got the screen credit for having directed the film, but he wasn't on the set much of the time. Quite often he just disappeared, and nobody knew where he went or what he did.

Adrian Conan Doyle thought the film was going to be called *Fog*, but it wasn't, except as an alternative title in some countries. The head of advertising at Columbia Pictures had come up with the title *A Study in Terror*, alluding to *A Study in Scarlet*.

Henry E. Lester, on the other hand, was satisfied. He had wanted John Neville, one of England's leading classical actors, for Holmes in Cohen's musical, and this time Neville did land the role. Lester also had a lot to say regarding the script. "Oh, no, no," he would insist, on numerous occasions. "Sherlock Holmes wouldn't do that!" The script was changed accordingly. Lester had moved to London, so he was close at hand for the filming. The reason he had relocated from New York was that Sir Nigel Films needed him to live in the United Kingdom in order to comply with the rules for the British film quota system, which applied to the films the company coproduced.

Sherlockians feared the worst. A film about Holmes and Jack the Ripper, made by the nudie-girlie company Compton?

Tony Howlett, one of the founders of the Sherlock Holmes Society of London, wrote in the *Sherlock Holmes Journal*: "What a surprise it is to welcome a really good Sherlock Holmes film." He thought it the best Holmes film to have been made since Basil Rathbone's *Hound of the Baskervilles* in 1939. "Quite outstanding is the manner in which the period atmosphere has been authentically captured and superbly photographed in restrained color. Never before have we had a Holmes film that really got the feel of the age as this one does." Howlett found Neville's portrayal one of the best ever done, and at long last there was a credible Watson, played by the Welsh actor Donald Houston. "Some Holmesians," Howlett concluded, "may take me to task for praising this bloodcurdling film so highly. I don't care. I am quite unrepentant. I loved every moment of it."

*   *   *

The big hit on American television at the time was *Batman*. So when *A Study in Terror* was shown in the United States, the promotional posters had copy completely different from those that had accompanied the film's British release. "Here comes the original caped crusader!" the American poster read, "POW! BIFF! AIEEE! BANG! CRUNCH!"

73

IN CHICAGO, THE seventy-three-year-old actor Basil Rathbone stepped into the WGN-TV studio.

Two decades earlier he had decided to run away from Sherlock Holmes, only to find that he was running in circles, and after each complete turn he saw that the detective stood there waiting for him, beckoning him to return. In the end Rathbone had given up and given in.

He had even written to the producer Alexander H. Cohen and asked whether the *Baker Street* musical could be of interest to him and Ouida. "It's a tempting thought," Basil wrote. The producer had replied that it had been written for the younger Holmes, and it was a singing lead.

The return of Sherlock Holmes was something that had kept on happening ever since the 1940s, whether Basil Rathbone was willing or unwilling. Not that he thought that it was all predestined, but there were things in life—and death—that couldn't be explained. He had a lot of experience in the occult and extrasensory perception, or ESP. A long time ago, after a dinner with Adrian Conan Doyle, Adrian had asked Rathbone if he wanted to speak with Adrian's father. Rathbone had been interested. "You have to come and live at my house for six months," said Adrian, "and become completely acclimated to all the necessary conditions before you are allowed to make contact." Rathbone unfortunately had not had the six months to spare, but he wished he had.

He sat down in front of the camera.

The detective was returning to him, like a ghost from the past. The whole series of Universal's fourteen Sherlock Holmes films was to be broadcast biweekly, all of them with introductions, bridges, and a variety of commentary by the actor playing the leading part, Basil Rathbone.

He could close his eyes and see the sets before him. The Victorian times, the World War II sets, and the pieces of scenery representing the other subgenres his Holmes films had passed through. He could close his eyes and get a *feeling* of Holmes.

Now it was time to produce those 107 segments.

74

Janry 5, 1968, was a bitterly cold winter's day in New York. At Cavanagh's Restaurant, preparations were under way for the Baker Street Irregulars' annual dinner. Since Edgar W. Smith's death in 1960, the society had been led single-handedly—though with the advice of a few others—by Julian Wolff, who was also the editor of the *Baker Street Journal*. The group's founder, Christopher Morley, had died in 1957, but his old traditions lived on. Toasts were still raised to characters from the Holmes stories, Sherlockian speeches were given, and the announcement of the names of the select handful of men to be admitted to the leading Sherlock Holmes society was still observed as a special moment. The average age of the men was rather high, although there were exceptions. A young Canadian, Christopher Redmond, had been just sixteen years old when he had been invested as a member in the BSI two years before, and he was at the center of a nascent movement of young people with an interest in all things Holmes. Most of them, however, would have to wait to be elected to the society.

Dinnertime was approaching. The members were starting to arrive. On the pavement outside they were met by something quite unexpected. Six female college students, all still in their teens, were marching up and down in front of the restaurant. Dressed in animal-patterned fake furs, miniskirts, fishnet stockings, and high heels—apart from the one hobbling about on crutches—they paraded with the banners they had prepared in their hotel room a short while earlier. The messages were clear: "We want in!" "BSI unfair to women." "Let us in from the cold." They were shivering and really did want to be let in from the freezing cold. They soldiered on.

Passersby stared at the women, and many of the BSI's older members cast surprised glances in their direction, while the restaurant's staff kept an eye on them. At one point the protesters saw a well-built policeman heading toward them. The leader of the group, Evelyn Herzog, was sent forward to represent them.

"If you want us to leave, we'll leave!" she said.

"You wouldn't stop people from entering the restaurant, would you?"

No, they said, they would not.

"Good enough," he said, and then walked away.

The protest had started back at a Catholic women's college in Connecticut. Evelyn Herzog and her friends had been discussing Sherlock Holmes stories at length; they thought this was a very good reason to get together and socialize. Herzog contacted the BSI to apply for membership, but that, it turned out, was not possible. The *Baker Street Journal* had, however, mentioned a Holmes pastiche that she had written for the college newspaper; that snippet had, in turn, prompted a funeral director from Oklahoma to try everything possible to make contact with the Dominican sisters who ran the school in order to get hold of a copy—he was a truly steadfast collector. The young women had then began writing to him. He was the funniest man ever to have set foot in the undertaking business and, from what they could gather, a leading Sherlockian expert. When it came to their college, he was of the opinion that it was so Catholic that if you were not a virgin when you arrived then you were sure to be one by the time you left.

Herzog and her group also became friends with William S. Baring-Gould, the BSI member who had written the Sherlock Holmes biography that had become a minor success in the early 1960s. When the women got to know him, he was busy working on an annotated edition of the Sherlock Holmes stories. Each of the BSI members was given an alias—a name or phrase from the Holmes stories called an investiture. Baring-Gould's alias was "Gloria Scott," the name of a ship featured in the title of one of the short stories. When Herzog and her friends wrote to him, they called him Gloria.

Their friendship with Baring-Gould did not last long. He died just a few months later, at age fifty-four, and never got to witness the publication of his magnum opus, in two large volumes, *The Annotated Sherlock Holmes*.

By then the women had acquired a taste for the Sherlockian world, and they wanted more. They decided to travel to New York in January and do what people their age did: demonstrate. So there they were, out on the pavement, freezing.

Up in the dining room, BSI leader Julian Wolff was red in the face. He took the portly Oklahoman undertaker, whose name was John Bennett Shaw, to one side.

"Shaw," Wolff hissed, "your goddamn girls are down there. Do something!"

Shaw headed down the steps, taking his younger friend Peter E. Blau, who had also exchanged letters with the young women, and approached Herzog and her friends, who were still outside in the ice-cold January evening.

"Come into the downstairs bar," Shaw said, "and we will buy you drinks."

It was just as much fun talking Sherlock Holmes with the young ladies as it was with the BSI members upstairs.

A manifesto was composed on a paper bag. The demonstration had not been held for these women's own sake; they simply wanted the BSI to be able to invite women who actually deserved the honor to join as members. Shaw took the short manifesto with him when he returned to the dinner upstairs.

He read it aloud.

It was greeted with silence. The Baker Street Irregulars were not ready for such a radical change in their traditions.

It was 8:00 a.m. on May 1, 1968. On a cliff edge by the Reichenbach Falls in Switzerland, a deerstalker-capped Briton—Sir Paul Gore-Booth, permanent undersecretary of state at the Foreign Office—was engaged in a deadly struggle with Professor Moriarty. After a while they took a break from their struggles, before it was time for another fight. A whole succession of news teams wanted pictures of the historic moment.

The Sherlock Holmes Society of London had flown to Switzerland on a weeklong pilgrimage during which the members dressed around the clock in Victorian clothing to represent various characters from the tales of Sherlock Holmes and Dr. Watson.

Among the members was Tony Howlett, who as a young lawyer had been a constant presence during the preparations for the Holmes exhibition of 1951. The following year Howlett had married Freda Pearce, the Marylebone library assistant from whom he had been unable to wrest his gaze. Howlett—now wearing his Mycroft Holmes disguise—had, along with the Swiss tourist board, arranged the whole tour, which meant he was responsible for ensuring that things went smoothly and for keeping the forty travelers and attendant media in line. Freda's old colleague Jack Thorne was also there, as Merridew, the character "of abominable memory," plucked from "The Empty House."

Thorne was asked to sneak around behind fountains or slip into cars' trunks while the television crew was filming. He was supposed to be a villain, after all.

The place was crawling with people in historical costumes. Michael and Mollie Hardwick posed as the Grand Duke and Duchess from "A Scandal in Bohemia." The society's chairman, Sir Paul Gore-Booth, and his wife were costumed as Sherlock Holmes and Irene Adler. Sir Paul, however, had some commitments from which he could not escape at the start of the trip, so Tony Howlett had had to play the detective until he arrived, just to keep the photographers happy.

On its arrival at Geneva Airport, the party had been spectacularly welcomed, with great fanfare, and the same treatment had followed it throughout the trip. Even on the flight down, the members had given interviews to journalists of various nationalities. The journalists themselves were also obliged to dress in Victorian attire. The tourist board made sure that the traveling party rode around in old horse-drawn carriages or classic motorcars as much as possible. Flag-waving children and folk-dancing troupes met the party. The event was generating huge publicity throughout the world.

During the first evening's banquet Irene Adler's jewels were "stolen," and Swiss television and radio audiences were able to assist in solving the mystery.

One day the group visited the Château de Lucens. The castle's medieval keep towered above them. The serpentine road from the village up to the castle had taken them past a scattering of houses and sheds, but for the most part they were surrounded by nature. Spring had come a lot further here than back home in England. It was practically summer already.

In front of the castle was a red sports car, a Lamborghini Miura. The lord of the manor had been a motorcar enthusiast from a very young age. He emerged to greet them in the courtyard, a tall, slim, elegant gentleman in a gray suit. In a suitable display of chivalry, he kissed each of the ladies on the hand. His hands gesticulated wildly as he spoke.

The castle was home to the Sir Arthur Conan Doyle Foundation, and the man in the suit was the author's youngest son, Adrian Conan Doyle.

75

"ADRIAN CONAN DOYLE is a very difficult person to deal with," said Henry E. Lester to the man sitting before him. "He is addle-headed and I am the only one who can hold the reins on him. I control him and he will do what I say."

They were seated in Lester's London home at Eaton Place. A prominent Los Angeles attorney had come to visit him.

The attorney represented Princess Nina, and he wanted to know all about Lester's involvement in the Sir Nigel Films project to produce a film based on Conan Doyle's two volumes of Brigadier Gerard stories, coproduced by Lester's old friend Gene Gutowski. It seemed that Lester was going to earn a lot of money, and the estate would get a very much smaller portion of the income.

"It is only due to my ability," Lester said, "that the estate will be able to make any money at all out of the two works, which have lain idle for some seventy years until I saw their possibilities, resurrected them, and worked on them."

Lester had for a long time been irritated by Nina's constant harassment. Everything was going well with Sir Nigel Films, and no extra supervision was necessary, at least not by "a third-class heir," as he had defined her. He was not going to let her or anyone else stop him from making the deal for the new movie. All these actions just made his life hard; working with Adrian was complicated enough.

"He is so difficult to deal with," said Lester, "that, at one time, for a period of some four or five months he and I did not speak to each other.

"Adrian Conan Doyle," Lester continued, "is living in a castle in Switzerland surrounded by the mementos of his father whom he venerates, and he is content to leave the motion picture, television, radio, stage, and other activities of the estate completely in my hands."

And in those hands so much of the Sherlock Holmes business had
been laid during the whole of the 1960s.

With Sir Nigel Films, Adrian had intended to ensure that he was coproducer of the films, which would give him more influence over their
content. He really did not approve of the way Denis had handled those
Universal films during the 1940s. Denis had been too relaxed, and the
results had been, according to Adrian, disastrous.

Unfortunately, things had not turned out as Adrian intended. However much he edited the scripts—especially for the Brigadier Gerard
film—his coproducer did not adhere to his changes. The payments
were not all that significant, either. It was several years before the
films began to turn a profit, and sometimes there were no payments
at all to the coproducers. The old licenses had been more lucrative
than being a coproducer.

As a result of Nina's complaints against Adrian, it was decided that
the heirs would employ a well-known Swiss company, Fides Union
Fiduciaire, to act as a trustee of the estate alongside Adrian. Nina's
debt to Adrian and Jean was significantly reduced and then completely
cleared. Adrian's shares in Sir Nigel Films were compulsorily purchased
by the estate, which meant that both Jean and Nina were represented
on the board.

By then, however, Adrian's mind was elsewhere. With the help of
the authorities in the Swiss canton of Vaud, he had been given access
to the castle in the village of Lucens and had established a foundation
in his father's name.

And now, on April 28, 1968, he stood greeting the Sherlock Holmes
folks in the courtyard. Adrian could tolerate the British society much
better than he endured its American counterpart. Its members paid
homage not only to the detective but also to his creator. The editor
of the society's magazine, the *Sherlock Holmes Journal*, was Lord Donegall, who happened to be an acquaintance of Adrian's and lived not
far from Lucens. The Sherlock Holmes Society of London was thus
most welcome.

Adrian took the members into the castle, allowing them a glimpse
of Holmes and Watson's sitting room. It was a fairly exact replica of
the room featured in the 1951 exhibition. The famous room itself had
been relocated from New York to the Sherlock Holmes, a newly opened

London pub on Northumberland Street, just south of Trafalgar Square, where the public could see it.

The castle visit provided excellent photo opportunities for the assembled press when two members of the Holmes society, dressed as Holmes and Watson, settled into the easy chairs by the room's fireplace. Adrian needed all the publicity he could get. The Sherlock Holmes–related parts of the château were open to the public and run along the lines of a museum.

The so-called manuscript room, where he stored his father's documents, was locked. Precisely what belonged to Adrian and what was owned by the foundation was somewhat fluid, since there had never been a full inventory of the contents. Via an intermediary, Adrian had spent two years negotiating with the University of Texas, hoping that it would buy the entire foundation, including the castle (to which he did not have title); the exhibited papers and objects; and his own comprehensive collection of weapons, armor, and instruments of torture. The university had been interested mainly in his father's old letters and original manuscripts. Adrian had wanted $1 million for the lot. Of course, nothing could be permanently removed from the foundation, but if the university were to borrow items for, say, forty years at a time, this would circumvent the rules that the canton had insisted upon.

But then some useless so-and-so at the canton offices had written a warning letter to the university, which had withdrawn in fright at the news that Adrian's ownership of the castle could be called into question. Through his intermediary—manuscript dealer Lew D. Feldman in New York—Adrian hoped to find another buyer for his father's documents, on condition that the deal ensured a personal payment of at least half a million dollars directly to Adrian himself. The foundation was not to be involved. All he needed to do was simply adjust things so that foundation property was transferred to his private belongings. That was one of the benefits of having no inventory.

Aʟᴍᴏsᴛ ꜰɪꜰᴛᴇᴇɴ ᴍɪʟʟɪᴏɴ Britons were glued to their screens each Monday evening during the autumn of 1968, watching Peter Cushing play the detective and Nigel Stock his companion, Dr. Watson.

One of the viewers was Peter Cushing. He was suffering. This was not like watching his performances in the Hammer horror films or in anything else he had appeared in over his long career. He could not convince himself that the man on his screen was Peter Cushing as Sherlock Holmes. The only thing on his mind was the image of Peter Cushing trying to remember his lines.

The television series was his worst nightmare.

When planning the 1968 programs, the BBC had made contact with Douglas Wilmer, wondering whether he might consider making a second series. Because of budget constraints, however, the rehearsal time for each hour-long episode would be cut from fourteen days to ten.

"It cannot be done," was his reply. "Or at any rate, not by me."

The BBC wanted to go ahead with the series anyway, since it had paid a large sum for the rights and wanted to exploit them a little further. It also attempted to get John Neville. Neville's theater commitments were unfortunately difficult to fit with the TV series' schedule.

The new series was to have quite a different style from its predecessor. It was to be harder and sharper edged, dripping with suspense, mysteries, and Victorian violence, each episode a thriller with macabre, almost gothic overtones. The crimes, preferably, would have some sexual element. With all this in mind, the choice of Peter Cushing to play the lead seemed appropriate. He had played Sherlock Holmes before, in Hammer Films' 1959 version of *The Hound of the*

Baskervilles, and had been involved in many of the company's gothic horror pictures.

All signs pointed to an exceptional television series. It would not merely rely on standard studio techniques; 90 percent was to be shot with real film cameras on location.

The production began with the recording of the two-part episode *The Hound of the Baskervilles*. By the time the cast and crew returned to the BBC they had gone more than £13,000 over budget. The BBC's drama department could not stand for this. The producer was to be fired. The original script editor had left during the recording of the first episode, and his replacement had to take care of the production work too. The BBC realized that it would cost too much to fire the producer, so he was allowed to stay on, although the other crew members were instructed not to listen to him.

The budget had to be kept, so the scripts were all rewritten to enable most of the scenes to be recorded in the studio instead of shot, as planned, on location. One of the stories was too expensive to record at all, and an entirely different script was inserted at the last minute instead.

Peter Cushing was horrified. He was a friendly, sympathetic soul who rarely caused problems for those around him, but the chaotic shoots and the accelerated tempo almost pushed him over the edge. He hardly had time to breathe, let alone learn his lines. He was also very wary regarding what one should or should not do to Conan Doyle's texts. He was a great admirer of the Holmes stories and kept a careful eye out during the filming to be sure the script felt true to the originals. He had even taken three months off ahead of filming in order to scan the fifteen scripts for any faults or errors. This would be the perfect Sherlock Holmes series, and he would be the perfect Sherlock Holmes. He wanted it all to resemble a living Sidney Paget illustration.

The viewers had no idea of what was going on behind the scenes. What they saw was a pleasant and innocently harmless TV series—there was no sign of the gothic overtones or sexually charged crime that had been proposed early on. Peter Cushing was good in his portrayal, and nothing of his own worries shone through. The series was well received by many viewers, and the BBC contemplated another sequel—this time with brand-new stories. They had, however, turned down the chance to make televised versions of Adrian Conan Doyle's and John Dickson Carr's short stories. Adrian got his own back by forbidding the BBC to create any plots of its own.

Peter Cushing, meanwhile, decided that he would never again record an entire television series. He said to his friend Douglas Wilmer that he would rather sweep Paddington Station for a living than go through it again.

77

IT WAS EARLY September 1969, and Adrian was visiting Pinewood Studios outside London to see how work was progressing on the film he was coproducing. Shooting of *The Private Life of Sherlock Holmes* had been under way for a few months.

He had been annoyed when Billy Wilder gave him the script so late that he had scarcely had time to check it before filming started. He got over it fairly quickly, however, and was pretty pleased with Wilder's work, especially when he was invited to watch a few selected scenes. Wilder was a master of slightly cerebral comedy and had a mantel full of Oscars at home. The Holmes picture wasn't going to be a comedy as such but neither was it a serious film.

Plans for such a film had been around throughout most of the 1960s. The production team had held off for a while, hoping that Peter O'Toole might become free to play Sherlock Holmes to Peter Sellers's Dr. Watson. Any thoughts of Sellers's participation came abruptly to an end after his near-fatal heart attack during the filming of Wilder's film *Kiss Me, Stupid*, which led him to publicly say some really nasty things about the director. In the end, the Holmes and Watson roles went to lesser-known actors, because Wilder had come to feel that famous faces might distract cinema audiences from the impression his wished to give.

Adrian walked among the sets and looked around the 221b sitting room. It felt like home. This was his father's work—a work without end. Adrian had every reason to feel proud. Every detail mentioned in the stories had been reproduced in the sitting room. Billy Wilder was an extremely diligent filmmaker and had found several of the artifacts himself while trawling through antique shops.

Adrian spoke to Robert Stephens, who was playing the detective and at that moment was wearing a dressing gown. Outside, Adrian inspected Baker Street as it was in the 1890s. The set designer had spent four months and £80,000 of the film's budget on re-creating a 150-yard stretch of the road. Everything was perfect, even up close. Not merely sets, these were practically real houses.

Adrian couldn't fail to enjoy going back in time. The 1960s weren't really for him, aside from the fast cars, of course. He longed for a bygone age of gentlemen and chivalry.

One of the actors, Christopher Lee, had been involved in Sherlock Holmes productions several times before. The role of Sherlock Holmes's brother, Mycroft, was supposed to have been played by another actor, but he had fallen ill, and Lee stood in. Tall and thin, Lee was quite a departure from Conan Doyle's description in the original stories of Mycroft as a rather portly gentleman.

Wilder had based the plot on four separate episodes, arranging them like four movements of a symphony. The whole script actually took its tempo from a particular piece of music, Miklós Rózsa's Violin Concerto, Op. 24. This was in no way an ordinary Sherlock Holmes film. This was an analytical study of Holmes's personality, a film that sought to get to the bottom of his drug abuse and his aversion to women. It presented a very human Holmes. It also turned the spotlight on Holmes's friendship with Dr. Watson, who was played by Colin Blakely. Wilder had actually wanted to go even further, making the detective homosexual and using that as the explanation for his addiction, but the director had chosen a middle way, leaving Holmes's sexual preference open to speculation instead.

The Private Life of Sherlock Holmes was Billy Wilder's pride and joy. It was to be the most important film of his life. He was a perfectionist, and the demands he made on the actors were extremely high. Every line was to be delivered exactly as it was written. He watched Robert Stephens like a hawk. When Stephens did not appear sufficiently emaciated for the role, Wilder insisted that he lose yet more weight.

It was to be a long film, up to three or perhaps even four hours, and would be shown with an intermission in cinemas. The four episodes took a lot of energy, time, and money to shoot. Apart from Baker Street, the production team had built a model of an ocean liner so large that it did not fit in the studio's huge tank but was instead shipped over to the Isle of Wight and launched there. They built a mechanical Loch Ness monster that was to be featured in the film, but it sank to the bottom of the loch during its maiden voyage. The night of the Loch Ness shoot, the actors sat in front of the television set at their little hotel in Inverness to watch the first human set foot on the moon.

The £10 million budget was soon exceeded, and the schedule did not hold, either. Robert Stephens suffered a nervous breakdown after filming in Scotland, and everything was put on hold for ten days while he recovered. The film company, Mirisch, kept a close eye on each stage of the filming but did not understand the movie and worried that the whole thing would turn into a fiasco. It started making demands of Wilder and insisted that the film be shortened, so as not to scare off potential audiences. Wilder saw no way out other than to start hacking at his own creation. Each edit was like a knife to the chest. He saw how the greatness of the piece trickled away, how his symphony fell apart. He started cutting the most bizarre moments. The first and third episodes—"The Case of the Upside-Down Room" and "The Dreadful Business of the Naked Honeymooners" (with attendant ocean liner)— were cut out altogether, even though the material had already been filmed. Several other long tranches were removed at the same time. In the end, the length came in at a shade over two hours.

Robert Stephens's portrayal of Sherlock Holmes was complex. It showed a man struggling to keep others at arm's length, who endeavored not to reveal his own feelings. Yet reveal his feelings was precisely what he did. Yes, he teased Watson, but it was obvious that he was both very fond of his companion and rather dependent on him.

In one of the deleted scenes, Billy Wilder gave an explanation as to why Holmes refused to speak of the women in his life. It was a flashback to long-ago events in Oxford, where Holmes fell in love with a woman who, it turned out, worked as a prostitute. Afterward, Holmes never trusted any woman, yet he still managed to get duped in the film. The leading female character got him to drop his guard, and he walked into a trap and was thus shown to be naïve by his meddling older brother, Mycroft. Toward the end of the film, Holmes found solace in cocaine. This was a romantic and nuanced portrait of the detective, typical of Wilder and reflecting social change in the wider world. It was, however, a mutilated masterpiece, the biggest creative failure in Billy Wilder's career to date, and it hit him hard.

Robert Stephens was not rewarded with the boost in stature that Billy Wilder had promised him, but for the actor who played Mycroft it was a high point. *The Private Life of Sherlock Holmes* meant much to Christopher Lee's career.

After the premiere, on October 28, 1970, cinema audiences were not interested in the film, in spite of the praise of several critics who judged it to be one of the best films of the year. Very few people seemed to realize that this was not a Sherlock Holmes film but rather a film about Sherlock Holmes. For the first time, Holmes had become a really credible figure, and Colin Blakely had portrayed an equally realistic Watson. It was a modern way of presenting Conan Doyle's creation.

His son Adrian, though, never got to see the completed film. He had died suddenly, at the age of fifty-nine, in his castle in Switzerland.

On the desk of Henry E. Lester's suite in Park Lane, London, lay a film script. It was a revised draft of something called *Elementary, My Dear Watson*, written by John Haggarty and Gene Gutowski. The two of them had worked together on *The Adventures of Gerard*, the 1970 movie based on Conan Doyle's short stories about Brigadier Gerard.

One hundred and thirty-three pages, punch-bound between covers with Sherlockian images, the draft was copyrighted by Compton–Sir Nigel Films Ltd. Compton was the company that had produced *A Study in Terror*. Below the byline it said "in association with Henry E. Lester."

It started with Professor Moriarty in disguise—as Queen Victoria—at a Wild West show. There were numerous bizarre and close-call attempts by Moriarty to end the lives of Holmes and Watson. The plot involved Lenin and Trotsky, and in the final scene Moriarty attempted to escape to Russia in a hot-air balloon loaded with sacks of money.

It was the strangest Sherlock Holmes screenplay ever to have been written. Now, after Adrian's death, Sir Nigel Films faced an uncertain future, and *Elementary, My Dear Watson* was never to be made into a movie.

One thing, however, was certain. The 1970s had started, a new era in which anything was possible. Sherlock Holmes could go everywhere and do anything. The only limit was the imagination of the men and women who wanted to reshape the famous detective into a form that suited their purposes. With the eccentric Conan Doyle brothers out of the way, anything could happen.

Part 6

1971–1980

78

A LEGAL NOTICE was published in the business pages of the London
Times. As trustee of the estate of Sir Arthur Conan Doyle, the
Swiss firm Fides Union Fiduciaire made public its intention to sell off
the estate's assets. These included valuable copyrights; income from
current film, television, and radio contracts; and other items. Interested
parties should submit their bids within one month, by 4:00 p.m. on
May 7, 1971, at the latest, and should include a check for 2 percent of
the total value of the bid. The winning bid would be announced two
weeks later, at which point unsuccessful bidders would have their
deposits refunded.

After Adrian's death his wife, Anna; his sister, Jean; and his sister-
in-law, Nina, agreed to sell the estate. The trust company, however,
had not been interested in a sale. It wanted to continue exploiting the
rights. Nina then sued the company in order to obtain an audit that
would make clear what the estate actually contained and to bring
about a sale after that.

On the same day as the notice appeared in the Times, Nina submitted another writ, this time seeking to halt the sale. There was still no
inventory of what the estate comprised, or at least Fides didn't want
to provide it. Nor was there any reference to who owned the fifty-six
large cases full of Conan Doyle's original documents, which remained
in the possession of Adrian's middleman in New York, Lew D. Feldman.

The case was not resolved until January 1972; it was heard behind
closed doors to protect the interests of the bidding parties.

The copyright on Conan Doyle's works was due to expire in 1980, fifty
years after the author's death. This was the case in Britain and most
of the world, at least, though in America the copyright situation was
more tangled and ambiguous. Whoever bought the estate had only

eight years to exploit the rights in full. It had been calculated that one might expect an income of around £30,000 a year for the remainder of the period.

The best opening bid came from an international company that handled intellectual property rights on behalf of several successful authors, including Ian Fleming and Agatha Christie. Its bid was £175,000.

A bid was accepted, and the deal was made on January 25, 1972. A few days later the people concerned gathered at the Fides Union Fiduciaire offices in Geneva to go through letters and accounting ledgers. The buyer had borrowed from the Royal Bank of Scotland to finance the purchase. The bank's representative was present, as was the buyer's new literary agent, Jonathan Clowes.

The price had been a shade over £17,000 higher than the international company had bid. The contract was 747 pages long and covered all current contracts binding the estate. Jean and Anna weren't happy to learn the buyer's identity.

The assets of the estate had been purchased by Princess Nina Mdivani Harwood.

The first thing Nina did after the purchase was to move all the assets to her newly established company on the Isle of Man, Baskervilles Investments Ltd., while ensuring that the company itself would be run from Jersey. No unnecessary taxes would be paid in England.

The security for the loan was in three parts: First, and above all, was the copyright on Conan Doyle's works. Second was the land around Windlesham, which was about to be sold, including the gardener's cottage in which Denis and Nina at one time had planned to live when they moved back to England. Third were the pawnshop tickets for Nina's jewels, which valued them at £100,000. In addition, Nina's husband, Tony Harwood, was expecting a significant sum of money in the near future, as his wealthy father was very ill. So there was plenty of collateral.

Now the task at hand was to make Sherlock Holmes a source of income.

After Baskervilles Investments' first year in business, income was double what it had been when Fides and Adrian had been in charge. Literary agent Jonathan Clowes actively negotiated new contracts with publishers and film and television companies. In order to be able to offer a complete Holmes package, he had negotiated a repurchase of the rights to *A Study in Scarlet* on behalf of Baskervilles Investments. They had been in the hands of publishers Ward, Lock & Co. since 1886.

Clowes was also working on a whole range of projects that might lead to something in the future. One of those was to have a publisher produce new Sherlock Holmes paperbacks in the United Kingdom with fresh designs by contemporary graphic masters.

Furthermore, Salvador Dalí—who had been a close friend of Princess Nina's sister, Roussie—had agreed to illustrate a Christmas-themed book containing "Silver Blaze," "The Sussex Vampire," and "The Blue Carbuncle." Unfortunately it never resulted in a published book.

There also were plans to start publishing children's books, the first a Sherlock Holmes alphabet book. And there was to be a pub—a prototype concept that could be sold to other countries—serving Baskervilles Investments' own brands of whiskey, Worcestershire sauce, mustard, and so forth. Other food items, such as Mrs. Hudson's Christmas and Dundee cakes, were under study, and Holmes's toffees and Professor Challenger's science-fiction puzzle biscuits were being considered.

In January 1973, the Royal Shakespeare Company expressed an interest in staging William Gillette's old play *Sherlock Holmes*. Baskervilles Investments' view on this was expressed in an internal report: "The nature of the play, the strong trend to nostalgia, the strength of the RSC seem to make such a revival of the greatest possible interest now and Baskervilles will do all in its power to back it." The report concluded:

> It is essential to make use of all possible media to revive interest at any and all levels. Only by playing them all simultaneously will this be made to happen in such a way as to appear spontaneous when in fact it is the product of a sustained and very strenuous effort devoted to highly sophisticated planning in the field of literary economics.

Baskervilles Investments looked upon Sir Nigel Films' projects of the 1960s—*A Study in Terror*, *The Private Life of Sherlock Holmes*, and *The Adventures of Gerard*—as commercial disasters. Now the company invested money in a new film project that aimed to create something that would meet the needs of the under-thirty demographic. It was to be a highly commercial, low-cost, witty interpretation that would still maintain the Holmes tradition. The company had found a great team, and the prospects were extremely favorable. It would be a low-budget version of *The Hound of the Baskervilles*, made in association with the pop master Andy Warhol and his filmmaker, Paul Morrissey, who were at the moment making farcical films about Frankenstein and Dracula. After *Hound*, the plan was to have Warhol and Morrissey continue with films of *A Study in Scarlet*, *The Sign of Four*, and *The Valley of Fear*.

At the same time, Nina was trying to register "Sherlock Holmes" as a trademark, and in so doing secure the rights to sell licenses for the use of the character. She had bought the assets of Conan Doyle's literary estate with the intention of making large sums of money, which would enable her to sustain the lifestyle to which she had become accustomed. It was just a case of making sure the investment paid off.

The only problems were Nina's overdraft, the interest on the loan, and the fact that all her expenses had to be approved by the Royal Bank of Scotland. As well as Baskervilles Investments' loan, she had taken out a personal loan with the bank. The bank was keeping an eye on everything and did not allow just any old expenses. When she needed to travel long distances, necessitating the rental of a Rolls-Royce, the expenses were not permitted to exceed £2,000, which was to include the cost of a driver.

It wasn't easy being Princess Nina Mdivani Harwood.

79

O N MARCH 6, 1973, the scriptwriters of the Writers Guild of America went on strike. They demanded that the fee paid by television and film companies for an hour's worth of material be increased from $4,500 to $12,000. The TV producers didn't take the strike terribly seriously, since it began just after the scripts for the current season had been handed over. They wouldn't need next season's scripts for months. In April the dispute was extended to include live broadcasts and the soaps. It looked as if the conflict was going to last.

Outside the Goldwyn Studio in Hollywood, some scriptwriters were demonstrating. Among them was Nicholas Meyer. Three hours a day, four days a week, he held a placard against his shoulder and marched along the sidewalk in a giant oval. When he completed one oval, he would start the next lap.

Meyer was bored. When he wasn't demonstrating, he wasn't able to spend time writing scripts. What was he supposed to do? Just sit at home?

"Well, since you can't write screenplays," his girlfriend said, while washing the dishes, "now you've got ample time to write that novel you're always talking about."

He stood next to her, drying the plates and glasses. She was right. It was time to write that book.

Fifteen years earlier, when Nicholas Meyer was thirteen years old, inspired by the Broadway hit *My Fair Lady*, he had attempted to write a musical himself, about the detective on Baker Street. It had not gone too well, but it was his first foray into the world of Sherlock Holmes.

At high school a friend had once asked whether his father, a psychiatrist, was a Freudian. Nicholas had had no idea. So he had asked his father. He found out far more than he expected. His father had told him how he observed patients, how he noted the details about their clothes, how they moved, and how they spoke. These clues helped him establish why the patients were not as happy as they would like to be.

At this point Nicholas had said that this sounded rather like detective work.

"Very like detective work," his father conceded.

Years passed. The thought of his father, the psychiatrist, as a Sherlock Holmes–like figure remained. How much had Conan Doyle actually known about Sigmund Freud? Both were doctors. Both had connections with cocaine. Conan Doyle had had Sherlock Holmes use it, while Freud had written of its use as an anesthetic during eye surgery. And Conan Doyle had been an ophthalmologist—after having studied in Vienna, where Freud lived. It all made sense.

Nicholas Meyer began reading Sherlockian texts, the kind that treated Sherlock Holmes as a real person. He tracked down obscure pamphlets about Holmes and women, Holmes and music, and any number of conceivable combinations. His friends were perplexed. Why was he wasting his time on that kind of thing? He didn't have a good answer. All he knew was that he might, one day, write about a meeting between Sherlock Holmes and Sigmund Freud.

Meyer finished drying the dishes, and his thoughts became more focused. He sat down and started writing, using his portable Smith Corona electric typewriter. He had no plan, no framework for the plot. He just wrote. The introductory chapter was soon complete, and he began writing what was supposed to be Dr. Watson's description of events. Writing Watson's words on a typewriter just did not feel right. Meyer picked up his legal pad and started writing by hand instead. It slowed the tempo but improved the novel. In the evenings he would read what he had written to his girlfriend, before typing it all up and making further alterations. He pretended he was editing Dr. Watson's text, so he threw in the occasional footnote with a comment to that effect.

When he finished the book, Meyer felt, for the first time, that he had written something fit for publication. All that remained was to convince someone else that he had done just that.

80

In mid-August 1973, Nina's husband, Tony Harwood, was arrested at Heathrow Airport for currency smuggling. He was carrying more than £7,000 in cash at the time.

In the weeks leading up to Harwood's arrest, two large checks payable to Baskervilles Investments had gone missing. More than $20,000 was to be paid to the Royal Bank of Scotland's account. Harwood claimed not to have a clue where the checks could have gone.

He had also, via literary agent Jonathan Clowes, pressured a publisher into agreeing to a short-term loan of £8,000 by using future royalties as collateral.

He then promptly bought a Rolls-Royce.

At around the same time, the Royal Shakespeare Company started producing William Gillette's 1899 play *Sherlock Holmes*. Members of the company had expressed a desire to revive plays that were well on the way to being forgotten about. Not only that, they had an actor, John Wood, whose resemblance to a certain detective was striking.

It was to be the theater troupe's Christmas production. No one imagined it would be anything more than that.

Nicholas Meyer's novel, *The Seven-Per-Cent Solution,* was about how Dr. Watson lured Sherlock Holmes to Vienna, where the young Sigmund Freud attempted to cure the detective of his cocaine addiction. Drugs might have been in fashion at the time Meyer was trying to sell his novel, but when he made contact with his agent he was told that Sherlock Holmes most certainly was not. The agent did not even want to read the manuscript.

Meyer knew just a single person in the world of publishing. So he stuffed the manuscript into his briefcase and bought a ticket to New

York. When he got there, rain was coming down in sheets. He tracked down the large publishing house where his acquaintance worked.

"He doesn't work here anymore," the receptionist informed him.

Meyer realized that he ought to have phoned ahead before crossing the entire country.

"Is he still in the publishing business?" Meyer asked.

She said she thought he was, and gave him the address of another Manhattan publisher. He hurried off, leaving a puddle of rainwater in front of the sparkling counter in the reception area. By the time he finally caught up with his contact, he was wet through.

"Oh," said the publisher, when Meyer had taken off his soaking-wet raincoat and told him he had written a novel.

"What do you mean, 'Oh'?"

"This is a nonfiction house," his friend explained.

"Oh," said Meyer.

He went back to Hollywood. At a party he met a Los Angeles lawyer who was related to a literary agent; she fell in love with the book and found a suitable publisher. Before long, Meyer managed to convince the publisher to buy the rights to the manuscript.

There was only one catch. The publisher had to get the nod from the holders of the rights to Sherlock Holmes first.

More than two decades earlier, when Tony Harwood was twenty-five, he had taken an ocean liner to Europe with his friend James Merrill. Both were poets, and they had known each other since their school days. Merrill was the more successful of the two and was well on the way to being published. Harwood, meanwhile, was the more worldly-wise. He had spent a lot of time living abroad, but for the last year he had rented and furnished a loft apartment in Manhattan. Merrill had never heard of such living arrangements; this was something new.

Harwood was tall and slim, with an olive complexion; he wore colorful tweeds and scarves that dragged on the floor. His snobbery when it came to French porcelain and English furniture had been unbearable even when he was still in school, but he was somehow so bold that he seemed to stand apart from mundane things. Harwood was the sort of person normally found only in Evelyn Waugh novels.

The two poets arrived in Europe and hired a little black Citroën. Harwood had first use of the car; he would drive down to meet some friends in Spain, and then it would be Merrill's turn to use the car over the summer. Harwood had never got around to taking his driving test and it was only thanks to a stressed French bureaucrat mistaking his driving school enrollment for a license that he got hold of the necessary permits. With a healthy spin of the wheels, he was off.

Speeding along the European country roads was lovely. The landscape was different from back home, as were the people. Harwood later told Merrill about a little incident in some remote Spanish village on his journey southward. The car had just grazed a small child, and Harwood had been terribly shaken, but it turned out not to be too serious—he had watched in the rearview mirror as the child got up.

While Tony Harwood was in Spain, James Merrill continued around Europe on his own until his boyfriend, Claude, could no longer stand it at home in New York and made his way to France to be reunited with Merrill. Claude, who ran a book-printing company, had printed a posthumous text by Gertrude Stein a few years before, and had then started exchanging letters with Stein's partner, Alice B. Toklas. Hence, Merrill and Claude spent a lot of time with Toklas during their visit to Paris. Stein and Toklas had always been terribly fond of male couples, especially if they were in some way involved in the world of literature.

There was a message waiting for Merrill when he returned to the hotel after one of his visits to Toklas. According to the concierge it was from "la Princesse Canada." James dialed the number and was surprised when a familiar voice answered. It was Tony Harwood. His female companion, it turned out, was Princess Conan Doyle, which explained the concierge's mistake. Did Merrill want to eat dinner with them? Certainly.

They picked him up in a magnificent Bentley.

"It's a vulgar restaurant," Harwood said. "But Paris, too, has a vulgar streak."

Harwood was dressed in a tuxedo. Nina Conan Doyle wore a loosely cut gown of tangerine silk, made to measure by one of the more voguish Parisian fashion houses. She was overweight and wore too much makeup, including shocking red lipstick, and had steel-gray hair and large, expressive eyes.

"All my husbands have liked fat women," she said. "They do not want to go to bed with a pencil."

The enormous diamonds around her neck sparkled in harmony with the surface of the Seine. Merrill remarked that it was a truly extraordinary necklace.

"For you, darlings, for you!" Nina exclaimed. As far as she was concerned, clothes and jewelry were a statement—and as such they should be bold and dramatic. For years Nina had been involved in a struggle with Coco Chanel over her late sister Roussie's jewels. Chanel had visited Roussie's deathbed and had been alone with her for a short while. When she left the room, Chanel claimed that Roussie had briefly regained consciousness and insisted that Chanel take the jewelry from her bedside table. Chanel had then taken the lot and left.

The Parisian autumn evening was becoming night, and the dinner was almost over. Tony Harwood and Nina were about to leave France to join Nina's husband, Denis, in Ceylon. The three of them would then travel north, from maharaja to maharaja, all the way to the Himalayan foothills.

Harwood and Nina had first met in Paris. Nina fell for his poetry; it was so clean, so beautiful. They had spent the mornings shopping in all the swankiest stores. Nina then returned most of her purchases in the afternoons. Harwood was so preoccupied with Nina that he was no longer able to find the time to write poetry. In a shop selling leather articles, they were deep in conversation while Nina tested the flexibility of a riding whip. Suddenly it snapped in two.

Nina went over to the shop assistant, "Put it on my bill," she instructed, "and have it delivered to the hotel."

She linked arms with Harwood, twenty years her junior, and walked out of the shop to the chauffeur waiting outside.

It was then that Harwood realized he could not live without her. They were soul mates. A bond like theirs simply must not be broken. When they got to Ceylon, Nina would ask Denis for a divorce.

It wasn't until long after Harwood's trip to Spain that James Merrill heard about the driver of a black Citroën who had hit and killed a child in a remote village. He had not even stopped. Influential friends in Madrid had pulled a few strings to ensure that Tony Harwood could continue as before. It was as though he were a fictional character, with no responsibilities or duties except to entertain and to terrify.

★   ★   ★

Nicholas Meyer had no choice but to wait. The negotiations with Baskervilles Investments took time. The publication of his Holmes book was delayed.

Meanwhile, the editor at the publishing house wanted Meyer to modernize the language. Meyer would have none of it. It was important to retain precisely the wording that Conan Doyle would have used had he written the same story. Meyer had even included a handful of deliberate continuity errors and other mistakes to make the text resemble the originals even more closely.

In the middle of work on the book, the editor left his post to join a rival firm. Meyer's publisher now seemed completely uninterested in helping Meyer out of his copyright predicament.

An editor at Dutton, another publisher, approached him. A friend of theirs, who was a literary agent, had gotten her hands on a copy of the manuscript and passed it along to Dutton. The editor was keen to take it on, and started to make higher and higher bids to Meyer. The author hesitated, but in the end he said yes. Considering the complicated copyright situation that had arisen, the original publisher had no hesitation in agreeing to cancel the contract.

Discussions with Baskervilles Investments started again, from scratch. It took eight months of negotiations to establish exactly what proportion of the royalties would be payable to the company.

Derek Jarman was a director, artist, and performer in London's gay scene in the late 1960s. An American named Tony Harwood had taken him under his wing and become his mentor.

The American was always impeccably turned out. Silver wind jackets, black polo necks, velvet breeches, and court shoes with diamond buckles were his sartorial staples. His flat, with its view of London's rooftops, revealed his tastes. Its furnishings included a bed, a glass table with three Plexiglas-cube chairs, and a silver crystal vase containing a yellow iris. It was strictly shoes off inside, so no marks would be left on the carpets. Whichever way you looked, you saw your own reflection in the gray-tinted mirrored walls.

Tony Harwood traveled the globe with his wife, Princess Nina. Both of them were interested in theosophy, and wherever they went they were searching for occult knowledge.

Nina's eyesight was deteriorating, and Harwood had become her eyes on the world. They were now based at a London hotel, which was perfect for trips out to the countryside, where they would occasionally spend a weekend at the estate belonging to Nina's friend Barbara Cartland.

In the early 1950s, Nina had persuaded her then husband, Denis Conan Doyle, to employ Harwood as his secretary, which he had done for a few years. Denis usually did as Nina told him.

Harwood saw himself as an author. That was his trade. He wrote collections of poetry, which he then printed himself, and plays that were never staged. He rented the flat for the purpose of having somewhere to work while Nina was at the hotel or out shopping. He would sit cross-legged on a silver cushion, typing away, with a cup of strong coffee beside him. The stereo played Maria Callas or Stravinsky and occasionally the Beatles or Lovin' Spoonful. Before returning to the hotel, he would make soup for Nina, which he transported in a plastic bag for her to eat in the hotel room.

At first Nina had no idea where Harwood's flat was, and this remained the case until she hired a private detective, who snooped around Harwood for a month, finding out exactly how he spent his days.

Harwood's protégé, Derek Jarman, had his own key to the flat, which he used as both a breathing space and a geographically perfect starting point for heading out into London's nightlife. Not only that, there was something that Jarman was desperate to have access to: a bathtub.

The flat also had another very important function. It was the place Harwood took his fleeting romantic partners. The younger they were, the more in love Harwood would be.

The audience at London's Aldwych Theatre one evening in spring 1974 was full of expectation as it waited for the performance to begin. The production of the play *Sherlock Holmes* by the Royal Shakespeare Company had become an unexpected success and was to continue in London until August. It was more than seventy years since its first West End staging, just a stone's throw away on the same street, at the Lyceum Theatre.

The whole production was excellent; it had been carefully built on Gillette's old methods of presenting the piece, but discreetly inserted details humorously brought the play into the modern era. Before the first act got under way, the cellist in the orchestra played a low and lugubrious melody. This continued until the curtain was raised and the thick London fog poured in from the wings.

It was at that point the audience realized it had in fact been listening to the theme music from the James Bond films.

At the Park Lane Hotel, New York, that same spring, Harwood was going through the mail. Nina was now effectively blind, and he took care of the day-to-day running of Baskervilles Investments. He read some of the letters aloud for her, but she did not need to hear everything. There were so many letters from the Royal Bank of Scotland, lawyers, and agents—all complaining about missing checks, overdrawn accounts, and loans in arrears. He kept working away, struggling to bring in yet more money to fund their lifestyle, and had recently been involved in the Royal Shakespeare Company's plans to bring its successful production to Broadway. Nina had approached Andy Warhol to do the sets, and he had been interested, but in the end it had come to nothing.

There were also new Sherlock Holmes books being written, the licensing fees for which provided welcome extra income for Harwood and Nina. The most important of these was Nicholas Meyer's novel, even if it had taken a long time to persuade him and his publisher to deliver as large a cut as possible of the royalties to Baskervilles Investments. The long delay had, however, the effect that everything regarding Meyer's novel and RSC's play now went according to Baskervilles Investments' internal plan—to put as many major Sherlock Holmes projects as possible on the market simultaneously.

Harwood had concluded that he and Nina required a monthly income of £3,000 in order to live a decent life. In addition to that, Harwood had other expenses of which Nina was not aware. He was busy furnishing a dream apartment in New York on behalf of his lover, a young lawyer named Robert. He had funded the swank yet Spartan interior—the dimmable lighting alone cost $5,000—by purloining a number of Nina's sapphires. What Robert's personal taste may have been was of no great significance.

81

Nicholas Meyer's editor at Dutton was Juris Jurjevics, who had been born in Latvia and had immigrated to the United States. Three weeks after returning from the war in Vietnam, Jurjevics had begun his publishing career in New York.

Jurjevics had had dealings with Meyer before, when Meyer had written a book about the making of the movie *Love Story*. It had been Jurjevics who had managed to persuade Meyer to go with Dutton, and he was absolutely convinced that *The Seven-Per-Cent Solution* had every chance of being a success. Slowly but surely he had built up enthusiasm for the book within the large publishing house. Before long, more than twenty colleagues in various departments had read it, and all were impressed.

The sales manager told Jurjevics about what had happened when he had shown the manuscript at a meeting of army reservists. Normally the participants at this gathering would not display any interest in what he was reading, but this time had been different. All of them had wanted to flip through the book. The sales manager was surprised. Was Sherlock Holmes still "in"? Oh, yes, several of those present told him; they had Conan Doyle's complete Sherlock Holmes stories on their bedside tables.

The sales manager not only recounted this to Jurjevics but sent carbon copies of his memo to all of the senior staff within the company. The enthusiasm spread as they began to realize that interest in Sherlock Holmes in all likelihood extended far beyond the members of the Sherlockian societies. The publishers hoped for sales in the region of twenty-five thousand copies, plus a decent contract with a paperback publisher. Such figures would represent fantastic success.

Jurjevics and his colleagues began doing some market research. It turned out that sales of Conan Doyle's Sherlock Holmes books had risen in recent years. A complete collection had even featured on the best-seller list just a year earlier. They also discovered that an old stage version of Sherlock Holmes had been a roaring success in London and was making its way to Broadway. This was the pivotal moment. They had no remaining doubts—this was a book they were going to give huge support to.

The advertising budget for the book was set at $20,000. A retired former head of publicity at Dutton, Elliott Graham, was brought in for a six-month assignment, during which he was to concentrate solely on promoting Meyer's book. The advertising campaign was sketched out. Subsidiary rights began to be sold—book-club licenses, serializations, television and film rights; there were plenty of areas where money could be made besides mere book sales. Fifteen hundred preview copies were printed and distributed at a big booksellers' convention in Washington, DC. Dutton's stand was filled with piles of *The Seven-Per-Cent Solution*.

Elliott Graham set about sending preview copies of the book to newspapers in all corners of the country, even though the book's release date—set for August 26, 1974—remained a long way off. He sent copies to a long list of members of the various Sherlockian societies. Nothing could inflate the prices of subsidiary rights as much as mentions in the local press. It was the sort of thing that impressed potential buyers.

The preview copies seemed to do the trick. Enthusiasm for the book spread to retailers, and the orders flowed in.

A number of Sherlockians wrote to Dutton offering to help spread the word about the book. Jurjevics told his colleague Graham that he had been in touch with a man in New Mexico named John Bennett Shaw, a former undertaker, bookseller, and oil prospector who was a significant collector of Sherlock Holmes material. "He's in touch with Sherlockians all over the world," Jurjevics explained, "and is sending us a helpful list."

Sherlockian magazines started publishing glowing reviews, and several members of the Baker Street Irregulars wrote about the book for their local newspapers.

The book's release was still weeks away, but the publisher decided to print an extra twenty-five thousand copies. Either they would sell out, or the company would be wading through books for the next few years.

On August 26, the book was in the shops. Dr. John H. Watson was credited as the author, and Nicholas Meyer as the editor. In the introduction Meyer explained how he had unearthed Watson's previously unpublished manuscript.

On September 15, the book made the *New York Times* best-seller list. The following week it had dropped off. The publishers were nervous. Was their investment about to fail? The reports from the retailers were good, however. Elliott Graham continued to distribute review copies, not only to regular critics but to anyone who might conceivably write about the book. The recipient of each copy also received a personal letter. At the time of its release, there had been only a few reviews, but shortly afterward there were more than two hundred in newspapers all over the country.

At the book's release, the advertising campaign got under way, with the slogan "Elementary, my dear Freud." In late September the book started climbing the *New York Times* best-seller list. Dutton ordered a third print run, of another twenty-five thousand copies. The more the publisher sold, the more it spent promoting the book. As soon as the marketing department saw that sales were good in a particular city, the book was supported with more advertising in that area, which made the book sell even more copies. Eventually *The Seven-Per-Cent Solution* became the second-best-selling book in the United States. It remained on the *New York Times* best-seller list for forty weeks.

In the summer of 1974, even before Nicholas Meyer's book was released, one could sense that another Sherlock Holmes boom was in the offing. Michael Harrison, who had written *In the Footsteps of Sherlock Holmes* in 1958, had returned with a new, successful guidebook to Sherlock Holmes's world, *The London of Sherlock Holmes*. Nonfiction books that treated the detective as a real person were no longer the preserve of obscure small presses but had recently, and in a short time, won a broader audience. The new regime in charge of Conan Doyle's copyright may have been anything but generous in its negotiations, but at least it had no problem with the Sherlockian world and saw no reason Sherlock Holmes could not take precedence over Conan Doyle.

The original stories were also selling well. William S. Baring-Gould's *Annotated Sherlock Holmes* had, since its publication in 1967, shortly after Baring-Gould's death, sold ninety thousand copies. And Doubleday's *Complete Sherlock Holmes* had sold 350,000 over the past twenty years, with forty thousand of those sales occurring in 1973 alone.

Nicholas Meyer was not the only one to use Conan Doyle's fictional world as the setting for a novel of his own. The English writer John Gardner planned to release his first Holmes-related book, *The Return of Moriarty*, just two months after Meyer's book. Gardner's project had started with a book club that wanted to release a novel about Professor Moriarty and had approached the copyright owners for permission. Once the rights were secured, the book club found an interested publisher. The only thing missing was an author. The publisher asked John Gardner. He accepted the offer, but was not interested in the kind of humorous book the club had had in mind. Instead, he produced a serious book about a Godfather-like criminal in late Victorian London.

Sherlock Holmes was back on everyone's lips. On November 12, 1974, it was time for the Royal Shakespeare Company's production of William Gillette's play to stage its premiere on Broadway. The return of the seventy-five-year-old drama had been widely covered in the American press. When the company brought the curtain down for the last time, the play had been performed 471 times in its yearlong Broadway run. It was a resounding success.

In Santa Fe, New Mexico, John Bennett Shaw fielded questions from journalists about the Holmes craze. "There was a great revival in 1951," Shaw said, "and a little one in the sixties, but this is the largest I've seen in forty years."

Holmes was back, in all manner of places. The detective appeared in advertisements, films, television, plays, and even the world of fashion. Houndstooth-patterned cloaks and deerstalker hats were all the rage once again. People could not get enough of Holmes.

A year later, a very long queue formed outside a New York City cinema. Was everyone there to see *Jaws*? A television crew was sent to the scene. This was so unusual that it even made the news. For it was no brand-new Hollywood blockbuster but in fact the 1939 version of *The Hound of the Baskervilles*, featuring Basil Rathbone and Nigel Bruce in the leading roles. The thirty-six-year-old black-and-white picture had drawn great audiences in cinemas across the country. The interest in Sherlock Holmes was insatiable.

And Nicholas Meyer's book went on to become an international success, selling more than two million copies.

82

No one wanted control of the Conan Doyle rights more than Mr. Montezuma Jones. Things had become rather complicated, and Mr. and Mrs. Montezuma Jones had barricaded themselves in an uptown hotel in Manhattan ever since. Those were, of course, not their real names.

Montezuma Jones—or, as he really was, Tony Harwood—launched Baskervilles Investments projects, negotiated, and did whatever else he could from the hotel room. He felt that he was constantly being obstructed. This was not too surprising, considering that he had been banned from all involvement in such matters two years earlier.

Interest had accumulated on the loan Nina had originally taken with the Royal Bank of Scotland in order to set up Baskervilles Investments and purchase the Conan Doyle estate, and she was unable to make any repayments. The checks she wrote for purchases of objets d'art and expensive dresses all bounced.

Baskervilles Investments' income was not as large as the bank had hoped. The outflows were much larger, above all the funds spent on legal representation. The bank declared that the security against the loan had not been all that secure after all. Tony Harwood's large inheritance from his wealthy father had been converted to a monthly stipend, despite the pleas Harwood made during the last months of his father's life.

Ultimately the situation deteriorated to the point that the bank appointed a receiver to run Baskervilles Investments. The man nominated, William G. Mackey, took control of the company's activities. No decisions were to be taken unless Mackey was consulted first. Anthony Harwood and Princess Nina Mdivani Conan Doyle Harwood were not to involve themselves in the running of the company under any circumstances. Mackey had permission to sell rights as he saw fit, in the best interests of the bank—or, if he deemed it the best course of action, to sell the whole enterprise to the highest bidder.

Nina sued the bank in an attempt to get rid of the official receiver, but without success. For two years she and Tony had tried to find another bank somewhere on the planet that was prepared to pay off their debt to the Royal Bank of Scotland, so that they could regain control of the Conan Doyle rights. There was no time to lose, since the copyright would lapse in four years, at which point the company would be worthless.

Tony became more and more frustrated. Mackey and his advisors were trashing the Sherlock Holmes brand, selling licenses to all sorts of people, with no regard to quality and often for a pittance. They had no knowledge of how best to extract the maximum possible from film companies and publishers. They did not understand the importance of timing and that sometimes you have to be patient and wait for the right moment.

While running the company—as Nina's mouthpiece, since he had lacked any statutory authority of his own—Tony had turned down an offer worth £10,000 to arrange a London run for a Sherlock Holmes musical, in the hope of a better offer. The bank had been furious at that. The same thing happened when he turned down other deals. It was all about timing, timing, and more timing. The bank did not understand such things.

Mackey just wanted to get everything over with as quickly as possible. It was all quick deals, bad results. Tony was not kept informed at all. The bank had forced him and Nina to begin parting with some of their most treasured possessions to make repayments on the loan, while Mackey knew full well that future deals would be able to clear the whole debt.

This was a Sherlock Holmes boom the like of which had never been seen before, and the loan ought to have been cleared at any moment. Gene Wilder had just premiered his comedy *The Adventure of Sherlock Holmes' Smarter Brother* to good reviews. At first the film company Twentieth Century Fox had thought that Wilder wanted to make a film version of Gillette's play. That would have meant that it already owned the rights, having purchased them in 1932 as the basis for the second Basil Rathbone film. A closer look at Wilder's script revealed this not to be the case, however, meaning that the studio would have to pay for a license. That could mean a substantial fee for the receiver handling Baskervilles Investments.

A film of Nicholas Meyer's novel *The Seven-Per-Cent Solution* was under way, bringing in yet more money to pay off the loan. Meyer himself was hard at work on another Sherlock Holmes novel, *The West End Horror*, partly in response to pressure from Dutton.

There also was the porn film *The Adventures of Surelick Holmes*—surely that company should also be paying for intellectual property rights?

The money ought by now to be cascading into Baskervilles Investments' coffers, but Mackey's bookkeeping showed only small deposits. Tony was simultaneously enraged, desperate, and depressed. He wrote letter after letter to the law firms, literary agents, and others who were involved in the great mess. He changed his own legal representation every time he felt he wasn't getting anywhere. The receiver for Baskervilles Investments constantly complained that the results were getting worse and worse because the money was rapidly swallowed up by legal fees, paid to lawyers attempting to clear up the mess that Tony had created.

To top it all, Tony had been forced to part with his beloved Rolls-Royce, and for less than it was worth. Hotel bills were piling up, as were threatening letters from senior management. He placed brown envelopes, unopened, in a drawer.

It was January 26, 1976. Tony Harwood was fifty years old. His world was upside down.

And then his heart stopped.

83

Theories about the true identity of Jack the Ripper had seen a revival in Britain in the 1970s. Long newspaper articles were published on the subject. The BBC had shown drama-documentaries about the bestial murders. Donald Rumbelow's book *The Complete Jack the Ripper* had become a best seller. One rumor held that the truth was somehow connected to leading figures of late nineteenth-century English society. In fact, it went so far as to claim that Prince Eddy—son of the future king Edward VII—was the murderer.

This material was too good not to make into a film. The ideas featured in the drama-documentaries could form the basis of the dramatization. The one to solve the mystery would be none other than the greatest detective of the age, Sherlock Holmes.

Actor Christopher Plummer, who had been a candidate for the role of the detective in the *Baker Street* musical, donned the deerstalker and the houndstooth cape. James Mason was Watson. Both played their characters in a way that suited 1970s thinking. Sherlock Holmes was no longer snobby and impersonal. He was passionate and caring, not reserved in the slightest, and even shed a tear as the film drew to a close. Sherlock Holmes had never cried on-screen before.

James Mason, meanwhile, followed the trend established in recent decades, portraying Watson as intelligent, sympathetic, and far more involved in the investigations themselves. The film as a whole made no attempt to portray the victims or the perpetrator in a flattering light, in contrast to the first Holmes film about Jack the Ripper, *A Study in Terror*, of 1965. It was important that it felt realistic.

The film, released in 1979, was called *Murder by Decree*. It made a widespread contribution to the new interest in conspiracy theories about Jack the Ripper.

★   ★   ★

The year before, there had been a new version of *The Hound of the Baskervilles* in cinemas, with Peter Cook as Holmes and Dudley Moore as Watson. The seeds of the production had been planted in the early 1970s, when Baskervilles Investments put money into a grand film venture—Andy Warhol and Paul Morrissey were to make a Holmes film, maybe a whole series. Very few of Baskervilles Investments' initial ideas were ever realized—especially after Nina's financial problems became critical—and for many years this project had been going nowhere.

It was Cook and Moore who had approached Morrissey. They had written a script for a Sherlock Holmes film based on one of their old TV sketches, and they wanted him to direct it. He was the kind of hip director who would be perfect for the film. Morrissey decided to rewrite the script, turning it into something that probably was closer to his original idea for a Holmes movie a few years previously. He added his own touches of humor, which were very much inspired by the Carry On films, the famous British series of low-budget comedies. Some of England's top comedians were hired to participate in the film.

The production that Nina, Tony Harwood, and Jonathan Clowes had once had such high hopes for turned out to be a catastrophe. The film was awful.

The Sherlock Holmes boom, which had been heralded by Nicholas Meyer's novel and the Royal Shakespeare Company's play, continued apace. Meyer was invited to write the script for the film version of his novel, in which Holmes was played by Nicol Williamson, Watson by Robert Duvall, and Professor Moriarty by none other than Sir Laurence Olivier.

Dutton was not alone among American publishers in issuing what were ostensibly recently discovered manuscripts by Dr. Watson. Every new Sherlock Holmes novel published was now introduced with the author's fictional account of how he or she had come across the manuscript. The quality was uneven. The most important thing was to cash in while the boom was still going and there was still money to be made. Buying a license was no problem, regardless of what one intended to publish. The rights were now under the auspices of a new company. Baskervilles Investments had been out of the picture for some time.

Following Tony Harwood's death in early 1976, Nina's situation had become hopeless. There was simply no way for her to repay the loan.

It was at this point that the fifty-three-year-old television producer Sheldon Reynolds stepped into the London office of Baskervilles Investments' receiver, William G. Mackey. In 1954 Reynolds's thirty-nine half-hour episodes about Sherlock Holmes had been a success in the United States. This time, instead of just securing a license to produce a new TV series, Reynolds went for something bigger. He intended to buy the whole company, including the rights to all of Conan Doyle's works.

Reynolds managed to negotiate the purchase; all he lacked was financing. Since he had no money of his own, he approached banks and private investors, but he had no luck. Just one week before the option was going to expire, the family of his wife stepped in. Hungarian-born, Andrea Reynolds was fifteen years younger than her husband. One of her mother's marriages had been to an heir to the Pfizer pharmaceuticals empire, and upon his death Andrea's mother had inherited a fortune.

On August 25, 1976, the Conan Doyle rights were transferred from Baskervilles Investments to Sheldon Reynolds. Andrea's mother paid some $200,000, and her first husband, Andrea's father, the Swiss banker André Milos, became the copyright owner. Sheldon and Andrea Reynolds managed the business from Sheldon's New York office, and he got a percentage of the profits, if there were any. There were just a few years left until the copyrights would expire altogether.

At about the same time, the United States had accepted international copyright law for new books; the rules were to go into effect on January 1, 1978. Some of the clauses in the new American legislation also affected older books. First, the length of the copyright term was extended: whereas it had once been possible to renew the original twenty-eight-year copyright term for only twenty-eight extra years, the renewal was extended to forty-seven years, giving copyright owners a possible total of seventy-five years of protection from the year of publication. Heirs of an author whose copyrights had been transferred and whose works were not in the public domain were given the possibility of reclaiming those copyrights and extending them, in what the law described as a "termination right." Spouses, children, or grandchildren were regarded as heirs, but no other relatives were, which meant there was only one person who could recapture the Conan Doyle copyright. The only surviving child was Conan Doyle's daughter Jean. Her half sister, Mary, had died in the summer of 1976 at the age of eighty-seven.

Dame Jean was aware of the changes in the US copyright law. She knew that she had the right to recapture US copyrights. Such a recapture could take effect after a two-year waiting period.

She hesitated. She had retired from a long career in the Royal Air Force but stayed active in several areas, particularly military service charities. Handling the Conan Doyle rights had never tempted her.

She thought about it during 1977–78, and then finally decided she couldn't decline to act the way the new US copyright act empowered her to. It would allow her to be true to her father's memory and what she thought her father and his work stood for. For the past several years she had seen how others, inside and outside the family, had handled the Conan Doyle rights—first her sister-in-law Nina and Nina's husband Tony Harwood, then the Royal Bank of Scotland, and most recently Sheldon Reynolds. Certainly Sherlock Holmes had become popular again during these years, but at what cost? Dame Jean definitely did not care for some of the uses to which her father's characters had been bent, and if she could put a stop to such pastiches as *Sherlock Holmes in Dallas* (a reexamination of the JFK assassination case, done by an immortal Sherlock Holmes) it would be worth it.

In early 1977 Dame Jean had made contact with the magazine *Baker Street Miscellanea* in order to put some things straight regarding a recently published Conan Doyle biography. The contributing editor responsible for the book reviews section was Jon L. Lellenberg, a member of the Baker Street Irregulars, who worked at the Pentagon. Dame Jean and Lellenberg later met each other in person in London, in the autumn of that year. Lellenberg offered to help her get an American copyright lawyer, Saul Cohen, another member of the BSI. Half a dozen other BSI members were also included in the preparations for the new era, forming a group dubbed the Friends of Dame Jean Conan Doyle. Dame Jean was more interested in quality control where her father's characters were concerned than in revenue, so she loved the idea of this support group, consisting of BSI members who had values equivalent to hers and who had abilities in various areas.

In November 1979 Cohen served a host of termination notices on previous licensees, including Sheldon Reynolds and his father-in-law, André Milos. In exactly two years' time Dame Jean would become owner of her father's remaining US copyrights.

"You standing or sitting?" asked the caller.

Film director Val Guest informed the person on the line that he was currently standing. "Well, sit," the caller instructed him. "Now, how would you like to make a Sherlock Holmes and Doctor Watson TV series in Warsaw?"

Warsaw? Behind the Iron Curtain? With the KGB sniffing around?

"It's a matter of foreign currency," the caller went on. "They need foreign currency desperately and this is one way they can get it."

Sheldon Reynolds was the one who had hatched the plan. Polish state television would provide the studio and the production team. Reynolds would bring the actors and the most important technicians. The shooting would start the following month. Time was very tight. It was now 1980, and the copyright was going to expire at the end of the year. Reynolds's plan was to create new works, which would have their own, longer, copyright terms.

Val Guest, along with Sheldon and Andrea Reynolds, took up residence in an American, undeniably capitalist, hotel in the center of the city. This was to be their home for the next four months.

Guest arrived at the studio at seven each morning. Costume director Andrea Reynolds, often looking as if she had stepped from a fashion spread from *Vogue*, would be ready to work. On the studio lot, a huge backdrop had been constructed to represent Baker Street. The Poles, armed only with photographs, had created something stunningly authentic, with hansom cabs and gas lanterns. Guest had the largest crew the film industry had seen since the filming of *Ben-Hur*. He was told that this was Communism. Unemployment could not exist. Wherever he went, along "Baker Street" or around the set, he was met by sellers of everything from caviar to Polish złotys.

Many of the scripts were recycled from the 1954 television series. Anthony Burgess, the author of *A Clockwork Orange*, was script consultant. With accomplished actors Geoffrey Whitehead and Donald Pickering as Holmes and Watson, it had the makings of a good series. Unfortunately, a number of things happened.

Whitehead had brought his family to avoid being away from them for half a year, and his wife was going to play some small parts in the series, but these plans had to be altered when her mother was killed in a car accident back home in England.

Pickering had accepted the role because it was an American TV company. He hoped that the series would never be shown in the United Kingdom. He also managed to fall out with Reynolds—they didn't talk for six months—and he couldn't stand Reynolds's wife.

Worst of all, Sheldon Reynolds became embroiled in a currency-exchange dispute with the Polish authorities. Andrea spent two days in custody, during which she was assaulted and forced to shower in scalding water, until Sheldon wired $30,000 to the prosecutor.

All the film negatives were confiscated, and all that Reynolds had to show for the effort was a single cutting copy of the series. He did manage to sell it in a handful of European countries, but not Britain. In the United States it was broadcast only on some small TV stations.

A few months later, the copyright expired in most of the world. Fifty years had passed since the author's death.

Part 7

1981–1997

84

THE BOY WAS about fourteen years of age; his task not at all complicated. He arrived at the house early in the morning, went straight
into the library, and picked up where he had left off the day before—
that gap on the second shelf, where he had pulled out a Sherlockian
anthology from the 1940s, or any of the other gems. He put the book
back and continued working from shelf to shelf, pulling books down,
flipping through them, or reading for hours. He felt it was like being
trapped on a desert island that he never wanted to leave. The house
was wonderfully quiet.

The telephone rang, and the boy sat down at the house owner's
desk—he loved to do that and pretend the collection was his. This was
his job for a couple of weeks every summer, answering the phone,
taking down messages, and collecting the mail, and all while he spent
time in the largest Sherlock Holmes collection in the world. He picked
up the receiver.

"John Bennett Shaw residence. Mitch Cullin speaking."

Santa Fe, New Mexico, in the early 1980s still felt like a small town. It
had fewer than fifty thousand inhabitants, though to that total could
be added all the tourists. Wealthy Texans and others came there for
vacations to look at the breathtaking scenery and the enchanting
azure sky, in which suddenly clouds could appear over the mountains
and produce the magical pink-looking rain that fell onto the scrubby
piñon trees.

Other tourists came there to walk around the historic downtown
and to delve into the rich supply of culture—Santa Fe had an unusual
number of artists and galleries for a city of its size. The architecture
had been regulated since the early twentieth century, and an ordinance
from the 1950s decreed that new houses had to reflect the traditional

flat-roofed adobe styles of the Pueblos or from the days of the New Mexico Territory.

Mitch Cullin lived, not in an adobe, but in an apartment with his father—a journalist, documentary filmmaker, gambler, and a bit of a hustler. His parents had divorced when Mitch was five, and he bounced back and forth between them so often that he didn't really have a chance to make many close friends. It didn't bother him, however, because the kids at school liked him anyway—even if he didn't feel he had much in common with them. When he got home in the afternoon he liked to keep to himself. His parents were avid readers, and he became an avid reader, too.

All those hours he spent in his bedroom, reading or listening to music, gave him time to redecorate as soon as he had a new interest. When he was twelve he had draped his stereo in a lacy doily and put an oil-burning lamp on top of it. The walls were covered with pictures of Basil Rathbone and other persons reminding him of a time long gone. Dressed in a robe, Mitch lounged in his big velvety chair, smoking a briar pipe with Prince Albert tobacco. His father peeked in through the door and nodded approvingly. Mitch had become immersed in the world of Sherlock Holmes.

On Sundays he watched reruns of the old Universal films with Basil Rathbone and Nigel Bruce. It was hard to accept that the old man introducing the films was Rathbone himself. Mitch taped the audio off the television with a cassette recorder so he could listen to it in bed at night, reimagining the scenes in his head. His weekly allowance was spent at a local grocery store where he found cassette tapes with radio shows from the 1950s, with John Gielgud as Sherlock Holmes and Ralph Richardson as Watson.

One afternoon Mitch's father came home from work and showed him an article in a local newspaper. It was about a Sherlockian scholar who had the largest Holmes collection in the world. Neither father nor son had heard about this extraordinary man, John Bennett Shaw, before. By pure coincidence, Shaw happened to live less than a mile away.

Twelve-year-old Mitch found Shaw's number in the phone book. He fetched the phone in the living room and stretched the cord to the dining-room table. He was nervous but at the same time excited. A woman answered and called Shaw to the phone.

He was the first Sherlockian Mitch had ever spoken to. In fact, Mitch hadn't realized that there were Sherlockians and Sherlock Holmes societies until he had read that article in the newspaper.

It was just a short phone call, but Shaw was cordial and friendly and suggested that Mitch should come over on the following Saturday to visit him and his library.

Mitch was ecstatic.

Mitch could have walked to Shaw's house. He loved to explore the area on foot, hiking through the endless arroyos that formed secret routes around the city. His father wanted to drop him off in the car, so along the Old Pecos Trail they went, before veering off into dirt roads that led them past piñon trees and juniper bushes. The brown adobes were all single story and low to the ground, and the vegetation was so scant and the expanse of land so vast that it felt as if there was more sky here than anywhere else. They stopped at 1917 Fort Union Drive. The house was not especially big, just a typical Santa Fe adobe.

John Bennett Shaw's wife, Dorothy, answered the door and led Mitch back to the library, where Shaw was sitting behind his desk. It had been a few days, spent in great excitement and anticipation, since the phone call, and maybe Mitch had expected things, but he had not anticipated that John Bennett Shaw would be so large. Shaw instantly reminded Mitch of Nero Wolfe. Shaw's hair was white and combed back, and his eyes betrayed a kind of sparkle that was disarming. He was almost seventy but didn't seem like an old man. He was funny, very funny; he laughed easily; and when he spoke to Mitch it was as if he were speaking to another adult. He showed the boy all kinds of things in his collection. There were many books in the library, all of them connected to Sherlock Holmes, and the collection held pretty much any other object on which the detective's face could be printed or applied. Mitch had a wonderful time. Shaw told him that he was welcome to stop by again, on another Saturday morning.

John Bennett Shaw said that he collected with the selectivity of a vacuum cleaner. He knew exactly what he was doing: assembling a massive collection of everything Sherlock Holmes in order to show Holmes's position in the world of popular culture. If Shaw heard of something

Sherlock, he had to have it, and generally people gave it to him. The majority of his collection was kept in another adobe, a large shed in the yard. That was also where he kept all his correspondence, because he needed a lot of space to store it.

For a whole generation of Sherlockians, no one was as important as Shaw. During recent years he had been going to universities all around the United States, giving popular three-day workshops on Sherlock Holmes, and he tried to encourage every attendee. His address could be found widely, and numerous people with an incipient interest in Sherlock Holmes wrote to him, wanting to know more about the detective, what organizations there were to join, and anything about the Sherlockian world, because that was what Shaw wanted people to do. He was the mainspring of the Sherlock Holmes universe and was eager to make sure that newcomers hooked up with others. If it was possible that one person could make the worldwide interest in Sherlock Holmes continue as well as grow, that person was John Bennett Shaw.

Ever since that first meeting, Mitch had visited Shaw at least three times a month. The older man became his mentor.

Dorothy Rowe Shaw was wonderful—a lovely, kind, and funny woman. She helped her husband in his collecting and was always look-ing for Sherlock Holmes–related things in all kinds of shops. Dorothy had built a beautiful miniature of 221b Baker Street, with all the correct furniture and all the details from Conan Doyle's stories. Sometimes the retired couple and the young teenager traveled together to film festi-vals or Sherlock Holmes seminars, but mostly John Bennett Shaw and Mitch spent the time in Shaw's library. Almost everything they talked about involved Sherlock Holmes. Mitch showed Shaw short stories and screenplays that he had begun to write, which often had a Holmes theme. The older man was always encouraging. He trusted Mitch and let him borrow books or anything else he wanted to study more closely. And he came up with the idea that Mitch should house-sit—or rather library-sit—when he and Dorothy were away on vacation.

Mitch hung up. The phone call had been from a Sherlockian who wanted to visit Shaw later that month. Mitch wrote down the message.

There were often visitors to the house, Sherlockian pilgrims who came from far and near. One day Shaw invited Mitch to join a dinner with an Englishman who had come to see him and his collections. The man had been there before, but Mitch had never met him. The Englishman was about thirty years old but looked younger, wore dark jeans, and carried a plastic shopping bag wherever he went. In the bag he kept a notebook. He was finishing his work on a huge Conan Doyle bibliography that he had coedited with another man. He had been traveling on sleeping buses from collector to collector to find the last details.

It was a golden evening for Mitch. The Englishman seemed shy at first, but when he relaxed he was terribly funny.

A long time ago Mitch had understood that John Bennett Shaw knew everything about Sherlock Holmes. This Englishman, Richard Lancelyn Green, however, knew even more.

85

A T THE AGE of sixty-nine, in November 1981, Dame Jean Conan
Doyle regained ownership of a long list of her father's works
published from 1907 to his death in 1930. The copyright applied only
to the United States, but this had consequences across the globe. As
soon as someone started a Sherlock Holmes production that might
conceivably be sold or shown in the United States, the initiator had
to take account of the fact that certain stories remained under
copyright.

There was a school of legal thought that argued that the copyright
applied not only to the stories but also to the characters that the series
was based on. The characters of Holmes and Watson themselves were
covered in this scenario. It was not a foregone conclusion, but it might
stand up in court.

Dame Jean was able to use this to influence the many pastiches that
were being published. She did not approve of all of them, although she
was by no means rabid in the way her brother Adrian had been. She
was a member of the Sherlock Holmes Society of London and appreciated the affection shown to her father's creation. She was a kindly
person, but one with quite particular opinions. For one, she thought
that a talented author ought to be able to invent his own characters.
There were far too many mediocre writers attempting to make a living
off the back of Sherlock Holmes.

She had sharply disapproved of the references to powerful society
figures in *Murder by Decree*. She definitely did not like *The Seven-Per-Cent
Solution*. What she really wanted was for people to read the original stories, for them to meet Sherlock Holmes as her father had created him.

Sheldon Reynolds tried hard to convince Dame Jean that he should
represent her in the United States. He had the experience from the
years when he had owned the rights. Dame Jean turned him down,

preferring to work with the BSI members who had helped her regain the rights. During the first two years the publisher and owner of Manhattan's Mysterious Bookshop, Otto Penzler—together with literary agent Nat Sobel, under the name Mysterious Literary Agency—handled the US rights, and after that Jon L. Lellenberg served as literary agent for Dame Jean.

The publishing and entertainment industries quickly acknowledged the new owner of the US Conan Doyle rights. The first deal was already in place at the time the recapture of the rights became effective in November 1981. The American film producer Sy Weintraub and his company Lorindy were planning a series of films based on the Holmes stories, to be filmed in England. During the 1960s Weintraub had produced a long series of Tarzan adventures, and he wanted to find another popular character around whom to make films.

Lorindy had approached Dame Jean's American lawyer in June 1981, and its representatives met her in her home in England in September. Lorindy wished to acquire the rights to all sixty stories and to turn at least six of them into feature-length films. They were to be shot for all markets—cinema, television, cable, and video.

Lorindy paid $45,000 for the rights, but for Dame Jean the price was not the big consideration.

"My great object is to see something of quality," she said. "To me the most important thing is to have some influence on my father's work."

What made things complicated was a letter that Dame Jean had received from a British television company, Granada.

86

THE SENIOR EXECUTIVES at Granada used to meet once a month to discuss future plans over dinner. Late one such evening the conversation turned to possible dramatizations. Producer Michael Cox mentioned that Conan Doyle's Sherlock Holmes stories were now free. It was the spring of 1981 and the UK copyright had expired. Wasn't it about time to make a television series? It had been many years since anyone had done so in Britain.

Granada had a proud tradition of adapting works by classic authors, such as Charles Dickens, Jane Austen, and H. G. Wells, to name but three. It had recently achieved international success with its version of Evelyn Waugh's *Brideshead Revisited*. That series had also set new standards for how to stage an expensive production and succeed in the United States as well as Britain.

A lot rested on the recording technology. Normally, outdoor scenes would be shot on film, while indoor shots would be recorded on ordinary tape. A whole day's filming outdoors might yield only three or four minutes of film, while recording in the studio, which allowed the use of several cameras at the same time and eliminated the need to adjust the lighting before each scene, could result in as much as twenty minutes of usable material from a day's shoot. It all came down to the budget. *Brideshead Revisited* had been shot entirely on film, which was what the Americans preferred. That meant that there was no visible difference in quality between indoor and outdoor scenes, and the series as a whole was vastly improved.

If Granada was going to make a Sherlock Holmes series, it would be of the same high quality as *Brideshead*. It would be the best Sherlock Holmes series ever. It would, however, take an advance sale to America to secure a larger production budget. The Granada folks also knew that the Americans would be picky about who played the leading role. There were two British actors in the frame: Jeremy Irons and Anthony Andrews, both of whom had had their breakthrough in *Brideshead*. Plucking just one of them from the cast of a successful production did not feel right. Michael Cox and his boss needed to find another English actor, someone the American viewers might have seen.

"Someone like Jeremy Brett," the manager said.

Jeremy Brett lived right under the Hollywood sign in Los Angeles. He was appearing in US television series and had occasionally been seen on the American stage. He had recently played Dr. Watson in a newly written Sherlock Holmes play. Most of his experience, though, had been in British theaters. He possessed the necessary attributes to play Holmes: the voice, the presence, the energy, and the posture of a gentleman. And he was a classically trained actor with many Shakespearean roles behind him. This was exactly the kind of actor they needed. Michael Cox and Granada's casting director began compiling a list of people like Jeremy Brett.

They never did find anyone who was like him on all fronts. The only remaining name, therefore, was Jeremy Brett's own. But would he be prepared to accept the role? A backward glance at those who had played Sherlock Holmes in the past revealed that those who had done so most successfully had failed to subsequently leave the role behind them.

There was one more problem with Jeremy Brett as Holmes. His wife was an executive producer at the same US network that was going to show the series, and she was very reluctant to mix her private and professional lives. After discussions with her colleagues, she was fortunately able to give a positive response. They did not want to stand in the way of such perfect casting.

It also emerged that Brett had decided that his Hollywood career had not been the success he had hoped for, and he was ready to return to his homeland. Even more important: while reading Conan Doyle's stories, Brett had discovered a character quite unlike the one he had expected, one that presented great opportunities for a skilled actor. He was positively eager to take on the role.

Thanks to the American sale, the budget was increased by 20 percent. This meant better casting in the minor roles, more horse-drawn carriages, better stunts, and more extras. It also meant that they could find and film in the perfect locations, even when that meant higher travel costs.

Granada wanted to re-create Baker Street, including commercial premises and other period features. The series would be a perfect re-creation of the 1890s, right down to the smallest details. There was space available for the erection of a length of road on old railway sidings behind the studio in Manchester. The company was prepared to invest a quarter of a million pounds on the street alone.

Michael Cox wanted to employ the best scriptwriters he could find and task them with faithfully adapting Conan Doyle's short stories for television. The whole Sherlockian scene of the 1970s had been one giant step away from the original adventures, and Cox longed to revive the author's vision.

And then Cox wrote to Dame Jean Conan Doyle, telling her of his plans. She was encouraging but careful to point out that there was a complicating factor. While her father's works were indeed free from copyright in England, if the series were to be shown in the United States, other rules would apply. The later stories were still under copyright. And she was negotiating with other companies, one of which sought exclusive US rights.

Michael Cox showed the letter to the people at Granada. They ignored it.

Granada's competitor, the American film company Lorindy, found a perfect Sherlock Holmes one cold January night in 1982. Weintraub had delegated some of the producing responsibilities to a British producer, who now sat at home on his sofa watching a BBC detective drama. The film was terrible, but the actor who played the police inspector—who attempted to emulate the methods of Sherlock Holmes—was good. The British producer turned to his wife and said, "That's our Holmes!"

The actor was Ian Richardson. He went to be interviewed for the part. For a moment the representatives of the American company were slightly dismayed—Richardson was much shorter than he had seemed in the BBC drama.

"I wore lifts," Richardson explained.

Sy Weintraub liked him and signed him for six films.

Everything went along perfectly until March, when Weintraub heard for the first time about Granada's plans to export its Sherlock Holmes television series to the United States. Weintraub's lawyer wrote to Granada and informed the company that Lorindy had exclusive US television rights to Sherlock Holmes. A distribution of Granada's series in the United States would violate those rights, and Weintraub threatened to sue the British television company if it marketed its series there. In a sort of reverse lawsuit, Granada sued Weintraub, Lorindy, and Dame Jean in the US District Court for the Southern District of New York—just to get the court to declare in advance whether Granada had the right to do as it wanted.

Weintraub was furious. He had paid a lot of money for the US rights, and there was a risk that Granada was going to get the same rights for free and steal his productions' thunder. This was all happening in the middle of the shooting of the first film, an adaptation of *The Sign of Four*, at the Shepperton Studios in Surrey. Picking up on the many intrigues going on in the background, the actors and the crew soon felt that something was wrong. As is often the case, the drivers who ferried around the cast and crew were the ones who seemed to know all about what was happening. Early in the mornings when they drove the cast to the studio they could tell them that a couple of the technical staff members had had to leave, and that Trevor Howard, who was a real star and was to play a cameo role, suddenly had been removed and replaced. One morning there was a rumor that Ian Richardson was to be dubbed, because he sounded too British, but fortunately that never happened. And there was almost a mutiny among the cast when the drivers claimed that the actor playing Dr. Watson was not going to get to play the part in the rest of the films.

The last rumor was true. A new actor played Watson when the second film, *The Hound of the Baskervilles*, was shot later that autumn. Since it was filmed on location at Dartmoor, the original Watson couldn't participate; he needed to be back in London every night to play in a revival of the musical *Guys and Dolls*.

Ian Richardson had prepared his role in detail. He had read all the stories and put together a file on all aspects of the detective's life—his habits, moods, sayings, clothes, and much more. He became a walking Sherlockian encyclopedia, and he edited the scripts so his lines would

be more true to the character and the books than the American phrases
he was supposed to say originally.

There were other things he couldn't stop. The Americans spent a
huge amount of money building a separate bedroom for Watson, to
explicitly show that he didn't share a bedroom with Holmes, in order
to avoid any suggestiveness.

"What are you worried about?" asked Richardson.

He also wanted to do more about Holmes's cocaine habit, but the
Americans wouldn't have it. One thing they did allow him was to smoke
a lot, as long as it was a meerschaum pipe.

"But Holmes smoked all sorts of pipes," said Richardson. "Briars,
clays—but not a monstrosity like a meerschaum!"

Weintraub just pointed to the pipe and said, "This is the image of
Sherlock Holmes. You will smoke a meerschaum."

The suit in New York went on and on. The first year the lawyers
concentrated on discussing whether a New York court was the correct venue for the suit. Lorindy was a Florida corporation, Weintraub
lived in California, and Dame Jean was in Kent, England. She had not
been to the United States since she had accompanied her father on a
lecture tour in 1923.

The following year the lawyers argued about whether the letters
that Lorindy's lawyer originally had sent to Granada were an "abuse
of copyright," for which Granada sought damages.

In November 1984 it was finally settled that it was OK to bring the
case in a New York court, which meant that Lorindy's lawyers could
now file an answer to Granada's complaint from 1982.

Eventually there was an out-of-court settlement for a huge sum of
money. Granada was allowed to distribute its TV series in the United
States, which meant that Weintraub and Lorindy saw no reason to
continue their own series. Weintraub was able to cover his production
costs for the two Sherlock Holmes films that had been released in 1983.
He even made a profit.

Meanwhile, Weintraub hadn't allowed Ian Richardson to go away
to play another role while the court case was pending, and Richardson
had lost out on the chance to play the emperor Joseph II in *Amadeus*;
this upset the actor terribly. In an odd sort of way, he heaved a sigh
of relief when Weintraub decided to make no more Sherlock Holmes

movies. Richardson didn't want to get too associated with the part of the detective.

He had nothing to fear regarding the two films they had already made. Nothing was made of the original plans for a theatrical release. They premiered in the United States on cable in late 1983 and were released on video in the United Kingdom the following year.

Michael Cox at Granada had never given up on his plans. The preparations had continued, even without the security of an American deal. The original stories were studied in detail. Every usable detail about Holmes and Watson was entered in a log. Clothes, mannerisms, opinions—it was all contained on the log's seventy pages. And it was 100 percent Conan Doyle.

An actor was chosen for the role of Dr. Watson: David Burke, whom Cox had worked with before and who enjoyed a successful career in the theater.

Shooting began in the summer of 1983, and anyone who might have had reservations about Jeremy Brett as Sherlock Holmes would soon be proved wrong. Brett turned out to be perfect for the role. He had exactly the same expectations for the project as Michael Cox had had all along. Wherever he went, Brett carried a complete edition of Conan Doyle's Holmes stories, which was full of underlining and notes. Brett was constantly comparing the TV script with the original. Everything had to be just right. The production team made sure that angles and scenography matched Sidney Paget's illustrations for the *Strand Magazine*. The deerstalker appeared only in the countryside scenes, as it would have in the 1890s. In town Holmes always stuck to the ordinary formal clothes expected of a Victorian gentleman.

Brett was generous in his praise for colleagues who did a good job, whether it was a case of a tricky camera move or an attractive light setting. He sent flowers when someone had something to celebrate. He kept tabs on everyone—whose car had just broken down, who had a sick child. Cox had heard in advance that Brett could be difficult to work with, but in this production Brett was loved and respected by all. In fact, the only time Brett became angry was when he himself failed to deliver a line exactly as he had intended. A few episodes into filming, Brett asked to be allowed more time to practice his lines and prepare himself ahead of the next episode. His request was granted.

Extending the shoot was expensive, but it allowed Brett to polish his interpretation of the role. It was an interpretation that drew on elements from Douglas Wilmer, with whom Brett had socialized back in the 1960s, as well as Christopher Plummer's more emotional big-screen detective. Above all, Jeremy Brett made the role of Sherlock Holmes his very own.

87

W HAT GRANADA WAS planning, and what Sy Weintraub had failed to do—to create a Sherlock Holmes series faithfully based on Conan Doyle's stories that would be loved by many millions of viewers—had already been done successfully, beginning in 1979, by another television company.

The director of that series, Igor Maslennikov, had not expected to be occupied with Sherlock Holmes films for several years of his life. He had tried to end the series on more than one occasion by making the "last" episode. Now he knew exactly what to expect every time he entered his Lenfilm office in Leningrad, where he was also the head of the creative division for television films. On his desk there were countless protest letters from the Soviet people. He read one of them:

> Comrade Maslennikov, I understand you are planning on finishing this series. It's unfair and unjust! You have no right to do that!!! If you started a thing, then do it until the very end! We are announcing to you that the audience will not rest until you film all the Memoirs of Sherlock Holmes. We will be sending letters to you until you give up and agree to continue working on the series. Comrade Maslennikov! Please understand this and stop torturing the audience with your merciless words "It's the last movie."

Igor Maslennikov looked at his desk. His other television plans had been postponed; his ideas and projects were piling up. All he was doing was continuing to work on the Sherlock Holmes films.

Soviet citizens loved England. For more than a century they had been fascinated with what they thought of as "Englishness," brought to them through Soviet filmmakers' versions of Shakespeare, Robin Hood,

Three Men in a Boat, *Ivanhoe*, Agatha Christie, Oscar Wilde, and George Bernard Shaw. Some films and TV series were also purchased from England, and in the early 1970s *The Forsyte Saga* had been very popular among viewers and had made its contribution to the Russian perception of good old England.

There had been Sherlock Holmes adaptations for Soviet television in the late 1960s and early 1970s, but nothing really memorable, and nothing that could fully satisfy the Sherlock Holmes–craving Soviet people. The stories had been enormously popular in printed form ever since they were first published in Russia in the 1890s, often just a few weeks after the original publication in England. For the Russians in the early twentieth century, Holmes was pronounced *Ghol'mz*, though this later changed to *Kholmes*.

In 1978 two screenwriters, Valery Frid and Yuly Dunsky, produced the script for a television film in their spare time. The two men had known each other since school; they had studied film together and later met again in the forced-labor camps of the Gulag, where they started writing scripts, always together. They knew all about friendship.

The film was, in translation, called *Sherlock Holmes and Dr. Watson*. From the title it was obvious that it would have an ingredient that had been missing from previous Russian Holmes productions. The screenwriters gave Dr. Watson a winning personality and concentrated on the friendship between him and Holmes. It was much less a drama or a crime story than a comedy.

They presented the script to Igor Maslennikov, who liked it. The state television broadcaster in the Soviet Union, Central Television, then ordered the Lenfilm studio to make a TV film of it.

Maslennikov knew from the beginning who should play Holmes. It was just a question of shaving the man clean and forcing him to tidy his hair.

No way, said the producers at the television company when they heard who Maslennikov had in mind.. "The man's one of the worst troublemakers in Moscow."

"But think of the Sherlock Holmes he will make!' said Maslennikov. There were so many things that coincided between this actor and the famous detective: the power of imagination, how both got carried away and excited, a sense of humor, the eccentricity, the self-important manner, their ability to fight back, their persistence of body and mind, an indomitable energy and enthusiasm. And do not forget the similar design of their skulls!

The actor's name was Vasily Livanov. His father had been an actor who had had a long career at the Moscow Art Theatre; an apprentice of Stanislavsky, he had once been described as the Russian Laurence Olivier. His mother, who was an artist, had worked with Vladimir Mayakovski. Their home often hosted Moscow's intellectual elite, such as Nobel Prize winner Boris Pasternak, sitting in a chair reading his latest creation to the family and their friends. As a boy Vasily Livanov had discovered Sherlock Holmes and had been so impressed that he had even written a fan letter to Conan Doyle. Born in 1935, young Vasily wasn't aware that Conan Doyle had been dead for many years by then.

Livanov studied to be an artist, but having finished art school he changed his mind and decided to be an actor. At twenty-four years old, he made his film debut. He played a geologist whose scenes were filmed during a cold Siberian winter storm; the director decided to record Livanov's voice live, outshouting the snowstorm. Livanov lost his voice for a couple of weeks. He had had a normal baritone, but when he was finally able to talk again, his voice had changed completely. It was hoarse. And it was to become his most important asset.

For many years Livanov was the voice behind some of the most popular Russian cartoon characters, such as Astrid Lindgren's Karlsson-on-the-Roof. And now he—and his voice—became famous and loved as Sherlock Holmes. Moscow traffic police even began to look indulgently upon him. If "Comrade Holmes" acted a bit rashly behind the wheel, it was probably just because he was racing toward yet another of his adventures.

The search for a Holmes was a quick one, mostly a matter of persuading the producers. Finding a Watson on the other hand was not easy at all. Finally they found Vitaly Solomin, an actor who had grown up in a wooden house in southeastern Siberia and had played mostly Russian heroes. However, with a red mustache, a starched collar, a tweed suit, a tie with a pin—and a stiff upper lip—he was utterly convincing as the young English military doctor. Subtle and warm, he brought a human dimension to the films, and many saw him as the true star of the series.

London also played a big role. The designers used photos from the Sherlock Holmes pub in London to re-create the interior of the sitting room at 221b Baker Street. Lenfilm's warehouses were full of furniture and objects that had been expropriated from the wealthy houses of Saint Petersburg during the revolution. The production got access to shooting locations at a number of beautiful places, such as a country villa that had belonged to Tsar Alexander II and the astonishing interior of the palace that became the House of Scientists social club. One important exterior—used when they shot the scenes on Baker Street—was found in Riga, and another was found in foggy Leningrad, where the river Neva was used for the steamboat chase in *The Sign of Four*. It was not exactly London, but neither did it have a Russian feel, thanks to clever camera angles.

The film team tried to be true to the original texts, but there were hindrances. "You have been in Afghanistan, I perceive," Sherlock Holmes says to Dr. Watson at their first meeting in *A Study in Scarlet*, so Livanov also said something like that in the first episode. When the Central Television staff evaluated the film before it could be broadcast, they reacted immediately. Soviet troops had just entered Afghanistan, and no references to that situation should be made. So "Afghanistan" became "the East."

Some things were incorrect in the Conan Doyle originals, so the film team felt they must correct them. The method a man employed to call his snake back—whistling—was changed to a tapping sound instead, since snakes can't hear but do rely on vibrations.

All the episodes were longer than an hour so that they could be called feature-length films and thereby get better financing. Two episodes, based on "The Speckled Band" and *A Study in Scarlet*, were broadcast in 1979; three more appeared the following year; and *The Hound of the Baskervilles* was shown in two parts in 1981.

The popularity of the series was so widespread that Sherlock Holmes and Dr. Watson even became part of Russian joke culture, the teller often mimicking the husky voice of Vasily Livanov.

Igor Maslennikov opened more letters requesting that the series continue. He found himself in a situation similar to what Conan Doyle had experienced. The tenacious grip of the detective had ensnared him too.

He kept asking himself, Why? What was the power of this fictional literary character? What was the charm of this hero of some short stories set in a past epoch and in a place so geographically far from the Soviet citizens? Was it because of his investigations? But nowadays they seemed naïve. His exploits? But he mostly sits in a chair, endlessly smoking a pipe and talking.

No, Maslennikov felt that the real reason was Holmes's attitude toward people. Those rooms on Baker Street imparted a feeling of comfort and stability and not only for Holmes and his faithful friend Watson. Every client could feel safe and secure within those walls, because Holmes was reliable. Sherlock Holmes was a defender of those who got into trouble. Conan Doyle had contrasted him with Scotland Yard in that Holmes was helping, not punishing.

Maslennikov was sure that this was the secret of the everlasting fascination of Sherlock Holmes—he was the living personification of loyalty and reliability, qualities that people always needed.

In Monte Carlo in February 1982, a big television festival was under way, and in the market section television companies from all over the world gathered to hawk their wares. In the Soviet stand a large, loud, and likable Russian was dispensing vodka to all and sundry and growling an invitation to take a look at his big new drama production. The man was Sherlock Holmes himself, Vasily Livanov. He was proud, because the festival magazine had published an article saying that the real Sherlock Holmes was a Soviet.

Someone had stopped at the stand, and Livanov invited him in. Although the series had been enormously popular for three years in the Soviet Union, it was practically unknown in the West. This was the first real chance for people from other countries to watch some scenes from one of the episodes. And if that wasn't enough, Livanov knew some other tricks too.

"Let us drink to Holmes," he said, pouring vodka into two glasses, "and Watson"—he raised his glass—"and even old Moriarty! *Na zdorovje!*"

Later that evening—it was the last day of the festival—the head of the British delegation approached the head of the Soviet delegation with a request. "I understand that your actor Livanov should sit with your delegation, but Sherlock Holmes should sit with us."

88

D URING THE SUMMER of 1984 the world's attention was turned to Los Angeles. The Summer Olympics were to start on July 28, and since early May the boycott of the games had grown. Fourteen Eastern bloc countries had announced their intention not to participate, citing security concerns and "chauvinistic sentiments and an anti-Soviet hysteria being whipped up in the United States." Most certainly it was also a reaction to what had happened in 1980, when US president Jimmy Carter had issued an ultimatum: if Soviet troops did not withdraw from Afghanistan within one month, the United States would boycott the Moscow Olympics. Soviet troops stayed where they were, and more than sixty countries stayed home from the games.

The opening ceremony in Los Angeles was a spectacular show. The composer and conductor John Williams's "Olympic Fanfare and Theme" may have raised a few goose bumps. A man flew into the Los Angeles Memorial Coliseum using a Bell Aircraft rocket pack, landing right in the center of his target circle.

"This is the most patriotic occasion I've ever attended," said producer-director Steven Spielberg when interviewed on TV. It had been a busy summer for Spielberg, who lived in Los Angeles. His latest film, *Indiana Jones and the Temple of Doom*, had opened at the end of May, and new films were being planned and produced. Michael Eisner, the president of Paramount Pictures, had sent him a screenplay to read.

Halfway through the script, Spielberg noticed something familiar. It was a reference to a film he had seen before. It called for a close-up of an adventurous young man, who is crawling through the darkness in a deserted structure. Next to him are his trusted companion, providing support and comic relief, and a beautiful young woman, to represent the love interest.

The camera pulls back. The three appear to be inside some ancient temple or pyramid. Some bizarre ritual is going on below them—mummies are carried by men with shaved heads, and certain doom is waiting.

Wait a second. A temple? Doom? An adventurous man, his trusted sidekick, and a pretty woman? Spielberg realized that he had directed the film, it was in the cinemas right now, and it was called *Indiana Jones and the Temple of Doom*.

The screenplay he was reading was for another film, by twenty-five-year-old writer Chris Columbus. Spielberg knew him, having executive-produced Columbus's script of *Gremlins* a few years earlier.

Columbus had got the idea for the film when reading some Dickens novels. He had become completely inspired by the romance of the Victorian period and had filled his screenplay, which was set in 1870, with Dickensian names like Waxflatter and Cragwitch, Badcock and Bobster, Snelgrove and Mrs. Dribb. Any references to Spielberg's movies were purely coincidental, said Columbus.

Spielberg had finished reading the script. He loved it, not only because of the homage to his own film. He called Eisner at Paramount and told him exactly what the studio chief wanted to hear. Spielberg would be delighted to be the executive producer of the movie *Young Sherlock Holmes*.

It was Friday, and John Bennett Shaw was looking forward to the week-end. It was time for a meeting of the Brothers Three of Moriarty.

The idea had come to Shaw in 1971, shortly after he and Dorothy had moved to Santa Fe. One of the first things he had noticed was the existence of a town called Moriarty one hour south of his new home. If there ever was a reason to found a Sherlockian society, this was it. He called it the Brothers Three of Moriarty, in honor of Professor James Moriarty and his two brothers, at least one of whom was also named James Moriarty. It had been proposed in Sherlockian circles that the third brother also had that name, since it would be silly for a mother to call only two of three sons James.

As its emblem the society used a cattle brand showing three J's (the middle one crooked, representing the evil professor). Shaw and his friends registered the brand officially with the state, as one does where cattle are raised. Moriarty, with its 750 inhabitants, was pure cattle country. The annual dinners had to take place on a Thursday—and the group chose the Thursday before Halloween. They were held at the Frontier Saloon in Moriarty, and the owner had explained that on Fridays and Saturdays the saloon was full of cowboys, and "if they discover there are people in the back room who can read, they'll shoot you."

On this summer day the annual meeting was still months away. A nice dinner with Sherlockian friends was the event of the weekend.

Suddenly something happened that threatened Shaw's plans. Steven Spielberg called. The two men had met before. Spielberg had a house in Santa Fe, and Shaw was the kind of person who knew a lot of people.

Would it be possible for Shaw to review a script? Spielberg was worried about its tone. Had Columbus really managed to capture the Victorian era and the proper Sherlock Holmes feeling? The movie was to be about an imaginary first meeting between Holmes and Watson when they were still young and solved a mystery together at a boarding school. The thing that was most important to Columbus was to explain why Holmes became so cold and calculating later in life, why he was alone for the rest of his days. Columbus let Holmes be a youngster ruled by emotions and fall deeply in love, and as a result of what happens in the film he becomes a different person.

And it should be noted that Shaw must review the script within two days.

Shaw tried to dodge the assignment. After all he had an important dinner to think about. Spielberg insisted, and said that he would charter a jet to fly the script from Los Angeles to Albuquerque on the same day, and then would have the cabby wait until Shaw had finished checking it.

Shaw accepted, and now he had another great anecdote to tell his friend Mitch, the youngest member of the Brothers Three of Moriarty.

Dame Jean Conan Doyle wasn't keen about the first draft of *Young Sherlock Holmes*. It was hideously bloodthirsty, full of inappropriate gore. This was meant to be a movie aimed first and foremost at young people. She would not permit this screenplay to be made into a movie.

Paramount executive Michael Eisner saw no other solution than to go to London and meet with Dame Jean.

★   ★   ★

Michael Eisner was doing everything he could to get this production going. Steven Spielberg, his executive producer, had hired the British best-selling author Jeffrey Archer to doctor the script, to anglicize it, and to rewrite some scenes to give it a more authentic feel. Archer had promised to have the script completed in four weeks, while at the same time he was touring the United States to promote his latest novel.

It was a strange time for Eisner. In early August he had been approached about another job—as the head of Walt Disney Productions. He felt that his own tastes and the Disney tradition would be a perfect match. While negotiating to leave Paramount, he was still making important decisions for the studio, as if he intended to stay.

Eisner arrived in London and took Dame Jean to lunch at the restaurant of her choice, the Connaught Hotel in Mayfair. He asked her what they needed to do to make the screenplay acceptable to her. She told him, and Paramount made the changes. The film could finally be made.

One September afternoon, just a few weeks after having officially started the production of *Young Sherlock Holmes*, and right in the middle of a big Hollywood shuffle in which three studios replaced their chief executives and numerous lower-level executives had shifted sides, Michael Eisner issued his statement of resignation.

It was the Thursday before Halloween. John Bennett Shaw and the Brothers Three of Moriarty were on their annual trip to Moriarty. When Mitch Cullin had joined them for the first time a few years earlier, the young boy had been really nervous. Shaw had explained to him that the townspeople thought that the invading members were odd. Luckily, no member had gone missing in action while in Moriarty—yet.

From the group's beginnings, Shaw had thought about how the Napoleon of crime could be memorialized in Moriarty. A life-size statue of the professor, making an obscene gesture? It would probably be shot to pieces by the local cowboys. No, they needed a memorial that couldn't be vandalized.

There were sixty members in the society, and many of them had been able to attend tonight's dinner: the Unhappy Birthday You Bastard

Moriarty celebration, as it was called. Maybe it couldn't be proved that Professor Moriarty was born on Halloween, but that mattered little.

There were more than 150 Sherlockian societies in the world, most of them in the United States. Not all of them were like the Brothers Three of Moriarty—but then again, not all of them were led by John Bennett Shaw.

The dinner was finished, with all its toasts, papers, readings, and singing, and the members and guests went outside to an open lot next to the saloon. This was the climax of the evening. The members contributed to the Moriarty memorial in a beautifully arranged ceremony, not too far in quality from the opening of the Summer Olympics. Shaw had wanted a memorial that wouldn't be vandalized, and there it was, the Moriarty Memorial Manure Pile, on which was deposited manure that the members had brought to the Frontier Saloon dinner. Manure from horses, mules, donkeys, cows, geese, and one or two more exotic animals, such as camels and kangaroos, donated by Sherlockian societies from all over the world.

Any inhabitants of Moriarty within range could hear the strange men and women in their deerstalkers singing, "Unhappy Birthday, You Bastard."

One special person was missing that evening: Mitch. He was sixteen now, and his intense fixation on Sherlock Holmes had waned during the last few years and finally all but evaporated. Thomas Pynchon's *Gravity's Rainbow* and Marcel Proust's *Remembrance of Things Past* were now his literature of choice. Punk music, foreign cinema, and other natural preoccupations of an adolescent were so much more interesting than Sherlock Holmes and the Sherlockian world.

One day on one of his frequent visits to Nicholas Potter Bookseller, a Santa Fe bookstore specializing in rare and collectible editions, Shaw was happy to run into his friend Mitch in the store. He hadn't seen him for some time. They talked for a while, and then Shaw noticed what Mitch was doing—selling some rare books from his Holmes collection. In fact, Mitch was divesting himself of all his Holmes books.

"Hold on," said Shaw. "Let me have a look."

He rummaged through the box, extracting four or five books, and told the owner he would like to buy them. Mitch seemed amused and pleased—he actually owned a few books that John Bennett Shaw wanted for his library!

John understood, of course. Mitch was moving forward in his life. He had seen it with many other young people interested in Sherlock Holmes. They were on loan to the Sherlockian world for a few years, but then the real world needed them back. John and Mitch had been dear friends during a period of their lives, and John just hoped it had meant as much to Mitch as it had to him. They said good-bye, and John Bennett Shaw walked away with his latest additions to the world's largest Sherlock Holmes collection.

That was the last time they met.

89

THERE WAS A new mouse in the house.

Of course, if you worked at Disney, you were never surprised to see mice wherever you looked. The mouse was, after all, the company's most famous symbol.

The mouse that Michael Eisner saw when he was walking down the corridor in the old animation building was the latest rodent knocking on the door to the magic kingdom.

A few days before Eisner had resigned from Paramount, the chief executive officer at Walt Disney Productions, Walt's son-in-law Ron Miller, had quit, outmaneuvered by Walt's nephew, Roy E. Disney, who had a seat on the board of directors. Eisner immediately took over the job. During his last two months at Paramount he had been occupied with Sherlock Holmes and the prospect of a blockbuster movie with Steven Spielberg as executive producer. Now he entered something completely different.

The Disney company was a Sleeping Beauty world. Everything was frozen in time. A few years earlier the Smithsonian Institution had planned an exhibition about the history of industrial arts in the entertainment industry, and the show's curator had called a production executive at Disney.

"We have heard that you still possess nineteen-thirties black and brass upright editing machines and a nonmotorized Oxberry camera stand," the curator said. "Would Disney be willing to donate these items for the exhibit?"

"But we're still using them," the Disney executive replied.

The curator was baffled. "You're kidding, right?"

He was not.

★ ★ ★

There were nearly fifty storyboards featuring the new mouse, a detective, name of Basil. Disney's animated film projects always started with storyboards, cartoonlike drawings that mapped out the plot. The two animators, Ron Clements and John Musker, were nervous. Would the executives be able to follow the story?

It seemed they would not.

"We should begin with a script," said Eisner, "just like with our other movies." And then he continued into the next room filled with mice on storyboards.

Disney's animated films were no longer the successful part of the company—especially after *The Black Cauldron*, an expensive and poorly received fiasco—and were not generating nearly as much in profits as the live-action features. Besides, most of the company's money came from the theme parks.

Eisner's first proposal when he began working at Disney was that they get rid of the animation unit. They should license the characters, let the films be done in some country far away, and just get the revenue, risking nothing. Eisner had new ideas, and they all involved live actors and filmmakers and real scripts. The animation unit seemed mostly to be a bunch of white-haired old men who needed an awful lot of years to make a new movie, using the same equipment as they had when they had come to Disney as young men many decades ago. They didn't even have electric pencil sharpeners.

Roy E. Disney put his foot down. The animation unit was the heart and soul of Disney. He convinced the new executives to at least visit the old animation building, and they were there now.

Basil of Baker Street was presented as a pitch, but Clements and Musker, who were among the younger men at the unit, had in reality been working on it for three years.

The first idea of the film had come in the 1970s when Ron Clements had walked into a bookstore and noticed the children's books about Basil of Baker Street by American writer Eve Titus.

Titus had originally been a concert pianist, playing mostly on cruise ships. Then she had started writing children's books, many of which featured mice as the central characters. Among the twenty books she wrote, five were about Basil of Baker Street, the first one appearing in 1958 and the last one in 1982.

The mouse Basil—named after Basil Rathbone—lived in the basement of the Holmes residence on Baker Street, where he was assisted
in his detective work by Dr. Dawson. The criminal acts were usually
the work of Professor Ratigan.

Over the years, Eve Titus came into contact with more and more
Sherlockians, some of whom were reflected in the characters portrayed
in her later books. She named many of the mice after the Sherlockians,
with slight alterations. Vincent Starrett, Julian Wolff, Peter E. Blau,
Ellery Queen, John Dickson Carr, and John Bennett Shaw had all made
appearances, albeit with slightly "mousified" names. Lord Adrian, the
explorer mouse featured several times, was clearly based on Conan
Doyle's youngest son.

Eve Titus even dedicated the books to Adrian Conan Doyle, in the
hope that her stories might become a bridge, leading children to Sherlock Holmes himself.

Adrian wrote to her and said that he was fond of the little rodent
characters.

Ron Clements immediately felt that these books could be turned into a
Disney film. The only problem was that the studio was already working on *The Rescuers*, another animated film with mouse detectives. A
few years later, when ideas for new projects were needed, Clements
casually mentioned Basil, and the proposal got a thumbs-up. The rights
were bought from Eve Titus.

First Clements and his colleagues, influenced by *Monty Python*, tried
to give the story a wacky angle; they had John Cleese in mind for the
voice of Basil. Six months later they showed their progress to the head
of the studio. He didn't like it at all. It lacked the warmth that a Disney
movie should have.

They had made the story straighter and were anxiously waiting to
hear what the executives in the hallway had to say.

"OK, we got that scene in the bar, right?" one of the executives
said, looking at a storyboard that depicted a bar on the docks. The
scene included a song, which had actually already been scored by the
composer Henry Mancini, but the executive had a better idea. "So
why can't we just go to Michael Jackson and say, 'Michael, take that
sequence and make it your own'?"

Jackson's involvement did not happen. But overall the response to Basil was good.

"This has possibilities," one of the executives said. "Paramount's doing a picture called *Young Sherlock Holmes*. It's still in the works, but it's good. This story's in that vein. So we'll keep going on it."

Eisner felt that the story lacked dramatic structure—a beginning, a middle, and an end—something he had always pressed for at Paramount. It was, however, cute and had potential. Roy E. Disney didn't want to risk losing some of the company's most talented animators. They needed something to do, so he pressed for a green light.

"How much more time do you need?" Eisner asked the animators.

"Two years," Clements said.

"I want it in one. How much will it cost?"

"About twenty-four million dollars."

"Nope," Eisner said. "Twelve million dollars."

If that could be done, and if it still would be quality animation, there was a future for animated films at Disney.

G RANADA'S SHERLOCK HOLMES TV series did not turn out to be quite
the success for which producer Michael Cox had been hoping.
Thirteen episodes had been broadcast, and the season was brought to
a close with the struggle between Sherlock Holmes and Professor Moriarty at the Reichenbach Falls, filmed on location in Switzerland.

While the show was critically acclaimed, it was not successful in
terms of viewing figures. It was going to take more than just good
production to turn Jeremy Brett into the Sherlock Holmes of his age.

All signs seemed to indicate that Granada might end up not resurrecting the master detective after he disappeared into eternity by the
Swiss waterfall. It was an ending of which Conan Doyle himself would
no doubt have approved.

Cox went back to his regular job as head of drama series at Granada.
Brett returned to his wife in the United States. She had recently been
diagnosed with cancer, and the couple wanted to spend as much time
together as possible. David Burke, who had played Dr. Watson, resumed
his career in the theater.

A few months later, in December 1985, *Young Sherlock Holmes* opened
in movie theaters. The new executives at Paramount weren't happy.
Eisner's old project was not a success.

One positive thing, however, was that it was nominated for an Academy Award for visual effects. For the first time in a film, there had
been a fully computer-generated, photorealistic animated character:
a knight composed of elements from a stained-glass window. It had
been scanned and painted directly onto film using a laser. John Las-
seter, a computer animator at Lucasfilm, who had created the effect,
had many ideas how computers could be used in filmmaking. He was
soon about to form a new company, Pixar.

★   ★   ★

The team making Basil of Baker Street had also employed computer technology, using it to animate the climactic fight that takes place in the interior of Big Ben—an homage to a scene in Hayao Miyazaki's animated film *The Castle of Cagliostro*. The studio had put together plot drawings of computer-graphic settings for the turning gears, and then the camera department exposed animations on top of the colored line plots. Ron Clements and John Musker saw the possibilities in the technology, but the producer didn't feel the effects fitted the overall look of the film. The pastels and charcoals were pinned next to the plotted line drawings and were more or less forgotten—until that day in September 1984 when Roy E. Disney was showing Michael Eisner and two other executives around the studio and they studied the storyboards. Disney happened to pass one of the animators and noticed the drawings.

"Glad to see we're putting some computer images into the mix," Disney said.

And that settled it.

The film opened in July 1986 with the title *The Great Mouse Detective*. When *Young Sherlock Holmes* was released half a year earlier and proved no big success, panic had set in among the executives at Disney. Sherlock Holmes doesn't sell? We must remove any reference to Sherlock Holmes in the marketing! There will be no British-sounding "Basil" or "Baker Street" in the title, and no deerstalker, meerschaum pipe, or magnifying glass on the poster, even if those things were constantly shown in the film. Instead, the poster would feature a mouse in a blue suit, swinging on a rope.

When Disney had approached Eve Titus to buy the film rights she had been flattered. She was no businesswoman and sold the rights far too cheaply, hoping that the film might lead to an upswing in sales of the books. Her name was, however, hardly mentioned in connection with the film, and the studio did not allow her to take part in its launch.

The books did not experience any renaissance. Many American filmgoers probably went to see the movie expecting it to feature Mickey Mouse. And those who managed to find the old books didn't recognize many similarities with the film. Except for the setting of Victorian

London and the three major characters, hardly anything remained from Titus's work.

For many youngsters the movie did, however, prove a bridge to Sherlock Holmes, just as Eve Titus had hoped when she wrote the books many years ago.

The film was well received by critics and was a moderate box-office success. The executives realized that it was possible to produce animated films with extreme cost control. Instead of closing the animation department, *The Great Mouse Detective* spurred Walt Disney Productions to start a whole new line of animated films. Roy E. Disney shared the new optimism and had already asked his animators to start working on a new project, a film that was to be called *The Little Mermaid*.

Eventually word reached Jeremy Brett, David Burke, and Michael Cox that Granada did want a second season after all.

Brett was ready to reprise the role, even if he wasn't in top form. His wife had died from her illness. Cox found another producer to take over his post on the series during filming, taking a backseat role. There were plenty of good stories left to adapt, as long as they stuck to the forty or so that were not still protected by American copyright. Pretty much all the important actors from the first season were available—except Dr. Watson. David Burke did not want to be away from his family for long periods, which shooting in Manchester would have entailed. Burke also felt an element of frustration at playing second fiddle to Brett, when he was used to playing leading roles onstage. At about the same time, he received an offer from the Royal Shakespeare Company, where he would be able to work alongside his wife. That was the end of it. They would have to find a new Watson.

It would be difficult to get closer to Conan Doyle's original than David Burke had managed to do. Burke did suggest a capable replacement: his friend Edward Hardwicke.

It was somehow quite fitting that a different Watson turned up in Granada's version of "The Empty House," which was broadcast in July 1986. Perhaps the loss of his friend Holmes had hit Watson so hard, one imagined, that he had become this slightly older and somewhat more serious man that Hardwicke portrayed.

Michael Cox had stepped back, and the new producer, June Wyndham-Davies, gradually introduced her own ideas about how the episodes ought to be filmed. Being faithful to the original was now of secondary importance; the main thing was to deliver a good-looking production.

Viewing numbers were much improved compared with the first season, and the new episodes were among the most popular programs in Britain that summer. The critics' reviews got better and better. Sherlock Holmes became what Sunday evenings were made for.

Following the second season, the series was sold to several European countries, to be broadcast during the centenary year 1987, one hundred years after the first Sherlock Holmes story was published.

The way Jeremy Brett played the detective—obsessive, mischievous, and volatile—impressed many, even some of the most hardened Basil Rathbone devotees, who had never countenanced anyone else in the role. For all those who appreciated Brett, it stood clear: it takes a genius to play a genius.

91

IT WAS A freezing day in late February 1987 on the banks of the Thames in London's dockland. The actor playing Tonga, four feet one inch tall, was in full costume, ready to shoot poisoned darts, although at the moment he was reading a paper and listening to his Walkman. Jeremy Brett was sitting unperturbed next to him, occasionally contributing to some conversation around him, but mostly casting his eyes down at the page of script for the next shot.

The Granada people had surveyed the river from Kew to Greenwich six or seven times, and found that only one stretch of about 150 yards remained as it had been in Holmes's day. There was nowhere else to point the camera. When they had located the perfect spot to shoot the scenes for the new Sherlock Holmes film, they found that overnight someone had started erecting a crane that totally ruined the skyline.

Nor was recording the sound an easy task. Drills, airplanes, and motorboats droned. They would have to go to some quieter mooring at lunchtime or in late afternoon and rerecord the sound. It was preferable to avoid post-synchronization back in Manchester, if they could, even if viewers would never be able to hear the difference.

It was 9:20 a.m. and time for the first shot of the day, of Holmes, Watson, and the Scotland Yarder on board the police launch. They shot it over and over again to get it right.

Granada had wanted to develop its techniques and try something completely new with Sherlock Holmes: produce a full-length film for television and shoot the whole thing on thirty-five-millimeter film. The use of film promised an excellent finished product but also meant large investments in equipment, as well as a larger crew. When the producers had planned the first series in 1981, they had thought of making *The Sign of Four* as a two-hour pilot episode. A script was written, but it had been logistically so difficult that they decided not to do it. Now, in 1986, the same script was dusted off. With some changes it could be used as a special program for the hundred-year jubilee in 1987.

That was when Jeremy Brett collapsed. His manic-depressive tendencies, including dramatic mood swings, had surfaced, and he was persuaded to go into the hospital for his own safety. He was admitted under his real name, Huggins, and the illness was successfully kept secret for several months. Then the headlines appeared. TV SHERLOCK IN A MENTAL HOME, the *Sun* shouted. Journalists claimed that he had gone mad after his wife's death. The truth was far more complicated. Brett had thrown himself into his work so wholeheartedly that he had never had time to grieve. Sherlock Holmes was a character that could easily take one over.

Brett's technique was to gain a complete understanding of the character he was playing. He couldn't simply pretend to be Holmes; he had to *become* the detective. With Conan Doyle's creation as a platform, Brett filled in the gaps, emphasizing the detective's theatrical and unpredictable elements. His Holmes would burst into hearty laughter, or jump over furniture or up onto a mantelpiece, "with no regard for his personal safety," Michael Cox noted. Brett wanted to plot out every conceivable facet of Holmes's personality. The only way to make the detective human was to show the chinks in his armor.

The biggest of those weaknesses that Brett had identified was the fact that Holmes needed Watson more than the reverse. Holmes could be distant and arrogant toward clients and witnesses, but his relationship with Watson gave him warmth and charm that had scarcely been explored by those who had played Holmes before. Granada's series had become a discourse about friendship. The viewers loved this about it.

Just as Watson was there for Holmes in the series, Edward Hardwicke was always on hand when Brett was struggling. He was a crutch that enabled Brett to get through the worst periods.

Brett had a whole barrage of medicines to keep him stable. He hated them but could not cope without them. He returned to the set but was a mere shadow of his former self.

On the set on the Thames, various shots were made with different boats, many of which had been borrowed from the historic ship collection at the nearby Saint Katharine Docks. A quarter past one was lunchtime—just as a snow squall swept up the river from the east. Everyone was worried; the team didn't have time to lose half of a day's filming. The whole 103-minute production had to be finished during six or seven weeks of filming. Luckily, the snow suddenly disappeared, and Holmes and Watson, in top hats, boarded a small black wherry propelled by a gent in the stern with a single oar. Also on the boat was Toby, the tracker dog, a border collie whose real name was Emma. And flat in the boat lay Emma's owner, to keep Emma happy in the midst of the dramatic steam-launch chase.

Then it was time for tea.

92

"HELLO, HELLO," SAID Michael Caine to the elderly woman in the lift, very politely, as he always did when meeting her, going up or going down.

It was late September 1988, and the well-known actor had recently moved to temporary lodgings in London's Chelsea after a long time in America.

"Hello, hello," he said again, next time they met. The woman replied in a similar polite manner, going up or going down.

Caine had just filmed something called *Without a Clue*, starring Ben Kingsley as Dr. Watson, a doctor who not only solved crimes but also wrote down his recollections. Watson had invented a fictional detective named Sherlock Holmes, and when people demanded to meet Holmes, he hired an alcoholic actor, Michael Caine, to play the role. It was a charming film, obviously written with lots of affection for Conan Doyle.

"Hello, hello." The woman was in the lift again, going down.

"You've played Sherlock Holmes, haven't you?" she asked. It was the first time they had got past the pure hello-hello exchange.

"Yes, I have," said Caine. The film would soon open at the cinemas.

"American newspapermen are going to come over here and interview you, aren't they?"

"Yes," said Caine.

"One of them is going to interview *me*."

Caine looked down at the old woman and gave her an understanding smile—and thought, She's a bit dotty.

"And why would they be interviewing *you*?" he asked.

The woman looked up at him.

"Because I am Conan Doyle's daughter."

They had reached the ground floor, and Dame Jean Conan Doyle walked out of the lift smiling, leaving Michael Caine behind.

After *The Sign of Four* had wrapped, Granada continued shooting further Sherlock Holmes episodes. For Michael Cox the production soon turned into misery. It started with Jeremy Brett, when he turned up for the first rehearsal with a new haircut, short and totally non-Victorian, looking as if he had cut it himself.

"I simply fancied a change," Brett said.

The first episode cost a lot, having been shot at Bangor racecourse in Wales, with a multitude of horses and an army of extras. They now had to save money to keep to the budget for the whole season. In the second episode they had a location problem, since the story took place in Cornwall. How to find nearby locations that could resemble the Cornish surroundings, instead of traveling 350 miles and staying there for two weeks, running up the extreme costs of travel and subsistence? Cox was confident that his colleagues responsible for the episode would fix it. When it was too late he discovered that their solution was to go to Cornwall anyway.

They had to find a way to save even more money during the rest of the episodes. In the end they skipped the last two planned one-hour episodes and chose instead to make one two-hour *Hound of the Baskervilles*. That would be cheaper, but it still had to be done on a shoestring. Street scenes from earlier episodes were reused; everything that was expensive to film was cut from the script. Going to Dartmoor was out of the question, so they had to find a moor that was closer to home. A Granada production of this novel could have been the best in history, but it was a failure. The reviews were bad for the first time during the Brett series. Basil Rathbone's 1939 version was far superior by comparison.

Despite all this, the series continued to do well overseas, and Granada wanted more episodes. Several famous actors had made cameo appearances, and—the odd weaker episode notwithstanding—the series had been a great success. When Brett and Hardwicke enacted the duo in a play, the fans flocked to see it, many waiting at the stage door afterward to get autographs. Jeremy Brett had become something of a heartthrob, especially among younger women.

*   *   *

When Dame Jean was nine years old she had been to a stage performance of *The Speckled Band* with her father and found it terribly
exciting. In that production the theater company had used a prop for
the snake. When the play had been put on originally, the company
had used a real snake, but audiences had complained, thinking it was
a false one. So they had switched to a fake snake that seemed more
real than a real one.

Almost seventy years later Dame Jean saw the two-man play *The
Secret of Sherlock Holmes*, written by Jeremy Paul, one of the Granada
scriptwriters, with Brett and Hardwicke in their famous roles. Dame
Jean thought it very elegantly written, fascinating in its way, something
that would have amused her father greatly. Conan Doyle didn't mind if
liberties were taken on the stage, providing the play was in good hands.

She liked Jeremy Brett's portrayal of Holmes—eventually. In the
early episodes of the series she hadn't liked him at all. He was far too
arrogant, she felt, too mannered, too high-strung altogether. Holmes
for her was a very cool character. Fortunately Brett's Holmes had
evolved from a rather unpleasant man into an endearing man. She told
Brett that, and he became so happy that he chose to celebrate with a
bottle of champagne.

Dame Jean respected and appreciated the use of her father's actual
stories and the efforts to get the period and its ways right. She loved
Edward Hardwicke's splendid Watson, just as she had liked David
Burke's version of the good doctor. And even when she didn't like
Brett's Holmes portrayal, she respected the actor's evident sincerity.

Brett didn't like the Michael Caine film *Without a Clue*, thinking it
was silly, maybe because he had hoped that his own Holmes would
lead to a proper feature film. Dame Jean loved it. She had read the
screenplay before the use of the characters was licensed.

"My father would have loved the joke here!" she told her American
representative, and she attended the London premiere.

Dame Jean was constantly asked for permission to use the characters.
Paramount Television approached her American representative for permission to use them in an episode of *Star Trek: The Next Generation*. The
character Data played Sherlock Holmes in a holodeck, virtual-reality

drama. *Star Trek* was greatly popular in the United States, and that episode (and another one later on) became many young Americans' first real meeting with Sherlock Holmes; the image of Data as the detective was engraved on their memories.

There was one group to whom Dame Jean Conan Doyle had become less interested in giving permission: authors writing new Sherlock Holmes stories. The quality of some of these pastiches was simply too poor, and she feared that readers might forget they were not reading the genuine article and get the impression that Sherlock Holmes stories were always so lackluster. More important, it was also a question of too much attention. The Sherlock Holmes centenary year, 1987, Dame Jean felt, had brought enough attention to her father and his creations. It was time for her to call a stop to new pastiches. She couldn't prevent British books, but if the British writers wanted the US market, they needed Dame Jean's permission.

This affected Michael Hardwick, Adrian Conan Doyle's favorite scriptwriter. Dame Jean had nothing against the novels about Sherlock Holmes that Hardwick had written during the past few years, as they had captured her father's style very well. Hardwick was, however, trying to write one a year, almost seeking a monopoly on pastiches, and Dame Jean didn't want her father's character dominated by any single writer. Hardwick took her decision very hard.

At the same time, she allowed other pastiche writers, in particular a Canadian woman, L. B. Greenwood, to publish new books about Sherlock Holmes. There was no exact set of rules.

Dame Jean saw herself as a protector of Sherlock Holmes's reputation. She was not a Sherlockian, and Holmes wasn't even her favorite character in her father's fictive worlds. She liked Brigadier Gerard and Professor Challenger much better, but she had real affection for Holmes. Like her father, she found him to be a terrible nuisance, taking up far too much of her time. She could well understand why her father wanted to push him over the Reichenbach Falls, and she would have happily done so herself from time to time.

93

THE TOURISTS LOOKED out through the tram windows when they approached what appeared to be the graffiti-smeared Berlin Wall. Two men in border-guard uniforms boarded. One of them approached a man and demanded, in German-accented English, to see his briefcase and admonished him for smiling.

The tourists were asked to leave the tram. The tour resumed on foot. They had each paid £6.95 to do this.

When the Cold War was still under way, there had been guard dogs, too, and visiting tourists had been frisked. Fathers had been taken off the trams, while their children said, "Don't take my daddy away." The guards had threatened to lock people up.

After the real wall in Berlin came down the previous November, the staff at Granada Studios had toned much of this down, and now such performances were reserved for corporate clients who specially requested them.

The forty tourists continued. They could choose between going to Coronation Street, where the British soap opera of that name was filmed, or they could go a century back in time to the Baker Street that Granada had built for the Sherlock Holmes TV series—even though the century-old feeling had been erased when the Victorian shops were converted into souvenir stalls and cafés.

The Berlin Wall replica between the two streets had been built for a Granada spy series, and it also served a second purpose, to screen off the adjacent Science and Industry Museum.

Visitors could also stroll along Downing Street and sit on the back benches in a life-size House of Commons set. The tour was closed on Mondays, making way for new episodes of *Coronation Street* to be filmed.

★   ★   ★

Visiting Sherlock Holmes at Baker Street was popular. A couple of years earlier, in the spring of 1989, there had been an advertisement in *Country Life*: "Investor/sleeping partner required with $4 million. World famous London landmark for sale. May suit titled person with cultural and historical interests."

The advertisement was the work of an entrepreneur who wanted to set up a Sherlock Holmes museum at 239 Baker Street. He had even asked the Westminster City Council to renumber Baker Street, so the present 239 would become 221b. The entrepreneur had noticed that there were seventeen steps leading up to the first floor in this very house, exactly as in Holmes's house in Conan Doyle's stories. He did not, however, mention that the interior of the house, including the seventeen steps, had been completely rebuilt after the World War Two bombing that had gutted almost all of Baker Street.

The entrepreneur got permission to put up a sign saying 221b, but he still wanted to renumber the street. In the spring of 1990 the museum opened.

The Sherlock Holmes Society of London avoided all association with the museum.

The Abbey National Building Society objected to the entrepreneur's wish to renumber the street and resented that he called the house 221b. Abbey National's address was 219–229 Baker Street, and the society had a special relationship with Sherlock Holmes, not only because it had housed the successful 1951 exhibition. What mattered more was that all letters addressed to Sherlock Holmes on Baker Street had been delivered to it ever since the 1930s, when its headquarters came to encompass the famous address.

From the 1950s onward, Abbey National had had a specific secretary whose job included receiving, and replying to, all Sherlock Holmes–related correspondence. This task meant telling the letter writers that Holmes had moved to Sussex to concentrate on beekeeping, which precluded taking on any new cases. There was no money to be made in this, but it did generate goodwill and a significant amount of publicity. It also had been a special privilege for the various holders of the position over the years.

Most of the letters came from America or Japan, though the stream of missives from Eastern Europe, and the former Soviet Union in particular, had swollen since the wall fell. Letters from Yugoslavia arrived regularly, but they naturally tailed off when the unrest in the Balkans began.

Some writers were applying for the job of housekeeper. Others were concerned about Holmes's drug problem, and a few asked his opinion on controversial subjects, such as abortion. A young chemistry student wrote a few times each year, presenting various pieces of information about herself and her study habits. Some of the letters were pure fan mail. Children were responsible for a large proportion of the incoming post, although their queries tended to be rather more straightforward: "Why do you wear such an ugly hat?" Sherlock Holmes's secretary had to come up with an answer to that one, too.

Every letter was answered. The largest haul came at Christmas, when an abundance of greeting cards arrived. Another spike followed around Holmes's birthday, January 6, when the secretary usually had to spend the whole day giving interviews to American radio stations.

Back at Granada's version of Baker Street the third Sherlock Holmes series was about to be filmed. The production team was obliged to pay £1,000 per day to hire its own set.

It was 1991, and Jeremy Brett had made up his mind: this would be his last season. It was time to escape the clutches of Sherlock Holmes.

94

I N A FINE palm court at 24 Fifth Avenue in Manhattan, on Saturday, January 12, 1991, the Baker Street Irregulars' annual cocktail party was under way. Both nonmembers and women were welcome at this event. The annual dinner itself—and membership—remained men-only affairs.

When Christopher Morley had founded the society back in the 1930s, he may not have at first intended for it to be an exclusively male group. Some of his other inventions were open to both sexes, and several women participants had attended the very first BSI lunch. That was the time when the ladies and gentleman had played sardines together.

Yet the BSI did become a men-only club. Men and women alike had solved the crossword that originally served as an entrance exam, yet it was only the men who had been invited to that first dinner. And, like so much else that occurred in the society's early proceedings, the single-sex membership became a tradition.

Six decades had passed since then, and for the last few years the BSI had had a new leader. He became fourth person to hold the office since the 1930s: Christopher Morley, Edgar W. Smith, Julian Wolff, and now Thomas L. Stix Jr.

The night before, at the BSI dinner, Stix had revealed the year's new members. The six gents had, one way or another, earned their places in the world's leading Sherlock Holmes society. That wasn't the end of it, however. Stix had a surprise up his sleeve at the cocktail party. In the Baker Street Irregulars' world, governed as it was by old traditions, he wanted to break what he regarded as the fustiest, most ridiculous tradition of them all. How he would do it was something few could have foreseen.

Tom Stix Jr. rose to speak, and it was noted that he was visibly moved. The conversation in the room tailed off. What was going on?

Stix announced that a woman was to be added to the ranks of the Baker Street Irregulars. That woman was none other than Dame Jean Conan Doyle.

The applause could have gone on forever. "Bravo!" was shouted from the crowd. Dame Jean was awarded the investiture simultaneously in London. This was indeed a historic moment in the Sherlockian world. In the almost sixty-year history of the BSI, two women had previously been invested, but neither of those elections had marked the start of a new, equal era. Now it felt as if the door had been opened. Evelyn Herzog was present, sitting at one of the tables. In the late 1960s, she and her friends had stood on the freezing pavement outside a Manhattan restaurant to protest the ban on women members. They had long since formed their own society, the Adventuresses of Sherlock Holmes. But this was what she had been fighting for back then, and now it was happening. Herzog was overcome with joy, and tears ran down her cheeks.

Dame Jean was just the beginning. It was time to redress a very old injustice. In 1934, Katherine McMahon had submitted a flawless solution to the Sherlock Holmes crossword. The other persons, men, who did so had been invited to become members, but McMahon had not received an invitation—until now. She was still alive and became the second woman to be admitted that Saturday afternoon. John Bennett Shaw, whose health wasn't all that good, was back home in Santa Fe and personally informed Katherine McMahon about the honor.

It still wasn't over. Stix spoke up again, informing those present that Edith Meiser had also been invested as a member. Meiser, one of those most responsible for keeping interest in Sherlock Holmes alive after Conan Doyle's death, was by then ninety-three years old and had joined some of the BSI members for lunch the previous day. The room echoed to warm applause. This was the biggest thing to have happened to the society since its inception.

Tom Stix Jr. took a moment to catch his breath. Then he continued, with a tremor in his voice, as this was an emotional moment—things getting closer to home, more personal. When Evelyn Herzog heard the next name, she was dumbfounded and confused, as though she could not believe what she was hearing. It felt like an eternity before she composed herself enough to stand. She felt as if her feet never touched the ground as she floated over to Stix to collect her certificate.

As she returned to her seat, she accidentally pushed a fellow member, who was taking photos and blocking her way, almost sending him to the floor. The world was shaking, and Herzog really did need to sit down again. She peeked into the envelope to make sure that it truly did contain a certificate of membership.

She then heard Stix continue, investing two more distinguished women—and members of the Adventuresses of Sherlock Holmes—Susan Rice and Julia Carlson Rosenblatt.

For the rest of the afternoon, Herzog kept a tight grip on the envelope, worried that she might lose it. As she walked home from the event, she was very careful indeed. Each time she came to cross a street, she looked in both directions. She did not want to become famous for being the woman who was run over within hours of becoming a BSI member.

At the following year's annual dinner, each table had a female representative.

95

Jeremy Brett changed his mind. He wanted to continue as Sherlock Holmes. By then, however, Michael Cox had already signed up for other projects and could no longer keep a watchful eye on the production. Instead, it fell into the hands of the schedulers. They wanted the new episodes to follow the same two-hour format popularized by the detective drama *Inspector Morse*.

The first of the new Holmes films—*The Master Blackmailer*, based on Conan Doyle's "Charles Augustus Milverton"—was a success. It filled in gaps in the short story's plot and explicitly said things that had only been implied. The schedulers were so pleased, in fact, that they commissioned a further two films, to be screened over the Christmas season of 1992. It was a fateful decision that came as a complete surprise to the producer June Wyndham-Davies. The short-story plots, normally barely enough to fill an hour-long episode, were now to be stretched to double that length. Newly written side plots with supernatural and gothic undertones were added. The productions lacked focus and offered little in the way of detective work; quite simply, they were no longer Sherlock Holmes stories.

Dame Jean was very disappointed, and Jeremy Brett promised, "No more!" He had had no intention of allowing the original stories to be distorted into such dreadful pastiches. He had not even brought his complete Sherlock Holmes edition with him—there was no point in comparing these scripts with the originals.

In 1994 Granada returned to the one-hour format. The new shows were not well received: Jeremy Brett was no longer himself; the producer had no regard for Conan Doyle's originals; besides, they had already filmed most of the good stories. While the programs were broadcast, Jeremy Brett was in the hospital for long periods, forced into care by a combination of heart problems, wrongly prescribed medication, and manic depression. While recording one of the episodes, he had been so ill that Sherlock Holmes's part in the story had had to be played instead by his brother Mycroft.

Toward the end of his career as Holmes, Brett became consumed with the idea of "completing the Canon" ("the Canon" being the term the Sherlockians used for Conan Doyle's Holmes stories)—he wished to play Holmes in all the sixty stories. No actor had ever done that. Over ten years, Brett had appeared in just over two-thirds of them. His health and the stories themselves put a stop to it—many of them didn't fit the one-hour television format.

Over the same decade there was another, much smaller production team that almost from the start had had as a realistic, yet magical, goal to do all the stories. Bert Coules was the series originator and head writer. Clive Merrison played Sherlock Holmes, and Michael Williams was Dr. Watson.

They were producing their program for BBC radio. It was popular, and they were, in fact, nearly finished.

In September 1995, Jeremy Brett died, at the age of sixty-two. At his memorial service, a violinist played the haunting tune heard in the Granada version of "The Final Problem," in the scene in which Sherlock Holmes dies.

96

IN THE SPRING of 1994, a new novel about Sherlock Holmes was published. There was nothing sensational about that—ever since the boom in the 1970s there had been a constant stream of Holmes pastiches. Initially most had come from American authors, but since the Granada series began, and the centenary year had brought even more focus on the detective, the British pastiches had grown in number.

In this new novel, *The Beekeeper's Apprentice*, the main character was not Holmes but Mary Russell, a fifteen-year-old girl, who in 1915 stumbles on the retired detective with his colony of bees in the Sussex Downs and becomes a detective in the Holmes mold.

The author, Laurie R. King, had written the book in the autumn of 1987—all of it with a Waterman fountain pen—and then collected rejection slips for two years while she finished another novel about Russell and Holmes (later to become the third in the series). Then she wrote a contemporary crime novel, which was quickly sold to a publisher and won an Edgar Award for best first novel.

The award, bestowed by the Mystery Writers of America, opened the door, and Russell and Holmes finally made their entry. Readers took Mary Russell into their hearts. Some of them became ardent Russell fans, and thanks to a new way of communicating they realized that there were other equally devoted readers out there.

The Internet, as it was becoming known, brought a great many opportunities for those interested in Sherlock Holmes to find one another and to carry out a continuous exchange of information, opinions, and small talk. The World Wide Web had grown rapidly; by 1996 there were thirty million users globally, and the total was growing by 10 percent every month.

The first mailing list for Sherlock Holmes fans, the Hounds of the Internet, or Hounds-L, had been established in 1992, when the Internet barely existed. The list was dedicated to the discussion of Sherlockian topics, but mainly the Holmes stories by Conan Doyle. Pastiches, films, and trivia were also among the matters about which the members wrote to one another.

There were other mailing lists, newsgroups (such as alt.fan.holmes), and forums dedicated to the study of Sherlock Holmes. Mary Russell fans, wherever they lived in the world, could communicate through the mailing list Russ-L. Having a core of fans was becoming increasingly important for any author.

The Internet provided not just new ways for people to get in touch with one another but also a quick way to find facts and read or download texts. In late 1994 Chris Redmond, the Canadian Sherlockian who in the late 1960s had been the youngest member of the Baker Street Irregulars, created the Sherlockian Holmepage (later renamed Sherlockian.Net), a collection of all sorts of necessary information for serious Sherlockians as well as incidental visitors.

The Sherlockian world had passed the boom caused by the Granada series, yet it was thriving. A large number of Sherlockian magazines were published, and thanks to desktop-publishing technology, even simple fanzines could attain a polished, professional look, as long as one refrained from mixing all those funny fonts that were available—what in typography was called the "ransom note effect."

Many of the oldest Sherlockian societies were still active, and other organizations had recently been launched. The Arthur Conan Doyle Society, founded in 1989, focused on the non-Sherlockian part of Conan Doyle's life and authorship, something that pleased honorary member Dame Jean Conan Doyle.

The Brothers Three of Moriarty were preparing for yet another pile of dung to be beautifully arranged in a New Mexican parking lot. In 1991 they had reason to do something extra for their Unhappy Birthday You Bastard Moriarty celebration—a hundred years had passed since the death of the evil professor at the Reichenbach Falls. John Bennett Shaw, who was now nearly eighty, used to tell all sorts of anecdotes about mailmen carrying stinking, leaking packages sent as contributions by Sherlockians all over the country. That was an inspiration for the other members. This time they would go all the way—they would collect animal droppings from all of the fifty states. Letters were sent to the governors; a few of them replied personally, others delegated the matter to their agriculture departments. Animal feces had soon been received from a number of states. Then the members sent the dung request to President Bush, and five weeks later a reply arrived from the White House. "Because of the great number of similar requests received for Presidential messages, I'm sorry that it is not possible for us to comply with all of them."

Three years later John Bennett Shaw passed away. He had been the most important figure in the Sherlockian world for at least the last twenty years.

In 1966 Shaw had staged an exhibition of what he considered to be the one hundred basic books, pamphlets, and periodicals relating to Sherlock Holmes. There was no catalog of the display, and he received many requests for a list of the items. Some ten years later he made that list, *The Basic Holmesian Library*, and now and then he revised it. For new and old Sherlock Holmes enthusiasts it became the necessary guide, in which every facet of the Sherlockian world was represented. It acted as a snapshot of the Sherlockian book world and made old Sherlockian scholarship live on. Shaw was careful to point out that it was a selection: "Please remember that while I have listed but one hundred items I have not listed some three thousand!"

At a Baker Street Irregulars dinner in the late 1960s, John had met a young librarian, Ronald Burt De Waal, who declared his intention to "compile a world bibliography on Sherlock Holmes." He had originally been inspired by an *Esquire* article by William S. Baring-Gould, from which he had learned that there was a whole world of Sherlockians out there.

"He is mildly insane," Shaw thought, and then: "Good heavens, I hope he does it."

The meeting led De Waal to spend ninety-seven days in Shaw's library, working on his bibliographical project. He continued with the project for years. It was basically a list of Shaw's collection, with additions from other collectors—more than six thousand items. Shaw thought he and De Waal were a perfect pair: Shaw was a blotter-type collector, and De Waal was obsessed with listing and describing it all.

De Waal's *World Bibliography of Sherlock Holmes and Dr. Watson* was published in 1974. An enlarged bibliography came six years later, and in 1994 the Sherlock Holmes world had grown so much that De Waal's third bibliography on the subject expanded to four volumes with a total of fourteen hundred pages. It listed twenty-five thousand items that were somehow related to Sherlock Holmes. And yet it was far from complete.

When Shaw died, his collection had already found a new home. In the mid-1980s he had arranged for its transfer to the University of Minnesota, a process that was completed a decade later.

Dame Jean's life would also end soon, within six months. She knew this because the doctors had told her so, and she was relieved, as the Parkinson's disease was getting worse. The cancer was a better alternative.

Jean had been a careful guardian of her father's literary estate, and her home was almost a Conan Doyle museum, containing variant editions of her father's writings, Sidney Paget illustrations, family portraits, and busts. The portrait of Napoleon gazing over from Saint Helena to the guardship on the horizon was one of Conan Doyle's favorite pictures and a long time ago used to hang in his billiard room. Among the great number of the books that had been in her father's library were copies inscribed by such authors as H. G. Wells and J. M. Barrie.

The subject of one imposing portrait over the fireplace was not related to Arthur Conan Doyle. The gentleman in military uniform was Dame Jean's much beloved husband, Air Vice Marshal Sir Geoffrey Bromet. After marrying him in the 1960s, she had preferred to be known as Jean Bromet, using the name Conan Doyle only in connection with the handling of her father's writings and in her contacts with the Sherlockian world. Geoffrey's death in 1983, when he was ninety-two years old, had devastated her. She would still get tears in her eyes when speaking about him, many years later.

Defiant of her infirmities, Jean kept up her support of the Sherlock Holmes Society of London in the mid-1990s. She was a patron of the new Sherlock Holmes museum in Meiringen, Switzerland, and in 1994 she unveiled a portrait of her father at the Sherlock Holmes pub. She very much disliked the entrepreneur's Sherlock Holmes Museum on Baker Street, especially since she had heard that the staff told visitors that the house was the former lodgings of her father, but the Sherlock

Holmes pub was something completely different. She had always liked to go there and now she had one more reason, bringing friends to lunch to show them the portrait.

On one occasion a gentleman at the next table asked her, "Can you tell me who that is in that picture?"

"Yes, that's my father," she replied, with a mischievous grin.

The man looked from her to the portrait and back again. "By God, it is!"

Dame Jean was very practical about her approaching departure. She wanted to see an end to the old litigation with her sister-in-law Nina— and Nina's estate, after her death ten years previously—litigation which for twenty-five years had kept Sir Arthur Conan Doyle's papers locked away. Dame Jean's other sister-in-law, Anna, had passed away in 1990, so she would see to it that Conan Doyle's papers would be divided among her own and Anna's heirs.

Dame Jean died in November 1997. With her death the last member of Sir Arthur Conan Doyle's immediate family was gone.

Her father's papers had finally been returned to the family. The American Conan Doyle copyrights, with some years still to run, were bequeathed to the Royal National Institute for the Blind. Dame Jean had struggled with eyesight problems and always thought about what she could do for others. When the institute realized that her bequest was not a lump sum but something requiring considerable management on an ongoing basis, it sold the rights back to Dame Jean's residual beneficiaries. Jean had chosen her cousin Charles Foley, a great-nephew of Conan Doyle, as the executor of her estate, and now he was one of the relatives who owned the US rights. Jon L. Lellenberg continued to be the US literary agent. The heirs were more open to broader uses of the Sherlock Holmes characters than Dame Jean had been.

Two years after Dame Jean's death, a statue was unveiled outside the Baker Street underground station. It depicted the most famous detective in the world. Unlike most statues, it was not turned toward the street but had its back to the traffic instead. This was intended to reduce the likelihood of tourists being run over as they posed for photographs in front of Sherlock Holmes.

It wasn't the first statue of the detective. Meiringen in Switzerland had one. Japan did too—there was huge interest in Sherlock Holmes in Japan, which had the world's largest Sherlock Holmes society, and a lot of books on the subject were published in Japanese editions. There was also a statue in Edinburgh, located just a few yards from where Conan Doyle was born.

But now, finally, Sherlock Holmes had come home.

Part 8

1998–2016

97

L ate one evening in May 1998, Michael Valle was at his night job at a large law firm in Los Angeles. Valle had been trying to make it in Hollywood as a screenwriter for ten years.

"Which fictional character," he asked one of the attorneys, "has been portrayed on film the most number of times?"

They were playing movie trivia. They challenged each other with a question every day.

The attorney thought about it and responded. "I would say either Sherlock Holmes or Dracula."

The correct answer was indeed Sherlock Holmes, but the attorney's answer made Michael Valle think. What if Sherlock Holmes were to encounter Dracula? That would be a very interesting premise.

He checked every video guide he could locate but found no movie in which Holmes meets Dracula. So he went ahead and started writing a script.

Bringing Holmes and Dracula together in the same story wasn't a new idea, at least not in literature. It had been done by crime writer Loren D. Estleman in *Sherlock Holmes vs. Dracula* and by science-fiction and fantasy writer Fred Saberhagen in *The Holmes-Dracula File*, both books published in 1978.

Valle's agent sent out his third and final draft, and it was very well received. Several producers read it and submitted it to various studios. Within five days the script was being read all over town.

In late 1999 much of the world was preoccupied with the Y2K problem—the threat that the world's computer systems would suffer a massive disruption when the millennium turned. But in Hollywood Michael Valle was celebrating. On November 4, Disney, Universal, and Columbia had all made bids to buy his screenplay. The offers kept getting higher and higher. And then, that very afternoon, Chris Columbus—the writer of *Young Sherlock Holmes*, who had become one of Hollywood's top filmmakers—informed Columbia Pictures that he wanted to direct the film. Columbia then made an offer of $700,000—plus an additional $300,000 if the film was made—for Valle's 260-page script about two of the world's greatest fictional characters. The film was to be titled *Sherlock Holmes and the Vengeance of Dracula*.

Valle's story began where Bram Stoker's *Dracula* left off. In 1891 an unsuspecting Professor Moriarty brings Dracula's sarcophagus with him to London. The count is determined to exact his revenge on Abraham Van Helsing and the other survivors from the little excursion to Transylvania. When one of them is found dead under suspicious circumstances, the victim's female cousin turns to Sherlock Holmes and Dr. Watson. Holmes quickly realizes that he faces an opponent with no regard for the very laws of nature in which he himself has placed all his trust. Holmes understands that the only way to defeat Dracula is by building an alliance with Moriarty.

It had the makings of a huge Hollywood production. It was an affectionate, playful reworking of fiction, yet full of blockbuster potential.

A few days into the New Year, it was obvious that the threat of malfunctioning computers had been significantly exaggerated. On the Sherlock Holmes front, however, there was a pressing danger, albeit perhaps a minor one. Without any living immediate Conan Doyle family member, there was no one to guard the author. He was slowly becoming more and more fictional himself. In Britain, a new miniseries was in the process of transforming public perceptions of Conan Doyle and the creation of Holmes.

The miniseries was called *Murder Rooms: The Dark Beginnings of Sherlock Holmes* and concerned Dr. Joseph Bell, played by Ian Richardson (who had played Holmes in the early 1980s), and his student Arthur Conan Doyle, portrayed by Charles Edwards. The fictional Bell and Conan Doyle solved crimes together, and Bell was just the kind of detective genius that Sherlock Holmes would later become. The program implied that Conan Doyle had completely based his leading man on his old lecturer, that Holmes was a clone of Bell. Needless to say this wasn't true; despite Bell's renowned powers of observation, he was no solver of crimes. Some reviewers expressed their concern that viewers might regard this fictional work as fact.

Conan Doyle had been used with increasing regularity in fiction and film over the past two decades. *Twin Peaks* creator Mark Frost had written two dark gothic novels with Conan Doyle as the main character. Several authors had extrapolated on Conan Doyle's interest in spiritualism. Conan Doyle had also been paired with escapologist extraordinaire Harry Houdini to form a crime-solving duo. In two films he had been duped by little girls who had posed for photographs with images of fairies cut out from magazines and then claimed that the fairies were actually real. The last was perhaps the least believable tale, but it was in fact the only example of the fictive portrayals of Conan Doyle that was true.

There wasn't much left to do in the genre. Over the years Holmes had been both a mouse and a dog, both superintelligent and insane. He had struggled against Nazis, met most of the celebrities of his day, died, and been resurrected. What else could be done with the character? Letting Conan Doyle himself experience adventures and pitting Holmes against evil incarnate in the form of Dracula were two things that had not been done on film or television before.

Work on *Sherlock Holmes and the Vengeance of Dracula* continued. Then Chris Columbus withdrew. He had agreed to make the first film from the enormously successful Harry Potter books by J. K. Rowling—a film that, in structure and setting, was more than a little reminiscent of *Young Sherlock Holmes*.

Time passed. Perhaps they could hold out for Chris Columbus to return as director? On Academy Awards night in 2001, scriptwriter Michael Valle, only forty-two years old, died of cancer.

A year later it was announced that Jude Law was to play Sherlock Holmes. By autumn 2003 the film had a new producer, but the script was no longer credited to Valle. It was attributed instead to a man most famous for writing the scripts for *Nightmare Creatures* and *Total Recall II*.

But soon the production got mired in "development hell," a state of perpetual planning from which it would never emerge. It would never become a film; it would only almost become one. With *Sherlock Holmes and the Vengeance of Dracula* a nonstarter, it seemed as though the last chance for a big Hollywood film about the detective was gone.

★   ★   ★

Was it no longer possible to make a major film about one of literature's greatest figures?

In November 2000 a new studio executive started working at Warner Brothers; he was immediately responsible for buying the Harry Potter book series for the studio. At about this time he also started thinking about another project: he felt that there must be a way to reinvent Sherlock Holmes. The images he saw in his head were different from those he had seen in previous films; he envisioned a much more modern, more bohemian character, who dressed more like an artist or a poet. It could be what Valle's script had promised but never succeeded in being. His project was in the end even going to have a number of things in common with *Sherlock Holmes and the Vengeance of Dracula*—call them genre clichés: a slight supernatural touch, explosions in gasworks, gas used as a weapon, battling atop scaffolding, a giant thug, and Holmes ending up wanted for arrest by Inspector Lestrade.

At the moment the project was, however, still just an idea in Lionel Wigram's head.

98

IT WAS A September morning in 2001, and Mitch Cullin, now thirty-three years old and an author, had reason to celebrate. He had been up all night writing and had finished part one of his sixth novel. He was used to publishing a new book every nine months, but this one was taking just forever, and his entire existence seemed designed to tear the writing process to pieces. Among the disruptions had been the illnesses of both his parents, a painful breakup with his partner, the use of various antidepressants, and too much drinking. Finally he had found a way into the writing of the novel again, and he felt that his sole audience, the one person he was writing it for, would like it. So Cullin went out of his office, opened a bottle of wine, felt happy, and turned on the TV—and watched as the second plane flew into the tower.

When John Bennett Shaw died in 1994, Cullin was living in Houston, Texas. He had formed his own life away from his family and was sharing a small apartment with his boyfriend and taking evening classes in creative writing at the University of Houston. He went to bars and clubs on the weekends and wrote during the week, mostly in the middle of the night, then watched VHS tapes of classic Japanese cinema until dawn.

Shaw was a memory of a distant past. Cullin had become another person, spending his days in the company of greatly talented and like-minded mentor friends. Shaw's death didn't really have any impact on him. Soon after, however, Cullin had an idea. Someday he would write something in Shaw's honor.

Four years later Cullin had moved to Arizona and begun making outlines of books and stories he wanted to write. One of them was a novella, which he called *The Moon Reflects the Sun*, about a famous

elderly novelist, now living as a beekeeper in the English countryside. The man finds one of his old unfinished manuscripts, something of a highly personal nature, but he doesn't remember writing
it and can't recall the exact events that precipitated its creation. He
decides to attempt to finish writing the manuscript as a way to jog
his memory.

"What is he like, this old man?" asked a fellow writer friend, when
they were out having drinks.

Cullin thought about it.

"Just imagine him to be someone like an elderly Sherlock Holmes
type," he said, at the same time hearing his own words.

Of course! Cullin realized that it was Sherlock Holmes he should
write about. Not a retired novelist, but a ninety-three-year-old former
master detective. He immediately started reworking the outline. This
was the book he would write in John Bennett Shaw's honor.

First there was a practical problem: Cullin had sold his Holmes
books when he was a teenager, so he needed to buy Conan Doyle's
Holmes stories again. Reading them, he was amazed at how little he
remembered, considering the detailed knowledge he had acquired as a
boy. More important, he used William S. Baring-Gould's *Sherlock Holmes
of Baker Street* and Jack Tracy's *The Encyclopaedia Sherlockiana* to get
everything Holmes-related right. The most exciting research was about
beekeeping, a subject Cullin had wanted to know more about anyway.

On another level the idea of the book was something else, something
that had increasingly interested Cullin: the notions that sometimes
terrible things happen for no logical reason whatsoever and that as
humans we have a very difficult time accepting that reality. We want
concrete answers, even in the worst of situations. His inspiration had
been a 1995 film by Hirokazu Koreeda in which the husband of the
protagonist may or may not have killed himself. His wife is left to
struggle with the circumstances of his death, which she does in a highly
profound, poetic manner. Cullin thought that this way of pondering
both life and death had some serious merit to it, and he wanted to
explore it in his own writing.

The concept for the book was ambitious, and it would be a thick volume. In the first section there would be four or five short pieces, one of
them a nonfiction account of the history of beekeeping in Sussex, and
none of them linked to any of the others. The second part, a novella,

should reveal that all the previous pieces are linked to its narrative. Maybe he would have pulled this off had his mental state been better, but Cullin decided, after having written the Holmes narrative, that he should weave one of the short stories, "The Glass Armonica," into the novella and skip the others, or else the book might never be finished.

There was someone waiting for it to be finished. Cullin knew that his sole audience, as he thought of him, had read almost every Holmes pastiche ever written, so he entertained an idea of writing him a literary novel about his favorite character that would be unlike any of the pastiches he had digested in his lifetime. It would be something original, a unique approach that wasn't intended to ape Conan Doyle yet was still correct in its relevant Holmes details.

Then it was September 11, 2001, and Mitch Cullin was trying to understand what he just had seen on television. It was surreal. The whole world had come to a standstill. Writing fiction and being creative felt wholly irrelevant and meaningless. He and everyone he knew had been thrown off balance. It was several months before he could resume his work.

Finally he was able to sit down and begin the second section of the book. He wrote: "Holmes woke, gasping. What had happened?"

If the 9/11 terrorist attacks hadn't occurred, those words would not have been written. This was how Cullin was feeling and thinking after the attack. What had happened? It was something he kept asking himself, something he was trying to make sense of. And that way a piece of 2001 reality leaked into his story of bygone times.

There were also other recent events he worked into the story, most important the onset of his father's dementia. And of course he included his own memories of a young boy's curiosity in exploring an elderly man's library and manuscripts—an elderly man who had become a good friend and who had been mentoring that boy.

John Bennett Shaw had passed away seven years ago, but when Cullin wrote the book it was with Shaw in mind. He imagined Shaw as his sole audience. And that day when he finally finished writing the book, which now had the title *A Slight Trick of the Mind*, he knew that Shaw would have been delighted with the result.

Cullin had no one else to celebrate with, so he took himself—and his thoughts of Shaw—out to lunch and had a slice of pizza.

99

IN THE MID-1980s, Andrea Reynolds had found herself in the public
eye. She had left television producer Sheldon Reynolds for a British
(originally Danish) society figure she had known since the early 1960s.
His name was Claus von Bülow, and he was then about to stand trial
a second time for the attempted murder of his wife, Sunny, with an
insulin overdose. A few years earlier he had been sentenced to thirty
years of imprisonment for the crime but had appealed the verdict.
Throughout the second court case, Andrea Reynolds had been at his
side, though not literally—the judge had banished her from the courtroom, so she watched the proceedings on the closed-circuit TV feed
in a news station's van outside the courthouse.

The trial concluded with von Bülow being found not guilty of all
charges. The story became a best-selling book, and the film version
that followed featured Jeremy Irons and Glenn Close in the two leading
roles, while Andrea was played by professional shrew-depicting actress
Christine Baranski.

Reynolds and von Bülow had since gone their separate ways, and
she had married a British aristocrat and distant relative of the queen.
Now known as Andrea Plunket, she ran a bed-and-breakfast outside
New York City. She also considered it her lifework to claim ownership
of the American rights to the Sherlock Holmes stories.

After Dame Jean Conan Doyle's death, Andrea Plunket began her
struggle to demonstrate that things had not been correctly handled
when Dame Jean had reclaimed the American rights in 1979. In 2001
she started suing different plaintiffs—Dame Jean's and Anna Conan
Doyle's heirs in the first case, Jon L. Lellenberg and one of the Conan
Doyle licensees in another case—in two different jurisdictions of the
US federal courts. She lost each time, including at the appellate level.
In the third and final court ruling she was barred from any further

attempts to claim the rights. This didn't stop her from repeatedly claiming to be the rightful owner of the Conan Doyle rights, a claim she made online and elsewhere: as soon as anyone wanted to use the character Sherlock Holmes, she averred, a license fee was to be paid to her.

She was not the only one making such claims. Opposite the museum on Baker Street a shop selling Sherlock Holmes memorabilia had existed for many years. That company, too, claimed to own the rights to the Sherlock Holmes brand and would license the rights to anyone prepared to pay.

In the late 1990s British copyright law had changed, and the protection of copyright was extended from fifty to seventy years after the death of the author. This meant the Sherlock Holmes stories were again under copyright protection for a few years. As the last British copyright holder, Andrea Plunket reclaimed that position and asserted a number of European trademark claims.

At the same time in the United States, a copyright term extension act had been signed into law by President Bill Clinton in October 1998. It was nicknamed the Sonny Bono Act, in memory of the late congressman—of Sonny and Cher fame—who had been one of twelve sponsors of a similar bill. Some called it the Mickey Mouse Protection Act because the Walt Disney Company had been lobbying for its adoption in order to delay the entry of the earliest Mickey Mouse movies into the public domain.

For Dame Jean's residual beneficiaries this all meant that those Conan Doyle stories that were still under US copyright got twenty further years of protection. To deal with this, once Dame Jean's estate was finally closed, they formed a company, Conan Doyle Estate Ltd., to take ownership and manage the rights. Dame Jean's cousin Charles Foley retired from the management role, and three other relatives continued as directors.

When Dame Jean had managed to end the old litigation with Nina's estate, a wealth of old Conan Doyle documents—correspondence, diaries, even unpublished manuscripts—had been released and returned to the family. The fifty-six crates Adrian Conan Doyle had tried to sell in New York had, for many years, been stored under lock and key at the offices of a lawyer in London. John Dickson Carr's biography of Conan Doyle had included a long, detailed, yet incomplete list of them, but they had remained an unattainable treasure for any Conan Doyle biographer.

A number of attempts had been made in the biography genre since Carr's book. In the 1960s, Adrian had collaborated with Pierre Nordon, a young Frenchman, who had written his doctoral thesis about Conan Doyle. Nordon had been given access to the documents, which at the time had been kept in Adrian's archive at the castle. A reworked, more popular version of this biography was later translated into English.

In the mid-1970s the celebrity biographer Charles Higham had written a fanciful account of Conan Doyle's life that was so riddled with inaccuracies that Dame Jean had felt obliged to write to the editor of the London *Times* and point this out. In the decades that followed, more books were published, but it was difficult for writers to create something new with Conan Doyle's archive hidden away. Daniel Stashower, author of the Conan Doyle biography *Teller of Tales*, published in 1999, was one of the most successful, winning both Edgar and Agatha awards for his work.

One man who hoped to write the definitive Conan Doyle biography was Andrew Lycett, who had earlier written books about Ian Fleming and Rudyard Kipling. The thought had occurred to him in the late 1990s, and he made contact with a representative of Conan Doyle's estate, hoping to be given access to the family archives. He was informed that they were in the process of being organized.

Richard Lancelyn Green, the world's leading expert on Sherlock Holmes and Conan Doyle, was also planning a biography of the great author. His was to be on an altogether larger scale than any of the other efforts. He had spent three decades on its preparation, and it was to comprise three thick volumes.

Inspired by his father, a member of the Sherlock Holmes Society of London, Green had been interested in all things Conan Doyle since childhood. His interest soon reached almost manic proportions. As a youth he had re-created part of the Baker Street flat in the loft of his family's manor house. His mother had assisted by asking local antique dealers to identify suitable Victorian objects. Even as a teenager Green had been busy compiling a comprehensive bibliography of Conan Doyle's works. Fifteen years later, the project was complete, and he and his friend John Gibson, a fellow collector and Conan Doyle specialist, produced a seven-hundred-page meticulously detailed bibliography of every single word ever published by Conan Doyle. That was the book Richard Lancelyn Green had been working on when a teenage Mitch Cullin had met him at John Bennett Shaw's home.

Over the years, Green had built up an unrivaled collection. It wasn't simply an assemblage of mint-condition first editions or every conceivable knickknack relating to the detective; it also included an enormous quantity of documents from the Conan Doyle family, some of them bought directly from the author's relatives. Green had known Nina Mdivani and had acquired some things from her, and at auction he had managed to purchase Denis's old letters and all the paperwork accumulated during Nina's years of involvement with the rights. He had also bought a large collection of family photographs that had been divided among the siblings' relatives following Lady Conan Doyle's death.

Many of the pieces were in place for the great biography, what was to be his magnum opus. What was missing was the almost mythical family archive. Outside the family very few had any knowledge of what was going on. Green had, however, understood from Dame Jean that at least some of it would be bequeathed to the British Library. But what was taking so long?

100

SHERLOCK HOLMES AND Dr. Watson were camping. They pitched their tent under the stars and went to sleep. Sometime in the middle of the night Holmes woke Watson up and said, "Watson, look up at the stars, and tell me what you see."

Watson replied, "I see millions and millions of stars."

Holmes said, "And what do you deduce from that?"

Watson replied, "Well, if there are millions of stars, and if even a few of those have planets, it's quite likely there are some planets like Earth out there. And if there are a few planets like Earth out there, there might also be life."

And Holmes said, "Watson, you idiot, it means that somebody stole our tent."

It was 2002 and a man from Blackpool, England, had submitted a joke to an experiment being conducted by psychologist Dr. Richard Wiseman of the University of Hertfordshire. During one year, people around the world had been able to judge the submitted jokes on an Internet site as well as contribute quips of their own. It was not a writing contest; anyone could submit any old joke he or she had once heard. Forty thousand jokes had been sent in, and at the experiment's end the scientists would unveil the world's funniest joke.

The joke the Blackpool man submitted didn't win, but it ended up second. It was a joke about Sherlock Holmes, Dr. Watson, and a missing tent. It had been around for some years, and no one really knew where it originally came from. But people in Russia knew. There they remembered it well. It was one of the many jokes that had been told in the 1980s, after the success of Igor Maslennikov's TV series. And it was always recounted in a hoarse voice sounding something like the rasp of Vasily Livanov.

★   ★   ★

There was a call from London.

"Mr. Maslennikov?" It was a woman's voice. Its owner was a Russian, married to an Englishman, he was later told.

"Yes," he answered.

"Igor?"

"Igor."

"It's Dartmoor's Sherlock Holmes society, the Baskerville Hounds." The Hounds were a scion group of an international Holmes society called the Franco-Midland Hardware Company (named after a business referred to in "The Stockbroker's Clerk"). They focused on only one thing—studying *The Hound of the Baskervilles*. "Our president Philip Weller would like to ask you to meet with us. My name is Tanya. Please, write down my London telephone number."

"I'm sorry," said Maslennikov, "but I do not understand anything."

"Dartmoor's Sherlock Holmes society, the Baskerville Hounds, love your movies and want to meet you. We are ready to come to Saint Petersburg."

They hung up. Maslennikov still didn't understand. Lenfilm had tried to sell the Sherlock Holmes series internationally in 1982, but nothing had happened after that. The West had never been won. And yet here he was, about to meet fans from England!

In Russia the success had continued. Lenfilm had made new films until 1986, eleven episodes in all. Since then there had been many reruns, and the series had somehow become a national cultural treasure.

On a September evening in 2003, Igor Maslennikov was on his way to Strelna, on the outskirts of Saint Petersburg. The English had arranged to meet him at the Baltic Star hotel, next to the newly restored Constantine Palace. Tanya and someone from the Baskerville Hounds would be waiting for him there.

The seventy-two-year-old director entered the hotel. There they were, not two, but eighteen persons—from Germany, France, Japan, and of course, good old England—led by a gentleman, Mr. Philip Weller, the president of the society. Apparently this society had a lot of "branch offices" worldwide.

They exchanged gifts. Maslennikov was given a huge bottle of whiskey and a certificate that declared he was an honorary member of the Baskerville Hounds. He gave the visitors copies of a DVD with the Russian films.

They talked for a while. Tanya interpreted.

"How come you know our movies about Sherlock Holmes so well?" Maslennikov wondered, still amazed.

"We have all of them."

"But they have not been sold in the West! Our TV did not meet the western standards."

"Your films have been shown on channels all over Eastern Europe and in the GDR as well."

"Yes, they have," said Maslennikov.

"West Berlin watched TV of East Germany."

"Well . . ."

"Not only watching, but also recording it on VHS tapes."

And there they were, in a Saint Petersburg hotel, the foreign fans of the twenty-year-old Soviet television series. Perhaps they were among the first fans from the West, but they would not be the last.

Soon DVD versions of the series would be sold and distributed all over the world, and the number of fans would grow.

Soon Igor Maslennikov's creation would be widely recognized as one of the best Sherlock Holmes adaptations ever made.

The cultural context would, however, stay in Russia. No one abroad would understand how synonymous the legendary words "porridge, sir" (from Lenfilm's version of *The Hound of the Baskervilles*) would be with England and Englishness. And no one would tell the tent joke in a really hoarse Livanovian voice.

101

O N MARCH 14, 2004, a large spread appeared in the *Sunday Times* describing a forthcoming auction at Christie's. The objects to be sold were in large part the contents of the Conan Doyle archive.

Richard Lancelyn Green had been informed about the auction in advance and had done everything in his power to try to prevent it from going ahead. This was not, he maintained, in accordance with Dame Jean's wishes. If the auction took place, large portions of the family archive would be spread among private collectors, in many cases placing the items out of reach of interested researchers.

In the weeks after the newspaper article, Green changed. He was by nature a friendly person, although shy and reserved, with a gentle voice. Friends who spoke to him on the phone noted that the impending auction had hit him hard.

On March 28, the fifty-year-old Richard Lancelyn Green was found dead at his home.

Green's tragic death was quickly sensationalized, given titillating coverage in the newspapers to amuse readers.

The cause of death was garroting with a shoelace. It was not possible to determine whether Green himself was responsible, although his friends—and the police—felt that suicide was the most likely explanation.

For those journalists who loved to link Sherlock Holmes to mysterious deaths or revel in conspiracy theories and talk of some "curse of Conan Doyle," this was all too good to resist. The media attention lasted for weeks, coming even from highbrow newspapers and radio programs. Later a BBC documentary about the events was broadcast.

While the Green tragedy was unfolding, the auction at Christie's was also widely reported. The auction had been arranged by Anna Conan

Doyle's heirs, and had been preceded by arrangements in the family regarding the objects owned by Anna and Dame Jean respectively. Two days before the auction, the British Library sent out a press release, stating that it was in touch with the consignors and executors to make sure that the sale didn't include any of the material that was due to it under the terms of Dame Jean's will. The library had been assured that that was the case.

The British Library bought many important documents at the sale and subsequently acquired those that had not sold. While this was undoubtedly good news for Conan Doyle researchers, it also served to make Green's early passing yet more tragic.

With the help of the newly acquired collections at the British Library and access to parts of Richard Lancelyn Green's collection, and with the assistance of Dame Jean's executor, Charles Foley (whom he later criticized in the afterword of his book), Andrew Lycett was able to complete his biography of Arthur Conan Doyle, *Conan Doyle: The Man Who Created Sherlock Holmes*, in 2007. That same year Conan Doyle Estate Ltd. authorized publication of a unique selection of Conan Doyle's letters, primarily those written to his mother. The book, *Arthur Conan Doyle: A Life in Letters*, edited by Jon L. Lellenberg, Daniel Stashower, and Charles Foley, won the Edgar Award for best critical/biographical work and also received further acclaim and awards.

It was two days after Richard Lancelyn Green's death. Nicholas Utechin, the editor of the *Sherlock Holmes Journal*—published by the Sherlock Holmes Society of London—got a phone call from Green's sister. She asked him to come and help her identify the most important items in her brother's collection, so that they might be immediately removed and put into safekeeping.

Utechin had known Green since the late 1970s but had been in his home only once. Green lived in the two lower floors of a London town house. The income he got from renting out the top two floors was what he lived—and collected—on, London rents being what they were.

First Utechin and Green's sister had a look at the ground floor. Nothing was there, no visible trace of manic collecting. Any normal non-Sherlockian could have been living here.

They went down to the basement, along with the packers, to a corridor filled with books—in crates, shelves, and piles. Any other collector would have considered these things a first-rate collection, but Utechin knew that he should just pass them by. He continued to the room on the right.

There they were: all the first editions of Conan Doyle's books. For any Sherlock Holmes and Conan Doyle enthusiast, seeing these volumes would bring a moment of joy. For Utechin, however, it was impossible to feel anything approaching that on this sad occasion. It was not just a collection; at least thirty years of passion and hard work were behind the accumulation of the books. All collectors knew that the volumes you loved most were the ones that you had to search for, to fight for, as if each and every one of them had been a kind of Holy Grail. Other volumes could be equally fine and precious, but for a collector each item had a story, of lesser or greater importance, that added a personal value to the book. Without their collector the books were no longer buzzing with such memories. It was a silent library. As long as it was kept together, however, it would bear the distinct memory of Richard Lancelyn Green.

Utechin then noticed the shelves of Sherlockian scholarship. He told the packers that everything on those shelves should be taken. In his own collection at home Utechin was proud to have two first editions of H. W. Bell's *Sherlock Holmes and Dr Watson: The Chronology of Their Adventures*, from 1932, with green boards. On one of Green's shelves he found nine copies! These were from a total print run of five hundred copies. And all of the nine copies had a thin dust jacket. Utechin had not even known that the book had originally appeared in a dust jacket.

Utechin and the packers continued. It was an almost impossible task. Everywhere there were books and innumerable rare or original documents connected to the life of Conan Doyle or the world of Sherlock Holmes. Green had never had any problems locating items among all his documents, but his system was utterly opaque for any outsider.

There were important items missing. Utechin knew of some extremely rare and valuable things in the collection, and they simply were not there. He took a break upstairs and then noticed it: between two old chairs stood a two-foot-tall, light gray filing cabinet. Green's sister had the key.

Utechin lifted up one after another of the most coveted items in the Sherlockian world.

For the first time he held in his hands a copy of *Beeton's Christmas Annual* from 1887, in which *A Study in Scarlet* was originally published.

He noticed something glimmering: the silver cigarette case, inscribed "From Sherlock Holmes 1893" that Conan Doyle had given illustrator Sidney Paget as a wedding present.

He kept looking. And there it was, the signed copy of *The Adventures of Sherlock Holmes*—featuring not only Conan Doyle's signature, but also those of Dr. Joseph Bell, George Newnes of the *Strand Magazine*, and William Gillette himself.

Even on such a sad day, it was impossible not to be stunned.

It turned out that Richard Lancelyn Green's collection would be kept together; the memory of the person and his achievement would live on. Green had bequeathed his collection to the city of Portsmouth, which had once been so helpful during his research into Conan Doyle's first years as an author. Once everything had been gathered from all of Green's rooms—as well as from a second flat that he kept—the items filled nine hundred large archival boxes, eventually to be scrutinized and cataloged.

102

"So what's going on with Sherlock?" Terry Gilliam asked.

Sitting at a little corner table inside a tapas bar were Mitch Cullin; the director Terry Gilliam, of Monty Python fame; and the producer who together with Gilliam had made Cullin's novel *Tideland* into a film. It was November 2004. Outside the bar it was cold, very cold. They were in Regina, Canada, where they had shot the film, a city that had taken its name in honor of Queen Victoria, Victoria Regina—or just *V. R.*, as Sherlock Holmes had written on his wall in bullet holes.

Cullin told the filmmakers about the phone call he had received the day before from his agent.

"Oh, Mitch, I have some terrible news," the agent had said, and then told Cullin about another book that was to be published at the same time as *A Slight Trick of the Mind*. It was a novella about the retired Sherlock Holmes, living with his bees in Sussex, on the cusp of the modern age, more literary than mystery.

"Well, you know, what can you do? These things happen," said Cullin. If only it hadn't been Michael Chabon, one of the greatest authors of the day, who had written it.

Cullin expected Gilliam to say something like, "Ah, don't worry about it, it'll work out fine." He didn't.

Instead he grinned wildly, cackling with that insane laugh of his, and sputtered, "Oh, you're screwed! Chabon's good! He's real good!"

The only positive thing was that Cullin hadn't yet learned about Caleb Carr's forthcoming Sherlock Holmes book. Thinking back on that evening in the tapas bar, Cullin was sure that had Carr been mentioned, Gilliam would have gladly pointed out that Cullin's book was destined to become a thin layer of mayo between two mighty slices of Texas toast.

*　　*　　*

When Cullin had finished writing his Sherlock Holmes novel in 2002 and sent it to the publishers of his previous book, they had mostly been perplexed. It was a fine novel, yes, but publishable? Not really. Cullin felt, on the one hand, that it was the most commercial thing he had ever produced. On the other hand, he realized that there was hardly any market for Sherlock Holmes books anymore. He hadn't been in touch with the Sherlockian world since the mid-1980s and wasn't even sure if there were still any Sherlockians out there. Maybe it had all died off after John Bennett Shaw's passing. Stranger things had happened.

Cullin, who had always been his own agent, tried publishers in England and Japan instead. No one was interested. The British editor he contacted thought that the UK audience would have problems accepting this novel about an old Sherlock Holmes for one main reason: it was written by an American.

The book was probably never going to be published. Cullin was OK with that. He had decided to stop writing fiction, and the unpublished manuscript, stashed in a box at the back of his bedroom closet, was a fine note to conclude his fiction career. He had written it to grapple with themes he thought were important, and it was of less importance that anyone else read it.

He was tired of the solitude, the poverty, and the continual battles he had to endure to get his books published on his own terms. It wasn't fun anymore. So he moved to Los Angeles and got a part-time job stocking shelves at a grocery store late at night after the store had closed. Then he walked home to his small studio apartment with the beer he had bought in the store and watched TV until the morning.

On the very day he was fired from his grocery-store job, Cullin had received an e-mail from Terry Gilliam. The financial backing was now in place; Gilliam could start filming Cullin's novel *Tideland*. That same week a New York agent left a message on his answering machine. Cullin's editor in England had sent him the Holmes manuscript.

Cullin called him. The agent loved the story.

"If you'd let me, I'd really love to represent you and this book," the agent said.

Cullin disliked literary agents. But he had nothing to lose, so he shrugged and said, "Sure, if you think you can sell it."

"I don't think I can sell it," the agent replied. "I know I can."

A couple of weeks later there was a bidding war for the novel. A film option followed, prior to the book's publication, and then, because Cullin had held on to his foreign rights, he was able to sell the book abroad to quite a few foreign publishers throughout 2004 and 2005. The only two holdouts were Japan and the United Kingdom, the two countries in which the novel was set.

Something had happened in the Sherlockian publishing world. There had been small-press publishing ever since the 1930s, when members of the Baker Street Irregulars and London's original Sherlock Holmes Society had distributed privately printed pamphlets, booklets, and the occasional full-length book, in print runs of a few hundred copies at most, though often, obviously, in runs of precisely 221 copies.

That way of sharing one's own writings and also interesting essays, pastiches, and parodies by others continued for many years. In the Sherlockian world the written word was a means to enjoying the company of others, even when geographical distances sometimes made it difficult to meet in person.

In the 1980s and '90s several more-professional outlets for publishing nonmainstream Holmes material emerged. Gaslight Publications, Gasogene Press, and Calabash Press were three of the most important small-press publishers in this field. In the early 2000s the Baker Street Irregulars—now led by Michael F. Whelan—began publishing very high-quality books and soon became one of the two major Sherlockian small-press publishers. The other was Wessex Press.

Steven Doyle and Mark Gagen had formed Wessex Press in 1996 and immediately purchased Gasogene Press and renamed it Gasogene Books, an imprint of Wessex Press. Two years later they published the first of ten volumes of *The Sherlock Holmes Reference Library*, edited by Leslie S. Klinger, a Los Angeles lawyer and member of the Baker Street Irregulars. The book series was a scholarly annotated edition of all of Conan Doyle's Sherlock Holmes stories, including the apocrypha (articles, spoofs, and other texts on Holmes written by Conan Doyle). Much had happened in Sherlockian research since William S. Baring-Gould had published his best-selling *Annotated Sherlock Holmes* in the 1960s, so it was undeniably time for a new, definitive annotated edition. By the early 2000s the publisher W. W. Norton was in negotiation with Wessex Press for licensing the rights to the *Reference Library*. Norton wanted to do it in three lavishly illustrated volumes for a more mainstream audience. *The New Annotated Sherlock Holmes* appeared in November 2004 to enormous critical acclaim. It was a forceful indication that Sherlock Holmes was once again on the main stage of popular culture.

Sherlock Holmes had gone mainstream before, especially in the 1970s, and now it was happening again. Everything seemed to come at once.

In the same month the Norton book came out, Pulitzer Prize–winning author Michael Chabon published *The Final Solution: A Story of Detection*. Five months later came Mitch Cullin's *A Slight Trick of the Mind*. In July 2005 the English author Julian Barnes, who had previously won the Man Booker Prize, published *Arthur & George*, based on the true events in the case of George Edalji. And finally *The Italian Secretary*, a Sherlock Holmes pastiche by the best-selling author Caleb Carr, also appeared in 2005.

Sherlock Holmes was not for the fans only, and these books had shown how the master detective could be brought to a wide audience as popular or literary entertainment. It was only a question of time before Hollywood would realize that, too.

There was a message from Michael Chabon, totally out of the blue.

Mitch Cullin read it, and he noticed that suddenly he was smiling and a tingling feeling had arisen somewhere and everywhere in his upper body. Chabon wrote:

> Well, I finally got up the nerve to read *A Slight Trick of the Mind*. I was fully prepared, and indeed in my darkest heart hoping, to disdain it or at least dismiss it. But it's wonderful, damn it, and I'm loving it. Congratulations. You have done Sir Arthur, and Holmes, a great honor.

103

J OHN WATKISS, A forty-five-year-old British artist living in Burbank, California, had worked on some special projects during his career. In his early twenties he had made a short experimental film with Derek Jarman that got banned by the Thatcher government because of its anticapitalist undertones. After that he moved into the graphic-novel world of Dark Horse Comics, and then DC Comics and Marvel Comics. Someone suggested he should go to Hollywood, and so he did, ending up at Disney, where he set the visual style of the 1999 film *Tarzan*. More Disney work followed, plus he worked on the storyboards for the movie *Sky Captain and the World of Tomorrow* and painted a mural for the Ford Motor Company Museum.

And here he was, in 2006, working on the sketches for a rough-looking character, a young, muscular man with a sword in one hand and a pistol in the other. It was concept art for a film—meant not to visualize the scenes as a help for the director and the designers but to get a movie deal in the first place.

It was very much a question of chiaroscuro—strong contrasts between dark and light. Watkiss used dramatically staged ink-and-tone drawings, a lot of mood, plenty of action. This was not like any Sherlock Holmes he had ever seen. At the same time it was a Holmes that Conan Doyle had hinted about: a man who was quite happy to spend two weeks lying on his sofa doing nothing between cases.

This Holmes was a skilled amateur boxer—Conan Doyle had been a great fan of pugilism and had even based several short stories, a novel, and a play on it. Holmes was also a competent participant in the martial arts of bartitsu and singlestick as well as fencing. A man of action, he was a modern character that kids of today could relate to, both as a misfit and as an individual who went his own way.

It was a friend at DC Comics who had recommended Watkiss. The person looking for an illustrator had been an executive at Warner Brothers but had recently transitioned to the role of independent producer. Lionel Wigram was his name. He had been a fan of Sherlock Holmes since he was a kid.

Wigram asked Watkiss to do storyboard illustrations, setting the atmosphere and tone. For this Wigram was prepared to pay $5,000 of his own money. Wigram had written a story, and he needed Watkiss to draw up the scenes.

When he saw what Watkiss had drawn, Wigram realized it was what he had imagined, only better. Wigram bound the drawings in comic-book form, twenty-five pages with almost no text, and brought the book to Warner Brothers. He felt that a written story would not be sufficient to make the studio executives understand. When they looked at the illustrations they wouldn't give a moment's thought to Jeremy Brett or deerstalkers or pipes.

What the executives saw was a superhero. They had almost run out of comic superheroes to adapt for film by now, but this character had never been used in that way. This was the original superhero, a man whose superpower was his brain.

Warner Brothers bought the story—and, even more, the look of it—and paid for a writer to come on board and do a draft. The usual development process started, and a couple of drafts later everybody felt it was a pretty cool movie.

At that point the British director Guy Ritchie read it and liked it and wanted to do it. Now it would definitely be a different kind of Sherlock Holmes movie.

While the Sherlock Holmes character was in the process of being totally remade in the United States, the popularity of the Russian depiction—more true to the original—continued to grow. Appreciation for it had also flourished abroad. In February 2006 the actor Vasily Livanov became an honorary MBE (Member of the Order of the British Empire) for his portrayal of Sherlock Holmes.

One year later a statue featuring life-size figures of Sherlock Holmes and Dr. Watson was unveiled in Moscow on the Smolenskaya embankment, 120 years after the publication of *A Study in Scarlet*. Vasily Livanov was present as the honorary guest. His friend Vitaly Solomin, who had played Dr. Watson, had died in 2002.

It had taken the sculptor four months and nearly a ton of bronze to make the statue. Sherlock Holmes was standing, pipe in hand, while his irreplaceable companion, Dr. Watson, looked up at him from a bench. In a city that was dominated by formal monuments to statesmen, often with a controversial legacy, this would be a welcome addition.

The sculptor had based his work on the illustrations of Sidney Paget. When the spectators looked closely, however, they noticed that the faces of Holmes and Watson were more familiar than that. They were the faces of Vasily Livanov and Vitaly Solomin.

Back in the United States things were happening with Holmes in the film world.

It was commonplace in Hollywood for the production of two very similar films to begin simultaneously, at two competing studios. The phenomenon was known as "twin films," and the theme could be anything from volcanic eruptions or asteroids to animated ants or penguins.

In the summer of 2008 it was made known that Sherlock Holmes could be added to that list. Sacha Baron Cohen, best known as the writer and star of *Borat*, was to play the detective in a comedy. Robert Downey Jr., meanwhile, was to appear in a film with a more action-adventure profile. The latter film gained even more stardust with the casting of Jude Law as Dr. Watson. This was a big-budget production of Sherlock Holmes, the like of which few Sherlockians had ever expected to witness. *Sherlock Holmes and the Vengeance of Dracula* had come to nothing, and more than two decades had passed since the last Sherlock Holmes cinema opening.

Warner Brothers had actually had plans for a Holmes movie in the early 1990s, although it was foremost a Dr. Watson story. The concept had appealed to the studio—and to Dame Jean's American representative—but Warner couldn't get the one specific actor it wanted for the lead and wasn't interested in alternatives for the role.

And while everything went smoothly in the production of the Guy Ritchie movie, the Sacha Baron Cohen comedy had problems. It turned out to be mostly a trial balloon without much air in it, so Conan Doyle

Estate Ltd. said no thanks to the idea. Without the rights sewn up for it, the film company would have problems finding any financiers.

The Warner Brothers film, entitled simply *Sherlock Holmes*, premiered on Christmas Day, 2009. Some of the critics feared that this was not a film that Sherlock Holmes enthusiasts would like. Sir Arthur Conan Doyle, they were sure, would be spinning in his eighty-year-old grave.

This was not necessarily so—not if one cast an eye over the history of Sherlock Holmes. For practically all of his existence, the detective had also lived another, parallel life. The first Holmes parodies emerged in the early 1890s, and later that decade the character was further developed by William Gillette. Parallel Holmes was born, a literary figure whose roots stretched almost as far back as those of the original Holmes.

Robinson Crusoe, Don Quixote, Hamlet, the Three Musketeers, and Robin Hood had all been reimagined. The new versions generally were not criticized for departing from the original. Why, then, was it so important that Sherlock Holmes did not?

This playing with the detective, this continuing of the story, was, for many Sherlockians, every bit as popular as the original. As long as it contained at least a modicum of affection toward the original, and a few nods in that direction, many of the Sherlockians would be sold. Throughout the history of film, there had indeed been some very dull Holmes films. A filmmaker's attempt to remain close to the original did not necessarily make for a good film.

The Guy Ritchie film picked up a number of aspects of the original stories, things that could be used in a blockbuster movie. Holmes the man of action was one of them. The humor present in the dialogue between Holmes and Watson—a slightly ironic tone that teased the other's strengths and weaknesses—could also be traced to the original stories. In fact, Conan Doyle's tales of Holmes and Watson had formed a template for modern buddy films.

Furthermore, Sherlock Holmes and Dr. Watson were portrayed as fairly young in the Ritchie film. When they first met in *A Study in Scarlet*, Holmes was twenty-seven, Watson a couple of years older. Most of the cases took place while Holmes was between thirty-five and forty-five years old. It was of course possible to make them much older—everything was possible in parallel Holmes development—but the fact that they had often been played by older actors didn't necessarily make this accurate.

Sherlockians were a playful breed, seldom irritated by strange interpretations. Sure, they might turn up their noses at certain things, but ultimately they were just happy that there was still such interest in this master detective invented more than 120 years ago. Their motto "to play the game" was about accepting the conceit that Sherlock Holmes and Dr. Watson once existed; from that point one could go about researching the characters and the stories in an almost academic way. The motto was just as much about seeing the whole thing as a game, albeit a game treated delightfully seriously.

One of those Sherlockians, one of the foremost experts on the subject, had been a consultant for the film—Leslie S. Klinger, the Los Angeles attorney who had edited *The New Annotated Sherlock Holmes*.

Conan Doyle Estate Ltd. had been involved early on and had been paid for the use of the character Sherlock Holmes, but it had not exerted any other influence on the film.

To avoid Andrea Plunket and her trademark claims, Warner Brothers had also paid her—a fee that it could certainly afford, since the film grossed in excess of half a billion dollars. The project had been a great success, and Robert Downey Jr. picked up a Golden Globe for best actor in a motion picture musical or comedy.

A sequel was already being talked about, and on a talk-show sofa Robert Downey Jr. joked that it might provide a closer examination of Holmes and Watson's relationship—in bed. Andrea Plunket immediately appeared in the press to declare that she would not countenance any such sequel. She would rescind the rights in that case. Warner Brothers wisely ignored her.

It was January 2010 and the Sherlock Holmes world had once again seen the master detective receiving the attention he deserved. Nothing could be bigger than a Hollywood film, after all.

Right then, in a Welsh film studio, the recording of a new television series had just got under way.

It had started on a train, a few years earlier. Mark Gatiss and Steven Moffat's idea about a new Sherlock Holmes, brought into the modern world, was about to become a reality.

104

In Monte Carlo two men and one woman were having lunch at a restaurant.

The woman kept on about it; "Tell me all about Sherlock Holmes," she beseeched.

What was going on? She had never shown the slightest interest in the great detective. And *all* about Sherlock Holmes? Where to begin?

They had discussed the subject on the train so many times, for so many years. Someone ought to update and modernize Sherlock Holmes, just as had been done in the Basil Rathbone films.

The woman was Sue Vertue, a television producer since 1991 and married to one of the men, Steven Moffat. The other man was Mark Gatiss.

Moffat had just said to Vertue, "Someone should do that, and it's really annoying because it should be us."

"Why don't you?" asked Vertue, because she thought this idea was actually realistic.

The two men talked. There was no end to their knowledge and no stop button in sight. Vertue jotted down questions on a napkin. Who are these characters? What do they call each other? Is John married?

The more Moffat and Gatiss talked about Sherlock Holmes the more excited they got. What would be the modern equivalents of objects, events, and phenomena from the Victorian days? An abundance of ideas popped up.

The lunch was soon finished, and they had other things to do. It was the Monte Carlo Television Festival, and they were there for an awards show.

A second lunch followed, now at the Criterion restaurant in London's Piccadilly Square, the very establishment where Watson once met his old friend Stamford in *A Study in Scarlet*, which led to Watson meeting Holmes and then to 120 years of popularity for the dynamic duo. Steven Moffat, Mark Gatiss, and Sue Vertue were systematizing and fleshing out their ideas over a nice meal. It was Vertue who had chosen the restaurant. She knew of its iconic significance.

During the lunch they realized that nowadays Watson would have written his stories as a blog. The telegrams in the Holmes stories were now text messages. And it was unavoidable that Holmes and Watson would call each other anything else than Sherlock and John.

That was what changed it all, that transition from Holmes to Sherlock. That was the key element in presenting their relationship. It meant that they were equal, and John was the co-lead. The series was to be as much about him as about Sherlock and the adventures.

The trio approached the head of drama at BBC Wales. After they had pitched the TV series for an hour, it was time for the head of drama to say something.

"Modern Sherlock Holmes? Yes."

That was easy. Now they just had to do it.

By September 2008 the first script was finished. It would be a one-hour pilot. They planned to have a six-episode series. They needed to write more scripts.

A few weeks later, Vertue and Moffat saw the actor Benedict Cumberbatch in the film *Atonement*. Gatiss knew him, and the trio agreed that Cumberbatch should come in and do a reading for them. They needed no time for consideration. No other Sherlock was possible—Cumberbatch was perfect.

Then the hunt for John started. A number of actors came in, and they put each next to Cumberbatch, but there was never electricity. One day Martin Freeman stood there and just looked ordinary, which of course was what he specialized in when it came to acting. When Freeman said his lines, Cumberbatch suddenly changed his own way of acting, only slightly, but his Sherlock definitely became funnier and warmer.

In January 2009 they shot the pilot episode. Afterward it was shown to sample audiences—they praised it but also had some complaints. They thought the Scotland Yarders were too stupid, and they were asking for Moriarty. The BBC was happy with the pilot and wanted a series. The station had just broadcast the first season of the English remake of *Wallander*, starring Kenneth Branagh, and those episodes were ninety minutes long. This had proved to be a perfect format, so the BBC commissioned a series of three ninety-minute episodes of *Sherlock*.

Moffat and Gatiss had to rework the whole series. They needed to introduce Moriarty earlier than previously planned, but with the extra time they could make so much more of the relationship between Sherlock and John—they didn't have to spend every minute of each episode on the progress of the investigation.

They still wanted to start with the same episode, "A Study in Pink," but instead of inserting extra scenes into the pilot episode they decided to do it all over again. They would have a new script, a more modern 221b Baker Street flat, more location shots from London, a better camera, a new director (the previous one wasn't available), and thirty minutes more, to make it even better.

It was January 2010 and time to start the filming of the three episodes.

105

SHERLOCK HOLMES WAS suddenly the talk of the town. He was influencing men's fashion. Hollywood was making impressive films about him. But most significant, one of the cleverest and most widely discussed TV series of recent years was the one Hartswood Films had produced for the BBC about Sherlock Holmes.

From the first episode, *Sherlock* was a hit. The audience was treated to the same experience as the *Strand* readers of the 1890s. The Victorians had been given the opportunity to behold the most cutting-edge, modern literature of their day. The viewers of 2010 enjoyed the same, except that this was cutting-edge, modern television. This was a series capable of keeping far more than just dedicated Sherlockians glued to their television sets.

Many Holmes enthusiasts were pleased to see that Benedict Cumberbatch and Martin Freeman were so young, even younger than the actors in the Guy Ritchie film. After more than a century, Holmes and Watson were being portrayed by actors who were roughly the same age as their literary role models had been when they first met.

And then there was the emphasis on the duo's names, Sherlock and John. The shift from surnames to first names had given the characters a new lease on life. Their friendship took center stage. It had been a common thread throughout Granada's television series, and a comic device in Guy Ritchie's film, but here it formed the basis for the storytelling itself. The friendship between Sherlock and John was what brought the television series to life.

Not only did the episodes contain clever, witty nods to the original stories, but later seasons also incorporated references to beloved Sherlockian classics like Vincent Starrett's sonnet "221B" and William S. Baring-Gould's Holmes biography. Furthermore, the series built on earlier film versions, not least the Rathbone pictures from the 1940s.

Billy Wilder's *Private Life of Sherlock Holmes*, above all, influenced the characterization of Sherlock's brother, Mycroft. And the producers made their TV series with the same thought in mind that Wilder had had with his film: it was not a detective story, but a story about a detective.

Within hours after the first *Sherlock* episode aired, in July 2010, fan fiction was being posted to a variety of Internet communities.

Fan fiction and fandoms, or fan subcultures, had been around for a very long time but mainly as underground movements that distributed photocopied fanzines among friends and communicated through correspondence. When accessibility to computers and the Internet rose in the late 1990s and early 2000s, most of these fan activities ended up online. And that was when young Harry Potter entered the stage. The growing popularity of J. K. Rowling's books, especially after the first film came out in 2001, meant an enormous surge in activity among the fans. They wanted to do more than just discuss the stories; they wanted to create others themselves.

During these years of early online fandom, copyright holders were extremely protective. Warner Brothers, which thought the fans were stealing its property rather than celebrating—and even promoting—it, used to send cease-and-desist letters to the owners of websites publishing any fan work about the characters in the Harry Potter universe; and the company wrote threatening letters to teenagers all over the world, insisting they hand over domain names that somehow could be connected to the Harry Potter series. Film companies, accompanied by law enforcement, could turn up at a fan convention and close the vendor room for several hours. Entire web communities risked being deleted if the wrong material ended up there.

Finally the great infringement war was over. Precedent was established for what "fair use" meant, and its definition was expanded: if the use was not making money and it was some kind of creative transformation, the original creators wouldn't usually go after it. Copyright holders began to accept fan fiction, and started to cooperate with fans more and more, interacting with them and even encouraging fandom. The fandoms had become important for the continued success of books, films, and TV series—for their ratings, their popularity, and spreading news of them by word of mouth.

After ten years, the Harry Potter fandom still existed, but many of its hundreds of thousands of fans were actively searching for other popular-culture phenomena to form fandoms around. *Doctor Who* had been a cult science-fiction television series in the United Kingdom since the 1960s, and its fandom had grown significantly since the BBC had revived the series in 2005, after a sixteen-year interregnum. In 2008 one of the contributing writers of the *Doctor Who* series, Steven Moffat, took over as head writer. Another of the writers was Mark Gatiss. After *Doctor Who* fans watched the first trailer for *Sherlock* they started flooding over to this new series, forming a new fandom.

Some weeks after the third episode of *Sherlock* had been broadcast, a whole country was still talking about the detective. The scene was a tapas restaurant in Soho, London. A man had taken the author Anthony Horowitz out for lunch, having hinted that he had an interesting proposition to put to him.

And he had. Over lunch, he revealed that he represented the estate of Sir Arthur Conan Doyle. "How would you feel," the man asked Horowitz, "about writing the first new Sherlock Holmes novel for almost a century?"

That was how Horowitz—not entirely correctly—recalled the event when he was interviewed for the *Scotsman*. Conan Doyle Estate's US representative, Jon L. Lellenberg, didn't agree with that wording—ever since the early 1980s he had licensed new Holmes novels. There was nothing new about that.

But the involved UK parties kept to their story: this was the estate's first commission for a new Holmes novel. It became a unique selling point for Horowitz's pastiche, *The House of Silk*. The media interest that followed such a commission was high. Whatever the book's literary qualities, it certainly gained bigger sales by all the extra publicity and by having Conan Doyle Estate's newly designed logotype printed on the cover. The endorsement gave the book an aura of the extraordinary —instead of just one more Sherlock Holmes pastiche—and it sold hundreds of thousands copies all over the world.

The man at the tapas restaurant who represented Conan Doyle Estate Ltd. was satisfied. Anthony Horowitz actually knew him quite well, since he was Horowitz's own literary agent—who also happened to be representing the Conan Doyle operation in the United Kingdom.

The same agent had previously got another of his clients, the author Andrew Lane, to write a series of young-adult thriller novels about young Sherlock Holmes. The spectacular thing was how the seal of approval from Conan Doyle Estate Ltd. could help a book reach success.

It took merely three episodes of *Sherlock* to make Benedict Cumberbatch a star. He had done good work before, but now his name was on everybody's lips—if people could only remember it correctly.

In February 2011 Cumberbatch was starring in *Frankenstein*, a play at the National Theatre in London, at the South Bank on the Thames. He and actor Jonny Lee Miller alternated in the roles of Victor Frankenstein and the Creature.

It was seven in the morning when Kristina Manente arrived at the ticket line, two and a half hours before the day's seats could be obtained. The twenty-two-year-old American had become obsessed with the *Sherlock* episodes, and having noticed that Cumberbatch was in a play, she wanted to check it out. As a child she had loved the Disney movie about Basil, *The Great Mouse Detective*, which had introduced Sherlock Holmes to her.

Approximately thirty people were already in the line (this was before the real hype started and fans had to wait all night for tickets), and Manente sat down along the wall, doing her Latin homework—she was studying for a master's degree in medieval history at King's College.

Suddenly the man behind her started making a fuss. The people in front of Manente, some young Frenchwomen, had let someone join them. Manente told the man to calm down. People do save spaces for friends.

It turned out the Frenchwomen were *Sherlock* fans, and Manente continued chatting with them until they all had their tickets. The Frenchwomen told Manente all about Cumberbatch and his other work. Manente hadn't made many friends in London yet, so on a whim she asked one of the women for her phone number so they could meet up that evening after the show.

And that way Kristina Manente was introduced into *Sherlock* fandom. She met other fans through her French friend, discovered the blogger platform Tumblr, and followed her new *Sherlock* friends on Twitter. To make it easier to follow them, she made a Twitter list and named it the Baker Street Babes.

"It sounds like a group," one of the women tweeted back. Manente replied that she had an idea for a Sherlock Holmes podcast and that it would actually be a good name.

There was one big podcast in the Sherlockian world, *I Hear of Sherlock Everywhere*, produced by Scott Monty and Burt Wolder, which had been around since 2007. Manente had had a radio show while she was an undergrad and was itching to do something again.

A few months later the first Baker Street Babes podcast went live, featuring Kristina Manente and two other women: Ardy from Germany, and Katherine from England.

The group grew, adding Marie, Turk, Jenn, Maria, Amy, Sarah, and Taylor—from the United States, the United Kingdom, Germany, and France. Some of them had come over from Mary Russell fandom; Laurie R. King had by now published ten books about Mary Russell, and the young girl had grown into a woman—and married Sherlock Holmes. It was sometimes difficult to find hours for the recording of the show, when all the American and European participants were awake and available to produce it together online.

Something was going on in the Sherlock Holmes world. These enthusiasts were not only Cumberbatch and *Sherlock* fans; they had a much broader perspective on the Sherlock Holmes universe than that. And their perspective was new, as was readily obvious in their tagline:

Central London overfloweth with gorgeous, intelligent women with a thirst for murder. The Baker Street Babes: The Web's Only All Female Sherlock Holmes Podcast. Eat your heart out, Sir Arthur Conan Doyle.

106

E VERYTHING WAS DIFFERENT NOW.
    In May 2011 the *Sherlock* team started filming a second season. Three new ninety-minute films were to be made. The pressure the team members felt to make something equivalent to the first series— preferably even better—was huge.

When they had shot the first three episodes more than a year ago, nobody had cared about them. They had just been another film crew out on the streets. Not many had known who Benedict Cumberbatch was. Now there were hordes of fans during the location shoots, well behaved and respectful, of course, but making it more difficult for the actors and director.

The team had twenty-two days to film each episode and started with "The Hounds of Baskerville," the second to be broadcast. They shot most of it in the Cardiff studio and on suitable locations in Wales. There were also some scenes shot on Dartmoor—unusual for film and TV adaptations of the novel. A couple of days into the shooting they left the horror beyond and went to the glittering British Academy of Film and Television Arts (or BAFTA) awards ceremony at the Grosvenor House Hotel in London. Martin Freeman won the best supporting actor award for his role as John H. Watson. *Sherlock* was also named best drama series. The team had all the reasons in the world to celebrate—fittingly, on Conan Doyle's birthday, May 22.

They kept on winning awards. In Britain, Canada, the United States— and the Prix Europa award.

One day the American TV network CBS approached the producer Sue Vertue and her colleagues at Hartswood Films with a view to making a US version of the British series. The answer was no.

★   ★   ★

Sherlock Holmes was everywhere.

A second fast-paced movie with Robert Downey Jr. as Sherlock Holmes and Jude Law as Dr. Watson opened in December 2011, *Sherlock Holmes: A Game of Shadows*. This one introduced brother Mycroft (played by Sherlock Holmes enthusiast Stephen Fry), Professor Moriarty (Jared Harris), and the most impressive Reichenbach Falls ever seen—with even a gothic castle plunked on top of it.

When it came to books, the scale and breadth of the array of new Holmes stories were almost impossible to grasp. Never before had as many Sherlock Holmes pastiches been produced as emerged in the period following the success of the BBC series. This was partly because it had become easier to get published in an era of print-on-demand and e-books but was thanks also to several best-selling and praised titles in the genre. In America, Lyndsay Faye was feted for her 2009 novel *Dust and Shadow*, a story that pitted Holmes against Jack the Ripper.

The popularity of Holmes was evident also in other genres. There was a constant stream of new graphic novels about Holmes, both adaptations of the original stories and pastiches.

In a parallel development, the subject took off in computer and video games. The very first personal-computer game about Sherlock Holmes, named *Sherlock*, had appeared in 1984, a text-based adventure in which Holmes interacted with the other characters by asking questions, persuading them, and challenging them with proof. Computer games had evolved since then. For a while it was trendy to have scenes played by live actors. Then came the point-and-click adventures with VGA graphics. And since 2007 a Ukrainian company, Frogwares, had dominated the market with its Sherlock Holmes series, developed primarily for video-game consoles. Its 2012 game *The Testament of Sherlock Holmes* channeled a much darker side of Holmes, presenting a complex, adult story that also tried to be true to the character's roots. Video games had become more than just games—they were stories in their own right.

The movies, books, and video games flourished. And an abundance of fan-created products available through the Internet had recently joined them.

"I hear of Sherlock everywhere," his brother, Mycroft, told Watson in "The Greek Interpreter." It was still true.

★   ★   ★

On January 1, 2012, the first of the new *Sherlock* episodes was broadcast. "A Scandal in Bohemia" had been turned into "A Scandal in Belgravia," referring to the London district, and the adventuress Irene Adler—"To Sherlock Holmes she is always *the* woman"—was now a ruthless and brilliant dominatrix. Almost eleven million viewers watched the episode in the United Kingdom.

It was January 14, the day before the last episode of the second season. The Baker Street Babes podcast had grown a lot since Kristina Manente had come up with the idea less than a year earlier. The website Sherlockology, which was devoted entirely to the series, and the Baker Street Babes were at the center of online *Sherlock* fandom. Seldom had a television episode caused so much emotion—before it was broadcast.

Moffat and Gatiss had sent tweets and given answers in interviews that implied that Sherlock would die. The fandom freaked.

There were innumerable Tumblr blog posts declaring, "We're all going to die on Sunday!"

It was pretty much mass hysteria, because people were *expecting* Sherlock to die.

107

THERE WAS AN old man in an armchair.

The scene was set in Mycroft Holmes's peculiar gentleman's association, the Diogenes Club, and the old man making a cameo appearance was Douglas Wilmer. It was same Wilmer who had portrayed the detective for a generation of Sherlock Holmes–loving Brits who had grown up in the 1960s. Not least among his admirers had been Richard Lancelyn Green, who as a teenager had written fan letters to the actor and had gone on to become his close friend many years later. Wilmer enjoyed his connection with the world of Sherlock Holmes and had a great many friends in the Sherlockian societies. It was perhaps not surprising, then, that the bow tie he wore in the scene at the Diogenes Club was the club tie of the Baker Street Irregulars—blue, purple, and mouse-colored, the three colors with which Holmes's dressing gown, on different occasions in the original stories, had been described. The theory was that the colors in fact described the same dressing gown but that it had faded over the years.

It was January 15, 2012, and "The Reichenbach Fall" episode of *Sherlock* was being broadcast. Very few of the viewers had the color of Holmes's dressing gown on their minds. There were more alarming things going on.

A few hours later the Internet was alive with reactions. The meeting between Sherlock and Moriarty had elicited an emotional response from many fans. Mika Hallor—a self-confessed pop-culture nerd—had seen on blogs that people were calling for fans to wear black armbands in a show of support, just as readers were supposed to have done when the short story "The Final Problem" was published in the 1890s. Hallor, though, didn't think it was appropriate. Back then the readers hadn't known that Sherlock Holmes would later return, so their grief was real and justified. The energy and commitment now being corralled could be directed into a rather more contemporary response, she felt. The TV series employed both social media and graffiti—by using those elements the fans should be able to do something creative and fun, instead of gloomy and passive.

Her idea was for *Sherlock* fans to attempt to clear Sherlock's name from the spurious accusations made by Moriarty during "The Reichenbach Fall." Hallor aimed to start a movement, built on distributing flyers, stickers, tags, tweets, and blog entries, to demonstrate support for Sherlock.

She thought that she would have to rely on her friends to spread the message online—a few hundred people at most. She had underestimated the *Sherlock* fans' commitment.

The response was immediate. Her Tumblr post was "liked" and re-blogged several thousand times within just a few hours. By the following day, the total number of responses was over ten thousand.

Without any further involvement from Hallor herself, the campaign —under the banner "Believe in Sherlock," with the attendant hashtag #believeinsherlock—had spread across Facebook, Twitter, and the blogosphere. Messages such as "I believe in Sherlock" and "Moriarty was real" spread not only across Britain but also to several countries where the episode hadn't even been shown yet.

Fans from towns small and large began to find one another thanks to the movement. Imagine thinking you're all alone in some backwater in Texas, Finland, or the Philippines, and the next thing you know you find a flyer in the supermarket. More and more photos popped up on the Internet from big meet-ups around the world. The difficult part about Internet fan culture was that you found people with the same interests, but often those people were on the other side of the world. When #believeinsherlock took to the streets, though, it turned out that the fans were *everywhere*.

Not only had the fans taken Sherlock and John into their hearts; they had also, to a large extent, made these characters their own. Even more fan fiction was published online—including spin-offs that were only vaguely reminiscent of the traditional genre of the Sherlock Holmes pastiche. The fan fiction was mainly about the relationship between these two friends, a relationship that often went one step further—into "slash," the term used for fan fiction with a sexual relation between two persons of the same sex. "Johnlock" was what it was called when Sherlock and John interacted in this way. "Sheriarty" was Sherlock and Moriarty; "Mystrade" meant Mycroft and Lestrade. The list of possible combinations could go on forever.

This wave of creativity was not, though, restricted to the written word. Around the globe, gifted artists uploaded fan art based on the characters from the series. Skilled individuals also created fan vids—videos using spliced-together clips from the series to create new story lines, usually posted on YouTube.

Occasionally some of the fans' bright ideas spread far beyond the *Sherlock* fandom and became Internet memes. One such example, "Otters Who Look Like Benedict Cumberbatch"—four pairs of photos in a Tumblr post by Red Sharlach—soon became an Internet phenomenon; finally, Benedict Cumberbatch made an appearance on the Graham Norton Show during which he made faces to demonstrate the striking resemblance. In the fandom world Sherlock was more and more often illustrated as an otter—and John as a hedgehog (that's another story).

The Granada series, too, got some new fan treatment. The interest surrounding *Sherlock*, and the long wait for the next series, made lots of Holmes-hungry fans widen their search to the annals of television and film history, where they discovered Jeremy Brett, Basil Rathbone, and others playing their versions of the much-loved detective.

Thanks to DVDs and the Internet, a new generation of Sherlockians was able to discover old series and films. Above all, the new fans were reading the original stories, spurring an increase in sales of Conan Doyle's books.

This torrent of new Sherlock Holmes fans also provided broad support for the action brought by Arthur Conan Doyle expert John Gibson, who was attempting to save the author's former home, Undershaw, from complete redevelopment. Young, deerstalker-clad fans gathered in Trafalgar Square in an attempt to save the old house. There really was something special about Sherlock Holmes and his devotees.

108

Amerian television producer Rob Doherty was in one of many
meetings with his producing partner, Carl Beverly. They were
trying to come up with new projects and to zero in on something both
of them liked.

"Oh," said Beverly, in an oh-by-the-way way. "I've been thinking
about Sherlock in the present day in New York City."

In the days that passed after that meeting, Doherty kept on thinking
about this updated Sherlock Holmes. He had always fancied Holmes;
he had watched the Basil Rathbone movies with his mother when
he was a kid, had liked the Jeremy Brett series, and had read about
Holmes in comic books. In one of his favorite Batman comics, the
Caped Crusader meets Sherlock Holmes. He loved the fact that the
TV series *House*, starring Hugh Laurie, was basically a brilliant Holmes
adaptation—the creators of that series had even placed clues to this
connection here and there in the scripts.

Doherty started reading Conan Doyle's books for the first time as
an adult, and he really liked some of the details that had been over
his head when he was young, especially Holmes's dabbling in drugs.
Doherty continued his research, reading essays written by psychiatrists
and psychologists, some touting theories that Holmes was bipolar,
had Asperger's syndrome, or didn't feel comfortable in the company
of women.

Doherty laughed to himself. "Well, Watson should be a woman."
Holmes being forced into such a living situation—that would be
something!

He couldn't get that idea, a joke, really, out of his head. He thought
about it. What would it really change if Watson were a woman? Their
way of working? Their being roommates for some practical reason?
Their friendship?

And that was how it started, what soon was to become the CBS series *Elementary*.

Each episode was forty-two minutes long. The creators had to make a decision about what to focus on. For a CBS show like this—in the same police-consultant genre as *The Mentalist*, *Lie to Me*, *Castle*, and *Numbers* (styled *NUMB3RS*)—it was important to have a case presented and closed in each episode. Should they base the series on Conan Doyle's stories? Not a chance—then they would have no time to explore what Doherty thought of as the mythological aspects of the show: the relationship between Holmes and Watson as they become friends, partners, and excellent investigators.

It was a different kind of Sherlock Holmes TV series. It was about a detective, a former drug addict, played by Jonny Lee Miller, who had hit bottom and discovered he was not a machine, and what that meant to a mind like his. Dr. Joan Watson, played by Lucy Liu, was his recovery coach, who got more and more involved in his investigations, finally becoming a real companion to him and coming into her own as a detective, working both with him and on her own.

Each season had twenty-four episodes, and in the last episode of the second season, the forty-eighth, Jonny Lee Miller beat the record for the actor who had portrayed Sherlock Holmes the most times in films or on television. Ronald Howard had played the detective thirty-nine times in the 1950s; Jeremy Brett had done so in forty-one episodes; and Eille Norwood had been the star of forty-seven Sherlock Holmes silent movies between 1921 and 1923.

109

I T WAS MAY 22, 2014, and Conan Doyle was celebrating his 155th birthday, provided he was still around as the spirit he had expected to become after death.

If his spirit that day was at all present in the United States Court of Appeals for the Seventh Circuit in Chicago, Illinois, it didn't show which side it was on, either by levitating tables or through automatic writing.

On one side was Leslie S. Klinger, the Los Angeles lawyer, whose wife had given him William S. Baring-Gould's *Annotated Sherlock Holmes* in the late 1960s, the beginning of his huge interest in the detective, which led to his becoming a member of the Baker Street Irregulars and writing and editing a number of books about Holmes.

On the other side was Conan Doyle Estate Ltd., the company that had been formed by Anna Conan Doyle's and Dame Jean's heirs, which was the US copyright holder of Conan Doyle's last ten stories about Sherlock Holmes.

It was time for the oral argument. The sound of rustling papers was picked up by one of the microphones. Someone in the room was coughing. One of the three judges was Richard Posner, seventy-five years old, the author of nearly forty books on law and economics and identified as the most cited legal scholar of the twentieth century. Coincidentally, ten years ago Posner had reviewed Klinger's *New Annotated Sherlock Holmes* for the *New Republic*. Among other things, he had written, "The Holmes stories and the Holmes persona seem to me wildly overrated, and this annotated edition an eccentric venture." People in the Sherlockian world feared for what this might mean to the case.

The attorney representing Conan Doyle Estate Ltd. began. "There are two reasons the district court decision in this matter should be reversed," he said, his voice soft and precise. "The first is that it was an advisory opinion. Mr. Klinger's entire action asks for advice on what the law would be on a hypothetical future state of facts, if he finishes the book that he has started, and if he finishes that book in a certain manner."

Judge Posner interrupted: "But didn't you tell him that if he went ahead with it you were going to"—Posner chuckled—"either sue him or tell Amazon and the other booksellers not to carry his book?"

"Yes, we did, Your Honor . . ."

Judge Posner continued to interrupt the attorney's oral argument with further questions.

In 2011 Leslie S. Klinger and Laurie R. King had published *A Study in Sherlock*, a collection of new pastiches written by prominent, contemporary authors. In June that year the two of them and their publisher, Random House, had been approached by Jon L. Lellenberg, the US agent for Conan Doyle Estate Ltd. He demanded that they enter into a copyright license agreement, and he threatened to sue them if they didn't. In the end Random House agreed to pay $5,000 for such a copyright license.

Klinger and King decided to create a sequel; they felt that the first book had been successful enough to warrant a second volume of newly written Holmes stories, by a new set of authors. Conan Doyle Estate Ltd. heard of their plans and sent a message to their publisher, which this time was Pegasus Books:

If you proceed instead to bring out *Study in Sherlock II* unlicensed, do not expect to see it offered for sale by Amazon, Barnes & Noble, and similar retailers. We work with those companies routinely to weed out unlicensed uses of Sherlock Holmes from their offerings, and will not hesitate to do so with your book as well.

Pegasus refused to publish the book unless Klinger and King obtained a license from Conan Doyle Estate Ltd. Unlike Random House, Pegasus Books—a smaller house—was not prepared to pay for that license. King and Klinger, who were outraged that Random House had paid previously, assured Pegasus that they'd take care of the problem.

Instead of getting such a license, they sued Conan Doyle Estate Ltd., agreeing that Klinger would act as the plaintiff. They sought a

declaratory judgment that anyone was free to use material in the fifty
Sherlock Holmes stories that were no longer under copyright, including,
of course, the names and fundamental elements of Holmes, Watson,
and many other inhabitants of their world.

Conan Doyle Estate Ltd. initially defaulted, and the district court
ruled in the editors' favor, but fearing that a simple victory would
allow the company to challenge future books, King and Klinger still
wanted a declaratory judgment on the merits. In the end the company
responded. It argued that the fictional characters of Holmes and Watson were not available for all to use.

> The facts are that Sir Arthur continued creating the characters in the
> copyrighted ten stories, adding significant aspects of each character's
> background, creating new history about the dynamics of their own
> relationship, changing Holmes's outlook on the world, and giving him
> new skills. And Sir Arthur did this in a non-linear way. Each of the
> ten stories is set at various points earlier in the two men's lives—and
> even late stories create new aspects of the men's youthful character. In
> other words, at any given point in their fictional lives, the characters
> depend on copyrighted character development.

The company iterated that it was not a question of which story
elements you could or could not use, but that "a complex literary
personality can no more be unraveled without disintegration than a
human personality." As soon as you used the friendship, the emotions,
the warmth that were to be found only in the still-copyrighted stories,
you were infringing the copyright.

The company added, "Although basic principles of copyright law
apply, the outcome depends on the facts of when and where a character was created." Was Sherlock Holmes a complete character already
before the last ten stories were published, or did he become one by
the publication of those stories?

The district court's ruling had been a victory for creators. It stated
that creators were free to use the characters of Holmes and Watson
without licensing them from Conan Doyle Estate Ltd. The court cau-
tioned that "character elements" that appeared exclusively in the ten
post-1922 stories by Conan Doyle (those that remained in copyright)

were still protected by copyright. However, elements from the fifty pre-1923 stories were in the public domain. "Sherlock Holmes belongs to the world," Klinger said after the district court's ruling. "This ruling clearly establishes that."

Asked to comment about the court's limitation regarding the post-1922 stories, Klinger said, "We never disputed that. If an author wants to write about a character that appears only in one of those stories, the Estate's permission is required. We cherish the remaining ten stories and we respect the Estate's right to control them."

That was in December 2013. One month later Conan Doyle Estate Ltd. appealed to the Seventh Circuit Court of Appeals. And here they were now. The oral argument had been going on for twelve minutes.

"Suppose he said he's going to write a book," said Judge Posner to the counsel for the company. "And it's going to make no modifications in the public domain characters of Watson and Holmes, it's just going to have them investigate some other crime. They are going to be the same people. Does that violate anything? Does it? Yes or no?'

"If the—"

"Yes or no? And no 'ifs.'"

"The answer is no," the counsel said, before going back to his argument that Klinger should have presented a fully written book first, in order for the company to be able to determine whether there were any infringing elements in it.

"That's your first point," said Judge Posner. "Your second point, which is much more ambitious, is about this completion of the character and no one can use the character until he is completed. That is a very aggressive attempt to enlarge copyright law. That is your argument. Even if there is no infringement in the conventional sense." Posner continued, stating that the company's position was that until there were no more Conan Doyle stories about Sherlock Holmes and Watson in copyright, nobody could use those characters in any book, article, or story. "Right? That is your second argument."

"It is," the counsel said. "And I would say, in theory it may be possible to separate the protectable—in practice it's not, because the fully developed Sherlock Holmes character—"

"Oh, come on," interrupted Judge Posner. And the oral argument went on.

★ ★ ★

Seven minutes later, Judge Posner said:

"You seem totally unable to give an example of a lawful work using Holmes and Watson that wasn't simply a reproduction of the non-copyrighted early stories. If you could give us an example, maybe we'd understand. You want to reserve everything. And in fact you are creating what would be an irresistible temptation for any copyright owner, to keep publishing variants of his original work in order to perpetuate the copyrights of those original works. That is the game that is being played here."

The counsel went back to his previous argument, that Klinger should have brought the company a real book.

"You have still not given us an example," Judge Posner continued, "of a work that modifies the characters that were in the early stories and yet does not infringe the later stories."

When the counsel didn't supply an example, the judge said: "I asked you a very specific question. You refused to answer it." Then he added, "If you can't give me an example, I just can't accept your argument."

"It would be to create," said the counsel finally, "a new story using Sherlock Holmes and to stay away from the emotions that he had developed and was developing through his life in the copyrighted stories, from the relationships that he had that changed and matured from his maturity, from his warmth going from a colder person to a warmer person. If you stay away from those things and stay away from his attitude toward new technology . . . Without having a book in front of us, we tried to say what you would need to stay away from, the best we could."

Four minutes later it was time for Leslie S. Klinger's counsel to speak. There still had been no rising or rotating tables, no sign of the spirit of the author. Maybe Sir Arthur Conan Doyle was really dead after all.

"If the Conan Doyle Estate," he said, "had said at the outset what its counsel seems to have said a few moments ago we would not be in this courtroom."

Klinger's counsel meant that Conan Doyle Estate Ltd. had never before indicated that Klinger and King could use the characters so long as they avoided copyright-protected material. Rather, the company had simply insisted that any use of the characters had to be licensed. The publisher Pegasus Books, which had been prepared to sign a contract for the book, "backed down in the face of this threat by the Conan Doyle Estate, which we pointed out in our brief is the business model of the Conan Doyle Estate. Appellant plays on the fog of uncertainty that it has succeeded in erecting around the copyright issues, such that producers and motion picture companies and television networks are willing to pay a licensing fee rather than bear the burden of a lawsuit, which Mr. Klinger chose to do."

On June 16, the US Court of Appeals for the Seventh Circuit upheld and affirmed the judgment of the district court.

A few weeks later Klinger filed a petition asking the court to require that Conan Doyle Estate Ltd. pay the legal fees and costs incurred to date by Klinger and King in the case, amounting to about $30,000 for the appeal. In response, the company filed a motion on July 3, 2014, asking the Supreme Court to grant an emergency stay, delaying the finality of the Seventh Circuit's order. Conan Doyle Estate Ltd. was going to ask the Supreme Court of the United States to overturn the Seventh Circuit's decision—and meanwhile it would lose significant licensing fees because Sherlock Holmes was so popular at present.

The company's motion was denied. And on November 3, 2014, the Supreme Court—which mostly accepted cases that had a constitutional bearing—denied its petition for the Court to hear its appeal.

Judge Posner, awarding Klinger almost $31,000 in attorneys' fees, wrote in an opinion on the case:

> The Doyle estate's [i.e., the company's] business strategy is plain: charge a modest license fee for which there is no legal basis, in the hope that the "rational" writer or publisher asked for the fee will pay it rather than incur a greater cost, in legal expenses, in challenging the legality of the demand. The strategy had worked with Random House; Pegasus was ready to knuckle under; only Klinger (so far as we know) resisted. In effect he was a private attorney general, combating a disreputable business practice—a form of extortion—and he is seeking by the present motion not to obtain a reward but merely to avoid a loss. He has performed a public service—and with substantial risk to himself, for had he lost he would have been out of pocket

for the $69,803.37 in fees and costs incurred at the trial and appellate
levels ($30,679.93 + $39,123.44). The willingness of someone in Klinger's
position to sue rather than pay Doyle's estate a modest license fee is
important because it injects risk into the estate's business model. As a
result of losing the suit, the estate has lost its claim to own copyrights in
characters in the Sherlock Holmes stories published by Arthur Conan
Doyle before 1923. For exposing the estate's unlawful business strategy,
Klinger deserves a reward but asks only to break even.

Judge Posner concluded, "It's time the estate, in its own self-interest,
changed its business model."

Klinger also filed a motion in the district court, asking for the $39,000-
plus in fees and costs incurred in the lower court. Ultimately, Conan
Doyle Estate Ltd. settled regarding those fees and costs, and the district
court motion was withdrawn.

Six months later in New Mexico, where Mitch Cullin had been born
forty-seven years before, a place that belonged to his past, a suit was
filed against him; his publisher, Penguin Random House; the film company Miramax; and director Bill Condon. It had not come ten years
ago, when A Slight Trick of the Mind had been published, but it came
now, a few weeks before the film Mr. Holmes—based on the book, with
Ian McKellen playing the elderly Holmes—was to have its premiere.
Conan Doyle Estate Ltd. had sued them for copyright infringement
and now, following the court decision that it was against the law to
use anything from the last ten stories, demanded damages and a share
of profits from the film.
    "We admire both the book and the movie, and we have told the
defendants that," the suit read. "But much of the setting, plot and
especially the character and emotional makeup of Sherlock Holmes
as an older man, come straight from copyrighted stories."
    There had been only a few actual references in the book that could be
tied to copyrighted stories—it could be claimed that these constituted
fair use—and in the film none of those references were even included.
The fact that the retired Sherlock Holmes became a beekeeper in Sussex
could already be found in "The Second Stain" from 1904. Conan Doyle
Estate Ltd. claimed that the entire book—and thus the movie—was

impossible without the still-protected stories from *The Case-Book of Sherlock Holmes*.

Finally a settlement was made between Conan Doyle Estate Ltd. and Mitch Cullin's publisher, and another was made with the movie-makers and distributors.

What would Conan Doyle have said of this meticulous protection of his stories, still going on in a millennium so far in the future on the day he passed away? Only the spiritualists that kept in touch with him would know.

One thing at least was certain. Cullin's old hometown Santa Fe was known as a spiritual, magical city, a place for healing, set in an area where anything could happen under that blue heaven and those pink rain clouds. And that day when the suit against Cullin and his associates was filed by Conan Doyle Estate Ltd.'s lawyer, who happened to live in Santa Fe, there were rotating, rising tables all over town.

Maybe it was Conan Doyle, finally having had enough—either of lawsuits or of people infringing his copyrights. Who knows? Or maybe it was just the imagination of the city's creative inhabitants.

The day the suit was filed against Cullin in 2015 just happened to be, again, May 22, but now Conan Doyle's 156th birthday. And someone, identity unknown, was present.

110

"Have you thought about donating your papers?" Leslie S. Klinger asked Mitch Cullin during a lunch.

Cullin had not. Who would be interested? He was still very much alive and creatively active—nowadays concentrating on photography instead of fiction.

"Nonsense," said Klinger. He was sure that the Sherlock Holmes Collections at the University of Minnesota would be interested.

A few months later, in his home studio, Cullin found himself surrounded by his entire life as a writer. He had decided to end his career as a novelist. After *A Slight Trick of the Mind* had been turned into the film *Mr. Holmes*, he had felt some sort of completion.

So he was packing, eight boxes, weighing four hundred pounds in total.

Wherever he looked there were piles of memories: an endless number of notebooks; screenplays, published manuscripts, and unpublished manuscripts; letters; doodles showing things that would make the archivist blush.

Only a small part of it was related to Sherlock Holmes. Cullin hadn't been a Sherlockian since he was a teenager back in Santa Fe, and only one of his novels had featured Sherlock Holmes.

Cullin finished packing and then ran over to the local CVS pharmacy to buy some water and toilet paper. He came home only ten minutes later to find that FedEx had already come and taken the boxes away.

He felt lighter—four hundred pounds lighter.

There they were, together again. Cullin and his old friend and mentor John Bennett Shaw—not in person but as neighbors, in a long row of archive shelves.

And they were not alone. So many of the others were there, even Conan Doyle himself in some original *Hound of the Baskervilles* manuscript pages. There were William Gillette's scrapbooks and photo album, a big Frederic Dorr Steele collection, the radio scripts of Edith Meiser, the entire collection and correspondence of Vincent Starrett, the William S. Baring-Gould collection, and so much more. Important parts of the Sherlockian world and history were here, in one location, and in the middle of it all was a large chunk of Mitch Cullin's creative and personal past.

111

For Emmanuelle Berthault, February 24, 2014, began much like any other day at work, within the stout walls of the nineteenth-century bastion Fort de Saint-Cyr, part of the fortifications built to defend Paris. The archives of Cinémathèque Française, comprising forty thousand films, were housed there.

The archive had been founded in 1936 by a young man named Henri Langlois, who, with the help of a few friends, had amassed a small number of films that might otherwise have been lost. The collection grew very rapidly, but was threatened by the German occupation during World War Two, when the Nazis ordered the destruction of any films recorded before 1937. Langlois and his associates smuggled large amounts of material out of the country for safekeeping until the war was over.

One of Emmanuelle Berthault's duties was to categorize the films in the enormous collection, something she undertook very carefully, in alphabetical order. Now, she had arrived at the letter *S*.

Occasionally, Berthault would come across films that had been wrongly cataloged earlier and that the archive was therefore unaware it possessed. Sometimes two separate films were filed under a single label, a trick Langlois had made regular use of in order to conceal valuable films during the war years. It was in a pile of film cans marked "Sherlock Holmes" that she made an unexpected discovery.

The cans turned out to contain not a single film, but several. There were a German production—*Der Mann, der Sherlock Holmes War*, from 1937—and a 1954 episode of the Sheldon Reynolds TV series. These films were also preserved in other archives around the world, so it was simply a case of updating the catalog. Between these two talking pictures, however, Berthault found five cans containing reels of a duplicate negative. At first she was confused, but as she watched the opening frames of the film she had no difficulty in identifying it. She saw the title of the film, the name of the director, and the production company—but, above all, its famous leading actor.

Recording these details was so straightforward, and the discovery made in such mundane circumstances, that Berthault did not immediately realize the significance of her find. It was only later, once it had sunk in, that she understood that what she had uncovered was the Sherlockian Holy Grail.

Another city, another sacred item. The visitor walked between the artifacts that had been lent to the museum. The exhibit was truly amazing!

The visitor was an American and had been a Sherlockian as long as she could remember, had even written some scholarly articles. The visitor was an old man, a member of the Sherlock Holmes Society of London. The visitor was a young woman who had become fascinated by the whole Holmes phenomenon through the new BBC series. The visitor could be anyone, just an ordinary museum visitor. The interest in Sherlock Holmes was everywhere, everything, everyone.

The visitor studied in detail Sidney Paget's original illustrations and noted the delicate pencil work. And the cigarette case that Conan Doyle had once given to Paget as a wedding present. And—this was astonishing—several handwritten manuscripts and two well-preserved copies of the extremely rare *Beeton's Christmas Annual* from 1887. Accompanying these was a host of other items illustrating the breadth of this icon of popular culture.

The visitor then turned around and saw it—finally—a small piece of paper in a showcase. There it was, the one item that had started it all, in an era that was so remote, and yet seemed so very near in our hearts. The piece of paper was on public display for the first time in more than sixty years.

It was the autumn of 2014, and a six-month exhibition at the Museum of London had just opened. The lead curator, Alex Werner, had never spent so much time giving interviews. *Sherlock Holmes: The Man Who Never Lived and Will Never Die* was the largest British exhibition on the detective since the display during the Festival of Britain in 1951. And in the United States another big Sherlock Holmes exhibition—a more interactive one—was on tour.

Through the glass the visitor studied every word of the old, fragile document. At the top the author had crossed out the initial title, "A Tangled Skein." The visitor read farther down: "Reserved—sleepy eyed young man—philosopher—Collector of rare Violins—An Amati—Chemical Laboratory." They were the first preliminary ideas for what was to become so dear to so many—something that had become such an important part of the visitor's life. "I am a Consulting detective." These were Conan Doyle's notes when he was preparing to write *A Study in Scarlet,* and the visitor could look at them forever, knowing they were the big bang that had created all Sherlockian life since.

The Paris discovery was not unveiled until October 2014. Céline Ruivo at the French archive made contact with film-restoration expert Robert Byrne, of the San Francisco Silent Film Festival, who in turn asked his good friend film professor Russell Merritt to provide Sherlockian expertise. Merritt had been invested as a member of the Baker Street Irregulars as far back as 1960 and had even been "mousified" by Eve Titus, featuring in the Basil of Baker Street books as Russmer.

The day of the world premiere of the digitally restored film had arrived: January 31, 2015. The venue was the Cinémathèque Française in Paris. Deerstalkers punctuated the crowd. The orchestra, featuring a grand piano, a violin, and percussion, was ready to accompany the silent film, which was almost two hours long.

In just a few minutes the film would appear on the silver screen. For the first time almost in living memory, it would be possible to see William Gillette performing in the role of Sherlock Holmes. William Gillette, aside from Conan Doyle, was the single most important person in the success and immortality of Sherlock Holmes. In a line of direct descent, he was the forebear of a century of Sherlock Holmes productions on film, television, radio, and the stage—a history that had gone from Holmes to Sherlock and back again. Sherlock Holmes lived on, not merely in his current incarnation, but in parallel, in all those myriad forms he had taken to date. Such was the interest in Holmes and the path that led to today's popular portrayal of Holmes and Watson's adventures. Such was the power of these fictional characters. Such was our love for them.

The film that had been unearthed was the near-mythical 1916 film *Sherlock Holmes* based on Gillette's own play. The film, it had been feared, might have been lost forever.

"The stage is set, the curtain rises, we are ready to begin," a Sherlock from the future or the past would say.

AUTHOR'S THANKS

W ITHOUT THE EARLIER research in the field, this book would have been all but impossible to write. I mean not just the great, broad works but also, and perhaps above all, the articles and books written by Sherlock Holmes and Conan Doyle experts over the last eight decades that examine the tiniest details in great depth. I have found mountains of facts, ideas, and inspiration in the hundreds of such sources and adapted them for the story I wanted to tell.

My own original research also crops up throughout the book, above all in the chapters that deal with the decades after Conan Doyle's death. Richard Lancelyn Green bequeathed his incredibly comprehensive collection to the city of Portsmouth, which in turn established the Arthur Conan Doyle Collection—Lancelyn Green Bequest. Thanks to the generosity and expertise of the senior archivist Michael Gunton, I have been able to illuminate a whole series of significant events that had until now been mostly unknown. Being able to immerse myself in the Conan Doyle family history on location was a wonderful feeling, as was spending the evenings wandering home through the streets once pounded by Conan Doyle himself.

I have also been assisted in my archival research by the British Library, Amy Hurst at the Shakespeare Birthplace Trust, Céline Ruivo of Cinémathèque Française, Mazie Bowen at University of Georgia Special Collections Library, Peggy Perdue at the Arthur Conan Doyle Collection at the Toronto Public Library, and Timothy Johnson at the Sherlock Holmes Collections at the University of Minnesota. Julie McKuras dug out necessary documents at the last institution. Uwe Sommerlad went to the Artur Brauner–Archive at the Deutsches Filminstitut in Frankfurt am Main to find exciting facts about *Sherlock Holmes und das Halsband des Todes*. Tamar Zeffren helped me by going through documents concerning the musical *Baker Street* in the Alexander H. Cohen papers at the New York Public Library. To complete my knowledge about the musical projects during the 1960s, Dana Cameron went to Boston University's Howard Gotlieb Archival Research Center to check some additional facts in the Richard Condon collection.

This book was originally published—in a shorter version—in Swedish in 2013, and when the time came for an English edition, I received great support, corrections, and suggestions from, among others, Mickey Fromkin, Roger Johnson, Jon L. Lellenberg, Christopher Redmond, Susan Rice, and Nicholas Utechin. Peter E. Blau has been a constant source during my research—there is hardly anything Sherlockian he can't provide information about. Elena Ahlmark studied Russian material that I wasn't able to read myself and contributed useful comments. Mitch Cullin generously and abundantly shared his memories with me, and his beautiful way of describing people, places, and events shines through in the chapters about him.

Many friends and acquaintances in the Sherlockian world have provided me with information and other material that I could not have managed without: Nils Andersson, Dan Andriacco, John Baesch, Phil Bergem, Kate Brombley, Vinnie Brosnan, Bert Coules, Susan Dahlinger, Steven Doyle, Alistair Duncan, John Gibson, Leah Cummins Guinn, Jim Hawkins, Paul Herbert, Evelyn Herzog, Don Hobbs, Jens Byskov Jensen, Robert Kirby, Anastasia Klimchynskaya, Leslie S. Klinger, Luke Benjamen Kuhns, Matt Laffey, Palle Schantz Lauridsen, Michele Lopez, Andrew S. Malec, Kristina Manente, Russell Merritt, Nicholas Meyer, Scott Monty, Alexander Orlov, Carrie Parris, Andrew Peck, Robert Pohle, Ashley Polasek, Charles Prepolec, Brian W. Pugh, Betsy Rosenblatt, Monica Schmidt, Alexander Sedov, Andrew Solberg, Patricia Stiehle, Randall Stock, Catarina Tjällberg, Jean Upton, and Bill Vande Water. Birgitta Larsson, Bengt Malmberg, Fredrik Tersmeden, and John Tibbetts have also provided useful information. I have been encouraged and assisted by countless other friends on Twitter and Facebook.

To my literary agents, Carina Brandt and Elin Hellström: I love having you as my cicerone guides on our present voyage throughout the literary world.

Thanks too to Daniel Stashower, who, through his Conan Doyle biography *Teller of Tales*, inspired me and demonstrated how to write exciting prose about people's lives. And Jenny Lingstam: I am so glad you sent that tweet in February 2012 that started the whole thing off!

Ted Bergman has been my constant support during various Sher-lockian projects over the past twenty-five years, and the work on this book has been no exception.

In two decades of friendship, Per Olaisen has never been afraid to use the red pen on my work, and for that I am eternally grateful. No one else knows my words—and my intentions—as well as Per.

Steven Rothman is not just the editor of the *Baker Street Journal*. His knowledge is vast—and his hundreds of e-mails to me contributed details about which I had no idea. And that was before he even had a chance to read anything of what I wrote, before the book was translated into English and I rewrote important sections of it. His comments and constant support—not least during and after the revision—have been crucial for this book to become a reality. I would not have succeeded without Steven.

Morgan Malm. Well, without Morgan Malm, there would be no *The Life and Death of Sherlock Holmes*. It is a privilege indeed to have a reader who can get to work on a freshly completed chapter and give exactly the response that is required, based on Sherlockian expertise and a large dollop of wisdom. The hard part is not criticizing what is on the page. The trick is to critique that which has been left out.

Publishers are experts in refining and communicating. That is pre-cisely why I was so grateful to end up in the capable hands of my accomplished colleagues at Piratförlaget for the original Swedish edition of the book. It has been truly fascinating to participate in the publishing of a book from an author's perspective.

Thanks also to Michael Gallagher, who gave my words a wonderful treatment when translating the original Swedish book into English.

Having Otto Penzler as editor and publisher for the English version of the book is not just a tremendous honor; it has also meant that important parts of the book were rewritten and the entire manuscript was expertly revised.

My wife, Christina, is not only an extremely understanding partner; she is also the love of my life, and my rock in all of the crazy adven-tures I undertake in the world of books.

Huge thanks to all of you!

SOURCES

Chapter 1

ON THE TRAIN JOURNEYS AND THE THOUGHTS BEHIND THE TELEVISION SERIES:

Steven Moffat, foreword to *Sherlock Holmes on Screen: The Complete Film and TV History*, by Alan Barnes (London: Titan Books, 2011), pp. 6–7.

Guy Adams, *Sherlock: The Casebook* (London: BBC Books, 2012), pp. 2–7.

Steven Moffat, introduction to *A Study in Scarlet*, by Arthur Conan Doyle (London: BBC Books, 2011), pp. vii–xii.

Mark Gatiss, introduction to *The Adventures of Sherlock Holmes*, by Arthur Conan Doyle (London: BBC Books, 2011), pp. vii–x.

Ian Cullen, "Mark Gatiss and Steven Moffat Clue Us In about 'Sherlock,'" *Monsters & Critics* (website), October 24, 2010.

Will Harris, "A Chat with Steven Moffat and Mark Gatiss," *Premium Hollywood* (website), October 23, 2010.

ON THE ANNUAL DINNER:

Roger Johnson, "Annual Dinner 2006," *Sherlock Holmes Journal*, Summer 2006, pp. 162–63.

Mark Gatiss, "The Adventure of the Missing Transcript," unpublished speech given at the annual dinner of the Sherlock Holmes Society of London, January 7, 2006.

Chapter 2

Harriet Richardson, *Building Up Our Health: The Architecture of Scotland's Historic Hospitals* (Edinburgh: Historic Scotland, 2010), p. 21 [about the Royal Infirmary].

"Sherlock Holmes, the Original, Dead" (Bell's obituary, originally published in the *New York Times*, October 5, 1911), in *Sir Arthur Conan Doyle: Interviews and Recollections*, ed. Harold Orel (New York: St. Martin's Press, 1991), p. 76 [Joseph Bell's appearance].

Ely M. Liebow, *Dr. Joe Bell: Model for Sherlock Holmes* (Madison, WI: Popular Press, 2007), chaps. 1 and 8 [the classes, and recollections from several of Bell's students (the potent drug, the chronic alcoholism, the noncommissioned officer, the cutty pipe)].

Arthur Conan Doyle, *Memories and Adventures* (Cambridge: Cambridge University Press, 2012), pp. 23, 25 [Conan Doyle's time as a university student].

Harry How, "A Day with Dr Conan Doyle" (originally published in the *Strand Magazine*, August 1892), in *Interviews and Recollections*, ed. Orel, pp. 66–67 [Joseph Bell about his methods].

Chapter 3

Jon L. Lellenberg, Daniel Stashower, and Charles Foley, eds., *Arthur Conan Doyle: A Life in Letters* (London: Penguin Books, 2008), pp. 160–71 [about Conan Doyle's Southsea home, and the letters to Mary Doyle].

"Sherlock Holmes, the Original, Dead," in *Interviews and Recollections*, ed. Orel, p. 78 [the golf-course anecdote].

Conan Doyle, *Memories and Adventures*, p. 25 [about Bell].

Arthur Conan Doyle, "My First Book" (originally published in *McClure's*, August 1894), in *Interviews and Recollections*, ed. Orel, pp. 91–96 [about childhood writings and early success as an author, and the "glossy locks" quote].

Andrew Lycett, *Conan Doyle: The Man Who Created Sherlock Holmes* (London: Phoenix, 2008), pp. 65, 73–74 [about the short stories that were accepted].

Chapter 4

Portsmouth Evening News (UK), January 8, 1886 [weather forecast].

Portsmouth Evening News (UK), January 11, 1886 [match report].

Portsmouth Evening News (UK), July 1, 1882 [the Miscellaneous Wants notice]

Geoffrey Stavert, *A Study in Southsea: The Unrevealed Life of Doctor Arthur Conan Doyle* (Portsmouth, UK: Milestone Publications, 1987), chaps. 1–5 [about Conan Doyle's time in Southsea].

Conan Doyle, *Memories and Adventures*, pp. 68, 70 [about the exchange of services, income taxes].

Chapter 5

Lellenberg, Stashower, and Foley, *A Life in Letters*, pp. 205–7 [the Greenwich dinner and Conan Doyle's writing plans].

Conan Doyle, *Memories and Adventures*, pp. 71–78 [Conan Doyle's stories in the mid-1880s, the "individuality" quote].

Stavert, *Study in Southsea*, pp. 62–65, 70, 77 [Conan Doyle meets Louisa Hawkins].

Chapter 6

The Conan Doyle Collection: Wednesday 19th May 2004 (London: Christie's, 2004), pp. 38–39 [early notes for *A Study in Scarlet*, as well as his sources of inspiration].

Conan Doyle, *Memories and Adventures*, pp. 74–75 [Bell as inspiration for *A Study in Scarlet*].

Conan Doyle's page of notes written for *A Study in Scarlet* still exists and has been reproduced in various books about him and Sherlock Holmes, including Stavert, *Study in Southsea*, p. 78.

Chapter 7

Edmund Gurney, Frederic W. H. Myers, and Frank Podmore, *Phantasms of the Living* (Cambridge: Cambridge University Press, 2011), pp. 194–95 [Jeannie Gwynne's childhood experience].

John Sutherland, *The Stanford Companion to Victorian Fiction* (Stanford, CA: Stanford University Press, 1989), p. 350 [about Jeannie Gwynne].

Coulson Kernahan, "Personal Memories of Sherlock Holmes" (first published in *London Quarterly and Holborn Review*, October 1934), in *Interviews and Recollections*, ed. Orel, p. 42 [quotes from Bettany, asking his wife to read].

Conan Doyle, *Memories and Adventures*, p. 75 [letter from the publisher].

Richard Lancelyn Green, introduction to *The Uncollected Sherlock Holmes*, by Arthur Conan Doyle (Harmondsworth, UK: Penguin Books, 1983), p. 43 [Conan Doyle asking for royalty].

Stavert, *Study in Southsea*, p. 117 [advertisement in the *Bookseller*].

Chapter 8

Allan Beveridge, "What Became of Arthur Conan Doyle's Father? The Last Years of Charles Altamont Doyle," *Journal of the Royal College of Physicians of Edinburgh* 36, no. 3 (2006): pp. 264–70 [Charles Doyle at Sunnyside].

Charles Doyle's sketchbook, with the drawings of fairies, was published as *The Doyle Diary* (New York: Ballantine Books, 1979).

Chapter 9

Green, introduction to *Uncollected Sherlock Holmes*, by Conan Doyle, pp. 46, 50 [on the writing of *A Study in Scarlet*].

Jon Lellenberg and Daniel Stashower, "A. Conan Doyle, *Nineteenth Century* Man," *Saturday Review of Literature*, 2014, pp. 3–8 [about Conan Doyle being inspired by *Nineteenth Century*].

Lycett, *Man Who Created Sherlock Holmes*, p. 42 [about Conan Doyle's childhood visit to London].

Lellenberg, Stashower, and Foley, *A Life in Letters*, pp. 257–70 [about *Micah Clarke*, ophthalmologist career].

Yorkshire Evening Post, January 19, 1895 [about the note on the mantelpiece].

Chapter 10

Tom Steel, *The Langham: A History; Opened 1865–Re-Opened 1991* (London: Langham, 1990), pp. 1–15 [about the history of the Langham Hotel].

Peter Henderson, *Practical Floriculture: A Guide to the Successful Cultivation of Florists' Plants, for the Amateur and Professional Florist* (New York: Orange Judd Company, 1892), p. 247 [about the plants at the Langham].

Prentice Mulford, "The Raw American," *Lippincott's Magazine*, June 1873 [about the Langham's popularity with Americans].

Conan Doyle, *Memories and Adventures*, pp. 78–79 [Conan Doyle's recollections of the dinner].

Obituary of Thomas P. Gill, *Times* (London), January 20, 1931 [biographical information about Gill].

Merlin Holland, *Oscar Wildes familjealbum* (Stockholm: Norstedts, 1998), pp. 63, 106, 125–26 [about Wilde].

"Conan Doyle's Dilemma," *New-York Tribune*, February 12, 1905 [interview with Stoddart regarding the damaged buttonhole].

Oscar Wilde, *The Complete Works of Oscar Wilde* (Oxford: Oxford University Press, 2005), vol. 3, pp. xxxii–xxxiii [about *The Picture of Dorian Gray*].

Lycett, *Man Who Created Sherlock Holmes*, p. 157 [the writing of *The Sign of Four*].

Christopher Roden, introduction to *The Sign of the Four*, by Arthur Conan Doyle (Oxford: Oxford University Press, 1993), pp. xi–xli [the writing of *The Sign of Four*].

Green, introduction to *Uncollected Sherlock Holmes*, by Conan Doyle, pp. 48–49 [Conan Doyle's letter to Stoddart].

Chapter 11

Green, introduction to *Uncollected Sherlock Holmes*, by Conan Doyle, pp. 50–51 [Conan Doyle's letters to Stoddart].

Chapter 12

Christopher Redmond, *In Bed with Sherlock Holmes: Sexual Elements in Arthur Conan Doyle's Stories of the Great Detective* (Toronto: Simon & Pierre, 1984), p. 44 [the theory that Mary Morstan is based on Conan Doyle's wife Louisa].

Lycett, *Man Who Created Sherlock Holmes*, pp. 150–63 [Conan Doyle's life in 1889–90].

Green, introduction to *Uncollected Sherlock Holmes*, by Conan Doyle, pp. 49–50 [the publishing of *The Sign of Four*].

Roden, introduction to *Sign of Four*, by Conan Doyle, pp. xvi [on the contract with Lippincott's].

Lellenberg, Stashower, and Foley, *A Life in Letters*, p. 274 [on *Micah Clarke*].

Conan Doyle, *Memories and Adventures*, pp. 81, 88 [the journey to Berlin].

Quotes are taken from Arthur Conan Doyle, *The Sign of Four* (Oxford: Oxford University Press, 1993).

Chapter 13

Carl Olof Josephson, "Några judiska bokhandlare och bokförläggare i gårdagens Stockholm" [Some Jewish Booksellers and Publishers in the Stockholm of the

Past], in *Det judiska Stockholm*, ed. David Glück, Aron Neuman, and Jacqueline Stare (Stockholm: Jewish Museum, 1998), pp. 142–58 [about the history of Stockholm's booksellers].

Ted Bergman, *Sherlock Holmes i Sverige: En Bibliografi* [Sherlock Holmes in Sweden: a Bibliography] (Stockholm: Författares Bokmaskin, 1991), p. 5 [about the advertisement in the Swedish booksellers' journal].

Obituary of Ernst Nordin, *Dalpilen* (newspaper, Falun, Sweden), March 16, 1897 [biographical information about Ernst Nordin].

William B. Todd and Ann Bowden, *Tauchnitz International Editions in English, 1841–1955: A Bibliographical History* (New York: Bibliographical Society of America, 1988), pp. vii–xi, 189–92, 398–99 [about the history of Tauchnitz and its publications].

Johan Svedjedal, *Bokens samhälle: Svenska Bokförläggareföreningen och svensk bokmarknad, 1887–1943* (Stockholm: Svenska Bokförläggareföreningen, 1993), part 1, p. 47 [about Swedish publishers' attitudes toward the Bern Convention].

The details about Ejnar Cohn and family come primarily from *Stockholms adresskalender* [Stockholm directory of addresses] for the years in question.

Ernst Nordin and Viktor Josephson both died in the late 1890s; neither lived to be forty. The bookshop was taken over by Josephson's widow, Ann-Sofi, who ran it for ten years before it became part of Nordiska Bokhandeln. The Josephsons' oldest son, Ragnar, later became a professor of art history, director of the Royal Dramatic Theatre, and a fellow of the Swedish Academy. His brother Gunnar Josephson was proprietor of Sandbergs Bokhandel and father of two sons: Carl Olof Josephson (also a bookseller) and Erland Josephson (famous Swedish actor).

Chapter 14

Lellenberg, Stashower, and Foley, *A Life in Letters*, pp. 277–89 [about the Conan Doyles' time in Vienna].

Lycett, *Man Who Created Sherlock Holmes*, p. 165 [about the Conan Doyles' last days in Southsea].

Mary Ann Gillies, *The Professional Literary Agent in Britain, 1880–1920* (Toronto: University of Toronto Press, 2007), pp. 27, 29 [on how Watt established his agency].

Peter D. McDonald: *British Literary Culture and Publishing Practice, 1880–1914* (Cambridge: Cambridge University Press, 1997), pp. 138, 150 [Newnes's quote, and Watt's letter to Conan Doyle].

Green, introduction to *Uncollected Sherlock Holmes*, by Conan Doyle, pp. 52–53 [about H. Greenhough Smith].

Chapter 15

McDonald, *British Literary Culture*, pp. 138, 140 [about the contact between Watt and Conan Doyle].

S. S. McClure, excerpt from *My Autobiography*, published in *Interviews and Recollections*, ed. Orel, pp. 52–53 [about the meeting between Lang and McClure].

Strand Magazine, "A Description of the Offices of the Strand Magazine," December 1892, pp. 594–606 [the description of Greenhough Smith's and Boot's office].

Ann Byerly, "Sidney Paget: Victorian Black-and-White Illustrator," *Baker Street Miscellanea*, no. 35 (1983), pp. 1–16 [about the choice of illustrator].

Chapter 16

Details regarding the artistic colony around Holland Park Road come from a swarm of facts found in small ads for rooms to let, art courses, and so forth, in London newspapers of the day.

Much of the remainder of the chapter is based on facts in Byerly, "Sidney Paget."

The dialogue between Sidney Paget and the messenger boy is pure fiction.

Chapter 17

Conan Doyle, *Memories and Adventures*, pp. 81, 88 [about the illness and the idea of a writing career].

Lycett, *Man Who Created Sherlock Holmes*, pp. 173–75 [the illness and the move].

McDonald, *British Literary Culture*, p. 138 [exchanges with Watt].

McClure, excerpt from *My Autobiography*, in *Interviews and Recollections*, ed. Orel, pp. 52–53 [about S. S. McClure].

Lellenberg, Stashower, and Foley, *A Life in Letters*, pp. 292–305 [about the bids that flooded in, the writing factory, and "The Copper Beeches"].

Chapter 18

J. M. Barrie, "My Evening with Sherlock Holmes," in *My Evening with Sherlock Holmes*, ed. John Gibson and Richard Lancelyn Green (London: Ferret Fantasy, 1981), pp. 15–17.

G. B. Burgin, *Memoirs of a Clubman* (London: Hutchinson & Co, 1921), pp. 95–111 [about the *Idler*].

Lycett, *Man Who Created Sherlock Holmes*, pp. 184–85 [about Conan Doyle's social life].

Lellenberg, Stashower, and Foley, *A Life in Letters*, p. 305 [about the dinner at the Idlers' Club].

Burnley Express, December 10, 14, and 17, 1892 [advertisements for Joseph Baron's story "The Man Who 'Bested' Sherlock Holmes"; Conan Doyle "emphatically pronounced it good"].

Chapter 19

Liebow, *Dr. Joe Bell*, pp. 150–51, 172–73 [about Bell's medical career and the rumors that he was the inspiration for Holmes].

Green, introduction to *Uncollected Sherlock Holmes*, by Conan Doyle, pp. 17–23 [about the exchanges between Conan Doyle and Bell].

How, "A Day with Dr Conan Doyle," in *Interviews and Recollections*, ed. Orel, pp. 62–67 [the article that Harry How wrote after his visit, including a letter from Joseph Bell].

Chapter 20

"A Description of the Offices of the Strand Magazine" [most of the chapter's guided tour is based on this article].

Reginald Pound, *The Strand Magazine, 1891–1950* (London: Heinemann), 1966, pp. 29–30, 56–57 [about the idea for the magazine, about Greenhough Smith].

Chapter 21

Lellenberg, Stashower, and Foley, *A Life in Letters*, p. 319 [Conan Doyle's letter to his mother explaining that he was writing the last Sherlock Holmes story].

Jerome K. Jerome, excerpt from *My Life and Times*, in *Interviews and Recollections*, ed. Orel, pp. 101–2 [about the visit to Norway].

Green, introduction to *Uncollected Sherlock Holmes*, by Conan Doyle, pp. 54–56, 59–66 [about Sidney Paget and Sherlock Holmes's death].

Lycett, *Man Who Created Sherlock Holmes*, pp. 196–204 [about the comic opera, the lecture, the trip to Switzerland, father's death, and wife's illness].

Pound, *Strand Magazine, 1891–1950*, p. 45 [about Newnes's message to the shareholders].

Mattias Boström, "The Leak," *Baker Street Journal*, 2012/no. 3, pp. 6–12 [about the leak to the press].

Sheffield Evening Telegraph (UK), November 15, 1893 [about the judge in South Africa].

Roger Johnson and Jean Upton, *The Sherlock Holmes Miscellany* (Stroud, UK: History Press, 2012), p. 57 [about the single-act play at the Court Theatre].

Glasgow Herald, November 20, 1893 [about plans of theater impresario, Austin Fryer, to stage a four-act Holmes play, which never came to fruition].

London Standard, July 6, 1893 [about the Ramsgate murder].

Yorkshire Evening Post, August 30, 1893 [about contemporary cases to which it was wished Sherlock Holmes could be called].

Bristol Mercury (UK), September 28, 1893 [about the Hampton Rocks mystery].

Manchester Evening News (UK), September 5, 1893 [about contemporary cases to which it was wished Sherlock Holmes could be called].

Bath Chronicle and Weekly Gazette (UK), September 28, 1893 [about the Hampton Rocks mystery].

Liebow, *Dr. Joe Bell*, p. 187 [on Bell as expert witness].

Conan Doyle, *Memories and Adventures*, pp. 99–100 [about the reactions to Sherlock Holmes's death].

Chapter 22

Lellenberg, Stashower, and Foley, *A Life in Letters*, pp. 227–28, 353–54, 377, 390, 392, 394–95, 399 [about Grant Allen, the construction of Undershaw, Conan Doyle's horses, Paget's visit, the hunt, and the banjo playing].

Georgina Doyle, *Out of the Shadows: The Untold Story of Arthur Conan Doyle's First Family* (Ashcroft, BC: Calabash Press, 2004), pp. 111–12 [about the boarding-school football matches and diary entries on Paget's visit].

Bram Stoker, "Sir Arthur Conan Doyle Tells of His Career and Work, His Sentiments towards America, and His Approaching Marriage" (originally published in *New York World*, July 28, 1907), in *Interviews and Recollections*, ed. Orel, pp. 155–62 [description of Undershaw].

Manchester Evening News (UK), October 12, 1897 [about the potato thieves].

Evening Telegraph (Dundee, Scotland), February 11, 1897 [about the bicycle thief].

Peggy Perdue, "'Did You Notice Nothing Curious about That Advertisement?'" *Baker Street Journal*, Christmas annual, 2009, pp. 5–8 [about Holmes in early advertisements].

Jon L. Lellenberg, "Bangsian Sherlockiana," *Baker Street Miscellanea*, no. 39 (1984), pp. 31–36 [about John Kendrick Bangs].

Christopher Redmond, *Welcome to America, Mr. Sherlock Holmes: Victorian America Meets Arthur Conan Doyle* (Toronto: Simon & Pierre, 1987), pp. 20–21, 27–28 [about the American trip].

Byerly, "Sidney Paget," p. 12 [about Paget after the death of Holmes].

Alistair Duncan, *An Entirely New Country: Arthur Conan Doyle, Undershaw and the Resurrection of Sherlock Holmes (1897–1907)* (London: MX Publishing, 2011), pp. 36–37 [about the play rumor].

Chapter 23

S. E. Dahlinger, "The Sherlock Holmes We Never Knew," *Baker Street Journal*, 1999/ no. 3, pp. 7–27 [about William Gillette and his play].

Duncan, *An Entirely New Country*, p. 55 [about Henry Irving].

Arthur Conan Doyle to Bram Stoker, ca. December 1897, Shakespeare Birthplace Trust Collections, Stratford-upon-Avon, England [about Conan Doyle's theatrical agent, the initial contact with Tree, and Irving's interest in the play].

Arthur Conan Doyle to Bram Stoker, August 20, 1897, Arthur Conan Doyle Papers, Harry Ransom Center, University of Texas, Austin [praising *Dracula*].

Henry Zecher, *William Gillette, America's Sherlock Holmes* (n.p.: Xlibris, 2011), pp. 44–46, 291 [about Nook Farm and Gillette's visit to Undershaw].

Georgina Doyle, *Out of the Shadows*, pp. 107, 120 [about Louisa's piano playing, the children's upbringing].

Chapter 24

Christopher Morley, *Thorofare* (New York: Harcourt, Brace and Company, 1942), pp. 151–54 [about the children's games].

Helen McK. Oakley, *Three Hours for Lunch: The Life and Times of Christopher Morley* (New York: Watermill Publishers, 1976), pp. 1–19 [about Kit's childhood].

Steven Rothman, introduction to *The Standard Doyle Company: Christopher Morley on Sherlock Holmes*, ed. Rothman (New York: Fordham University Press, 1990), pp. 1–6 [about Kit's childhood].

The News (Frederick, MD), November 12, 1900 [about Gillette's tour in Baltimore].

Zecher, *William Gillette*, p. 295 [about the gas-chamber scene].

Alan Barnes, *Sherlock Holmes on Screen: The Complete Film and TV History* (London: Titan Books, 2011), p. 216 [about *Sherlock Holmes Baffled* and the Mutoscope].

Richard J. Sveum, "100 Years Ago," *Friends of the Sherlock Holmes Collections*, 2002/no. 2, p. 2 [about Mark Twain's novel].

Chapter 25

Lellenberg, Stashower, and Foley, *A Life in Letters*, pp. 419–81 [Conan Doyle's letters to his mother from June 1899 to June 1901].

Philip Weller, ed., *The Hound of the Baskervilles: Hunting the Dartmoor Legend* (Tiverton, UK: Devon Books, 2001), pp. 12–14 [about the meeting with Robinson and how the novel came about].

Lycett, *Man Who Created Sherlock Holmes*, p. 273 [about falling out with Hornung].

Green, introduction to *Uncollected Sherlock Holmes*, by Conan Doyle, pp. 77, 89–98 [about Raffles and the origins of *The Hound of the Baskervilles*].

Chapter 26

Zecher, *William Gillette*, pp. 323–24, 337 [about the king's visit to the theater and Saintsbury's tour].

Coventry Evening Telegraph (UK), February 11, 1902 [about the Dutch production].

Sunderland Daily Echo and Shipping Gazette (UK), February 7, 1902 [about set building ahead of the provincial tours].

Yorkshire Evening Post, February 22, 1902 [about foreign productions of Gillette's play].

Mattias Boström, "The Three Plays—Sherlock Holmes in Stockholm 1902," in *Scandinavia and Sherlock Holmes*, ed. Bjarne Nielsen (New York: Baker Street Irregulars, 2006), pp. 209–21 [about Walter Christmas].

Dahlinger, "The Sherlock Holmes We Never Knew" [about the king reading *The Hound of the Baskervilles*].

Lellenberg, Stashower, and Foley, *A Life in Letters*, pp. 502, 506–7 [Conan Doyle knighted].

Chapter 27

Lellenberg, Stashower, and Foley, *A Life in Letters*, pp. 510, 512, 517–18 [about the offer from *Collier's*, Jean's plot idea, and the many letters to Conan Doyle].

Richard Lancelyn Green, introduction to *The Return of Sherlock Holmes*, by Arthur Conan Doyle (Oxford: Oxford University Press, 1993), pp. xx–xxii, xxv–xxvii [about Hornung, Fletcher Robinson, the letter from Roosevelt, Wodehouse's parody, and McClure's request].

Green, introduction to *Uncollected Sherlock Holmes*, by Conan Doyle, pp. 99–101, 104–5 [about Greenhough Smith's criticism, "The Dancing Men," and the letters to beekeeper Holmes].

P. G. Wodehouse, *Performing Flea* (London: Herbert Jenkins, 1953), p. 31 [young Wodehouse reading Conan Doyle].

Kevin Telfer: *Peter Pan's First XI: The Extraordinary Story of J. M. Barrie's Cricket Team* (London: Sceptre), 2010, p. 192 [about playing cricket with Wodehouse].

McClure, excerpts from *My Autobiography*, in *Interviews and Recollections*, ed. Orel, pp. 53–54 [about S. S. McClure].

Chapter 28

ON FREDERIC DORR STEELE:

Andrew Malec, introduction to *The Return of Sherlock Holmes*, by Arthur Conan Doyle (New York: Mysterious Press, 1987).

Robert G. Steele, "Frederic Dorr Steele: A Biographical Sketch," *Baker Street Miscellanea*, no. 67 (1991): pp. 1–11.

Frederic Dorr Steele, "Veteran Illustrator Goes Reminiscent," *Baker Street Miscellanea*, no. 67 (1991): pp. 31–39.

Frederic Dorr Steele, "Sherlock Holmes in Pictures," in *221b: Studies in Sherlock Holmes*, ed. Vincent Starrett (New York: Macmillan Company, 1940), pp. 129–37.

New-York Tribune, February 7, 1903 [news item announcing Steele's son's death].

ON SIDNEY PAGET:

Byerly, "Sidney Paget."

Chapter 29

Lycett, *Man Who Created Sherlock Holmes*, pp. 317–19 [about the Edalji case].

Lellenberg, Stashower, and Foley, *A Life in Letters*, pp. 534, 538 [about his wife's death and the Edalji case].

ABOUT CONAN DOYLE'S WEDDING:

Gloucester Citizen (UK), September 18, 1907.

Surrey Mirror (UK), September 20, 1907.

Leamington Spa Courier (UK), September 20, 1907.

Manchester Courier and Lancashire General Advertiser (UK), September 20, 1907.

Chapter 30

ON CONAN DOYLE'S PROTEST:

Harald Thornberg to G. Herbert Thring, January 5, 1909; February 1, 1909, Society of Authors Papers, British Library, London, England (hereafter, "Society of Authors Papers").

A. S. Watt to G. Herbert Thring, January 14, 1909, Society of Authors Papers.
A. P. Watt to G. Herbert Thring, March 4, March 6, March 11, March 12, March 17, March 18, 1909, Society of Authors Papers.
Copenhagen lawyer Ulf Hansen to G. Herbert Thring, September 7, 1909, Society of Authors Papers.
"'Sherlock Holmes' Fortællinger" [Conan Doyle's protest], *Nationaltidende* (Copenhagen), September 6, 1909.

OTHER SOURCES:

Nils Nordberg, *The Misadventures of Sherlock Holmes, World Detective* (Nykøbing, Denmark: Sherlock Holmes Museet, 2005) [about the origins of the German series].
Barnes, *Holmes on Screen*, pp. 220–22 [about *Sherlock Holmes i Livsfare*].
"The Influence of Suggestion: Banning 'Sherlock Holmes.,'" *Aberdeen Journal*, February 4, 1910 [Swiss railway bookstalls prohibiting the sale of Sherlock Holmes].

Chapter 31

Oakley, *Three Hours for Lunch*, pp. 1, 30–31 [about Chris].
Rothman, introduction to *Standard Doyle Company*, ed. Rothman, pp. 6–7 [about Chris at Oxford].
Michael J. Crowe, introduction to *Ronald Knox and Sherlock Holmes: The Origin of Sherlockian Studies*, ed. Michael J. Crowe (Indianapolis: Gasogene Books, 2011), pp. 1–32 [about Ronald Knox and his Sherlock Holmes lecture, and the letter from Conan Doyle to Knox].
Lycett, *Man Who Created Sherlock Holmes*, pp. 349–52 [about Conan Doyle 1912].

Chapter 32

Lellenberg, Stashower, and Foley, *A Life in Letters*, pp. 594–99, 602–5 [about visit to Canada, Conan Doyle at the outbreak of war, the application quote, and the meeting with Masterman].
Lycett, *Man Who Created Sherlock Holmes*, pp. 372–74 [about Conan Doyle at the outbreak of war and about the meeting with Masterman].
Philip M. Taylor, *British Propaganda in the 20th Century: Selling Democracy* (Edinburgh: Edinburgh University Press, 1999), pp. 35–36 [about the propaganda effort].
Gary S. Messinger, *British Propaganda and the State in the First World War* (Manchester, UK: Manchester University Press, 1992), pp. 62–63 [about Kipling's role in the propaganda effort].
Adrian Conan Doyle to the Earl Jellicoe (Foreign Office), August 6, 1955 [about Admiral Jellicoe photograph at Windlesham].
Jon L. Lellenberg, *Nova 57 Minor: The Waxing and Waning of the Sixty-First Adventure of Sherlock Holmes* (Bloomington, IN: Gaslight Publications, 1990), p. 81 [about Arthur Whitaker].

R. Dixon Smith, "'The Speckled Band': The Story, the Play, and the Snake," in *The Illustrated Speckled Band*, ed. Leslie S. Klinger (Indianapolis: Gasogene Books, 2012), pp. 89–100 [about the play].

Mattias Boström, afterword to *Sherlock Holmes i Skräckens dal* [The Valley of Fear], by Arthur Conan Doyle (Lund, Sweden: Bakhåll, 2010), pp. 179–89 [the inspiration for *The Valley of Fear*].

Chapter 33

Vincent Starrett, *Born in a Bookshop: Chapters from the Chicago Renascence* (Norman: University of Oklahoma Press, 1965), pp. 147–48 [the conversation between Starrett and Roosevelt].

Chapter 34

Wake, Wild & Boult to G. Herbert Thring, October 2, 1914; January 8, 1915, Society of Authors Papers [on the row with the Frenchmen].

Arthur Conan Doyle to A. P. Watt, October 4, 1914, Society of Authors Papers [on the row with the Frenchmen].

"How Moving Pictures Are Made: A Cinema Studio at Bexhill," *Bexhill-on-Sea Observer* (UK), June 15, 1912 [interview with G. Tréville about the filming of the French films].

"Picture Making on the Marina," *Bexhill-on-Sea Observer*, July 13, 1912 [about the filming of the French films].

"Bexhill Cinema Factory," *Bexhill-on-Sea Observer*, August 10, 1926 [about Conan Doyle insisting upon having English actors in the French films].

"Film-Making at Bexhill," *Bexhill-on-Sea Observer*, August 21, 1926 [about the filming of the French films].

Barnes, *Holmes on Screen*, pp. 62–64, 275–76, 295 [about the French films and both of Samuelson's films].

"Biografväsendets utveckling" [The Growth of the Cinema Business], *Nya Dagligt Allehanda* (Stockholm), May 9, 1909 [about sound effects and music during showings of silent movies].

Thierry Saint-Joanis, *Le Guide du Film* Sherlock Holmes *(1916)* (Saint-Sauvier: Societé Sherlock Holmes de France, 2015), p. 16 [the *Motography* quotes about recording the Gillette film].

Chapter 35

Arthur Conan Doyle, "Sherlock Holmes on the Screen," in *The Uncollected Sherlock Holmes* (Harmondsworth, UK: Penguin Books, 1983), pp. 295–304 [Conan Doyle's and Eille Norwood's speeches during the dinner, as well as Green's comments].

Barnes, *Holmes on Screen*, pp. 13–17 [about Stoll's films].

Scott Allen Nollen, *Sir Arthur Conan Doyle at the Cinema* (Jefferson, NC: McFarland & Company, 1996), pp. 67–74 [about Stoll's films].

Lycett, *Man Who Created Sherlock Holmes*, pp. 377–85 [about Conan Doyle's visit to the front line and his path to spiritualism].

Chapter 36

Birgit Th. Sparre, *Fackelrosor* (Stockholm: Gebers, 1968), pp. 154–60 [Sparre's memories of meeting Conan Doyle, including quotes from Conan Doyle and Flammarion].

Lycett, *Man Who Created Sherlock Holmes*, pp. 402–3, 414, 428–31 [about Pheneas, Conan Doyle's children, and the photographs of fairies].

Georgina Doyle, *Out of the Shadows*, pp. 244–45 [about Conan Doyle's children].

Chapter 37

Pound, *Strand Magazine, 1891–1950*, pp. 56–58 [about Greenhough Smith].

Green, introduction to *Uncollected Sherlock Holmes*, by Conan Doyle, p. 137 [about Frank Wiles].

H. Greenhough Smith, "Some Letters of Conan Doyle," *Strand Magazine*, October 1930, pp. 390–95 [about "Thor Bridge"].

Conan Doyle, "Mr. Sherlock Holmes to His Readers," in *Uncollected Sherlock Holmes*, pp. 317–22 [the quote from the farewell piece].

"Sherlock Holmes skulle också tro på spiritismen!" [Sherlock Holmes Would Also Believe in Spiritualism!], *Svenska Dagbladet* (Stockholm), October 23, 1929 [quote from Copenhagen].

Chapter 38

Mattias Boström, "Mästerdetektivens skapare" [The Creator of the Master Detective], in *Tretton kriminella klassiker—författarporträtt*, ed. Jan Broberg (Lund, Sweden: BTJ Förlag, 2005), pp. 103–18 [about Conan Doyle's visit to Stockholm].

Lycett, *Man Who Created Sherlock Holmes*, pp. 350, 441–43, 444, 450 [about Oscar Slater].

Lady Conan Doyle to unknown person, October 27, 1929, unknown location of the letter—information received from Richard Lancelyn Green [Lady Conan Doyle's views regarding Oscar Slater].

Rolf Carleson, *Vidare går min väg* (Stockholm: Bokförlaget Excelsior, 1967), p. 25 [Conan Doyle's letter to Carleson just before the former's death].

Chapter 39

Edith Meiser, "We Never Called Him Sherlock," *Serpentine Muse*, Winter 1983, pp. 7–13 [about her visit to London].

"Adventures on the Air: Edith Meiser in Conversation with John Bennett Shaw," *Baker Street Miscellanea*, no. 36 (1983), pp. 10–24 [about her visit to London].

"Chamber of Horrors Hoax," *Evening Telegraph* (Dundee, Scotland), March 5, 1903 [about the letters to Madame Tussaud's].

Chapter 40

Barnes, *Holmes on Screen*, pp. 149–52 [about the film *The Return of Sherlock Holmes*].

Huntingdon (PA) *Daily News*, November 12, 1924 [anecdote about cigarette card].

Christopher Redmond, ed., *Quotations from Baker Street* (Waterloo, ON: published privately, 2009), p. 51 [Wodehouse quote].

"Sherlock Holmes's Latest!" *Northampton Mercury* (UK), November 15, 1901 [Potson quote].

Chapter 41

Oakley, *Three Hours for Lunch*, pp. 42–44, 97, 102–3; Rothman, introduction to *Standard Doyle Company*, ed. Rothman, p. 13 [sources on Morley].

Jon L. Lellenberg, ed., *Irregular Memories of the 'Thirties* (New York: Baker Street Irregulars, 1990), pp. 14–15, 31–32 [about the foreword to the Holmes edition and Morley's lunches].

Charles A. Beckett, "Edith Meiser: The Other Woman in Sherlock Holmes' Life," in *Return with Us Now . . .* , 2009/no. 5, pp. 1, 3–4 [on Meiser].

Frederick Nolan, *Lorenz Hart: A Poet on Broadway* (Oxford: Oxford University Press, 1994), pp. 61–66 [about *The Garrick Gaieties*].

"Adventures on the Air: Edith Meiser in Conversation with John Bennett Shaw" [on Meiser].

Chapter 42

John Nieminski and Jon L. Lellenberg, eds., *"Dear Starrett—" / "Dear Briggs—"* (New York: Baker Street Irregulars, 1989), pp. ii–v [about Briggs in London].

Frederic Dorr Steele, "Reminiscent Notes," in *Sherlock Holmes—A Play*, by William Gillette (Santa Barbara, CA: Helan Halbach, 1974), pp. xxvi–xxvii [about Briggs in London].

Robert G. Steele, "Frederic Dorr Steele: A Biographical Sketch" [Steele after World War I, and the conversation between Steele and John Barrymore].

Andrew Malec, "Frederic Dorr Steele and Gray Chandler Briggs," *Baker Street Miscellanea*, no. 67 (1991): pp. 12–23 [the correspondence between Steele and Briggs].

Andrew Malec, "Frederic Dorr Steele and Gray Chandler Briggs, Part II," *Baker Street Miscellanea*, no. 68 (1991): pp. 1–12 [the correspondence between Steele and Briggs].

Andrew Malec, *The Other Master: Frederic Dorr Steele—A Commemorative Essay* (Minneapolis: Sherlock Holmes Collections, University of Minnesota, 1984) [about Steele].

Barnes, *Holmes on Screen*, pp. 175–77 [about the John Barrymore film].

Starrett, *Born in a Bookshop*, pp. 46, 49, 122–23 [childhood memories and the meeting on the train].

Susan Rice, *The Somnambulist and the Detective: Vincent Starrett and Sherlock Holmes* (Huddersfield, UK: Northern Musgraves, 2010) [about Starrett].

In the original quote (in *Born in a Bookshop*) from Vincent Starrett's teacher, he is referred to not as Vincent, but as Charles—the name he was known by in his youth.

Chapter 43

Bliss Austin, "William Gillette on the Air," *Baker Street Miscellanea*, no. 29 (1982): pp. 1–9 [transcript of the opening scene of the radio show].

"Times Square Theater Now Radio Studio," *Pittsburgh Press*, March 2, 1930 [about technology in the studio].

Zecher, *William Gillette*, pp. 531–35 [about William Gillette, Edith Meiser, and the radio show].

Meiser, "We Never Called Him Sherlock" [about the poll of critics and radio producers].

Chapter 44

Nieminski and Lellenberg, eds., *"Dear Starrett—" / "Dear Briggs—"* [correspondence between Starrett and Briggs].

Crowe, introduction to *Knox and Holmes*, ed. Crowe, pp. 1–32 [the publishing of Knox's essay].

S. C. Roberts, "How It All Began," *Sherlock Holmes Journal*, July 1954, pp. 3–4 [how Knox's essay inspired Roberts to write about Sherlockian things].

Maurice Campbell, "The First Sherlockian Critic—1902," *Sherlock Holmes Journal*, September 1952, pp. 3–5, 24 [about Frank Sidgwick].

D. F. O. Dangar, "In Memoriam," *Alpine Journal*, 1978, pp. 267–68 [about T. S. Blakeney].

The editor of the *Bookman* was Arthur Bartlett Maurice, and his articles can be found in S. E. Dahlinger and Leslie S. Klinger, eds., *Sherlock Holmes, Conan Doyle and The Bookman* (Indianapolis: Gasogene Books, 2010).

EARLY SHERLOCKIAN BOOKS:

Vincent Starrett, *The Private Life of Sherlock Holmes* (New York: Otto Penzler Books, 1993).

T. S. Blakeney, *Sherlock Holmes: Fact or Fiction?* (New York: Otto Penzler Books, 1993).

H. W. Bell, *Sherlock Holmes and Dr Watson: The Chronology of Their Adventures* (London: Constable & Co, 1932).

S. C. Roberts: *Doctor Watson* (London: Faber & Faber, 1931).

Chapter 45

Lellenberg, ed., *Irregular Memories of the 'Thirties* [about the founding of the Baker Street Irregulars, including quotations].

Chapter 46

Tom Curtin, "Thrill Adventures," *Radio Digest*, March 1932, pp. 10–11 [about Nina meeting the Bolshevist leader].

Nina Mdivani, *My Book*, unpublished manuscript, Arthur Conan Doyle Collection, Lancelyn Green Bequest, Portsmouth City Council, Portsmouth, England (hereafter, "Lancelyn Green Bequest") [about visits to Windlesham and her thoughts on her mother- and father-in-law].

Georgina Doyle, *Out of the Shadows*, pp. 245, 265–67 [about racing cars and the Mdivani family].

Philip Porter, "Kindred Spirits," *Classic and Sportscar*, June 1989, pp. 70–72 [about Adrian and Denis as racing enthusiasts].

"Conan Doyle's Sons in Motor Smash," *Evening Telegraph* (Dundee, Scotland), August 12, 1931 [about the accident in Oxford].

"Prince Alexis Killed in Crash," *San Antonio Light*, August 2, 1935 [about Alexis Mdivani's death].

"Prince Dead," *San Antonio Light*, March 16, 1936 [about Serge Mdivani's death].

"Princess Nina Mdivani," *Nottingham Evening Post* (UK), June 4, 1936 [about the couple's engagement].

"Princess's Romance," *Nottingham Evening Post*, August 17, 1936 [about Denis and Nina's wedding].

"Princess's Wedding," *Nottingham Evening Post*, August 18, 1936 [report from the wedding].

"Son of Conan Doyle Engaged," *St. Louis Post-Dispatch*, June 26, 1931 [about Adrian and Miss Isabelle Bridges].

"Marriage Not to Hinder Motor Racing Career, Says Adrian Conan Doyle," *Winnipeg Tribune*, August 1, 1936 [about Adrian and Miss Rita Cooper].

The car Chitty Bang Bang was the inspiration for Ian Fleming when he wrote his children's book *Chitty-Chitty-Bang-Bang: The Magical Car* (1964), which later was turned into both a film and a stage musical.

Chapter 47

Lady (Jean) Conan Doyle, "Conan Doyle Was Sherlock Holmes" (originally appeared in *Pearson's Magazine*, December 1934), in *Interviews and Recollections*, ed. Orel, pp. 83–85 [about her idea that Conan Doyle used himself as the model for Holmes].

Lycett, *Man Who Created Sherlock Holmes*, p. 454 [Lady Conan Doyle's contact with her deceased husband].

John Lamond, *Arthur Conan Doyle: A Memoir* (London: John Murray, 1931).

Arthur Conan Doyle's last will and testament, Lancelyn Green Bequest.

Adrian Conan Doyle to Denis Conan Doyle, October 25, 1937, Lancelyn Green Bequest [about the discord between Nina and Lady Conan Doyle].

Georgina Doyle, *Out of the Shadows*, p. 274 [Lady Conan Doyle's illness].

Adrian Conan Doyle to Denis Conan Doyle, February 15, 1938, Lancelyn Green Bequest [about the shares].

Barnes, *Holmes on Screen*, pp. 261–63 [about *The Sleeping Cardinal*].

Nollen, *Conan Doyle at the Cinema*, pp. 113–20 [about Wontner's films].

Chapter 48

"Wide Reactions to Czech Crisis: No Hint of Panic in England," *Advertiser* (Adelaide, Australia), September 15, 1938 [about the state of affairs in London].

Adrian Conan Doyle to Denis Conan Doyle, September 28, 1938, Lancelyn Green Bequest [about the state of affairs in London].

Adrian Conan Doyle to Denis Conan Doyle, April 3, 1938, Lancelyn Green Bequest [about Ufa].

Denis Conan Doyle to Lady (Jean) Conan Doyle, April 29, 1938, Lancelyn Green Bequest [about Ufa].

Frederick Kohner, *The Magician of Sunset Boulevard: The Improbable Life of Paul Kohner, Hollywood Agent* (Palos Verdes, CA: Morgan Press, 1977) [about Paul Kohner].

Amanda J. Field, *England's Secret Weapon: The Wartime Films of Sherlock Holmes* (London: Middlesex University Press, 2009), pp. 66, 102 [about the Fox contract].

Paul Kohner to Victor Orsatti, January 26, 1939, Lancelyn Green Bequest [about work preparing for the Fox contract].

Michael Pointer, *The Public Life of Sherlock Holmes* (Newton Abbot, UK: David & Charles), 1975, p. 76 [about Fox executives' dinner, including quotations].

Denis Conan Doyle to Lady (Jean) Conan Doyle, October 10, 1938, Lancelyn Green Bequest [about the plans for the American tour].

Adrian Conan Doyle to Denis Conan Doyle, October 23, 1938, Lancelyn Green Bequest [about the date for Lady Conan Doyle's operation and about the séances].

Adrian Conan Doyle to Denis Conan Doyle, August 1938, Lancelyn Green Bequest [about the snakeskins].

Margaret Shipley, "Adventure Spices Life of Writer," *Arizona Republic*, March 2, 1952 [about the first meeting between Adrian and Anna].

The three men at Twentieth Century Fox were film company director Darryl F. Zanuck, scriptwriter Gene Markey, and director Gregory Ratoff.

Chapter 49

Field, *England's Secret Weapon*, pp. 61–100 [about the filming of *The Hound of the Baskervilles*].

Barnes, *Holmes on Screen*, pp. 253–56 [about the 1939 film *The Hound of the Baskervilles*].

Nigel Bruce, "Extracts from the Unpublished Autobiography of Nigel Bruce," *Sherlock Holmes Journal*, Winter 1988, pp. 8–13.

Nicholas Utechin, "My Father as Watson," *Sherlock Holmes Journal*, Winter 1988, pp. 6–8 [interview with Nigel Bruce's daughter, Pauline Page].

"A Closer Look at the Second Mrs. Rathbone," *The Baz: the Basil Rathbone Blog*, December 7, 2012 [about Ouida Rathbone's early life].

Paul Kohner to Victor Orsatti, January 26, 1939, Lancelyn Green Bequest [about the MGM negotiations].

Denis Conan Doyle to A. S. Watt, September 28, 1939, Lancelyn Green Bequest [about forthcoming American trip].

ABOUT THE CONTRACTUAL NEGOTIATIONS:

Paul Kohner to Rudolf Jess (telegrams), December 6, 1938; December 7, 1938; December 12, 1938; December 22, 1938; December 29, 1938; January 9, 1939, Lancelyn Green Bequest.

Rudolf Jess to Paul Kohner (telegrams), December 8, 1938; December 13, 1938; December 30, 1938; January 8, 1939; January 24, 1939; Lancelyn Green Bequest.

Paul Kohner to Rudolf Jess, December 8, 1938, Lancelyn Green Bequest.

Julian Johnson (Fox) to Paul Kohner, December 24, 1938; July 8, 1939, Lancelyn Green Bequest.

Rudolf Jess to Paul Kohner, January 12, 1939; May 2, 1939, Lancelyn Green Bequest.

A. S. Watt to Denis Conan Doyle, February 23, 1939, Lancelyn Green Bequest.

Denis Conan Doyle to Victor Orsatti, August 8, 1939, Lancelyn Green Bequest.

Chapter 50

Robert G. Steele, "Frederic Dorr Steele: A Biographical Sketch" [Steele's life during the 1930s].

Lellenberg, ed., *Irregular Memories of the 'Thirties* [about the Baker Street Irregulars dinner, including the conversation between Edgar W. Smith and Denis].

Denis Conan Doyle to Lady (Jean) Conan Doyle, November 15, 1939; December 4, 1939; January 1, 1940; February 10, 1940; April 17, 1940; May 14, 1940, Lancelyn Green Bequest [reports from his US tour, about his political career, plans for Denis and Nina's future in London, the BSI dinner, Twentieth Century Fox, Fitelson, the radio show, plans for a Broadway production].

Denis Conan Doyle to A. S. Watt, December 5, 1939; May 4, 1940, Lancelyn Green Bequest [the Fox contract for the Gillette play, Fitelson, the canceled NBC contract].

Adrian Conan Doyle to Denis Conan Doyle (telegram), June 27, 1940, Lancelyn Green Bequest [about the death of Lady Conan Doyle].

Adrian Conan Doyle to Denis Conan Doyle, July 9, 1940; July 30, 1940; December 4, 1940, Lancelyn Green Bequest [about the death of Lady Conan Doyle, her will, cleaning up Windlesham, Denis's political career].

Chapter 51

Adrian Conan Doyle to Denis Conan Doyle, October 17, 1940; October 25, 1940, Lancelyn Green Bequest [about the bombs and the war situation at Windlesham].

Georgina Doyle, *Out of the Shadows*, pp. 269–70 [about Mary as warden].

Bruce, "Extracts from Unpublished Autobiography" [about Bruce and the radio show].

Utechin, "My Father as Watson" [interview with Nigel Bruce's daughter Pauline Page].

Meiser, "We Never Called Him Sherlock" [the conversation between Edith Meiser and Denis].

"Adventures on the Air: Edith Meiser in Conversation with John Bennett Shaw" [about the radio show].

Edith Meiser to Denis Conan Doyle, ca. February 10, 1941; ca. April 21, 1941, Lancelyn Green Bequest [about a role for Nina, and enclosing adaptations for Denis to have a look at].

Denis Conan Doyle to Edith Meiser, February 26, 1941 [about the role for Nina].

Victor Orsatti to Denis Conan Doyle, December 9, 1940, Lancelyn Green Bequest [plans of a film based on "The Speckled Band"].

Basil Rathbone to Denis Conan Doyle, December 13, 1940, Lancelyn Green Bequest [suggests a meeting when Denis returns to Hollywood].

Denis Conan Doyle to Basil Rathbone, December 29, 1940, Lancelyn Green Bequest [possible film deals and the plans for a Broadway production].

Denis Conan Doyle to H. William Fitelson, June 15, 1941, Lancelyn Green Bequest [about beer ad].

H. William Fitelson to Denis Conan Doyle, June 24, 1941, Lancelyn Green Bequest [about beer ad].

Donald Friede (of Myron Selznick & Co) to Denis Conan Doyle, August 6, 1941; September 5, 1941, Lancelyn Green Bequest [about Warner Brothers].

Denis Conan Doyle to Frank Orsatti, June 16, 1941, Lancelyn Green Bequest [Denis is not satisfied with the Orsatti brothers].

Chapter 52

Jon L. Lellenberg, ed., *Irregular Records of the Early 'Forties* (New York: Baker Street Irregulars, 1991) [including the correspondence with Roosevelt].

Denis Conan Doyle to William Fitelson, July 14, 1942, Lancelyn Green Bequest [about the meeting with Tom McKnight].

Field, *England's Secret Weapon*, pp. 101–15 [about the Universal contract and the war effort].

Godfrey B. Courtney, "General Clark's Secret Mission," *Life*, December 28, 1942, pp. 75–76, 78–80 [about the Allies' landing].

Edgar W. Smith, "From the Editor's Commonplace Book," *Baker Street Journal*, 1946/no. 1, pp. 65–66 [about the landing].

Ted Bergman, "Sherlock Holmes ger trygghet i svåra tider" [Sherlock Holmes Provides Security in Difficult Times], *Sydsvenskan* (Sweden), October 17, 1992 [about the landing].

Chapter 53

Lellenberg, ed., *Irregular Records of the Early 'Forties*, pp. 128–29 [Smith's letter to Starrett].

Lellenberg, *Nova 57 Minor* [about the newly discovered story].

Terry DeLapp (Universal) to Denis Conan Doyle, October 8, 1942, Lancelyn Green Bequest [includes a summary of the meeting about Denis's PR efforts].

Adrian Conan Doyle to Denis Conan Doyle, February 26, 1943; March 19, 1943, June 12, 1943, Lancelyn Green Bequest [about unpaid dues, marketing in various states, General Motors, and tax issues].

Adrian Conan Doyle to Denis Conan Doyle (telegram), March 15, 1943, Lancelyn Green Bequest [about his health].

Chapter 54

Adrian Conan Doyle to Denis Conan Doyle, August 20, 1943; January 9, 1944; May 26, 1944; February 23, 1945, Lancelyn Green Bequest [about military training, his illness, Ellery Queen's book, and his time in hospital].

Bruce, "Extracts from Unpublished Autobiography" [about Nigel Bruce and the films].

Field, *England's Secret Weapon*, pp. 139–49 [about Universal's Sherlock Holmes films 1943–45].

H. William Fitelson to Denis Conan Doyle, August 15, 1941, Lancelyn Green Bequest [about Pola Negri].

Denis Conan Doyle to H. William Fitelson, January 29, 1944 [about the radio scripts].

Richard Lancelyn Green, "Tilting at Windmills: Denis Conan Doyle and the Baker Street Irregulars," *Baker Street Journal*, Christmas annual, 2002, pp. 13–27 [about Ellery Queen's book].

Lellenberg, ed., *Irregular Records of the Early 'Forties*, pp. 135, 159 [about President Roosevelt and the BSI].

Franklin Delano Roosevelt, "Sherlock Holmes Was an American!" in *A Sherlock Holmes Compendium*, ed. Peter Haining (London: W. H. Allen, 1980), pp. 101–02 [Roosevelt's theories about Holmes's background].

Jon L. Lellenberg, ed., *Irregular Proceedings of the Mid 'Forties* (New York: Baker Street Irregulars, 1995), pp. 222–25 [about President Truman accepting an honorary membership in the BSI].

Chapter 55

Robert G. Steele, "Frederic Dorr Steele: A Biographical Sketch" [about the last months in Steele's life].

Green, *Tilting at Windmills*, pp. 45–64 [about the Limited Editions Club].

Chapter 56

Adrian Conan Doyle to Denis Conan Doyle, December 5, 1940; September 29, 1944; December 17, 1944; January 8, 1945; January 9, 1945; March 19, 1945; March 30, 1945; May 1, 1945; February 2, 1946; June 21, 1946, Lancelyn Green Bequest [about the latest meeting between Adrian and Denis, keeping the missing copyright a secret, ancient contracts, transforming the estate into a company, expected Holmes boom after the war, John Dickson Carr, new taxation rules, Denis in England, Adrian's workload].

Green, *Tilting at Windmills*, pp. 29–34 [about Edgar W. Smith's plans].

Peter Ruber, introduction to *The Final Adventures of Solar Pons*, by August Derleth (Shelburne, ON: Mycroft & Moran), 1998 [about Derleth].

Chapter 57

Jeffrey Marks: *Anthony Boucher: A Biobibliography* (Jefferson, NC: McFarland & Company, 2008), pp. 23–24, 78–86 [about Boucher's involvement in the radio show].

Julie McKuras, "Edith Meiser: A Fascinating and Beautiful Woman," unpublished speech given at the conference Gillette to Brett II, Indianapolis, on November 17, 2007 [about Edith Meiser's career and personal life].

"Adventures on the Air: Edith Meiser in Conversation with John Bennett Shaw" [about Meiser leaving the radio show].

Bruce, "Extracts from Unpublished Autobiography" [Bruce's feelings about Meiser and Rathbone].

Utechin, "My Father as Watson" [interview with Nigel Bruce's daughter Pauline Page].

Basil Rathbone, *In and Out of Character* (New York: Limelight Editions, 1989), pp. 178–88 [about Rathbone leaving the Holmes films, including the quote].

Barnes, *Holmes on Screen*, pp. 56–58 [about the final Rathbone film, *Dressed to Kill*].

William Nadel, "Edith Meiser and Sherlock Holmes on the Radio," in *Edith Meiser and Her Adventures with Sherlock Holmes* (Minneapolis: Sherlock Holmes Collections, University of Minnesota, 1999), pp. 8–9 [about Bruce and Meiser].

Chapter 58

Adrian Conan Doyle to Denis Conan Doyle, May 14, 1945; August 31, 1945; August 1, 1946; November 26, 1946; December 10, 1946, Lancelyn Green Bequest [about Emil Ludwig, Pearson, Italian castles, sorting old documents, John Dickson Carr].

Chapter 59

"Police Aid in Excess Speed," *Barrier Miner* (Broken Hill, New South Wales), May 24, 1948 [about the snakebite].

Jon L. Lellenberg, ed., *Irregular Crises of the Late 'Forties* (New York: Baker Street Irregulars, 1999), pp. 153–54 [about the snakebite].

"Secret Drink Lured Python Down Chimney," *Sunday Times* (Perth, Australia),
    December 4, 1938 [about Adrian's missing snake].
Douglas G. Greene, *John Dickson Carr: The Man Who Explained Miracles* (New York:
    Otto Penzler Books, 1995), pp. 310–21 [about work on the biography, including
    "Daddy prowling" quote and quote from the BSI dinner].
Adrian Conan Doyle to Denis Conan Doyle, January 24, 1947; March 4, 1947; April
    17, 1947; April 22, 1947; April 27, 1947; June 14, 1947; October 4, 1948; January 21,
    1949; April 26, 1949, Lancelyn Green Bequest [about John Dickson Carr and
    the writing of the biography, Winston Churchill, a film based on *The White
    Company*, paper shortage, Adrian moving to Tangier, Whitaker writing to
    Pearson, the swordfish season].
Denis Conan Doyle to Ray Stark, January 15, 1947, Lancelyn Green Bequest [about
    Hitchcock, who was interested in filming "The Lost Special"].
Irving Wallace, *The Sunday Gentleman* (New York: Simon & Schuster, 1965), pp. 392–
    415 [the journalist who wrote about Dr. Joseph Bell].
Lellenberg, *Nova 57 Minor* [about "The Case of the Man Who Was Wanted"].
Adrian Conan Doyle to Arthur Whitaker, January 21, 1949, Lancelyn Green Bequest
    [demanding evidence].
Denis Conan Doyle to Gerald Churcher, March 12, 1951, Lancelyn Green Bequest
    [about the payment to the *Cosmopolitan*].
"Death of Noted Local Ornithologist," *Gloucester Citizen* (UK), July 12, 1949 [about
    Arthur Whitaker].
Georgina Doyle, *Out of the Shadows*, pp. 284–90 [about Mary's reaction to the
    biography, about Adrian's move].
Sven Åhman, "Den levande Sherlock Holmes" [The Living Sherlock Holmes],
    Dagens Nyheter (Stockholm), August 4, 1946 [about Edgar W. Smith's office].
Green, *Tilting at Windmills*, pp. 45–64 [about Edgar W. Smith's problems].
Jens Byskov Jensen, "Snogen der bed Adrian Doyle" [The Snake That Bit Adrian
    Doyle], speech, given at Sherlock Holmes Club of Denmark, January 7, 2012
    [about toasting the snake].

Chapter 60

"Sherlock Holmes Collection: How It All Began," Westminster Libraries and
    Archives website [about the 1951 exhibition].
"Memories of the Exhibition," Westminster Libraries and Archives website [the
    elderly woman quotation].
Greg Darak, "The Second Return of Sherlock Holmes," *Sherlock Holmes Journal*,
    Diamond Jubilee supplement, 2011, pp. 1–5 [about the founding of the Sherlock
    Holmes Society of London].
Nicholas Utechin, "The Society: A Discursive History," *Sherlock Holmes Journal*,
    Summer 2001, pp. 40–48 [about the founding of the Sherlock Holmes Society
    of London].

Anthony Howlett, "In the Beginning: Memories of 1951," *Sherlock Holmes Journal*, Summer 2001, pp. 48–49 [about the 1951 exhibition].

John Bergquist, "50 Years Ago," *Friends of the Sherlock Holmes Collections*, 2001/no. 4, pp. 3, 7 [about the 1951 exhibition and the founding of the Sherlock Holmes Society of London].

Sherlock Holmes: Catalogue of an Exhibition Held at Abbey House, Baker Street, London, May–September 1951 (London: Wightman and Company, 1951) [list of all exhibited objects].

Adrian Conan Doyle to Geoffrey Stephens (Marylebone Library), January 2, 1951, Lancelyn Green Bequest [offers to help with the exhibition—if he gets paid].

Geoffrey Stephens (Marylebone Library) to Adrian Conan Doyle, March 1, 1951 [explains that they can't afford to pay Adrian].

Georgina Doyle, *Out of the Shadows*, pp. 293, 301–3, 308–16 [about Denis's health, Jean's work on the exhibition].

"Holmes Has a Visitor," *Daily Graphic*, July 18, 1951 [about Queen Mary visiting the exhibition, including quotation].

Richard Lancelyn Green, ed., *The Sherlock Holmes Letters* (Iowa City: University of Iowa Press, 1986), p. 225 [letter from George Edalji to the organizer of the Sherlock Holmes exhibition].

Chapter 61

Adrian Conan Doyle, *Djungel och djuphav* [Swedish translation of *Heaven Has Claws*] (Stockholm: Tidens Bokklubb, 1956), pp. 79–85 [about the ruins in the jungle].

"Ruins of Palace Believed to Be Link with Sheba," *West Australian* (Perth), July 2, 1951 [about Adrian's find].

Adrian Conan Doyle to Denis Conan Doyle, August 10, 1951; August 12, 1951, Lancelyn Green Bequest [about the New York City (NYC) exhibition].

Edgar W. Smith to Harold J. Sherman (Fitelson and Mayers), August 1, 1951, Lancelyn Green Bequest [about the NYC exhibition].

Jensen, "Snogen der bed Adrian Doyle" [about Anna's career].

Chapter 62

Adrian Conan Doyle, "U.S. Report 1952," Lancelyn Green Bequest [about the preparations for the NYC exhibition].

Henrik V. Ringsted, *London i lup* (Copenhagen: Thaning & Appels Forlag), 1953, p. 71 [about the death of Jum-Jum].

"Can't Fool Old Sherlock—Mrs. Adrian Conan Doyle Says She Is Kept Informed," *Kansas City* (MO) *Times*, February 27, 1952 [about Anna traveling on SS *America*].

Des Moines (IA) *Register*, "Mrs. Roosevelt Attends Holmes Exhibit," July 6, 1952 [Eleanor Roosevelt at the opening of the NYC exhibition].

Adrian Conan Doyle to Nina Mdivani, November 17, 1951; October 30, 1952 [about Denis's economies and health, and disagreements between the brothers].

Adrian Conan Doyle to Denis Conan Doyle, September 1, 1951; December 21, 1951;
    January 3, 1952; January 16, 1952; January 28, 1952; February 2, 1952; February 10,
    1952; February 22, 1952; February 26, 1952; March 4, 1952; March 5, 1952; March
    13, 1952; April 2, 1952; April 11, 1952; June 3, 1952; June 7, 1952; June 16, 1952; June
    18, 1952; July 25, 1952; October 30, 1952; November 9, 1952; November 10, 1952;
    December 18, 1952; December 20, 1952 [about preparations for the NYC exhibi-
    tion, Mr. Shapiro, disagreements on who should be executors of the will, Denis's
    hotel bill, Fitelson, Rathbone has helped Anna, Universal Studios considering
    legal action, Denis's criticism regarding the NYC exhibition, Eleanor Roosevelt,
    reasons why the NYC exhibition failed, Tony Harwood, Adrian being shadowed
    by Secret Service, Adrian realizing that Denis had taken all US money].
Denis Conan Doyle to William Fitelson, November 10, 1952, Lancelyn Green Bequest
    [about Denis's health].
Denis Conan Doyle to Adrian Conan Doyle, December 12, 1952; December 16,
    1952, Lancelyn Green Bequest [about Denis's fraud, Tony Harwood, Nina's
    innocence, Adrian cheating on his wife].

Chapter 63

Greene, *John Dickson Carr*, pp. 350, 354–62 [about working on the Holmes stories].
Herbert Brean, "How Holmes Was Reborn," *Life*, December 29, 1952, pp. 62–66
    [about the idea of new Holmes stories].
Adrian Conan Doyle to Denis Conan Doyle, unknown date in 1952 [about Tage
    Ekelöf's Swedish book]; July 25, 1952; October 23, 1952; November 9, 1952; Novem-
    ber 10, 1952; January 2, 1953; March 13, 1953, Lancelyn Green Bequest [about the
    writing of Adrian's and Carr's Holmes stories, no contract with the estate for
    the new stories, Carr beginning to drink, Adrian asking Denis for plot ideas].
Ted Bergman, ed., *Two Two One B*, no. 4 (1990) [about Tage Ekelöf's book].
Denis Conan Doyle to Adrian Conan Doyle, December 16, 1952 [criticizing Adrian's
    decision to write new Holmes stories].
Adrian Conan Doyle, *Djungel och djuphav* [*Heaven Has Claws*], p. 9 [about Tangier].
Earle F. Walbridge, quoted in "From the Editor's Commonplace Book," *Baker Street
    Journal*, 1955/no. 2, pp. 125–26 [mention of *The Exploits*]. The original Franklin
    D. Roosevelt quotation reads "a date that will live in infamy."
The name of Carr's novel that concludes at the London exhibition is *The Nine
    Wrong Answers*.
Tage Ekelöf's book is now one of the rarest and most expensive Swedish detective stories.
The two closing quotes from Holmes are taken from "The Greek Interpreter" and
    The Sign of Four, respectively.

Chapter 64

R. P. Watt to Gerald Churcher, November 7, 1951, Lancelyn Green Bequest [about
    Bruce's interest in the TV series].

Nigel Bruce to Denis Conan Doyle (telegram), December 21, 1951, Lancelyn Green Bequest [expressing desire to appear in the TV series].

René de Chochor to Adrian Conan Doyle and Denis Conan Doyle, March 20, 1953, Lancelyn Green Bequest [quote from de Chochor visiting Fitelson, and about the economics of a TV series].

René de Chochor to Adrian Conan Doyle, March 26, 1953; June 3, 1953, Lancelyn Green Bequest [about the copyright situation, sponsors, "The Black Baronet"].

Denis Conan Doyle to H. William Fitelson, November 11, 1951, Lancelyn Green Bequest [about Walt Disney].

René de Chochor to Denis Conan Doyle, April 13, 1953, Lancelyn Green Bequest [about "The Black Baronet"].

Brenda Loew, ed., *Playbills to Photoplays: Stage Performers Who Pioneered the Talkies* (n.p.: New England Vintage Film Society, 2010), p. 134 [about Nigel Bruce in Mexico].

Adrian Conan Doyle to Denis Conan Doyle, April 2, 1952; July 25, 1952; August 7, 1952; March 13, 1953; June 5, 1953, Lancelyn Green Bequest [about newspaper strips, Roy Rogers, merchandising].

Adrian Conan Doyle, "U.S. Report 1952," Lancelyn Green Bequest [about comic strips].

Chapter 65

Greg Darak, "Treasures from the BSI Trust Archives: The Basil Rathbone–Edgar Smith Correspondence," *For the Sake of the Trust*, Fall 2012, pp. 1, 4–5 [about the Christmas present].

S. E. Dahlinger and Glen S. Miranker, "Rathbone Returns! A Misadventure Called Sherlock Holmes," *Baker Street Journal*, Christmas annual, 2007 [about the Rathbone play]

"A Closer Look at the Second Mrs. Rathbone," *The Baz* [about Ouida Rathbone's early life].

Mattias Boström, "Ouida Before Rathbone," *Baker Street Journal*, 2017/no. 2 [about Ouida Rathbone's correct name and early career].

Chapter 66

Adrian Conan Doyle to Denis Conan Doyle, June 5, 1953; June 13, 1953; June 15, 1953; July 3, 1953; September 22, 1953; October 13, 1953; October 20, 1953; November 10, 1953; November 11, 1953; November 20, 1953; February 8, 1954; June 29, 1954, Lancelyn Green Bequest [about Denis's latest hotel bill, the new Holmes stories are written thanks to Adrian's father, Universal film at a cinema, US tax authorities, the failure of the Rathbone play, the Universal deal, discussions with Sheldon Reynolds].

René de Chochor to Adrian Conan Doyle and Denis Conan Doyle, September 6, 1953; September 14, 1953; September 16, 1953; September 20, 1953; September 28, 1953; October 5, 1953; October 7, 1953; October 14, 1953; October 19, 1953; November 10, 1953; November 17, 1953, Lancelyn Green Bequest [about Reynolds's TV series negotiations, Universal film at a cinema, the Reynolds contract].

René de Chochor to Denis Conan Doyle, June 5, 1953; January 11, 1954, Lancelyn Green Bequest [about Denis's contacts with Sheldon Reynolds, parallel negotiations with Universal and Reynolds].

Adrian Conan Doyle to René de Chochor, June 25, 1953, Lancelyn Green Bequest [about Sheldon Reynolds].

Denis Conan Doyle to René de Chochor, July 10, 1953; September 24, 1953; October 6, 1953; November 8, 1953; September 6, 1954, Lancelyn Green Bequest [about Sheldon Reynolds and the preparations for a TV series, Meiser and Giacoia's strips, Denis's contacts with Reynolds].

McKuras, "Edith Meiser" [about Edith Meiser's career and personal life].

"Adventures on the Air: Edith Meiser in Conversation with John Bennett Shaw" [about Meiser and the comic strips].

Barnes, *Holmes on Screen*, pp. 178–85 [about Sheldon Reynolds's TV series].

Russell Merritt, "Holmes and the Snake Skin Suits: Fighting for Survival on '50s Television," in *Fan Phenomena: Sherlock Holmes*, ed. Tom Ue and Jonathan Cranfield (Bristol, UK: Intellect Books, 2014), pp. 28–42 [about Éclair's studio].

Nicole de Bedford, *Nicole Nobody: The Autobiography of the Duchess of Bedford* (London: W. H. Allen, 1975), pp. 160–62 [about Archie Duncan and his tea].

René de Chochor to Adrian Conan Doyle, February 9, 1956, Lancelyn Green Bequest [about Adrian not being able to sell the TV rights for *The Exploits of Sherlock Holmes*].

Chapter 67

Nina Mdivani, *My Book*, Lancelyn Green Bequest [about Denis's death in India, including all quotations].

Chapter 68

Felix Barker, "Hounds of the Baskervilles," *Evening News* (London), October 13, 1958 [interview with Peter Cushing during the filming, including quotations].

Jesse L. Lasky Jr., *Whatever Happened to Hollywood?* (New York: Funk & Wagnalls, 1975), pp. 280–82 [about the train journey, including conversation].

Henry E. Lester to Vincent Starrett, January 17, 1962, Sherlock Holmes Collections, University of Minnesota, Minneapolis (hereafter, "Sherlock Holmes Collections") [about Lester's longtime friendship with Adrian and Denis].

Gene Gutowski, *With Balls and Chutzpah: A Story of Survival* (Bloomington, IN: iUniverse, 2011), pp. 177–78, 181, 182, 187–89 [about Gutowski and Lester's visit in London in 1959 and Gutowski's involvement in CCC-London].

Tim Bergfelder, *International Adventures: German Popular Cinema and European Co-Productions in the 1960s* (New York and Oxford: Berghahn Books, 2005), pp. 125–37 [about CCC-London and the production of the Christopher Lee film].

Henry E. Lester to Artur Brauner, August 3, 1961; October 30, 1961; November 10, 1961; December 17, 1961; May 16, 1962; April 25, 1963, Artur Brauner-Archive at Deutschen Filminstitut, Frankfurt, Germany (hereafter, "Artur Brauner-Archive") [about Brauner's early interest, complains about the suggestion of Christopher Lee as Holmes, rights sold to the musical, Gutowski's difficulties, late advance payments, Michael Hardwick, the film title *Fog* is mentioned].

Film contract between CCC and the Conan Doyle estate, dated September 18, 1961, Artur Brauner-Archive [contract for *Sherlock Holmes und das Halsband des Todes*].

C. E. Fielding (Crawley & de Reya, solicitors) to Artur Brauner, May 1, 1962, Artur Brauner-Archive [problems in a possible future agreement with Hammer Films, *Sherlock Holmes contra Jack the Ripper*].

Adrian Conan Doyle to Artur Brauner, May 13, 1962; June 8, 1962, Artur Brauner-Archive [about the choice of actors, Michael Hardwick will write the script, criticizes the objections to Hardwick's script].

Henry E. Lester to Michael and Mollie Hardwick, May 30, 1962, Artur Brauner-Archive [about Hardwick's script which is not good enough].

Henry E. Lester to René de Chochor, June 8, 1962, Artur Brauner-Archive [criticizing Hardwick's script].

Henry E. Lester to theatrical agent Margaret "Peggy" Ramsay, June 26, 1962, Artur Brauner-Archive [about the Hardwick script].

Henry E. Lester to Artur Brauner (memorandum), June 30, 1962, Artur Brauner-Archive [about the Hardwick script being reworked by Fisher, Lee, and Lester].

Artur Brauner to Otto Joseph (solicitor for the Conan Doyle estate), July 24, 1962, August 20, 1962, Artur Brauner-Archive [complaining that the Conan Doyle estate criticizes everything CCC does].

Henry E. Lester to Alexander H. Cohen, July 12, 1962; September 14, 1962, Alexander H. Cohen Papers, New York Public Library, New York (hereafter, "Cohen Papers") [about filming on location in Ireland, and the second CCC film to be produced with a start in January 1963].

Chapter 69

Jon L. Lellenberg, "An Interview with Michael Harrison," *Baker Street Miscellanea*, no. 41 (1985): pp. 14–29 [about Harrison, including quotations].

Jon L. Lellenberg, "An Interview with Michael Hardwick," *Baker Street Miscellanea*, no. 25 (1981): pp. 11–17 [about the Hardwicks].

Chris Redmond, e-mail correspondence with the author, fall 2015 [about Baring-Gould and the importance of his Holmes biography].

Peter E. Blau, e-mail correspondence with the author, spring 2016 [about Sabine Baring-Gould's childhood, referring to research by Laurie R. King].

Chapter 70

"Soviet Court Will Study the Sherlock Holmes Case," *Des Moines* (IA) *Register*, August 15, 1959 [about the Russian royalty money].

"Conan Doyle's Estate Loses Case in Russia," *St. Louis Post-Dispatch*, August 17, 1959 [about the Russian royalty money].

"Holmes Gets the Needle," *Arizona Republic*, August 24, 1959 [about the Russian royalty money].

"Re: Sir Arthur Conan Doyle, Deceased; Opinion," summary about the Conan Doyle estate, November 3, 1964, Lancelyn Green Bequest [about the increased income].

"Record of a conversation with Mr. Churcher, the U.K. representative of the Conan Doyle estates, when Mr. Adrian Conan Doyle's difficulty in obtaining a Soviet visa was discussed," Lord Jellicoe, November 21, 1955, National Archives [about visa trouble].

"Elementary, My Dear Nikolai," *St. Louis Post-Dispatch*, April 29, 1956 [about Adrian filing a complaint with Bulganin].

Adrian Conan Doyle to Sir Anthony Eden (Foreign Office), January 10, 1955; January 14, 1955, National Archives [about claim against Russia, and the Russian zone in Austria].

Henry E. Lester to Alexander Cohen, September 14, 1962, Cohen Papers [about Adrian and Lester's week in Cannes].

Court documents 1963 d.no. 1341, High Court of Justice, Chancery Division, Group B, between Nina Harwood and Adrian Conan Doyle, Lancelyn Green Bequest [about attempted recovery of moneys owed in Moscow, founding of Sir Nigel Films, the film project with Billy Wilder, obstacles to new film contracts].

Gordon Dadds & Co. to Gerald Churcher, November 12, 1962, Lancelyn Green Bequest [Jean declines involvement in Sir Nigel Films].

Barnes, *Holmes on Screen*, pp. 142–43 [about Billy Wilder's early Holmes plans].

Brian Cady, "The Private Life of Sherlock Holmes," TCM: Turner Classic Movies (website) [Billy Wilder quotation about doing it as a movie].

Nina Mdivani to Adrian Conan Doyle, August 12, 1955; March 16, 1970, Lancelyn Green Bequest [about the orchids and Adrian's disapproval of Universal's films].

Adrian Conan Doyle to Nina Mdivani, September 6, 1955; April 30, 1956, Lancelyn Green Bequest [about the orchids and Nina's proposal to sell the estate].

Nina Mdivani, *My Book*, Lancelyn Green Bequest [about the orchids and Tony Harwood].

Georgina Doyle, *Out of the Shadows*, pp. 323–27 [about Mary's attitude toward the legal wrangle between Adrian and Nina].

Court documents between J. Arthur Leve (representing Denis Conan Doyle's estate) and Adrian Conan Doyle, Supreme Court of the State of New York, Lancelyn Green Bequest [about Adrian's decision not to pay Nina her one-third share].

"Re: Sir Arthur Conan Doyle. Re: Estate of Denis Conan Doyle. Case to Counsel to Advise in Conference on Behalf of Princess Mdivani," compiled by Burton, Yeates, and Hart, May 9, 1963, Lancelyn Green Bequest [about Nina not being given any accounts].

Managing Director's Report to the Annual General Meeting of Sir Nigel Films
    Limited, December 4, 1964, Lancelyn Green Bequest [about film projects:
    The Private Life of Sherlock Holmes, Fog, Brigadier Gerard, The White Company].

Chapter 71

Carol Ilson, *Harold Prince: A Director's Journey* (New York: Limelight Editions, 2000),
    pp. 109–18 [about *Baker Street*].
David Paul Hellings, "Movie Review: Hound of the Baskervilles," Haddonfield Horror
    (website), May 2015 [about Kenneth Hyman's involvement in the Hammer film].
Salt Lake Tribune, December 23, 1961 [about Hyman and the policy from Lloyd's].
John C. Taylor to Alexander H. Cohen, April 3, 1961, Cohen Papers [about rights
    trouble with the Conan Doyle estate].
Notes by Alexander H. Cohen, April 28, 1961, Cohen Papers [about the different
    producers wanting the rights for a Holmes musical].
Alexander H. Cohen to Henry E. Lester, April 28, 1961; May 10, 1962; April 22, 1963;
    May 21, 1963; June 17, 1963; July 23, 1963, Cohen Papers [about rights trouble
    with the Conan Doyle estate, Lester reinstated as representative of the Conan
    Doyle estate, Rex Harrison, *The Sherlock Holmes Companion*, Richard Condon,
    trying to get Fritz Weaver for the Holmes part, rewriting the book].
Henry E. Lester to Alexander H. Cohen, August 6, 1961; August 9, 1961; November
    24, 1961; January 20, 1962; January 21, 1962; April 8, 1962; April 26, 1962; May 8,
    1962; August 24, 1962; September 14, 1962; March 29, 1963; May 10, 1963; May
    26, 1963; June 13, 1963; June 24, 1963; November 13, 1963, Cohen Papers [about
    the quality of Coopersmith's work, Kenneth Hyman, approved actors for the
    Holmes part, views on Coopersmith's book and the lyrics, Christopher Lee's
    interest in playing Holmes, Gregory Peck, *The Sherlock Holms Companion*,
    Richard Condon, Rex Harrison, the BBC series].
Agreement between the Conan Doyle estate and Alexander H. Cohen, November
    9, 1961, Cohen Papers [concerning the musical *Baker Street*].
Adrian Conan Doyle to Alexander H. Cohen, January 31, 1962; February 14, 1962;
    April 24, 1962; September 14, 1962; December 30, 1963, Cohen Papers [about
    René de Chochor as new agent in the agreement with Cohen, Adrian replaces
    Lester, disagreement with Lester is solved, Gregory Peck, approval of Fritz
    Weaver, additional option payment].
Adrian Conan Doyle to Henry E. Lester, January 14, 1962, Cohen Papers [Adrian is
    not at all happy with the musical, especially criticizing the music].
René de Chochor to Alexander H. Cohen, April 30, 1962, Cohen Papers [the dis-
    agreement with Lester has been solved].
Alexander H. Cohen to Adrian Conan Doyle, November 19, 1962; December 5,
    1962, Cohen Papers [about additional option payment, problems with the
    score, new composers].

Alexander H. Cohen to Peter O'Toole, April 12, 1963, Cohen Papers [trying to get O'Toole to play Holmes].

Alexander H. Cohen to Henry Lester (telegram), June 12, 1963, Cohen Papers [about Rex Harrison losing interest in the musical].

Barnes, *Holmes on Screen*, pp. 185–90 [about the BBC series with Wilmer as Holmes].

Douglas Wilmer, *Stage Whispers: The Memoirs* (Tenbury Wells, UK: Porter Press International, 2009), pp. 157–70 [about the BBC series with Wilmer as Holmes].

Johnson and Upton, *Holmes Miscellany*, pp. 83–84 [about Holmes on BBC Radio].

Richard Hewett, "Canon Doyle? Getting Holmes Right (and Getting the Rights) for Television," *Adaptation* 8, no. 2 (2015): pp. 192–206 [about the fidelity difference between UK and US adaptations].

"Mystery Casting in Baker Street," *Montreal Gazette*, October 3, 1964 [about the search for a Fritz Weaver look-alike].

Cliff Jahr, "Lord of the Flops" *New York*, October 8, 1979, pp. 40–44 [about Alexander H. Cohen's publicity stunts].

"Ms. of Conan Doyle Is Sold for $12,600," *New York Times*, December 19, 1964 [about the auction at Christie's].

"Sherlock Manuscript Brings $12,600," *Kansas City* (MO) *Times*, December 19, 1964 [about the auction at Christie's].

Tom Prideaux, "A Singing Holmes in Baker Street," *Life*, April 2, 1965, pp. 133–34, 137–38 [about Richard Burton's recording].

Murray Schumach, "Theater to Show Holmes Exhibits," *New York Times*, February 9, 1965 [about the manuscripts exhibited in the theater lobby].

Peter E. Blau and Randall Stock, e-mail correspondence with the author, spring 2016 [about *Baker Street*, the auction at Christie's, and the exhibition].

Chapter 72

Georgina Doyle, *Out of the Shadows*, pp. 323–27 [about Jean's wedding].

"Business Booms in Baker-Street," *Daily Mail* (UK), June 1965 [Adrian meeting a journalist at Brown's Hotel, including quotation].

John Hamilton, *Beasts in the Cellar: The Exploitation Film Career of Tony Tenser* (Godalming, UK: FAB Press, 2005), pp. 67–74 [about the production of *A Study in Terror*, including the quotations from the Compton shooting and the meeting with the Ford brothers].

Andrew Spicer and A. T. McKenna, *The Man Who Got Carter: Michael Klinger, Independent Production and the British Film Industry, 1960–1980* (London: I. B. Taurus, 2013), pp. 30–32 [about *A Study in Terror*—who wrote the screenplay and who came up with the original idea].

Tom Weaver, *Attack of the Monster Movie Makers* (Jefferson, NC: McFarland & Company, 1994) [interview with Herman Cohen, part of it about *A Study in Terror*].

Gary Coville and Patrick Lucanio, *Jack the Ripper: His Life and Crimes in Popular Entertainment* (Jefferson, NC: McFarland & Company, 1999), pp. 113–15 [about

A Study in Terror—who wrote the screenplay and who came up with the original idea].

Managing Director's Report to the Annual General Meeting of Sir Nigel Films Limited, December 4, 1964, Lancelyn Green Bequest [about the upcoming film projects for Sir Nigel Films].

"For the Commonplace Book," *Daily Telegraph* (London), May 3, 1963 [about the upcoming film projects for Sir Nigel Films].

Anthony Howlett, "A Study in Terror," *Sherlock Holmes Journal*, Winter 1965, pp. 88–89 [review of the film].

Barnes, *Holmes on the Screen*, pp. 283–84 [about the US release of *A Study in Terror*].

Chapter 73

Peter E. Blau, e-mail to the author, April 4, 2016 [about WGN-TV's Sherlock Holmes Theater in 1965, with the 107 recorded segments with Basil Rathbone].

Basil Rathbone to Alexander H. Cohen, January 31, 1963, Cohen Papers [Rathbone asking for a part in the musical].

Alexander H. Cohen to Basil Rathbone, February 4, 1963, Cohen Papers [Cohen explains that Rathbone doesn't fit their demands for the Holmes part].

Harvey Pack, "Basil Rathbone Believes in the Wonders of ESP," *Asbury Park* (NJ) *Press*, June 15, 1966 [about the proposal to make contact with the late Conan Doyle].

Chapter 74

Stephen Clarkson, "'The Strength and Activity of Youth': The Junior Sherlockian Movement," *Baker Street Journal*, Christmas annual, 2003 [about Christopher Redmond].

Susan Rice, "Dubious and Questionable Memories: A History of the Adventuresses of Sherlock Holmes," *Baker Street Journal*, Christmas annual, 2004 [about the young women who demonstrated in 1968].

John Bennett Shaw, "Who's Afraid of Julian Wolff?" *Baker Street Journal*, 1986/no. 2, pp. 85–89 [about the 1968 dinner].

"Tour of Switzerland in the Footsteps of Sherlock Holmes, 27th April to 5th May, 1968," supplement, *Sherlock Holmes Journal*, summer 1968 [about the Sherlock Holmes Society of London's pilgrimage to Switzerland].

A film from the trip to Switzerland, *In the Footsteps of Sherlock Holmes*, can be viewed at the British Pathé website: www.britishpathe.com/video/in-the-footsteps-of-sherlock-holmes.

Chapter 75

Court documents 1966 d.no. 876, High Court of Justice, Chancery Division, Group B, between Nina Harwood and Adrian Malcolm Conan Doyle and Another, April 29, 1966, Lancelyn Green Bequest [about attorney Morton Feiler's meeting with Henry E. Lester, including quotations].

Adrian Conan Doyle to Henry Lester, October 11, 1968, Lancelyn Green Bequest [about Adrian's alterations in the film script].

Henry Lester to Adrian Conan Doyle, November 3, 1969, Lancelyn Green Bequest [about film company profits that failed to materialize].

Heads of agreement, between Adrian Conan Doyle, Dame Jean Conan Doyle, Nina Harwood, and Henry Lester, November 7, 1965, Lancelyn Green Bequest [about Fides Union Fiduciaire].

Henry Lester to John C. Taylor, November 23, 1967, Lancelyn Green Bequest [about the foundation and the sale to Texas].

Adrian Conan Doyle to Lew Feldman, December 10, 1968; January 30, 1969, Lancelyn Green Bequest [about ownership of the Conan Doyle documents and the sale that did not take place].

Chapter 76

Barnes, *Holmes on Screen*, pp. 242–51 [about the series with Cushing as Holmes].

Tony Earnshaw, *An Actor, and a Rare One: Peter Cushing as Sherlock Holmes* (Lanham, MD: Scarecrow Press, 2001), pp. 29–63 [about the BBC series with Cushing].

Wilmer, *Stage Whispers: The Memoirs*, pp. 160–61 [quotations "It cannot be done . . ." and "I'd rather sweep . . ."].

Chapter 77

Brian Cady, "The Private Life of Sherlock Holmes," TCM: Turner Classic Movies (website) [about Peter Sellers's conflict with Billy Wilder].

Harold Heffernan, "Sellers Fires Ad at Billy Wilder," *Pittsburgh Press*, July 15, 1964 [about Peter Sellers's conflict with Billy Wilder].

Adrian Conan Doyle to Henry Lester, March 11, 1970, Lancelyn Green Bequest [about Adrian's verdict on the film].

Michael Billington, "The Case of the Slow-Witted Sleuth," *Guardian* (UK), November 29, 2002 [about Robert Stephens].

Barnes, *Holmes on Screen*, pp. 142–47 [about *The Private Life of Sherlock Holmes*].

David Stuart Davies, "The Private Life of Sherlock Holmes," *Sherlock Holmes Gazette*, no. 14 (1996): pp. 4–10 [about *The Private Life of Sherlock Holmes*].

Trevor Raymond, "Billy Wilder on Baker Street: The Making and Unmaking of a Movie," *Canadian Holmes*, 2003/no. 1, pp. 35–48 [about *The Private Life of Sherlock Holmes*].

Paul Herbert and Peter E. Blau, e-mail correspondence with the author, spring 2016 [about the film script *Elementary, My Dear Watson*].

Chapter 78

"The Estate of the Late Sir Arthur Conan Doyle—Creator of Sherlock Holmes," *Times* (London), April 7, 1971 [legal notice].

"Move to Halt Conan Doyle Estate Sale," *Times* (London), April 8, 1971 [Nina trying to stop the sale].

"Not Elementary," *Times* (London), April 14, 1971 [about the sale].

Court documents 1971 d.no. 359, High Court of Justice, Chancery Division, Group B, between Nina Harwood and Fides Union Fiduciaire, Lancelyn Green Bequest [about the interest in selling the estate].

Lycett, *Man Who Created Sherlock Holmes*, p. 462 [about Nina's purchase of the estate].

Sidney Pearlman (Nina's solicitor) to A. E. Drysdale (Royal Bank of Scotland), February 3, 1972; February 7, 1972; February 8, 1972, Lancelyn Green Bequest [about the purchase, company registration, and securities].

A. E. Drysdale to Superintendent of Branches, Royal Bank of Scotland, February 11, 1972, Lancelyn Green Bequest [about Tony's expected inheritance].

Jonathan Clowes to Sidney Pearlman, June 21, 1973, Lancelyn Green Bequest [about doubling incomes].

Cancellation of Agreement with Ward Lock & Co. Limited in Respect of "A Study in Scarlet," September 30, 1973, Lancelyn Green Bequest [about the repurchasing of rights for £3,000].

Baskervilles Investments Ltd: Report September 72–March 73, Lancelyn Green Bequest [about the company's plans].

Samuel French Limited to Sidney Pearlman & Greene, January 19, 1973, Lancelyn Green Bequest [about the Royal Shakespeare Company's interest in Gillette's play].

Deriaz, Kirker & Cie to Jonathan Clowes, July 20, 1972, Lancelyn Green Bequest [about registering trademarks].

Sidney Pearlman to Nina Mdivani, January 29, 1973, Lancelyn Green Bequest [about registering trademarks].

W. Lyall (Royal Bank of Scotland) to Nina Mdivani, December 4, 1973, Lancelyn Green Bequest [about overdrafts].

Sidney Pearlman to John Brown (Royal Bank of Scotland), October 19, 1973, Lancelyn Green Bequest [about Nina's restricted expenses].

Chapter 79

Nicholas Meyer, *The View from the Bridge: Memories of Star Trek and a Life in Hollywood* (New York: Plume, 2010), pp. 40–57 [about the writing of *The Seven-Per-Cent Solution*, including quotations].

Nicholas Meyer, "Seven-Per-Cent at Thirty: Memories and Reflections," *Baker Street Journal*, 2004/no. 2, pp. 26–30 [about the writing of *The Seven-Per-Cent Solution*].

Steven T. Doyle, "Together Again for the First Time: Forty Years of *The Seven-Per-Cent Solution*," *Baker Street Journal*, Christmas annual, 2015 [about the writing of *The Seven-Per-Cent Solution*].

Chapter 80

Regional General Manager to J. S. McFarlane (Royal Bank of Scotland), November 14, 1973, Lancelyn Green Bequest [about missing checks, currency smuggling, and Nina's failing eyesight].

Pointer, *Public Life of Sherlock Holmes*, pp. 105–6 [about the Royal Shakespeare Company and the James Bond theme].

Amy Hurst, of the Shakespeare Birthplace Trust, e-mail to author, January 25, 2013 [about the reasons for the RSC version].

Meyer, *View from the Bridge*, pp. 40–57 [getting *The Seven-Per-Cent Solution* published, including quotations].

Meyer, *"Seven-Per-Cent* at Thirty" [getting *The Seven-Per-Cent Solution* published].

James Merrill, *A Different Person: A Memoir* (New York: Alfred A. Knopf, 1993), pp. 3–17, 40, 58, 74, 160–64 [about Merrill and Tony Harwood's European trip, including quotations].

Patrick O'Higgins, *Madame: An Intimate Biography of Helena Rubinstein* (New York: Viking Press, 1971), pp. 266–67 [about Nina's jewelry].

Barbara Cartland, *In Search for Rainbows* (London: Arrow Books, 1973), p. 279 [Nina's quote about fat women].

Derek Jarman, *Dancing Ledge* (London: Quartet Books, 1984), pp. 78–82, 137 [about Harwood in the 1960s and Coco Chanel].

Tony Peake: *Derek Jarman* (London: Abacus, 2001), pp. 120–25, 209 [about Harwood in the 1960s and in New York].

"Authoress Barbara Cartland Loves Gold, Gold, Gold," *Cedar Rapids* (IA) *Gazette*, July 16, 1967 [about Nina visiting Barbara Cartland].

Tony Harwood to Brian Lewis, January 21, 1974, Lancelyn Green Bequest [about the plans for a Broadway version of Gillette's play].

Audrey Wood (International Famous Agency) to Nina Mdivani, April 22, 1974, Lancelyn Green Bequest [mentioning Andy Warhol's interest in doing the sets].

"Princess Nina Harwood," minutes of meeting, January 17, 1974, attended by Sidney Pearlman, J. G. Tomlins, Jonathan Clowes, and Royal Bank of Scotland representative R. B. Standring, Lancelyn Green Bequest [about Tony and Nina's financial needs].

Ian Calderon to Tony Harwood, September 30, 1974, Lancelyn Green Bequest [about the dimmable lighting].

Chapter 81

Thomas Weyr, "The Road to the Top for 'The Seven-Per-Cent Solution': Not at All Elementary," *Publishers Weekly*, October 27, 1975 [about publishing work at Dutton, including quotations].

"The Case of the Baker Street Boom," *Publishers Weekly*, July 8, 1974 [sales figures during the Holmes boom].

John Gardner, "An Interview with John Gardner, Conducted on May 1, 1981," *Baker Street Miscellanea*, no. 27 (1981): pp. 13–15, 33 [about Gardner].

"Sherlock Holmes Revival Booms," *Newark* (OH) *Advocate*, December 25, 1974 [interview with John Bennett Shaw].

"Sherlock Holmes: Zounds! The Super Sleuth Is Our Latest Literary Hero," *People*, 1974/no. 27, pp. 38–39 [about increased sales of deerstalkers].

WCBS-TV, New York, September 2, 1975, Lancelyn Green Bequest [news bulletin about the cinema queue].

Chapter 82

George T. Delacorte to Princess Nina Mdivani Harwood, December 9, 1975, Mdivani family papers, Hargrett Rare Book & Manuscript Library, University of Georgia, Athens [addressed to Mrs. Montezuma Jones].

Langdon Hammer: *James Merrill: Life and Art* (New York: Alfred A. Knopf, 2015), p. 568 [about Nina and Tony living as Mr. and Mrs. Montezuma Jones].

Sidney Pearlman to Nina Mdivani, April 5, 1974, Lancelyn Green Bequest [about bouncing checks].

Notice of Appointment of Receiver or Manager, pertaining to Baskervilles Investments, April 26, 1974, Lancelyn Green Bequest [William G. Mackey is appointed receiver].

Jonathan Clowes to Tony Harwood, May 9, 1974, Lancelyn Green Bequest [about implications of receivership].

E. J. N. Harris and S. E. Blake to Nina Mdivani, June 26, 1974, Lancelyn Green Bequest [about the writ against the bank].

Account by Nina Mdivani of Baskervilles Investments' affairs, July 2, 1974, Lancelyn Green Bequest [about the Broadway musical].

Tony Harwood to Anthony Lewis (at the *New York Times*), July 30, 1975, Lancelyn Green Bequest [about missing bank statements].

Tony Harwood to Audrey Wood (memorandum), October 27, 1975, Lancelyn Green Bequest [about how the receiver hid future deals, destroying the trademark].

Tony Harwood to Audrey Wood (memorandum), December 15, 1975, Lancelyn Green Bequest [about Gene Wilder's film].

Barnes, *Holmes on Screen*, pp. 11–13 [about Gene Wilder's film].

Tony Harwood to Audrey Wood (memorandum), January 8, 1976 [about the pornographic film].

Tony Harwood to Audrey Wood (memorandum), December 28, 1975, Lancelyn Green Bequest [about the receiver's incompetence].

Bernard R. Pollock to John Linsenmeyer, December 3, 1975, Lancelyn Green Bequest [about the receiver's legal costs].

Nina Mdivani to Andrew Walker, January 5, 1976, Lancelyn Green Bequest [about the sale of the couple's Rolls-Royce].

Jarman, *Dancing Ledge*, p. 160 [about brown envelopes in the drawer].

Chapter 83

Barnes, *Holmes on Screen*, pp. 83–85, 121–26, 196–200 [about *Murder by Decree*, the Cook/Moore film, and Reynolds's TV series].

Jon L. Lellenberg, "Rights and Copyrights," *Baker Street Miscellanea*, no. 21 (1980): pp. 26–28 [about the Conan Doyle rights in the 1970s].

Jon L. Lellenberg, e-mail correspondence with the author, autumn 2012 and spring 2016 [about the Conan Doyle rights in the 1970s and Dame Jean's regaining of the US copyright].

Alan M. Dershowitz, *Reversal of Fortune: Inside the von Bülow Case* (London: Penguin Books, 1986), pp. 214–15 [about Andrea Reynolds].

Andrea Reynolds, *My Claus von Bulow Affaire* (Bloomington, IN: iUniverse, 2013) [about her relation to Sheldon Reynolds].

Val Guest, *So You Want to Be in Pictures* (London: Reynolds & Hearn, 2001), pp. 171–73 [about Reynolds's TV series, including quotations].

Anthony Burgess to Ted Bergman, August 22, 1986, author's collection [confirming Burgess's involvement in Reynolds's TV series].

"Så här lever Sherlock Holmes och Doktor Watson privat" [This Is How Sherlock Holmes and Dr. Watson Live], *Husmodern* (Sweden), 1980/no. 44, pp. 14–15, 57 [interview with Geoffrey Whitehead and Donald Pickering, in connection with the Reynolds TV series being shown on Swedish TV].

Chapter 84

Mitch Cullin, e-mail correspondence with the author, spring 2016 [about his childhood and friendship with John Bennett Shaw].

Mitch Cullin, "'I couldn't quite justify taking liberties with the character without first making sure I had done my homework correctly': An Interview with Mitch Cullin, Author of *A Slight Trick of the Mind*," by Peter Wild, *Bookmunch* (blog), May 28, 2014 [about his early interest in Sherlock Holmes].

Beverly Stephen, "Spirit and Style Sum Up the Magic of New Mexico," *Montreal Gazette*, November 8, 1986 [about Santa Fe].

Chapter 85

Christopher Roden, "In Conversation with . . . Dame Jean Conan Doyle," *ACD*, 1990/no. 2 [Dame Jean's views about Holmes pastiches].

"U.S. Law Aids Holmes Champion," *Daily Telegraph* (London), January 8, 1981 [Dame Jean's views about Holmes pastiches].

Andrew Jay Peck, "Sherlock Holmes and the Law," *Baker Street Miscellanea*, no. 40 (1984): pp. 16–24 [about the withdrawal of Dame Jean's rights].

Jon L. Lellenberg, e-mail correspondence with the author, spring 2016 [about Dame Jean].

Barnes, *Holmes on Screen*, pp. 256–61 [about Lorindy's two TV movies].

"Doyle Daughter Sells Rights to Holmes Tales," *Gettysburg* (PA) *Times*, February 2, 1982 [Dame Jean's quotations about the Lorindy deal].

Chapter 86

Michael Cox, *A Study in Celluloid: A Producer's Account of Jeremy Brett as Sherlock Holmes* (Indianapolis: Gasogene Books, 2011), pp. 1–22 [about the Granada series].

Barnes, *Holmes on Screen*, pp. 21–27, 256–61 [about the Granada series and Lorindy's two TV movies].

David Stuart Davies, *Bending the Willow: Jeremy Brett as Sherlock Holmes* (Ashcroft, BC: Calabash Press, 2012) [about Brett and the Granada series].

Sharon Mail, *We Could Possibly Comment: Ian Richardson Remembered,* chap. 5 (Leicester, UK: Matador, 2009) [about Richardson in the Lorindy TV movies, including the quotations].

Peck, "Sherlock Holmes and the Law" [about the conflict between Lorindy and Granada].

Chapter 87

Igor Maslennikov, "Sherlock Holmes, Vasily Livanov and Others," Alek Morse (blog) [about the production of the Lenfilm TV series].

Igor Maslennikov, "Dear Sherlock Holmes's and Doctor Watson's Friends," Alek Morse (blog) [about the Lenfilm TV series; the original article includes the quoted protest letter].

Olga Fedina, *What Every Russian Knows (And You Don't)* (London: Anaconda Editions, 2013), pp. 104–14 [about the Lenfilm TV series].

Elena Korenévskaya, "Four Soviet Films in a British Boat," Russia beyond the Headlines (website), March 28, 2014 [about Russian adaptations of British literary classics].

Alexander Sedov, "From King Lear to Ten Little Indians," Alek Morse (blog), November 14, 2013 [about "Englishness" in Soviet cinema].

Dmitry Urnov, "An Enviable but Difficult Fate," in *Legend and Fact: Stories,* by Vassily Livanov (Moscow: Raduga Publishers, 1989), pp. 7–18 [about Vasily Livanov's career and the Moscow traffic police].

Martin Walker, "Vassily Holmes," *Guardian* (UK), August 17, 1987 [about the actor Vasily Livanov].

Valery Kichin, "Sherlock Holmes OBE," Russia beyond the Headlines (website), December 12, 2007 [about Livanov and the Lenfilm TV series, quotation about troublemaker].

Peter Haining, *The Television Sherlock Holmes* (London: Virgin Books, 1991), pp. 88–90 [about the Lenfilm TV series].

Stig-Arne Kristoffersen, *Ukraine: A Joke?* (published privately, 2010), p. 40 [about the Russian tradition of Sherlock Holmes jokes].

Peter Knight, "Year of Social Awareness," *The Age* (Melbourne), March 4, 1982 [about the International Television Festival in Monte Carlo, including the vodka quotation].

A. Koroleva, "Visiting Holmes," *221B Baker Street* (blog) [interview with Vasily Livanov, including the quotation from the British delegation].

Alexander Sedov, e-mail correspondence with the author, spring 2016.

Chapter 88

Joe Lapointe, "Review," *Detroit Free Press*, July 29, 1984 [about Spielberg and the opening ceremonies of the Olympics, including Spielberg quotation].

David Blum, "Steven Spielberg and the Dread Hollywood Backlash," *New York*, March 24, 1986, p. 56 [about Spielberg reading the script for *Young Sherlock Holmes*].

Leslie Bennetts, "Imagine Sherlock as a Boy . . . ," *New York Times*, December 1, 1985 [about *Young Sherlock Holmes*].

Jim Hawkins, "From a Little Adobe House to the Sherlock Holmes Collections," *Friends of the Sherlock Holmes Collections*, 2002/no. 3, pp. 1, 6 [about John Bennett Shaw reading the film script].

"Anglicizing the Script," *Courier-Journal* (Louisville, KY), August 15, 1984 [about Jeffrey Archer doctoring the script for *Young Sherlock Holmes*].

Jon L. Lellenberg, e-mail correspondence with the author, spring 2016 [about Dame Jean's views on the first draft of *Young Sherlock Holmes*].

Tony Schwartz, "Son of Hollywood's Hottest Stars: Behind the Quake at Paramount That Rocked the Business," *New York*, October 8, 1984, pp. 42–47, 49 [about Michael Eisner leaving Paramount].

Barbara Palmer, "Sherlockians Bid Holmes a Happy 130th," *USA Today*, January 6, 1984 [about the Brothers Three of Moriarty and Mitch Cullin].

Mitch Cullin, e-mail correspondence with the author, spring 2016 [about his last meeting with John Bennett Shaw].

Chapter 89

Tom Sito, *Drawing the Line: The Untold Story of the Animation Unions from Bosko to Bart Simpson* (Lexington: University Press of Kentucky, 2006), pp. 293–96 [about the phone call from the Smithsonian, Roy E. Disney, and Michael Eisner coming to Disney].

James B. Stewart, *DisneyWar: The Battle for the Magic Kingdom* (New York: Simon & Schuster, 2005), pp. 71–72, 84 [about Michael Eisner coming to Disney, his quotation regarding a script, and the conversation about time needed and cost].

Steve Hulett, *Mouse in Transition: An Insider's Look at Disney Feature Animation* (n.p.: Theme Park Press, 2014), chap. 15 [about Michael Eisner coming to Disney, quotation about Paramount].

John Musker and Ron Clements, "Animating Sherlock Holmes: *The Great Mouse Detective*," in *Sherlock Holmes: Behind the Canonical Screen*, ed. Lyndsay Faye and Ashley D. Polasek (New York: Baker Street Irregulars, 2015), pp. 233–38 [about the production of *The Great Mouse Detective*, quotation about Michael Jackson].

Jim Korkis, "How Basil Saved Disney Feature Animation: Part One," MousePlanet, February 23, 2011 [about the production of *The Great Mouse Detective*].

Michael Peraza, "Basil of Baker Street, Part 1," *Ink and Paint Club* (blog), March 24, 2010.

Brian J. Robb, *A Brief History of Walt Disney* (London: Robinson, 2014), pp. 225–28 [about *The Great Mouse Detective*].

Barnes, *Holmes on Screen*, pp. 69–71 [about *The Great Mouse Detective*].

Julie McKuras, "Basil of Baker Street," *Friends of the Sherlock Holmes Collections*, 2001/no. 1, pp. 1, 6 [about Eve Titus's children's books].

Vincent Brosnan, Peter E. Blau, Russell Merritt, Peggy Perdue, and Julie McKuras, e-mail correspondence with the author, spring 2013 [about Eve Titus].

Chapter 90

Cox, *Study in Celluloid*, pp. 78–84 [about the Granada series].

Barnes, *Holmes on Screen*, pp. 21–27, 152–55 [about the Granada series].

Davies, *Bending the Willow: Jeremy Brett as Sherlock Holmes* [about the Granada series].

Musker and Clements, "Animating Sherlock Holmes" [about the production of *The Great Mouse Detective*].

Michael Peraza, "Basil of Baker Street, Part 2," *Ink and Paint Club* (blog), March 25, 2010 [about the production of *The Great Mouse Detective*, quotation about computer images].

Jim Korkis, "How Basil Saved Disney Feature Animation: Part Two," MousePlanet (website), March 2, 2011 [about the production of *The Great Mouse Detective*].

Elizabeth Trembley, "Holmes' Encore!" *Armchair Detective*, 1992/no. 1, pp. 4–13 [interview with Jeremy Brett].

Chapter 91

Jessica McMahon, Catherine Cooke, and Nick Utechin, "Times of the 'Sign,'" *Sherlock Holmes Journal*, Summer 1987, pp. 42–46 [about the filming of Granada's *The Sign of Four*].

Barnes, *Holmes on Screen*, pp. 236–38 [about the Granada adaptation of *The Sign of Four*].

Cox, *Study in Celluloid*, pp. 107–17 [about the Granada adaptation of *The Sign of Four*].

Chapter 92

John C. Tibbetts, "Holmes in London, 1988," *Baker Street Miscellanea*, no. 57 (1989), pp. 32–43 [interview with Michael Caine, Dame Jean Conan Doyle, and Jeremy Brett, including the lift conversation].

Barnes, *Holmes on Screen*, pp. 87–88, 152–55 [about the Granada series].

Cox, *Study in Celluloid*, pp. 117–21, 139–50 [about the Granada series, including the haircut quotation].

Jean Conan Doyle, "An Interview with Jean Conan Doyle," transcript at John C. Tibbetts's website [about the 1921 performance of *The Speckled Band*, and Dame Jean's views on *The Secret of Sherlock Holmes*].

"Air Commandant Dame Jean Conan Doyle," *Times* (London), November 19, 1997 [about Dame Jean's attitude toward the Granada series].

"Michael Hardwick," *Times* (London), March 14, 1991 [about Dame Jean's attitude toward Hardwick's books].

Roden, "In Conversation with . . . Dame Jean Conan Doyle" [Dame Jean's views about Holmes pastiches].

Jon L. Lellenberg, e-mail correspondence with the author, fall 2015 [Dame Jean's views about *Without a Clue*, including the quotation, and giving permission to *Star Trek* and pastiche authors].

Chapter 93

"For Cold War Junkies, Berlin Wall in England," *Free Lance-Star* (Fredericksburg, VA), August 16, 1990 [about Granada Studios in Manchester].

Mattias Boström, "Yrke: Sekreterare till Sherlock Holmes" [Occupation: Sherlock Holmes's Secretary], *The Moor*, no. 36 (1992): pp. 10–11 [interview with the Sherlock Holmes secretary at Abbey National, including "ugly hat" quotation].

District Messenger (newsletter of the Sherlock Holmes Society of London), no. 146, November 20, 1994 [about the Sherlock Holmes museum at Baker Street].

Peter E. Blau, *Scuttlebutt from the Spermaceti Press*, June 1989; December 1989; February 1990; April 1990; June 1990; December 1990 [about the Sherlock Holmes museum at Baker Street, including *Country Life* quotation].

Alistair Duncan, *Close to Holmes* (London: MX Publishing, 2009), pp. 5–7 [about the Sherlock Holmes museum at Baker Street].

Cox, *Study in Celluloid*, pp. 153–54, 179 [about starting the production of a new Granada series].

Chapter 94

Steven Rothman and Evelyn Herzog, e-mail correspondence with the author, spring 2013 [about BSI's cocktail party, 1991].

Philip A. Shreffler, "Women," *Baker Street Journal*, 1991/no. 1, pp. 5–7 [about women being invested as members of BSI].

"The Adventuresses of Sherlock Holmes," *I Hear of Sherlock Everywhere*, podcast, episode 89, January 30, 2016 [about BSI's cocktail party, 1991].

Chapter 95

Cox, *Study in Celluloid*, pp. 52, 179–90, 211–16 [about the Granada series, quotation about "completing the Canon," and Brett's funeral].

Barnes, *Holmes on Screen*, pp. 59–60, 106–8, 113–18 [about the Granada series].

Elizabeth Wiggins, "No More! Cried Jeremy, after Dame Jean's Criticism," *Sherlock Holmes Gazette*, Autumn 1993, p. 9 [about Brett's attitude toward the two-hour episode].

Bert Coules, *221 BBC* (Indianapolis: Gasogene Books, 2014) [about the BBC radio series with Clive Merrison as Holmes].

Chapter 96

Laurie R. King, "Autobiography," Laurie R. King's website [about the writing of *The Beekeepers's Apprentice*].

John F. Farrell Jr., *Report of the 1991 Professor James Moriarty Memorial Committee* (published privately, 1993) [about the collecting of animal droppings].

John Bennett Shaw, *The Basic Holmesian Library* (printed privately, February 1983).

John Bennett Shaw, foreword to *The Universal Sherlock Holmes*, by Ronald B. De Waal (Toronto: Metropolitan Toronto Reference Library, 1994), p. xvi [about Shaw and De Waal].

Jon L. Lellenberg, "Dame Jean Conan Doyle," *Sherlock Holmes Journal*, Summer 1998, pp. 138–41 [obituary].

Tibbetts, "Interview with Jean Conan Doyle" [about Dame Jean's home].

Jean Upton, "Dame Jean Conan Doyle," Adventuresses of Sherlock Holmes website [about Dame Jean and the museum at Baker Street].

Chapter 97

Bert Coules, "Sherlock Kicks Ass!" *Sherlock Holmes: The Detective Magazine*, issue 35 (2000): pp. 14–15 [interview with Michael Valle].

Mattias Boström, "Holmes i helvetet" [Holmes in Hell], *Jury*, 2004/no. 3 [about *Sherlock Holmes and the Vengeance of Dracula*].

Barnes, *Holmes on Screen*, pp. 126–31 [about *Murder Rooms*].

Sarah Lyall, "Is That You, Sherlock?" *New York Times*, January 21, 2009 [about Lionel Wigram's original ideas for a Holmes movie].

Charles Prepolec, e-mail correspondence with the author, spring 2016 [about similarities between *Sherlock Holmes and the Vengeance of Dracula* and Guy Ritchie's *Sherlock Holmes*].

Chapter 98

Mitch Cullin, e-mail correspondence with the author, spring 2016 [about the writing of *A Slight Trick of the Mind*, including quotations].

Chapter 99

Dershowitz, *Reversal of Fortune* [about Claus von Bülow and Andrea Reynolds].

Lycett, *Man Who Created Sherlock Holmes*, afterword, pp. 457–67 [about Andrew Lycett's work on the biography].

Steven Rothman and Nicholas Utechin, eds., *To Keep the Memory Green: Recollections on the Life of Richard Lancelyn Green 1953–2004* (London and New York: Quartering Press, 2007), pp. 11, 17, 21–22, 90 [about Richard Lancelyn Green].

Chapter 100

Richard Wiseman, *Quirkology: The Curious Science of Everyday Lives* (London: Macmillan, 2007), chap. 5 [about the search for the world's funniest joke].

Igor Maslennikov, *The Baker Street on Petrogradskaya* (Saint Petersburg, Russia: Séance & Amfora, 2007), chap. 1 [about the meeting between Maslennikov and the Baskerville Hounds].

Alexander Sedov, e-mail correspondence with the author, spring 2016 [confirming that the tent joke existed in the Soviet Union in the 1980s].

Chapter 101

Utechin and Rothman, introduction to *To Keep the Memory Green*, ed. Rothman and Utechin, pp. 15–19 [about the death of Richard Lancelyn Green].

"'The Conan Doyle Collections' and the British Library," British Library, May 17, 2004 (press release).

Nicholas Utechin, "Packing Up," in *To Keep the Memory Green*, ed. Rothman and Utechin, pp. 183–90 [about Utechin visiting Richard Lancelyn Green's home after his death].

Chapter 102

Mitch Cullin, e-mail correspondence with the author, spring 2016 [about getting *A Slight Trick of the Mind* published, including all quotations].

Mitch Cullin, "Interview with Mitch Cullin," *Bookmunch* [about the publishing of *A Slight Trick of the Mind*, including the Chabon quotation].

Steven Doyle, e-mail correspondence with the author, spring 2016 [about Sherlock Holmes literature going mainstream].

Chapter 103

"About John," John Watkiss's website [about John Watkiss].

Jill Pantozzi, "Elementary," Nerdy Bird (website), January 4, 2010 [about Lionel Wigram and John Watkiss].

Charley Parker, "John Watkiss Concept Art for *Sherlock Holmes*," *Lines and Colors* (blog), December 27, 2009 [examples of the concept art for the film].

Borys Kit and Steven Zeitchik, "Guy Ritchie Signs On to Sherlock," *Hollywood Reporter*, June 3, 2008 [about Guy Ritchie as director of Warner Brothers' Sherlock Holmes movie].

Borys Kit, "Robert Downey Jr. to Play Sherlock," *Hollywood Reporter*, July 9, 2008 [about Robert Downey Jr. cast as Sherlock Holmes].

Seth Jones, "Silver, Downey and Wigram on 'Sherlock Holmes,'" CBR.com, December 22, 2009 [about the film *Sherlock Holmes*].

Edward Douglas, "CS on Location with Sherlock Holmes," ComingSoon.net, March 5, 2009.

Barnes, *Holmes on Screen*, pp. 192–96 [about Guy Ritchie's film].

District Messenger (newsletter of the Sherlock Holmes Society of London), no. 261, April 4, 2006 [about Livanov's honorary MBE].

"Monument to Sherlock Holmes and Dr. Watson," Dialogue of Cultures–United World website [about the Moscow statue].

Jon L. Lellenberg, e-mail correspondence with the author, spring 2016 [about the Watson film project in the early 1990s].

Mattias Boström, "En sherlockians syn på filmen *Sherlock Holmes*" [A Sherlockian's Views on the Film *Sherlock Holmes*], SherlockHolmes.se, January 5, 2010 [about Guy Ritchie's film and the parallel life of Sherlock Holmes].

Chapter 104

Steve Tribe, *Sherlock Chronicles* (London: BBC Books, 2014), pp. 13, 22–52 [about the lunches in Monte Carlo and London, the casting, and the pilot episode].

Michael Leader, "Steven Moffat and Mark Gatiss Interview: Sherlock," Den of Geek (website), July 21, 2010 [about the production of the first series of *Sherlock*].

Chapter 105

Heidi Tandy, "How Harry Potter Fanfic Changed the World (or at Least the Internet)," in *Fic: Why Fanfiction Is Taking Over the World*, ed. Anne Jamison (Dallas: BenBella Books, 2013), pp. 165–74 [about fan fiction in the early 2000s].

Anastasia Klimchynskaya, e-mail correspondence with the author, spring 2016 [about the development of fandom and fan fiction from Harry Potter and onward].

David Robinson, "Interview: Anthony Horowitz, Author of *The House of Silk*," *Scotsman* (Edinburgh), October 28, 2011 [about the meeting at the restaurant, including quotation].

Charlotte Williams, "Horowitz to Write Holmes Mystery for Orion," *Bookseller*, January 17, 2011 [about Horowitz's Sherlock Holmes pastiche].

Robert Kirby, e-mail to the author, April 11, 2016 [about the meeting at the restaurant; Robert Kirby, of United Agents, was the literary agent].

Kristina Manente, e-mail correspondence with the author, spring 2016 [about the forming of the Baker Street Babes, including quotations].

Chapter 106

Tribe, *Sherlock Chronicles*, p. 126 [about the different shooting situation during the second series].

"The Sherlockology Review of 2011," Sherlockology (website), December 31, 2011.

"Sherlock Scoops Top Prize at BAFTAs," Hartswood Films (UK), May 22, 2011 (press release).

Justin Andress, "The History of Sherlock Holmes in Video Games." Inverse (website), April 6, 2016.

Barnes, *Holmes on the Screen*, pp. 168–73 [about the BBC series].

Chapter 107

Mattias Boström, "Mika Hallor from Sweden Started the Movement #believeinsherlock," SherlockHolmes.se, March 11, 2012 [how the #believeinsherlock movement spread all over the world].

Chapter 108

Leslie S. Klinger and Rob Doherty, "It's Elementary: A Talk-Back with Rob Doherty," in *Sherlock Holmes: Behind the Canonical Screen*, ed. Faye and Polasek, pp. 239–46 [about the idea for *Elementary*, including the quotations].

Rob Doherty, transcript of interview by Ashley Polasek, July 29, 2012 [about the idea for *Elementary*].

Chapter 109

Darlene Cypser, "Adventures in Copyright," *Baker Street Journal*, 2014/no. 1, pp. 22–27 [about *Klinger v. Conan Doyle Estate Ltd.*].

Betsy Rosenblatt, "A 'Pretty Little Intellectual [Property] Problem': Understanding the 'Free Sherlock' Ruling," *Baker Street Journal*, 2014/no. 1, pp. 28–34 [about *Klinger v. Conan Doyle Estate Ltd.*].

Free Sherlock website, free-sherlock.com [legal documents regarding *Klinger v. Conan Doyle Estate Ltd.* can be found here].

Klinger v. Conan Doyle Estate Ltd., no. 14-1128 (7th Cir., 2014), Oral Argument, May 22, 2014, recording, www.ca7.uscourts.gov [the courtroom quotes in the chapter].

Klinger v. Conan Doyle Estate Ltd., no. 14-1128 (7th Cir., 2014), Appeal from the United States District Court for the Northern District of Illinois, Eastern Division, No. 13 C 1226, June 16, 2014 [the message from Conan Doyle Estate Ltd. to Pegasus Books].

Klinger v. Conan Doyle Estate Ltd., no. 1:13-cv-01226, In the United States District Court for the Northern District of Illinois Eastern Division, Conan Doyle's Response in Opposition to Plaintiff's Motion for Summary Judgment Pursuant to FRCP 56, filed September 10, 2013 ["The facts are that . . ." and the two following quotations].

"December 2013: Ruling," Free Sherlock! (website), December 27, 2013 [about the district court's ruling and Klinger's quotations after the ruling].

Klinger v. Conan Doyle Estate Ltd., no. 14-1128 (7th Cir., 2014), Motion for Award of Attorneys' Fees in an Appeal from the United States District Court for the

Northern District of Illinois, Eastern Division, No. 13 C 1226, August 4, 2014 [Judge Posner's quotation about the business strategy of Conan Doyle Estate Ltd.]

Ben Child, "Mr. Holmes and the Strange Case of the Alleged Copyright Infringement," *Guardian* (UK), May 26, 2015 [about Conan Doyle Estate Ltd. and its legal actions in connection with the film *Mr. Holmes*].

Derrick Belanger, "Bombshell Interview with Author Mitch Cullin," I Hear of Sherlock Everywhere (website), November 23, 2015 [about Conan Doyle Estate Ltd.'s legal action].

Jon L. Lellenberg, e-mail correspondence with the author, 2016 [about *Klinger v. Conan Doyle Estate Ltd.*, and about the legal action in connection with the film *Mr. Holmes*].

Leslie S. Klinger, e-mail correspondence with the author, 2016 [about *Klinger v. Conan Doyle Estate Ltd.*].

Chapter 110

Mitch Cullin, "The Mitch Cullin Papers," *Friends of the Sherlock Holmes Collections*, 2016/no. 2, pp. 1, 6 [about moving Cullin's archive to the Sherlock Holmes Collections in Minneapolis].

Chapter 111

Russell Merritt, Céline Ruivo, and Palle Schantz Lauridsen, e-mail correspondence with the author, spring 2015 [about finding Gillette's film, and the opening of the restored film in January 2015].

BIBLIOGRAPHY

Adams, Guy. *Sherlock: The Casebook*. London: BBC Books, 2012.

"Adventures on the Air: Edith Meiser in Conversation with John Bennett Shaw." *Baker Street Miscellanea*, no. 36 (1983): pp. 10–24.

"The Adventuresses of Sherlock Holmes." *I Hear of Sherlock Everywhere*. Podcast, episode 89, January 30, 2016. http://www.ihearofsherlock.com/2016/01/episode-89-adventuresses-of-sherlock.html.

Advertiser (Adelaide, Australia). "Wide Reactions to Czech Crisis: No Hint of Panic in England." September 15, 1938.

Åhman, Sven. "Den levande Sherlock Holmes" [The Living Sherlock Holmes]. *Dagens Nyheter* (Stockholm), August 4, 1946.

Andress, Justin. "The History of Sherlock Holmes in Video Games," Inverse (website), April 6, 2016. http://www.inverse.com/article/13880-the-history-of-sherlock-holmes-in-video-games.

Arizona Republic. "Holmes Gets the Needle." August 24, 1959.

Austin, Bliss. "William Gillette on the Air." *Baker Street Miscellanea*, no. 29 (1982): pp. 1–9.

Barker, Felix. "Hounds of the Baskervilles." *Evening News* (London), October 13, 1958.

Barnes, Alan. *Sherlock Holmes on Screen: The Complete Film and TV History*. London: Titan Books, 2011.

Bath Chronicle and Weekly Gazette (UK). September 28, 1893. Hampton Rocks mystery.

Beckett, Charles A. "Edith Meiser: The Other Woman in Sherlock Holmes' Life." *Return with Us Now . . .*, 2009/no. 5, pp. 1, 3–4.

Bedford, Nicole de. *Nicole Nobody: The Autobiography of the Duchess of Bedford*. London: W. H. Allen, 1975.

Belanger, Derrick. "Bombshell Interview with Author Mitch Cullin." I Hear of Sherlock Everywhere (website), November 23, 2015. http://www.ihearofsherlock.com/2015/11/bombshell-interview-with-author-mitch.html.

Bell, H. W. *Sherlock Holmes and Dr Watson: The Chronology of Their Adventures*. London: Constable & Co, 1932.

Bennetts, Leslie. "Imagine Sherlock as a Boy . . ." *New York Times*, December 1, 1985.

Bergfelder, Tim. *International Adventures: German Popular Cinema and European Co-Productions in the 1960s*. New York and Oxford: Berghahn Books, 2005.

Bergman, Ted. "Sherlock Holmes ger trygghet i svåra tider" [Sherlock Holmes Provides Security in Difficult Times]. *Sydsvenskan* (Sweden), October 17, 1992.

———. *Sherlock Holmes i Sverige: En bibliografi.* Stockholm: Författares Bokmaskin, 1991.

Bergman, Ted, ed. *Two Two One B*, no. 4 (1990). Special edition about the book *Nya Sherlock Holmes äventyr* by Tage Ekelöf.

Bergquist, John. "50 Years Ago." *Friends of the Sherlock Holmes Collections*, 2001/ no. 4, pp. 3, 7.

Beveridge, Allan. "What Became of Arthur Conan Doyle's Father? The Last Years of Charles Altamont Doyle." *Journal of the Royal College of Physicians of Edinburgh* 36, no. 3 (2006): pp. 264–70.

Bexhill-on-Sea Observer (UK). "Bexhill Cinema Factory." August 10, 1926.

———. "Film-Making at Bexhill." August 21, 1926.

———. "How Moving Pictures Are Made: A Cinema Studio at Bexhill." June 15, 1912.

———. "Picture Making on the Marina." July 13, 1912.

Billington, Michael. "The Case of the Slow-Witted Sleuth." *Guardian* (UK), November 29, 2002.

Blakeney, T. S. *Sherlock Holmes: Fact or Fiction?* New York: Otto Penzler Books, 1993 (first published 1932).

Blau, Peter E. *Scuttlebutt from the Spermaceti Press* (newsletter). June 1989; December 1989; February 1990; April 1990; June 1990; December 1990.

Blum, David. "Steven Spielberg and the Dread Hollywood Backlash." *New York*, March 24, 1986, p. 56.

Boström, Mattias. Afterword. *Sherlock Holmes i Skräckens dal* [The Valley of Fear], by Arthur Conan Doyle. Lund, Sweden: Bakhåll, 2010.

———. "En sherlockians syn på filmen *Sherlock Holmes*" [A Sherlockian's Views on the Film *Sherlock Holmes*]. SherlockHolmes.se, January 5, 2010. http://www.sherlock holmes.se/2010/01/05/en-sherlockians-syn-pa-filmen-sherlock-holmes.

———. "Holmes i helvetet" [Holmes in Hell]. *Jury*, 2004/no. 3.

———. "The Leak." *Baker Street Journal*, 2012/no. 3, pp. 6–12.

———. "Mästerdetektivens skapare" [The Creator of the Master Detective]. In *Tretton kriminella klassiker: Författarporträtt*, edited by Jan Broberg, pp. 103–118. Lund, Sweden: BTJ Förlag, 2005.

———. "Mika Hallor from Sweden Started the Movement #believeinsherlock," SherlockHolmes.se, March 11, 2012. http://www.sherlockholmes.se/2012/03/11/ mika-hallor-from-sweden-started-the-movement-believeinsherlock.

———. "Ouida Before Rathbone." *Baker Street Journal*, 2017/no. 2.

———. "The Three Plays—Sherlock Holmes in Stockholm 1902." In *Scandinavia and Sherlock Holmes*, edited by Bjarne Nielsen, pp. 209–21, New York: Baker Street Irregulars, 2006.

———. "Yrke: Sekreterare till Sherlock Holmes" [Occupation: Sherlock Holmes's Secretary]. *Moor*, no. 36 (1992): pp. 10–11.

Brean, Herbert. "How Holmes Was Reborn." *Life*, December 29, 1952, pp. 62–66.

Bristol Mercury (UK). September 28, 1893. Hampton Rocks mystery.

Bruce, Nigel. "Extracts from the Unpublished Autobiography of Nigel Bruce." *Sherlock Holmes Journal*, Winter 1988, pp. 8–13.

Burgin, G. B. *Memoirs of a Clubman*. London: Hutchinson & Co, 1921.

Burnley Express (UK), December 10, 14, and 17, 1892. Advertisements for Joseph Baron's story "The Man Who 'Bested' Sherlock Holmes."

Byerly, Ann. "Sidney Paget: Victorian Black-and-White Illustrator." *Baker Street Miscellanea*, no. 35 (1983): pp. 1–16.

Cady, Brian. "The Private Life of Sherlock Holmes." TCM: Turner Classic Movies website. http://www.tcm.com/tcmdb/title/87212/The-Private-Life-of-Sherlock-Holmes/articles.html.

Campbell, Maurice. "The First Sherlockian Critic—1902." *Sherlock Holmes Journal*, September 1952, pp. 3–5, 24.

Carleson, Rolf. *Vidare går min väg*. Stockholm: Bokförlaget Excelsior, 1967.

Carr, John Dickson. *The Life of Sir Arthur Conan Doyle*. London: John Murray, 1949.

Cartland, Barbara. *In Search for Rainbows*. London: Arrow Books, 1973.

"The Case of the Baker Street Boom." *Publishers Weekly*, July 8, 1974. Available at the Sherlock Holmes Collections, University of Minnesota.

Cedar Rapids (IA) *Gazette*. "Authoress Barbara Cartland Loves Gold, Gold, Gold." July 16, 1967.

Child, Ben, "Mr Holmes and the Strange Case of the Alleged Copyright Infringement." *Guardian* (UK), May 26, 2015.

Clarkson, Stephen. "'The Strength and Activity of Youth': The Junior Sherlockian Movement." *Baker Street Journal*, Christmas annual, 2003.

"A Closer Look at the Second Mrs. Rathbone." *The Baz: The Basil Rathbone Blog*, December 7, 2012. https://thegreatbaz.wordpress.com/2012/12/07/a-closer-look-at-the-second-mrs-rathbone.

The Conan Doyle Collection: Wednesday 19th May 2004. London: Christie's, 2004. Auction catalog.

"'The Conan Doyle Collections' and the British Library." British Library, May 17, 2004. Press release. Available at http://www.bestofsherlock.com/ref/british-library-press.htm.

Coules, Bert. "Sherlock Kicks Ass!" *Sherlock Holmes: The Detective Magazine*, issue 35 (2000): pp. 14–15.

———. *221 BBC*. Indianapolis: Gasogene Books, 2014.

Courier-Journal (Louisville, KY). "Anglicizing the Script." August 15, 1984.

Courtney, Godfrey B. "General Clark's Secret Mission." *Life*, December 28, 1942, pp. 75–76, 78–80.

Coventry Evening Telegraph (UK). February 11, 1902. Dutch version of William Gillette's play *Sherlock Holmes*.

Coville, Gary, and Patrick Lucanio. *Jack the Ripper: His Life and Crimes in Popular Entertainment*. Jefferson, NC: McFarland & Company, 1999.

Cox, Michael. *A Study in Celluloid: A Producer's Account of Jeremy Brett as Sherlock Holmes*. Indianapolis: Gasogene Books, 2011 (first published 1999).

Crowe, Michael J., ed. *Ronald Knox and Sherlock Holmes: The Origin of Sherlockian Studies*. Indianapolis: Gasogene Books, 2011.

Cullen, Ian. "Mark Gatiss and Steven Moffat Clue Us In about 'Sherlock.'" Monsters & Critics (website), October 24, 2010. www.monstersandcritics.com.

Cullin, Mitch. "'I couldn't quite justify taking liberties with the character without first making sure I had done my homework correctly': An Interview with Mitch Cullin, Author of *A Slight Trick of the Mind*." By Peter Wild. *Bookmunch* (blog), May 28, 2014. https://bookmunch.wordpress.com/2014/05/28/i-couldnt -quite-justify-taking-liberties-with-the-character-without-first-making-sure-i -had-done-my-homework-correctly-an-interview-with-mitch-cullin-author-of-a -slight-trick-of-the-mi.

———. "The Mitch Cullin Papers." *Friends of the Sherlock Holmes Collections*, 2016/ no. 2, pp. 1, 6.

Curtin, Tom. "Thrill Adventures." *Radio Digest*, March 1932, pp. 10–11.

Cypser, Darlene. "Adventures in Copyright." *Baker Street Journal*, 2014/no. 1, pp. 22–27.

Dahlinger, S. E. "The Sherlock Holmes We Never Knew." *Baker Street Journal*, 1999/ no. 3, pp. 7–27.

Dahlinger, S. E., and Leslie S. Klinger, eds. *Sherlock Holmes, Conan Doyle and The Bookman*. Indianapolis: Gasogene Books, 2010.

Dahlinger, S. E., and Glen S. Miranker. "Rathbone Returns! A Misadventure Called Sherlock Holmes." *Baker Street Journal*, Christmas annual, 2007.

Daily Graphic. "Holmes Has a Visitor." July 18, 1951.

Daily Telegraph (London). "For the Commonplace Book." May 3, 1963.

———. "U.S. Law Aids Holmes Champion." January 8, 1981.

Dalpilen (newspaper, Falun, Sweden). Ernst Nordin obituary. March 16, 1897.

Dangar, D. F. O. "In Memoriam." *Alpine Journal*, 1978, pp. 267–68.

Darak, Greg. "The Second Return of Sherlock Holmes." *Sherlock Holmes Journal*, Diamond Jubilee supplement, 2011, pp. 1–5.

———. "Treasures from the BSI Trust Archives: The Basil Rathbone–Edgar Smith Correspondence." *For the Sake of the Trust*, Fall 2012, pp. 1, 4–5.

Davies, David Stuart. *Bending the Willow: Jeremy Brett as Sherlock Holmes*. Ashcroft, BC: Calabash Press, 2012 (first published 1996).

———. "The Private Life of Sherlock Holmes." *Sherlock Holmes Gazette*, no. 14 (1996): pp. 4–10.

"December 2013: Ruling." Free Sherlock! (website), December 27, 2013. https://free -sherlock.com/2013/12/27/december-2013-ruling.

Dershowitz, Alan M. *Reversal of Fortune: Inside the von Bülow Case*. London: Penguin Books, 1986.

"A Description of the Offices of the Strand Magazine." *Strand Magazine*, December 1892, pp. 594–606.

Des Moines (IA) *Register*. "Mrs. Roosevelt Attends Holmes Exhibit." July 6, 1952.

———. "Soviet Court Will Study the Sherlock Holmes Case." August 15, 1959.

District Messenger (newsletter of the Sherlock Holmes Society of London). No. 146, November 20, 1994. Sherlock Holmes Museum on Baker Street.

———. No. 261, April 4, 2006. Livanov's honorary MBE.

Doherty, Rob. Transcript of interview by Ashley Polasek, at the Television Critics Association Summer Tour in Los Angeles, July 29, 2012.

Douglas, Edward. "CS on Location with Sherlock Holmes." ComingSoon.net, March 5, 2009. www.comingsoon.net.

Doyle, Adrian Conan. *Djungel och djuphav*. Stockholm: Tidens Bokklubb, 1956. Swedish translation of Conan Doyle, *Heaven Has Claws* (New York: Random House, 1953).

Doyle, Arthur Conan. *Memories and Adventures*. Cambridge: Cambridge University Press, 2012 (first published 1924).

———. *The Sign of Four*. Oxford: Oxford University Press, 1993 (first published 1890).

———. *The Uncollected Sherlock Holmes*. Harmondsworth, UK: Penguin Books, 1983.

Doyle, Charles Altamont. *The Doyle Diary*. New York: Ballantine Books, 1979.

Doyle, Georgina. *Out of the Shadows: The Untold Story of Arthur Conan Doyle's First Family*. Ashcroft, BC: Calabash Press, 2004.

Doyle, Jean Conan. "An Interview with Jean Conan Doyle." By John C. Tibbetts. Transcript available at http://www.johnctibbetts.com/PDFs/Jean%20Conan%20Doyle%20Int.pdf.

Doyle, Steven, and David A. Crowder. *Sherlock Holmes for Dummies*. Hoboken, NJ: Wiley Publishing, 2010.

Doyle, Steven T. "Together Again for the First Time: Forty Years of *The Seven-Per-Cent Solution*." *Baker Street Journal*, Christmas annual, 2015.

Duncan, Alistair. *Close to Holmes*. London: MX Publishing, 2009.

———. *An Entirely New Country: Arthur Conan Doyle, Undershaw and the Resurrection of Sherlock Holmes (1897–1907)*. London: MX Publishing, 2011.

———. *The Norwood Author: Arthur Conan Doyle and the Norwood Years (1891–1894)*. London: MX Publishing, 2010.

Earnshaw, Tony. *An Actor, and a Rare One: Peter Cushing as Sherlock Holmes*. Lanham, MD: Scarecrow Press, 2001.

Evening Telegraph (Dundee, Scotland). February 11, 1897. London constable deduces man is a bicycle thief.

———. "Chamber of Horrors Hoax." March 5, 1903.

———. "Conan Doyle's Sons in Motor Smash." August 12, 1931.

Farrell, John F., Jr. *Report of the 1991 Professor James Moriarty Memorial Committee*. Published privately, 1993.

Fedina, Olga. *What Every Russian Knows (And You Don't)*. London: Anaconda Editions, 2013.

Field, Amanda J. *England's Secret Weapon: The Wartime Films of Sherlock Holmes*. London: Middlesex University Press, 2009.

Free Lance-Star (Fredericksburg, VA). "For Cold War Junkies, Berlin Wall in England." August 16, 1990.

Free Sherlock website, free-sherlock.com. Legal documents regarding *Klinger v. Conan Doyle Estate Ltd.* can be found here.

"From the Editor's Commonplace Book." *Baker Street Journal*, 1955/no. 2. Earle F. Walbridge quoted on *The Exploits of Sherlock Holmes*.

Gardner, John. "An Interview with John Gardner, Conducted on May 1, 1981." *Baker Street Miscellanea*, no. 27 (1981): pp. 13–15, 33.

Gatiss, Mark. "The Adventure of the Missing Transcript." Unpublished speech given at the annual dinner of the Sherlock Holmes Society of London, January 7, 2006.

———. Introduction. *The Adventures of Sherlock Holmes*, by Sir Arthur Conan Doyle. London: BBC Books, 2011.

Gettysburg (PA) Times. "Doyle Daughter Sells Rights to Holmes Tales." February 2, 1982.

Gibson, John, and Richard Lancelyn Green, eds. *My Evening with Sherlock Holmes*. London: Ferret Fantasy, 1981.

Gillies, Mary Ann. *The Professional Literary Agent in Britain, 1880–1920*. Toronto: University of Toronto Press, 2007.

Glasgow Herald. November 20, 1893. Theater impresario Austin Fryer's plans to stage a Holmes play (which never was produced).

Gloucester Citizen (UK). September 18, 1907. Arthur Conan Doyle's wedding to Jean Leckie.

———. "Death of Noted Local Ornithologist." July 12, 1949.

Green, Richard Lancelyn. Introduction. *The Return of Sherlock Holmes*, by Arthur Conan Doyle. Oxford: Oxford University Press, 1993.

———. Introduction. *The Uncollected Sherlock Holmes*, by Arthur Conan Doyle. Harmondsworth, UK: Penguin Books, 1983. Green compiled the book and provided a 140-page introduction.

———. "Tilting at Windmills: Denis Conan Doyle and the Baker Street Irregulars." *Baker Street Journal*, Christmas annual, 2002.

Green, Richard Lancelyn, ed. *The Sherlock Holmes Letters*. Iowa City: University of Iowa Press, 1986.

Greene, Douglas G. *John Dickson Carr: The Man Who Explained Miracles*. New York: Otto Penzler Books, 1995.

Guest, Val. *So You Want to Be in Pictures*. London: Reynolds & Hearn, 2001.

Gurney, Edmund, Frederic W. H. Myers, and Frank Podmore. *Phantasms of the Living*. Cambridge: Cambridge University Press, 2011 (first published 1886).

Gutowski, Gene. *With Balls and Chutzpah: A Story of Survival*. Bloomington, IN: iUniverse, 2011.

Haining, Peter. *The Television Sherlock Holmes*. London: Virgin Books, 1991.

Hamilton, John. *Beasts in the Cellar: The Exploitation Film Career of Tony Tenser*. Godalming, UK: FAB Press, 2005.

Hammer, Langdon. *James Merrill: Life and Art*. New York: Alfred A. Knopf, 2015.

Harris, Will. "A Chat with Steven Moffat and Mark Gatiss." Premium Hollywood (website), October 23, 2010. http://www.premiumhollywood.com/2010/10/23/a-chat-with-steven-moffat-and-mark-gatiss-sherlock.

Hawkins, Jim. "From a Little Adobe House to the Sherlock Holmes Collections." *Friends of the Sherlock Holmes Collections*, 2002/no. 3, pp. 1, 6.

Heffernan, Harold. "Sellers Fires Ad at Billy Wilder." *Pittsburgh Press*, July 15, 1964.

Hellings, David Paul. "Movie Review: Hound of the Baskervilles." Haddonfield Horror (website), May 2015. http://www.haddonfieldhorror.com/2015/05/movie-review-hound-of-baskervilles.html.

Henderson, Peter. *Practical Floriculture: A Guide to the Successful Cultivation of Florists' Plants, for the Amateur and Professional Florist*. New York: Orange Judd Company, 1892.

Hewett, Richard. "Canon Doyle? Getting Holmes Right (and Getting the Rights) for Television." *Adaptation* 8, no. 2 (2015): pp. 192–206.

Higham, Charles. *The Adventures of Conan Doyle: The Life of the Creator of Sherlock Holmes*. New York: W. W. Norton & Company, 1976.

Holland, Merlin. *Oscar Wildes familjealbum*. Stockholm: Norstedts, 1998. Swedish translation of Holland, *The Wilde Album* (New York: Henry Holt, 1998).

Howlett, Anthony. "In the Beginning: Memories of 1951." *Sherlock Holmes Journal*, Summer 2001, pp. 48–49.

———. "A Study in Terror." *Sherlock Holmes Journal*, Winter 1965, pp. 88–89.

Hulett, Steve. *Mouse in Transition: An Insider's Look at Disney Feature Animation*. N.p.: Theme Park Press, 2014. Also published at http://www.cartoonbrew.com/untold-tales/mouse-in-transition-the-arrival-of-jeffrey-katzenberg-chapter-15-106992.html.

Huntingdon (PA) *Daily News*. November 12, 1924. Anecdote about cigarette card.

Ilson, Carol. *Harold Prince: A Director's Journey*. New York: Limelight Editions, 2000.

"The Influence of Suggestion: Banning 'Sherlock Holmes.'" *Aberdeen Journal*, February 4, 1910.

Jahr, Cliff. "Lord of the Flops." *New York*, October 8, 1979, pp. 40–44.

Jarman, Derek. *Dancing Ledge*. London: Quartet Books, 1984.

Jensen, Jens Byskov. "Snogen der bed Adrian Doyle" [The Snake That Bit Adrian Doyle]. Speech given at the Sherlock Holmes Club of Denmark, January 7, 2012. http://sherlockholmesklubben.dk/wp-content/uploads/2014/04/Snogen-der-bed-Adrian-Doyle.pdf.

Johnson, Roger. "Annual Dinner 2006." *Sherlock Holmes Journal*, Summer 2006, pp. 162–63.

Johnson, Roger, and Jean Upton. *The Sherlock Holmes Miscellany*. Stroud, UK: History Press, 2012.

Jones, Seth. "Silver, Downey and Wigram on 'Sherlock Holmes.'" CBR.com, December 22, 2009. http://www.cbr.com/silver-downey-and-wigram-on-sherlock-holmes.

Josephson, Carl Olof. "Några judiska bokhandlare och bokförläggare i gårdagens Stockholm" [Some Jewish Booksellers and Publishers in the Stockholm of the Past]. In *Det judiska Stockholm*, edited by David Glück, Aron Neuman, and Jacqueline Stare. Stockholm: Jewish Museum, 1998.

Kansas City (MO) *Times*. "Can't Fool Old Sherlock: Mrs. Adrian Conan Doyle Says She Is Kept Informed." February 27, 1952.

————. "Sherlock Manuscript Brings $12,600." December 19, 1964.

Kichin, Valery. "Sherlock Holmes OBE." Russia beyond the Headlines (website), December 12, 2007. http://rbth.com/articles/2007/12/13/sherlok_holmes.html.

King, Laurie R. "Autobiography." Laurie R. King's website. http://laurierking.com/author-pages/autobiography. Also published in *Contemporary Author*, vol. 207.

Kit, Borys. "Robert Downey Jr. to Play Sherlock." *Hollywood Reporter*, July 9, 2008. http://www.hollywoodreporter.com/news/robert-downey-jr-play-sherlock-115374.

Kit, Borys, and Steven Zeitchik. "Guy Ritchie Signs On to Sherlock." *Hollywood Reporter*, June 3, 2008. http://www.hollywoodreporter.com/news/guy-ritchie-signs-sherlock-113088.

Klinger, Leslie S., ed. *The Illustrated Speckled Band: The Original 1910 Stage Production in Script and Photographs.* Indianapolis: Gasogene Books, 2012.

Klinger, Leslie S., and Rob Doherty. "It's Elementary: A Talk-Back with Rob Doherty." In *Sherlock Holmes: Behind the Canonical Screen*, edited by Lyndsay Faye and Ashley D. Polasek, pp. 239–46. New York: Baker Street Irregulars, 2015.

Klinger v. Conan Doyle Estate Ltd., no. 1:13-cv-01226, In the United States District Court for the Northern District of Illinois Eastern Division, Conan Doyle's Response in Opposition to Plaintiff's Motion for Summary Judgment Pursuant to FRCP 56, filed September 10, 2013.

Klinger v. Conan Doyle Estate Ltd., no. 14-1128, US Court of Appeals for the Seventh Circuit. Oral Argument, May 22, 2014. Recording at www.ca7.uscourts.gov .http://media.ca7.uscourts.gov/sound/2014/rt.14-1128.14-1128_05_22_2014.mp3.

Klinger v. Conan Doyle Estate Ltd., no. 14-1128, US Court of Appeals for the Seventh Circuit. Appeal from the United States District Court for the Northern District of Illinois, Eastern Division, No. 13 C 1226, June 16, 2014.

Klinger v. Conan Doyle Estate Ltd., no. 14-1128, US Court of Appeals for the Seventh Circuit. Motion for Award of Attorneys' Fees in an Appeal from the United States District Court for the Northern District of Illinois, Eastern Division, no. 13 C 1226, August 4, 2014.

Knight, Peter. "Year of Social Awareness." *The Age* (Melbourne), March 4, 1982.

Kohner, Frederick. *The Magician of Sunset Boulevard: The Improbable Life of Paul Kohner, Hollywood Agent.* Palos Verdes, CA: Morgan Press, 1977.

Korenévskaya, Elena. "Four Soviet Films in a British Boat." Russia beyond the Headlines (website), March 28, 2014. http://rbth.com/arts/2014/03/28/four_soviet_films_in_a_british_boat_35445.html.

Korkis, Jim. "How Basil Saved Disney Feature Animation: Part One." Mouse-Planet, February 23, 2011. https://www.mouseplanet.com/9534/How_Basil_Saved_Disney_Feature_Animation_Part_One.

———. "How Basil Saved Disney Feature Animation: Part Two."MousePlanet, March 2, 2011. https://www.mouseplanet.com/9549/How_Basil_Saved_Disney_Feature_Animation_Part_Two.

Koroleva, A. "Visiting Holmes." *221B Baker Street* (blog). http://221b-bakerst.livejournal.com/620135.html. Translation by Alexander Sedov of an article originally published in *Komsomolskaya Pravda* (USSR), September 18, 1984.

Kristoffersen, Stig-Arne. *Ukraine: A Joke?* Published privately, 2010.

Lamond, John. *Arthur Conan Doyle: A Memoir.* London: John Murray, 1931.

Lapointe, Joe. "Review." *Detroit Free Press,* July 29, 1984.

Lasky, Jesse L., Jr. *Whatever Happened to Hollywood?* New York: Funk & Wagnalls, 1975.

Leader, Michael. "Steven Moffat and Mark Gatiss Interview: Sherlock." Den of Geek (website), July 21, 2010. www.denofgeek.com.

Leamington Spa Courier (UK). September 20, 1907. Conan Doyle's wedding to Jean Leckie.

Lellenberg, Jon L. "Bangsian Sherlockiana." *Baker Street Miscellanea,* no. 39 (1984): pp. 31–36.

———. "Dame Jean Conan Doyle." *Sherlock Holmes Journal,* Summer 1998, pp. 138–41.

———. "An Interview with Michael Hardwick." *Baker Street Miscellanea,* no. 25 (1981): pp. 11–17.

———. "An Interview with Michael Harrison." *Baker Street Miscellanea,* no. 41 (1985): pp. 14–29.

———. *Nova 57 Minor: The Waxing and Waning of the Sixty-First Adventure of Sherlock Holmes.* Bloomington, IN: Gaslight Publications, 1990.

———. "Rights and Copyrights." *Baker Street Miscellanea,* no. 21 (1980): pp. 26–28.

Lellenberg, Jon L., ed. *Irregular Crises of the Late 'Forties.* New York: Baker Street Irregulars, 1999.

———, ed. *Irregular Memories of the 'Thirties.* New York: Baker Street Irregulars, 1990.

———, ed. *Irregular Proceedings of the Mid 'Forties.* New York: Baker Street Irregulars, 1995.

———, ed. *Irregular Records of the Early 'Forties.* New York: Baker Street Irregulars, 1991.

Lellenberg, Jon, and Daniel Stashower. "A. Conan Doyle, *Nineteenth Century* Man." *Saturday Review of Literature,* 2014, pp. 3–8.

Lellenberg, Jon L., Daniel Stashower, and Charles Foley, eds. *Arthur Conan Doyle: A Life in Letters.* London: Penguin Books, 2008.

Liebow, Ely M. *Dr. Joe Bell: Model for Sherlock Holmes.* Madison, WI: Popular Press, 2007 (first published 1982).

Loew, Brenda, ed. *Playbills to Photoplays: Stage Performers Who Pioneered the Talkies.* N.p.: New England Vintage Film Society, 2010.

London Standard. July 6, 1893. Murder in Ramsgate.

Lyall, Sarah. "Is That You, Sherlock?" *New York Times*, January 21, 2009.

Lycett, Andrew. *Conan Doyle: The Man Who Created Sherlock Holmes.* London: Phoenix, 2008 (first published 2007).

Mail, Sharon. *We Could Possibly Comment: Ian Richardson Remembered.* Leicester, UK: Matador, 2009.

Malec, Andrew. "Frederic Dorr Steele and Gray Chandler Briggs." *Baker Street Miscellanea*, no. 67 (1991): pp. 12–23.

———. "Frederic Dorr Steele and Gray Chandler Briggs, Part II." *Baker Street Miscellanea*, no. 68 (1991): pp. 1–12.

———. Introduction. *The Return of Sherlock Holmes*, by Arthur Conan Doyle. New York: Mysterious Press, 1987.

———. *The Other Master: Frederic Dorr Steele—A Commemorative Essay.* Minneapolis: Sherlock Holmes Collections, University of Minnesota, 1984.

Manchester Courier and Lancashire General Advertiser (UK). September 20, 1907. Conan Doyle's wedding to Jean Leckie.

Manchester Evening News (UK). September 5, 1893. Sherlock Holmes's involvement desired in police cases.

———. October 12, 1897. Police use observation and deduction to catch potato thieves.

Marks, Jeffrey. *Anthony Boucher: A Biobibliography.* Jefferson, NC: McFarland & Company, 2008.

Maslennikov, Igor. *The Baker Street on Petrogradskaya*, chap. 1. Saint Petersburg, Russia: Séance & Amfora, 2007. The published book is in Russian. The chapter and the book title have been translated by Alexander Sedov; the translated text, "How Russian Film Director Meets the Baskerville Hounds," is available at http://221b-bakerst.livejournal.com/619989.html.

———. "Dear Sherlock Holmes's and Doctor Watson's Friends." Alek Morse (blog). http://alek-morse.livejournal.com/3028.html. Translation by Alexander Sedov of an article originally published in *Avrora* (USSR), July 1985.

———. "Sherlock Holmes, Vasily Livanov and Others." Alek Morse (blog). http://alek-morse.livejournal.com/76395.html. Translation by Alexander Sedov of an article originally published in *Avrora* (USSR), no. 7, 1981.

McDonald, Peter D. *British Literary Culture and Publishing Practice, 1880–1914.* Cambridge: Cambridge University Press, 1997.

McKuras, Julie. "Basil of Baker Street." *Friends of the Sherlock Holmes Collections*, 2001/no. 1, pp. 1, 6.

———. "Edith Meiser: A Fascinating and Beautiful Woman." Unpublished speech given at the conference Gillette to Brett II, Indianapolis, on November 17, 2007.

McMahon, Jessica, Catherine Cooke, and Nick Utechin. "Times of the 'Sign.'" *Sherlock Holmes Journal*, Summer 1987, pp. 42–46.

Meiser, Edith. "We Never Called Him Sherlock." *Serpentine Muse*, Winter 1983, pp. 7–13.

"Memories of the Exhibition." Westminster Libraries and Archives website. http://www.westminsteronline.org/holmes1951/memories/index.htm.

Merrill, James. *A Different Person: A Memoir*. New York: Alfred A. Knopf, 1993.

Merritt, Russell. "Holmes and the Snake Skin Suits: Fighting for Survival on '50s Television." In *Fan Phenomena: Sherlock Holmes*, edited by Tom Ue and Jonathan Cranfield, pp. 28–42. Bristol, UK: Intellect Books, 2014.

Messinger, Gary S. *British Propaganda and the State in the First World War*. Manchester, UK: Manchester University Press, 1992.

Meyer, Nicholas, "*Seven-Per-Cent* at Thirty: Memories and Reflections." *Baker Street Journal*, 2004/no. 2, pp. 26–30.

———. *The View from the Bridge: Memories of Star Trek and a Life in Hollywood*. New York: Plume, 2010.

Miller, Russell. *The Adventures of Arthur Conan Doyle*. London: Pimlico, 2009.

Moffat, Steven. Foreword. *Sherlock Holmes on Screen: The Complete Film and TV History*, by Alan Barnes. London: Titan Books, 2011.

———. Introduction. *A Study in Scarlet*, by Arthur Conan Doyle. London: BBC Books, 2011.

Montreal Gazette. "Mystery Casting in Baker Street." October 3, 1964.

"Monument to Sherlock Holmes and Dr. Watson." Dialogue of Cultures–United World website. http://www.ethnoworld.ru/en/projects/projects-in-russia/monument-to-sherlock-holmes-and-dr-watson.

Morley, Christopher. *Thorofare*. New York: Harcourt, Brace and Company, 1942.

Mulford, Prentice. "The Raw American." *Lippincott's Magazine*, June 1873.

Musker, John, and Ron Clements. "Animating Sherlock Holmes: *The Great Mouse Detective*." In *Sherlock Holmes: Behind the Canonical Screen*, edited by Lyndsay Faye and Ashley D. Polasek, pp. 233–38. New York: Baker Street Irregulars, 2015.

Nadel, William. "Edith Meiser and Sherlock Holmes on the Radio." In *Edith Meiser and Her Adventures with Sherlock Holmes*, pp. 8–9. Minneapolis: Sherlock Holmes Collections, University of Minnesota, 1999.

Nationaltidende (Denmark). "'Sherlock Holmes' Fortællinger." September 6, 1909.

Newark (OH) *Advocate*. "Sherlock Holmes Revival Booms." December 25, 1974.

News (Frederick, MD). November 12, 1900. William Gillette's tour in Baltimore.

New York Times. "Ms. of Conan Doyle Is Sold for $12,600." December 19, 1964.

New-York Tribune. February 7, 1903. Death of Frederic Dorr Steele's son.

———. "Conan Doyle's Dilemma." February 12, 1905.

Nieminski, John, and Jon L. Lellenberg, eds. "*Dear Starrett—*" / "*Dear Briggs—*." New York: Baker Street Irregulars, 1989.

Nolan, Frederick. *Lorenz Hart: A Poet on Broadway*. Oxford: Oxford University Press, 1994.

Nollen, Scott Allen. *Sir Arthur Conan Doyle at the Cinema*. Jefferson, NC: McFarland & Company, 1996.

Nordberg, Nils. *The Misadventures of Sherlock Holmes, World Detective*. Nykøbing, Denmark: Sherlock Holmes Museet, 2005.

Nordon, Pierre. *Conan Doyle*. Translated into English from the French by Frances Partridge. London: John Murray, 1966.

Northampton Mercury (UK). "Sherlock Holmes's Latest!" November 15, 1901.

Nottingham Evening Post (UK). "Princess Nina Mdivani." June 4, 1936.

———. "Princess's Romance." August 17, 1936.

———. "Princess's Wedding." August 18, 1936.

Nya Dagligt Allehanda (Stockholm, Sweden). "Biografväsendets utveckling" [The Growth of the Cinema Business]. May 9, 1909.

Oakley, Helen McK. *Three Hours for Lunch: The Life and Times of Christopher Morley*. New York: Watermill Publishers, 1976.

O'Higgins, Patrick. *Madame: An Intimate Biography of Helena Rubinstein*. New York: Viking Press, 1971.

Orel, Harold, ed. *Sir Arthur Conan Doyle: Interviews and Recollections*. New York: St. Martin's Press, 1991.

Pack, Harvey. "Basil Rathbone Believes in the Wonders of ESP." *Asbury Park* (NJ) *Press*, June 15, 1966.

Palmer, Barbara. "Sherlockians Bid Holmes a Happy 130th." *USA Today*, January 6, 1984.

Pantozzi, Jill. "Elementary." Nerdy Bird (website), January 4, 2010. http://thenerdybird .com/elementary.

Parker, Charley. "John Watkiss Concept Art for *Sherlock Holmes*." *Lines and Colors* (blog), December 27, 2009. http://linesandcolors.com/2009/12/27/john-watkiss -concept-art-for-sherlock-holmes.

Peake, Tony. *Derek Jarman*. London: Abacus, 2001.

Pearson, Hesketh. *Conan Doyle*. London: Unwin Paperbacks, 1987 (first published 1943).

Peck, Andrew Jay. "Sherlock Holmes and the Law." *Baker Street Miscellanea*, no. 40 (1984): pp. 16–24.

Peraza, Michael. "Basil of Baker Street, Part 1." *Ink and Paint Club* (blog), March 24, 2010. http://michaelperaza.blogspot.se/2010/03/basil-of-baker-street-part-1 .html.

———. "Basil of Baker Street, Part 2." *Ink and Paint Club* (blog), March 25, 2010. http://michaelperaza.blogspot.se/2010/03/basil-of-baker-street-part-2.html.

Perdue, Peggy. "'Did You Notice Nothing Curious about That Advertisement?'" *Baker Street Journal*, Christmas annual, 2009.

Pittsburgh Press. "Times Square Theater Now Radio Studio." March 2, 1930.

Pointer, Michael. *The Public Life of Sherlock Holmes.* Newton Abbot, UK: David & Charles, 1975.

Porter, Philip. "Kindred Spirits." *Classic and Sportscar,* June 1989, pp. 70–72.

Portsmouth Evening News (UK). July 1, 1882. Miscellaneous Wants notice.

———. January 8, 1886. Weather forecast.

———. January 11, 1886. Cricket match report.

Pound, Reginald. *The Strand Magazine, 1891–1950.* London: Heinemann, 1966.

Prideaux, Tom. "A Singing Holmes in Baker Street." *Life,* April 2, 1965, pp. 133–34, 137–38.

Pugh, Brian W. *A Chronology of the Life of Sir Arthur Conan Doyle, May 22nd 1859 to July 7th 1930.* Revised and expanded edition. London: MX Publishing, 2012.

Rathbone, Basil. *In and Out of Character.* New York: Limelight Editions, 1989 (first edition published 1962).

Raymond, Trevor. "Billy Wilder on Baker Street: The Making and Unmaking of a Movie." *Canadian Holmes,* 2003/no. 1, pp. 35–48.

Redmond, Christopher. *In Bed with Sherlock Holmes: Sexual Elements in Arthur Conan Doyle's Stories of the Great Detective.* Toronto: Simon & Pierre, 1984.

———. *Welcome to America, Mr. Sherlock Holmes: Victorian America Meets Arthur Conan Doyle.* Toronto: Simon & Pierre, 1987.

Redmond, Christopher, ed. *Quotations from Baker Street.* Waterloo, ON: published privately, 2009.

———, ed. *Sherlock Holmes Handbook.* 2nd ed. Toronto: Dundurn Press, 2009.

Reynolds, Andrea. *My Claus von Bulow Affaire.* Bloomington, IN: iUniverse, 2013.

Rice, Susan. "Dubious and Questionable Memories: A History of the Adventuresses of Sherlock Holmes." *Baker Street Journal,* Christmas annual, 2004.

———. *The Somnambulist and the Detective: Vincent Starrett and Sherlock Holmes.* Huddersfield, UK: Northern Musgraves, 2010.

Richardson, Harriet. *Building Up Our Health: The Architecture of Scotland's Historic Hospitals.* Edinburgh: Historic Scotland, 2010.

Ringsted, Henrik V. *London i lup.* Copenhagen: Thaning & Appels Forlag, 1953.

Robb, Brian J. *A Brief History of Walt Disney.* London: Robinson, 2014.

Roberts, S. C. *Doctor Watson.* London: Faber & Faber, 1931.

———. "How It All Began." *Sherlock Holmes Journal,* July 1954, pp. 3–4.

Robinson, David. "Interview: Anthony Horowitz, Author of *The House of Silk.*" *Scotsman* (Edinburgh), October 28, 2011.

Roden, Christopher. "In Conversation with . . . Dame Jean Conan Doyle." *ACD,* 1990/no. 2.

———. Introduction. *The Sign of the Four,* by Arthur Conan Doyle. Oxford: Oxford University Press, 1993.

Roosevelt, Franklin Delano. "Sherlock Holmes Was an American!" In *A Sherlock Holmes Compendium,* ed. Peter Haining, London: W. H. Allen, 1980.

Rosenblatt, Betsy. "A 'Pretty Little Intellectual [Property] Problem': Understanding the 'Free Sherlock' Ruling." *Baker Street Journal,* 2014/no. 1, pp. 28–34.

Rothman, Steven, ed. *The Standard Doyle Company: Christopher Morley on Sherlock Holmes*. New York: Fordham University Press, 1990.

Rothman, Steven, and Nicholas Utechin, eds. *To Keep the Memory Green: Recollections on the Life of Richard Lancelyn Green, 1953–2004*. London and New York: Quartering Press, 2007.

Ruber, Peter. Introduction. *The Final Adventures of Solar Pons*, by August Derleth. Shelburne, ON: Mycroft & Moran, 1998.

"Så här lever Sherlock Holmes och Doktor Watson privat" [This Is How Sherlock Holmes and Dr. Watson Live]. *Husmodern* (Sweden), 1980/no. 44, pp. 14–15, 57.

Saint-Joanis, Thierry. *Le Guide du Film* Sherlock Holmes *(1916)*. Saint-Sauvier: Societé Sherlock Holmes de France, 2015.

St. Louis Post-Dispatch. "Conan Doyle's Estate Loses Case in Russia." August 17, 1959.

———. "Elementary, My Dear Nikolai." April 29, 1956.

———. "Son of Conan Doyle Engaged." June 26, 1931.

Salt Lake Tribune. December 23, 1961. Kenneth Hyman gets insurance policy from Lloyd's.

San Antonio Light. "Prince Alexis Killed in Crash." August 2, 1935.

———. "Prince Dead." March 16, 1936.

Schumach, Murray. "Theater to Show Holmes Exhibits." *New York Times*, February 9, 1965.

Schwartz, Tony. "Son of Hollywood's Hottest Stars: Behind the Quake at Paramount That Rocked the Business." *New York*, October 8, 1984, pp. 42–47, 49.

Sedov, Alexander. "From King Lear to Ten Little Indians." Alek Morse (blog), November 14, 2013. http://alek-morse.livejournal.com/77420.html.

Shaw, John Bennett. *The Basic Holmesian Library*. Published privately, February 1983.

———. Foreword. *The Universal Sherlock Holmes*, by Ronald B. De Waal. Toronto: Metropolitan Toronto Reference Library, 1994, p. xvi.

———. "Who's Afraid of Julian Wolff?" *Baker Street Journal*, 1986/no. 2, pp. 85–89.

Sheffield Evening Telegraph (UK). November 15, 1893. Judge in South Africa advises police to study the Sherlock Holmes stories.

Sherlock Holmes: Catalogue of an Exhibition Held at Abbey House, Baker Street, London, May–September 1951. London: Wightman and Company, 1951.

"Sherlock Holmes Collection: How It All Began." Westminster Libraries and Archives website. www.westminsteronline.org/holmes1951/history/began.html.

"Sherlock Holmes: Zounds! The Super Sleuth Is Our Latest Literary Hero." *People*, 1974/no. 27, pp. 38–39.

"The Sherlockology Review of 2011." Sherlockology (website), December 31, 2011. http://www.sherlockology.com/news/2011/12/31/the-sherlockology-review-of-2011-311211.

"Sherlock Scoops Top Prize at BAFTAs." Hartswood Films, May 22, 2011. Press release. http://www.hartswoodfilms.co.uk/press/2011/sherlock-scoops-top -prize-at-baftas.

Shipley, Margaret. "Adventure Spices Life of Writer." *Arizona Republic*, March 2, 1952.

Shreffler, Philip A. "Women." *Baker Street Journal*, 1991/no.1, pp. 5–7.

Sito, Tom. *Drawing the Line: The Untold Story of the Animation Unions from Bosko to Bart Simpson*. Lexington: University Press of Kentucky, 2006.

Smith, Edgar W. "From the Editor's Commonplace Book." *Baker Street Journal*, 1946/no. 1, pp. 65–66.

Smith, H. Greenhough "Some Letters of Conan Doyle." *Strand Magazine*, October 1930, pp. 390–95.

Sparre, Birgit Th. *Fackelrosor*. Stockholm: Gebers, 1968.

Spicer, Andrew, and A. T. McKenna. *The Man Who Got Carter: Michael Klinger, Independent Production and the British Film Industry, 1960–1980*. London: I. B. Taurus, 2013.

Starrett, Vincent. *Born in a Bookshop: Chapters from the Chicago Renascence*. Norman: University of Oklahoma Press, 1965.

———. *The Private Life of Sherlock Holmes*. New York: Otto Penzler Books, 1993 (first published 1933).

Stashower, Daniel. *Teller of Tales: The Life of Arthur Conan Doyle*. London: Penguin Books, 2000.

Stavert, Geoffrey. *A Study in Southsea: The Unrevealed Life of Doctor Arthur Conan Doyle*. Portsmouth, UK: Milestone Publications, 1987.

Steel, Tom. *The Langham: A History; Opened 1865–Re-Opened 1991*. London: Langham, 1990.

Steele, Frederic Dorr. "Reminiscent Notes." In *Sherlock Holmes: A Play*, by William Gillette. Santa Barbara, CA: Helan Halbach, 1974.

———. "Sherlock Holmes in Pictures." In *221b: Studies in Sherlock Holmes*, edited by Vincent Starrett, pp. 129–37. New York: Macmillan Company, 1940.

———. "Veteran Illustrator Goes Reminiscent." *Baker Street Miscellanea*, no. 67 (1991): pp. 31–39.

Steele, Robert G. "Frederic Dorr Steele: A Biographical Sketch." *Baker Street Miscellanea*, no. 67 (1991): pp. 1–11.

Stephen, Beverly. "Spirit and Style Sum Up the Magic of New Mexico." *Montreal Gazette*, November 8, 1986.

Stewart, James B. *DisneyWar: The Battle for the Magic Kingdom*. New York: Simon & Schuster, 2005.

Sunday Times (Perth). "Secret Drink Lured Python Down Chimney." December 4, 1938.

Sunderland Daily Echo and Shipping Gazette (UK). February 7, 1902. Sets built for provincial tours of William Gillette's play *Sherlock Holmes*.

Surrey Mirror (UK). September 20, 1907. Conan Doyle's wedding to Jean Leckie.

Sutherland, John. *The Stanford Companion to Victorian Fiction*. Stanford, CA: Stanford University Press, 1989.

Svedjedal, Johan. *Bokens samhälle: Svenska Bokförläggareföreningen och svensk bokmarknad 1887–1943*. Stockholm: Svenska Bokförläggareföreningen, 1993.

Svenska Dagbladet (Stockholm). "Sherlock Holmes skulle också tro på spiritismen!" [Sherlock Holmes Would Also Believe in Spiritualism!] October 23, 1929.

Sveum, Richard J. "100 Years Ago." *Friends of the Sherlock Holmes Collections*, 2002/no. 2, p. 2.

Tandy, Heidi. "How Harry Potter Fanfic Changed the World (or at Least the Internet)." In *Fic: Why Fanfiction Is Taking Over the World*, edited by Anne Jamison, pp. 165–174. Dallas: BenBella Books, 2013.

Taylor, Philip M. *British Propaganda in the 20th Century: Selling Democracy*. Edinburgh: Edinburgh University Press, 1999.

Telfer, Kevin. *Peter Pan's First XI: The Extraordinary Story of J. M. Barrie's Cricket Team*. London: Sceptre, 2010.

Tibbetts, John C. "Holmes in London, 1988." *Baker Street Miscellanea*, no. 57 (1989), pp. 32–43.

Times (London). January 20, 1931. Thomas P. Gill obituary.

———. "Air Commandant Dame Jean Conan Doyle." November 19, 1997.

———. "The Estate of the Late Sir Arthur Conan Doyle—Creator of Sherlock Holmes." April 7, 1971. Legal notice.

———. "Michael Hardwick." March 14, 1991.

———. "Move to Halt Conan Doyle Estate Sale." April 8, 1971.

———. "Not Elementary." April 14, 1971.

Todd, William B., and Ann Bowden. *Tauchnitz International Editions in English, 1841–1955: A Bibliographical History*. New York: Bibliographical Society of America, 1988.

"Tour of Switzerland in the Footsteps of Sherlock Holmes, 27th April to 5th May, 1968." Supplement, *Sherlock Holmes Journal*, Summer 1968.

Trembley, Elizabeth. "Holmes' Encore!" *Armchair Detective*, 1992/no. 1, pp. 4–13.

Tribe, Steve. *Sherlock Chronicles*. London: BBC Books, 2014.

Upton, Jean. "Dame Jean Conan Doyle." Adventuresses of Sherlock Holmes website (the obituary is no longer available at the website, but can be found at archive .org). https://web.archive.org/web/20130730124603/http://www.ash-nyc .com/DameJean.htm.

Urnov, Dmitry. "An Enviable but Difficult Fate." In *Legend and Fact: Stories*, by Vassily Livanov, pp. 7–18. Moscow: Raduga Publishers, 1989.

Utechin, Nicholas. "My Father as Watson." *Sherlock Holmes Journal*, Winter 1988, pp. 6–8.

———. "The Society: A Discursive History." *Sherlock Holmes Journal*, Summer 2001, pp. 40–48.

Walker, Martin. "Vassily Holmes." *Guardian* (UK), August 17, 1987.

Wallace, Irving. *The Sunday Gentleman*. New York: Simon & Schuster, 1965.

Watkiss, John. "About John." John Watkiss's website. http://www.johnwatkissfineart .com/about-john.

Weaver, Tom. *Attack of the Monster Movie Makers*. Jefferson, NC: McFarland & Company, 1994. (The Herman Cohen interview can also be found at http:// www.hermancohen.com/interview-attack5.html.)

Weller, Philip, ed. *The Hound of the Baskervilles: Hunting the Dartmoor Legend*. Tiverton, UK: Devon Books, 2001.

West Australian (Perth). "Ruins of Palace Believed to Be Link with Sheba." July 2, 1951.

Weyr, Thomas. "The Road to the Top for 'The Seven-Per-Cent Solution': Not at All Elementary." *Publishers Weekly*, October 27, 1975. Available at the Sherlock Holmes Collections, University of Minnesota.

Wiggins, Elizabeth. "No More! Cried Jeremy, after Dame Jean's Criticism." *Sherlock Holmes Gazette*, Autumn 1993, p. 9.

Wilde, Oscar. *The Complete Works of Oscar Wilde*. Vol. 3. Oxford: Oxford University Press, 2005.

Williams, Charlotte. "Horowitz to Write Holmes Mystery for Orion." *Bookseller*, January 17, 2011.

Wilmer, Douglas. *Stage Whispers: The Memoirs*. Tenbury Wells, UK: Porter Press International, 2009.

Winnipeg Tribune. "Marriage Not to Hinder Motor Racing Career, Says Adrian Conan Doyle." August 1, 1936.

Wiseman, Richard. *Quirkology: The Curious Science of Everyday Lives*, chapter 5. London: Macmillan, 2007.

Wodehouse, P. G. *Performing Flea*. London: Herbert Jenkins, 1953.

Yorkshire Evening Post. August 30, 1893. Contemporary cases in which Sherlock Holmes's involvement was desirable.

———. January 19, 1895. Conan Doyle's to-do list on the mantelpiece.

———. February 22, 1902. Foreign versions of Gillette's play.

Zecher, Henry. *William Gillette, America's Sherlock Holmes*. N.p.: Xlibris, 2011.

Documents in Arthur Conan Doyle Collection— Lancelyn Green Bequest, Portsmouth City Council, Portsmouth, England

Baskervilles Investments Ltd: Report September 72–March 73.

Cancellation of Agreement with Ward Lock & Co. Limited in Respect of "A Study in Scarlet." September 30, 1973.

Court documents, 1966 d.no. 876, High Court of Justice, Chancery Division, Group B, between Nina Harwood and Adrian Malcolm Conan Doyle and Another. April 29, 1966.

Court documents, 1971 d.no. 359, High Court of Justice, Chancery Division, Group B, between Nina Harwood and Fides Union Fiduciaire. April 27, 1971.

Court records, 1958, from J. Arthur Leve (representing Denis Conan Doyle's estate) versus Adrian Conan Doyle, Supreme Court of the State of New York. March 3, 1958.

Court records, 1963 d.no. 1341, High Court of Justice, Chancery Division, Group B, between Nina Harwood and Adrian Conan Doyle. September 23, 1963.

Daily Mail (UK). "Business Booms in Baker-Street." June 1965.

Doyle, Adrian Conan. "U.S. Report 1952." Thirteen-page report written on board the SS *America* and sent to Denis Conan Doyle.

Doyle, Arthur Conan. Will and testament.

Heads of agreement, between Adrian Conan Doyle, Dame Jean Conan Doyle, Nina Harwood and Henry Lester. November 7, 1965. (About Fides Union Fiduciaire.)

Managing Director's Report to the Annual General Meeting of Sir Nigel Films Limited, December 4, 1964.

Mdivani, Nina. July 2, 1974. Account of Baskervilles Investments' affairs.

Mdivani, Nina. *My Book.* Unpublished manuscript.

Notice of Appointment of Receiver or Manager. April 26, 1974. Regards Baskervilles Investments.

"Princess Nina Harwood." January 17, 1974. Minutes of meeting attended by Sidney Pearlman, J. G. Tomlins, Jonathan Clowes, and Royal Bank of Scotland representative R. B. Standring.

"Re: Sir Arthur Conan Doyle, Deceased—Opinion." November 3, 1964. Sixteen-page summary about the Conan Doyle estate.

"Re: Sir Arthur Conan Doyle. Re: Estate of Denis Conan Doyle. Case to Counsel to Advise in Conference on Behalf of Princess Mdivani." May 9, 1963. Compiled by Burton, Yeates, and Hart.

WCBS-TV, New York. September 2, 1975. News bulletin about cinema queue.

Correspondence in Arthur Conan Doyle Collection— Lancelyn Green Bequest, Portsmouth City Council, Portsmouth, England

Nigel Bruce to Denis Conan Doyle (telegram), December 21, 1951.

Ian Calderon to Tony Harwood, September 30, 1974.

René de Chochor to Adrian Conan Doyle, March 36, 1953; June 3, 1953; February 9, 1956.

René de Chochor to Adrian Conan Doyle and Denis Conan Doyle, March 20, 1953; September 6, 1953; September 14, 1953; September 16, 1953; September 20, 1953; September 28, 1953; October 5, 1953; October 7, 1953; October 14, 1953; October 19, 1953; November 10, 1953; November 17, 1953.

René de Chochor to Denis Conan Doyle, April 13, 1953; June 5, 1953; January 11, 1954.

Jonathan Clowes to Tony Harwood, May 9, 1974.

Jonathan Clowes to Sidney Pearlman, June 21, 1973.

Terry DeLapp (Universal) to Denis Conan Doyle, October 8, 1942.

Deriaz, Kirker & Cie to Jonathan Clowes, July 20, 1972.

Adrian Conan Doyle to René de Chochor, June 25, 1953.

Adrian Conan Doyle to Denis Conan Doyle, October 25, 1937; February 15, 1938; April 3, 1938; unknown date in August 1938; September 28, 1938; October 23, 1938; July 9, 1940; July 30, 1940; October 17, 1940; October 25, 1940; December 4, 1940; December 5, 1940; February 26, 1943; March 19, 1943; June 12, 1943; August 20, 1943; January 9, 1944; September 29, 1944; December 17, 1944; January 8, 1945; January 9, 1945; February 23, 1945; March 19, 1945; March 30, 1945; May 1, 1945; May 14, 1945; August 31, 1945; February 2, 1946; June 21, 1946; August 1, 1946; November 26, 1946; December 10, 1946; January 24, 1947; March 4, 1947; April 17, 1947; April 22, 1947; April 27, 1947; June 14, 1947; October 4, 1948; January 21, 1949; April 26, 1949; August 10, 1951; August 12, 1951; September 1, 1951; December 21, 1951; January 3, 1952; January 16, 1952; January 28, 1952; February 2, 1952; February 10, 1952; February 22, 1952; February 26, 1952; March 4, 1952; March 5, 1952; March 13, 1952; April 2, 1952; April 11, 1952; June 3, 1952; June 7, 1952; June 16, 1952; June 18, 1952; July 25, 1952; August 7, 1952; October 23 1952; October 30, 1952; November 9, 1952; November 10, 1952; December 18, 1952; December 20, 1952; unknown date in 1952 (about Ekelöf's book); January 2, 1953; March 13, 1953; June 5, 1953; June 13, 1953; June 15, 1953; July 3, 1953; September 22, 1953; October 13, 1953; October 20, 1953; November 10, 1953; November 11, 1953; November 20, 1953; February 8, 1954; June 29, 1954.

Adrian Conan Doyle to Denis Conan Doyle (telegrams), June 27, 1940; March 15, 1943.

Adrian Conan Doyle to Lew Feldman, December 10, 1968; January 30, 1969.

Adrian Conan Doyle to Henry Lester, October 11, 1968; March 11, 1970.

Adrian Conan Doyle to Nina Mdivani, November 17, 1951; October 30, 1952; September 6, 1955; April 30, 1956.

Adrian Conan Doyle to Geoffrey Stephens (Marylebone Library), January 2, 1951.

Adrian Conan Doyle to Arthur Whitaker, January 21, 1949.

Denis Conan Doyle to René de Chochor, July 10, 1953; September 24, 1953; October 6, 1953; November 8, 1953; September 6, 1954.

Denis Conan Doyle to Gerald Churcher, March 12, 1951.

Denis Conan Doyle to Adrian Conan Doyle, December 12, 1952; December 16, 1952.

Denis Conan Doyle to Lady (Jean) Conan Doyle, April 29, 1938; October 10, 1938; November 15, 1939; December 4, 1939; January 1, 1940; February 10, 1940; April 17, 1940; May 14, 1940.

Denis Conan Doyle to H. William Fitelson, June 15, 1941; July 14, 1942; January 29, 1944; November 11, 1951; November 10, 1952.

Denis Conan Doyle to Edith Meiser, February 26, 1941.

Denis Conan Doyle to Frank Orsatti, June 16, 1941.

Denis Conan Doyle to Victor Orsatti, August 8, 1939.

Denis Conan Doyle to Basil Rathbone, December 29, 1940.

Denis Conan Doyle to Ray Stark, January 15, 1947.

Denis Conan Doyle to A. S. Watt, September 28, 1939; December 5, 1939; May 4, 1940.

A. E. Drysdale to Superintendent of Branches, Royal Bank of Scotland (memorandum), February 11, 1972.

H. William Fitelson to Denis Conan Doyle, June 24, 1941; August 15, 1941.

Donald Friede (of Myron Selznick & Co) to Denis Conan Doyle, August 6, 1941;
September 5, 1941.

Gordon Dadds & Co to Gerald Churcher, November 12, 1962.

E. J. N. Harris and S. E. Blake to Nina Mdivani, June 26, 1974.

Tony Harwood to Anthony Lewis (*New York Times*), July 30, 1975.

Tony Harwood to Brian Lewis, January 21, 1974.

Tony Harwood to Audrey Wood (memoranda), October 27, 1975; December 15,
1975; December 28, 1975; January 8, 1976.

Rudolf Jess to Paul Kohner, January 12, 1939; May 2, 1939.

Rudolf Jess to Paul Kohner (telegrams), December 8, 1938; December 13, 1938;
December 30, 1938; January 8, 1939; January 24, 1939.

Julian Johnson (Fox) to Paul Kohner, December 24, 1938; May 2, 1939.

Paul Kohner to Rudolf Jess (telegrams), December 6, 1938; December 7, 1938;
December 12, 1938; December 22, 1938; December 29, 1938; January 9, 1939.

Paul Kohner to Rudolf Jess, December 8, 1938.

Paul Kohner to Victor Orsatti, January 26, 1939.

Henry Lester to Adrian Conan Doyle, November 3, 1969.

Henry Lester to John C. Taylor, November 23, 1967.

W. Lyall (Royal Bank of Scotland) to Nina Mdivani, December 4, 1973.

Nina Mdivani to Adrian Conan Doyle, August 12, 1955, March 16, 1970.

Nina Mdivani to Andrew Walker, January 5, 1976.

Edith Meiser to Denis Conan Doyle, ca. February 10, 1941; ca. April 21, 1941.

Victor Orsatti to Denis Conan Doyle, December 9, 1940.

Sidney Pearlman to John Brown (Royal Bank of Scotland), October 19, 1973.

Sidney Pearlman to A. E. Drysdale (Royal Bank of Scotland), February 3, 1972;
February 7, 1972; February 8, 1972.

Sidney Pearlman to Nina Mdivani, January 29, 1973; April 5, 1974.

Bernard R. Pollock to John Linsenmeyer, December 3, 1975.

Basil Rathbone to Denis Conan Doyle, December 13, 1940.

Regional General Manager to J. S. McFarlane (Royal Bank of Scotland), November
14, 1973.

Samuel French Limited to Sidney Pearlman & Greene, January 19, 1973.

Edgar W. Smith to Harold J Sherman (Fitelson and Mayers), August 1, 1951.

Geoffrey Stephens (Marylebone Library) to Adrian Conan Doyle, March 1, 1951.

A. S. Watt to Denis Conan Doyle, February 23, 1939.

R. P. Watt to Gerald Churcher, November 7, 1951.

Audrey Wood (International Famous Agency) to Nina Mdivani, April 22, 1974.

Documents and correspondence in Artur Brauner-Archive at Deutschen Filminstitut—DIF e.V., Frankfurt, Germany

Film contract between CCC and the Conan Doyle Estate, film contract, dated
     September 18, 1961.

Artur Brauner to Otto Joseph (solicitor for the Conan Doyle Estate), July 24, 1962;
     August 20, 1962.

Adrian Conan Doyle to Artur Brauner, May 13, 1962; June 8, 1962.

C. E. Fielding (Crawley & de Reya, solicitors) to Artur Brauner, May 1, 1962.

Henry E. Lester to Artur Brauner, August 3, 1961; October 30, 1961; November 10,
     1961; December 17, 1961; May 16, 1962; April 25, 1963.

Henry E. Lester to Artur Brauner (memorandum), June 30, 1962.

Henry E. Lester to René de Chochor, June 8, 1962.

Henry E. Lester to Michael and Mollie Hardwick, May 30, 1962.

Henry E. Lester to Margaret "Peggy" Ramsay (theatrical agent), June 26, 1962.

Documents and correspondence in Alexander H. Cohen Papers, New York Public Library, New York

Agreement between the Conan Doyle Estate and Alexander H. Cohen, November
     9, 1961.

Notes by Alexander H. Cohen, April 28, 1961.

René de Chochor to Alexander H. Cohen, April 30, 1962.

Alexander H. Cohen to Adrian Conan Doyle, November 19, 1962; December 5, 1962.

Alexander H. Cohen to Henry E. Lester, April 28, 1961; May 10, 1962; April 22, 1963;
     May 21, 1963; June 17, 1963; July 23, 1963.

Alexander H. Cohen to Henry E. Lester (telegram), June 12, 1963.

Alexander H. Cohen to Peter O'Toole, April 12, 1963.

Alexander H. Cohen to Basil Rathbone, February 4, 1963.

Henry E. Lester to Alexander H. Cohen, August 6, 1961; August 9, 1961; November
     24, 1961; January 20, 1962; January 21, 1962; April 8, 1962; April 26, 1962; May 8,
     1962; July 12, 1962; August 24, 1962; September 14, 1962; March 29, 1963; May
     10, 1963; May 26, 1963; June 13, 1963; June 24, 1963; November 13, 1963.

Adrian Conan Doyle to Alexander H. Cohen, January 31, 1962; February 14, 1962;
     April 24, 1962; September 14, 1962; December 30, 1963.

Adrian Conan Doyle to Henry E. Lester, January 14, 1962.

Basil Rathbone to Alexander H. Cohen, January 31, 1963.
John C. Taylor to Alexander H. Cohen, April 3, 1961.

Correspondence in Society of Authors Papers, British Library, London, England

Arthur Conan Doyle to A. P. Watt, October 4, 1914.
Ulf Hansen (lawyer in Copenhagen) to G. Herbert Thring, September 7, 1909.
Harald Thornberg to G. Herbert Thring, January 5 and February 1, 1909.
Wake, Wild & Boult to G. Herbert Thring, October 2, 1914; January 8, 1915.
A. P. Watt to G. Herbert Thring, March 4, March 6, March 11, March 12, March 17, March 18, 1909.
A. S. Watt to G. Herbert Thring, January 14, 1909.

Documents and correspondence in "Infringement of Copyrights by the Soviet Union in Relation to the Works of Conan Doyle," National Archives, Kew, Richmond, England

"Record of a conversation with Mr. Churcher, the U. K. representative of the Conan Doyle estates, when Mr. Adrian Conan Doyle's difficulty in obtaining a Soviet visa was discussed." Lord Jellicoe, November 21, 1955.
Adrian Conan Doyle to Sir Anthony Eden (Foreign Office), January 10, 1955; January 14, 1955.
Adrian Conan Doyle to the Earl Jellicoe, August 6, 1955.

Correspondence in Sherlock Holmes Collections, University of Minnesota, Minneapolis

Henry E. Lester to Vincent Starrett, January 17, 1962.

Correspondence in Mdivani family papers, Hargrett Rare Book and Manuscript Library, University of Georgia, Athens

George T. Delacorte to Princess Nina Mdivani Harwood, December 9, 1975. (Addressed to "Mrs. Montezuma Jones.")

Correspondence in Arthur Conan Doyle Papers, Harry Ransom Center, University of Texas, Austin

Arthur Conan Doyle to Bram Stoker, August 20, 1897.

Correspondence in Shakespeare Birthplace Trust Collections, Stratford-upon-Avon, England

Arthur Conan Doyle to Bram Stoker, ca. December 1897.

Correspondence in author's collection

Anthony Burgess to Ted Bergman, August 22, 1986.

INDEX